Nicholson's

COMPLETE LONDON

With full colour street maps

The deluxe edition of the famous Nicholson pocket guide

ROBERT NICHOLSON PUBLICATIONS
COMMUNICA-EUROPA

© Robert Nicholson Publications Limited
24 Highbury Crescent
London N5 1RX.

London map
© Robert Nicholson Publications Limited
based upon the Ordnance Survey map with
the sanction of the Controller of Her Majesty's
Stationery Office, Crown Copyright reserved.

London Underground map by kind
permission of London Transport.

All other maps
© Robert Nicholson Publications Limited

Printed in England by
Jolly & Barber Ltd, Rugby

Great care has been taken throughout
this book to be accurate, but the
publisher cannot accept responsibility
for any errors which appear.

NE-4/77-17-Lu75.

Contents

Street maps
Street index   16
Theatres and cinemas map   28
Shopping map   29
Underground map   30
Bus maps   31
Parking   34
Sightseeing
Information centres   35
London maps and guides   35
Telephone services   35
Viewpoints   36
Daily ceremonies   36
Annual events   36
Thames river map   38
London tours   42
River trips   42
Canal trips   42
Charter boats   43
Day trips from London   43
Historic London
Historic buildings   44
Great houses and gardens near London   50
Houses of famous people   52
Commemorative plaques   53
Statues   54
Modern outdoor sculpture   55
Abbeys and cathedrals   55
Churches   56
The Wren churches of London   57
Modern architecture   59
Museums and parks
Museums and galleries   61
Parks and gardens   63
Botanic gardens and arboreta   65
Zoos and aquaria   65
Aviaries and wildfowl reserves   66
Birdwatching   66
Nature reserves   67
Children's London
Looking at London   68
Museums for children   69
Animals in parks   69
Nature trails   70
Hill figures   70
Fossil hunting   70
Brass rubbing   71
Traction engines   71
Windmills   71
Learning   72
Scouts and guides   72
Helping others   72
Playgrounds   73
Fairs   73
Children's theatre   73
Children's holidays   73
For parents   74
Children's shopping   74
Children's clothes   75
Scholar's London
Reference libraries   75
Student's London   78
Politcal and minority interest groups   79
Travel and holiday information
Passports   80
Inoculations and vaccinations   80
Money: currency exchange   81
Lost property   81
Embassies   81
Commonwealth offices   82
Institutes of culture   82
Tourist offices   83
Travel agents and tour operators   83
Unusual holidays   83
Passenger shipping lines   85
Car ferries   86
Taxis and mini cabs   86
Car hire   87
Coach hire   87
Buses and coaches   87
Coach stations   87
Rail terminals   87
Airports   88
Air terminals   88
Airlines   88
Specialist air charter   88
Helicopter charter   88
Accommodation
Hotel booking agents   89
Hotels: luxury   89

Hotels: medium prices   90
Hotels: low prices   91
Hostels   91
Lodgings 92
Motels   92
Hotels near Heathrow airport   92
Hotels near Gatwick airport   92
Estate agents   92
Eating and drinking
Tipping   93
Restaurants   93
Vegetarian and health food   100
Carveries   100
Inexpensive eating   100
Unusual eating   101
Outdoor eating   101
Afternoon teas   102
Pubs   102
Musical pubs   104
Drag pubs   104
Open air pubs   105
Theatre pubs   105
Wine bars   105
Night life and clubs
Dinner dancing   106
Night clubs   107
Jazz clubs   107
Discotheques   107
Dance halls   108
Ticket agents   108
Theatres, cinemas and music
Theatres   108
Opera, ballet and musicals   110
Poetry   110
Concert halls   110
Cinemas   111
Radio and T.V. shows   112
Church music   112
Lunchtime concerts   112
Open air music   112
Festivals   113
Sport
Ticket agents: sport   114
Sports stadiums   113
Sport   114
Shopping
Consumer protection   119
Children's clothes   119
Men's clothes   119
Women's clothes   121
Specialist shops and services   124
Markets   142
Home services   143
Night services   144
Business information services   145
Business and secretarial services   145
Social services
Police stations   146
Hospitals   146
Cry for help   147
Charities   152
Voluntary social work   152
Lavatories   152
Crisis page   154

Symbols

L	lunch
D	dinner
B	buffet
£	meal without wine for under £3.00 per person
££	meal without wine for under £6.00 per person
£££	meal without wine for over £6.00 per person
Children	Children welcome, sometimes with a reduction in price
Reserve	It is advisable to reserve
A	Access card accepted
Ax	American Express
B	Barclaycard
Cb	Carte Blanche
Dc	Diners Club
E	Eurocard
M	Membership necessary

| **1** | **2** | **3** | **4** | **5** | **6** |

Melrose ter · Poplar gro
Cromwell gro
Shepherd's Bush la
Melrose gdns
Minford gdns
Westwick gdns
Anley rd
Netherwood rd
Lakeside rd
Addison gdns
Charecroft way
Richmond way
Sinclair PO
Woodstock gro
Hansard ms
Addison
Larne gdns
Upper Addison gdns
gdns
Norland sq
Portland rd
Clarendon rd
Notting Hill
Ladbroke
Lansdowne ms
Boyne ter
Holland Park avenue
Holland Park

Dewhurst rd
Sterndale rd
Dunsany rd
Augustine rd
Applegarth rd
Brook grn
Bolingbroke rd
Fielding rd
Irving rd
Redan st
Masbrough rd
Caithness rd
Blythe rd
Aynhoe rd
Girdlers rd
Brook grn
Holland rd
Milson rd
Ceylon rd
Faroe rd
Gratton rd
Hazlitt rd
Hazlitt mews
Porten rd
Sinclair rd
Russell gdns
Russell gdns
Elsham rd
Addison
Holland rd
Russell rd
Holland road
Addison rd
Abbotsbury rd
Holland vils rd
Holland pk ms
Holland pk
Holland pk ms
Holland pk
Holland Park
King George VI Hostel
Holland wlk
Sheldrake pl
Duchess of
Upper Phillimore gdns
Phillimore Pl
Essex Vil

Kensington Olympia Station
PO
Maclise rd
Olympia
Blythe rd
Addison cres
Addison cres
Oakwood ct
Ilchester pl
Napier rd
Napier pl
Holland mews
Melbury rd
Holland pk rd
Commonwealth Institute
Melbury ct
Phillimore gdns
Stafford ter
Phillimore

Hammersmith road
Kensington high street
St Pauls Sch
Edith rd
Auriol rd
Munden st
South Combe st
Vernon st
Vernon mews
Bishop King's rd
Gorleston st
Cumberland cres
Addison Br
Earsby st
St Mary Abbots ter
St Mary Abbots pl
Edwardes sq
Edwardes sq
Edwardes sq ms
Pembroke rd
Warwick gdns
PO
Pem broke pl
Pater st
Cope pl
Abingdon rd
Abingdon vil
Wrights la
Allen st

Gliddon rd
Fitzgeorge av
Fitz James av
Gunterston rd
Edith rd
Olgibston rd
Gwendwr rd
Talgarth rd
Matheson rd
North End cres
Stanwick rd
Stonor rd
Fenelon place
Pembroke gdns
Pembroke gdns
Edwardes sq ms
Pembroke vils
Earl's wlk
Pembroke sq
Pembroke rd
Scarsdale villas
Stratford rd
Lexham gdns
Hadley
Shaftesbury mews
Lexham gdns
Marl

Barons Court Station
Barton rd
Baron's Ct rd
Comeragh rd
Gledstanes rd
Vereker rd
Castle town
Charleville rd
Fairholme rd
Perham rd
Chalfont st
North End road
Beaumont av
Beaumont cres
West Kensington Station
Mund st
Lanfrey pl
Edith vils
Edith vils
West Cromwell road
Clonyms
Warwick road
Phillbeach gdns
Longridge rd
Nevern rd
Nevern pl
Templeton pl
Cromwell cres
Logan pl
Logan mews
Earl's Court road
WC
Redfield la
Wallgrave rd
Childs place
Childs street
Kenway rd
Knaresborough pl
Scarsdale

St Andrews rd
Greyhound rd
Normand ms
Queen's clo gdns
Turneville rd
Archel rd
Chesson rd
Bramber rd
Star rd
Fane street
West Kensington
Earl's Court Exhibition
Nevern sq
Trebovir rd
Hogarth rd
Earls Court Station
Penywern rd
Earl's Ct gdns
Barkston gdns
Laverton gdns
Hesper ms
Courtfield gdns
Collingham gdns
Courtfield
Cour

Normand Park
Lillie rd
Normand rd
Jerviston
Clem Atlee ci
Lillie road
Chestnut cl
Sedlescombe rd
Eardley cres
Kempsford gdns
Earl's Ct sq
Earl's Ct sq
Bramham gdns
Bolton gdns
Earl's Court
Wetherby ms
Bolton gdns
Collingham gdns

St Thomas's way
Mirabel rd
Fabian rd
Hartismere rd
Estcourt rd
Haldane rd
Tournay rd
Epirus rd
Racton rd
Anselm rd
Halford rd
Armadale rd
Knivett rd
Waite st
Tamworth st
Ongar rd
Merrington rd
Hildyard rd
Seagrave rd
Eustace
Old Brompton road
Rickett st
Rosmead yard
West Brompton Station
Princess Beatrice Hospital
Wharfedale st
Coleherne rd
Coleherne ms
Westgate ter
Redcliffe close
Red cliffe
gardens
Redcliffe gdns
Bolton gdns
Earls court ter
Harcourt ter
The Little Boltons

Miles ¼ ½ ¾
Metres 500 1000 1500
Continued on map **4**

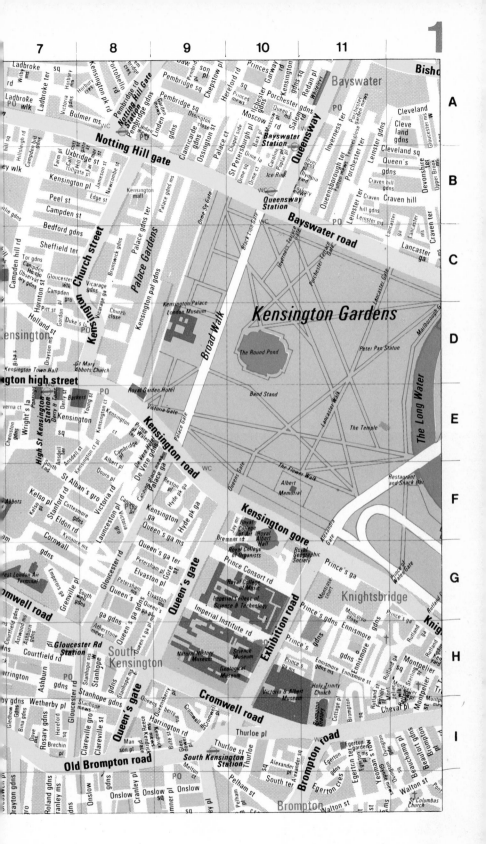

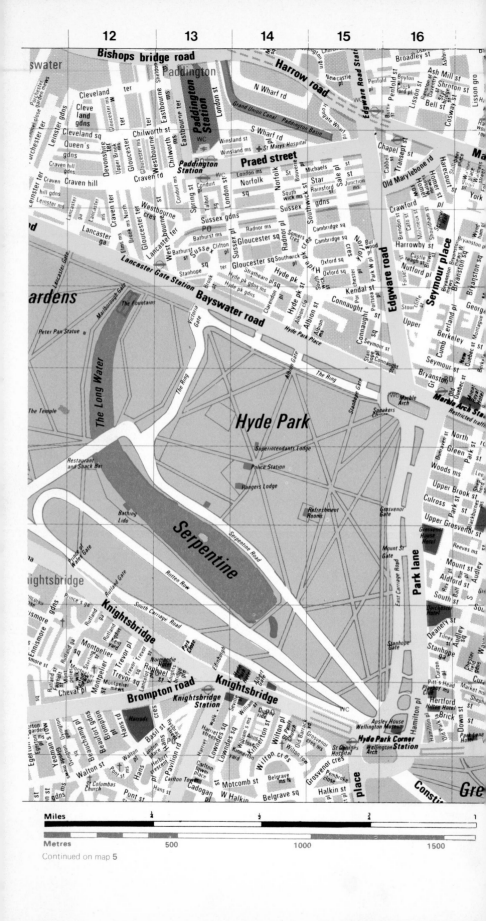

Continued on map 5

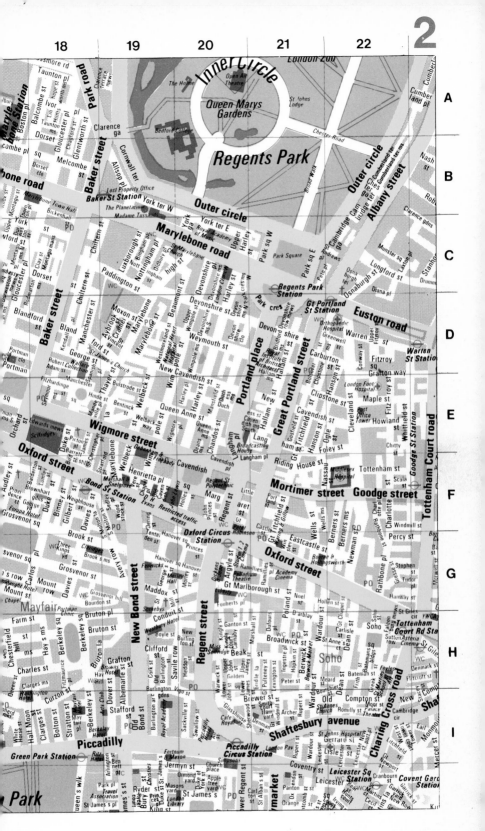

18   19   20   21   22

A
B
C
D
E
F
G
H
I

Marylebone Station
Taunton pl
Boston st
Balcombe st
Ivor
Taunton pl
Gloucester pl
Glentworth st
Baker street
Park road
Terrace mews
The Home
Inner Circle
Open Air Theatre
London Zoo
St Johns Lodge
Cumberland pl
Nash st
Rob

Dorset sq
Melcombe
Clarence ga
Bedford College
Queen Marys Gardens
Cumber land pl

combe pl
Dorset sq
Dorset clo
Cornwall ter
Allsop pl
Regents Park
Chester Road
Clarence gdns

bone road
Marylebone Town Hall
Bickenhall
Baker St Station
Lost Property Office
The Planetarium
Madame Tussauds
York ter W
Baker street
Outer circle
Outer circle
Munster sq
Longford st

York st
ford st
Chiltern st
Luxborough st
Nottingham st
Bingham pl
Didbury pl
Gloucester
Marylebone road
York ter E
Royal Academy of Music
York ga
York ter E
Upper Harley
Park sq W
Park Square
Park sq E
St Andrews
Cambridge
Osnaburgh st
Munster sq
Longford st
Stanho

Dorset
Clay st
Montagu mans
Paddington st
Devonshire ms
Church st
Marylebone high st
Devonshire clo
Devonshire st
Harley st
Park cres
Regents Park Station
Gt Portland St Station
Osnaburgh st
Diana pl
Drummo

Blandford
Baker street
Bland
Manchester st
Moxon st
Aybrook
Cramer
Marylebone
ford st
Beaumont st
Devonshire st
Devonshire ms
Weymouth st
Portland place
Great Portland street
Carburton
Greenwell
Warren st
Euston road
Warren St Station

George st
Robert
Walters
Adam st
Kendal st
St James's Church
New Cavendish st
Wimpole st
Harley st
Hallam
New
Bridford ms
British
Hallam st
Clipstone st
Clipstone st
Hanson st
Maple st
Conway st
Fitzroy sq
Grafton way

Portman
clo
Portman
Fitzhardinge
Manchester
sq
George st
Thayer st
Bulstrode st
Hinde st
Bentinck
Welbeck st
Wimpole st
Mansfield st
Duchess st
Cavendish st
Gt Titchfield st
Ogle st
Foley st
Cleveland st
Howland st
Tottenham st
Tottenham Court road
Goodge St Station

Orchard
Edwards mews
Schinges
Duke st
Picton st
Christopher pl
Welbeck st
Debenham & Freebody
Wigmore street
Queen Anne st
Welbeck
pole st
Queen Anne's Gate
Chandos st
Langham
Broadcasting House
Langham pl
Riding House st
Nassau
Middlesex Hospital
Chitty st
Scala

Oxford street
Audley
Gee
Brownhart
Gilbert st
Binney st
Weighhouse st
Bond St Station
Henrietta pl
Marshall
Snelgrove
Vere st
Regent st Polytechnic
Little
Port
land st
Mortimer street
Wells st
Berners st
Berners ms
Newman st
Goodge street
Charlotte st
Windmill st
Percy st

Europa Hotel
Grosvenor sq
Davies
Brook st
Brook s ms
Dering st
Tenter den st
Hanover sq
Princes st
Eastcastle st
Margaret st
Castle st
Robinson
PO
Bourne & Hollingsworth
Oxford street
Rathbone pl
Rathbone st
Hanway st
Stephen st
Tudor st

svenor sq
Charles st
Mount
Mount st
Chapel
Three Kings yard
Grosvenor st
Avery row
Grosvenor hill
Bourdon st
New Bond street
Maddox st
Hanover sq
Hanover st
George st
Morley Hall
Gt Marlborough st
Liberty
Regent street
Palladium Theatre
Ramillies st
Ramillies pl
Noel st
D'arblay st
Poland st
Hollen st
Academy Cinema
Soho
Bateman's bldgs
St Giles
Tottenham Court Rd Sta

Mayfair
Farm st
Mount st
Portman
Clinic
Bruton pl
Berkeley sq
Bruton st
Berkeley la
Conduit st
Clifford
Westbury Hotel
Boyle st
New Burlington st
Heddon st
Kingly st
Ganton st
Carnaby
Beak st
Broadwick st
Marshall st
Wardour st
Dean
Carlisle st
Soho
Sutton row
Falconberg
Astoria Cinema
YWCA
Tottenham Court Rd Sta

Chesterfield ms
Charles st
Clarges ms
Hay's ms
Berkeley st
Fitzmaurice pl
Grafton st
Browns Hotel
Albemarle st
Burlington gdns
Vigo st
Sackville st
Swallow st
Warwick st
Upper James st
Golden
Lexington st
Peter st
Brewer st
Bridle la
Pulteney st
Ingestre pl
Hopkin st
Berwick st
Berwick st
Wardour st
Old Compton st
Bateman st
Greek st
Frith st
Foley
Denmark st

Washington Hotel
Charles st
Curzon st
Bolton st
Stratton st
May fair
Berkeley st
Old Bond st
Royal Academy
Burlington Arcade
Glasshouse st
Sherwood st
Denman st
Archer st
Old St Anne's Church
Romilly st
Compton st
Palace cir
Cambridge cir
Earl st
New Compt

White Horse st
Hall Moon st
Clarges st
Piccadilly
Ritz Hotel
Arlington st
Green Park Station
Fortnum & Mason
Jermyn st
St James's
Duke st
Church place
Piccadilly
Café Royal
London Pav
Rupert st
Gerrard st
Lisle st
Litchfield
Newport
Shaftesbury avenue
Charing Cross road
Sha

Park
Bennett st
Park pl
Travel Association
St James's pl
Ryder st
Bury
Duke st
King st
Ormond yard
Duke of York st
Apple tree yard
St James's
St James's sq
Charles II st
Carlton st
PO
Regent st
lower
Waterloo pl
Haymarket
Panton st
Orange
Coventry st
Leicester
Whitcomb st
Leicester Sq Station
Cranbourn st
Leicester Sq Station
Martins la
St Martins
New Row
Cecil
Covent Garden Station

Continued on map 6

A
B
C
D
E
F
G
H
I

Bride st
Wheelwright st
Ponder st
Ellington st
Offord st
Corn st
Arundel sq pl
Offord rd
Barnsbury gro
St Clements st
PO
Bufford d
Gifford st
Tilloch st
Carnoustie drive
Huntingdon st
Hemingford rd
Arundel pl
Randells rd
Pembroke st
Gifford st
Belitha vlls
Offord rd
Highb
st rd
Freeling st
Story st
Thornhill cres
Barnsbury ter
Barnsbury sq
Barnsbury pk
Laycock st
Bingfield st
Thornhill
Hemingford rd
Lambert st
Lofting rd
Thornhill rd
Bewdley st
Havelock st
Stanmore
Bemerton st
Twyford st
Ripplevale gro
Lofting rd
Brooksby st
Islington pk
PO
Copenhagen st
Luard st
Treaty st
Edward sq
Martina st
Shirley
Everilda st
Richmond cres
Richmond
Malvern ter
Sheen gro
Lonsdale sq
Barn
sbury st
College cross
College cross
York way
Boadicea st
Richmond avenue
Pulteney ter
Roxminton ter
Gainford st
Milner sq
Waterloo ter
Almeida st
Cirnan st
Carnegie st
Copenhagen st
PO
Dewey rd
Stone field st
Cloud esley
Liverpool road
Gibson st
Moon Studd st
Florence st
Cross
All Saints st
Charlotte ter
Barnsbury rd
Cloudesley rd
Theberton st
Dagmar ter
Wharfdale rd
Grand Union Canal
Cave st
Barnsbury gro
Cloudesley
Moon st
Dagmar ter
Railway st
Northdown st
Wynford rd
Muriel st
Maygood st
Denmark gro
Cloudesley pl
Barford st
St Alban's
St Marys path st
Keystone cres
Southern st
Calshot st
Hall Moon cres
Dewey rd
Diquin st
Batchelor
Ritchie
Gaskin st
Florence st
Killick st
Collier st
Rodney st
Donegal st
Culpeper st
W Conduit st
Mantell st
Parkfield st
WC
Essex road
Affleck st
Cumming st
Penton st
Grant st
 Wharf court
Tibbury st
Islington
Cynthia st
Hermes st
Wharton st
Penton gro
White Lion st
Parkfield st
Camden pas
Charlton
Camden wk
Cruden st
Raleigh
Queen's Head st
Windsor
Pentonville road
Penton rise
Claremont st
Islington High st
Duncan ter
St Peter street
Rheidol
Priebe st
Penton rise
Weston st
Claremont sq
Bevin
Medford st
Torrens st
Duncan
Gerrard rd
Grantbridge st
Allingham st
Packington st
King's Cross road
Percy
Cir
Gt Percy st
Muddleton st
St Mark's Church
Field st
Angel Station
Devonia rd
Noel rd
Burgh st
Frome st
Wharton st
Prideaux
Cruikshank
Inglebert st
Chadwell st
PO
Colebrook row
Vincent ter
Danbury st
Lloyd
River st
Ella st
Quick st
Sidsley
Provence st
Baldwin ter
Lloyd Baker
Amwell st
Myddelton pas
Metropolitan Water Board
Hardwick
Owen st
Owen's row
Nelson pl
Rochter st
Coombs street
Baldwin ter
Margery st
Finsbury Town Hall
Sadlers Wells Theatre
Friend st
Oakley cres
Hemington st
City Garden row
Wenlock Basin
Attneave st
Wilmington sq
Gloucester
Green Lloyds ter
Wynyatt st
Spencer st
Hall st
Haverstock st
Graham st
City Road Basin
Wharf road
Mount Pleasant Post Office
Exmouth mkt
Myddelton st
Rawstone st
Pickard st
Moreland st
Wenlock rd
Sturt st
Farringdon road
Clerkenwell avenue
Pine st
Northampton rd
Whiskin st
Meredith st
Wycliff
Northampton
Ash st
Sebastian st
St John street
City road
Micawber st
Shepherdess wlk
Rosebery
WC
Clerkenwell
Bowling Grn la
Corporation row
Northampton Sq
Northampton College
Goswell road
St Barnabas Church
Dingle rd
Taplow st
Windsor ter
Whitefriar ter
Murray
Eyre st hill
Garner st
Ray st
Pear Tree ct
Sans wlk
Aydon st
Percival st
Malta st
Lever st
PO
Central street
Hull
Underwood st
Nile st
Clerkenwell road
Vine st
Haywards pl
Compton st
Cyrus st
Seward st
Lever st
Paton st
Shepherdess pl
Hatton wall
br
Clerkenwell Aylesbury grn
Dallington st
Pear tree st
Norman
Morris row
Albemarle way
Northburgh st
Bastwick st
Radnor st
Cayton st
Moorfields PO
Peerless st
Hospital
Britannia st
Farringdon Rd Station
Broad yd st
Britton st
Gt Sutton st
Gee st
Mitchell row
Lizard st
Bath
Baldwin st
Cross st
Turnmill st
Briset st
Albion pl
St Johns la
PO
Helmet row
St Lukes Church
Crescent row
Baltic st
Old street
East
Cowcross
The Charterhouse
St Bartholomews Medical School
Garrett st

Continued on map 1

1   2   3   4   5   6

St Thomas's way
Cotcourt rd
Racton rd
Anselm rd
ton rd
Hild
yard rd
Princess Beatrice Hos
Coleherne m
Red
cliffe
Coleherne ter
Cole
Re
The Boltons

Mirabel rd
Fabian rd
Haldane rd
Hartismere rd
Tournay rd
Epirus rd
Shorrolds rd
Armadale rd
Knivett rd
Halford rd
Tamworth
Ongar
Mickletwaite rd
Seagrave rd
Westgate ter
cliffe
sq
Redcliffe ms
Harcourt ter
The Little Boltons

Dawes road
Bishops rd
Eustace rd
Walham gro
field rd
Finborough rd
Cath
cart rd
Redcliffe gardens
Tregunter rd
Cathcart rd

Burnthwaite rd
Darlan rd
Jordan pl
Vanston pl
Farm la
PO
Brompton Cemetery
cett st
Faw
Hollywood rd
Seymour wlk
Redcliffe rd
Gilston rd
Pri
The Boltons

Elmstone rd
Marbledown rd
Shottendane rd
Poulton pl
Barclay rd
Aigon
pl
Effie rd
WC
Fulham Broadway Station
Stamford Bridge
Chelsea
Football Ground
Chapel
Sitting pl
Burial gd
Redcliffe pl
PO
St Stephens Hospital
Limerston st
Cam

Novello st
Campana rd
Basuto rd
Crondace rd
Eel Brook Common
Favart rd
Effie rd
Musgrave cres
Kemp son rd
Blake gdns
Tyrawley rd
Moore pk rd
Water
ford rd
Britannia
rd
Maxwell
Rumbold
Holmead
Wandon
Kings road
Hortensia rd
Gunter gro
Fernshaw rd
Edith gro
Edith ter
Slaidburn
Langton
Netherton
St Marks Coll
Gertrude st
Shalcomb
Hobury
Lamont rd
WC
Ann la
Riley
rd
Apollo
pl

Quarrendon rd
Chipstead st
Perrymead st
Rycroft st
Bowerdean st
Studdridge st
Harwood road
Stokenchurch st
Avalon rd
Harwood ter
Edith row
Soth
ann
Michael rd
Meek st
Lots
rd
Telcott rd
Upcerne rd
Uverdale rd
Burnaby st
ema rd
Ashurnham rd
Stadium st
Cremorne rd
Lots rd
Edith gro

Clancarty rd
Beltran rd
Ashcombe st
Marlborough st
Friston st
Woolneigh st
Wandsworth bridge road
Cresford
rd
Bovingdon rd
Sandilands rd
Pearscroft rd
Langford rd
Broughton rd
Stephendale rd
Bagley's la
Ful mead rd
Imperial rd
Elswick st
Embden st
Dock

De Morgan rd
Hamble st
Althea st
Edenvale rd
Kilkie st
Quarrin st
Townmead rd
Fulham Power Station
Snow bury rd
Canbury rd
Hazlebury rd
Oakbury rd
Rosebury rd
Gilsted rd
Furness
Glenrosa st
Lindrop st
Byam st
Tilbury st
Elbe st
River Thames
St Marks Church
PO
Battersea Chu
Morga

Ismailia rd
Kelmscott
Vicarage cres
Westbridge rd
Granfield st
Parkham st
Studley
Sisley
Condray st
Bolingbroke wlk
Winstead st
Randall st
Hyd
Westb

York road
Mendip rd
Chatfield rd
Steel works rd
York pl
Vicarage cres
Lombard rd
Harroway
Holman rd
Gwynne rd
Yelverton rd
Badric st
Tottenridge
Orville rd
Battersea High st
Trott st
Orbel st
Henning
Edna st
Shuttleworth rd
Inworth st
Octavia st
Baltern st
Stanmer st
Banbury
Coles town st
Surrey la
Orbel st
Ursula st
Goulden st
Bullen st
Bridge l a
Simpson st
Winders rd
Home rd
PO
Abercrombie st
Frere
Atten
Atbin st
Row ena cres
PO

Petergate
Usk rd
Wynter st
Hibb
st
Hope st
Mendip rd
Holgate av
Benham
Stock wood
Wayland
Darien rd
Plough rd
Winstanley rd
Knox st
Currie st
Meyrick rd
Darien rd
Lavender rd
Ingrave st
Mantua st
Kambala rd
Musjid rd
Heaver rd
Kambala rd
Patience rd
Khyber rd
Candahar rd
Afghan rd
Kerrison rd
Falcon rd
Cabul
Wayford st
Shifting ton st
Stein
forth
Latchmere rd
Creek
Lavender
rd
Bar
Bentfield
Vernon st
Wye st
Falcon rd

Miles

Metres   500   1000   1500

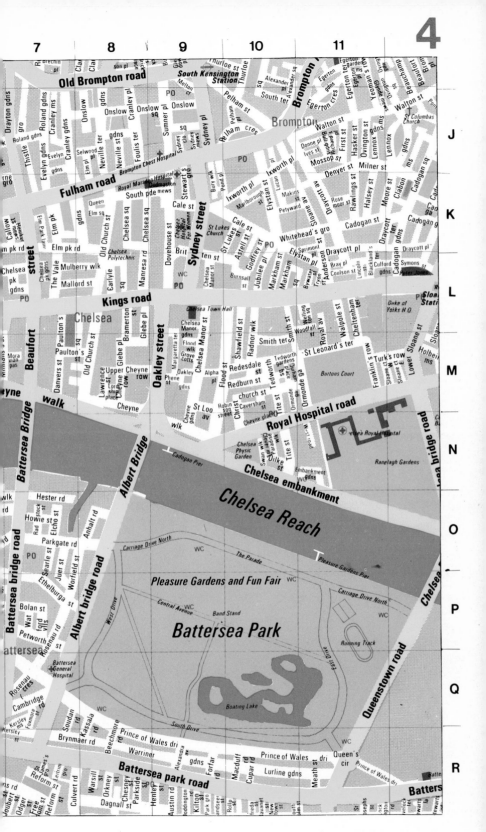

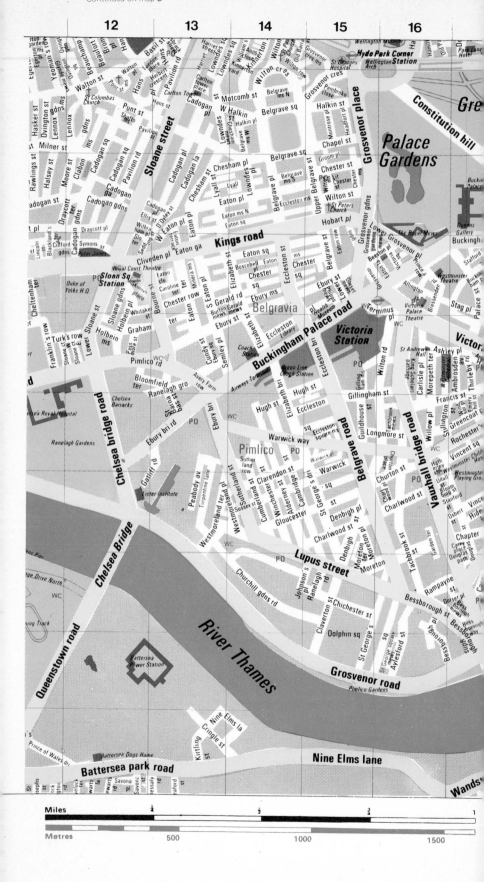

12   **13**   **14**   **15**   **16**

Wellington Museum
Hyde Park Corner Station
Hyde Park Corner
Wellington Arch
St Georges Hospital

Constitution hill

Gre

Palace Gardens

Buckingham Palace

Queens Gallery

Buckingham

Harriet st
Harriet walk
Wilton cres
Wilton pl
Grosvenor cres
Old Barr
Pembroke close

William s
Anniston
mews

Lowndes sq
Kinnerton
Yard

Motcomb st
Halkin st
Grosvenor gdns

Belgrave
ms N

Carlton
tower place
Carlton Towers

W Halkin
st
Halkin st
Halkin pl

Montrose pl
Headfort pl

Belgrave sq

St Columbas Church

Chapel st

Groom pl

The Royal Mews

Stafford

Walton st
Hans pl

Cadogan
pl

Belgrave sq

Belgrave
ms W

Chester st

Beeston pl

Westminster Theatre

Hans st
Shafto
Punt st

Chesham pl
Chesham st
Lyall st

Belgrave
ms S

Chester st

W Eaton pl
St Peters Church

Allington

Pavilion st

Cadogan
la

Lyall

Lowndes
st

Wilton st

Grosvenor place

Victoria Palace Theatre

Sloane street

Cadogan sq

Cadogan
gdns

Chesham st

Eaton pl

Belgrave
ms

Lower Grosvenor pl

Stag pl

Milner st

Cadogan
gdns

Draycott
ter gdns

Eaton ms N
Eaton sq

Upper Belgrave st
Wilton st

Hobart pl

Cheltenham
terrace

Victor

Rawlings st

Hasker st
Ovington st
Lennox gdns
Lennox

Cadogan
gdns

Ellis st
D Oyley st

Eaton ms S

Eaton
row

Terminus
pl

Halsey st
Moore st
Clabon
ms

Cadogan st

Draycott pl

Wilbraham pl
Seddings ter

W Eaton pl
Eaton ter

Kings road

Eaton
cio

Eaton sq
Chester
sq

Boscobel pl
Chester
ms

Chester row

Eccleston
st

Belgrave
pl

Health Museum

Victoria
Palace
Theatre

St Andrews
Hall

Franklin s row
BlackLand's
Lincoln
gdns

Symons st

Peter Jones

Cliveden pl
Eaton ga

Eaton sq

Chester
sq

Chester

Belgravia

Ebury
ms

Ashley pl

Cadogan
pl

Draycott pl

Royal Court Theatre

Sloane Sq Station

Sloane gdns
Holbein pl
Bourne st

Caroline ter
Chester row
Chester row

S Gerald rd

Minera ms

Ebury ms

Ebury st

Lower
Belgrave st

Eaton
la

Eccleston
bri

Carlisle pl
Morepeth ter

Thirleby rd

Duke of
Yorks H.Q

S Eaton pl

Burton Gerald
mews

Elizabeth st

Eccleston
st

PO

St Andrews
Hall

Ambrosden

Chelsea
ter

Holbein
ms

Graham

ter

Semley pl
Cundy st
Elizabeth st

Eccleston
bri

Buckingham Palace road

Wilton rd

Gillingham
pl

WC

Willow pl
Stillington
Emery
Stanford

Francis st

Turk's row
Sloane ct
Lower Sloane st

Pimlico rd

Avery Farm
row

Coach
Station

Green Line
Coach Station

Victoria Station

St Andrews
Hall

Greencoat pl

Rochester

Pimlico rd

Bloomfield
ter

Ranelagh gro

Barna
bas st

Hugh st
Eccleston

Gillingham st

Vincent st

Westmister
Playing Gro

Chelsea bridge road

Chelsea
Barracks

Ebury bri

Hugh st
Elizabeth st

Longmore st

Belgrave road

Churton st

Vincent sq

Ebury bri rd

PO

WC

Hugh st

Eccleston
square

Warwick way

Ecceston
square

PO

Warwick
sq

Guildhouse

Chapter

Chelsea Royal Hospital

Ranelagh Gardens

Pimlico

Suther
land
row

Clarendon
st

Winchester
st

Alderney
st

Warwick
sq

St George's
dri

PO

Oshert
Rampayne

Garden ter

Gatliff rd

Lister institute

Peabody av
Turpentine lane

Westmoreland ter

Sutherland
st

Cumberland st

Cambridge
st

Denbigh pl

Charlwood st

Tachbrook st

Lupus street

Moreton st

WC

Churchill gdns rd

Gloucester
st

Charlwood st
Denbigh

Moreton pl

Moreton

Bessborough st

Lupus street

PO

Chelsea Bridge

Johnson s
Ranelagh

Claverton
st

Chichester st

St George s
sq

Aylesford st

Bessborough st

Bessborough

WC

Dolphin sq

Grosvenor road

Pimlico Gardens

Queenstown road

Battersea
Power Station

River Thames

Nine Elms la
Cringle st

Kirtling st

Prince of Wales dri

Battersea Dogs Home

Battersea park road

Nine Elms lane

Wands

Miles   ¼   ½   ¾   1

Metres   500   1000   1500

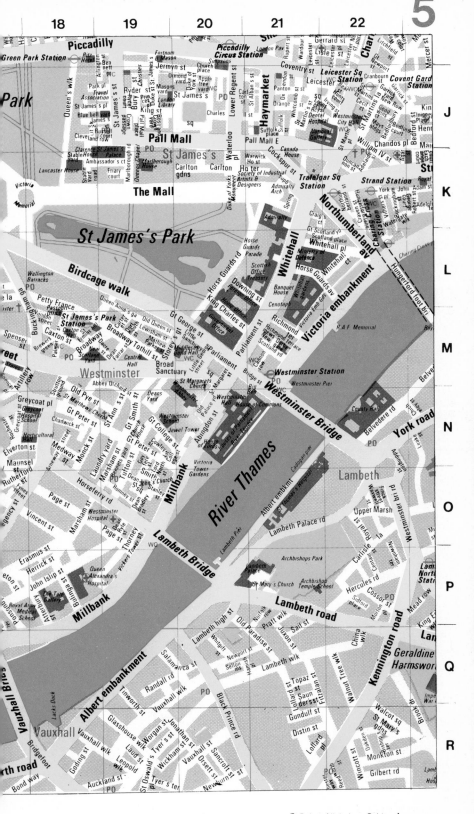

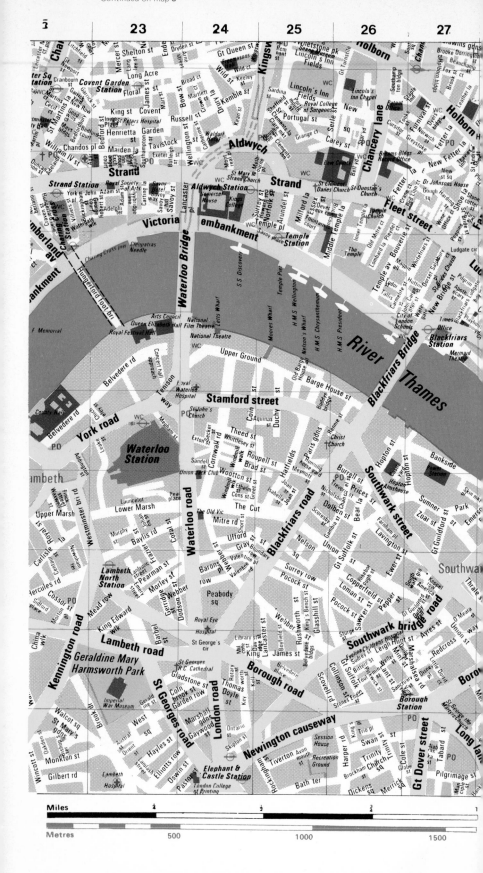

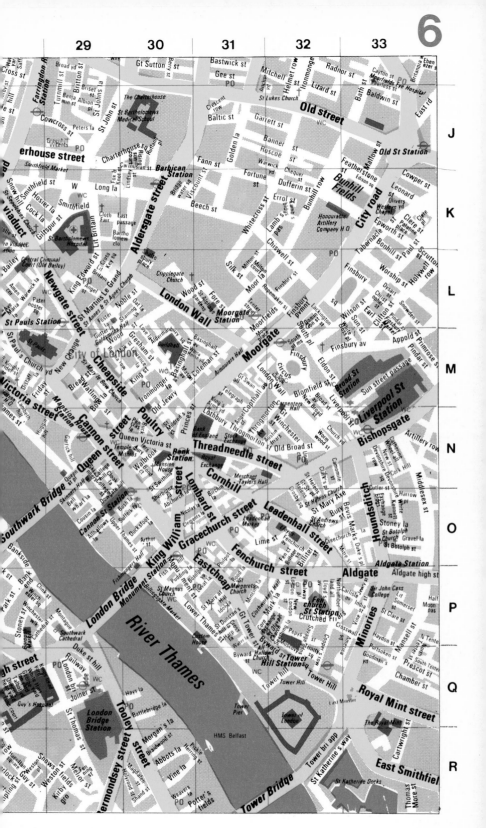

29   **30**   **31**   **32**   **33**

J

K

L

M

N

O

P

Q

R

Farringdon R Station
Cross rd
War Saff
Broad yd st
Britton st
Gt Sutton st
Benj st
PO
Bastwick st
Gee st
PO
Mitchell st
Helmet row
Ironmonger
Lizard st
Radnor st
Bath st
Britannia
Eben ezer s
Cayton st PO
Moorfields
Peerless st
Eye Hospital
East rd

Cowcross st
Turnmill st
Benja min st
Briset st
St Johns
St Bartholomews Medical School
Crescent row
Baltic st
Garrett st
St Lukes Church
Old street
WC
Baldwin st

erhouse street
Greenhill Rents
PO
Peters la
Charterhouse
Charterhouse sq
Rising sun
Carthusian st
St Bartholomews Hospital
Banner
Roscoe st
Banner st
Warwick
Golden la
Old St Station
Featherstone
Cowper st
Leonard
Edson st

Smithfield Market
Long la
Barbican Station
Fann st
Fortune st
Dufferin st
Dufferin st Bunhill row
Bunhill Fields
City road
Tabernacle st
Bonhill st
Worship st
Westers yd
Scrutton
Clere st
Paul st
Epworth st

Snow hill
Smithfield
Cock la
Gtspur st
Cloth Fair
East passage
Bartho mew clo
Beech st
Whitecross st
Lamb pass
Lamb st
Chiswell st
Honourable Artillery Company H Q
Finsbury
Wilson st
Sun st
Earl st
Clifton st
Snowden st
Holywell row

viaduct
St Sepulchres Church
Viaduct
St Bartholomews Hospital
Lt Britain
King Edward st
Silk st
Milton courts
Milton st
Ropemaker st
Finsbury sq
Finsbury av
Appold st
Primrose st
Pindar st

Bailey
Central Criminal Court (Old Bailey)
St Martins Le Grand
Noble st
Wood st
Fore st
Moorgate Station
Moorfields
Telegraph
South pl
Eldon st
Broad St Station
Sun street passage
Liverpool St Station
Bishopsgate

Newgate street
Angel st
St Anne & St Agnes Chapel
Gutter la
Aldermanbury
Basinghall st
London Wall
Blomfield WC
New Broad
Liverpool st
Artillery row

Victoria street
St Pauls Station
Paternoster sq
St Pauls
City of London
Cheapside
Poultry
Old Jewry
Gt Swan
Throgmorton
Old Broad st
Church yd

Magpie alley
Friday st
New Change
Bread st
Watling st
Queen Victoria st
Bank Station
Mansion House
Royal Exchange
Cornhill
Threadneedle street
Bank of England
Stock Exchange
Winchester
Warp wood st
Bishopsgate

Queen Victoria st
Queen street
King st
Ironmonger la
Cheapside
Wilbrook
Lombard street
Gracechurch street
Leadenhall street
St Mary Axe
Bury
Bevis Marks
Duke s st
Houndsditch
Cutler st
Harrow st
Middlesex st

Southwark Bridge
Queen street
Cannon St Station
Cannon street
King William street
Eastcheap
Fenchurch street
Lime st
Fenchurch St Station
Aldgate Station
Aldgate
Aldgate high st
Sir John Cass College
Lt Somerset st
Half Moon pas

River Thames
London Bridge
Monument Station
Lower Thames street
Custom House
Byward st
Tower Hill Station
Minories
Mansell st
Prescot st
Chamber st

Southwark Cathedral
London Bridge Station
Toolley street
Tower Pier
Tower of London
Tower Hill
Royal Mint street
The Royal Mint
Cartwright st

gh street
Duke st hill
Railway app
Bermondsey street
HMS Belfast
Tower Bridge
St Katherine way
St Katherine Docks
East Smithfield
Thomas More st

Guy's Hospital
Snaws st
Weston st
Morgan s la
Abbots la
Vine la
Weavers la
Potter's fields

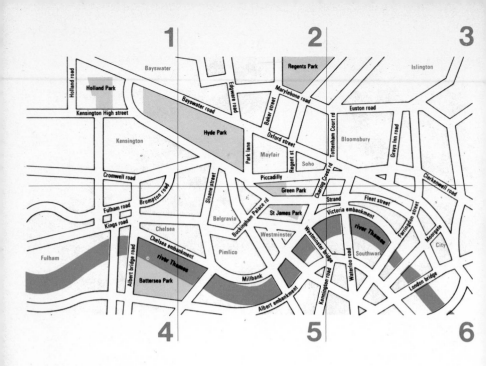

1   **2**   **3**

Bayswater — Regents Park — Islington — Holland road — Holland Park — Marylebone road — Baker street — Euston road — Kensington High street — Bayswater road — Edgware road — Tottenham Court rd — Grays Inn road — Hyde Park — Oxford street — Bloomsbury — Park lane — Kensington — Regent st — Clerkenwell road — Mayfair — Soho — Charing Cross rd — Cromwell road — Brompton road — Piccadilly — Fleet street — Farringdon street — Green Park — Strand — Moorgate — Sloane street — St James Park — Victoria embankment — City — Fulham road — Belgravia — Buckingham Palace rd — Westminster — river Thames — Kings road — Chelsea — Southwark — Albert bridge road — Chelsea embankment — Pimlico — river Thames — Westminster bridge — Kennington road — Waterloo road — London bridge — Fulham — Battersea Park — Millbank — Albert embankment

4   **5**   **6**

Street index

Abbey Orchard st SW1 5 M 19
Abbotsbury rd W14 1 B 4
Abbots la SE1 6 R 30
Abchurch la EC4 6 O 30
Abercrombie st SW11 4 R 6
Abingdon rd W8 1 E 6
Abingdon st SW1 5 N 20
Abingdon villas W8 1 E 6
Acfold rd SW6 4 M 2
Acton st WC1 3 E 28
Adam & Eve mews W8 1 E 6
Adam's row W1 2 G 17
Adam st WC2 6 K 23
Addington st SE1 5 N 22
Addison av W11 1 A 4
Addison Bri pl W14 1 E 3
Addison cres W14 1 C 3
Addison gdns W14 1 A 2
Addison rd W14 1 B 4
Addle hill EC4 6 M 28
Adelaide st WC2 5 K 22
Adeline pl WC1 3 G 23
Affleck st N1 3 E 29
Afghan rd SW11 4 R 5
Agar st WC2 5 K 22
Agdon st EC1 3 H 30
Airlie gdns W8 1 B 7
Air st W1 2 I 20
Albany st NW1 2 C 22
Albemarle st W1 2 I 19
Albemarle way EC1 3 I 29
Albert bri SW3 & SW11 4 N 8
Albert Bri rd SW11 4 P 7
Albert embkmt SE1 &
SE11 5 O 21
Albert pl W8 1 F 8
Albert st NW1 3 A 24
Albion clo W2 2 D 14
Albion mews W2 2 D 15
Albion pl EC1 6 J 29
Albion st W2 2 D 15
Aldenham st NW1 3 B 25
Aldermanbury sq EC2 6 M 30
Alderney st SW1 5 O 14
Aldersgate st EC1 6 K 30
Aldford st W1 2 G 16
Aldgate EC3 6 P 33
Aldgate High st EC3 6 P 33
Aldwych WC2 6 J 24

Alexander pl SW7 1 I 10
Alexander sq SW7 1 I 10
Alexandra av SW11 4 R 9
Alfreda st SW11 4 R 10
Alfred mews WC1 3 F 23
Alfred pl WC1 3 F 23
Allen st W8 1 E 6
Allhallows la EC4 6 O 29
Allingham st N1 3 F 33
Allington st SW1 5 L 16
All Saints st N1 3 C 29
Allsop pl NW1 2 B 19
Almeida st N1 3 D 33
Alpha pl SW3 4 M 9
Althea st SW6 4 P 1
Ambassador's ct SW1 5 K 18
Ambrosden av SW1 5 M 17
Amen cnr EC4 6 L 28
America sq EC3 6 Q 33
America st SE1 6 P 27
Ampton st WC1 3 F 27
Amwell st EC1 3 F 29
Anchor yd EC1 3 I 32
Anderson st SW3 4 L 11
Angel ct EC2 6 N 31
Angel mews N1 3 F 31
Angel st EC1 6 L 29
Anhalt rd SW11 4 O 8
Anley rd W14 1 A 1
Ann la SW10 4 M 6
Anns clo SW1 2 I 14
Ansdell st W8 1 E 7
Ansdell ter W8 1 E 7
Anselm rd SW6 1 I 2
Apollo pl SW10 4 M 6
Apothecary st EC4 6 L 27
Applegarth rd W14 1 B 1
Apple Tree yd SW1 5 J 20
Appold st EC2 6 M 33
Aquinas st SE1 6 N 25
Archel rd W14 1 H 1
Archer st W1 2 I 21
Argon mews SW6 4 K 2
Argyle sq WC1 3 E 27
Argyle st WC1 3 E 27
Argyll rd W8 1 D 6
Argyll st W1 2 G 20
Arlington rd NW1 3 A 24
Arlington st SW1 2 I 19
Arlington way EC1 3 F 30
Armadale rd SW6 4 J 2
Arne st WC2 3 I 24
Arneway st SW1 5 N 18

Arthur st EC4 6 O 30
Artillery la E1 6 N 33
Artillery row SW1 5 M 17
Artizan st E1 6 O 33
Arundel pl N1 3 A 33
Arundel sq N7 3 A 33
Arundel st WC2 6 K 25
Ashbridge st NW8 2 A 16
Ashburn gdns SW7 1 H 7
Ashburnham rd SW10 4 M 5
Ashburn mews SW5 1 H 7
Ashburn pl SW7 1 H 7
Ashby st EC1 3 H 31
Ashcombe st SW6 4 O 1
Ashley pl SW1 5 M 16
Ash Mill st NW1 2 A 16
Astell st SW3 4 K 10
Astwood mews SW5 1 H 7
Atherstone mews SW7 1 H 8
Atherton st SW11 4 R 6
Atterbury st SW1 5 P 18
Attneave st WC1 3 G 28
Aubrey rd W8 1 B 6
Aubrey wlk W8 1 B 6
Auckland st SE11 5 R 19
Audley sq W1 2 H 17
Augustine rd W14 1 B 1
Augustus st NW1 3 B 23
Auriol rd W14 1 E 1
Austinfriars EC2 6 N 31
Austin rd SW11 4 R 9
Austral st SE11 6 R 23
Avalon rd SW6 4 M 2
Ave Maria la EC4 6 L 28
Avery Farm row SW1 5 M 13
Avery row W1 2 G 19
Avonmore rd W14 1 E 3
Avonmouth st SE1 6 R 25
Aybrook st W1 2 D 19
Aylesbury st EC1 3 I 29
Aylesford st SW1 5 Q 16
Aynhoe rd W14 1 C 1
Ayres st SE1 6 Q 27

Back hill EC1 3 H 28
Baden pl SE1 6 R 28
Badric rd SW11 4 Q 4
Bagley's la SW6 4 N 2
Bainbridge st WC1 3 H 23
Bakers al SE1 6 R 30
Bakers row EC1 3 H 28
Baker st W1 & NW1 2 D 18
Balcombe st NW1 2 A 18

Balderton st W1	2	F	18
Baldwin pl EC1	3	I	27
Baldwins gdns EC1	3	I	27
Baldwin st EC1	6	J	33
Baldwin ter N1	3	G	33
Balfern st SW11	4	Q	6
Balfe st N1	3	D	28
Balfour pl W1	2	G	17
Baltic st EC1	6	J	31
Banbury st SW11	4	Q	6
Bank end SE1	6	P	28
Bankside SE1	6	N	27
Banner st EC1	6	J	31
Barbel st SE1	6	Q	23
Barclay rd SW6	4	K	1
Barford st N1	3	D	32
Bark pl W2	1	A	10
Barker st SW10	4	K	5
Barkston gdns SW5	1	H	5
Barmore st SW11	4	Q	3
Barnby st NW1	3	B	24
Barnsbury gro N7	3	A	32
Barnsbury pk N1	3	B	33
Barnsbury rd N1	3	D	31
Barnsbury sq N1	3	B	32
Barnsbury st N1	3	C	33
Barnsbury ter N1	3	B	32
Baron's Ct rd W14	1	F	1
Barons pl SE1	6	P	24
Baron st N1	3	E	30
Barrett st W1	2	E	18
Barter st WC1	3	H	24
Bartholomew clo EC1	6	K	29
Barton rd W14	1	F	1
Basil st SW3	2	I	13
Basinghall av EC2	6	M	31
Basinghall st EC2	6	M	30
Bastwick st EC1	3	I	31
Basuto rd SW6	4	L	1
Batchelor st N1	3	E	31
Bateman st W1	2	H	22
Batemans bldgs W1	2	H	22
Bath st EC1	6	J	33
Bath ter SE1	6	R	25
Bathurst mews W2	2	C	13
Bathurst st W2	2	C	13
Battersea bri SW3 & SW11	4	N	7
Battersea Bri rd SW11	4	P	7
Battersea Church rd SW11	4	O	6
Battersea High st SW11	4	P	5
Battersea Pk rd SW8 & SW11	4	R	8
Battishill st N1	3	D	33
Battlebridge la SE1	6	Q	30
Battle Bri rd NW1	3	C	27
Bayham pl NW1	3	A	25
Bayham st NW1	3	A	25
Bayley st WC1	3	G	23
Baylis rd SE1	6	O	23
Bayswater rd W2	1	B	10
Beak st W1	2	H	20
Bear all EC4	6	K	28
Bear gdns SE1	6	O	28
Bear la SE1	6	O	26
Bear st WC2	5	J	22
Beauchamp pl SW3	2	I	12
Beauchamp st EC1	3	I	27
Beaufort gdns SW3	2	I	12
Beaufort st SW3	4	M	7
Beaumont av W14	1	F	2
Beaumont cres W14	1	G	2
Beamont pl WC1	3	D	23
Beaumont st W1	2	D	19
Bedford av WC1	3	G	23
Bedfordbury WC2	5	J	22
Bedford ct WC2	5	J	22
Bedford gdns W8	1	C	7
Bedford pl WC1	3	G	24
Bedford row WC1	3	I	26
Bedford sq WC1	3	G	23
Bedford st WC2	6	J	23
Bedford way WC1	3	F	24
Beechmore rd SW11	4	R	8
Beech st EC1	6	K	31
Beeston pl SW1	5	L	15
Belgrave mews N SW1	5	J	14
Belgrave mews S SW1	5	K	14
Belgrave mews W SW1	5	J	14
Belgrave pl SW1	5	K	14
Belgrave rd SW1	5	N	15
Belgrave sq SW1	5	J	14
Belgrave st SW1	3	D	27
Belgrave yd SW1	5	L	15
Belitha villas N1	3	B	32
Bell st NW1	2	A	16
Bell yd WC2	6	K	26
Bellwharf la EC4	6	O	29
Beltran rd SW6	4	N	1
Belvedere bldgs SE1	6	Q	25
Belvedere pl SE1	6	Q	25
Belvedere rd SE1	5	N	22
Benfield st SW11	4	R	3
Benham st SW11	4	R	2
Bennett st SW1	2	I	19
Bennetts yd SW1	5	O	19
Benjamin st EC1	6	J	29
Bentinck st W1	2	E	19
Berkeley mews W1	2	D	17
Berkeley sq W1	2	H	18
Berkeley st W1	2	I	18
Bermondsey st SE1	6	R	29
Bernard st WC1	3	F	25
Berners mews W1	2	G	22
Berners rd N1	3	E	32
Berners st W1	2	G	22
Berry pl EC1	3	H	31
Berry st EC1	3	I	30
Berwick st W1	2	H	21
Bessborough gdns SW1	5	P	17
Bessborough mews SW1	5	P	17
Bessborough pl SW1	5	P	16
Bessborough st SW1	5	P	16
Bessborough way SW1	5	P	17
Betterton st WC2	3	I	23
Bevin way WC1	3	E	29
Bevis marks EC3	6	O	33
Bewdley st N1	3	B	33
Bickenhall st W1	2	B	18
Bidborough st WC1	3	D	26
Billing pl SW10	4	K	4
Billing rd SW10	4	K	4
Billiter sq EC3	6	O	32
Billiter st EC3	6	O	32
Bina gdns SW5	1	I	7
Bingfield st N1	3	B	30
Bingham pl W1	2	C	19
Binney st W1	2	F	18
Birchin la EC3	6	O	31
Birdcage walk SW1	5	L	18
Bird st W1	2	F	18
Birkenhead st WC1	3	D	27
Bishop King's rd W14	1	D	2
Bishop's Bri rd W2	2	A	12
Bishopsgate EC2	6	N	33
Bishops rd SW6	4	J	1
Bishop's terr SE11	5	R	22
Bittern st SE1	6	Q	26
Blackburnes mews W1	2	F	17
Blackfriars bri EC4	6	M	26
Blackfriars la EC4	6	L	27
Blackfriars rd SE1	6	O	25
Blackland's ter SW3	4	L	11
Black Prince rd SE11	5	Q	20
Blake gdns SW6	4	L	2
Blandford st W1	2	D	18
Blithfield st W8	1	F	6
Blomfield st EC2	6	M	32
Bloomburg st SW1	5	O	17
Bloomfield ter SW1	5	M	12
Bloomsbury pl WC1	3	H	25
Bloomsbury sq WC1	3	H	24
Bloomsbury st WC1	3	G	23
Bloomsbury way WC1	3	H	24
Blue bell yd SW1	5	J	19
Blythe rd W14	1	A	1
Boadicea st N1	3	C	29
Boddys bri SE1	6	N	26
Bolan st SW11	4	P	7
Boldero st NW8	2	A	17
Bolingbroke rd W14	1	B	1
Bolingbroke wlk SW11	4	O	6
Bolsover st W1	2	E	21
Bolton gdns SW5	1	H	5
Boltons the SW10	4	J	6
Bolton st W1	2	I	18
Bond ct EC4	6	N	30
Bond way SW8	5	R	17
Bonhill st EC2	6	L	33
Borough High st SE1	6	Q	27
Borough rd SE1	6	Q	25
Boscobell pl SW1	5	L	14
Boston pl NW1	2	A	17
Boswell ct WC1	3	H	25
Boswell st WC1	3	H	25
Botolph la EC3	6	P	31
Boundary row SE1	6	O	25
Bourchier st W1	2	I	22
Bourdon st W1	2	G	18
Bourne st SW1	5	L	13
Bouverie pl W2	2	B	14
Bouverie st EC4	6	L	26
Bovingdon rd SW6	4	M	2
Bowerdean st SW6	4	N	1
Bow la EC4	6	M	29
Bowling Grn la EC1	3	H	29
Bowling Grn pl SE1	6	R	28
Bow st WC2	3	J	24
Boxworth gro N1	3	C	31
Boyfield st SE1	6	Q	25
Boyle st W1	2	H	19
Boyne Ter mews W11	1	A	6
Boyton pl NW1	2	A	16
Brad st SE1	6	N	24
Braidwood st SE1	6	R	30
Bramber rd W14	1	H	1
Bramerton st SW3	4	L	8
Bramham gdns SW6	1	H	5
Bray pl SW3	4	L	11
Bread st EC4	6	M	29
Breams bldgs EC4	6	K	26
Brechin pl SW7	1	I	7
Bremner rd SW7	1	G	10
Brendon st W1	2	C	16
Bressenden pl SW1	5	L	16
Brewer st W1	2	I	21
Brewers grn SW1	5	M	18
Brewhouse yd EC1	3	I	30
Brick ct WC2	6	K	25
Brick st W1	2	I	17
Bride st N7	3	A	33
Bridford mews W1	2	D	21
Bridgefoot SE11	5	R	18
Bridge la SW11	4	Q	6
Bridge st SW1	5	M	21
Bridgewater sq EC1	6	K	30
Bridgeway st NW1	3	B	25
Bridle la W1	2	H	21
Briset st EC1	6	J	29
Britannia rd SW6	4	L	2
Britannia st WC1	3	E	28
Britannia wlk N1	3	I	33
Britten st SW3	4	K	9
Britton st EC1	3	J	29
Broad ct WC2	6	J	24
Broadley st NW8	2	A	16
Broadley ter NW1	2	A	17
Broad sanctuary SW1	5	M	19
Broad St av EC2	6	M	32
Broad wlk NW1	2	B	21
Broadwall SE1	6	N	25
Broadway SW1	5	M	18
Broadwick st W1	2	H	21
Broad yd EC1	3	I	29
Brockham st SE1	6	R	26
Bromfield st N1	3	E	31
Brompton pl SW3	2	I	12
Brompton rd SW1 & SW3	1	I	11
Brompton sq SW3	1	I	11
Brook dr SE11	5	R	23
Brooke ct EC1	3	I	27
Brook grn W6	1	C	1
Brook mews north W2	2	B	12
Brooksby st N1	3	B	33
Brook's mews W1	2	G	18
Brook st W1	2	G	18
Brook st W2	2	C	13
Broughton rd SW6	4	O	1
Brownhart gdns W1	2	F	18
Brownlow mews WC1	3	G	27
Brownlow st WC1	3	I	26
Brown st W1	2	C	16
Brunswick gdns W8	1	C	8
Brunswick sq WC1	3	F	26
Bruton la W1	2	H	18
Bruton pl W1	2	H	18
Bruton st W1	2	H	18
Bryanston mews W1	2	C	17
Bryanston mews west W1	2	C	17
Bryanston pl W1	2	C	17
Bryanston sq W1	2	C	17
Bryanston st W1	2	E	16
Brynmaer rd SW11	4	R	7
Buckingham ga SW1	5	L	17
Buckingham Pal rd SW1	5	M	14
Buckingham pl SW1	5	L	17
Buckingham st WC2	5	K	22
Bucklersbury EC4	6	N	30
Bucknall st WC2	3	H	23
Bulinga st SW1	5	P	18
Bullen st SW11	4	Q	5
Bull gdns SW3	4	J	11
Bull Inn ct WC2	6	K	23
Bulmer mews W11	1	A	8
Bulstrode st W1	2	E	19
Bunhill row EC1	6	K	32
Burgh st N1	3	F	33
Burleigh st WC2	6	K	23
Burlington ar W1	2	I	19
Burlington gdns W1	2	I	19
Burlington st W1	2	H	19
Burnaby st SW10	4	M	4
Burne st NW1	2	A	16
Burnett st SE11	5	R	19
Burnsall st SW3	4	L	10
Burns rd SW11	4	R	7
Burnthwaite rd SW6	4	K	1
Burrell st SE1	6	O	26
Burton mews SW1	5	L	13

Street		Grid
Burton st WC1	3	E 25
Burwood pl W2	2	C 15
Bury pl WC1	3	H 24
Bury st EC3	6	O 33
Bury st SW1	5	J 19
Bury wlk SW3	4	K 9
Bush la EC4	6	O 30
Bute st SW7	1	I 9
Byam st SW6	4	O 2
Byng pl WC1	3	E 24
Byward st EC3	6	Q 32
Bywater st SW3	4	L 11
Cabbell st NW1	2	B 16
Cabul rd SW11	4	R 5
Cadogan gdns SW3	5	K 12
Cadogan ga SW1	5	K 12
Cadogan la SW1	5	K 13
Cadogan pl SW1	5	K 13
Cadogan sq SW1	5	J 12
Cadogan st SW3	4	K 11
Caithness rd W14	1	C 1
Caledonia st N1	3	D 28
Caledonian rd N1	3	B 30
Cale st SW3	4	K 9
Callcott st W11	1	B 7
Callow st SW3	4	K 7
Calshot st N1	3	D 29
Calthorpe st WC1	3	G 27
Calvert bldgs SE1	6	Q 28
Cambria st SW6	4	M 3
Cambridge cir WC2	2	I 22
Cambridge ga NW1	2	C 22
Cambridge pl W8	1	E 8
Cambridge rd SW11	4	Q 7
Cambridge sq W2	2	C 15
Cambridge st SW1	5	O 14
Cambridge ter NW1	2	B 22
Camden pas N1	3	E 32
Camden st NW1	3	A 25
Camden wlk N1	3	E 32
Camera pl SW10	4	L 6
Camley st NW1	3	B 27
Camomile st EC3	6	N 32
Campana rd SW6	4	L 1
Campden gro W8	1	C 7
Campden hill W8	1	C 6
Campden Hill gdns W8	1	B 7
Campden Hill rd W8	1	C 7
Campden Hill sq W8	1	A 6
Campden Ho clo W8	1	G 7
Campden st W8	1	B 7
Candahar rd SW11	4	R 5
Canning pl W8	1	F 8
Canning pl mews W8	1	F 9
Cannon row SW1	5	M 21
Cannon st EC4	6	N 29
Capper st WC1	3	E 23
Carburton st W1	2	D 22
Cardington st NW1	3	C 24
Carey pl SW1	5	O 17
Carey st WC2	6	J 26
Carlisle av EC3	6	P 33
Carlisle la SE1	5	P 22
Carlisle pl SW1	5	M 16
Carlisle st W1	2	H 22
Carlos pl W1	2	G 18
Carlton gdns SW1	5	K 20
Carlton Ho ter SW1	5	K 20
Carlton Tower pl SW1	5	J 13
Carlton st SW1	5	J 21
Carlyle sq SW3	4	L 8
Carmelite st EC4	6	L 26
Carnaby st W1	2	H 20
Carnegie st N1	3	C 30
Carnoustie st N1	3	B 30
Caroline pl W2	1	B 10
Caroline ter SW1	5	L 13
Carteret st SW1	5	M 19
Carter la EC4	6	M 28
Carthusian st EC1	6	J 30
Carting la WC2	6	K 23
Cartwright gdns WC1	3	E 25
Castle la SW1	5	L 17
Castle yd SE1	6	N 26
Castlereagh st W1	2	C 16
Castletown rd W14	1	F 1
Cathcart rd SW10	4	J 5
Cathedral st SE1	6	P 29
Catherine pl SW1	5	L 17
Catherine st WC2	6	J 24
Catherine Wheel all E1	6	N 33
Cato st W1	2	C 16
Causton st SW1	5	P 17
Cavendish pl W1	2	F 20
Cavendish sq W1	2	F 20
Caversham st SW3	4	M 10
Cave st N1	3	D 30
Caxton st SW1	5	M 18
Cayton st EC1	3	I 33
Cecil ct WC2	5	J 22
Cedarne rd SW6	4	L 2
Centaur st SE1	5	P 22
Central av SW11	4	P 9
Central st EC1	3	I 31
Ceylon rd W14	1	C 2
Chadwell st EC1	3	F 30
Chadwick st SW1	5	N 18
Chagford st NW1	2	A 18
Challoner st W14	1	G 1
Chalton st NW1	3	D 25
Chamber st E1	6	Q 33
Chancel st SE1	6	O 26
Chancery la WC2	6	J 26
Chandos pl WC2	5	J 22
Chandos st W1	2	E 20
Chantry st N1	3	F 33
Chapel mkt N1	3	E 30
Chapel pl W1	2	F 19
Chapel side W2	1	A 10
Chapel st NW1	2	B 16
Chapel st SW1	5	J 15
Chapter st SW1	5	O 17
Charecroft way W12	1	A 2
Charing Cross rd WC2	2	I 22
Charles II st SW1	5	J 20
Charles st W1	2	H 17
Charleville rd W14	1	G 1
Charlotte pl W1	2	F 22
Charlotte st W1	2	F 22
Charlotte ter N1	3	D 30
Charlton pl N1	3	E 32
Charlwood pl SW1	5	O 16
Charlwood st SW1	5	O 16
Charrington st NW1	3	B 26
Charterhouse mews EC1	6	J 30
Charterhouse sq EC1	6	J 30
Charterhouse st EC1	6	J 28
Chatfield rd SW11	4	R 2
Cheapside EC2	6	M 29
Chelsea bri SW1	5	P 12
Chelsea bri rd SW1	5	N 12
Chelsea embkmt SW3	4	N 10
Chelsea Manor gdns SW3	4	L 9
Chelsea Manor st SW3	4	M 9
Chelsea Pk gdns SW3	4	L 7
Chelsea sq SW3	4	K 8
Cheltenham ter SW3	4	L 11
Cheney rd NW1	3	D 27
Chenies mews WC1	3	E 23
Chenies st WC1	3	F 23
Cheniston gdns W8	1	E 7
Chepstow pl W2	1	A 9
Chequer st EC1	6	K 32
Chesham mews SW1	5	J 14
Chesham pl SW1	5	K 13
Chesham st SW1	5	K 13
Chesney st SW11	4	R 8
Chesson rd W14	1	H 1
Chesterfield gdns W1	2	H 17
Chesterfield hill W1	2	H 17
Chesterfield st W1	2	H 17
Chester ga NW1	2	B 22
Chester mews SW1	5	K 15
Chester rd NW1	2	A 21
Chester row SW1	5	L 13
Chester ter NW1	2	B 22
Chester Ter mews NW1	2	B 22
Chester sq SW1	5	L 14
Chester st SW1	5	K 15
Chester way SE11	5	R 21
Chestnut clo SW6	1	I 1
Cheval pl SW7	2	I 12
Cheyne gdns SW3	4	M 9
Cheyne pl SW3	4	N 10
Cheyne row SW3	4	M 8
Cheyne wlk SW3 & SW10	4	M 8
Chicheley st SE1	6	N 23
Chichester st SW1	5	P 15
Childs pl SW5	1	G 5
Childs st SW5	1	G 5
Chiltern st W1	2	D 18
Chilworth mews W2	2	B 13
Chilworth st W2	2	B 13
China wlk SE11	5	Q 22
Chipstead st SW6	4	M 1
Chiswell st EC1	6	L 32
Chitty st W1	2	E 22
Christchurch st SW3	4	M 10
Christopher st EC2	6	L 33
Church clo W8	1	D 8
Churchill Gdns rd SW1	5	P 14
Church pl SW1	5	J 20
Church st W2	2	A 15
Churchway NW1	3	D 25
Church yd EC2	6	N 32
Churton pl SW1	5	N 16
Churton st SW1	5	N 16
Circus mews W1	2	B 17
Circus pl EC2	6	M 32
City Garden row N1	3	G 32
City rd EC1	6	K 33
Clabon mews SW1	5	K 12
Clancarty rd SW6	4	N 1
Clanricarde gdns W2	1	B 9
Clare mkt WC2	6	J 25
Claremont clo N1	3	F 30
Claremont sq N1	3	E 30
Clarence gdns NW1	3	B 23
Clarence ga NW1	2	A 19
Clarence pas NW1	3	C 27
Clarence Ter mews NW1	2	A 19
Clarendon pl W2	2	D 14
Clarendon rd W11	1	A 5
Clarendon st SW1	5	O 14
Clareville gro SW7	1	I 8
Clareville st SW7	1	I 8
Clarges mews W1	2	H 18
Clarges st W1	2	I 18
Clark's pl EC2	6	N 32
Claverton st SW1	5	P 15
Clay st W1	2	C 18
Clem Attlee cl SW6	1	I 1
Clements la EC3	6	O 30
Clere pl EC2	6	K 33
Clere st EC2	6	K 33
Clerkenwell clo EC1	3	I 29
Clerkenwell grn EC1	3	I 29
Clerkenwell rd EC1	3	I 28
Cleveland gdns W2	2	A 12
Cleveland row SW1	5	J 19
Cleveland sq W2	2	B 12
Cleveland st W1	2	E 22
Cleveland ter W2	2	A 12
Clifford st W1	2	H 19
Clifton pl W2	2	C 13
Clifton st EC2	6	L 33
Clink st SE1	6	P 28
Clipstone ms W1	2	E 21
Clipstone st W1	2	E 22
Cliveden pl SW1	5	L 13
Cloak la EC4	6	N 29
Cloth fair EC1	6	K 29
Cloudesley pl N1	3	D 31
Cloudesley rd N1	3	D 31
Cloudesley sq N1	3	D 32
Cloudesley st N1	3	D 31
Clover mews SW3	4	N 10
Cluny mews SW5	1	G 3
Cobourg st NW1	3	C 24
Cock hill E1	6	N 33
Cock la EC1	6	K 28
Cockspur st SW1	5	K 21
Coin st SE1	6	N 24
Colebeck mews SW7	1	H 7
Colebrook row N1	3	F 32
Coleherne mews SW10	1	I 5
Coleherne rd SW10	1	I 5
Coleman st EC2	6	M 31
Colestown st SW11	4	Q 6
Cole st SE1	6	R 27
Colet gdns W14	1	E 1
Coley st WC1	3	G 27
College cross N1	3	C 33
College hill EC4	6	N 29
College pl NW1	3	A 26
College st EC4	6	N 29
Collier st N1	3	D 29
Collingham gdns SW5	1	H 6
Collingham pl SW5	1	G 6
Collingham rd SW5	1	H 6
Collins yd N1	3	E 33
Collinson st SE1	6	Q 26
Colnbrook st SE1	6	Q 24
Comeragh mews W14	1	F 1
Comeragh rd W14	1	F 1
Compton pl WC1	3	E 26
Compton st EC1	3	I 30
Concert hall appr	6	M 23
Condray st SW11	4	O 6
Conduit mews W2	2	B 13
Conduit pl W2	2	B 13
Conduit st W1	2	H 19
Connaught pl W2	2	D 15
Connaught sq W2	2	D 15
Connaught st W2	2	D 15
Cons st SE1	6	O 24
Constitution hill SW1	5	J 16
Conway st W1	2	D 22
Coombs st N1	3	G 32
Cooper's row EC3	6	P 32
Copenhagen st N1	3	B 29
Cope pl W8	1	E 6
Copperfield st SE1	6	P 26
Copthall av EC2	6	M 31
Coptic st WC1	3	H 24
Coral st SE1	6	O 23
Coram st WC1	3	F 25
Cork st W1	2	H 19

Cornhill EC3	6	N	31
Corn st N7	3	A	32
Cornwall gdns SW7	1	G	7
Cornwall rd SE1	6	N	24
Cornwall ter NW1	2	B	19
Corporation row EC1	3	H	29
Cosmo pl WC1	3	G	25
Cossor st SE1	5	P	22
Cosway st NW1	2	A	16
Cottage pl SW7	1	I	11
Cottesmore gdns W8	1	F	7
Coulson st SW3	4	L	11
Counter ct SE1	6	Q	28
Counter st SE1	6	Q	30
Courtfield gdns SW5	1	H	6
Courtfield rd SW7	1	H	7
Cousin la EC4	6	O	29
Covent gdn WC2	6	J	23
Coventry st W1	5	J	21
Cowcross st EC1	6	J	29
Cowley st SW1	5	N	19
Cowper st EC2	6	K	33
Craig's ct SW1	5	K	21
Cramer st W1	2	D	19
Cranbourn st WC2	5	J	22
Cranbury rd SW6	4	O	1
Crane st EC4	6	K	26
Cranleigh st NW1	3	B	25
Cranley gdns SW7	4	J	7
Cranley mews SW7	4	J	7
Cranley pl SW7	4	J	8
Craven hill W2	2	B	12
Craven Hill gdns W2	1	B	11
Craven rd W2	2	B	12
Craven st WC2	5	K	22
Craven ter W2	2	C	12
Crawford pl W1	2	B	16
Crawford st W1	2	C	17
Creechurch la EC3	6	O	33
Creed la EC4	6	M	28
Creek st SW11	4	R	3
Cremorne rd SW10	4	M	5
Crescent row EC1	6	J	31
Cresford rd SW6	4	M	2
Creswell gdns SW10	1	I	6
Cresswell pl SW10	4	J	6
Crestfield st WC1	3	D	27
Crinan st N1	3	C	28
Cringle st SW8	5	R	13
Crockford pl NW1	2	A	16
Cromer st WC1	3	E	26
Cromwell cres SW5	1	F	4
Cromwell gro W6	1	A	1
Cromwell mews SW7	1	I	9
Cromwell pl SW7	1	I	9
Cromwell rd SW7 & SW5	1	G	7
Crondace rd SW6	4	M	1
Crosby row SE1	6	R	28
Crosby sq EC3	6	O	32
Cross Key sq EC1	6	L	29
Cross la EC3	6	P	31
Cross st N1	3	D	33
Crosswall EC3	6	P	32
Crown ct WC2	6	J	24
Crown pas SW1	5	J	19
Crowndale rd NW1	3	A	25
Cruden st N1	3	E	33
Cruikshank st WC1	3	F	29
Crutched friars EC3	6	P	32
Cubitt st WC1	3	F	28
Culford gdns SW3	4	L	11
Culpeper st N1	3	E	30
Culross st W1	2	F	16
Culvert rd SW11	4	R	7
Cumberland cres W14	1	E	2
Cumberland gdns WC1	3	F	29
Cumberland mkt NW1	3	B	23
Cumberland pl NW1	3	A	23
Cumberland st SW1	5	O	14
Cumberland ter NW1	3	A	23
Cumming st N1	3	E	29
Cundy st SW1	5	M	13
Cupar rd SW11	4	R	10
Cureton st SW1	5	P	17
Currie rd SW11	4	R	3
Cursitor st EC4	6	J	26
Curzon pl W1	2	H	16
Curzon st W1	2	I	17
Cutler st E1	6	O	33
Cut the SE1	6	O	24
Cynthia st N1	3	E	29
Cyrus st EC1	3	I	30
Dacre st SW1	5	M	19
Dagmar ter N1	3	D	33
Dagnall st SW11	4	R	8
Dallington st EC1	3	I	30
Danbury st N1	3	F	32
Danvers st SW3	4	M	7
D'arblay st W1	2	H	21
Darien rd SW11	4	R	3
Darlan rd SW6	4	K	1
Dartmouth st SW1	5	M	19
Daventry st NW1	2	A	16
Davidge st SE1	6	Q	24
Davies st W1	2	G	18
Dawes rd SW6	4	J	1
Dawson pl W2	1	A	9
Dean Bradley st SW1	5	O	19
Deanery st W1	2	H	16
Dean Farrar st SW1	5	M	19
Dean Ryle st SW1	5	O	19
Deans mews W1	2	E	20
Dean Stanley st SW1	5	O	19
Dean st W1	2	H	22
Dean's yd SW1	5	N	19
De Morgan rd SW6	4	P	1
Denbigh pl SW1	5	O	15
Denbigh st SW1	5	O	15
Denman st W1	2	I	21
Denmark gro N1	3	D	31
Denmark st WC2	3	H	23
Denyer st SW3	4	J	11
Derby ga SW1	5	M	21
Dering st W1	2	F	19
Derry st W8	1	E	7
De Vere gdns W8	1	F	8
Devereux ct WC2	6	K	25
Devonia rd N1	3	F	33
Devonshire clo W1	2	D	20
Devonshire pl W1	2	C	20
Devonshire mews north W1	2	D	20
Devonshire mews south W1	2	D	20
Devonshire mews west W1	2	C	20
Devonshire row EC2	6	N	33
Devonshire Row mews W1	2	D	21
Devonshire sq EC2	6	N	33
Devonshire st W1	2	D	20
Devonshire ter W2	2	B	12
Dewey rd N1	3	D	31
Dewhurst rd W14	1	B	1
Diana pl W1	2	D	22
Dickens sq SE1	6	R	26
Dignum st N1	3	D	31
Dilke st SW3	4	N	10
Dingley pl EC1	3	I	32
Dingley rd EC1	3	I	32
Disney pl SE1	6	Q	27
Distaff la EC4	6	M	28
Distin st SE11	5	R	21
Doddington rd SW11	4	R	9
Dodson st SE1	6	P	24
Dolben st SE1	6	O	25
Dolphin sq SW1	5	Q	15
Dombey st WC1	3	H	26
Dominion st EC2	6	L	32
Donegal st N1	3	E	29
Donne pl SW3	4	J	11
Doric way NW1	3	D	25
Dorrington st EC1	3	I	27
Dorset clo NW1	2	B	18
Dorset mews SW1	5	L	15
Dorset pl SW1	5	P	17
Dorset rise EC4	6	L	27
Dorset sq NW1	2	B	18
Dorset st W1	2	C	18
Doughty mews WC1	3	G	27
Doughty st WC1	3	G	27
Douglas path SW1	5	O	17
Douglas st SW1	5	O	17
Douro pl W8	1	F	8
Dovehouse st SW3	4	K	9
Dove mews SW5	1	I	7
Dover st W1	2	I	19
Dowgate hill EC4	6	O	29
Downing st SW1	5	L	20
Down st W1	2	I	17
Dowrey st N1	3	C	32
D'Oyley st SW1	5	K	13
Draycott av SW3	4	K	11
Draycott pl SW3	4	K	11
Draycott ter SW3	4	K	11
Drayson mews W8	1	D	7
Drayton gdns SW10	4	J	7
Drummond cres NW1	3	C	25
Drummond st NW1	3	C	23
Drury la WC2	3	I	24
Duchess of Bedford's wlk W8	1	C	6
Duchess mews W1	2	E	20
Duchess st W1	2	E	20
Duchy st SE1	6	N	25
Dudmaston mews SW3	4	K	8
Dufferin st EC1	6	K	32
Dufours pl W1	2	H	21
Duke of York st SW1	5	J	20
Duke's la W8	1	D	8
Duke's pl EC3	6	O	33
Duke's rd WC1	3	D	25
Duke st SW3	4	N	10
Duke st W1	2	E	18
Duke St hill SE1	6	Q	29
Duke st St. James's SW1	5	J	19
Duncannon st WC2	5	K	22
Duncan st N1	3	F	32
Duncan ter N1	3	F	31
Dunraven st W1	2	F	16
Dunsay rd W14	1	B	1
Duplex ride SW1	2	I	14
Durham pl SW3	4	M	10
Durweston ms W1	2	C	17
Durweston st W1	2	C	17
Dyers bldgs EC1	6	J	27
Dyott st WC1	3	H	23
Dysart st EC2	6	L	33
Eagle st WC1	3	I	25
Eardley cres SW5	1	H	4
Earlham st WC2	1	I	23
Earls Ct gdns SW5	1	G	5
Earls Ct rd W8 & SW5	1	G	5
Earls Ct sq SW5	1	H	5
Earlstoke st EC1	3	G	31
Earl st EC2	6	L	33
Earls wlk W8	1	E	5
Earnshaw st WC2	3	H	23
Earsby st W14	1	E	2
Eastbourne mews W2	2	A	13
Eastbourne ter W2	2	A	13
East Carriage rd W1	2	G	16
Eastcastle st W1	2	G	21
Eastcheap EC3	6	P	31
East dri SW11	4	Q	11
East Harding st EC4	6	K	27
Eastminster EC3	6	Q	33
East pas EC1	6	K	30
Easton st WC1	3	G	29
East rd N1	6	J	33
East Smithfield E1	6	R	33
Eaton clo SW1	5	L	13
Eaton ga SW1	5	L	13
Eaton la SW1	5	L	16
Eaton mews SW1	5	K	14
Eaton mews north SW1	5	K	14
Eaton pl SW1	5	K	14
Eaton row SW1	5	L	15
Eaton sq SW1	5	K	14
Eaton ter SW1	5	L	13
Ebenezer st N1	3	I	33
Ebury bri SW1	5	N	13
Ebury Bri rd SW1	5	N	13
Ebury mews SW1	5	L	14
Ebury sq SW1	5	M	13
Ebury st SW1	5	M	13
Eccleston bri SW1	5	M	15
Eccleston mews SW1	5	K	14
Eccleston pl SW1	5	M	14
Eccleston sq SW1	5	N	15
Eccleston Sq mews SW1	5	N	15
Eccleston st SW1	5	L	14
Eck st N1	3	D	30
Edenvale rd SW6	4	P	1
Edge st W8	1	B	8
Edgware rd W2	2	D	16
Edith gro SW10	4	L	5
Edith rd W14	1	E	1
Edith row SW6	4	M	3
Edith ter SW10	4	L	5
Edith villas W14	1	F	2
Edna st SW11	4	Q	6
Edwardes sq W8	1	E	5
Edwardes Sq mews W8	1	E	5
Edwards mews W1	2	E	18
Edward sq N1	3	C	29
Effie pl SW6	4	K	2
Effie rd SW6	4	K	2
Egerton cres SW3	4	J	11
Egerton gdns SW3	1	I	11
Egerton gdn ms SW3	1	I	11
Egerton pl SW3	1	I	11
Egerton ter SW3	1	I	11
Elbe st SW6	4	O	2
Elcho st SW11	4	O	7
Eldon rd W8	1	F	7
Eldon st EC2	6	M	32
Elia st N1	3	F	32
Elizabeth bri SW1	5	M	14
Elizabeth st SW1	5	L	14
Ellington st N7	3	A	33
Elliotts row SE11	6	R	23
Ellis st SW1	5	K	12
Elm Pk gdns SW10	4	K	7
Elm Park la SW3	4	K	7
Elm Pk rd SW3	4	K	7
Elm pl SW7	4	J	8
Elms mews W2	2	C	12

Elmstone rd SW6	4	K	1
Elm st WC1	3	H	27
Elsham rd W14	1	B	3
Elswick st SW6	4	O	2
Elthiron rd SW6	4	M	1
Elvaston mews SW7	1	G	9
Elvaston pl SW7	1	G	8
Elverton st SW1	5	N	17
Ely pl EC1	6	J	28
Elystan pl SW3	4	L	11
Elystan st SW3	4	K	10
Embankment gdns SW3	4	N	11
Embden st SW6	4	M	2
Emerald st WC1	3	H	26
Emerson st SE1	6	O	27
Emery Hill st SW1	5	N	17
Emery st SE1	6	P	23
Emperors ga SW7	1	G	7
Endell st WC2	3	I	23
Endsleigh gdns WC1	3	D	24
Endsleigh pl WC1	3	E	24
Endsleigh st WC1	3	E	24
Enford st W1	2	B	17
Ennismore gdns SW7	1	H	11
Ennismore Gdns mews SW7	1	H	11
Ennismore st SW7	1	H	11
Epirus rd SW6	4	J	1
Epworth st EC2	6	K	33
Erasmus st SW1	5	P	17
Errol st EC1	6	K	32
Essex rd N1	3	E	33
Essex st WC2	6	K	25
Essex villas W8	1	D	6
Estcourt rd SW6	1	I	1
Esterbrooke st SW1	5	O	17
Ethelburga st SW11	4	P	7
Ethelm st SE1	6	O	24
Eustace rd SW6	4	J	2
Euston bldgs NW1	3	D	23
Euston rd NW1	3	D	22
Euston sq NW1	3	D	24
Euston st NW1	3	D	23
Evelyn gdns SW7	4	J	7
Everilda st N1	3	C	30
Eversholt st NW1	3	C	25
Everton bldgs NW1	3	C	23
Ewer st SE1	6	P	26
Exchange bldgs E1	6	O	33
Exchange ct WC2	6	K	23
Exeter st WC2	6	K	23
Exhibition rd SW7	1	H	10
Exmouth mkt EC1	3	G	29
Exton st SE1	6	N	24
Eyre St Hill EC1	3	H	28
Fabian rd SW6	4	J	1
Fairholme rd W14	1	G	1
Fairholt st SW7	1	I	11
Falconburg ct W1	2	H	22
Falconburg mews W1	2	H	22
Falcon gro SW11	4	R	4
Falcon rd SW11	4	R	4
Fane st W14	1	H	2
Fann st EC1	6	J	31
Farmer st W8	1	B	8
Farm la SW6	4	J	2
Farm pl W11	1	B	7
Farm st W1	2	H	17
Farnham pl SE1	6	O	26
Faroe rd W14	1	B	2
Farringdon rd EC1	3	H	28
Favart rd SW6	4	L	1
Fawcett st SW10	4	K	5
Featherstone st EC1	6	J	33
Fenchurch av EC3	6	O	32
Fenchurch st EC3	6	O	31
Fen ct EC3	6	O	32
Fenelon pl W14	1	F	3
Fenning st SE1	6	R	29
Fernsbury st WC1	3	G	29
Fernshaw rd SW10	4	L	5
Fetter la EC4	6	K	26
Fielding rd W14	1	B	2
Field pl EC1	3	F	30
Field st WC1	3	E	28
Finborough rd SW10	4	J	5
Finck st SE1	6	O	22
Finsbury av EC2	6	M	32
Finsbury circus EC2	6	M	32
Finsbury mkt EC2	6	L	33
Finsbury pvmnt EC2	6	L	32
Finsbury sq EC2	6	L	33
Finsbury st EC2	6	L	32
First st SW3	4	J	11
Fisher st WC1	3	H	25
Fish St hill EC3	6	P	30
Fitzalan st SE11	5	Q	21
Fitz George av W14	1	E	1
Fitzhardinge st W1	2	E	18
Fitz James av W14	1	E	2
Fitzmaurice pl W1	2	H	18
Fitzroy pl NW1	2	D	22
Fitzroy st W1	2	E	22
Fitzroy sq W1	2	D	22
Flaxman ter WC1	3	D	25
Fleet la EC4	6	L	28
Fleet st EC4	6	K	26
Flitcroft st WC2	3	H	23
Flood st SW3	4	M	9
Flood wlk SW3	4	M	9
Floral st WC2	6	J	23
Florence st N1	3	D	33
Foley st W1	2	E	21
Fore st EC2	6	L	31
Forfar rd SW11	4	R	9
Forset st W1	2	C	16
Fortune st EC1	6	K	31
Fosbury mews W2	1	B	11
Foster la EC2	6	L	29
Fouberts pl W1	2	G	20
Foulis ter SW7	4	J	8
Fountain ct WC2	6	K	25
Fox & Knot st EC1	6	K	29
Fox ct EC1	6	J	27
Foxmore st SW11	4	Q	7
Francis st SW1	5	N	16
Franklin's row SW3	4	M	11
Frazier st SE1	6	P	23
Frederick st WC1	3	F	28
Freedom st SW11	4	R	7
Freeling st N1	3	B	30
Frere st SW11	4	R	6
Friary ct SW1	5	K	19
Friday st EC4	6	M	28
Friend st EC1	3	G	31
Friston st SW6	4	O	1
Frith st W1	2	H	22
Frome st N1	3	F	33
Fulham bdy SW6	4	K	2
Fulham rd SW3, SW10 & SW6	4	L	4
Fulmead st SW6	4	N	2
Fulton mews W2	1	B	11
Fulwood pl WC1	3	I	26
Furness rd SW6	4	O	2
Furnival st EC4	6	J	27
Fynes st SW1	5	O	17
Gainford st N1	3	C	31
Galen pl WC1	3	H	24
Galsen yd WC1	3	F	26
Gambia st SE1	6	O	26
Ganton st W1	2	H	20
Garden mews W2	1	A	9
Garden row SE1	6	Q	24
Garden ter SW1	5	P	16
Garlick hill EC4	6	N	29
Garnault mews EC1	3	G	30
Garrett st EC1	6	J	31
Garrick st WC2	5	J	22
Garrick yd WC2	5	J	22
Garway rd W2	1	A	10
Gaskin st N1	3	D	33
Gate st WC2	3	I	25
Gatliff rd SW1	5	O	12
Gayfere st SW1	5	N	19
Gaywood st SE1	6	R	24
Gee st EC1	3	I	31
George ct WC2	5	K	22
George Inn yd SE1	6	Q	28
George st W1	2	D	17
George yd W1	2	F	18
Geraldine st SE11	6	Q	23
Gerald mews SW1	5	L	14
Gerald rd SW1	5	L	13
Gerrard rd N1	3	F	32
Gerrard st W1	2	I	22
Gerridge st SE1	6	P	23
Gertrude st SW10	4	L	6
Gibson sq N1	3	D	32
Gifford st N1	3	A	30
Gilbert pl WC1	3	H	24
Gilbert st SE11	5	R	22
Gilbert st W1	2	F	18
Gillingham mews SW1	5	M	15
Gillingham st SW1	5	N	15
Gillray sq SW10	4	M	6
Gilstead rd SW6	4	N	2
Gilston rd SW10	4	J	6
Giltspur st EC1	6	K	28
Girdlers rd W14	1	C	1
Gladstone st SE1	6	Q	23
Glasshill st SE1	6	P	25
Glasshouse st W1	2	I	20
Glasshouse wlk SE11	5	R	19
Glazbury rd W14	1	E	1
Glebe pl SW3	4	L	8
Gledhow gdns SW5	1	I	7
Gledstanes rd W14	1	G	1
Glendower pl SW7	1	I	9
Glenrosa st SW6	4	O	2
Glentworth st NW1	2	A	18
Gliddon rd W14	1	E	1
Globe st SE1	6	R	27
Gloucester mews W2	2	B	12
Gloucester mews west W2	2	A	12
Gloucester pl W1	2	A	18
Gloucester Pl mews W1	2	D	17
Gloucester rd SW7	1	I	7
Gloucester sq W2	2	C	14
Gloucester st SW1	5	O	14
Gloucester ter W2	2	C	12
Gloucester wlk W8	1	C	7
Glynde ms SW3	1	I	11
Godfrey st SW3	4	K	10
Goding st SE11	5	R	18
Godson st N1	3	E	30
Golden la EC1	6	J	31
Golden sq W1	2	H	20
Goldington st NW1	3	B	26
Golford pl NW1	2	A	17
Goode st EC1	3	H	29
Goodge st W1	2	F	22
Goodman's yd E1	6	Q	33
Goods way NW1	3	B	27
Goodwins ct WC2	5	J	22
Gordon pl W8	1	D	7
Gordon sq WC1	3	E	24
Gordon st WC1	3	E	24
Gore st SW7	1	G	9
Gorleston st W14	1	E	2
Gosfield st W1	2	E	21
Goswell rd EC1	3	H	31
Gough sq EC4	6	K	27
Gough st WC1	3	G	27
Goulden st SW11	4	Q	5
Gower ct WC1	3	E	24
Gower mews WC1	3	G	23
Gower pl WC1	3	D	24
Gower st WC1	3	E	23
Gracechurch st EC3	6	O	31
Grafton pl NW1	3	D	25
Grafton st W1	2	H	19
Grafton way W1	2	E	22
Graham st N1	3	G	32
Graham ter SW1	5	M	12
Granby ter NW1	3	B	24
Granfield st SW11	4	P	5
Grange ct WC2	6	J	25
Grantbridge st N1	3	F	33
Grant st N1	3	E	30
Granville sq WC1	3	F	28
Grape st WC2	3	H	23
Gratton pl W1	1	C	2
Gravel la E1	6	O	33
Grays Inn rd WC1	3	G	27
Grays Inn sq WC1	3	I	27
Gray st SE1	6	O	24
Gt Castle st W1	2	F	20
Gt Central st NW1	2	B	17
Gt Chapel st W1	2	H	22
Gt College st SW1	5	N	19
Gt Cumberland pl W1	2	D	16
Gt Dover st SE1	6	R	27
Gt George st SW1	5	M	20
Gt Guildford st SE1	6	P	27
Gt James st WC1	3	H	26
Gt Marlborough st W1	2	G	20
Gt Newport st WC2	2	J	22
Gt Ormond st WC1	3	G	26
Gt Percy st WC1	3	F	29
Gt Peter st SW1	5	N	19
Gt Portland st W1	2	E	21
Gt Pulteney st W1	2	H	21
Gt Queen st WC2	3	I	24
Gr Russell st WC1	3	H	23
Gt St Helens EC3	6	O	32
Gt St Thomas Apostle EC4	6	N	29
Gt Scotland yd SW1	5	L	21
Gt Smith st SW1	5	N	19
Gt Suffolk st SE1	6	P	26
Gt Sutton st EC1	3	I	30
Gt Swan all EC2	6	M	31
Gt Titchfield st W1	2	F	21
Gt Tower st EC3	6	P	31
Gt Turnstile WC2	3	I	26
Gt Winchester st EC2	6	N	29
Gt Windmill st W1	2	I	21
Greek st W1	2	I	22
Green ter EC1	3	G	30
Greencoat pl SW1	5	N	17
Greencoat row SW1	5	N	17
Greenhill rents EC1	6	J	29
Green st W1	2	F	17
Greenwell st W1	2	D	22
Greet st SE1	6	O	24
Grenville pl SW7	1	G	7
Grenville st WC1	3	G	26

Gresham st EC2	6	M 30
Gresse st W1	2	G 22
Greville st EC1	6	J 28
Greycoat pl SW1	5	N 18
Greycoat st SW1	5	N 17
Greyhound rd W14	1	G 1
Greystoke pl EC4	6	J 27
Groom pl SW1	5	K 15
Grosvenor cres SW1	5	J 15
Grosvenor Cres mews SW1	2	I 15
Grosvenor gdns SW1	5	L 15
Grosvenor gdns mews SW1	5	L 15
Grosvenor hill W1	2	G 18
Grosvenor pl SW1	5	J 15
Grosvenor rd SW1	5	Q 15
Grosvenor sq W1	2	F 17
Grosvenor st W1	2	G 18
Grove cotts SW3	4	M 9
Guildhouse st SW1	5	N 15
Guilford st WC1	3	G 26
Gundulf st SE11	5	R 21
Gunter gro SW10	4	L 5
Gunterstone rd W14	1	E 1
Gutter la EC2	6	M 29
Guy st SE1	6	R 28
Gwendwr rd W14	1	F 1
Gwynne pl WC1	3	F 28
Gwynne st SW11	4	Q 4
Gye st SE11	5	R 18
Haldane rd SW6	1	I 1
Halford rd SW6	4	J 2
Half Moon cres N1	3	D 30
Half Moon st W1	2	I 18
Halkin pl SW1	5	J 14
Halkin st SW1	5	J 15
Hallam mews W1	2	E 21
Hallam st W1	2	E 21
Hall st EC1	3	G 31
Halsey st SW3	4	K 11
Ham yd W1	2	I 21
Hamble st SW6	4	P 1
Hamilton pl W1	2	I 16
Hamilton sq SE1	6	R 28
Hamish pl SE11	5	Q 20
Hammersmith rd W14 & W6	1	D 2
Hampstead rd NW1	3	C 23
Hand ct WC1	3	I 26
Handel st WC1	3	F 26
Handley st SW11	4	O 5
Hankey pl SE1	6	R 28
Hanover sq W1	2	G 19
Hanover st W1	2	G 20
Hansard mews W14	1	A 3
Hans cres SW1	2	I 13
Hans pl SW1	5	J 12
Hans rd SW3	2	I 12
Hans st SW1	5	J 13
Hanway st W1	2	G 22
Harbledown rd SW6	4	L 1
Harcourt st W1	2	B 16
Harcourt ter SW10	4	J 5
Hardwick st EC1	3	G 29
Harewood av NW1	2	A 17
Harewood row NW1	2	A 17
Harleton st SW11	4	P 6
Harley gdns SW10	4	J 6
Harley pl W1	2	E 20
Harley st W1	2	E 20
Harp all EC4	6	K 27
Harp la EC3	6	P 31
Harper rd SE1	6	R 26
Harpur st WC1	3	H 26
Harriet st SW1	2	I 13
Harriet wlk SW1	2	I 13
Harrington gdns SW7	1	H 7
Harrington rd SW7	1	I 9
Harrington sq NW1	3	A 24
Harrington st NW1	3	B 23
Harrison st WC1	3	E 27
Harroway rd SW11	4	Q 4
Harrowby st W1	2	C 16
Harrow pl E1	6	O 33
Harrow rd W2	2	A 14
Hartismere rd SW6	4	J 1
Harwood rd SW6	4	L 2
Harwood ter SW6	4	M 2
Hasker st SW3	4	J 11
Hastings st WC1	3	E 26
Hatfields SE1	6	N 25
Hatherley st SW1	5	N 16
Hatton gdn EC1	3	I 28
Hatton wall EC1	3	I 28
Hatton yd EC1	3	I 28
Havelock st N1	3	B 29
Havelock ter SW8	5	R 12
Haverstock st N1	3	G 32
Hayes pl NW1	2	A 17
Hay hill W1	2	H 18
Hayles st SE11	6	R 23
Haymarket SW1	5	J 21
Hays la SE1	6	Q 30
Hay's mews W1	2	H 17
Hazlebury rd SW6	4	O 1
Hazlitt mews W14	1	C 2
Hazlitt rd W14	1	C 2
Headford pl SW1	5	J 15
Heathcote st WC1	3	F 27
Heaver rd SW11	4	R 4
Heckfield pl SW6	4	K 1
Heddon st W1	2	H 20
Helmet row EC1	3	I 32
Hemingford rd N1	3	B 31
Heniker mews SW3	4	K 7
Henley st SW11	4	R 9
Henning st SW11	4	P 5
Henrietta pl W1	2	F 19
Henrietta st WC2	6	J 23
Herbal hill EC1	3	H 28
Herbert cres SW3	2	I 13
Herbrand st WC1	3	F 25
Hercules rd SE1	5	P 22
Hereford rd W2	1	A 10
Hereford sq SW7	1	I 7
Hermes st N1	3	E 30
Hermit st EC1	3	G 31
Herrick st SW1	5	P 18
Hertford st W1	2	I 16
Hesper mews SW5	1	H 6
Hester rd SW11	4	O 7
Hibbert st SW11	4	R 1
Hide pl SW1	5	O 17
Highbury Sta rd N1	3	B 33
High Holborn WC1	3	I 23
Hildyard rd SW6	1	I 3
Hillgate pl W8	1	B 7
Hillgate st W8	1	B 8
Hillsleigh rd W8	1	B 7
Hill st W1	2	H 17
Hinde st W1	2	E 18
Hobart pl SW1	5	K 15
Hobury st SW10	4	L 6
Hofland rd W14	1	B 2
Hogarth rd SW5	1	G 5
Holbein mews SW1	5	M 12
Holbein pl SW1	5	M 12
Holborn EC1	6	J 27
Holborn bldgs EC4	3	I 27
Holborn circus EC1	6	J 27
Holborn viaduct EC1	6	K 28
Holford sq WC1	3	F 29
Holgate av SW11	4	R 2
Holland gdns W14	1	C 3
Holland mews W14	1	D 4
Holland pk W11	1	A 5
Holland Pk av W11	1	A 5
Holland Pk gdns W14	1	A 4
Holland Pk mews W11	1	A 5
Holland Pk rd W14	1	D 4
Holland rd W14	1	B 3
Holland st W8	1	D 7
Holland Villas rd W14	1	B 3
Holland wlk W8	1	C 6
Hollen st W1	2	G 22
Holles st W1	2	F 20
Hollywood rd SW10	4	K 6
Holman rd SW11	4	Q 4
Holmead rd SW6	4	L 3
Holyrood st SE1	6	R 30
Holywell row EC2	6	L 33
Home rd SW11	4	Q 5
Homer row W1	2	B 16
Homer st W1	2	B 16
Hope st SW11	4	R 2
Hopkin st W1	2	H 21
Hopton st SE1	6	N 26
Horbury cres W11	1	A 8
Horbury mews W11	1	A 7
Hornton st W8	1	D 7
Horseferry rd SW1	5	O 18
Horse Guards av SW1	5	L 21
Horse Guards pde SW1	5	L 21
Horse Guards rd SW1	5	L 20
Hortensia rd SW10	4	L 4
Hosier la EC1	6	K 28
Houghton st WC2	6	J 25
Houndsditch EC3	6	O 33
Howard st WC2	6	K 25
Howick pl SW1	5	M 17
Howie st SW11	4	O 7
Howland st W1	2	E 22
Hudsons pl SW1	5	M 15
Hugh st SW1	5	M 14
Hull st EC1	3	I 32
Hungerford Foot bri WC2 & SE1	6	L 23
Hungerford la WC2	5	K 22
Hunter st WC1	3	F 26
Huntingdon st N1	3	A 31
Huntley st WC1	3	E 23
Hunts ct WC2	5	J 22
Huntsworth mews NW1	2	A 18
Hutton st EC4	6	L 27
Hyde la SW11	4	O 6
Hyde Pk cnr SW1	2	I 16
Hyde Pk cres W2	2	C 15
Hyde Pk gdns W2	2	D 14
Hyde Pk Gdns mews W2	2	C 14
Hyde Pk ga SW7	1	F 9
Hyde Pk pl W2	2	D 14
Hyde Pk sq W2	2	C 14
Hyde Pk st W2	2	D 14
Idol la EC3	6	P 31
Ifield rd SW10	4	J 4
Ilchester gdns W2	1	A 10
Ilchester pl W14	1	C 4
Imperial Institute rd SW7	1	G 9
Imperial rd SW6	4	N 2
India st EC3	6	P 33
Ingestre pl E1	2	H 21
Inglebert st EC1	3	F 30
Ingrave st SW11	4	R 3
Inigo pl WC2	6	J 23
Inner Circle NW1	2	A 21
Inner Temple la EC4	6	K 26
Insurance st WC1	3	F 29
Inverness pl W2	1	B 11
Inverness ter W2	1	B 11
Inworth st SW11	4	Q 6
Irongate Wharf rd W2	2	A 15
Ironmonger la EC2	6	M 30
Ironmonger row EC1	3	I 32
Irving rd W14	1	B 2
Irving st WC2	5	J 22
Isabella st SE1	6	O 25
Islington grn N1	3	E 32
Islington High st N1	3	F 31
Islington Pk st N1	3	B 33
Ismailia rd SW6	4	P 1
Italian wlk SE11	5	R 18
Iverna ct W8	1	E 7
Iverna gdns W8	1	E 6
Ives st SW3	4	J 11
Ivor pl NW1	2	A 18
Ivybridge la WC2	6	K 23
Ixworth pl SW3	4	K 10
James st W1	2	E 18
James st WC2	6	J 23
Jameson st W8	1	B 8
Jay mews SW7	1	F 10
Jay's bldgs N1	3	D 30
Jerdan pl SW6	4	K 2
Jermyn st SW1	2	J 19
Jervis rd SW6	1	H 1
Jewry st EC3	6	P 33
Joan st SE1	6	O 25
Jockeys fields WC1	3	I 26
Johanna st SE1	6	O 23
John Adam st WC2	5	K 22
John Carpenter st EC4	6	L 26
John Islip st SW1	5	P 18
John Princes st W1	2	F 20
Johns mews WC1	3	H 27
Johnson's pl SW1	5	P 15
John st WC1	3	H 27
Joiner st SE1	6	Q 29
Jonathan st SE11	5	R 19
Joubert st SW11	4	R 7
Jubilee pl SW3	4	L 10
Judd st WC1	3	E 26
Juer st SW11	4	O 7
Junction mews W2	2	B 15
Juxon st SE11	5	Q 21
Kambala rd SW11	4	R 4
Kassala rd SW11	4	Q 8
Kean st WC2	6	J 24
Keeley st WC2	6	J 24
Kell st SE1	6	Q 24
Kelso pl W8	1	F 7
Kelway st W14	1	G 2
Kemble st WC2	6	J 24
Kempsford gdns SW5	1	I 4
Kempson rd SW6	4	L 2
Kendall pl W1	2	D 18
Kendal st W2	2	D 15
Kendrick mews SW7	1	I 9
Kendrick pl SW7	1	I 8
Kennet Whf la EC4	6	N 28
Kennington rd SE1 & SE11	5	Q 22
Kensington Church st W8	1	D 8
Kensington ct W8	1	E 8
Kensington Ct pl W8	1	F 8

Street	No	Grid	
Kensington Gdns sq W2	1	A	10
Kensington ga W8	1	F	9
Kensington gore SW7	1	F	10
Kensington High st W8 &			
W14	1	D	4
Kensington mall W8	1	B	8
Kensington Pal gdns W8	1	D	8
Kensington Pk rd W11	1	A	8
Kensington pl W8	1	B	7
Kensington rd W8 & SW7	1	E	8
Kensington sq W8	1	E	7
Kent yd SW7	2	H	12
Kentish bldgs SE1	6	Q	28
Kenway rd SW5	1	G	5
Keppel row SE1	6	P	27
Keppel st WC1	3	F	23
Kerrison rd SW11	4	R	5
Kersley mews SW11	4	Q	7
Kersley st SW11	4	Q	7
Keystone cres N1	3	D	28
Keyworth st SE1	6	Q	24
Khyber rd SW11	4	R	5
Kilkie st SW6	4	P	1
Killich st N1	3	D	28
Kilton st SW11	4	R	9
King Charles st SW1	5	L	20
King Edward st EC1	6	L	29
King Edward wlk SE1	6	P	23
King James st SE1	6	Q	25
Kingly ct W1	2	H	20
Kingly st W1	2	H	20
King's Arms yd EC2	6	M	31
King's Bench st SE1	6	P	25
King's cross N1	3	D	27
King's Cross rd WC1	3	F	28
King's Head yd SE1	6	Q	28
Kings mews WC1	3	H	27
King's pl SE1	6	R	26
King's rd SW1	5	L	14
King's rd SW3, SW10 &			
SW6	4	L	4
Kings Scholars pas SW1	5	M	16
King st EC2	6	M	30
King st SW1	5	J	19
King st WC2	6	J	23
Kingsway WC2	6	J	25
King William st EC4	6	O	30
Kinnerton st SW1	2	I	14
Kinnerton yd SW1	2	I	14
Kipling st SE1	6	R	28
Kirby gro SE1	6	R	29
Kirby st EC1	3	I	28
Kirtling st SW8	5	R	13
Knaresborough pl SW5	1	G	6
Knightrider st EC4	6	M	28
Knightsbridge SW1 &			
SW7	2	I	14
Knightsbridge grn SW1	2	H	13
Knivett st SW6	4	J	2
Knox rd SW11	4	R	3
Knox st W1	2	B	17
Kynance mews SW7	1	F	7
Lackington st EC2	6	L	32
Ladbroke gro W11	1	A	6
Ladbroke rd W11	1	A	6
Ladbroke sq W11	1	A	7
Ladbroke ter W11	1	A	7
Ladbroke wlk W11	1	A	7
Lakeside rd W14	1	A	1
Lambert st N1	3	B	32
Lambeth bri SW1	5	P	20
Lambeth High st SE1	5	Q	20
Lambeth hill EC4	6	N	28
Lambeth Palace rd SE1	5	O	21
Lambeth rd SE1	5	P	21
Lambeth wlk SE11	5	Q	21
Lambs bldgs EC1	6	K	32
Lambs Conduit pas WC1	3	H	26
Lambs Conduit st WC1	3	H	26
Lamb's pass EC1	6	K	32
Lamlash st SE11	6	R	23
Lamont rd SW10	4	L	6
Lancaster ga W2	1	C	11
Lancaster mews W2	2	C	12
Lancaster pl WC2	6	K	24
Lancaster ter W2	2	C	12
Lancelot pl SW7	2	I	12
Lancing st NW1	3	D	25
Landon pl SW3	2	I	13
Landseer st SW11	4	R	9
Lanfranc st SE1	6	P	23
Lanfrey pl W14	1	G	2
Langford SW6	4	N	2
Langham pl W1	2	F	20
Langham st W1	2	E	21
Langley st WC2	3	I	23
Langton clo WC1	3	F	28
Langton st SW10	4	L	5
Lansdowne mews W11	1	A	6
Lansdowne rd W11	1	A	6
Lansdowne ter WC1	3	G	26
Lant st SE1	6	Q	26
Latchmere rd SW11	4	R	6
Laud st SE11	5	R	19
Launcelot st SE1	6	O	23
Launceston pl W8	1	F	8
Laundry yd SW1	5	N	19
Laurence Pountney la EC4	6	O	30
Lavender rd SW11	4	R	3
Laverton mews SW5	1	H	5
Lavina gro N1	3	C	29
Lavington st SE1	6	O	26
Lawrence la EC2	6	M	30
Lawrence st SW3	4	M	8
Laycock st N1	3	B	33
Laystall st EC1	3	H	28
Layton rd N1	3	E	31
Leadenhall st EC3		O	32
Leake st SE1	6	N	23
Leather la EC1	3	I	28
Leeke st WC1	3	E	28
Lees pl W1	2	F	17
Leicester ct WC2	2	I	22
Leicester pl WC2	2	I	22
Leicester sq WC2	5	J	22
Leicester st WC2	2	I	21
Leigh Hunt st SE1	6	Q	26
Leigh st WC1	3	E	26
Leinster gdns W2	1	B	11
Leinster mews W2	1	B	11
Leinster ter W2	1	B	11
Leitrim gro SW11	4	R	7
Lennox gdns SW1	5	J	12
Lennox Gdns mews SW1	4	J	11
Leonard st EC2	6	K	33
Leopold wlk SE11	5	R	19
Lever st EC1	3	I	32
Lewisham st SW1	5	M	19
Lexham gdns W8	1	F	6
Lexham mews W8	1	F	6
Lexington st W1	2	H	21
Library st SE1	6	Q	24
Lidlington pl NW1	3	B	25
Lillie rd SW6	1	I	2
Limerston st SW10	4	L	6
Lime st EC3	6	O	31
Lincolns Inn fields WC2	3	I	25
Lincoln st SW3	4	L	11
Linden gdns W2	1	A	9
Linden mews W2	1	A	9
Lindrop st SW6	4	O	2
Lindsey st EC1	6	K	30
Linhope st NW1	2	A	18
Lisgar ter W14	1	E	3
Lisle st WC2	2	I	22
Lisson gro NW1	2	A	17
Lisson st NW1	2	A	16
Litchfield st WC2	2	I	22
Lithgow st SW11	4	Q	3
Little Boltons the SW10	4	J	6
Little Britain EC1	6	L	29
Little Chester st SW1	5	K	15
Little College st SW1	5	N	19
Little Dorrit ct SE1	6	Q	27
Little George st SW1	5	M	20
Little Portland st W1	2	F	21
Little Russell st WC1	3	H	24
Little St James's st SW1	5	J	18
Little Sanctuary SW1	5	M	20
Little Somerset st E1	6	P	33
Liverpool rd N1 & N7	3	D	32
Liverpool st EC2	6	N	33
Lizard st EC1	3	J	32
Lloyd Baker st WC1	3	F	29
Lloyd's av EC3	6	P	32
Lloyds row EC1	3	G	30
Lloyd sq WC1	3	F	29
Lloyd st WC1	3	F	29
Lockington rd SW8	4	R	11
Lockyer st SE1	6	R	28
Lofting rd N1	3	B	32
Logan mews W8	1	F	5
Logan pl W8	1	F	5
Lollard pl SE11	5	R	21
Lollard st SE11	5	Q	21
Loman st SE1	6	P	26
Lombard la EC4	6	L	26
Lombard rd SW11	4	P	4
Lombard st EC3	6	N	30
London bri SE1	6	P	29
London Bri st SE1	6	P	29
London mews W2	2	B	14
London rd SE1	6	Q	24
London st EC3	6	P	32
London st W2	2	B	13
London wall EC1 & EC2	6	L	31
Long Acre WC2	3	J	23
Longford st NW1	2	C	22
Long la EC1	6	K	29
Long la SE1	6	R	28
Longmoore st SW1	5	N	16
Longridge rd SW5	1	G	4
Long yd WC1	3	G	26
Longs ct WC2	5	J	22
Lonsdale pl N1	3	C	32
Lonsdale sq N1	3	C	32
Lord North st SW1	5	O	19
Lordship pl SW3	4	M	8
Lorenzo st WC1	3	E	28
Lorne gdns W11	1	A	3
Lothbury EC2	6	N	31
Lots rd SW10	4	M	5
Lovat la EC3	6	P	31
Love la EC2	6	L	30
Lower Belgrave st SW1	5	L	15
Lower Grosvenor pl SW1	5	K	16
Lower James st W1	2	I	20
Lower John st W1	2	I	20
Lower Regent st W1	5	J	20
Lower Marsh SE1	6	O	23
Lower Sloane st SW1	5	M	12
Lower Thames st EC3	6	P	30
Lowndes pl SW1	5	K	14
Lowndes sq SW1	2	I	13
Lowndes st SW1	5	J	13
Loxham st WC1	3	E	27
Luard st N1	3	B	30
Lucan pl SW3	4	K	10
Ludgate Bdy EC4	6	L	27
Ludgate circus EC4	6	L	27
Ludgate hill EC4	6	L	28
Ludgate sq EC4	6	L	28
Lumley ct WC2	6	K	23
Lumley st W1	2	F	18
Lupus st SW1	5	P	15
Lurline gdns SW11	4	R	10
Luxborough st W1	2	C	19
Lyall mews SW1	5	K	14
Lyall st SW1	5	K	13
Macclesfield rd EC1	3	H	32
Macduff rd SW11	4	R	10
Macklin st WC2	3	I	24
Mackworth st NW1	3	B	23
Maclise rd W14	1	C	2
Maddox st W1	2	G	19
Magdalen st SE1	6	R	30
Magpie all EC4	6	L	26
Maiden la WC2	6	J	23
Maidstone bldgs SE1	6	Q	28
Makins st SW3	4	K	10
Malet st WC1	3	F	24
Mallord st SW3	4	L	8
Mallow st EC1	6	J	33
Mall the SW1	5	K	19
Malta st EC1	3	H	30
Malvern ter N1	3	C	31
Manchester sq W1	2	E	18
Manchester st W1	2	D	18
Manciple st SE1	6	R	27
Mandeville pl W1	2	E	18
Manresa rd SW3	4	L	8
Mansell st E1	6	P	33
Mansfield st W1	2	E	20
Manson pl SW7	1	I	8
Mantell st N1	3	E	31
Mantua st SW11	4	R	4
Maple st W1	2	E	22
Marble arch W1	2	E	16
Marbledon pl WC1	3	D	26
Marchmont st WC1	3	F	25
Margaret st W1	2	F	20
Margaretta ter SW3	4	M	9
Margery st WC1	3	G	29
Marinefield rd SW6	4	N	2
Market mews W1	2	I	17
Markham sq SW3	4	L	10
Markham st SW3	4	L	10
Mark la EC3	6	P	32
Marlborough rd SW1	5	K	19
Marlborough st SW3	4	K	10
Marloes rd W8	1	F	6
Marshall gdns SE1	6	R	24
Marshall st W1	2	H	21
Marshalsea rd SE1	6	Q	27
Marsham st SW1	5	O	18
Martin la EC4	6	O	30
Mart st WC2	6	J	23
Martlett ct WC2	6	J	24
Marylebone High st W1	2	D	19
Marylebone la W1	2	E	19
Marylebone rd NW1	2	B	17
Marylebone st W1	2	D	19
Masbro rd W14	1	B	2
Mason's av EC2	6	M	31
Masons pl EC1	3	H	31
Masons yd SW1	5	J	19
Matheson rd W14	1	E	3
Mathew Parker st SW1	5	M	19

Matilda st N1 3 C 30
Matthews st SW11 4 R 6
Maunsel st SW1 5 N 17
Maxwell rd SW6 4 L 3
Mayfair pl W1 2 I 18
Maygood st N1 3 D 30
Mead row SE1 6 P 23
Meard st W1 2 H 22
Meath st SW11 4 R 11
Mecklenburgh pl WC1 3 G 27
Mecklenburgh sq WC1 3 F 27
Medburn st NW1 3 B 26
Medcalfe pl N1 3 F 30
Medway st SW1 5 N 18
Meek st SW10 4 M 4
Melbourne pl WC2 6 K 24
Melbury ct W8 1 D 5
Melbury rd W14 1 D 4
Melbury ter NW1 2 A 17
Melcombe pl NW1 2 B 17
Melcombe st NW1 2 B 18
Melior st SE1 6 R 29
Melrose gdns W6 1 A 1
Melrose ter W6 1 A 1
Melton ct SW7 1 I 9
Melton st NW1 3 D 24
Mendip rd SW11 4 R 1
Mepham st SE1 6 N 23
Mercer st WC2 3 I 23
Meredith st EC1 3 H 30
Merlin st WC1 3 G 29
Mermaid ct SE1 6 Q 28
Merrick sq SE1 6 R 26
Merrington rd SW6 1 I 3
Meymott st SE1 6 N 25
Meyrick rd SW11 4 R 3
Micawber st N1 3 H 33
Michael rd SW6 4 M 3
Micklethwaite rd SW6 4 J 3
Middlesex st E1 6 N 33
Middle Temple la EC4 6 L 25
Middle yd SE1 6 Q 29
Midhope st WC1 3 E 26
Midland rd NW1 3 D 26
Midborne gro SW10 4 J 6
Milcote st SE1 6 Q 24
Milford la WC2 6 K 25
Milk st EC2 6 M 30
Millbank SW1 5 P 18
Millman mews WC1 3 G 26
Millman st WC1 3 G 26
Mill st W1 2 G 19
Milman's st SW10 4 M 7
Milner pl N1 3 D 33
Milner sq N1 3 C 33
Milner st SW3 4 J 11
Milson rd W14 1 B 2
Milton ct EC2 6 L 31
Milton st EC2 6 L 31
Mincing la EC3 6 P 31
Minera mews SW1 5 L 13
Minford gdns W14 1 A 1
Minories EC3 6 P 33
Mint st SE1 6 Q 26
Mirabel rd SW6 4 J 1
Mitchell st EC1 3 I 32
Mitre rd SE1 6 O 24
Mitre st EC3 6 O 33
Mohammed all N1 3 A 28
Molyneux st W1 2 C 16
Monck st SW1 5 N 18
Moncorvo clo SW7 1 G 11
Monkton st SE11 5 R 22
Monmouth st WC2 3 I 23
Montague cl SE1 6 P 29
Montague pl WC1 3 G 24
Montague st WC1 3 G 24
Montagu mans W1 2 C 18
Montagu mews north W1 2 C 17
Montagu pl W1 2 C 17
Montagu sq W1 2 D 17
Montagu st W1 2 D 17
Montpelier mews SW7 2 I 11
Montpelier pl SW7 2 H 12
Montpelier sq SW7 2 H 12
Montpelier st SW7 2 I 12
Montpelier wlk SW7 2 H 12
Montreal pl WC2 6 K 24
Montrose ct SW7 1 G 11
Montrose pl SW1 5 J 15
Monument st EC3 6 P 30
Moon st N1 3 D 33
Moor la EC2 6 L 31
Moor pl EC2 6 M 31
Moor st W1 2 I 22
Moore Pk rd SW6 4 L 2
Moore st SW3 5 K 12
Moorfields EC2 6 L 31
Moorgate EC2 6 M 31
Mora st EC1 3 I 33

Moreland st EC1 3 H 31
Morepeth ter SW1 5 M 16
Moreton pl SW1 5 O 15
Moreton st SW1 5 P 16
Moreton ter SW1 5 P 15
Morgan's la SE1 6 R 30
Morgan's wlk SW11 4 O 6
Morley st SE1 6 P 23
Mornington av W14 1 F 2
Mornington cres NW1 3 A 24
Mornington pl NW1 3 A 24
Mornington ter NW1 3 A 24
Mortimer st W1 2 F 21
Morton pl SE1 5 P 22
Morwell st WC1 3 G 23
Moscow pl W2 1 A 10
Moscow rd W2 1 A 10
Mossop st SW3 4 J 11
Motcomb st SW1 5 J 14
Mount mills EC1 3 I 31
Mount pleasant WC1 3 H 28
Mount row W1 2 G 18
Mount st W1 2 G 19
Moxon st W1 2 D 19
Mulberry wlk SW3 4 L 8
Munden st W14 1 D 2
Mund st W14 1 G 2
Munster sq NW1 2 C 22
Muriel st N1 3 D 29
Murphy st SE1 6 O 23
Murray gro N1 3 H 33
Muscovy st EC3 6 P 32
Museum st WC1 3 H 24
Musgrave cres SW6 4 L 2
Musjid rd SW11 4 R 4
Myddelton pas EC1 3 F 30
Myddelton sq EC1 3 F 30
Myddelton st EC1 3 G 30
Mylne st 3 F 30

Napier pl W14 1 D 4
Napier rd W14 1 D 3
Napier ter N1 3 D 33
Narborough st SW6 4 O 1
Nassau st W1 2 F 22
Neal st WC2 3 I 23
Neal's yd WC2 3 I 23
Nebraska st SE1 6 R 27
Nelson pl N1 3 G 32
Nelson sq SE1 6 O 25
Nepaul rd SW11 4 R 5
Netherton gro SW10 4 K 5
Netherwood rd W14 1 A 1
Netley st NW1 3 C 23
Nevern pl SW5 1 G 4
Nevern rd SW5 1 G 4
Nevern sq SW5 1 G 4
Neville st SW7 4 J 8
New Bond st W1 2 G 19
New Bridge st EC4 6 L 27
New Broad st EC2 6 M 32
New Burlington st W1 2 H 20
Newburn st SE11 5 R 20
Newcastle pl W2 2 A 15
Newcastle st EC4 6 K 28
New Cavendish st W1 2 E 21
New Change EC4 6 M 29
Newcombe st W8 1 B 8
Newcomen rd SW11 4 R 3
Newcomen st SE1 6 Q 28
New Compton st WC2 3 I 23
New Fetter la EC4 6 J 27
Newgate st EC1 6 L 29
Newington causeway SE1 6 R 25
New London st EC3 6 P 32
Newman st W1 2 G 22
Newnham ter SE1 5 P 22
New North st WC1 3 H 25
New Oxford st WC1 3 H 23
Newport pl WC2 2 I 22
Newport st SE11 5 Q 20
New row WC2 5 J 22
New Scotland yd SW1 5 M 21
New sq WC2 6 J 26
New st EC2 6 N 33
New St sq EC4 6 K 27
Newton st WC2 3 I 24
Newtown st SW11 4 R 10
New Quebec st W1 2 D 17
Nicholas la EC4 6 O 30
Nicholson st SE1 6 O 25
Nile st N1 3 I 33
Nine Elms la SW8 5 R 15
Noble st EC2 6 L 30
Noel rd N1 3 F 32
Noel st W1 2 G 21
Norfolk cres W2 2 C 15
Norfolk pl W2 2 B 14
Norfolk row SE11 5 P 21
Norfolk sq W2 2 B 14

Norland pl W11 1 A 5
Norland sq W11 1 A 5
Normand mews W14 1 G 1
Normand rd W14 1 G 1
Norman st EC1 3 I 32
Northampton rd EC1 3 H 29
Northampton sq EC1 3 H 31
North Audley st W1 2 F 17
Northburgh st EC1 3 I 30
Northdown st N1 3 D 28
North End cres W14 1 E 2
North End rd W14 & SW6 1 F 2
Northington st WC1 3 H 27
North mews WC1 3 H 27
North row W1 2 E 17
North Tenter st E1 6 Q 33
Northumberland all EC3 6 P 32
Northumberland av WC2 5 K 22
Northumberland st WC2 5 K 22
North Wharf rd W2 2 A 14
Norwich st EC4 6 J 27
Nottingham pl W1 2 C 19
Nottingham st W1 2 C 19
Notting Hill ga W11 1 A 8
Novello st SW6 4 L 1
Nutford pl W1 2 C 16

Oakbury rd SW6 4 O 1
Oakden st SE11 5 R 22
Oakley cres EC1 3 G 32
Oakley gdns SW3 4 M 9
Oakley sq NW1 3 A 25
Oakley st SW3 4 M 9
Oakwood ct W14 1 C 4
Oat la EC2 6 L 30
Observatory gdns W8 1 C 7
Octavia st SW11 4 Q 6
Odger st SW11 4 R 7
Offord rd N1 3 A 32
Offord st N1 3 A 32
Ogle st W1 2 E 22
Old Bailey EC4 6 L 28
Old Barrack yd SW1 2 I 14
Old Bond st W1 2 I 19
Old Broad st EC2 6 N 32
Old Brompton rd SW7 & SW5 1 I 7
Old Burlington st W1 2 H 19
Oldbury pl W1 2 C 19
Old Cavendish st W1 2 F 19
Old Church st SW3 4 M 8
Old Compton st W1 2 I 22
Old Gloucester st WC1 3 H 25
Old Jewry EC2 6 N 30
Old Marylebone rd NW1 2 B 16
Old Mitre ct EC4 6 K 26
Old Palace yd SW1 5 N 20
Old Paradise st SE11 5 P 20
Old Park la W1 2 I 16
Old Pye st SW1 5 N 18
Old Quebec st W1 2 E 17
Old Queen st SW1 5 M 19
Old st EC1 3 I 32
Olivers yd EC1 6 K 33
Olympia yd W1 1 B 11
O'Meara st SE1 6 P 29
Ongar rd SW6 1 I 3
Onslow gdns SW7 4 J 8
Onslow sq SW7 4 J 9
Onslow st EC1 3 I 28
Ontario st SE1 6 R 24
Orange st WC2 5 J 21
Orbel st SW11 4 P 6
Orchard st W1 2 E 17
Orde Hall st WC1 3 G 26
Orient st SE11 6 R 23
Orkney st SW11 4 R 8
Orme ct W2 1 B 10
Orme la W2 1 B 10
Orme sq W2 1 B 10
Ormond mews WC1 3 E 26
Ormond yd SW1 5 J 20
Ormonde ga SW3 4 M 11
Orsett st SE11 5 R 20
Orville rd SW11 4 P 4
Osbert st SW1 5 O 17
Osnaburgh st NW1 2 C 22
Osnaburgh ter NW1 2 C 22
Ossington clo W2 1 A 9
Ossington st W2 1 B 9
Ossulston st NW1 3 C 26
Oswin st SE11 6 R 23
Outer circle NW1 2 B 20
Ovington gdns SW3 1 I 11
Ovington sq SW3 2 I 12
Ovington st SW3 4 J 11
Owen's ct EC1 3 G 31
Owen's row EC1 3 G 31
Owen st EC1 3 F 31

Oxendon st SW1	5	J	21
Oxford circus W1	2	G	20
Oxford sq W2	2	C	15
Oxford st W1	2	G	21
Packington st N1	3	E	33
Paddington Cres gdns W2	2	A	15
Paddington grn W2	2	A	14
Paddington W1	2	C	19
Page st SW1	5	O	18
Paget st EC1	3	G	31
Pakenham st WC1	3	G	28
Palace ct W2	1	B	9
Palace Gdns mews W8	1	B	9
Palace Gdns ter W8	1	C	8
Palace ga W8	1	F	9
Palace st SW1	5	L	17
Palatine pl EC2	6	K	33
Pall mall SW1	5	J	19
Pall Mall east SW1	5	J	21
Pall Mall pl SW1	5	J	19
Palmer st SW1	5	M	18
Pancras la EC4	6	N	30
Pancras rd NW1	3	C	27
Panton st SW1	5	J	21
Parade the SW11	4	O	10
Paradise wlk SW3	4	N	10
Pardon st EC1	3	I	30
Paris gdns SE1	6	N	25
Park cres W1	2	D	21
Park Cres mews west W1	2	D	21
Parker st WC2	3	I	24
Parkfield st N1	3	E	31
Parkgate rd SW11	4	O	7
Park gro SW11	4	R	9
Parkham st SW11	4	P	6
Park la W1	2	G	16
Park pl SW1	5	J	19
Park rd NW1	2	A	18
Park rd SE1	6	O	27
Parkside st SW11	4	R	8
Park sq NW1	2	C	21
Park Sq east NW1	2	C	21
Park Sq west NW1	2	C	21
Park st SE1	6	P	28
Park st W1	2	F	17
Park Village east NW1	3	A	23
Park wlk SW10	4	L	6
Park West pl W2	2	C	15
Parliament sq SW1	5	M	20
Parliament st SW1	5	M	20
Parry st SW8	5	R	17
Parthenia rd SW6	4	M	1
Passmore st SW1	5	M	12
Pastor st SE11	6	R	24
Paternoster row EC4	6	L	28
Paternoster sq EC4	6	L	28
Pater st W8	1	E	6
Patience st SW11	4	R	5
Paton st EC1	3	I	32
Paul st EC2	6	L	33
Paulton's sq SW3	4	L	7
Paulton's st SW3	4	M	7
Pavilion rd SW1	5	K	12
Pavilion st SW1	5	J	12
Pea grn SW10	4	N	6
Peabody av SW1	5	O	13
Pearman st SE1	6	P	23
Pearscroft ct SW6	4	N	2
Pearscroft rd SW6	4	N	2
Pear pl SE1	6	O	23
Pear Tree ct EC1	3	H	29
Peartree ct EC1	3	I	31
Peel st W8	1	B	7
Peerless st EC1	3	I	33
Pelham cres SW7	4	J	10
Pelham pl SW7	4	J	10
Pelham st SW7	4	J	10
Pembridge cres W11	1	A	8
Pembridge rd W11	1	A	8
Pembridge gdns W2	1	A	8
Pembridge pl W2	1	A	9
Pembridge sq W2	1	A	9
Pembroke clo SW1	5	J	15
Pembroke Gdn clo W8	1	E	4
Pembroke gdns W8	1	E	4
Pembroke mews W8	1	E	5
Pembroke pl W8	1	E	5
Pembroke rd W8	1	F	4
Pembroke sq W8	1	E	5
Pembroke st N1	3	A	30
Pembroke studios W8	1	E	4
Pembroke villas W8	1	E	5
Pembroke wlk W8	1	H	6
Penfold pl NW1	2	A	15
Penfold st NW1 & NW8	2	A	16
Pennant mews W8	1	G	6
Penryn st NW1	3	B	26
Penton gro N1	3	E	30
Penton rise WC1	3	E	29
Penton st N1	3	E	30
Pentonville rd N1	3	E	29
Penywern rd SW5	1	H	5
Pepper st SE1	6	P	26
Pepys st EC3	6	P	32
Percival st EC1	3	H	30
Percy circus WC1	3	F	29
Percy st W1	2	G	22
Percy yd WC1	3	F	28
Perham rd W14	1	G	1
Perrymead st SW6	4	M	1
Petergate SW11	4	R	1
Petersham mews SW7	1	G	8
Petersham pl SW7	1	G	8
Peters la EC1	6	J	29
Peter st W1	2	H	21
Peto pl NW1	2	C	22
Petty France SW1	5	L	18
Petworth st SW11	4	P	7
Petyward SW3	4	K	10
Phene st SW3	4	M	9
Philbeach gdns SW5	1	G	4
Phillimore gdns W8	1	D	6
Phillimore pl W8	1	D	6
Phillimore wlk W8	1	D	6
Philpot la EC3	6	O	31
Phipps mews SW1	5	L	15
Phoenix pl WC1	3	G	28
Phoenix rd NW1	3	C	25
Piccadilly W1	2	I	18
Piccadilly circus W1	2	I	20
Pickard st EC1	3	G	32
Pickle Herring st SE1	6	R	31
Pickwick st SE1	6	Q	26
Picton pl W1	2	E	18
Pilgrimage st SE1	6	R	27
Pilgrim st EC4	6	L	27
Pimlico rd SW1	5	M	12
Pindar st EC2	6	M	33
Pine st EC1	3	H	29
Pitt's Head mews W1	2	I	16
Pitt st W8	1	D	7
Platt st NW1	3	B	26
Playhouse yd EC4	6	M	27
Pleydel ct EC4	6	K	26
Plough st SW11	4	R	2
Plumtree ct EC4	6	K	28
Pocock st SE1	6	P	25
Poland st W1	2	H	21
Polygon rd NW1	3	C	25
Ponder st N7	3	A	31
Pond pl SW3	4	K	9
Pond yd SE1	6	O	27
Ponsonby pl SW1	5	P	17
Ponsonby ter SW1	5	P	17
Pont st SW1	5	J	12
Pont st mews SW1	5	J	12
Poplar gro W6	1	A	1
Poplar pl W2	1	B	10
Poppins ct EC4	6	L	27
Porchester gdns W2	1	A	10
Porchester Gdn mews W2	1	A	11
Porchester pl W2	2	C	15
Porchester sq W2	1	A	10
Porchester ter W2	1	B	11
Porlock st SE1	6	R	28
Porten rd W14	1	C	2
Portland pl W1	2	E	20
Portland rd W11	1	A	5
Portman clo W1	2	D	17
Portman mews south W1	2	E	17
Portman sq W1	2	D	17
Portman st W1	2	E	17
Portobello rd W11	1	A	8
Portpool la EC1	3	I	27
Portsea pl W2	2	D	15
Portsmouth st WC2	6	J	25
Portsoken st E1	6	Q	33
Portugal st WC2	6	J	25
Potter's fields SE1	6	R	30
Poulton pl SW6	4	K	1
Poultry EC2	6	N	30
Powis pl WC1	3	G	26
Praed st W2	2	B	14
Pratt wlk SE11	5	P	21
Prebend st N1	3	F	33
Prescot st E1	6	Q	33
Prices st SE1	6	O	26
Prideaux pl WC1	3	F	29
Primrose st EC2	6	M	33
Prince Consort rd SW7	1	G	10
Princedale rd W11	1	A	5
Prince of Wales dri SW11	4	R	8
Prince of Wales ter W8	1	E	8
Prince's gdns SW7	1	G	11
Prince's ga SW7	1	G	11
Prince's Gate mews SW7	1	H	10
Princes mews W2	1	A	10
Princes pl EC4	5	J	19
Prince's row SW1	5	L	16
Princes sq W2	1	A	10
Princes st EC2	6	N	30
Princes st W1	2	G	20
Princeton st WC1	3	H	26
Priory wlk SW10	4	J	6
Prospect ter WC1	3	F	27
Provence st N1	3	G	33
Providence ct W1	2	F	17
Pudding la EC3	6	P	30
Pulteney ter N1	3	C	31
Purchese st NW1	3	B	26
Quarrendon rd SW6	4	M	1
Queen Anne mews W1	2	E	20
Queen Anne's ga SW1	5	L	19
Queen Anne st W1	2	E	19
Queen Elm sq SW3	4	K	8
Queensberry mews SW7	1	I	9
Queensberry pl SW7	1	I	9
Queensborough ter W2	1	B	11
Queens circus SW11	4	R	11
Queens Clo gdns W14	1	G	1
Queens gdns W2	1	B	12
Queen's ga SW7	1	G	9
Queens Ga gdns SW7	1	G	8
Queens Ga mews SW7	1	F	9
Queens Ga pl SW7	1	G	8
Queens Ga Pl mews SW7	1	H	8
Queens Ga ter SW7	1	G	8
Queens Head st N1	3	E	33
Queen's Head yd SE1	6	Q	28
Queen's mews W2	1	A	10
Queen sq WC1	3	G	25
Queenstown rd SW8	4	Q	11
Queen st W1	2	H	17
Queen st EC4	6	N	29
Queen St pl EC4	6	N	29
Queen's wlk SW1	5	J	18
Queensway W2	1	A	11
Queen Victoria st EC4	6	M	28
Querrin st SW6	4	P	2
Quilp st SE1	6	Q	27
Quick st N1	3	F	32
Racton rd SW6	1	I	2
Radley mews W8	1	F	6
Radnor mews W2	2	C	14
Radnor pl W2	2	C	14
Radnor st EC1	3	I	32
Radnor wlk SW3	4	M	10
Radstock st SW11	4	O	7
Railway app SE1	6	Q	29
Railway pl EC3	6	P	32
Railway st N1	3	D	28
Rainsford st W2	2	B	15
Raleigh st N1	3	F	33
Ramillies pl W1	2	G	21
Ramillies st W1	2	G	21
Rampayne st SW1	5	P	16
Randall rd SE11	5	Q	19
Randall st SW11	4	P	6
Randalls rd N1	3	A	29
Ranelagh gro SW1	5	M	13
Ranelagh rd SW1	5	P	15
Ranston st NW1	2	A	16
Raphael st SW7	2	H	13
Rathbone pl W1	2	G	22
Rathbone st W1	2	G	22
Ravanet st SW11	4	R	10
Rawlings st SW3	4	K	11
Rawstorne pl EC1	3	G	31
Rawstorne st EC1	3	G	31
Ray st EC1	3	H	28
Redan pl W2	1	A	11
Redan st W14	1	B	1
Redburn st SW3	4	M	10
Redcliffe clo SW5	1	I	5
Redcliffe gdns SW10	4	J	5
Redcliffe mews SW10	4	J	5
Redcliffe pl SW10	4	K	5
Redcliffe rd SW10	4	K	6
Redcliffe sq SW10	1	I	5
Redcliffe st SW10	4	J	5
Redesdale st SW3	4	M	10
Redfield la SW5	1	G	5
Redhill st NW1	3	A	23
Red Lion ct EC4	6	K	26
Red Lion sq WC1	3	H	25
Red Lion st WC1	3	I	26
Reece mews SW7	1	I	8
Reedworth st SE11	5	R	22
Reeves mews W1	2	G	17
Reform st SW11	4	R	7
Regency st SW1	5	O	17
Regent sq WC1	3	E	26
Regent st SW1 & W1	2	H	20
Regnart bldgs NW1	3	D	24
Relton mews SW7	2	I	12
Remington st N1	3	G	32
Remnant st WC2	3	I	25

Street			
Rennie st SE1	6	N	26
Reston pl SW7	1	F	9
Rex pl W1	2	G	16
Rheidol ter N1	3	F	33
Richmond av N1	3	C	31
Richmond cres N1	3	C	31
Richmond ter SW1	5	M	21
Richmond Ter mews SW1	5	M	21
Richmond way W14	1	A	2
Rickett st SW6	1	I	3
Ridgmount gdns WC1	3	F	23
Ridgmount st WC1	3	F	23
Riding House st W1	2	F	21
Ring the W2	2	E	13
Ripplevale gro N1	3	B	31
Riseborough st SE1	6	P	26
Risinghill st N1	3	E	30
Rising Sun ct EC1 & NW1	6	J	30
Ritchie st N1	3	E	31
River st EC1	3	F	29
Robert Adam st W1	2	D	18
Robert st NW1	3	B	23
Robert st WC2	6	K	23
Robinson st SW3	4	M	9
Rochester row SW1	5	N	17
Rochester st SW1	5	N	17
Rockingham st SE1	6	R	25
Rocliffe st N1	3	G	32
Rodmarton mews W1	2	C	18
Rodney st N1	3	E	29
Roger st WC1	3	G	27
Roland gdns SW7	4	J	7
Rollo st SW11	4	R	10
Romilly st W1	2	I	22
Romney st SW1	5	O	19
Rood la EC3	6	P	31
Ropemaker st EC2	6	L	32
Rosary gdns SW7	1	I	7
Roscoe st EC1	6	J	31
Rose all SE1	6	O	28
Rose and Crown yd SW1	5	J	19
Rosebery av EC1	3	H	28
Rosebury rd SW6	4	O	1
Rosemoor st SW3	4	K	11
Rosenau cres SW11	4	Q	7
Rosenau rd SW11	4	P	7
Rosoman st EC1	3	H	29
Rossmore rd NW1	2	A	18
Rotary st SE1	6	Q	24
Rotten row SW7 & SW1	2	G	13
Roupell st SE1	6	N	24
Rowena cres SW11	4	R	5
Roxby pl SW6	1	I	4
Royal av SW3	4	L	11
Royal College st NW1	3	A	26
Royal Hospital rd SW3	4	N	10
Royal Mint st E1	6	Q	33
Royal st SE1	5	O	22
Rufford st N1	3	A	29
Rugby st WC1	3	H	26
Rumbold rd SW6	4	L	3
Running Horse yd SE1	6	O	25
Rupert st W1	2	I	21
Rushworth st SE1	6	P	25
Russell st WC1	5	J	19
Russell gdns W14	1	B	3
Russell rd W14	1	C	3
Russell sq WC1	3	F	24
Russell st WC2	6	J	23
Russia row EC2	6	M	30
Rutherford st SW1	5	O	17
Rutland gdns SW7	2	H	12
Rutland ga SW7	2	H	12
Rutland pl EC1	6	J	30
Rutland st SW7	1	I	11
Ryder ct SW1	5	J	19
Ryder st SW1	5	J	19
Ryecroft st SW6	4	M	1
Rysbracket st SW3	2	I	13
Sackville st W1	2	I	20
Saffron hill EC1	3	I	28
Sail st SE11	5	Q	21
St Albans gro W8	1	F	7
St Albans pl N1	3	D	32
St Alban's st SW1	5	J	21
St Alphage gdns EC2	6	L	31
St Andrew hill EC4	6	M	28
St Andrews pl NW1	2	C	22
St Andrews rd W14	1	G	1
St Andrew st EC4	6	K	27
St Anne's ct W1	2	H	22
St Ann's st SW1	5	N	19
St Barnabas st SW1	5	N	13
St Boltoph st EC3	6	O	33
St Bride st EC4	6	K	27
St Chads pl WC1	3	E	28
St Chads st WC1	3	E	27
St Christopher pl W1	2	E	18
St Clare st EC3	6	P	33
St Clements la WC2	6	J	25
St Clements st N7	3	A	32
St Cross st EC1	3	I	28
St Dunstan's hill EC3	6	P	31
St Erims hill SW1	5	M	18
St George's circus SE1	6	Q	24
St George's rd SE1	6	O	15
St George's rd SE1	6	Q	23
St George's sq SW1	5	O	15
St George Sq mews SW1	5	O	16
St George's st W1	2	G	19
St Giles circus WC2	3	H	23
St Giles High st WC2	3	H	23
St Helens pl EC3	6	N	32
St James's gro SW11	4	R	7
St James's pl SW1	5	J	18
St James's sq SW1	5	J	20
St James's st SW1	5	J	19
St James's wlk EC1	3	I	29
St Johns la EC1	3	I	29
St Johns sq EC1	3	I	29
St John st EC1	3	I	29
St Joseph's st SW8	4	R	11
St Katharine's way E1	6	R	32
St Leonard's ter SW3	4	M	11
St Loo av SW3	4	M	9
St Lukes st SW8	4	K	10
St Margaret st SW1	5	M	20
St Martins ct WC2	5	J	22
St Martins la WC2	5	J	22
St Martins le Grand EC1	6	L	29
St Martin's pl WC2	5	J	22
St Martin's st WC2	5	J	21
St Mary Abbots pl W8	1	E	4
St Mary at Hill EC3	6	P	31
St Mary axe EC3	6	O	32
St Mary's gdns SE11	5	R	22
St Marys path N1	3	D	33
St Michaels st W2	2	B	15
St Mildred's ct EC2	6	N	30
St Oswald's pl SE11	5	R	19
St Pancras way NW1	3	A	26
St Paul's Church yd EC4	6	M	28
St Petersburgh pl W2	1	B	10
St Peter's st N1	3	F	33
St Swithins la EC4	6	N	30
St Thomas' st SE1	6	Q	29
St Thomas's way SW6	1	I	1
St Vincent st W1	2	D	19
Salamanca pl SE1	5	Q	20
Salamanca st SE11	5	Q	19
Salem rd W2	1	A	10
Sale pl W2	2	B	15
Salisbury ct EC4	6	L	27
Salisbury st NW8	2	A	16
Sancroft st SE11	5	R	20
Sanctuary st SE1	6	Q	26
Sandell st SE1	6	N	24
Sandilands rd SW6	4	N	2
Sandland st WC1	3	I	26
Sandwich st WC1	3	E	26
Sans wlk EC1	3	H	29
Sardina st WC2	6	J	25
Saunder's st SE11	5	Q	21
Savage gdns EC3	6	P	32
Savile row W1	2	H	20
Savona pl SW8	5	R	12
Savona st SW8	5	R	12
Savoy hill WC2	6	K	23
Savoy pl WC2	6	L	25
Savoy st WC2	6	K	23
Savoy way WC2	6	K	23
Sawyer st SE1	6	P	26
Scala st W1	2	F	22
Scarsdale villas W8	1	F	6
Scholey st SW11	4	O	6
Scoresby st SE1	6	O	25
Scotland pl SW1	5	L	21
Scovell rd SE1	6	Q	25
Scrutton st EC2	6	L	33
Seacoal la EC4	6	L	28
Seaford st WC1	3	E	27
Seagrave rd SW6	4	J	3
Searle clo SW11	4	O	7
Seaton pl NW1	2	D	22
Sebastian st EC1	3	H	31
Secker st SE1	6	N	24
Sedding st SW1	5	L	12
Sedlescombe rd SW6	1	I	2
Sedley pl W1	2	F	19
Seething la EC3	6	P	32
Sekforde st EC1	3	I	29
Sellon mews SE11	5	Q	20
Selwood pl SW7	4	J	8
Selwood ter SW7	4	J	8
Semley pl SW1	5	M	13
Serle st WC2	6	J	25
Serpentine rd W2	2	G	14
Seville st SW1	2	I	14
Seward st EC1	3	I	31
Seymour mews W1	2	E	18
Seymour pl W1	2	C	16
Seymour st W1 & W2	2	D	16
Seymour wlk SW10	4	K	6
Shaftesbury av W1 & WC2	2	I	21
Shaftesbury mews W8	1	F	5
Shaftesbury pl EC1	6	L	30
Shafto mews SW1	5	J	12
Shalcomb st SW10	4	L	6
Shand st SE1	6	R	30
Shawfield st SW3	4	M	10
Sheen gro N1	3	C	31
Sheffield st WC2	6	J	25
Sheffield ter W8	1	C	7
Sheldon st W2	2	A	13
Sheldrake pl W8	1	C	6
Shelton st WC2	3	I	23
Shepherd mkt W1	2	I	17
Shepherd st W1	2	I	17
Shepherdess pl N1	3	I	33
Shepherdess wlk N1	3	H	33
Shepherd's Bush rd W6	1	A	1
Shepherd's pl W1	2	F	17
Sherborne la EC4	6	O	30
Sherwood st W1	2	I	20
Shillibeer pl W1	2	B	16
Shillington st SW11	4	R	5
Shipwright yd SE1	6	R	29
Shirley st N1	3	C	30
Shoe la EC4	6	K	27
Shorrolds rd SW6	4	J	1
Shorts gdns WC2	3	I	23
Short st SE1	6	O	24
Shottendane rd SW6	4	K	1
Shouldham st W1	2	C	16
Shropshire pl W1	3	E	23
Shroton st NW1	2	A	17
Shuttleworth rd SW11	4	Q	5
Sidford pl SE1	5	P	22
Sidmouth st WC1	3	F	27
Simpson st SW11	4	Q	5
Sinclair gdns W14	1	A	2
Sinclair rd W14	1	B	2
Skin Mkt pl SE1	6	O	27
Skinners la EC4	6	N	29
Skinner pl SW1	5	L	12
Skinner st EC1	3	H	30
Skipton st SE1	6	R	24
Slaidburn st SW10	4	L	5
Sleaford st SW8	5	R	13
Sloane av SW3	4	K	11
Sloane ct east SW3	5	M	12
Sloane ct west SW3	5	M	12
Sloane gdns SW1	5	L	12
Sloane sq SW1	5	L	12
Sloane st SW1	5	K	12
Sloane ter SW1	5	L	12
Smith sq SW1	5	O	19
Smith st SW3	4	L	10
Smith ter SW3	4	M	10
Smithfield st EC1	6	K	28
Smith's ct W1	2	I	21
Snowbury rd SW6	4	O	1
Snowden st EC2	6	L	33
Snow hill EC1	6	K	28
Snow's fields SE1	6	R	29
Soho sq W1	2	H	22
Soho st W1	2	H	22
Somers mews W2	2	C	14
Sotheron rd SW6	4	M	3
Soudan rd SW11	4	Q	7
Souldern st W14	1	C	1
Southampton bldgs WC2	6	J	26
Southampton pl WC1	3	H	25
Southampton row WC1	3	G	25
Southampton st WC2	6	J	23
S Audley st W1	2	G	17
S Carriage rd SW7	2	H	13
Southcombe st W14	1	D	2
South dri SW11	4	Q	9
South Eaton pl SW1	5	L	13
South end W8	1	F	7
Southern st N1	3	D	29
South Molton la W1	2	F	18
South Molton st W1	2	F	19
Southolm st SW11	4	R	10
South pde SW3	4	K	8
South pl EC2	6	M	32
South Pl mews EC2	6	M	32
South sq WC1	3	I	27
South st W1	2	H	17
South Tenter st E1	6	Q	33
South ter SW7	4	J	10
Southwark Bri SE1	6	O	28
Southwark Bri rd SE1	6	Q	26
Southwark gro SE1	6	P	27
Southwark st SE1	6	O	26
Southwell gdns SW7	1	G	8

Street	Grid
South Wharf rd W2	2 B 14
Southwick mews W2	2 B 14
Southwick pl W2	2 C 14
Southwick st W2	2 C 15
Spanish pl W1	2 D 18
Speech st SE1	6 R 24
Speedy pl WC1	3 E 26
Spencer pl SW1	5 M 17
Spencer st EC1	3 G 30
Spenser st SW1	5 M 17
Spicer st SW11	4 P 6
Sprimont pl SW3	4 K 11
Spring gdns SW1	5 K 21
Spring st W2	2 B 13
Stable yd SW1	5 K 18
Stable Yd rd SW1	5 K 18
Stadium st SW10	4 M 5
Stafford pl SW1	5 L 17
Stafford st W1	2 I 19
Stafford ter W8	1 D 6
Stag pl SW1	5 L 16
Stainer st SE1	6 Q 29
Stainforth rd SW11	4 R 6
Staining la EC2	6 L 30
Stalbridge st NW1	2 A 16
Stamford st SE1	6 N 24
Stanford rd W8	1 F 7
Stanford st SW1	5 O 17
Stanhope gdns SW7	1 H 8
Stanhope ga W1	2 H 16
Stanhope mews east SW7	1 H 8
Stanhope mews south SW7	1 H 8
Stanhope mews west SW7	1 H 8
Stanhope pl W2	2 D 15
Stanhope st NW1	3 C 23
Stanhope ter W2	2 C 13
Stanley pas NW1	3 C 27
Stanmer st SW11	4 Q 6
Stanmore st N1	3 B 30
Stanwick rd W14	1 F 3
Staple inn WC1	6 J 26
Starcross st NW1	3 C 23
Star rd W14	1 G 1
Star st W2	2 B 15
Star yd WC2	6 J 26
Steelworks rd SW11	4 R 2
Stephendale rd SW6	4 O 1
Stephen st W1	2 G 22
Sterling st SW7	2 H 12
Sterndale rd W14	1 B 1
Stewart's gro SW3	4 K 9
Stewarts la SW8	5 R 12
Stewarts rd SW8	5 R 12
Stillington st SW1	5 N 16
Stockwood st W1	4 R 2
Stokenchurch st SW6	4 M 1
Stonecutter st EC4	6 K 27
Stonefield st N1	3 D 32
Stones End st SE1	6 Q 26
Stoney la E1	6 O 33
Stoney st SE1	6 P 28
Stonor rd W14	1 F 3
Store st WC1	3 F 23
Storey's gt SW1	5 M 19
Story st N1	3 B 30
Stourcliffe st W1	2 D 16
Strand WC2	6 K 23
Strand la WC2	6 K 24
Stratford pl W1	2 F 19
Stratford rd W8	1 F 6
Stratford studios W8	1 F 6
Strathearn pl W2	2 C 14
Stratton st W1	2 I 18
Streatham st WC1	3 H 23
Strutton ground SW1	5 M 18
Studdridge st SW6	4 N 1
Studd st N1	3 D 33
Stukeley st WC2	3 I 24
Sturge st SE1	6 Q 26
Sturt st N1	3 H 33
Sudeley st N1	3 F 32
Sudrey st SE1	6 Q 26
Suffolk la EC4	6 O 30
Suffolk pl SW1	5 J 21
Suffolk st SW1	5 J 21
Sumner pl SW7	4 J 9
Sumner st SE1	6 O 27
Sunbury la SW11	4 O 5
Sun st EC2	6 L 33
Sun St pas EC2	6 M 33
Surrey la SW11	4 P 6
Surrey row SE1	6 P 25
Surrey st WC2	6 K 25
Sussex gdns W2	2 C 13
Sussex pl W2	2 C 14
Sussex sq W2	2 C 13
Sussex st SW1	5 O 14

Street	Grid
Sutherland row SW1	5 N 14
Sutherland st SW1	5 O 14
Sutton row W1	2 H 22
Swallow st W1	2 I 20
Swan st SE1	6 R 26
Swan wlk SW3	4 N 10
Swinton st WC1	3 E 28
Sydney clo SW7	4 J 9
Sydney grn EC1	3 G 31
Sydney mews SW7	4 J 9
Sydney pl SW7	4 J 9
Sydney st SW3	4 K 9
Symons st SW3	5 L 12
Tabard st SE1	6 R 27
Tabernacle st EC2	6 K 33
Tachbrook mews SW1	5 N 16
Tachbrook st SW1	5 O 16
Tadema rd SW10	4 M 5
Talbot sq W2	2 B 13
Talbot yd SE1	6 Q 28
Talgarth rd W14	1 F 1
Tallis st EC4	6 L 26
Tamworth st SW6	1 I 2
Tanswell st SE1	6 O 23
Taplow st N1	3 H 33
Taunton mews NW1	2 A 18
Taunton pl NW1	2 A 18
Tavistock pl WC1	3 E 25
Tavistock sq WC1	3 E 24
Tavistock st WC2	6 J 23
Taviton st WC1	3 E 24
Tedworth gdns SW3	4 M 10
Tedworth sq SW3	4 M 10
Telcott rd SW10	4 M 4
Telegraph st EC2	6 M 31
Temple av EC4	6 L 26
Temple pl WC2	6 K 25
Templeton pl SW5	1 G 5
Tenison way SE1	6 M 23
Tenniel clo W2	1 A 11
Tenter st EC2	6 L 31
Tenterden st W1	2 G 19
Terminus pl SW1	5 L 16
Tetbury pl N1	3 E 32
Thanet st WC1	3 E 26
Thavies inn EC4	6 K 27
Thayer st W1	2 E 19
Theberton st N1	3 D 32
Theed st SE1	6 N 24
Theobalds rd WC1	3 H 25
Thessaly rd SW8	5 R 13
Thirleby rd SW1	5 M 17
Thistle gro SW10	4 J 7
Thomas Doyle st SE1	6 Q 24
Thomas More st E1	6 R 33
Thoresby st N1	3 H 33
Thornedike st SW1	5 O 16
Thorney st SW1	5 O 19
Thornhaugh st WC1	3 F 24
Thornhill cres N1	3 B 31
Thornhill rd N1	3 B 32
Thornhill sq N1	3 B 31
Thornton pl W1	2 B 18
Thrale st SE1	6 P 27
Threadneedle st EC2	6 N 31
Three Kings yd W1	2 G 18
Three Tuns ct SE1	6 Q 28
Throgmorton av EC2	6 N 31
Throgmorton st EC2	6 N 31
Thurloe pl SW7	1 I 10
Thurloe sq SW7	1 I 10
Thurloe st SW7	1 I 9
Tilloch st N1	3 A 30
Tilney st W1	2 H 16
Tinworth st SE11	5 O 19
Tite st SW3	4 M 10
Tiverton st SE1	6 R 25
Tolmers sq NW1	3 D 23
Tompion st EC1	3 H 30
Tonbridge st WC1	3 E 26
Tooks ct EC4	6 J 26
Tooley st SE1	6 Q 30
Topaz st SE11	5 Q 21
Topham st EC1	3 H 28
Tor gdns W8	1 C 7
Torrens st N1	3 F 31
Torrington pl WC1	3 E 23
Torrington sq WC1	3 F 24
Tothill st SW1	5 M 19
Tottenham Ct rd W1	3 F 23
Tottenham st W1	3 F 23
Totteridge rd SW11	4 Q 4
Toulmin st SE1	6 Q 26
Tournay rd SW6	4 J 1
Tower bri E1	6 R 31
Tower Bri app E1	6 R 32
Tower ct WC2	3 I 23
Tower hill EC3	6 Q 32
Tower st WC2	2 I 22

Street	Grid
Townmead rd SW6	4 P 2
Transept st NW1	2 B 16
Trafalgar sq SW1 & WC2	5 K 22
Treaty st N1	3 C 29
Trebovir rd SW5	1 G 4
Tregunter rd SW10	4 J 5
Trevanion rd W14	1 E 2
Treveris st SE1	6 O 26
Trevor pl SW7	2 H 12
Trevor sq SW7	2 H 12
Trevor st SW7	2 H 12
Trinity Church sq SE1	6 R 26
Trinity sq EC3	6 Q 32
Trinity st SE1	6 R 26
Trio pl SE1	6 R 26
Trott st SW11	4 P 5
Tryon st SW3	4 L 11
Tudor pl	2 G 22
Tudor st EC4	6 L 26
Tufton st SW1	5 O 19
Turk's row SW3	4 M 11
Turpentine la SW1	5 O 13
Turneville rd W14	1 G 1
Turnmill st EC1	3 I 29
Twyford pl WC2	3 I 25
Twyford st N1	3 B 30
Tyer's st SE11	5 R 19
Tyer's ter SE11	5 R 19
Tynemouth st SW6	4 O 2
Tyrawley rd SW6	4 L 2
Tysoe st EC1	3 G 29
Udall st SW1	5 O 16
Ufford st SE1	6 O 24
Underwood st N1	3 I 33
Unicorn pas SE1	6 R 30
Union ct EC2	6 N 32
Union st SE1	6 O 25
University st WC1	3 E 23
Upcerne rd SW10	4 M 4
Upper Addison gdns W14	1 A 3
Upper Belgrave st SW1	5 K 15
Upper Berkeley st W1	2 D 16
Upper Brook mews W2	2 B 12
Upper Brook st W1	2 F 16
Upper Cheyne row SW3	4 M 8
Upper Grosvenor st W1	2 F 16
Upper ground SE1	6 M 24
Upper Harley st NW1	2 C 20
Upper James st W1	2 H 20
Upper John st W1	2 H 20
Upper marsh SE1	5 O 22
Upper Montagu st W1	2 B 17
Upper Phillimore gdns W8	1 C 6
Upper st N1	3 E 32
Upper St Martins la WC2	3 J 22
Upper Thames st EC4	6 M 28
Upper Wimpole st W1	2 D 20
Upper Woburn pl WC1	3 E 24
Ursula st SW11	4 Q 6
Usk rd SW11	4 R 1
Uverdale rd SW10	4 M 4
Uxbridge st W8	1 B 7
Valentine pl SE1	6 P 24
Valentine rd SE1	6 P 24
Vale the SW3	4 L 7
Vandon st SW1	5 M 18
Vanston pl SW6	4 J 2
Varndell st NW1	3 B 23
Vauxhall bri SW1	5 Q 17
Vauxhall Bri rd SW1	5 N 16
Vauxhall st SE11	5 R 20
Vauxhall wlk SE11	5 R 19
Vereker rd W14	1 F 1
Vere st W1	2 F 19
Vernon mews W14	1 E 2
Vernon rise WC1	3 E 28
Vernon sq WC1	3 E 29
Vernon st W14	1 E 2
Verona st SW11	4 R 3
Verulam st EC1	3 I 27
Vicarage cres SW11	4 P 4
Vicarage gdns W8	1 C 8
Vicarage ga W8	1 C 8
Victoria Embkmt EC4, SW1 & WC2	5 M 22
Victoria gdns W11	1 A 7
Victoria gro W8	1 F 8
Victoria rd W8	1 F 8
Victoria sq SW1	5 L 16
Victoria st SW1	5 M 17
Vigo st W1	2 I 20
Villiers st WC2	5 K 22
Vincent sq SW1	5 N 17
Vincent st SW1	5 O 18
Vincent ter N1	3 F 32
Vinehill EC1	3 H 28
Vine la SE1	6 R 30
Vine st EC3	6 P 33

Street			
Vine st bri EC1	3	I	29
Vine yd SE1	6	Q	27
Virgil pl W1	2	B	17
Viscount st EC1	6	K	31
Wakefield st WC1	3	F	26
Wakley st EC1	3	G	31
Walbrook EC4	6	N	30
Walcot sq SE11	5	R	22
Walham gro SW6	4	J	2
Wallgrave rd SW5	1	G	5
Walmer pl W1	2	B	17
Walmer st W1	2	B	17
Walnut Tree wlk SE11	5	Q	22
Walpole st SW3	4	L	11
Walton pl SW3	2	I	12
Walton st SW3	4	J	11
Wandon rd SW6	4	L	4
Wandsworth rd SW8	5	R	17
Wandsworth Bri rd SW6	4	O	1
Wansdown pl SW6	4	K	3
Wardour st W1	2	I	21
Warner st EC1	3	H	28
Warren st W1	2	D	22
Warriner gdns SW11	4	R	8
Warsill st SW11	4	R	8
Warwick ct WC1	3	I	26
Warwick gdns W14	1	E	4
Warwick Ho st SW1	5	K	21
Warwick la EC4	6	L	28
Warwick pl SW1	5	N	15
Warwick rd SW5 & W14	1	G	4
Warwick sq SW1	5	N	15
Warwick st W1	2	H	20
Warwick way SW1	5	N	14
Warwick yd EC1	6	J	31
Waterford rd SW6	4	L	2
Watergate EC4	6	L	27
Watergate wlk WC2	5	K	22
Waterloo bri SE1	6	L	24
Waterloo pl SW1	5	J	20
Waterloo rd SE1	6	O	24
Waterloo ter N1	3	C	33
Watford villas SW11	4	P	7
Watling st EC4	6	M	29
Watsons mews W1	2	B	16
Waverton st W1	2	H	17
Waxwell st SE1	5	O	22
Wayford st SW11	4	R	5
Wayland rd SW11	4	R	2
Weavers la SE1	6	R	30
Webber row SE1	6	P	23
Webber st SE1	6	P	24
Weighhouse st W1	2	F	18
Weirs pas NW1	3	D	26
Welbeck st W1	2	E	19
Welbeck way W1	2	E	19
Wellers ct NW1	3	C	27
Weller st SE1	6	Q	26
Wellesley ter N1	3	I	33
Wellington sq SW3	4	L	11
Wellington st WC2	6	J	24
Wells mews W1	2	F	22
Wells st W1	2	F	21
Wenlock rd N1	3	H	33
West rd SW3	4	N	11
Westbourne cres W2	2	B	12
Westbourne st W2	2	C	13
Westbourne ter W2	2	B	13
Westbridge rd SW11	4	O	6
W Central st WC1	3	H	24
W Conduit st N1	3	E	31
W Cromwell rd SW5 & W14	1	F	3
West dri SW11	4	P	8
West Eaton pl SW1	5	K	13
Westgate ter SW10	4	J	5
West Halkin st NW1	5	J	14
Westland pl N1	3	I	33
Westminster bri SW1	5	N	21
Westminster Bri rd SE1	5	O	22
Westmoreland pl SW1	5	O	14
Westmoreland st W1	2	D	19
Westmoreland ter SW1	5	O	13
Weston pl SE1	6	R	28
Weston rise WC1	3	E	28
Weston st SE1	6	R	29
W Smithfield EC1	6	K	29
West st WC2	2	I	22
West sq SE11	6	R	23
Westwick gdns W14	1	A	1
Wetherby gdns SW5	1	I	6
Wetherby mews SW5	1	I	6
Wetherby pl SW7	1	I	7
Weymouth st W1	2	D	20
Wharfdale rd N1	3	C	28
Wharfedale st SW10	1	I	5
Wharf rd N1	3	G	33
Wharton st WC1	3	F	28
Wheelwright st N7	3	A	31

Street			
Whetstone pk WC2	3	I	25
Whiskin st EC1	3	H	30
Whitaker st SW1	5	L	12
Whitcomb st WC2	5	J	21
White Hart yd SE1	6	Q	28
White Horse st W1	2	I	17
White Horse yd EC2	6	M	31
White Kennett st E1	6	O	33
White Lion st N1	3	E	30
Whitecross pl EC2	6	M	33
Whitefriars st EC4	6	L	27
Whitehall SW1	5	L	21
Whitehall ct SW1	5	L	22
Whitehall gdns SW1	5	L	21
Whitehall pl SW1	5	L	22
Whitehead's gro SW3	4	K	10
Whitfield st W1	2	E	22
Whitgift st SE11	5	Q	20
Whittlesey st SE1	6	N	24
Wickham st SE11	5	R	19
Wicklow st WC1	3	E	28
Wigmore pl W1	2	E	20
Wigmore st W1	2	E	19
Wilbraham pl SW1	5	K	12
Wilby mews W11	1	A	7
Wild ct WC2	6	J	24
Wild st WC2	6	J	24
Wilfred st SW1	5	L	17
William IV st WC2	5	J	22
William rd NW1	3	C	23
William's mews SW1	2	I	14
William st SW1	2	I	14
Willow pl SW1	5	N	16
Wilmington sq WC1	3	G	29
Wilson st EC2	6	L	33
Wilton cres SW1	5	J	14
Wilton mews SW1	5	K	15
Wilton pl SW1	2	I	14
Wilton rd SW1	5	M	16
Wilton row SW1	2	I	14
Wilton st SW1	5	K	15
Wimpole mews W1	2	D	20
Wimpole st W1	2	E	19
Winchester st SW1	5	O	14
Winchester sq SE1	6	P	28
Winchester wlk SE1	6	P	28
Wincott st SE11	5	R	22
Winders rd SW11	4	Q	5
Windmill la SE8	6	N	24
Windmill st W1	2	F	22
Windmill wlk SE1	6	O	24
Windsor pl SW1	5	N	17
Windsor st N1	3	E	33
Windsor ter N1	3	H	33
Wine Office ct EC4	6	K	27
Winsland mews W2	2	B	14
Winsland st W2	2	B	14
Winsley st W1	2	G	21
Winstanley rd SW11	4	R	3
Winstead st SW11	4	P	6
Winterton clo SW10	4	K	6
Woburn mews WC1	3	F	25
Woburn pl WC1	3	E	25
Woburn sq WC1	3	F	24
Woburn wlk WC1	3	E	25
Woodbridge st EC1	3	H	29
Woodfall st SW3	4	M	11
Woods mews W1	2	F	16
Woodstock gro W12	1	A	3
Woodstock st W1	2	F	19
Wood st EC2	6	L	30
Woolneigh st SW6	4	O	1
Wootton st SE1	6	O	24
Worfield st SW11	4	P	7
Worgan st SE11	5	R	19
Wormwood st EC2	6	N	32
Worship st EC2	6	L	33
Wren st WC1	3	G	27
Wright's la W8	1	E	7
Wyclif st EC1	3	H	30
Wye st SW11	4	R	4
Wyndham pl W1	2	C	17
Wyndham st W1	2	B	17
Wynford rd N1	3	D	30
Wynnstay gdns W8	1	E	6
Wynter st SW11	4	R	1
Wynyatt st EC1	3	G	31
Wyvern pl WC1	3	H	25
Yardley st WC1	3	G	29
Yelverton rd SW11	4	Q	4
Yeoman's row SW3	1	I	11
York ga NW1	2	B	20
York pl WC2	5	K	22
York pl SW11	4	Q	2
York rd SE1	5	N	22
York rd SW11	4	R	1
York st W1	2	C	17
York ter NW1	2	B	19
York way N1	3	C	28

Street			
Young st W8	1	E	8
Zoar st SE1	6	O	27

Cinemas	Tel. nos.
ABC 1 & 2	836 8861
Academy 1	437 2981
Academy 2	437 5129
Academy 3	437 8819
Astoria	580 9562
Berkeley 1 & 2	636 8150
Bloomsbury	837 1177
Carlton	930 3711
Casino Cinerama	437 6877
Centa	734 1449
Cinecenta 1, 2, 3 & 4	930 0631
Cineclub 24	636 3228
Classic	437 2380
Classic (Charing X rd)	930 6915
Classic (Moulin)	437 1653
Classic (Victoria)	834 6588
Classic Windmill	437 7413
Columbia	734 5414
Compton Cine Club	437 4555
Continentale	636 4193
Curzon	499 3737
Dilly Cine Club	437 6266
Dominion	580 9562
Empire	437 1234
Eros	437 3839
Gala Royal	262 2345
Jacey (Charing X rd)	437 4815
Jacey (Leicester sq)	437 2001
Jacey (Trafalgar sq)	930 1143
Leicester Square Theatre	930 5252
London Pavilion	437 2982
Metropole	834 4673
National Film Theatre	928 3232
Odeon Haymarket	930 2738
Odeon Leicester sq	930 6111
Odeon Marble Arch	723 2011
Odeon St Martin's Lane	836 0691
Plaza	839 6494
Prince Charles	437 8181
Rialto	437 3488
Ritz	437 1234
Scene 1, 2, 3, 4	439 4446
Studio 1 & 2	437 3300
Universal	930 8944
Warner 1, 2, 3 & 4	439 0791

Theatres	Tel. nos.
Adelphi	836 7611
Albery	836 3878
Aldwych	836 6404
Ambassadors	836 1171
Apollo	437 2663
Arts	836 3334
Cambridge	836 6056
Coliseum	836 3161
Comedy	930 2578
Covent Garden	240 1911/1066
Criterion	930 3216
Drury Lane	836 8108
Duchess	836 8243
Duke of York's	836 5122
Fortune	836 2238
Garrick	836 4601
Globe	437 1592
Haymarket	930 9832
Her Majesty's	930 6606
Jeanetta Cochrane Theatre	242 7040
Lit. Theatre Club	240 0660
Lyric	437 3686
Lyttelton	928 2252
May Fair	629 3036
Mermaid	248 7656
New London	405 0072
New Victoria	834 2544
Old Vic	928 7616
Open Space	580 4970
Palace	437 6834
Palladium	437 7373
Phoenix	836 8611
Piccadilly	437 4506
Players	839 1134
Price of Wales	930 9681
Queen Elizabeth H.	928 3191
Queen's	734 1166
Regent	323 2707
Royal Albert Hall	589 8212
Royal Festival Hall	928 3191
Royalty	405 8004
Sadler's Wells	837 1672
St. Martin's	836 1443
Savoy	836 8888
Shaftesbury	836 6596
Strand	836 2660
Talk of the Town	734 5051
Vaudeville	836 9988
Victoria Palace	834 1317
Westminster	834 0283
Whitehall	930 6692
Wigmore H.	635 2141
Wyndham's	836 3028

© Robert Nicholson Publications

Cinemas & Theatres Map

Not to scale

● Cinemas
■ Theatres

Stores   Tel. nos.

Aquascutum 734 6090
Army & Navy 834 1234
Asprey 493 6767
Austin Reed 734 6789
Barkers 937 5432
Bourne & Hollingsworth 636 1515
Building Centre 637 4522
C & A Modes 629 7272
Cartier 493 6962
Christie's 839 9060
Civil Service Stores 836 1212
Debenhams 580 3000
Design Centre 839 8000
Dickins & Jones 734 7070
D. H. Evans 629 8800
Fenwick 629 9161
Fortnum & Mason 734 8040
Foyles 437 5660
General Trading Company 730 0411
Habitat 351 1211
Habitat (Tott. Ct. rd) 387 9021
Hamleys 734 3161
Harrods 730 1234
Harvey Nichols 235 5000
Heals 636 1666
Imhof's 636 7878
Jaeger 734 4050
John Lewis 629 7711
Laura Ashley 730 1771
Liberty's 734 1234
Lillywhites 930 3181
Maples 387 7000
Marks & Spencer (Marble Arch) 486 6151
Marks & Spencer 437 3761
Mothercare 629 6621
Peter Jones 730 3434
Peter Robinson 636 7700
Selfridges 629 1234
Simpson 734 2002
Sotheby's 493 8080
Swan & Edgar 734 1616

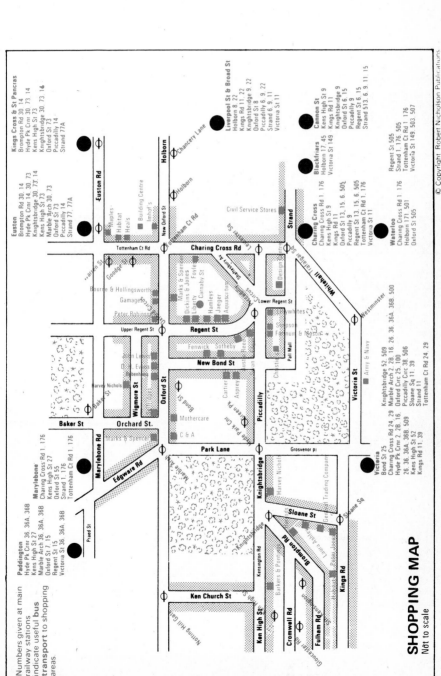

Numbers given at main railway stations indicate useful **bus transport** to shopping areas.

SHOPPING MAP
Not to scale

© Copyright Robert Nicholson Publications

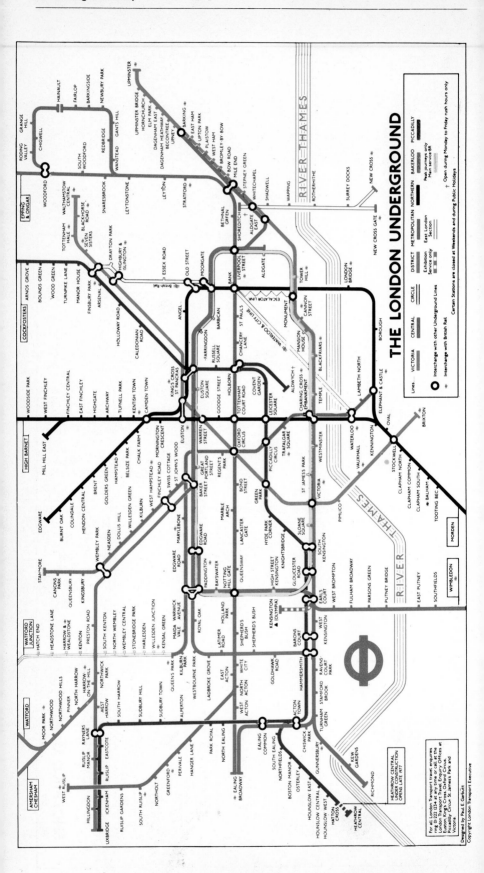

THE LONDON UNDERGROUND

For all London Transport travel enquiries ring 01-222 1234 at any time or call at the London Transport Travel Enquiry Offices at Euston, King's Cross, Oxford Circus, Piccadilly Circus, St James's Park and Victoria.

Designed by Paul E Garbutt
Copyright London Transport Executive

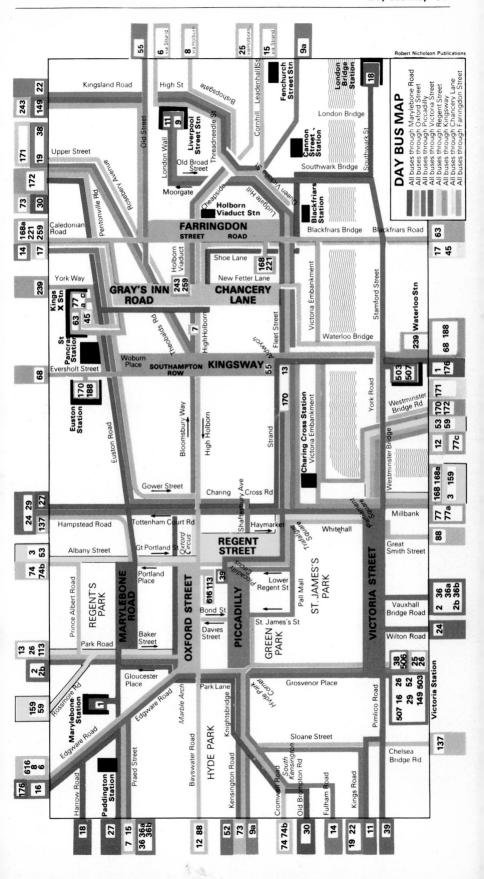

Robert Nicholson Publications

DAY BUS MAP

All buses through Marylebone Road
All buses through Oxford Street
All buses through Piccadilly
All buses through Victoria Street
All buses through Regent Street
All buses through Kingsway
All buses through Chancery Lane
All buses through Farringdon Street

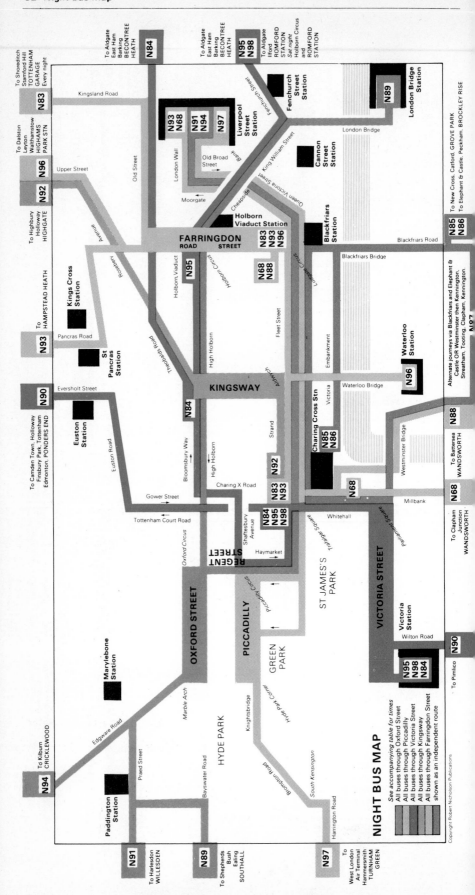

NIGHT BUS MAP

See accompanying table for times
All buses through Oxford Street
All buses through Piccadilly
All buses through Victoria Street
All buses through Kingsway
All buses through Farringdon Street
shown as an independent route

Copyright Robert Nicholson Publications

Night bus map timetable

Only routes indicated in red run on Saturday nights

N83	from Trafalgar Square (except Saturday nights)	00.52
		04.29
		05.32
	from Farringdon Street	01.49
	from Ludgate Circus	03.32
N83	(Saturday nights)	
	from Trafalgar Square	00.52
		04.29
		05.43
	from Farringdon Street	02.00
		06.56
	from Ludgate Circus	03.32
N84	from Trafalgar Square	00.39
	from Victoria Station	00.55
N85	about every ½ hour	
N86	about every ¼ hour	
N87	about every 20 minutes	
N88	about every 1-2 hours	
N89	about every hour	
N90	about every hour	
N91	from Liverpool Street	23.56
		02.32
		04.47
N92	about every ½ hour	
N93	from Trafalgar Square	23.54
		03.51
		04.50
	from Farringdon Street	00.54
		01.37
	from Ludgate Circus	02.58
N94	from Liverpool Street	00.37
		01.37
		03.32
		05.13
		05.40
	from Aldwych	03.00
N95	from Trafalgar Square	01.19
		02.07
	from Victoria	04.05
		04.52
	from Red Lion Square	06.10
	from Holborn (Kingsway) Station	06.36
N96	about every hour from	01.13
N97	about every ½ hour	
N98	from Victoria	02.43
		03.11
		03.37
		04.07
		05.26
	from Trafalgar Square	00.14
		00.43
		01.17
		05.05
		05.52
		06.02
	from Bank	00.16
	from Aldgate	23.55
N98	from Holborn Circus	00.55
		04.24
		05.16
		06.03
	from Bank	02.33
		03.33
		04.29
	from Aldgate Station	23.53
		01.03
N68	from Farringdon Street	00.38
		05.14
	from Ludgate Circus	03.10
		05.15
	from Trafalgar Square	01.41
		04.10

RED ARROW BUSES

Route 507 runs every day, 500 Monday to Saturday, and all other routes Monday to Friday only

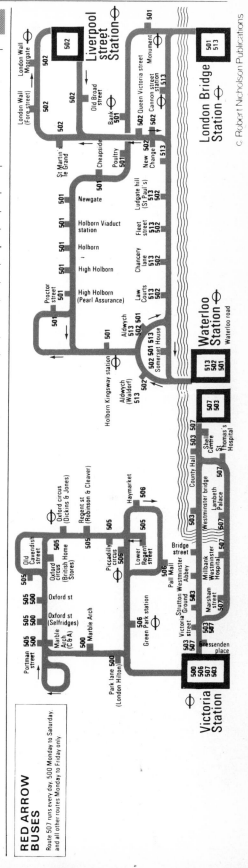

c. Robert Nicholson Publications

Parking

Charges vary according to the length of stay and the proximity to Central London. Most of these listed are National Car Parks, whose rates range from 37p-£3.00 for up to 9 hours. Underground and multi-storey car parks tend to be expensive, but are more secure than surface car parks, which mostly close at night. Some garages charge more for larger cars. Most have a cheap overnight rate.

Abingdon Street   **5 N 20**
SW1. 01-930 1621. Undercover. Capacity 250. *OPEN 24 hrs, 7 days a week.*

Aldersgate   **6 K 30**
Aldersgate St EC1. 01-606 2192. Undercover. Capacity 850. *OPEN 24 hrs, 7 days a week.*

Audley Square   **2 H 17**
W1. 01-499 1721. Undercover. Capacity 310. *OPEN 24 hrs, 7 days a week.*

Bayswater Road   **1 B 10**
Kensington Gardens W8. *OPEN 08.00-18.00 Mon-Sat. 08.30-18.30 Mon-Sat during summer.*

Bishopsgate   **6 N 33**
EC2. Open. Capacity 300. *OPEN 08.00-18.00 Mon-Sat. 08.00-14.00 Sun.*

Blackfriars   **6 N 26**
SE1. Open. Capacity 150. *OPEN 07.30-18.30 Mon-Fri.*

Broad Street Station   **M 32**
EC2. Open. Capacity 360. *OPEN 07.00-18.30 Mon-Fri. 08.00-14.00 Sat-Sun.*

Cadogan Place Gardens   **5 K 13**
SW1. 01-235 5106. Undercover. Capacity 349. *OPEN 24 hrs. 7 days a week.*

Cavendish Square   **2 F 20**
W1. 01-629 6968. Undercover. Capacity 545. *OPEN 07.00-23.00 Mon-Sat.*

Chiltern Street   **2 D 18**
W1. 01-486 4509. Undercover. Capacity 394. *OPEN 24 hrs, 7 days a week.*

Cumberland Garage   **2 E 16**
W1. Bryanston St, off Marble Arch. 01-493 6927. *OPEN 24 hrs, all week.*

Denman Street   **2 I 21**
W1. 01-437 6801. Undercover. Capacity 320. *OPEN 07.30-24.00 all week.*

Dolphin Square   **5 Q 15**
SW1. 01-834 1077. Undercover. Capacity 300. Petrol facilities. *OPEN 24 hrs, 7 days a week.*

Euston Station   **3 D 23**
NW1. 01-387 9114. Capacity 500. *OPEN 24 hrs, 7 days a week.*

Festival Hall   **6 M 23**
South Bank, SE1. Open. Capacity 529. *OPEN 7.00-23.00 Mon-Sat.*

Finsbury Square   **6 L 33**
EC2. 01-638 8055. Undercover. Capacity 320. Petrol facilities. *OPEN 08.00-20.00 Mon-Fri.*

Grosvenor Hill   **2 G 18**
W1. 01-499 4331. Undercover. Capacity 230. *OPEN 08.00-20.00 Mon-Fri.*

Harley Garage   **2 E 20**
Queen Anne Mews W1. 01-636 0838. Undercover. Capacity 400. *OPEN 24 hrs, 7 days a week.*

Hillgate House   **6 L 28**
Seacoal lane EC4. 01-248 5467. Undercover. Capacity 180. *OPEN 24 hrs, 7 days a week.*

Hilton Hotel   **2 I 16**
Park Lane W1. 01-629 6915. Undercover. Capacity 200. *OPEN 24 hrs, 7 days a week.*

Holborn   **3 H 24**
Museum St WC1. 01-836 2039. Undercover. Capacity 250. *OPEN 24 hrs, 7 days a week.*

Ironmonger Row   **3 I 32**
EC1. Open. Capacity 300. *OPEN 08.00-18.00 Mon-Fri.*

London Wall   **6 L 30**
Moorgate EC2. 01-628 7468. Undercover. Capacity 250. *OPEN 07.30-19.00 Mon-Fri. 07.30-13.30 Sat.*

Marylebone Road   **2 B 17**
W1. 01-935 6078. Undercover. Capacity 180. *OPEN 24 hrs, 7 days a week.*

Millman Street   **3 H 26**
Gt James St WC1. Open. Capacity 200. *OPEN 08.00-18.00 Mon-Fri.*

Minories   **6 P 33**
EC3. 01-709 0143. Undercover. Capacity 640. *OPEN 24 hrs, 7 days a week.*

Oakley Street   **4 M 9**
SW3. Open. Capacity 200. *Open 08.00-18.30 Mon-Sat.*

Old Burlington Street   **2 H 19**
W1. 01-437 2313. Undercover. Capacity 480. *OPEN 07.30-24.00 Mon-Fri. 07.30-12.00 Sat.*

Old Park Lane   **2 I 16**
W1. Undercover. Capacity 80. *OPEN 24 hrs all week.*

Park Lane   **2 G 16**
W1. 01-262 1814. Undercover. Capacity 1,100. *OPEN 24 hrs, 7 days a week.*

Paternoster Row   **6 L 28**
Ave Maria Lane EC4. 01-248 7527. Undercover. Capacity 277. *OPEN 24 hrs, 7 days a week.*

Piccadilly Circus   **2 I 21**
Brewer St W1. 01-734 9497. Undercover. Capacity 450. Petrol facilities. *OPEN 24 hrs, 7 days a week.*

Portman Square Garage   **2 D 17**
W1. 01-935 5310. Undercover. Capacity 440. *OPEN 24 hrs, 7 days a week.*

Queensway   **1 A 11**
W2. 01-727 6173. Undercover. Capacity 300. *OPEN 24 hrs, 7 days a week.*

Rochester Row   **6 N 33**
SW1. 01-828 4298. Undercover. Capacity 299. Petrol facilities. *OPEN 24 hrs, 7 days a week.*

Rodwell House   **6 N 33**
Strype St E1. 01-247 7923. Undercover. Capacity 225. *OPEN 24 hrs, 7 days a week.*

Royal Garden Hotel   **1 E 8**
Kensington High St W8. 01-937 8000 Ext 851. Undercover. Capacity 250. *OPEN 24 hrs, 7 days a week.*

Saffron Hill   **3 I 28**
EC1. 01-405 5871. Undercover. Capacity 400. *OPEN 07.00-22.00 Mon-Fri. 08.00-13.00 Sat.*

Semley Place   **5 M 13**
SW1. 01-730 3302. Undercover. Capacity 422. *OPEN 24 hrs, 7 days a week.*

Smithfield Central Markets   **6 K 28**
Giltspur St EC1. 01-248 1039. Undercover. Capacity 430. *OPEN 24 hrs, 7 days a week.*

Tower Hill   **6 Q 32**
Lower Thames St EC3. 01-626 2082. Undercover. Capacity 270. *OPEN 07.30-19.30 Mon-Fri. 07.30-13.30 Sat.*

Upper St Martin's Lane   **5 J 22**
WC2. 01-836 7451. Undercover. Capacity 220. *OPEN 08.00-24.00 Mon-Fri, 08.00-02.00 Sat*

Upper Thames Street   **6 M 28**
EC3. 01-283 7776. Undercover. Capacity 635. *OPEN 05.00-1930 Mon-Fri. 05.00-13.30 Sat.*

Vintry   **6 N 29**
Upper Thames St EC4. 01-236 3640. Undercover. Capacity 485. *OPEN 07.00-19.00 Mon-Fri*

Warner Street   **3 H 28**
EC1. Open. Capacity 250. *OPEN 08.00-18.30 Mon-Fri. 08.00-13.00 Sat.*

Warwick Way   **5 N 15**
SW1. 01-828 4520. Undercover. Capacity 465. *OPEN 24 hrs, 7 days a week.*

Water Garden   **2 C 15**
Burwood Place W2. 01-723 4940. Undercover. Capacity 300. *OPEN 24 hrs, 7 days a week.*

Wright's Lane   **1 E 7**
W8. Open. Capacity 200. *OPEN 08.00-18.00 Mon-Fri.*

Y.M.C.A.   **3 F 23**
Tottenham Court Rd W1. *OPEN 24 hrs all week.*

Young Street   **1 E 8**
Kensington W8. 01-937 7420. Undercover. Capacity 270. *OPEN 24 hrs, 7 days a week.*

Sightseeing

Information centres

These are the main sources of information available to the tourist about events, places or travel.

British Rail Travel Centre   **5 J 20**
4 Lower Regent St SW1. Personal callers only. British Rail's shop window in the West End. Booking centre for rail travel in Britain and rail-and-sea journeys to the Continent and Ireland. Several languages spoken. Smaller offices at: 14 Kingsgate Parade. Victoria St SW1, 407 Oxford St W1, 170b Strand WC2, 87 King William St EC4.

British Tourist Authority   **5 J 19**
64 St James's St SW1. 01-629 9191. Tourist information about Britain. Nine languages spoken. Literature, some free, some on sale. *OPEN Apr-Oct 09.00-18.00 Mon-Fri, 09.00-14.30 Sat. Nov-Mar 09.00-17.30 Mon-Fri, 09.00-12.30 Sat. CLOSED Sun.*

City of London Information Centre   **6 M 28**
St Paul's Churchyard EC4. 01-606 3030. Information and advice with specific reference to the 'Square Mile'. Free literature. Essential to get monthly 'Diary of Events' which lists a big choice of free entertainment in the City. *OPEN 09.30-17.00 Mon-Fri, 10.00-16.00 Sat (until 12.30 in winter). CLOSED Sun.*

Daily Telegraph Information Bureau
Telephone only 01-353 4242. General information service available *Mon-Fri 09.30-17.30.*

Guildhall Library   **6 M 30**
King St EC2. 01-606 3030. Will tell you anything historical about London. *OPEN 09.30-17.00 Mon-Sat.*

International Travellers' Aid   **3 H 23**
Head Office, YWCA, 16 Great Russell St WC1. 01-580 1478. To help any traveller in distress but particularly concerned with young people and mothers travelling with young children. Will meet and escort a traveller across London, but book in advance.

London Tourist Board Information Bureau   **5 K 15**
Give travel and tourist information. Also information on accommodation. Most languages spoken. 26 Grosvenor Gardens SW1. 01-730 0791. *OPEN summer 09.00-20.00, winter 09.00-18.00.*

Student Accommodation Bureau   **5 L 16**
8-10 Buckingham Palace Rd SW1. 01-730 9841. *OPEN summer only 08.00-23.00.* Personal callers only.
Victoria Station SW1   **5 M 15**
Opposite platform 15. *Open May-Sep 07.30-23.00. Oct-Apr 09.00-21.00. Closed Xmas.* Personal callers only.

Travel Enquiry Offices
London Transport offices for enquiries on travel (underground and buses) and general tourist information. Their booklet 'How to get there' (5p) is essential. Also free maps of underground and buses.
St James's Park Underground Station   **5 M 18**
01-222 1234. *24-hr telephone service.*
Oxford Circus Underground Station   **2 G 20**
Victoria Station Underground Station   **5 M 15**
Euston Station Underground Station   **3 C 24**
King's Cross Underground Station   **3 D 27**
Piccadilly Circus Underground Station   **2 I 20**
Green Line Coaches have an enquiry office giving details of London country buses at:
Eccleston Bridge, Victoria SW1.   **5 M 15**
01-834 6563.
All OPEN daily 08.00-18.00.

Telephone Services

Emergency calls 999

Directory enquiries
Great Britain 192
London 142

International calls
You can now dial direct to many European countries, Canada and the USA. If the exchange you want is not listed in the GPO Dialing instructions booklet, ask the operator to put you through to the relevant International Exchange operator.

Telegrams
Inland, Ships & Enquiries 190
International 557
International enquiries 559

Ships telephone service
For telephone calls to ships 100

Radiophone service 141

Recorded services
Bedtime stories *18.00-08.00* 246 8000
Children's London 246 8007
Dial-a-Disc *18.00-08.00 weekdays (19.00 during test matches), all day Sun.* 160, also:
Test matches *08.00-19.00 Mon-Sat.* 154
Financial Times share index & Business News summary 246 8026. Updated four times *daily.*
Gardening *08.00-1800* 246 8000
Motoring information
Details of roadworks and traffic delays within 50 miles of London 246 8021.
Daily recipe 246 8071. Dial this number on *Sun* for the 'Food market', an advisory service for shoppers.
Time: speaking clock 123
Daily events in and around London
Teletourist in English 246 8041
in French 246 8043
in German 246 8045
in Spanish 246 8047
in Italian 246 8049
Weather forecasts
London area 246 8091
Essex coast 246 8096
Sussex coast 246 8097
Kent coast 246 8098
Thames valley 246 8090
Bedford area 246 8099
For all other areas ring the Meteorological office 836 4311.

London maps and guides

London Street Finder 75p
The clearest, most up-to-date and easy to use street atlas of London available.
London Street Finder, Large Edition £2.25
A super de luxe version of the standard book. Plastic laminate cover, large scale and two colour maps, one-ways clearly marked.
Night Life 95p
Practical and 'hot spots' guide to London after dark. Coloured centre maps.
Student's London 75p
Essential information for the student, impecunious tourist or Londoner.
American's London £1.50
Written for Americans by Americans.
Parents' Guide to Children's London 95p
Everything to keep the kids happy and amused.
Guide to the Thames £1.25
A practical guide designed to enable the reader to get maximum pleasure from the river. Comprehensive text accompanied by large scale maps.
Sightseer's London 50p
A colourful map and guide.
London Map 50p
Highly detailed map and index of London.
2 London Maps 75p
Central London map and index. Greater London route-planning map, bus, underground and theatre, cinema and shopping maps.
Visitor's Map of London 50p
Handy fold-out map showing all the sights in 3D.

Viewpoints

A nice way of orientating oneself or seeing London with a fresh sense of alignment is to go to the top of one of the very tall, new buildings. Together with old favourites and natural viewpoints, these are the most outstanding

Alexandra Palace
On Muswell Hill N22. About 250 ft. View from the terrace over Kent, Surrey, Essex and Hertfordshire. Free.

Hampstead Heath
450 ft high. Constable's famous view of London. A more comfortable view from:

Jack Straw's Castle
North End Way NW3. 01-435 8885. Lunch and dinner in the restaurant with long views across London to the distant Kentish hills. *CLOSES 20.00 LD (Sun L only)*

Heathrow Airport, London
Roof of Queens' Building, Heathrow, Middx. A favourite for children. Aircraft continuously landing and taking off. *OPEN 10.00-dusk.* Small admission charge.

London Hilton   2 I 16
Park Lane W1. 01-493 8000. Roof bar at 320 ft. Lift. Fine views on Hyde Park, Buckingham Palace and Mayfair.

Post Office Tower   2 E 22
Cleveland St W1. 01-636 9361. The highest restaurant in London, revolving slowly and giving an ever-changing view over Regent's Park, central and outer London: from Epping Forest in the east to the Surrey hills in the west.

St Paul's Cathedral   6 M 28
EC4. Magnificent view of the City, the Wren churches, the Tower and London Pool. 335 ft. 727 steps. *OPEN Mon-Sat 10.45-15.15 (& 16.45-18.80 Summer only).* Small admission charge to see the galleries.

Daily ceremonies

These are the main ceremonies that occur daily throughout the year. For information about individual day's events dial Teletourist service (see under Information centres).

The Changing of the Queen's Guard   5 K 17
Buckingham Palace SW1
The new Guard, following the band, arrives from Chelsea or Wellington Barracks for ceremony lasting ½hr. Not held in bad weather. *Daily 11.30, alternate days in winter.*
The old Guard leaves St James's for Buckingham Palace at *11.15.* Small ceremony.

The Changing of the Queen's Life Guard   5 L 21
Horse Guards Arch, Whitehall SW1.
The ceremony popularly known as 'the changing of the Guard' lasts 20 mins. *11.00 (Sun 10.00).* The Guard is also inspected on foot at *16.00.*

The Changing of the Guard
Windsor Castle, Windsor Berks.
A new Guard relieves the old Guard *every day at 10.30.* A military band enlivens the pageant.

Ceremony of the Keys   6 Q 32
Tower of London EC3
The Chief Warder, with an escort of soldiers bearing arms, locks the West Gates and the Middle Tower and Byward Tower doors with traditional ceremony. *21.40* by written application to the Governor.

Annual events

The following list presents not only the most important annual events but also some of the more obscure London customs in order to cover as wide a field as possible. For exact dates, times and places, where not given, contact one of the centres given under 'Information centres'.

January

International Boat Show   1 H 4
Earls Court, Warwick Rd SW5. 01-385 1200. The latest pleasure craft, yachts and equipment. *Early Jan.*

Royal Epiphany Gifts   5 J 19
Chapel Royal, St James's Place, Marlborough Rd SW1. Picturesque ceremony, when two 'Gentleman Ushers' offer gold, frankincense and myrrh on behalf of the Queen. *11.30, 6th Jan.*

International Racing Car Show   1 D 2
Olympia. *Jan.*

Chinese New Year   2 I 22
Soho, Gerrard St W1. Papier-mâché dragon and lit-up festivities march through the centre of London's Chinese community. *Jan or Feb.*

February

English Folk Dance & Song Societies Festival   1 F 10
Royal Albert Hall, Kensington Gore SW7. 01-589 8212. *No fixed date.*

Cruft's Dog Show   1 D 2
Olympia. *Early Feb.*

International Furniture Show   1 H 4
Earls Court. *Feb.*

March

St David's Day
Windsor, Berks. Leeks given to the Welsh Guards. Generally attended by the Duke of Edinburgh. *1st Mar.*

Daily Mail Ideal Home Exhibition   1 D 2
Olympia. Very popular and always crowded.

St Patrick's Day
Pirbright, Surrey. Shamrocks given to the Irish Guards by the Queen Mother. *17th Mar.*

Royal Film Performance
A selected film gets royal patronage in aid of charity. Celebrities and glitter at one of the big cinemas. *No fixed date.*

Oranges & Lemons Service   6 K 25
St Clement Danes, Strand WC2. 01-242 8282.*No fixed date.*

Spring Antiques Fair   4 L 9
Chelsea Old Town Hall, Kings Rd SW3. 01-352 8101.*Mid Mar.*

Oxford v Cambridge Boat Race
River Thames, Putney to Mortlake. *Mar or April.*

John Stow Memorial Service
St Andrew Undershaft, Leadenhall St EC3. The Lord Mayor attends.*Mar or April, 11.30*

April

Butterworth Charity   6 K 29
St Bartholomew, The Great Smithfield EC1. 01-606 5171. Presentation of hot cross buns, traditionally to 'poor widows', now to children. *G. Fri following 11.00 service.*

Flower Show   6 J 23
Covent Garden Market WC2. *Easter Eve.*

Easter Sunday Parade   4 P 9
Battersea Park SW11. Colourful carnival procession preceded by a parade of old vehicles. *Easter Sun.*

Easter Procession & Carols   5 N 20
Westminster Abbey SW1. 01-222 1051. *Easter Mon.*

The Greyhound Derby
White City. *Mid April.*

London Harness Horse Parade   2 A 21
Regent's Park NW1. Fine horses and carts; brewer's vans and drays on parade. Judging *starts at 09.45* followed by a procession twice round the Inner Circle *at about 12.00. Easter Mon.*

Putney & Hammersmith Amateur Regattas
01-748 3632. Rowing regattas make exciting watching from the river banks.

Annual Spital Sermon   6 M 30
St Lawrence Jewry, Gresham St EC2. 01-638 0824. *No fixed date.*

Tower of London Church Parade   Q 32
Tower of London EC3. The Yeoman Warders in state dress are inspected, and parade before and after morning service on *Easter Sun. 11.00. Also Whit Sun & Sun before Xmas.*

May

May Day   2 I 15
Labour Party procession to Hyde Park W1. *1st May.*

Summer Art Exhibition   2 I 18
Royal Academy, Burlington House, Piccadilly W1. 01-734 9052.*May-end of July.*

Samuel Pepys Commemoration Service   6 P 32
St Olave's Hart St EC3. 01-488 4318. The Lord Mayor lays a wreath on Pepys' monument. *End of May or early June*

F.A. Cup Final
Empire Stadium, Wembley, Middx. 01-902 1234. The climax of the English football season. *2nd Sat in May.*

Chelsea Flower Show   4 N 11
Royal Hospital Grounds, Chelsea SW3. 01-730 7036. Superb flower displays. *For 3 days late May. No fixed date.*

Oak-Apple Day   4 N 11
Royal Hospital, Chelsea SW3. 01-730 7036. Chelsea Pensioners inspected. *29th May.*

Open Air Art Exhibition   5 L 22
Victoria Embankment Gardens WC2 (next to Embankment Underground station). Artists and their work on

exhibition. *2nd-14th May. Aug, Mon-Sat.*
The Terrace, Richmond Hill, Richmond, Surrey. Run by
Richmond Art Group. Fine views from terrace.
Weekends. May or June 10.00-20.00
Every Sunday morning on the Green Park side of
Piccadilly; a multitude of street artists set up their
pictures against the railings.
Rugby League Challenge Cup Final
Wembley. *Mid May.*

June

Antiquarian Book Fair
Europa Hotel, Grosvenor Sq W1.
Royal Ascot Races
A fashionable society event where hats attract more
attention than the horses.
The Garter Ceremony
Service, attended by the Queen at St George's Chapel,
Windsor, preceded by a colourful procession with the
Household Cavalry and Yeomen of the Guard.
Ceremony dates from 14th cent. *Mon afternoon of
Ascot week (usually third week in June).*
Antiques Dealers Fair & Exhibition   2 **G 16**
Grosvenor House, Park Lane W1. 01-499 6363. *Mid
June.*
Trooping the Colour   5 **L 21**
The route is from Buckingham Palace SW1 along the
Mall to Horse Guards Parade, Whitehall and back
again. Pageantry at its best for the Queen's official
birthday. *11.00, Sat nearest 11th June.*
Lord's Test Match
Lord's Cricket Ground, St John's Wood Rd NW8.
Tickets 01-289 1615. Prospects of play 01-286
8011.*June or July.*
Election of Sheriffs of the City of London
Guildhall EC2. 01-606 3030. Lord Mayor and Aldermen
in a colourful ceremony. Posies are carried traditionally
to ward off 'the plague'. *24th June.*
Open Air Exhibition
Heath St NW3. Organised by Hampstead Arts Council.
*Every weekend commencing 1st weekend June to 21st
Aug.*
All England Lawn Tennis Championships
All England Lawn Tennis & Croquet Club, Church Rd,
Wimbledon SW19. 01-946 2244. 'Wimbledon
Fortnight', the world's most famous championship.
Last week in June and first week July.

July

Road Sweeping by Vintners' Company   6 **N 29**
St James Garlickhythe, Garlick Hill EC4. 01-236 1863.
After the swearing in of the new master of the Vintners'
Company. Procession from the Vintners' Hall to St
James Garlickhythe, led by the wine porters who
sweep the road. Tradition dating from the reign of
Edward III. *About 16.00 on a Thur in July.*
Swan Upping   6 **P 29**
Starts: London Bridge (Temple stairs). *09.00-09.30.*
Ownership of the swans on the Thames is divided
between the Dyers Company, the Vintners Company
and HM the Queen. Each July a census of the swans on
the reaches up to Henley is taken, and the cygnets are
branded by nicking their beaks. *No fixed date.*
Royal Tournament March Past   5 **L 21**
Horseguards, Whitehall SW1. Colourful parade by all
troops taking part in the Royal Tournament. *15.00 Sun
before Tournament.*
Royal Tournament   1 **H 4**
Earls Court. 01-385 1200. Impressive military spectacle
with marching displays and massed brass bands. *Mid
July 2 weeks. No fixed date.*
Royal International Horse Show
Empire Pool, Wembley, Middx. 01-902 1234. Top-class
show jumping competition before Royalty. *Mid July.
No fixed date.*
Henry Wood Promenade Concerts   1 **F 10**
Royal Albert Hall, Kensington Gore SW7. 01-589 8212.
Concerts of classical music. Tickets by ballot only for
first and last nights. *Late July until Sep. No fixed date.*
Doggetts Coat & Badge Race
The Thames, London Bridge to Chelsea. Rowing race
for Thames Watermen, originated in 1715. Sometimes
called the 'Waterman's Derby'. *Mid July or early Aug.
No fixed date.*

August

Greater London Horse Show
Clapham Common SW4. *B Hol Sat & Mon.*
Bank Holiday Fair
Hampstead Heath (nr North End way) NW3. *B. Hol
Mon.*

September

London to Brighton Walk   5 **N 21**
Starts, Westminster Bridge SW1. Originated in 1903.
Early Sept 07.00.
Battle of Britain Week
Thanksgiving service at Westminster Abbey SW1. 01-
222 1051. Biggin Hill Flying Display. *Early Sept.*
**International Handicrafts & Do-It-Yourself
Exhibition**   1 **D 2**
Olympia. *Autumn*
Autumn Antiques Fair   4 **L 9**
Chelsea Old Town Hall, Kings Road SW3. 01-352 8101.
For 10 days. Mid Sep.
Last night of the 'Proms'   1 **F 10**
Royal Albert Hall, Kensington Gore SW7. 01-589 8212.
Now a tradition. Audience sing with the orchestra and
wave banners. Tickets by ballot only. *15th Sep or
nearest Sat.*
Christ's Hospital Boys March
'Bluecoats' march through the City. *St Matthew's Day;
on or near 21st Sep.*
Election of Lord Mayor of London
Procession from St Lawrence Jewry, Gresham St EC2,
to the Guildhall EC2. 01-606 3030. *Michaelmas Day.*

October

**Her Majesty's Judges & Queen's Counsels
Annual Breakfast**
After special service at Westminster Abbey there is a
procession to the House of Lords for the opening of the
Law term. *1st Oct.*
Harvest of the Sea Thanksgiving   6 **P 31**
St Mary at Hill, Lovat Lane EC3. 01-626 4184. Also a
fine display of fish at the church. *11.00, 2nd Sun in Oct.*
Costermongers' Harvest Festival   5 **K 22**
St Martin-in-the-Fields, Trafalgar Square WC2. 01-930
1862. Service attended by the 'Pearly Kings and
Queens', in their colourful regalia. *15.30, 1st Sun in
Oct.*
International Motor Show   1 **H 4**
Earls Court. Popular and crowded. *Oct.*
Trafalgar Day Service & Parade   5 **K 21**
Nelson's Column, Trafalgar Square WC2. Organised by
the Navy League. *Trafalgar Day 21st Oct.*
National Brass Band Festival   1 **F 10**
Royal Albert Hall, Kensington Gore SW7. 01-589 8212.
Concerts by the best of Britain's brass bands. *No fixed
date.*
Horse of the Year Show
Wembley Stadium, Empire Way, Wembley, Middx. 01-
902 1234. Fine show jumping. *Early Oct.*

November

London to Brighton Veteran Car Run: Start   2 **I 16**
Hyde Park corner W1. Vintage cars leave here for
Brighton. *08.00 1st Sun Nov.*
State Opening of Parliament   5 **N20**
The Queen, in the Irish state coach, is driven from
Buckingham Palace to the House of Lords. A royal
salute is fired in St James's Park. *Early Nov. No fixed
date.*
Guy Fawkes Day
Anniversary of the Gunpowder Plot of 1605. Private
and public firework displays. *Evening, 5th Nov.*
International Caravan and Camping Exhibition 1 **G4**
Earls Court. *For 10 days, Mid Nov.*
Admission of the Lord Mayor Elect
The Lord Mayor takes office. Colourful ceremony at
Guildhall including handing over of insignia by former
Lord Mayor. *Fri before Lord Mayor's show.*
Lord Mayor's Procession & Show
The newly elected Lord Mayor is driven in his state
coach from the Guildhall to the Law Courts to be
received by the Lord Chief Justice. The biggest
ceremonial event in the City. *2nd Sat Nov.*
Armistice Day
Poppies sold in the streets to raise money for ex-
servicemen. Service at the Cenotaph, Whitehall SW1
with a salute of guns. *11.00, 2nd Sun Nov.*
National Cat Club Championship Show   1 **D 2**
Olympia. *Nov.*
Royal Command Performance   3 **E 27**
London Palladium, Argyle St WC1. Variety show in aid
of charity occasionally attended by the Queen.

December

Royal Smithfield Show   1 **H 4**
Earls Court. *Early Dec.*
Richmond Championship Dog Show   1 **D 2**
Olympia. *Early Dec.*

(Continued on page 42)

Twickenham
Little survives of the 18th cent elegance of Twickenham, but Walpole's 'little plaything house', Strawberry Hill, which he gothicised in a whimsical manner, has been restored to his original plans. It is still as charming and convincing a case for the revival as when it was built. It now houses St Mary's Training College and can be viewed by appointment only. Alexander Pope, poet and satirist, lived in a house on the site of the convent in Cross Deep between the road and the river. He laid our large gardens on the other side of the road which were reached by a tunnel — his famous 'Grotto'. This survives but without the original lavish decorations of sea shells and fossils of which Pope was so proud.

Eel Pie Island
The hotel which used to stand on the island had a lively and varied history. In Edwardian days it held tea dances well attended by the jet-set. In the 1960s it housed a noisy nightclub from which many of the most famous groups (including the Rolling Stones) emerged. More recently it was taken over by a commune; after their eviction the hotel was razed to the ground. Luxury flats and houses are at present being built on the site. Access by boat or footbridge.

Isleworth
Some lovely 17th-18th cent houses and a 15th cent church. Syon house, refaced and with a redesigned interior by Robert Adam, still retains much of its original 16th cent structure. The most notable sight on this stretch of the river is a splendid, elegant boathouse complete with Ionic columns, attributed to Capability Brown.

Chiswick
The Georgian houses along the waterfront stretch from Kew bridge to Hammersmith. Originally there were three 18th cent mansions with grounds down to the river — Grove House, Sutton Court and Chiswick House. Only the latter remains. Lord Burlington and William Kent, who were largely responsible for the elegance of Chiswick, are buried in St Nicholas' Church. Chiswick Mall is still reminiscent of the wealthy riverside village it was in the 18th cent.

Fulham
Long ago a haunt of wild fowl, then a fertile 'garden' area, Fulham today is a mass of untidy buildings. The old Sandford Manor House (possibly the home of Nell

The River Thames

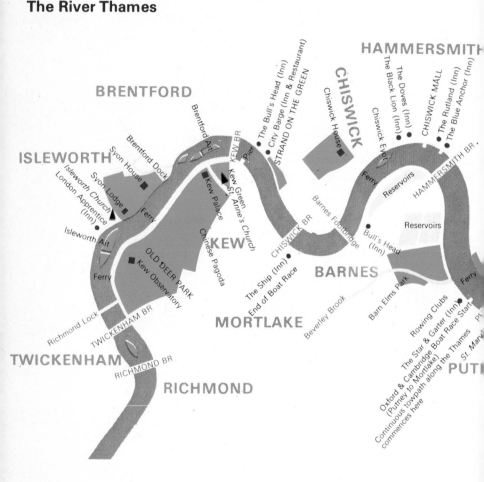

Richmond
A pleasant, almost rural, town which has had long associations with royalty. Richmond Palace, called the Palace of Shene before it was rebuilt by Henry VII in 1497, was a favourite of Elizabeth I. Other famous residents include Joshua Renolds, first president of the Royal Academy, who had a weekend house here and entertained many of the celebrated literary figures of his time. In this century, Leonard and Virginia Woolf lived at Suffield House and set up the Hogarth Press (publishing among other things the early works of T. S. Eliot). The Park of 2,000 acres has good herds of deer. Private shooting was stopped in 1904.

Kew
In the Old Deer Park is the Observatory built by Sir William Chambers to enable George III to watch the transit of Venus and Mercury. Kew is most famous for its gardens of exotic plants, trees and 'follies' built by order of Queen Charlotte in the late 18th cent. Gainsborough and Zoffany are buried in the churchyard on the Green. In 1892 Camille Pissarro, the Impressionist painter, made several studies of Kew and the nearby river.

Gwynne) is dominated by gasworks, and many other old buildings have been destroyed completely. North End House, 18th cent, was the home for a time of novelist Samuel Richardson and later of the pre-Raphaelite painter Burne-Jones. John Dwight, potter, was granted a licence to make stone and earthenware in 1671 and the pottery is still on the original site.

Fulham Palace is the oldest building in Fulham and has had an uninterrupted ecclesiastical history for over 1,200 years. Today it is the main residence of the Bishop of London. Hurlingham House, the only large 18th cent house which remains, has grounds to the river and is now an exclusive sports club.

Chelsea
The street with most notable literary and artistic connections in Chelsea is Cheyne walk. George Eliot spent her last few weeks here; Lloyd George lived at No. 10; Rossetti and Swinburne at No. 16; Whistler at No. 21 (also 96 and 101); Carlyle at No. 24; Mrs Gaskell was born at No. 93; Wilson Steer lived at No. 109 and J. M. W. Turner at 119. Tite street was very popular in the 19th cent — Whistler, Sargent, Augustus John and Oscar Wilde all lived here at some time. Both streets are near the river. The Chelsea China Works (which produced some excellent porcelain in the 18th cent) was in Lawrence street where Fielding and Smollett also lived at some time in that century. The nearby Apothecaries' Garden was established in 1673 and it was from here that cotton seeds were first sent to America in 1732. The waterfront is characterised by Geogian houses and, to the west, by houseboats.

Westminster
From the river the stretch from Vauxhall bridge to Blackfriars affords beautiful views of the north bank and its many impressive buildings. The Houses of Parliament and Westminster Abbey complement distant views of St Paul's. This part of the river particularly attracted the Impressionist painter, Monet, who came to London in 1899 on a second visit with the express intention of painting the river at that point. Many of the pictures were views from his bedroom window in the Savoy Hotel. Well known is that of the 'Houses of Parliament' 1904.

Associations with the area are mainly political, though the Abbey abounds in memorials of scientists, poets and many other notable figures. During World War 2 Parliament escaped damage, but the stained glass of the Henry VII chapel in the Abbey and the Deanery were both badly hit.

The Strand
The road runs parallel with the river from Whitehall to the edge of the City. In the Tudor period it was lined with aristocratic mansions whose gardens spread down to the river bank. Before that it had been a bridle path 'full of pits and sloughs'. During the 17th and 18th cent it was known for its preponderance of coffee houses.

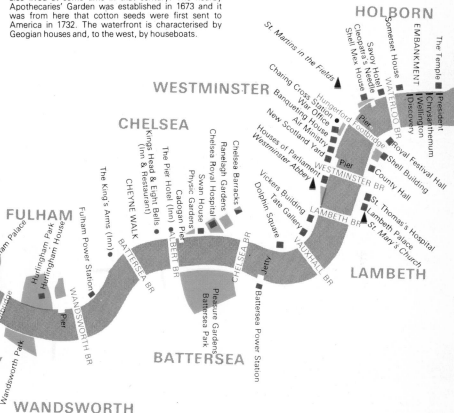

Putney
In 1647 Putney was the headquarters of Cromwell's Parliamentarian army. In the 19th cent Leigh Hunt, Swinburne, Gibbon and George Eliot lived here. There are always eights and sculls practising on the river which is famous at this point as the start of the Oxford and Cambridge Boat Race.

Wandsworth
Settled as far back as the palaeolithic age. Had a local silk industry until the 19th cent. With mechanisation the River Wandle became industrialised and lost what was left of its rural qualities.

Battersea
Away from the pleasure gardens the waterfront is very industrial, it is therefore surprising that in the vestry of the riverside church of St Mary is preserved the chair in which J. M. W. Turner sat and watched sunsets across the river. In this same church on the 18th August 1782, William Blake, poet, painter and mystic married Catherine Boucheron. The power station — a remarkable, if ugly landmark — was built in 1932-4.

Lambeth
The manor is first mentioned as having been owned by King Hardingcut before 1042. The palace, which was often used as a prison for ecclesiastic or political prisoners, was attacked by Wat Tyler and his mob in 1381. They burnt books and charters and drank the cellar dry. The palace had an even hotter night on 10th May 1940 when it was badly damaged during the biggest air raid on London of World War 2.

The City

The waterfront from the Temple to the Tower is mainly taken up by warehouses. World War 2 and many fires destroyed countless valuable buildings and fine churches, but old spires and tall office buildings still dominate the skyline. The most intensive bombing during World War 2 took place on the night of the 16th May 1940 when it was estimated that more than 100,000 bombs were dropped on the city. In the previous December (29th) about 60 fires were burning at once, reminding Londoners of the night in 1666 when the Great Fire broke out in Pudding lane near Eastcheap and spread rapidly throughout the City.

City waterfront

This used to be the most important docking area of London. The 'legal quays and wharfs' were here before the modern docks were built to the east. Queenhithe was the largest wharf and has a very long history. It was here that in the 12th cent Queen Maud built the first public lavatory for the 'common use of citizens'. Billingsgate and Customs House form a large complex of trade buildings and the street names between the waterfront and the city often indicate the type of trade which was originally carried out here.

Tower Bridge

The Gothic towers of the bridge are not purely ornamental, they contain the steam powered machinery which lifts the drawbridge. Since its installation in 1894 the machinery has only broken down twice — once at the official opening ceremony and once during the heat wave of 1968. A rather spectacular event happened in 1954 when the warning signal failed to sound and a bus had to 'leap' the gap as the bridge was raised. Regrettably with the closing of most of the London docks the bridge is opened so rarely that the steam system is no longer economic and an electrical one has been substituted.

Bankside (Southwark)

A narrow strip of thoroughfare forming the waterfront of Southwark. It was once an Elizabethan pleasure park, between the 'liberty of the Clink and the Paris garden'. Bear baiting and the theatre formed the central attractions. The 'Rose', 'Swan', 'Globe' and 'Hope' playhouses were here and there were large arenas for baiting, wrestling and cock fighting. The area rapidly became rowdy and vicious and was eventually known as the 'Stews'. In the 17th cent Samuel Pepys was a frequent visitor. Taverns were many — including the 'Anchor' (still there), the 'Cardinal's Cap', 'Falcon', 'Oliphant' and 'Crane'. Small cottages and wharves lined the waterfront. Sir Christopher Wren is said to have watched the rebuilding of St Paul's after the Great Fire of 1666 from one of the houses. The area is now dominated by Bankside power station.

Southwark

A warehouse area. Badly hit during the blitz and very largely rebuilt. In 1898, apparently, Southwark had a street lamp which supplied hot water, tea and cocoa if you 'put a penny in the slot'. The cathedral is built on an old site, probably of a Roman temple and certainly of two previous churches, the first of which was St Mary Overie, a nunnery. In 1905 the church (then St Saviour's) became a cathedral. A famous series of 19th cent stained glass windows commemorating dramatists like Shakespeare, Beaumont, Fletcher and Massinger (all associated with Bankside) were totally destroyed during World War 2. John Gower, the poet, is buried here.

Bermondsey

The name means 'island of Beormund' and describes the marshy beginnings of the area. St Saviour's Dock marks the western boundary of the Bermondsey waterfront and Cherry Garden Pier the eastern limit. The latter was a popular place for recreation in the 17th cent. The Church of St Mary Magdalen is on the site of one of the earliest Cluniac monasteries established in this country after the Norman conquest. The present church was built in 1680.

Rotherhithe

There are conflicting interpretations of this name but the most realistic translation is from the Anglo-Saxon 'rethra' for mariner and 'hythe' for haven. The catholic church at Dockhead was completely ruined by a V2 rocket. The present church was consecrated in 1960.

Deptford

According to a memorial in the church of St Nicholas on Deptford green, Christopher Marlowe who was killed in a fight at a tavern in Deptford is buried here. Drake's ship 'The Golden Hind' was kept in dry dock here for years until it finally collapsed. The dockyard was founded by Henry VIII in 1513.

Poplar
The main area of the original parish lies in the Isle of
Dogs which was for years an uninhabited and very
swampy peninsular. Millwall, on the west, was called
Marshwall until the 18th cent when seven windmills
were built there. The West India dock network now
cuts the Isle of Dogs from west to east making the area
quite literally an island. It was very badly hit during
World War 2 and has been largely rebuilt since then.

The docks
During World War 2 3,000 convoys sailed from London
and munitions from the States and Canada were
docked here in millions of tons. Bombing was extremely
heavy from August 1940 to 1945, beginning with air
raids, then in 1944 with flying bombs and finally late in
1944 with V2 rockets. The docks were a major objective
(the bombers following the Thames to the city naturally
approached over the docks).

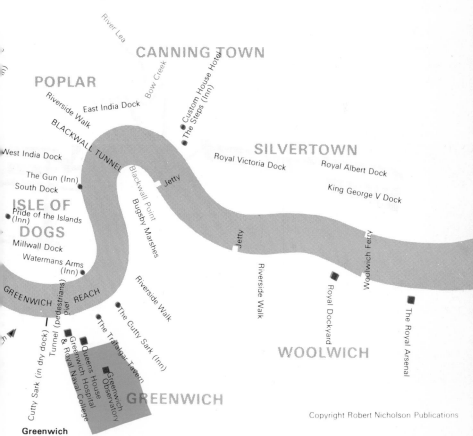

Copyright Robert Nicholson Publications

Greenwich
The church, which had a vast number of medieval
relics, was completely burnt out during World War 2,
and most were lost including the famous 'Tallis Organ'
(Thomas Tallis musician, 1510-85, is buried here).
In the park the Queen's House, a perfect example of
neo-classical architecture by Inigo Jones, houses the
Maritime Museum. Marked on the path in front of the
Observatory (also in the park but no longer in use) is the
zero meridian from which was calculated the
Greenwich Mean Time. In 1831 Charles Darwin,
grandson of Erasmus, set off aboard 'The Beagle' on a
scientific expedition to South America. The 'Cutty
Sark', one of the original tea-clippers and Chichester's
boat 'Gipsy Moth' are in dock near the pier.
Up to the 19th cent the only dock system in existence
was on the South Bank where the Great Howland dock
had been built in 1696 to take the Greenland whalers.
Most ships had to dock at the 'legal quays' where all
cargo had to be disembarked between dawn and dusk.
The India group of docks were opened in 1802 to cope

with increased traffic and combat the smuggling which
was rife as a result of the overcrowding at the legal
quays. The Royal docks followed from 1855. In 1909
the three companies which owned these dock areas
privately merged into the Port of London Authority,
which then had complete control.
After World War 2 the Old Granary at Shooter's hill
became the PLA's private radio station. Since then
international VHF and UHF have been installed centred
on Greenwich and known as the Thames Navigation
Service. Radar was introduced into the port system in
1955 and covers the whole river right down to the
estuary mouth.

Woolwich Royal Arsenal
Built as a look-out post to protect Greenwich Palace
and to serve as an armoury. Originally called the 'Royal
Warren' (presumably because it was a good site for a
royal rabbit hunt), it was renamed the Arsenal in 1805.
During World War 2 over 40,000 people were employed
there making armaments.

(Continued from page 37)

Annual Ice Show
Empire Pool, Wembley, Middx. 01-902 1234. Pantomime on ice. *Dec-Mar.*

Christmas Decorations
Regent St and Carnaby St W1. Gay illuminations to attract Christmas shoppers. *Best seen 16.00 onwards.* Also illuminated pine tree in Trafalgar Square, given by Norway each year. *Best seen 16.00 onwards; from about 10th Dec.*

Carol Singing   5   **K 22**
Trafalgar Square WC2. Recorded on tape. *Every evening from about 14th Dec.*

Tower of London Church Parades   6   **Q 32**
Tower of London EC3. The Yeomen warders in state dress are inspected and parade before and after morning service on the *Sun before Xmas 11.00. Also Easter Sun & Whit Sun.*

Westminster Carol Service   5   **M 20**
Carol services *on 26th, 27th and 28th Dec.*

New Year's Eve   5   **K 21**
Trafalgar Square WC2. Singing of 'Auld Lang Syne' by massed crowds also dancing around (sometimes in) the fountains.
St Paul's Cathedral EC4 ·   6   **M 28**
Gathering of Scots outside. *22.00-24.00. 31st Dec.*

Camping, Ourdoor Life and Travel Exhibition[1]   **D 2**
Olympia. *Dec-Jan.*

London tours

London tours: by coach

All coach tours start from the addresses given. Commentary given en route. Sightseeing tours to all the main tourist attractions, including Changing the Guard, Westminster Abbey, The City, St Paul's, Windsor Castle and Hampton Court. Also 'London by night'. There is a 24 hour service for travel enquiries: 01-222 1234.

American Express   5   **J 21**
6 Haymarket SW1. 01-930 4411.

Thomas Cook   2   **I 18**
45 Berkeley St W1. 01-491 7434.

Evan Evans   3   **G 23**
Metropolis House, 41 Tottenham Court Rd W1. 01-637 4171.

Frames   3   **F 25**
25 Tavistock place WC1. 01-387 3488

London Transport Tours   5   **M 14**
Victoria Coach Station SW1. 01-730 0202. Sightseeing tour *daily every hour* from Grosvenor Gdns and Eros, Piccadilly. Bright red open-topped buses are used. Covers 20 miles of the City and West End.

Red Rover Ticket
A day's unlimited travel on London's red buses for 50p adults, 25p children *weekdays after 09.30, Sat. Sun. B. Hol. any hour.* Available from travel enquiry offices, underground stations and garages.

London tours: by private guides

Autoguide   2   **I 14**
93 Knightsbridge SW1. 01-235 0806. Any sort of tour arranged, from a 1-hr shopping trip to a continental jaunt. Most European languages spoken.

Guides of Britain   2   **I 19**
71 Burlington Arcade W1. 01-493 3416. Guides to take you on an individual shopping tour. £9.00 per half day with car. Also chauffeur-driven guided tours throughout England – individually tailored.

Horse-drawn carriage tours of residential London   1   **G 8**
42 Kenning Place Mews. 01-584 7387. A pageant of English social history in London's only private carriage. Visit places you would otherwise never know were there. *1½ hrs from 09.00-12.00. £6.00 per person.*

London tours: walking

Off-beat Tours of London   2   **B 15**
66 St Michaels St W2. 01-262 9572. Small parties of people conducted by competent guide-lecturers on a gentle 1½ hr walk to unusual and out of the way parts of London. Many different walks. *Each tour 50p adults, 30p children.*

London Walks
20 Alexandra Rd N8. 01-889 7288. Meet at various underground stations for topical walks through London. *Weekdays May-Oct.* Topics include Dickens' London, Jack the Ripper, Ghosts of the West End. *Walks 1½-2 hrs. Students ½ price. Children free.*

River trips

The Thames is a fascinatingly beautiful river, never more so than as it passes through London. One of the best ways of appreciating the city is to take a boat trip. The buildings which line the banks range from decrepit warehouses to palaces; they conjure up a whole world of literary, historic and artistic associations. During the summer months daily services run from the following piers:

Greenwich 01-858 3996
The Tower 01-709 9697   6   **Q 31**
Charing Cross 01-839 5320   6   **L 23**
Westminster 01-930 2074   5   **M 21**
Putney 01-788 5104
Kew 01-940 3891
Richmond 01-940 2244
Hampton Court 01-977 5702
The tours start from the following piers, but travellers may join them at any of the other piers en route. Remember times of trips fluctuate according to the weather and the tides.

Charing Cross   6   **L 23**
Victoria Embankment WC2. 01-839 5320. Trips to the Tower *approx. every ½ hr;* to Greenwhich *every 45 mins.*

Greenwich
Westminster Tours, Greenwich Pier. 01-858 3996. Trips to Charing Cross *every ½ hr 11.00-17.00.*

Kew
Thompsons Launches. 01-940 3891. Trips to Westminster *every ½ hr 11.45-14.45;* to Richmond & Hampton Court phone 01-930 5947.

Putney
Putney Embankment. 01-788 5104. Trips to Kew *every ½ hr 11.30-16.30;* to Westminster *every ½ hr 12.30-15.00;* to Kew, Richmond & Hampton Court *every ½ hr 11.00-16.00.*

Richmond
01-940 2244. Trips to Hampton Court *11.00, 11.45, 14.30 & 15.30;* trips to Westminster *16.45 & 17.15.*

Tower Pier   6   **Q 31**
Tower Hill EC3. 01-709 9697. Trips to Greenwich approx. *every 25 mins;* to Westminster *every 25 mins.*

Westminster Pier   5   **M 21**
Victoria Embankment SW1. 01-930 2074. Trips to Kew *every ½ hr,* to Putney & Richmond and Hampton Court *every ½ hr.*

Useful telephone numbers:
From Westminster Pier, Thames Motor Boat 01-930 4097; Thompson Launches 01-930 5927; Wheelers Launches 01-930 4097.
From Tower Pier, Greenwich Pleasure Craft 01-858 6311; Thames Pleasurecraft 01-709 9697; Woods River Services 01-481 2711.

Steamer Services: Kingston – Oxford
Salter Bros, Follybridge, Oxford. Oxford 43421. Salters' steamers run *daily May-Sep.* Passengers may join/leave the boat at an advertised stop or lock. Arrangements have been made with British Rail for very favourably priced combined rail/river tickets to be issued from many of London's main-line and suburban stations, making it possible to incorporate a one-way river trip in a day's outing. Trips are also available from Oxford-Abingdon, Reading-Henley, Marlow-Windsor, Windsor-Staines.

Canal trips

Jason's Trip & Argonaut Gallery
Opposite 60 Blomfield Rd W9. 01-286 3428. The traditional narrow boats 'Jason' and 'Serpens' leave the Argonaut Gallery for 1½ hr return trips, with commentary, through Regent's Park and zoo to Hampstead Road locks. *Depart 11.00, 14.00, 18.00.* Night trips *depart 19.30.* Booked parties only £2.75 including supper and music.

Jenny Wren Cruises
Camden Lock, Commercial Place, Chalk Farm Rd NW1. 01-485 6210. 1½ hr round trips along Regent's Canal passing the Zoo and Little Venice. Up to 4 tours a day *daily from Easter to end Sep.* Also longer and evening trips.

Zoo Water Bus
British Waterways Board, Delamere Terrace W2. 01-286 6101. Boat leaves from the end of Delamere Terrace for ½ hr trip to the zoo. *On the hour 10.00-17.00 (Sun and B. Hols till 18.00).* Last return boat leaves zoo *17.45 (Sun and B. Hols till 18.45).* Visit to the zoo optional.

Charter boats

Boat Enquiries
7 Walton Well Rd, Oxford. Oxford 511161. Will arrange cruiser hire in England or abroad.

Catamaran Cruisers
West India Docks Pier, Cuba St, Isle of Dogs E14. 01-987 1185. Motor catamaran can be hired for private parties or business functions.

Alfred Crouch   **5 M 21**
Westminster pier SW1. 01-930 7912. Fully licensed, 120 passenger 'London Belle' for private hire, weddings, dances, etc. Departs from Westminster pier.

Thames Launches
Day time and evening cruises. 01-892 9041. The fully licensed launches are suitable for private or business entertain ment. Embark from Charing Cross or Westminster piers. Prices on application.

Thames Pleasure Craft
4 Highland Croft, Beckenham, Kent. 01-709 9697. Daytime and evening cruises. Fully licensed launches with dancing space. Embark from Tower pier. Price on application.

Inland Waterways Association
114 Regent's Park Rd NW1. 01-586 2556. Will supply a list of boat-hire firms for canals and rivers. 'Inland Waterways Guide' 75p by post.

Woods River Services
P.O. Box 177 SE3 9JA. 01- 481 2711. Modern all-weather passenger launches, 'Silver Dolphin' — 160 passenger, 'Silver Marlin' — 120 passenger. Fully fitted dance floor, film projector and licensed bar. Guided tours arranged. Prices on application.

Day trips from London

Cheap day excursion and special country afternoon tickets are available to most places by rail. Buses and coaches leave regularly from Victoria Coach Station. EC = early closing day.

Ashdown Forest
Excellent walking. High sandy country of heather and bracken with wind blown pine trees, silver birch and beeches in the valleys — each with its stream. 'Winnie-the-Pooh' country. Start from Crowborough, Hartfield, Forest Row or Three Bridges. London 30 miles.

Brighton, Sussex
Known as 'Little London by the sea', this once poor fishing village has been a lively, bustling seaside resort ever since the Prince Regent set up his court in the fabulous oriental-domed Pavillion. Fashionable shops, splended Regency terraces, good pubs and restaurants, cockle stalls, fairs and sport of all kinds. 5 miles of beach and two magical Victorian piers. Train 1 hr. *EC Wed or Thur.* London 48 miles.

Cambridge
A great university of spires, mellow colleges and riverside meadows, bordering the Cam. The famous 'Backs' and the lovely bridges are best seen by hiring a punt. The 20 or so colleges are from the 13th cent onwards including Trinity by Wren, Kings by James Gibbs and the modern Queens by Basil Spence. The city also contains the superb Fitzwilliam Museum, the notable Botanic Garden and some very fine churches. Train 1½ hrs. *EC Thur.* London 55 miles (A 10).

Canterbury, Kent
Pleasant old walled city on the River Stour, dominated by the magnificent Gothic cathedral, containing the shrine of Thomas à Becket (murdered 1170) and the tomb of the Black Prince. Good local museum in West Gate. Train 1½ hrs. *EC Thur.* London 56 miles (M2).

Chichester, Sussex
An old Roman city walled by the Saxons and graced by its beautiful 12th cent cathedral. Now mostly Georgian in character. Fine 16th cent Butter Cross, a medieval Guildhall and modern Festival Theatre, built 1962.

Excellent harbour for sailing. Train 1½ hrs. *EC Thur.* London 63 miles.

The Chilterns
A forty-mile-long ridge of chalk hills with fine views. Open downs, wheat fields, magnificent beech woods and charming villages. Start from Henley, Great Missenden, Stokenchurch, Wendover or Whipsnade. London 20-30 miles.

Colchester, Essex
England's first Roman city, with many visible remains: the city wall, a Mithraic temple, and arches, windows and doorways built from Roman bricks. Norman relics include Colchester castle (now housing a museum) and the ruins of the church of St Botolph. There is a small harbour and an oyster fishery. The famous 'Colchester Oyster Feast' takes place every year, *about 20th October.* Train 1 hr. *EC Thur.* London 52 miles.

Devil's Punchbowl, Surrey
A vast and impressive bowl scooped out of the high open hills. Good views. Start from Haslemere or Hindhead. Train 1 hr. London 30 miles..

Thaxted, Finchingfield and Great Bardfield
Perhaps the nicest of all Essex's villages. Thaxted's timbered houses and fine guildhall are dominated by a magnificent church begun in 1340 and finished in the Reformation period. Finchingfield is a charming village on the edge of the river Pant; nearby Great Bardfield has some splendid 17th cent buildings, a fine church and a windmill. It is now the centre of an artists' community. London 45 miles.

The North Downs
An outcrop of high chalk hills with magnificent views over the Weald of Kent. The Pilgrim's Way runs along the south face of the hills. Farming country with open beech and oak woods, and pleasant villages and pubs. Start from Dorking, Box Hill, Woldingham or Otford. London 15-20 miles.

Oxford
A university city of spires and fine college buildings on the Thames and the Cherwell and dating from the 13th cent. The Sheldonian Theatre by Wren, the Radcliffe Camera by Gibbs and the 15th cent Bodleian Library are particularly notable. Visit also the famous old Botanic Garden and the Ashmolean Museum. Train 1½ hrs. *EC Thur.* London 65 miles.

Southend-on-Sea
Traditionally the Cockney's weekend seaside resort. Carnivals and every sort of entertainment and attraction. Visit Westcliff-on-Sea nearby and Shoeburyness for cockle-beds, boats and paddling. Train 1 hr. *EC Wed.* London 40 miles (A127).

Stratford-on-Avon
The birthplace of William Shakespeare (1564-1616). The town is still Elizabethan in atmosphere with overhung gables and timbered inns. Visit the poet's birthplace in Henley St, his house at New Place, Anne Hathaway's cottage and the museum and picture gallery. The Shakespeare Memorial Theatre in Waterside is thriving and progressive. Train 2½ hrs. *EC Thur.* London 90 miles.

Thames Estuary
Unusual and sometimes tough walking along the tidal sea wall. Not everyone's cup of tea; it can be cold, windy or foggy. Take binoculars and wrap up well. Thousands of sea birds, a constant traffic of ships and the lonely marshes. Romantic and isolated but you have to be able to absorb the odd oil refinery or factory and accept that·commerce is part of it all. Start from Cliffe, Higham or Gravesend in Kent; Tilbury or Mucking in Essex. London 20-25 miles. (See 'Birdwatching' section.)

Winchester, Hants
The ancient Saxon capital of England set among lovely rolling chalk downland. The massive, square towered Norman cathedral, with its superb vaulted Gothic nave, contains the graves of King Canute, Izaac Walton and Jane Austen. The 'round table of King Arthur' is in the remains of the Norman castle. Train 1½ hrs. *EC Thur.* London 65 miles (A30).

Historic London

Historic buildings

This list cover the most important of the historic houses, notable buildings, monuments, characteristic streets and districts, and items of general historic interest. Look also under sections such as 'Churches' or 'Parks'.

Abbey Mills Pumping Station
Abbey Lane E15. An unusual building of cupolas and domes built in 1865 to pump the 83 miles of sewers draining the 100 sq miles of the city of London. This remarkable piece of drainage engineering was the work of the engineer Joseph Bazalgette and still survives intact and perfect after 100 years of use.

Admiralty Arch   **5 K 21**
Entrance to the Mall SW1. Massive Edwardian triple arch by Sir Aston Webb 1911. A memorial to Queen Victoria.

Albany   **2 I 19**
Piccadilly W1. Patrician Georgian mansion by Sir William Chambers 1770. Now privately-owned residences with quiet public forecourt.

Albert Memorial   **1 F 10**
Kensington Gore SW7. Statue of Prince Albert on a memorial to the Great Exhibition of 1851, by Sir George Gilbert Scott 1872.

Admiralty Arch   Albert Memorial

Annersly Lodge
Platts Lane NW3. A fine example of a house by C. F. A. Voysey, built 1895.

Apothecaries Garden   **4 N 10**
Swan Walk SW3. The 'Chelsea physic garden' since 1673. Seeds and plants exchanged on a world scale. *Appointment only.* 01-353 5678.

Apsley House   **2 I 16**
149 Piccadilly W1. 01-499 5676. Robert Adam 1771-78 but altered in 1828 by Wellington. Now the Wellington Museum containing paintings, silver plate, porcelain and extravagant military relics. *OPEN 10.00-18.00 Mon-Sat, 14.30-18.00 Sun. CLOSED New Year's, G. Fri, Xmas Eve, Xmas, Box.* Free.

Apsley House   Bank of England

Ball Court   **6 N 31**
Next to 39 Cornhill EC3. Straight out of Dickens. Simpson's chop house built in 1757.

Bank of England   **6 N 31**
Threadneedle St EC2. 01-601 4444. The vaults hold the nation's gold reserves. Outer walls are still the original design by Sir John Soane, architect to the Bank from 1788-1833. Rebuilt by Sir H. Baker 1925-33.

Bankside   **6 N 27**
Southwark SE1. Thames-side walk with the finest views of St Paul's and the City across the river. Here were Shakespeare's theatres; his Globe is marked by a plaque in Park St. Number 49 is reputed to be the house in which Wren lodged while St Paul's was being built.

Bayswater W2   **1 B 10**
Unpretentious Georgian squares and terraces built 1830-60.

Belgravia SW1   **5 J 14**
Handsome Regency squares and mews; Eaton Square, Chester Square, Belgrave Square. Designed and built by Thomas Cubitt, 1825 onwards.

Billingsgate   **6 P 30**
Lower Thames St EC3. Market building 1876. London's fish market. Once a port (nearly all fish now comes by land). Porters, famous for their strong language and their unique leather hats on which they carry fish boxes.

Blackheath SE3
High, open and grassy. Bordered by 18th cent houses including 'The Paragon', and the pleasant village of Blackheath.

Bloomsbury Squares WC1   **3 H 24**
Elegant Georgian houses and squares; Bedford Square, Russell Square, Tavistock Square. Built by Thomas Cubitt, mid 19th cent.

Bond Street W1   **2 H 19**
Mayfair's fashionable High Street. Originally laid out in the 1680s it no longer has any architectural distinction but is noted for its art dealers' galleries, fashion and quality shops.

Boston Manor House
Boston Manor Rd, Brentford, Middx. Tudor and Jacobean mansion with park and gardens. House *OPEN May-Sept 14.30-17.00 Sat only.* Small admission charge. Gardens *OPEN dawn-dusk daily.* Free.

Bridges
The tidal Thames has 17 bridges. Noteworthy ones in central London are:

Bridges: Albert Bridge   **4 N 8**
Unusual rigid chain suspension. Built by Ordish 1873.

Bridges: Chelsea Bridge   **P 12**
Original 1858. Rebuilt as suspension brigde by G. Topham Forrest & E. P. Wheeler in 1934.

Bridges: London Bridge   **6 P 29**
The site of many replacements. Wooden construction until 13th cent; the famous stone bridge that followed carried houses and shops. Granite bridge built in 1832 by Rennie was shipped off to Lake Havasu City, Arizona in 1971. Latest construction completed 1973.

Bridges: Tower Bridge   **6 R 31**
Victorian-Gothic towers with hydraulic twin drawbridge. Jones and Wolfe Barry 1894.

Bridges: Waterloo Bridge   **6 L 24**
Concrete. Fine design by Sir Giles Gilbert Scott 1940-5.

Bridges: Westminster Bridge   **5 N 21**
Graceful cast iron. Thomas Page 1862.

Brixton windmill
Blenheim gardens SW. Elegant windmill of the tower type, built 1816. Now restored by the GLC.

Brompton Cemetery SW10   **4 J 4**
Several extraordinary acres of ornamental Victorian marble tombs and memorials. The best of several fascinating London cemeteries.

Buckingham Palace   **5 K 17**
St James's Park SW1. 01-930 4832. The permanent London palace of the reigning Sovereign. Originally built 1705; remodelled by Nash 1825; refaced 1913 by Sir Aston Webb.

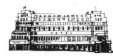

Burlington House   Charing Cross Hotel

Burlington Arcade   **2 I 19**
Piccadilly W1. 1819 Regency shopping promenade with original shop windows. Still employs a beadle to preserve the gracious atmosphere.

Burlington House   **2 I 19**
Piccadilly W1. Victorian-Renaissance façade on one of the great 18th cent palaces. Houses the Royal

Academy and various Royal Societies.

Cadogan Square SW1　　　　　　　　**5 J 12**
A typical 19th cent Chelsea square of red brick houses.

Canonbury Tower
Canonbury Place .N1. 1530. Tudor brick tower containing fine oak-panelled rooms and staircase. *Viewing by appointment only.* HQ of amateur theatre company.

Carlton House Terrace S.W.1　　　　　**5 K 20**
A magnificent sweep of columns by John Nash.

Carshalton House
Carshalton, Surrey. 01-642 0287. Fine early Georgian house. Water pavilion in the style of Vanbrugh. Now St Philomena's Convent Girls' School. *Open by appointment only.*

The Cenotaph　　　　　　　　　　　**5 L 21**
Whitehall SW1. Designed 1920 by Sir Edward Lutyens to honour the dead of World War 1.

Chandos House　　　　　　　　　　　**2 E 20**
Chandos St W1. Fine Robert Adam house built 1771.

Charing Cross WC2　　　　　　　　　**5 K 22**
The Charing Cross was the last of the stone crosses set up by Edward I to mark the funeral resting places of Queen Eleanor's body on its way to Westminster Abbey. Originally placed where Trafalgar Square now is, it was demolished in 1647 and the statue of Charles I now stands in its place. The stone cross in the station courtyard is a replica.

Charlton House
See under Greenwich.

Chelsea Royal Hospital　　　　　　　**4 N 11**
Chelsea embankment SW3. A hospital for old soldiers. Fine, austere building. 1682 by Wren. Stables 1814 by Sir John Soane. Museum *OPEN 10.00-12.00 & 14.00-16.30 Mon-Sat, 14.00-16.30 Sun. CLOSED G. Fri, Easter Sun, Xmas. Free.*

Chiswick House
Burlington Lane W4. 01-994 3299. Lovely Palladian villa built in the grand manner by 3rd Earl of Burlington 1725-30. Fine interiors and gardens by William Kent. *OPEN 09.30-13.00, 14.00-16.00; until 17.30 Mar, Apr & Oct; until 19.00 May-Sept. CLOSED Mon, Tues Oct-Mar, Xmas Eve, Xmas, Box. Small admission charge.*

Chiswick House　　　　　　The Queen's House

Chiswick Mall W4
17th-18th cent riverside houses.

The Citadel　　　　　　　　　　　　**5 K 19**
The Mall SW1. Creeper covered concrete. Built as a bomb-proof unit by the Admiralty 1940.

Clarence House　　　　　　　　　　　**5 K 18**
Stable Yard Gate SW1. Mansion by Nash 1825. Now the home of the Queen Mother.

Cleopatra's Needle　　　　　　　　　**6 L 23**
Victoria Embankment SW1. From Heliopolis. 1500 BC. Presented by Egypt and set up by the Thames 1878.

College of Arms　　　　　　　　　　**6 M 28**
Queen Victoria St EC4. 01-248 2762. Handsome late 17th cent building which houses the official records of English and Welsh heraldry and genealogy.

Covent Garden Market WC2　　　　　**6 J 23**
Originally designed by Inigo Jones as a residential square in 1638, the market buildings were erected in 1831. The glass Floral hall, 1859, is by E. M. Barry; other market halls 1831-3 by Chas. Fowler. The fine church of St Paul's (1633), the Royal Opera house and the Theatre Royal are imposing buildings.
The Market moved to Nine Elms in 1974 when the future of the area became a matter of controversy. The Covent Garden Community Association convinced Westminster Council, Camden and the GLC to develop the area commercially and residentially without destroying its unique character. A community centre has been set up at 45 Shorts Gdns WC2. 01-836 3355 and vacant plots have been converted into gardens. The GLC plan to restore the Central Market buildings and house the new Transport and Theatre museums in the flower market.

Crewe House　　　　　　　　　　　**2 H 17**
15 Curzon St W1. Georgian town house, 1735 by Edward Shepherd, who gave his name to Shepherd Market nearby. It was for many years the home of the Marquess of Crewe.

Cromwell House
104 Highgate Hill N6. 01-340 1108. Fine 17th cent house, typical of its period. *Open by appointment only.*

Crosby Hall　　　　　　　　　　　　**4 M 7**
Cheyne Walk SW3. 01-352 9663. 15th cent dining hall of city mansion — transplanted here in 1910. Fine timbered roof. Open to the public unless on hire. The Hall serves as a residence for postgraduate women students. *OPEN 10.00-12.00, 14.15-17.00 Mon-Sat, 14.15-17.00 Sun. CLOSED G. Fri, Xmas, Box. Free.*

Custom House　　　　　　　　　　　**P 31**
Lower Thames St EC3. Robert Smirke 1828. Badly damaged during the war; almost half the present building is new. The back is interesting, frigid and official but the Portland stone front, facing the Thames, is imposing.

HMS 'Discovery'　　　　　　　　　　**6 L 24**
Victoria Embankment WC2. 01-836 5138. Captain Scott's 1901-4 Antarctica vessel. Scott relics. *OPEN 13.00-16.30. CLOSED Xmas. Free.* Other moored ships nearby are HMS 'Chrysanthemum' and HMS 'President' (naval training vessels) and the 'Wellington' belonging to the Master Mariners. *OPEN 13.00-16.30 daily. CLOSED Xmas, New Year's. Free.*

Docks
The Port of London. A marvellous example of 19th cent industrial architecture, stretching from the Tower to Tilbury on the north bank of the Thames. The London and St Katharine Docks were bought by the GLC in 1968 for £1½ million. Taylor Woodrow & Co have obtained the lease of St Katharine's Dock, and have developed the site into a commercial and residential area. Also see 'Port of London' in this section and St Katherine-by-the-Tower under 'Modern Architecture'.

Downing Street SW1　　　　　　　　**5 L 20**
17th cent street houses built by Sir George Downing. No. 10 is the official residence of the Prime Minister, No. 11 of the Chancellor of the Exchequer.

Drapers Company Hall　　　　　　　**6 N 31**
Throgmorton Avenue EC2. City livery hall dating from 1667 but largely rebuilt in 1870. Fine staircase and collection of plate. For information on tours of all Livery Company Halls contact the Information Centre, St Paul's Churchyard EC4.

Eastbury Manor House
Barking, Essex. A fine Elizabethan manor house. *OPEN 10.00-12.00, 13.00-17.00 Tues. Free.*

'Ebonite' tower: Islington
Tileyard Rd, York Way N7. An elegant brick tower — a fine example of early industrial architecture, built 1870. 150 ft high it once contained meter testing water tanks with known constant pressures.

Eltham Palace
Off Court Yard, Eltham SE9. 01-850 3861. 15th cent Royal Palace until Henry VIII. Also remains of earlier Royal residences. Great Hall with hammer beam roof and a very fine 14th cent bridge over the moat. *OPEN Apr-Oct 10.30-18.00 Mon, Thur-Sun; Nov.Mar 10.30-16.00 Mon & Thur. Free.*

Fenton House
Hampstead Grove NW3. 01-435 3471. Built in 1693. Collection of early keyboard instruments and porcelain. Gardens. *OPEN 11.00-17.00 Wed-Sat, 14.00-17.00 Sun. CLOSED G. Fri, Xmas. Admission charge.*

Fitzroy Square W1　　　　　　　　　**2 D 22**
The south and east sides by Robert Adam 1790-4.

Flamsteed House
See Greenwich: Old Royal Observatory.

Fleet Street EC4　　　　　　　　　　**6 K 26**
London's 'Street of ink'. Has been associated with printing since the days of Caxton. All national and most provincial newspapers have their offices in or near it.

Fribourg & Treyer　　　　　　　　　**5 J 21**
34 Haymarket SW1. Fine old shop front. Unaltered, it has been a tobacconist since 1720.

Fulham Gasometer
Fulham Gasworks SW6. The oldest gas-holder in the world; built in 1830 by Winsor & Mindock. Diameter 100 ft, capacity ¼ million cu ft. An extraordinary piece of early industrial engineering.

Fulham Palace
Fulham Palace Rd SW6. 01-736 5821. Ex-residence of the Bishop of London. 16th cent building with riverside park.

Goldsmith's Hall　　　　　　　　　　**6 L 29**
Foster Lane EC2. Pre-Victorian classical style palazzo built in 1835 by Hardwick. Occasional exhibitions. For information on tours of all Livery Company Halls contact the Information Centre, St Paul's Churchyard EC4.

Goodwin's Court   5 J 22
St Martin's Lane WC2. A completely intact row of bow-windowed 17th cent houses. No. 3 once contained the offices of a famous London publishing company.

Gray's Inn   3 I 27
Holborn WC1. 01-242 8591. Entrance from passage next to 22 High Holborn. An Inn of Court since 14th cent. The Hall (16th cent) and 'Buildings' restored after bomb damage. Gardens were laid out by Francis Bacon. *Hall OPEN by written application to the Under Treasurer. Gardens OPEN Jun-Jul 12.00-14.00; Aug 08.00-18.00. CLOSED Sat, Sun, B. Hols. Free.*

Greenwich
Six miles downriver and associated with England's former sea power. The following are notable:

Greenwich: Charlton House
Charlton Rd SE7. 01-856 3951. Perfect small red brick Jacobean manor house on an 'H' plan, built 1607-12. Fine ceilings, staircase and some bizarre chimney-pieces. *OPEN by appointment only. Contact warden.*

Greenwich: The 'Cutty Sark'
King William walk SE10. 01-858 3445. Stands in dry dock. One of the great sailing tea-clippers, built 1869. 'Gipsy Moth IV', the boat in which Chichester sailed round the world in 1966 stands in dry dock next to the 'Cutty Sark'. *Both ships OPEN Apr-Sept 11.00-18.00 Mon-Sat, 14.30-18.00 Sun; Oct-Mar 11.00-17.00 Mon-Sat, 14.30-17.00 Sun. CLOSED New Year's, Xmas Eve, Xmas. Small admission charge.*

Greenwich: The Queen's House
Romney Rd SE10. 01-858 4422. Now part of the National Maritime Museum. Built by Inigo Jones 1619 for the Queen of Denmark. *OPEN 10.00-18.00 Mon-Sat, 14.30-1800 Sun in summer; 10.00-17.00 winter. CLOSED G. Fri, Xmas, Box, New Year's. Free.*

Greenwich: Royal Hospital
Greenwich SE10. 01-858 2154. Now the Royal Naval College, the site of the former Royal palace for the Tudor Sovereigns. A fine and interesting group of classical buildings by Webb 1664, Wren 1692 and Vanbrugh 1728. Chapel by James 'Athenian' Stuart 1789 and Painted Hall by Thornhill. *OPEN 14.30-17.00. CLOSED Thur. Free.*

Greenwich: Greenwich Market
A simple Georgian block with an interesting market.

Greenwich: Rotunda Museum
Woolwich Common SE18. Pavilion by Nash 1814. Little known museum full of guns of the Royal Artillery. *OPEN 10.00-12.45 & 14.00-17.00. Winter 16.00 (Sun 14.00-17.00). Free.*

Greenwich: Old Royal Observatory
Greenwich Park SE10. 01-858 4422. Formerly the Greenwich Observatory. Part of the National Maritime Museum and includes Flamsteed House. Designed by Wren and founded by Charles II in 1675. Time and astronomical instruments. *OPEN 10.00-18.00, Winter 17.00 (Sun 14.30-18.00, Winter 17.00.) CLOSED G. Fri, Xmas Eve, Xmas & Box.* also a Planetarium: phone for times of showing.

Greenwich: Vanburgh Castle
3 Westcombe Park Rd, Maze Hill SE3. 01-858 1604. Sir John Vanbrugh's own house 1717-26. *By appointment only.*

Guildhall   6 M 30
Off Gresham St EC2. 01-606 3030. 15th cent with façade by George Dance 1789 and later restorations by Sir Giles Gilbert Scott. The Great Hall is used for ceremonial occasions. Medieval groined vaulting in crypts. Library, Art Gallery, museum of clocks and watches. *Great Hall OPEN 10.00-17.00 Mon-Sat, 14.00-17.00 Sun, May-Sept & B. Hols. CLOSED New Year's, G. Fri, Xmas, Box. Free. Exhibition Hall OPEN 10.00-17.00 Mon-Fri, Wed until 19.00 CLOSED B. Hols. Free. Art Gallery OPEN 10.00-17.00 Mon-Sat. CLOSED B. Hols. Usually free.*

Guildhall

Jewel Tower

Wellington Arch

Gunnersbury Park
W3. 01-992 2247. Regency house of the Rotschilds. Museum of local history, including transport. Park. *OPEN Apr-Sep, Mon-Fri 14.00-17.00. Sat & Sun 14.00-18.00. Oct-Mar daily 14.00-16.00. CLOSED G. Fri, Xmas, Box.*

Hall Place
Bexley, Kent. Tudor mansion, 1540, in a park with rose garden, conservatories and fine water garden. *Mansion OPEN Apr-Oct 10.00-17.00 Mon-Sat, 14.00-18.00 Sun. Park OPEN every day during daylight. Free.*

Ham House
Petersham, Surrey. 01-940 1950. Superb 17th cent country house built on an 'H' plan. Lavish Restoration interior. Important collection of Stuart furniture. *OPEN Apr-Sept 14.00-18.00 Tues-Sun & B. Hols; Oct-Mar 12.00-16.00 Tues-Sun. CLOSED New Year's, G. Fri, Xmas, Box. Small admission charge.*

Hammersmith Mall
Upper & Lower Mall W6. Boathouses, riverside pubs and terraces of Georgian houses, including Kelmscott House, 1780, where William Morris lived and founded his printing press.

Hampstead Garden Suburb
Good pioneering suburban planning. Laid out by Sir Raymond Unwin, 1907.

Hampstead Village NW3
Still very much a village of Georgian houses and alleyways. Church Row, Holly Mount and Regency houses on Downshire Hill, including Keats' house, are notable. Keats' house *OPEN 10.00-18.00 Mon Sat, 14.00-17.00 Sun & B. Hol Mon. CLOSED New Year's, G. Fri, Easter Sat, Xmas, Box. Free.*

Hampton Court Palace
Hampton Court, Middx. 01-977 8441. Royal palace built 1514 for Cardinal Wolsey with later additions by Henry VIII and Wren. Sumptuous state rooms painted by Vanbrugh, Verrio and Thornhill. Famous picture gallery of Italian masterpieces. Orangery, mellow courtyards, the 'great vine' and the maze. The formal gardens are probably among the greatest in the world. Exotic plants from 16th cent. (The Mitre opposite). *OPEN 09.30-17.30 Mon-Sat, 11.00-17.30 Sun; Mar, Apr & Oct closes 16.30 Mon-Sat, 14.00-16.30 Sun; Nov-Feb closes 15.30, 14.00-15.30 Sun. CLOSED G. Fri, Xmas, Box. Admission charge.*

Henry VIII's Wine Cellar   5 L 21
Whitehall SW1. Genuine Tudor wine cellar built for Cardinal Wolsey. All that remains of Tudor Whitehall Palace. *OPEN Sat afternoons by pass from the Dept of the Environment, Room 4/58, Elizabeth House, York Rd SE1.*

Highgate N6 .
Here you stand level with the cross of St Paul's. A village full of 18th cent surprises.

Highgate Archway N6
Carries Hornsey Lane across Archway Rd. London's first 'fly-over'. Originally built in 1813 and replaced by present structure in 1897. From the top you see the whole of London laid out before you.

Highgate Cemetery
Swains Lane N6. Spookiest place in London. Egyptian catacombs reveal coffins within open tombs. Karl Marx's tomb. *OPEN 09.00-16.30 Mon-Sat, 14.00-16.00 Sun. Free.*

Holborn Viaduct EC1   6 K 28
William Haywood, 1869. Fine example of Victorian cast iron, and a pioneer traffic improvement scheme.

Holland House   1 C 6
Off Kensington High St W8. One wing only left of this mansion by Thorpe 1607. In Holland Park (50 acres).

Honourable Artillery Compound   6 K 32
City Rd EC1. Victorian castellated fortress (1857) hides the Georgian (1735) headquarters of the oldest regiment in the British Army. Supplies Guard of Honour for Lord Mayor's Shows and for Royalty visiting the City.

House of St Barnabas   2 H 22
1 Greek St W1. 01-437 1894. Early Georgian town house in Soho Square, with fine carvings and rococo plaster-work. *OPEN 14.30-16.15 Wed, .11.00-12.30 Thur. Free.*

Houses of Parliament   5 N 20
St Margaret St SW1. 01-219 3000. Victorian-Gothic building 1840-68 by Sir Charles Barry and A. W. N. Pugin. Westminster Hall was built in 1099 as the Great

Hall of William Rufus' new palace; the roof dates from the late 14th cent. House of Lords admission at St Stephen's entrance (Old Palace Yard side) or by Westminster Hall if wet. House of Commons admission only by permission from MP or by queueing outside St Stephen's entrance on day of debate. Tour of Parliament admission at Sovereign's Entrance, House of Lords. *When neither House is sitting OPEN 10.00-16.30 Sat, Easter Mon & Tues; Spring hol Mon & Tues; Aug Mon, Tues & Thur; Sept Thur. Conducted tours Sat. During sessions queue admitted from 16.15 Mon-Thur, 11.30 Fri to House of Commons, and from 14.40 Mon-Wed, 15.10 Thur to House of Lords. Westminster Hall OPEN when Parliament is in session but neither House is sitting, 10.00-13.00 Mon-Thur, 10.00-17.00 Sat. During recess 10.00-16.00 Mon-Fri, 10.00-17.00 Sat. CLOSED G. Fri, Xmas, Box.* All free.

Hyde Park Corner SW1 2 I 15
Consists of Construction Arch at the top of Constitution Hill, and the Ionic screen of three classical style triumphal arches at the entry to Hyde Park, by Decimus Burton, 1825. Wellington Museum *OPEN 10.00-18.00 Mon-Sat, 14.30-18.00 Sun. CLOSED New Year's, G. Fri, Xmas Eve, Xmas, Box.* Free.

Inns of Chancery 6 J 27
Before the 18th cent, a student of law had first to go through one of the nine Inns of Chancery then existing. They have now mostly disappeared. Staple Inn, High Holborn remains a fine Elizabethan building. Others survive only as names. Clifford Inn. Thavies Inn and Furnival Inn.

Jewel Tower
Old Palace yard SW1. 01-839 2201. 14th cent fragment of the old palace of Westminster. *OPEN 10.30-16.00 Mon-Sat. CLOSED Sun, New Year's, Xmas Eve, Xmas, Box.* Free.

Kensal Green Cemetery NW10
One of the first of the many cemeteries opened in 1833 to replace the completely unhygienic church graveyard: 70 acres of imposing graveyard architecture, tombs and ornamentation.

Kensington Palace 1 D 9
Kensington Gardens W8. Simple and charming building acquired by William III in 1689 as a palace. Exterior altered by Wren, interior by William Kent. Queen Victoria and Queen Mary born here. The warm brick Orangery was built 1704 by Hawksmoor. State apartments *OPEN Mar-Sept 10.00-18.00 Mon-Sat, 14.00-18.00 Sun; Oct 10.00-17.00 Mon-Sat, 14.00-17.00 Sun; Nov-Feb 10.00-16.00 Mon-Sat, 14.00-16.00 Sun. CLOSED G. Fri, Xmas, Box, New Year's.*

Kensington Palace Gardens W8 1 D 8
A street of prosperous town mansions in the grand Italianate style, laid out by Pennethorne in 1843, but continued by other famous architects. No. 8a is by Owen Jones and Decimus Burton; No. 12a James Murray; Nos. 18-20 by Banks and Barry; No. 13 by C. J. Richardson.

Kenwood House (Iveagh Bequest)
Hampstead Lane NW3. 01-348 1286. Robert Adam house and interior 1767-69. English 18th cent paintings and furniture. Fine Rembrandt, Hals and Vermeer. Gardens and wooded estate of 200 acres. *OPEN daily Apr-Sept 10.00-19.00; Oct 10.00-17.00; Nov-Jan 10.00-16.00; Feb-Mar 10.00-17.00. CLOSED G. Fri, Xmas Eve, Xmas.* Free.

Kew Palace
Kew, Surrey. Small red brick house in Dutch style. 1631. Souvenirs of George III and a collection of animal and bird pictures. *OPEN Apr-Oct 11.00-17.30 Mon-Sat, 14.00-18.00 Sun. Kew Gardens OPEN 10.00 daily until dusk, or 20.00 in summer. CLOSED Xmas.* 1p entrance.

Lambeth Palace
Lambeth Palace Rd SE1. 01-928 6222 (Library only). The London residence of the Archbishop of Canterbury. 15th cent. Fine medieval crypt and 17th cent hall. Portraits from 16th-19th cent. Library for

readers only, *OPEN 10.00-17.00 Mon-Fri. CLOSED at conference times, Easter, B. Hols and Xmas.*

Lancaster Gate W2 2 C 12
Area of fine stucco houses 1865, in and around Lancaster Gate (Queens Gardens, Cleveland Square and Gardens).

Lancaster House K K 18
Stable Yard, St James's SW1. Early Victorian London town house. Lavish state apartments and painted ceilings. Used for official functions.

Law Courts 6 K 25
Strand WC2. 01-405 7641. Massive Victorian-Gothic building, housing the Royal Courts of Justice. *OPEN to public 10.00-16.30 Mon-Fri. CLOSED Aug and Sept.*

Leadenhall Market 6 O 31
Gracechurch St EC3. Impressive Victorian glass and iron hall.1881, housing the poultry market.

Lincoln's Inn 3 I 25
Lincoln's Inn WC2. 01-405 1393. An Inn of Court. 17th cent. New Square, barristers' chambers and solicitors' offices. A chapel by Inigo Jones (1623) and the 15th cent Old Hall. Great Hall was built in 1845. The 'Stone Buildings' are by Sir Robert Taylor and were begun in 1774. Still has Dickens atmosphere. *Apply to Gatehouse in Chancery Lane for admission to Hall and Chapel. Mon-Fri. Free.*

Lincoln's Inn Fields WC2 3 I 25
7 acres of gardens laid out by Inigo Jones 1618. Once a famous duelling ground. Nos. 12-14 built 1792 by Sir John Soane. Nos. 57-8 built 1730 by Henry Joynes. Nos. 59 & 60 built 1640 by Inigo Jones. *OPEN Tues-Sat 10.00-17.00. CLOSED Sun, Mon & B. Hols.*

'Little Venice' 2 A 14
Harrow Rd W2. Artists, writers, converted barges and the Grand Union Canal.

Lloyds of London 6 O 32
Lime St EC3. World-famous international insurance market. Over 10,000 members are represented by underwriters conducting over £1,000m of business a year in 'The Room' which houses the Lutine Bell. *Apply in writing to Head of Information & Publicity, giving at least 3 weeks' notice.*

London Stone 6 O 30
Cannon St EC4. Set into the wall of the Bank of China opposite Cannon St Station. The Roman Millarium from which all road distances were measured.

London's Wall
Surviving parts of the medieval wall around the old city of London can still be seen at St Alphage on the north side of London Wall EC1; St Giles churchyard; Cripplegate EC1; Jewry St EC3; off Trinity Square EC3 and in the Tower of London.

Mansion House 6 N 30
Opposite Bank of England EC2. 01-626 2500. Official residence of the Lord Mayor. Palladian building by George Dance 1739. Completed 1752. *OPEN alternate Sat mornings by appointment.* Parties limited to 30.

Lancaster House   Mansion House

Marlborough House 5 K 19
Marlborough Gate, Pall Mall SW1. 01-839 3411. Designed by Wren 1710. Contains a painted ceiling by Genti Peschi which was originally designed for the Queen's House at Greenwich. The simple classical-style Queen's Chapel in the grounds is by Inigo Jones, 1626. *Not open to the public.*

Melbury Road W14 1 D 4
Near Holland Park. Contains several notable houses; No. 9 William Burgess' own house 1875-80; Nos. 8 & 11 are by Norman Shaw 1896 & 1877; and No. 1 Holland Park Road nearby is by Philip Webb.

The Monument 6 O 30
Monument St EC3. A 17th cent hollow fluted column by Wren to commemorate the Great Fire of London. Magnificent view. *OPEN Mar-Sept 09.00-17.40 Mon-Sat, 14.00-17.40 Sun; Oct-Mar 09.00-16.00 Mon-Sat. CLOSED Sun, Xmas, Box, G. Fri.* Admission charge.

Morden College
19 St Germain's Place, Morden Rd SE3. 01-858 3365. Characteristic Wren domestic architecture in 18th cent landscaped grounds.

Nelson's Column 5 K 21
Trafalgar Square SW1. 145-ft-high column by William Railton 1840. Weighs 16 tons. At the top a statue of Nelson by Bailey 1843.

Old Bailey 6 L 28
Old Bailey EC4. 01-248 3277. The Central Criminal

Court. On the site of old Newgate Prison. *Trials open to the public. Gallery OPEN 10.30-13.00 & 14.00-16.00 Mon-Fri. Minimum age 14. Free.*

Old Battersea House
30 Vicarage Crescent SW11. Originally the home of the potter William de Morgan. Reopened 1971 as the museum of de Morgan pottery and pre-Raphaelite painting.

Old Curiosity Shop　　　　　　　　　　**6 J 25**
13-14 Portsmouth St WC2. 01-405 9891. Tudor house built 1567 and now an antique shop. Immortalised by Dickens in 'The Old Curiosity Shop'. *OPEN daily Apr-Oct 09.00-17.30; Nov-Mar 09.30-17.30. Free.*

Old Palace
Old Palace Rd, Croydon, Surrey. 01-688 2027. Seat of the Archbishop of Canterbury for 1,000 years. Tudor chapel. *OPEN various afternoons during the year, 14.00-17.30. Conducted tours. Phone for details. Admission charge.*

Old St Thomas's Hospital Operating Theatre　　　　　　　　　　**6 Q 29**
St Thomas St, London Bridge SE1. A well-preserved early 19th cent operating theatre, located in the old chapel of St Thomas's Hospital (now the Chapter House of Southwark Cathedral). Owned by the Diocese of Southwark but write to the Counting House, Guy's Hospital SE1 for a permit to visit. *OPEN 12.30-16.00 Mon, Wed & Fri. Student rates. Admission charge.*

Old Swan House　　　　　　　　　　**4 N 10**
17 Chelsea Embankment SW3. Late 19th cent house by R. Norman Shaw.

Osterley Park House
Thornbury Rd, Osterley, Middx. 01-560 3918. Remodelled by Robert Adam 1761-78 on an already fine Elizabethan building built round a courtyard. The magnificent interiors with furniture, mirrors, carpets and tapestry all show the elegance and richness of Adam's genius. *OPEN Apr-Sept 14.00-18.00; Oct-Mar 12.00-16.00. Admission in morning by special arrangement. CLOSED Mon (except B. Hols), Xmas Eve, Xmas, Box, New Year's, G. Fri. Free. Park OPEN all year 10.00-dusk.*

Pall Mall SW1　　　　　　　　　　**5 J 20**
Early 19th cent opulence. This fine street and its surroundings express the confidence and wealth of the London of this period. Pall Mall itself contains two fine buildings by Sir Charles Barry; the Travellers Club, 1829-32 (Italian-Renaissance revival), and his more mature Reform Club, 1837-41.

Piccadilly Circus W1　　　　　　　　　　**2 I 20**
The confluence of six major thoroughfares. Fountains and statue of Eros by Gilbert 1892. Its fame is largely sentimental.

Pimlico SW1　　　　　　　　　　**5 N 15**
Laid out by Cubitt in the 1850s as a less grand neighbour to Belgravia.

Port of London　　　　　　　　　　**6 P 30**
Begins at London Bridge and includes the docks. London has been a port since AD 30. Principal cargoes are containers, grain, forest products, bulk wine and oil. Vessels of up to 10,000 tons can go up to London Bridge. The port is slowly being restructured.

Postmans Park　　　　　　　　　　**6 L 29**
Churchyard of St Botolph Without, Aldersgate EC2. Under an alcove are some remarkable 'art nouveau' tile tablets recording Victorian deeds of bravery (1880).

Prince Henry's Rooms　　　　　　　　　　**6 K 26**
17 Fleet St EC4. 01-353 7323. From 1610; oldest domestic building in London. Named after the son of James I. Fine plaster ceiling and carved oak panelling. *OPEN 13.45-17.00 Mon-Fri, 13.45-16.30 Sat. Free.*

Queen Anne's Gate SW1　　　　　　　　　　**5 L 19**
Quiet, completely preserved 18th cent street in its original state. Statue of Queen Anne near No. 13.

Regent's Canal　　　　　　　　　　**2 A 13**
Paddington Bridge W2 to Regent's Canal Dock E14. The canal was built by James Morgan in 1820 to connect Paddington with the Thames, thus allowing goods to be shipped direct from Birmingham to the Thames by the canal network. The best way to see the canal is to take a boat trip (see 'Canal trips').

Regent's Park Environs　　　　　　　　　　**2 B 21**
The park and the surrounding Regency architecture was planned almost entirely by John Nash, 1812-26. Particularly notable are Park Crescent, Park Square, Cambridge Terrace, York Terrace and Chester Terrace. Decimus Burton designed the façades of Cornwall and Clarence Terraces.

Roman Bath　　　　　　　　　　**6 K 24**
5 Strand Lane WC2. Disputed origin: restored in the 17th cent. *OPEN 10.00-12.30 Mon-Sat. CLOSED Sun, G. Fri, Xmas. Small admission charge.*

Royal Exchange　　　　　　　　　　**6 N 31**
Corner of Threadneedle St and Cornhill EC3. Built in

Royal Exchange

Somerset House

1884 by Tite. The third building on this site. Originally founded as a market for merchants and craftsmen in 1564, and destroyed in the Great Fire. The second building was also burnt down in 1838. Ambulatory containing statues and mural painting and courtyard. *OPEN 10.00-16.00 Mon-Fri, 10.00-12.00 Sat. CLOSED Sun & B. Hols.*

Royal Mews　　　　　　　　　　**5 K 16**
Buckingham Palace Rd SW1. The Queen's horses and carriages, including the Coronation coach. *OPEN 14.00-16.00 Wed & Thur. CLOSED Royal Ascot week. Admission charge.*

Royal Opera Arcade　　　　　　　　　　**5 J 21**
Between Pall Mall and Charles II St SW1. John Nash 1816, London's earliest arcade. Pure Regency; bow-fronted shops, glass domed vaults and elegant lamps.

Royal Society of Arts　　　　　　　　　　**6 K 23**
6-8 John Adam St WC2. Built 1774. Fine surviving example of Adam architecture, from the original Adelphi area (now almost entirely demolished).

St James's Palace　　　　　　　　　　**5 K 19**
Pall Mall SW1. Built by Henry VIII with many later additions. Still officially a Royal residence. Ceiling of Chapel Royal by Holbein. *No admission to palace. Entry to courtyards only.*

St James's Street SW1　　　　　　　　　　**5 J 19**
Contains some of its original 18th cent houses and shop fronts. Boodles (No. 28) 1775 by J. Crunden; Brooks's (No. 60) 1776 by Henry Holland.

St John's Gate　　　　　　　　　　**6 J 29**
St John's Lane EC1. Once a gateway to the Priory of the Knights Hospitallers of St John of Jerusalem. Built in 1504 it is the only monastic gateway left in London.

Skinners Hall　　　　　　　　　　**6 O 29**
8 Dowgate Hill EC4. 01-236 5629. 17th-18th cent buildings and quiet arcaded courtyard.

Smithfield EC1　　　　　　　　　　**6 K 29**
Once 'Smooth Field'. Historical site of tournaments, public executions, cattle market and the famous Bartholomew Fair. In north east corner original Tudor gatehouse built over 13th cent archway leading to Church of St Bartholomew the Great (see Churches). South-east side occupied by St Bartholomew's Hospital, London's oldest hospital, founded in 1123. Gateway (1702) bears London's only statue of Henry VIII. Smithfield Market is the largest meat market in the world (10 acres). The Italianate-style market buildings with some ornamental ironwork were designed by Horace Jones and erected between 1868 and 1899.

Soho　　　　　　　　　　**2 H 22**
An area bounded by Regent St, Oxford St and Charing Cross Rd. Lively and notorious but perfectly safe. Visit London's 18th cent streets full of fascinating foreign food shops, restaurants and night life of all sorts. Visit London's 'China town' around Gerrard St, and Carnaby St for the boutiques.

Somerset House　　　　　　　　　　**6 K 24**
Strand WC2. On the site of an unfinished 16th cent palace. By Sir W. Chambers 1776. Used to house the register of births, marriages and deaths in England and Wales, now holds the Registry of divorce, wills and probate and the Inland Revenue.

Spitalfields
This centre of silk weaving in England was established by the influx of Flemish and French weavers in the 16th and 17th cent. The industry reached its height at the end of the 18th and early 19th cent when about 17,000 looms were in use and a large area of East London was dependent on these family concerns. Fournier St is a good example of typical Dutch style houses of the time. The industry collapsed 100 years ago.

Stations
Some good examples of 19th cent 'railway architecture'.

King's Cross　　　　　　　　　　**3 D 27**
Euston Rd NW1. Functional. 1851, by Lewis Cubitt.

St Pancras　　　　　　　　　　**3 D 26**
Euston Rd NW1. Victorian Gothic. 1868, by Sir George Gilbert Scott.

Paddington　　　　　　　　　　**2 A 13**
Praed St W2. 1850-2. 'Railway cathedral' engineering at its best by Brunel; the Gothic ornament by Wyatt and Owen Jones; the Renaissance-style hotel by Hardwick.

Stock Exchange　　　　　　　　　　**6 N 31**
Old Broad St EC2. 01-588 2355. Entrance to public gallery at corner of Threadneedle St and Old Broad St,

showing the turmoil of 2,000 soberly dressed members milling below. Films shown in adjoining cinema. *Gallery OPEN 10.00-15.15 Mon-Fri. Last tour begins 14.30. CLOSED G. Fri, B. Hols, Xmas, New Year's. Free.* Parties up to 40, ring or write to P.R. Dept.

Strand WC2   **6 K 23**
Once a 'strand' — a walk along the river bordered in Stuart times with mansions and gardens down to the river. Their names still survive in the streets: Bedford, Buckingham, Villiers.

Syon House
Park Rd, Brentford, Middx. 01-560 0884. The exterior is the original convent building of the 15th cent, but the interior 1762-9 is by Robert Adam. The imaginative elegance and variety in each room is unsurpassed. Garden by Capability Brown. Do not miss Syon Lodge nearby — Crowther's showplace of acres of garden ornaments. *OPEN various times during the year, phone for details. Party visits can be arranged for mornings of open days. Admission charge. Garden Centre OPEN daily 10.00-18.00 or dusk.*

The Temple   **6 L 26**
Inner Temple, Crown Office Row EC4. 01-353 4355. Middle Temple, Middle Temple Lane EC4. 01-353 4355. Both are Inns of Court. Enter by Wren's gatehouse, 1685, in Middle Temple Lane. An extensive area of courtyards, alleys, gardens and warm brick buildings. Middle Hall 1570. The Temple Church is an early Gothic 'round church' built by the Templars. 12th-13th cent. *Inner Temple OPEN 10.00-11.30 & 14.30-16.00 Mon-Fri. CLOSED weekends, B. Hols & legal vacations. Middle Temple OPEN 10.00-12.00 & 15.00-16.30 Mon-Fri, 10.00-16.00 Sat. CLOSED Sun, B. Hols and during examinations.*

Temple of Mithras, Bucklesbury House   **6 N 30**
Queen Victoria St EC4. Originally found 18 ft underground in Walbrook and moved here with other Roman relics.

Thames Tunnels: Rotherhithe to Wapping
The first tunnel under the Thames built by Sir Marc Isambard Brunel (the elder) and completed in 1843 after many deaths by accident and illness. Now used by underground trains and still a perfect feat of engineering — withstanding over 100 years of train vibration. Original tunnel can be seen at Wapping station — also stairs and handrails.

Thames Tunnels: Blackwall by Binnie 1897 is now incorporated in a two-way system with the new tunnel, completed in 1967 under the direction of the GLC. For vehicles and pedestrians.

Thames Tunnels: Rotherhithe 1908. For vehicles and pedestrians.

Thames Tunnels: Greenwich (1902) and Woolwich (1912) pedestrians only.

The Tower of London   York Watergate   Nelson's Column

The Tower of London   **6 Q 32**
Tower Hill EC3. 01-709 0765. A keep, a prison and still a fortress. Famous for the Bloody Tower, Traitors' Gate, the ravens, Crown Jewels and the Yeomen warders. Norman Chapel of St John. *Museum OPEN Mar-Oct 09.30-17.00 Mon-Sat, 14.00-17.00 Sun; Nov-Feb 09.30-16.00 Mon-Sat. Admission charge. Jewel House OPEN Mar-Oct 09.30-17.45 Mon-Sat, 14.00-17.30 Sun; Nov-Feb 09.30-16.30 Mon-Sat. Admission charge.*

Trafalgar Square WC2   **5 K 21**
Laid out by Sir Charles Barry 1829. Nelson's column (granite) by William Railton 1840. Statue by Baily. Bronze lions by Landseer 1868. Fountains by Lutyens. Famous for political demonstrations and its pigeons.

Watermen's Hall   **6 P 31**
18 St Mary at Hill EC3 01-626 3911. Adam style front surviving from 1780. Unexpectedly beautiful amid drab surroundings. *Visits arranged in summer through City Information Centre, St Paul's Churchyard EC4. 01-606 3030.*

Whitefriars Crypt   **6 L 26**
30 Bouverie St EC4. 01-353 3030. 15th cent crypt belonging to a House of Carmelites. Discovered in 1895

and restored by the proprietors of the 'News of the World' and 'Sun' under whose offices it is buried. *Apply to newspaper for permission to view.*

Whitehall SW1   **5 L 21**
Wide thoroughfare used for ceremonial and State processions; contains the Cenotaph and several notable statues. Lined with Government offices.

Whitehall

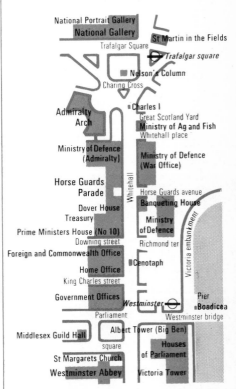

Whitehall: Old Admiralty
1725-8 by T. Ripley. Fine Robert Adam columnar screen 1760. The New Admiralty 1887 lies behind.

Whitehall: Scotland Yard
1888. An asymmetrical building by Shaw.

Whitehall: The War Office
1898-1907. William Young. Victorian-baroque.

Whitehall: The Horse Guards
1750-60. William Kent.

Whitehall: Banqueting House
1619-25 17th cent Palladian style by Inigo Jones. Rubens ceilings 1630. *Banqueting Hall OPEN 10.00-17.00 Tues-Sat, 14.00-17.00 Sun. CLOSED Mon (except B. Hol), Xmas, Box, New Year's, G. Fri. Changing of the Guard in the forecourt daily at 11.00 (Sun 10.00), at Buckingham Palace 11.30. London Tourist Board phone information 01-730 0791 during office hours, or 01-246 8041 24 hrs.*

Horse Guards   Banqueting House

Whitehall: Dover House
1755-8 by Paine. Entrance screen and rotunda 1787 by Henry Holland.

Whitehall: The Treasury
1846 Sir C. Barry. Victorian columned façade on Whitehall. Earlier façade overlooking Horse Guards Parade 1733-6 by William Kent.

Whitehall: The Foreign Office
Mid Victorian palazzo style by Gilbert Scott. Completed by Ministry of Housing 1920.

White House   **4 M 10**
35 Tite St Chelsea SW3. The house of Whistler the artist designed by William Godwin in 1879.

Whittington Stone
Highgate Hill N6, near junction with Dartmouth Park Hill. Milestone marking the spot where tradition says

young Dick Whittington rested on his way home from London and heard Bow Bells ring out. 'Turn again Whittington, thrice Lord Mayor of London', and returned to become London's most famous Mayor.

Woolwich Arsenal
Woolwich SE18. Fine example of early 18th cent ordnance architecture. Sir John Vanbrugh, 1716-19. *OPEN by appointment only.*

World War 2 Operational Headquarters   **5 L 21**
Whitehall SW1. 01-930 5422. A 6-acre honeycomb of rooms and corridors in the heart of government Whitehall, originally the secret war headquarters of Churchill's cabinet. War-time furnishings. *By appointment only. Write to the Chief Clerk, Cabinet Office, Whitehall SW1.*

York Watergate   **5 K 22**
Watergate Walk, off Villiers St WC2. Built in 1626 by Nicholas Stone as the watergate to York House, it marks the position of the north bank of the Thames before the construction of the Victoria Embankment in 1862. The arms and motto are those of the Villiers family.

Great houses and gardens near London

These are some of the great country houses within a 70-mile radius of London, dating from between the 11th and 19th cent. Each property has been selected as being characteristic of its period; many were designed by such famous architects as Inigo Jones, Christopher Wren and Robert Adam. The gardens and parks were laid out by various inspired landscape gardeners including Sir John Vanbrugh, William Kent, 'Capability' Brown and Humphrey Repton. Almost without exception they contain great richness of interior decoration and ornament, and often famous collections or works of art.

Recommended books

Historic Houses, Castles & Gardens. ABC Travel Guides. A complete and useful guide to all houses open to the public, with detailed opening times and tours available.
The English Garden Edward Hyams. Thames & Hudson. Lavishly produced and illustrated.
Gardens of England and Wales. Tells you what gardens are open to the public on any particular day of the year. From the National Gardens Scheme, 57 Lower Belgrave St SW1. 01-730 0355.
The National Trust Guide Robin Fedden & Rosemary Joekes. Jonathan Cape. A complete introduction to the buildings, gardens, coast and country owned by the National Trust, illustrated throughout.

Arundel Castle
Arundel, Sussex. Arundel 88 2118. An imposing feudal stronghold set among the beechwoods of the South Downs, overlooking the tidal River Arun. Built at the time of Edward the Confessor, it has been the home of the Dukes of Norfolk for the last 500 years. Completely restored in 1890 by the 15th Duke. Paintings by Van Dyck, Holbein and Gainsborough; important collection of portraits of the Howard family. London 45 miles (A29). *OPEN Apr-Jun 13.00-17.00 Mon-Thurs; Jun-Oct 12.00-17.00 Mon-Fri. Also Suns in Aug, Easter Mon, Spring B. Hol Mon 12.00-17.00. Admission charge.*

Audley End
Saffron Walden, Essex. Saffron Walden 2399. A great Jacobean mansion standing mellow and serene in its park near the road to Cambridge. Imposing as it now is, Audley End was once three times its present size. Built 1603-16, it served for a while as a royal country palace. In 1721 Vanbrugh demolished two thirds of the building. Fine state rooms — some decorated by Biago Rebecca in Adam style in 1776, extremely well restored. London 40 miles (A11). *OPEN Apr-Oct 10.00-17.30. CLOSED G. Fri & Mons except B. Hol. Admission charge.*

Blenheim Palace
Woodstock, Oxfordshire. Woodstock 811325. A great classical style ducal palace by Sir John Vanbrugh 1705-

22. The estate was given by Queen Anne to John Churchill, Duke of Marlborough for his victory over Louis XIV at Blenheim in 1704. Winston Churchill was born here. Fine paintings, tapestries and furniture. The park was landscaped first by Wise and later by Capability Brown in 1760, who dammed the small stream to create two great lakes, keeping Vanbrugh's original bridge, and forming a dam ingeniously separating the two levels of water. London 60 miles (A34). *OPEN Mar-Oct 11.30-17.00 daily. Admission charge.*

Bodiam Castle
Robertsbridge, Sussex. Staplecross 436. A romantic and lovely medieval castle completely surrounded by a wide moat. A mighty fortress built 1385 as a defence against the French. London 45 miles (A21). *OPEN Apr-Sept 10.00-19.00 daily; Oct-Mar 10.00-dusk Mon-Fri. Admission charge.*

Royal Pavilion, Brighton
Old Steine, Brighton, Sussex. Brighton 63005. A fantastic Oriental seaside 'villa', complete with onion domes and minarets, built for the Prince Regent (later George IV), by John Nash in 1822. The lavish Chinese

style staterooms are breathtaking; the original furniture has been returned from Buckingham Palace and the exemplary restorations after years of neglect are now complete. London 45 miles. (A23). *OPEN Jul-Oct 10.00-20.00 daily; until 17.00 in winter. Admission charge.*

Buscot Park
Faringdon, Berks. A charming late 18th cent house in the Adam style. Notable for its superb painted panels by the pre-Raphaelite painter Burne-Jones in the 'Sleeping Beauty' room. Also paintings by Reynolds, Murillo and Rembrandt. Pleasant park and lake. London 70 miles (A417). *OPEN Apr-Sept 14.00-18.00 Wed, First Sat & Sun in month; Oct-Mar 14.00-18.00 Wed. Admission charge.*

Claydon
Nr Wimslow, Buckinghamshire. Steeple Claydon 349. Built in 1752-68 as an ambitious effort by the 2nd Earl Verney to outdo the splendours of the Grevilles' rival seat at Stowe. Never completed, this remaining wing contains marvellous rococo state rooms decorated by the inspired carvings of a relatively unknown craftsman called Lightfoot. The Chinese Room is notable. Florence Nightingale Museum; also the remarkable Gubbay collection of 18th cent porcelain and furniture. London 45 miles (off A413). *OPEN Apr-Oct 14.00-18.00. CLOSED Mon, Fri except B. Hol Mon and Tues following B. Hol. Admission charge.*

Cliveden
Nr Maidenhead, Buckinghamshire. Burnham 5069. Superbly sited in wooded grounds overlooking the Thames. An imposing and famous country house built for the Duke of Sutherland in 1850 by Sir Charles Barry, in Italian palazzo style, replacing the two previous buildings destroyed by fire. Formal gardens with fine sculpture from the Villa Borghese and temples by Giacomo Leoni. London 25 miles (M4). *House OPEN Apr-Oct 14.30-17.30. CLOSED Mon, Tues, Thurs & Fri. Gardens OPEN Apr-Oct 11.00-18.30 Wed-Sun, B. Hols. Admission charge.*

Firle Place
Nr Lewes, Sussex. Glynde 256. Large 16th cent house pleasantly altered 1730. Notable for its outstanding collection of British and European old masters, furniture and porcelain. London 50 miles. *OPEN Jun-Sept 14.15-17.30 Wed & Thur, 18.30 Sun, B. Hols, Mon. Admission charge.*

Goodwood
Nr Chichester, Sussex. Chichester 527107. An 18th cent house planned by James Watt to have eight sides, of which only three were completed. Stables by Sir

William Chambers. A fine example of building in Sussex flint. Excellent paintings: some of Canaletto's London views and portraits by Van Dyck, Romney, Kneller and Stubbs. (The latter's depictions of the Lennox family are particularly lovely.) Magnificent Sevres porcelain, considered to be as fine as any in France; Gobelin tapestries; Louis XV and XVI furniture. Booking advisable for tickets for a visit which includes a tour of the state apartments, a Guide Book, plus luncheon or afternoon tea with the guide/hostess in the State Supper Room. London 50 miles. *OPEN Easter Sun-Sept 14.00-17.00 Sun, B. Hols, Mon. Admission charge.*

Hatfield
Hatfield, Hertfordshire. Hatfield 62823. A mellow and completely preserved Jacobean mansion with

magnificent interior built in 1607-11 by Robert Cecil, 1st Earl of Salisbury and still the home of the Cecil family. The Tudor Old Royal Palace nearby was the home of Queen Elizabeth I. Collection of 16th-, 17th- and 18th cent portraits, manuscripts and relics. London 20 miles (A1). *House OPEN 25th Mar-7th Oct 12.00-17.30 Tues-Sat & B. Hols, 14.00-17.30 Sun. CLOSED G. Fri. Admission charge.*

Heveningham Hall
Nr. Halesworth, Suffolk. Ubbeston 355. An imposing Georgian mansion by Sir Robert Taylor built in 1778-80 in a park by Capability Brown. The interior by James Wyatt is magnificent, and contains much original furniture. London 98 miles. *OPEN Apr-Oct 14.00-17.30 Wed, Thur, Sat, Sun & B. Hols; May-Sept also open Tues. Admission charge.*

Hever Castle
Nr Edenbridge, Kent. Edenbridge 2205. 13th cent moated castle once the home of Anne Boleyn who was courted here by Henry VIII. Excellent furnished rooms of the period and many fine portraits. A delightful garden and lake, landscaped by the first Viscount Astor in 1905 and containing a walled Italianate garden with statues, topiary and fountains. London 25 miles. *OPEN Apr-Sept 13.00-18.00 Wed, Sun, B. Hols. Admission charge.*

Hughenden Manor
High Wycombe, Buckinghamshire. High Wycombe 28051. Benjamin Disraeli's country seat from 1847 until his death in 1881, altered from its original Georgian to typical mid-Victorian. Museum of Disraeli relics and portraits. London 30 miles (A40). *OPEN Feb-Nov 14.00-18.00 Wed-Fri, 12.30-18.00 weekends and B. Hols. CLOSED G. Fri. Admission charge.*

Knebworth
Knebworth, Hertfordshire. Stevenage 812661. A successful and imaginative re-creation from the original Tudor built by the 1st Lord Lytton, the Victorian novelist in 1844. Pleasant garden. London 30 miles (A1). *OPEN Apr-Oct 14.00-17.00 Tues-Sun. Guided tours. Parties by arrangement. Admission charge.*

Knole
Sevenoaks, Kent. Sevenoaks 53006. A great Jacobean country house with a splendid park. The family home of the Sackvilles since 1566. The house and its richly decorated interior survive intact. It is a treasure house of robust gilded decoration and ornament, fine furniture, tapestries and paintings of 16th-18th cent. Many ancient oaks and beeches in the large park with a fine herd of deer (not to be fed). London 25 miles. *OPEN Apr 11.00-12.00 & 14.00-15.30 Wed-Sat; Nov 14.00-15.30 Sun; Apr-Oct 10.00-12.00 & 14.00-17.00 Wed-Sat & B. Hols, 14.00-17.00 Sun. Admission charge. Private gardens OPEN 1st Wed of month May-Sept. Guided tours for visitors to house only in mornings. Parties by arrangement.*

Leonardslee
Lower Beeding, Horsham, Sussex. Lower Beeding 212. Overlooking the South Downs and containing ancient 'hammer ponds' from the time when the Weald was a great iron producing area. Famous for conifers, azaleas, rhododendrons and camelias. Lovely views and woodland walks. London 30 miles. *OPEN last Sun Apr-first Sun Jun, Spring B.Hol, Wed, Thur and weekends in May; also 2-3 weekends in Oct for 'Autumn Tints' 10.00-18.00.*

Luton Hoo
Luton, Bedfordshire.
Luton 22955.
Imposing front of
original house designed
by Robert Adam 1767. Altered in
1903 and interior redecorated in French 18th cent style. Park and famous rose garden by Capability Brown. Particularly notable for the Wernher Collection, and important private collection of paintings, tapestries. English porcelain. Fabergé jewels and an unusual collection of momentoes and portraits of the Russian Imperial family. London 30 miles (M1). Exit 10. *OPEN G.Fri-last Sun Sept 11.00-18.00, 14.00-18.00 Sun. CLOSED Tues & Fri. Admission charge. Gardens OPEN Wed & Thur 11.00-18.00.*

Marble Hill House
Richmond Rd, Twickenham, Middx. 01-892 5115. Palladian-style house built in 1728 by Roger Morris, with interior and furnishings in period. Summer exhibition of paintings. *OPEN 10.00-17.00 every day except Fri. CLOSED G.Fri & Xmas. Free.*

Milton Manor
Abingdon, Berks. Steventon 287. Handsome 17th cent house. Fine rooms in lavishly 'Gothic' style. London 50 miles. *OPEN Easter-beginning Oct 14.00-18.00 weekends & B.Hols. Admission charge. Guided tours.*

Nyman Gardens
Handcross, Sussex. Handcross 321. One of the great Victorian gardens, originally designed by Colonel Messel. Consists of a heather garden, a sunken garden, a walled garden with herbaceous borders and a rose garden. The pinetum and the rhododendrons are features of great beauty and around the lawns are plants from foreign countries, many of which are rarely seen in England. London 40 miles (A23). *OPEN Apr-Oct 14.00-18.00 Tues-Sat & B.Hols, 11.00-18.00 Sun. CLOSED Fri.*

Parham
Pulborough, Sussex. Storrington 2866. Fine Elizabethan house in a great deer park facing the South Downs, with a superb Great Hall and Long Gallery, and a good collection of portraits. London 45 miles (A29). *OPEN Easter Sun-end of Sept 14.00-17.30 Sun, Wed, Thur & B.Hols. Admission charge. Gardens OPEN 13.00-17.00. Guided tours.*

Penshurst Place
Penshurst, Tunbridge Wells, Kent. A serene medieval house set amidst flat lawns. Built 1340 and enlarged during Queen Elizabeth's reign. Magnificent great hall

with carved timber roof, fine portraits of the Sidney family, early Georgian and Chippendale furniture, and a delightful formal walled garden with ponds and ancient apple trees. London 30 miles. *OPEN Easter Sat-Sept 12.30-18.00 Wed-Sun & B.Hols, also Tues from Jun. Guided tours. CLOSED Fri.*

Petworth
Petworth House, Sussex. Petworth 42207. An impressive 320-ft-long house, rebuilt late 17th cent and containing a range of magnificent state rooms. Famous for its splendid 'Carved Room' by the greatest carver in wood, Grinling Gibbons, and a most important collection of paintings including Van Dycks, Reynolds, many Dutch pictures and some particularly superb Turners. Fine deer park. London 50 miles. *OPEN Apr-Oct 16th 14.00-17.30 Wed, Thur, Sat & B.Hols. Extra rooms shown Tues. Admission charge.*

Rousham
Steeple Aston, Oxfordshire. Steeple Aston 40214. One of the best remaining examples of the work of William Kent, carried out 1738-40. Original interior decoration, painted ceilings and furniture within the Jacobean house. Kent's delightful classic garden beside the Cherwell, with statues (by Van Nost), glades and cascades, remain unaltered. London 65 miles. *OPEN Apr.-Sept 14.00-17.30 Wed, Sun & B. Hols. Guided tours. Garden OPEN all year 10.00-18.00. Admission charge.*

Sissinghurst Castle
Sissinghurst, Kent, Sissinghurst 250. The soft red-brick remains of the walls and buildings of a once extensive Tudor manor, enchantingly transformed by the late Victoria Sackville-West and Sir Harold Nicolson into numerous enclosed walled gardens. Each is different in character and outstandingly beautiful in its richness of flowers and shrubs. London 40 miles (A21). *OPEN 1st April-15th Oct 12.00-18.30 Mon-Fri, 10.00-18.30*

weekends & B. Hols. Admission charge. No dogs.

Stowe

Stowe School, nr Buckingham, Bucks. Buckingham 3165. Chiefly famous for its succession of notable landscape gardeners and garden architects. Bridgeman, Vanbrugh, James Gibbs, William Kent and Capability Brown. They produced the fine gardens, park, lake and Palladian bridges, temples and garden pavilions. London 55 miles. *OPEN (garden and part of house) during school Easter & summer hols, mid Jul-beginning Sept 10.00-18.00 daily.*

Uppark

Petersfield, Hants. Harting 317. Beautifully simple 17th cent house on the ridge of the South Downs, by William Talman 1690. Faultless 18th cent interiors retain
Repton. London 50 miles (A3). *OPEN Easter Sun-late Sept 14.00-18.00 Wed, Thur, Sun & B. Hols. Admission charge.*

The Vyne

Sherborne St John, Basingstoke, Hampshire. Bramley Green 337. Early 16th cent mansion with private chapel containing original glass. A classic-style portico was added in 1654. Fine Long Gallery with 'linenfold' carving on the panels throughout its length. 18th cent staircase by John Chute. London 45 miles (A30). *OPEN Apr-Sept 11.00-13.00 & 14.00-18.00 Wed, B. Hols, 14.00-18.00 Thur, Sat & sun. Admission charge.*

Waddesdon Manor

Nr Aylesbury, Buckinghamshire. Waddesdon 211. An extraordinary house built 1880-9 for baron Ferdinand de Rothschild by the French architect Bariel — Hippolyte Destailleur, in the style of a great chateau in Touraine.

The garden, fountains and large aviary of rare birds are enchanting. The house contains a superb collection of works of art, mostly of the 17th and 18th cent. Fine French furniture. Savonnerie carpets, 18th cent terracotta figures, and remarkable collections of Sèvres and Dresden porcelain. The paintings include Rubens 'Garden of Love', eight views of Venice by Guardi, many portraits by Gainsborough and Reynolds, including the latter's 'Pink Boy', and paintings by Watteau and Boucher. London 45 miles (A41). *OPEN late Mar-late Oct 14.00-18.00 Wed-Sun, 11.00-18.00 B. Hols. Admission charge.*

West Wycombe Park

High Wycombe, Buckinghamshire. High Wycombe 24411. Georgian house rebuilt 1745-71, by Sir Francis Dashwood. Still the home of the Dashwood family, it has good furniture, painted ceilings and frescoed walls. The landscaped grounds are dotted with garden buildings, including Roman and Greek temples, a flint mausoleum and, overlooking the River Thames, the cave where the notorious 18th cent drinking club, the Hell Fire Club, used to meet. London 30 miles (A40). *OPEN Jun, Jul, Aug & B. Hols 14.15-18.00. CLOSED weekends in Jun & Sat in Aug. Special guided tours by arrangements. Caves OPEN 11.00-19.00 Apr-mid Sept.*

Windsor Castle

Windsor, Berks. Windsor 63106. An imposing 800-year-old medieval fortress. 12th cent Round Tower built by Henry II. St George's chapel is fine 16th cent perpendicular. Magnificent state apartments. *OPEN Jan-mid March 10.30-15.00; mid Mar-mid Oct 10.30-17.00 (Sun from 13.00); mid Oct-Dec 10.30-15.00. CLOSED Sun, mid Oct-mid Mar and when the Queen is in residence — usually 6 weeks at Easter, 3 weeks in Jun and 3 weeks at Xmas. Admission charge.*

Woburn Abbey

Woburn, Bedfordshire. Woburn 666. The Duke of Bedford's 18th cent mansion, set in a fine 3,000-acre park landscaped by Humphrey Repton (part of which has been converted into a Safari Park). The house retains the quadrangular plan of the medieval monastery from which it also derived its site and name. Remodelling has occurred at different periods; the west front and the magnificent state apartments were done in 1747-60 by Henry Flitcroft; the south side, the lovely Chinese dairy and the orangery in 1802 by Henry Holland. Incomparable collection of pictures by Rembrandt, Van Dyck, Reynolds, Gainsborough, Holbein and a famous group of fine Canalettos. English

and French furniture, porcelain and silver. London 40 miles (M1). *Abbey and Park OPEN Mar 22-Aug 31 10.30-17.00 Mon-Sat, 10.00-17.30 Sun; Sept 1-Oct 24 11.00-16.30 Mon-Sat, 11.00-17.00 Sun; Oct 25-Mar 20 11.00-15.30 daily. Safari Park OPEN 10.00-17.30 weekdays, 10.00-18.00 weekends or until dusk in winter. Admission charge.*

Houses of famous people

These houses, open to the public, are those most worth visiting. Many others are now private houses with no facilities for entry and will be found in the next section, 'Commemorative plaques'.

Carlyle's house   **4 M 8**

24 Cheyne Row SW3. 01-352 7087. A modest 18th cent street house where Carlyle lived for 42 years until his death in 1881. *OPEN 11.00-13.00 & 14.00-18.00 Wed-Sat, 14.00-18.00 Sun. CLOSED Dec & G. Fri. Admission charge.*

Churchill's house

Chartwell, nr Westerham, Kent. Crockham Hill 368. A famous house full of recent political history. The water gardens, grounds and views of the Weald of Kent are memorable.

Darwin's house

Downe House, Downe, Kent. Charles Darwin's house where he lived and worked. *OPEN 13.00-18.00. CLOSED Mon, Fri except B. Hols. Admission charge.*

Dickens house   **3 G 27**

48 Doughty St WC1. 01-405 2127. 19th cent terrace house. Relics of Dickens' life and writings. He lived here from 1837 to 1839. *OPEN 10.00-17.00. CLOSED Sun, B. Hols. Admission charge.*

Disraeli's house

Hughenden Manor, High Wycombe, Buckinghamshire. Disraeli lived here from 1847 until his death in 1881. Contains much of his furniture, pictures, books and other relics. *OPEN Feb-Nov 14.00-18.00 Wed-Fri, 12.30-18.00 Sat, Sun & B. Hols. CLOSED G. Fri. Admission charge.*

Hogarth's house

Hogarth Lane, Gr West Rd W4. 01-570 7728. The 17th cent country villa of William Hogarth; relics and late impressions of his engravings. *OPEN 11.00-18.00 Mon-Sat, 14.00-18.00 Sun. CLOSED at 16.00 Oct-Mar, G. Fri, Xmas Eve, Box. Small admission charge.*

Henry James' house

Lamb House, Rye, Sussex. Georgian house with garden. Home of Henry James from 1898 to his death in 1916. Study with relics. *OPEN Apr-Oct 14.00-18.00 Wed, Sat. Small admission charge.*

Dr Johnson's house   **6 K 27**

17 Gough Square, Fleet St EC4. 17th cent house. Relics and contemporary portraits. He lived here from 1748 to 1759. *OPEN 10.30-17.00 Mon-Sat May-Sept; 10.30-16.30 Oct-Apr. CLOSED Sun, B. Hols. Small admission charge.*

Keats' house

Wentworth Place, Keats Grove NW3. 01-435 2062. The poet lived here during his prolific period 1818-20. *OPEN 10.00-18.00 Mon-Sat, 14.00-17.00 Sun. CLOSED G. Fri, Easter Sat, Xmas, Box, New Year's. Free.*

Kipling's house

Bateman's Burwash, Sussex. Burwash 882 302. The house built in 1634, contains Kipling's furniture and relics. The surroundings are described in 'Puck of Pook's Hill' and 'Rewards and Fairies'. *OPEN Mar-Oct 31 daily except Fri 14.00-17.30; Jun-Sept 30 11.00-12.30 Mon-Thur. CLOSED Fri except G. Fri afternoon. Admission charge.*

Shaw's Corner

Ayot St Lawrence, Welwyn. Stevenage 820307. London 25 miles. George Bernard Shaw lived here from 1906 until his death in 1950. *OPEN 11.00-13.00 & 14.00-18.00 or dusk. CLOSED Mon & Tues, G. Fri and from Nov 29-Jan 31. Admission charge.*

William Morris Gallery

Water House, Lloyd Park, Forest Rd E17. 01-527 5544. 18th cent house. Textiles, wallpapers, carpets, woodwork and designs by Morris, pre-Raphaelites and contemporaries, housed in Morris's boyhood home. *OPEN 10.00-17.00 Mon-Sat, 10.00-20.00 Tues & Thur; Apr-Sept 10.00-12.00, 14.00-17.00 & 1st Sun in month.*

CLOSED B. Hols. Free.
Wellington Museum   **2 I 16**
Apsley House, 149 Piccadilly W1. 01-499 5676. Known as 'No. 1 London'. Duke of Wellington's house. Built 1771-8 from designs by Robert Adam and altered 1828 by B. D. Wyatt. Contains Wellington relics, fine Spanish (Velasquez) and Dutch paintings, silver plate and porcelain. *OPEN 10.00-18.00 Mon-Sat, 14.30-18.00 Sun. CLOSED G. Fri, Xmas. Small admission charge.*
Wesley's house & chapel   **6 K 33**
47 City Rd EC1. 01-253 2262. John Wesley's possessions and personal relics. His tomb is in the chapel grounds. *OPEN 10.00-13.00 & 14.00-16.00. CLOSED Sun. G. Fri, Xmas, Box. Small admission charge.*
Wolfe's house
Quebec House, Westerham, Kent. Mainly 17th cent house where General Wolfe spent his early years. Contains a collection of 'Wolfiana'. *OPEN Mar-Oct 14.00-18.00 Tues, Wed, Sun, 10.00-13.00 & 14.00-18.00 B. Hols. CLOSED rest of year. Admission charge.*

Commemorative plaques

Blue plaques and tablets have been fixed by the GLC and the Corporation of London to many houses and buildings associated with famous persons. The following are some of the most well known.

Adam, Robert   **6 K 23**
Lived at 1-3 Robert St, Adelphi WC2.
Arnold, Matthew   **5 L 14**
Lived at 2 Chester Sq SW1.
Asquith, Herbert Henry   **2 F 20**
Lived at 20 Cavendish Sq W1.
Baden-Powell, Robert   **1 F 9**
Lived at 9 Hyde Park Gate SW7.
Baird, John Logie   **2 H 22**
First demonstrated television at 22 Frith St W1.
Baldwin, Stanley   **5 K 14**
Lived at 93 Eaton Sq SW1.
Barrie, Sir James   **1 B 10**
Lived at 100 Bayswater Rd W2
and at 1-3 Robert St, Adelphi WC2.   **6 K 23**
Beardsley, Aubrey   **5 O 14**
Lived at 114 Cambridge St SW1.
Bennett, Arnold   **5 J 12**
Lived at 75 Cadogan Sq SW1.
Berlioz, Hector   **2 E 19**
Stayed at 58 Queen Anne St W1.
Bligh, William   **5 P 21**
Commander of the 'Bounty' lived at 100 Lambeth Rd SE1.
Boswell, James   **2 E 21**
Lived and died on the site of 122 Great Portland St W1.
Browning, Elizabeth Barrett   **2 E 19**
Lived on the site of 50 Wimpole St W1,
and at 99 Gloucester Place NW1.   **2 A 18**
Brunel, Sir Marc Isambard   **4 M 8**
Lived 98 Cheyne Walk SW10.
Burne-Jones, Sir Edward Coley   **3 H 25**
Lived at 17 Red Lion Sq WC1.
Canaletto, Antonio   **2 H 20**
Lived at 41 Beak St W1.
Carlyle, Thomas   **3 F 27**
Lived at 33 Ampton St WC1.
Chamberlain, Joseph
Lived at 25 Highbury Place N5.
Chesterton, Gilbert Keith   **1 E 4**
Lived at 11 Warwick Gardens W14.
Chippendale, Thomas
and his son had their workshop near
61 St Martin's Lane WC2.   **5 J 22**
Churchill, Lord Randolph   **2 D 16**
Lived at 2 Connaught Place W2.
Clive of India, Lord   **2 H 18**
Lived at 45 Berkeley Sq W1.
Coleridge, Samuel Taylor
Lived at 7 Addison Bridge Place W14.   **1 E 3**
and on the site of 71 Berners St W1.   **2 G 22**
Constable, John
Lived at 40 Well Walk NW3.
Cook, Captain James
Lived in house on site of 88 Mile End Rd E1.
Darwin, Charles
Lived on the site of 110 Gower St WC1.   **3 D 23**
Defoe, Daniel
Lived on the site of 95 Stoke Newington Church St N16.
Dickens, Charles
Lived at 48 Doughty St WC1.   **3 G 27**
Disraeli, Benjamin
Born at 22 Theobalds Rd WC1.   **3 H 26**
and died at 19 Curzon St W1.   **2 H 17**

Du Maurier, George
Lived at 28 Hampstead Grove NW3,
and at 91 Great Russell St WC1.   **3 H 23**
Elgar, Sir Edward
Lived at 51 Avonmore Rd W14.   **1 E 3**
Eliot, George (Mary Ann Cross)
Lived at Holly Lodge, 31 Wimbledon Park Rd SW18,
and died at 4 Cheyne Walk SW3.   **4 M 8**
Faraday, Michael
Apprenticed at 48 Blandford St W1.   **2 D 18**
Fielding, Henry
Lived at 19-20 Bow St WC2,   **6 J 24**
and at Essex Hall, Essex St WC2.   **6 K 25**
Ford, Ford Madox
Lived at 80 Campden Hill Rd W8.   **1 C 7**
Franklin, Benjamin
Lived at 36 Craven St WC2   **5 K 22**
Freud, Sigmund
Lived at 20 Maresfield Gardens NW3.
Fry, Elizabeth
Prison reformer. Lived at St Mildred's Court, Poultry EC2.   **6 N 30**
Gainsborough, Thomas
Lived at 82 Pall Mall SW1.   **5 J 20**
Galsworthy, John
Lived at Grove Lodge, Hampstead Grove NW3,
and at 1-3 Robert St, Adelphi WC2   **6 K 23**
Garrett Anderson, Elizabeth
Lived at 20 Upper Berkeley St W1.   **2 D 16**
Gibbon, Edward
Lived on site of 7 Bentinck St, W1.   **2 E 19**
Gibbons, Grinling
Lived at 19-20 Bow St WC2.   **6 J 24**
Gladstone, William Ewart
Lived at 11 Carlton House Terrace SW1,   **5 K 21**
at 10 St James's Sq SW1,   **5 J 20**
and at 73 Harley St W1.   **2 E 20**
Greenaway, Kate
Lived and died at 39 Frognal NW3.
Handel, George Frederick
Lived and died at 25 Brook St W1.   **2 G 18**
Hardy, Thomas
Lived at 172 Trinity Rd SW17,
and at Adelphi Terrace WC2.   **6 K 23**
Hazlitt, William
Lived on the site of 6 Bouverie St EC4,   **6 L 26**
and died at 6 Frith St W1.   **2 I 22**
Holman-Hunt, William
Lived and died at 18 Melbury Rd W14.   **1 D 5**
Housman, A. E.
Lived at 17 North Rd N6.
Irving, Sir Henry
Lived at 15a Grafton St W1.   **2 H 19**
James, Henry
Lived at 34 De Vere Gardens W8.   **F 8**
Johnson, Dr Samuel
Lived at 17 Gough Sq, Fleet St EC4,   **6 K 27**
at Johnson's Court, Fleet St EC4,   **6 K 27**
and at Essex Hall, Essex St WC2   **6 K 25**
Keats, John
Lived at Wentworth Place, Keats Grove, NW3 and was born on the site of 'The Swan & Hoop Public House, 85 Moorgate EC2.   **6 M 31**
Kipling, Rudyard
Lived at 43 Villiers St WC2.   **5 K 22**
Kitchener of Khartoum
Lived at 2 Carlton Gardens SW1.   **5 K 20**
Lamb, Charles
Lived at 64 Duncan Terrace N1.   **3 F 32**
Lawrence, David Herbert
1 Byron Villas, Vale of Health, Hampstead Heath NW3.
Lived here in 1915.
Lawrence, T. E.
Lived at 14 Barton St SW1.   **5 N 19**
Lear, Edward
Lived at 30 Seymour St W1.   **2 D 16**
Lenin, Vladimir Ilvitch Ulyanov
Lived at 16 Percy Circus WC1.   **3 F 29**
Lind, Jenny
Lived at 189 Old Brompton Rd SW5.   **1 I 6**
Lloyd George, David
Lived at 3 Routh Rd SW18.
Lutyens, Sir Edwin Landseer
Lived at 13 Mansfield St W1.   **2 E 20**
Macdonald, Ramsay
Lived at 9 Howitt Rd NW3.
Mansfield, Katherine
Lived at 17 East Heath Rd NW3.
Marconi, Guglielmo
Lived at 71 Hereford Rd W2.   **1 A 10**
Marx, Karl
Lived at 28 Dean St W1.   **2 H 22**
Millais, Sir John Everett
Lived and died at 2 Palace Gate W8.   **1 F 9**

Morris, William
Lived at 17 Red Lion Sq WC1.   3 H 25
Mozart, Wolfgang Amadeus
Composed his first symphony at
180 Ebury St SW1.   5 M 13
Napoleon III
Lived at 1c King St SW1   5 J 19
Nelson, Lord (Horatio)
Lived on the site of 147 New Bond St W1,   2 G 19
and at 103 New Bond St W1.   2 G 19
Newton, Sir Isaac
Lived on the site of 87 Jermyn St SW1.   2 I 19
Nightingale, Florence
Lived and died on the site of 10 South St W1.   2 H 17
Palmerston, Lord (Henry John Temple)
Born at 20 Queen Anne's Gate SW1.   5 L 19
Lived at 4 Carlton Gardens SW1,   5 K 20
and at Naval and Military Club, 94 Piccadilly W1. 2 I 17
Pepys, Samuel
Born on site of Wall of Westminster Bank, Salisbury
Court EC4.   6 L 27
Lived at 12 & 14 (site) Buckingham St WC2.   5 K 22
Pitt, William
Lived at 10 St James's Sq SW1.   5 J 20
Pitt, William (The Younger)
Lived at 120 Baker St W1.   2 D 18
Reynolds, Sir Joshua
Lived and died on the site of Fanum House, Leicester
Sq WC2.   5 J 22
Rosebery, 5th Earl
Born at 20 Charles St W1.   2 H 17
Rossetti, Dante Gabriel
Born on the site of 110 Hallam St W1.   2 E 21
Lived at 17 Red Lion Sq WC1,   3 H 25
and at 16 Cheyne Walk SW3.   4 M 8
Ruskin, John
Born at 54 Hunter St WC1.   3 F 26
Lived on the site of 26 Herne Hill SE24.
Scott, Capt. Robert Falcon
Lived at 56 Oakley St SW3.   4 M 9
Shackleton, Sir Ernest (Henry)
Lived at 12 Westwood Hill SE26.
Shaw, George Bernard
Lived at Adelphi Terrace WC2.   6 K 23
Sheraton, Thomas
Lived at 163 Wardour St W1.   2 I 21
Sheridan, Richard Brinsley
Lived at 14 Saville Row W1,   2 H 20
and at 10 Hertford St W1.   2 I 16
St Thomas à Becket
Born in a house near here. 86 Cheapside EC2.   6 M 29
Stephenson, Robert
Died on the site of 35 Gloucester Sq W2.   2 C 14
Stuart, Charles Edward, Prince
Stayed in a house in Essex St WC2   6 K 25
Swinburne, Algernon Charles
Lived at 16 Cheyne Walk SW3,   4 M 8
and died at 11 Putney Hill SW15.
Tagore, Rabindranath
Lived at 3 Villas on the Heath, Vale of Heath NW3.
Thackeray, William Makepeace
Lived at 16 Young St W8,   1 E 8
and at 36 Onslow Sq SW7.   4 J 9
Trollope, Anthony
Lived at 39 Montagu Sq W1.   2 D 17
'Twain, Mark' (Samuel L. Clemens)
Lived at 23 Tedworth Sq SW3.   4 M 10
Wallace, Edgar
Lived at 6 Tressilian Crescent SE4.
Walpole, Sir Robert
Lived at 5 Arlington St SW1.   2 I 19
Wells, H. G.
Lived at 13 Hanover Terrace NW1.
Wesley, John
Lived at 47 City Rd EC1.   6 K 33
Whistler, James Abbot McNeil
Lived at 96 Cheyne Walk SW10.   4 M 8
Whittington, Richard ('Dick')
House of Whittington stood at 20 College Hill EC4 in
1423, and 'Dick' was born and buried in the church of
St Michael, Royal College Hill EC4.   6 N 29
Wilberforce, William
Lived at 111 Broomwood Rd SW11,
and at 44 Cadogan Place SW1.   5 K 13
Wilde, Oscar
Lived at 34 Tite St SW3.   2 M 10
Wolfe, General James
Lived at Macartney House, Greenwich Park SE10.
Wood, Sir Henry
Lived at 4 Elsworthy Rd NW3.
Wyndham, Sir Charles
Lived at 43 York Terrace NW1.   2 B 19
Yeats, William Butler
Lived at 23 Fitzroy Rd NW1.

Statues

*London has over 400 outdoor statues. The great
majority of them are quite undistinguished; these are
the best and most interesting.*

Achilles   2 I 16
Hyde Park W1. Westmacott, 1822. Erected to honour
Wellington. London's first nude statue.
Alfred the Great   6 R 26
Trinity Church Sq SE1. Origin unknown but it possibly
came from Westminster Hall, in which case it dates
from 1395 and is by far the oldest statue in London.
Queen Anne   6 M 28
In front of St Paul's Cathedral EC4. After Bird, 1712.
This is a copy (1886) of the original. Surrounding the
Queen are figures representing England, France,
Ireland and North America.
Queen Anne   5 L 19
Queen Anne's Gate SW1. Origin uncertain but
probably by Francis Bond early 18th cent; believed to
have originally stood over the portico of the church of
St Mary-le-Strand.

Queen Anne   Boadicea   George Canning   Nurse Cavell

Boadicea   5 N 21
Westminster Bridge SW1. Thornycroft, 1902. Famous
group showing the ancient British Queen with her
daughters in her war chariot.
George Canning   5 M 20
Parliament Sq SW1. Westmacott, 1832. Fell over while
in the sculptor's studio and killed a man.
Nurse Cavell   5 J 22
St Martin's Place WC2. Frampton, 1920. Simple and
impressive memorial to the nurse who was shot for
assisting prisoners to escape during World War 1.
Charles I   5 K 21
Trafalgar Sq SW1. Le Sueur, 1633. The oldest
equestrian statue in London and one of the finest.
Ordered to be destroyed during the Civil War and
hidden until the Restoration. It was erected on its
present site between 1675 and 1677.
Crimea Memorial   5 J 20
Waterloo Place SW1. Bell, 1859. Figures of Guards cast
from melted down cannon taken in battle. A pile of
actual cannons decorate the back. Memorial includes a
statue of:
Florence Nightingale   5 J 20
Waterloo Place SW1. Waller, 1915. She is shown
holding an oil lamp, whereas the famous lamp which
gave her the name 'The lady with the lamp' was
actually a candle lantern.

Charles I   Florence Nightingale   Oliver Cromwell   King Edward

Oliver Cromwell   5 N 20
Old Palace Yard SW1. Thornycroft, 1899.
Queen Elizabeth I   6 K 26
St Dunstan in the West, Fleet St EC4. Originally stood
over Lud Gate. Made during the Queen's lifetime in
1586, it is one of London's oldest statues.
Eros   2 I 20
Piccadilly Circus W1. Gilbert, 1893. Officially the Angel
of Christian Charity. It is part of the memorial to the
Victorian philanthropist Lord Shaftesbury. Made in
aluminium.
George III   5 K 21
Cockspur St SW1. Wyatt, 1836. The best statue of this
king, on a fine spirited horse.
George IV   5 K 21
Trafalgar Sq WC2. Chantrey, 1843. Rides without
boots on a horse without saddle or stirrups. Was
originally intended for the top of Marble Arch.
George V   5 N 20
Old Palace Yard SW1. Reid Dick, 1947.

Sir Henry Irving   **5 J 21**
By the side of the National Portrait Gallery, St Martin's
Place WC2. Brock, 1910. London's only statue of an
actor.
James II   **5 J 22**
Outside National Gallery, Trafalgar Sq WC2. Grinling
Gibbons, 1686. One of London's finest statues. Shows
the king in Roman costume.

Eros   George III   George IV   George V

Dr Samuel Johnson   **6 K 25**
St Clement Danes churchyard, Strand WC2. Fitzgerald,
1910.
Abraham Lincoln   **5 M 20**
Parliament Sq SW1. Saint-Gaudens, 1920. Replica of
the one in Chicago.
Nelson   **5 K 21**
On column in Trafalgar Sq WC2. Baily, 1843. The
statue is 16 ft high; weighs 16 tons. Made of stone, it
was hoisted into position in three pieces.
Peter Pan   **2 D 12**
Kensington Gardens W2. Frampton, 1912. Charming
fairy figure. Erected overnight as a surprise for the
children.
Richard I   **5 N 20**
Old Palace Yard SW1. Marochetti, 1860.
Franklin D. Roosevelt   **2 F 17**
Grosvenor Square W1. Reid Dick, 1948.
Sir Joshua Reynolds   **2 I 19**
Forecourt of Burlington House, Piccadilly W1. Drury,
1931.
Royal Artillery Memorial   **2 I 16**
Hyde Park Corner SW1. Jagger. London's best war
memorial, with its great stone howitzer aimed at the
Somme where the men it commemorates lost their
lives. The bronze figures of soldiers are possibly the
finest sculptures to be seen in the streets of London.
Captain Scott   **5 K 20**
Waterloo Place SW1. Lady Scott, 1915. 'Scott of the
Antarctic' modelled by his widow.

Sir Joshua   James II   Sir Henry Irving   Abraham Lincoln
Reynolds

William Shakespeare   **5 J 22**
Leicester Sq WC2. After Scheemakers, 1740. Copy
(1874) of the memorial in Westminster Abbey for which
David Garrick is said to have posed.
Victoria Memorial   **5 K 17**
In front of Buckingham Palace SW1. Brock, 1911.
Impressive memorial to Queen Victoria which includes
a fine dignified figure of the Queen, the best of the
many statues of her.
George Washington   **5 J 21**
Outside National Gallery. Trafalgar Sq WC2. Replica of
the statue by Houdon in the Capitol at Richmond,
Virginia, and presented by that State in 1921.
Duke of Wellington   **6 N 31**
Outside Royal Exchange EC3. Chantrey, 1844. Like the
same sculptor's statue of George IV, his horse has no
saddle or stirrups and he wears no boots.
Duke of Wellington   **2 I 16**
Hyde Park Corner SW1. Boehm, 1888. Equestrian
statue of the Duke. The memorial is distinguished by
four well-modelled figures of soldiers in full kit. The
Duke rides his favourite horse 'Copenhagen' and he
looks towards Apsley House, in which he lived.
William III   **5 J 20**
St James's Sq SW1. Bacon, 1807. First proposed in
1697 but not erected until 1808. Beneath one of the
horse's hooves is the mole-hill over which the horse
stumbled, killing the King.

Richard I   Royal Artillery Memorial   Captain Scott   William
                                                            Shakespeare

Duke of York   **5 K 20**
On column, Carlton House Terrace SW1. Westmacott,
1834. Cost £30,000 and was paid for by deducting a
day's pay from every officer and man in the British
Army.

Modern outdoor sculpture

*This is a depressingly short list of good modern outdoor
sculpture — a reflection of a sad lack of public
confidence and private commission. Well worth visiting
however is the summer exhibition of outdoor sculpture
in various London parks.*
Arts Council (of Great Britain) Shop   **2 I 20**
25 Sackville St W1. 01-734 4318. The Arts Council
organises many of the most important sculpture
exhibitions in London, the major ones being held at the
Hayward and Serpentine Galleries which both have
outdoor facilities. The shop stocks a large collection of
catalogues and literature on sculpture. Hayward
Gallery, South Bank SE1. 01-928 3144. Serpentine
Gallery, Kensington Gardens W2. 01-402 6075.
Geoffrey Clarke (b. 1924)
Thorn Building, Upper St Martin's Lane WC2   **2 I 22**
Bronze relief.
Sir Jacob Epstein (1880-1959)
Convent of the Holy Child, 11 Cavendish   **2 F 20**
Sq W1. Bronze 'Madonna and Child', 1952.
St James's Park Undergrounf Station.   **5 L 18**
Fine sculpture of 'Day and Night'.
Elizabeth Frink (b. 1930)
Carlton Towers Hotel, Cadogan Sq SW1.   **5 J 13**
Beaten copper relief on façade.
Dame Barbara Hepworth (1903-1975)
John Lewis Store, Oxford St W1. Bronze relief. **2 F 19**
State House, High Holborn WC1.   **3 I 23**
Fine abstract 'Meridian'.
Bernard Meadows (b. 1915)
TUC Building, Gt Russell St WC1.   **3 H 23**
Bronze group.
Henry Moore (b. 1898)
Time & Life Building, New Bond St W1.   **2 G 19**
Fine stone relief.
Times Building, Printing House Sq EC4.   **6 M 27**
Bronze sun dial of vertical and horizontal arcs, giving
accurate solar time. 1967.
Abingdon St Gardens   **5 N 20**
'Knife Edge 2'.

Abbeys and cathedrals

St George's R.C. Cathedral, Southwark   **6 P 29**
Lambeth Rd (opp. Imperial War Museum) SE1. 01-928
5256. By A. W. Pugin, 1848. Spire never completed.
Burnt out in last war and interior finely rebuilt.
St Paul's Cathedral   **6 M 28**
EC4. 01-236 4128. Wren's greatest work; built 1675-
1710 replacing the previous church destroyed by the
Great Fire. Superb dome, porches and funerary
monuments. Contains magnificent stalls by Grinling
Gibbons. Ironwork by Tijou, paintings by Thornhill and
mosaics by Salviati and Stephens. *OPEN Apr-Sept
07.45-19.00; Oct-Mar 07.45-17.00. Crypt & galleries
OPEN 10.45-15.15 Mon-Sat.*

St Paul's Cathedral   Southwark Cathedral   Westminster Abbey

Southwark Cathedral   6 Q 27
Borough High St SE1. 01-407 2939. Much restored.
Built by Augustinian Canons 1206. Beautiful early
English choir and retrochoir. Tower built c. 1520, nave
by Blomfield 1894-97. Contains work by Comper (altar
screen).

Westminster Abbey   5 M 20
(The Collegiate Church of St Peter in Westminster)
Broad sanctuary SW1. 01-222 1051. Original church by
Edward the Confessor 1065. Rebuilding commenced by
Henry III in 1245 who was largely influenced by the new
French cathedrals. Completed by Henry Yevele and
others 1376-1506 (towers incomplete and finished by
Hawksmoor 1734). Henry VII Chapel added 1503; fine
perpendicular with wonderful fan vaulting. The Abbey
contains the Coronation Chair, and many tombs and
memorials of the Kings and Queens of England and
their subjects. Starting place for pilgrimage to
Canterbury Cathedral. *Abbey OPEN 09.00-17.00 Mon-
Fri. Royal Chapels OPEN various times as are the
Chapter House & Chamber of the Pyx & Museum.*

Westminster Roman Catholic Cathedral   5 M 16
Ashley Place SW1. 01-834 7452. Early Christian
Byzantine-style church by J. F. Bentley, 1903. The
most important Roman Catholic church in England.
Fine marbled interior.

Churches

*London's churches fared badly in both the 'Great Fire'
of 1666 and the blitz of World War 2. Yet those
remaining, restored or rebuilt, are not only surprisingly
numerous but form a remarkably fine collection well
worth visiting. Here are some of the most interesting.*

All Hallows-by-the-Tower   6 Q 32
Byward St EC3. 01-481 2928. Foundations date from
675, audaciously restored by Lord Mottistone after
bombing. Fine copper steeple. Crypt museum with
Roman pavement — *visits Sat/Sun or by arrangement
with Verger*. Headquarters of Toc H.

All Hallows London Wall   6 L 30
83 London Wall EC2. 01-588 3388. Small 13th cent
church rebuilt 1765-7 by Dance junior. Restored 1962
by David Nye as centre for church art. Occasional
exhibitions still held. Charming interior.

All Saints Margaret Street   2 F 20
Margaret St W1. 01-636 9961. Gothic Revival
masterpiece. Butterfield 1859. Paintings by Ninian
Comper. Fine musical tradition.

All Souls Langham Place   2 F 20
Langham Place W1. 01-580 3522. John Nash 1822-4.
Corinthian columns with needle spire. Restored after
bomb damage.

The Annunciation Bryanston Street   2 E 16
Bryanston St W1. 01-262 4329. Sir Walter Tapper 1914.
Gothic-style interior with baroque furnishings.

Brompton Oratory   1 I 11
Brompton Rd SW7. 01-589 4811. Large Italian
Renaissance-style church designed by H. Gribble, 1884.
Fine marbled interior and original statues from the
Cathedral of Siena.

Capel Bedyddwyr Cymreig   2 G 21
31 Eastcastle St W1. Highly imaginative Welsh Baptist
chapel.

Christ the King   3 E 24
Gordon Sq WC1. 01-387 0670. The University church,
formerly known as the Catholic Apostolic church.
Cruciform, cathedral-like building by Raphael Brandon,
1853. (West front and tower unfinished.)

Chapel Royal of St John   6 Q 32
White Tower, Tower of London EC3. The oldest church
in London, c. 1085, original Norman.

Chelsea Old Church, All Saints   4 M 8
Chelsea Embankment SW3. 01-352 5627. Rebuilt after
severe bombing. 14th cent chapels, one restored by Sir
Thomas More 1528. Original Jacobean altar table and
rails; many historic monuments.

Christchurch Spitalfields
Commercial St E1. Fine church by Hawksmoor, 1723-5,
recently partly restored. Notable tower and spire, and
lofty interior. Crypt a shelter for the destitute.

Christ Church Newgate Street   6 L 29
Newgate St EC1. Wren 1691. Only the tower (1704) and
four walls remain.

Church of the Holy Sepulchre   6 K 28
Holborn Viaduct EC1. 01-248 1660. Rebuilt in 15th cent,
altered by Wren in 1667, and again altered in the 18th
and 19th cent. Tombs of Sir Henry Wood and Captain
John Smith.

Grosvenor Chapel   2 G 17
South Audley St W1. 01-499 1684. 'Colonial'-looking
chapel built 1730. Decorations by Comper added in
1912.

The Guards Chapel   5 L 18
Wellington Barracks, Birdcage Walk SW1. Original
chapel (1838) destroyed during the war with the loss of
121 lives. New chapel, finished 1963, is austere but
complements the original surviving apse. *OPEN 10.00-
16.00.*

Holy Trinity   5 L 12
Sloane St SW1. 01-730 2442. By Sedding in 1890.
London's most elaborate church of the 'Arts and Crafts'
movement.

Notre Dame de France   2 I 22
5 Leicester Place WC2. 01-437 9363. First church 1865,
rebuilt 1955 after bombing. Circular. Large Aubusson
tapestry, mural by Jean Cocteau and statue of Our
Lady by Georges Sanpique.

Queen's Chapel of the Savoy   6 K 23
Savoy Hill, Strand WC2. Late perpendicular style built
1508. Some 13th and 15th cent glass.

The Queen's Chapel, St James's Palace   5 K 19
Marlborough Rd SW1. Built by Inigo Jones 1623. Fine
restored woodwork and coffered ceiling. *OPEN on
application to the Administrative Officer, Marlborough
House, SW1.*

St Alban Holborn   3 I 27
Brooke St EC1. Originally by Butterfield 1859. Restored
after bomb damage. Soaring arches. Huge mural by
Hans Feilbusch.

St Alban Wood Street   6 L 30
Wood St EC2. Wren. Only the tower remains 1697-8
(modern pinnacles).

St Andrew Holborn   6 J 27
Holborn Circus EC1. 01-353 3544. Largest of Wren's
parish churches, 1686. Restored 1961 after bombing.
Pulpit, font, organ and tomb of Thomas Coram, from
the chapel of the 18th cent Foundling Hospital.

St Andrew-by-the-Wardrobe   6 M 27
Queen Victoria St EC4. Fine city church by Wren, 1685-
95. Restored after bomb damage, 1959-61.

St Andrew Undershaft   6 O 32
Leadenhall St EC3. Rebuilt 1532. Altar rails by Tijou,
font by Nicholas Stone. Monument to John Stow,
London's first historian.

St Anne's Soho   2 H 22
57 Dean St W1. Steeple only, by Cockerell 1802-6. The
church, by Wren, was destroyed by bombing.

St Anne & St Agnes   6 M 30
Gresham St. EC2. 01-606 4986. Wren, 1676-87.
Attractive church restored after bomb damage.

St Augustine Watling Street   6 M 29
Watling St EC4. Wren, 1687. Only tower remains after
bombing, with new spire after the original design. Now
incorporated into new cathedral choir school.

St Barnabas Pimlico   5 N 13
St Barnabas St SW1. 01-730 5054. By Thomas Cundy
Jnr, 1849. Fine medieval-type shrine of St Barnabas.

St Bartholomew-the-Great   6 K 29
West Smithfield EC1. 01-606 5171. Norman choir of
Augustinian Priory 1123 with later Lady Chapel; the
only pre-Reformation font in City. Tomb of founder
(who also founded St Bartholomew's Hospital and
other fine monuments.

St Bartholomew-the-Less   6 K 29
West Smithfield EC1. 01-606 7777. Inside 'Barts'
hospital (serves as its chapel). Tower and west end
medieval, rest rebuilt 1789 and 1823. Octagonal
interior.

St Benet Guild Welsh Church   6 M 28
Queen Victoria St EC4. 01-723 3104. Attractive church
by Wren 1677-85. Brick with stone dressings.

St Botolph Aldersgate   6 K 30
Aldersgate EC1. Nathaniel Wright, 1788, with additions
in 1831. Charming interior.

St Botolph Aldgate   6 O 33
Aldgate High St EC3. 01-283 1670. Rebuilt 1741-4 by
Dance senior. Restored by Bentley 1890s and again
1966. Fine monuments. Lies north and south. Renatus
Harris organ (1674). Peal of 8 bells (18th cent). Crypt is
used for down-and-outs.

St Botolph Bishopsgate   6 N 33
Bishopsgate EC2. 01-588 1053. Rebuilt 1725-9 by
James Gold. Baroque steeple at east end. Large
churchyard.

St Bride   6 L 27
Fleet St EC4. 01-353 1301. Wren, 1670-84. Famous
spire 1701-4. Restored after bomb damage. Fine city
church.

St Clement Danes   6 K 25
Strand WC2. 01-242 8282. First built for the Danes, 9th
cent. Spire by Gibbs. Rebuilt by Wren 1681. Destroyed
in air raids 1941 and rebuilt and rededicated in 1958 as
the central church of the R.A.F. Bells ring 'Oranges and
Lemons' every 3 hrs. Fine moulded plaster roof.

St Clements Nr Eastcheap   6 Q 30
Clements Lane, King William St EC4. 01-248 6121.
Wren 1687. Restored by Butterfield 1872, and by
Comper 1933. Notable 17th cent woodwork and fine

The Wren Churches of London

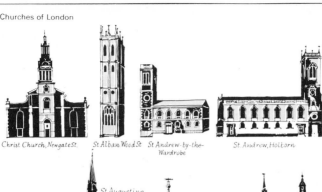

Christ Church, Newgate St.

St Alban Wood St

St Andrew-by-the-Wardrobe

St. Andrew, Holborn

St Anne and St Agnes

St Augustine Watling St.

St Benet Paul's Wharf

St Bride, Fleet St.

St. Clement Danes

St. Clement, Eastcheap

St Dunstans in the East

St Edmund

St James Garlickhithe

St Lawrence Jewry

St. Magnus

St. Margaret Lothbury

St Margaret Pattens

St. Martin Ludgate

St Mary Abchurch   St Mary Aldermary

St. Mary-at-Hill

St Mary le Bow

St Mary Somerset

St. Michael Cornhill

St Michael Paternoster Royal

St Olave Old Jewry

St. Peter, Cornhill

St Stephen, Walbrook

St.Vedast

organ 1695.

St Cyprian   **2 A 19**
Clarence Gate NW1. Outstanding example of a complete church by Comper, in his early style, 1903.

St Dunstan-in-the-East   **6 P 31**
St Dunstan's Hill EC3. Only the delicately poised spire by Wren remains, 1696-1701.

St Dunstan-in-the-West   **6 K 26**
Fleet St EC4. 01-242 6027. Octagonal church by John Shaw 1831-3. Restored in 1950. Fine lantern-steeple clock with 'striking jacks', from old church. Orthodox chapel with icon screen brought from Antim Monastery in Bucharest.

St Dunstan All Saints, Stepney
White Horse Rd E1. 01-790 4120. The Mother church of East London, late 15th cent. Mostly rebuilt. Fine interior. Notable Saxon crucifix.

St Edmund the King   **6 N 30**
Lombard St EC3. 01-623 6970. Rebuilt by Wren, 1690, and lies north and south, like the pre-'fire' church. Restored after slight damage in both world wars. Fine woodwork, distinctive steeple.

St Ethelburga   **6 N 33**
68-70 Bishopsgate EC2. 01-588 3596. Tiny church, late 14th cent, restored by Comper. Fine mural by Hans Feibusch (1693) on East Wall. One of the City 'Guild Churches' whose special concern is with mental and spiritual health.

St George Bloomsbury   **3 H 24**
Bloomsbury Way WC1. 01-636 5572. Hawksmoor, 1731. Statue of George I on top of steeple. Restored in 1870. Six-column Corinthian portico. Classical interior.

St George's Hanover Square   **2 G 19**
Hanover Sq W1. 01-629 0874. Classical church by John James 1721-4. Restored by Blomfield in 1894. Original of 'Last Supper' by Kent.

St George's-in-the-East
Cannon Street Rd E1. Remarkable church by Hawksmoor 1715-23. Modern rebuilding (1964) within the bomb-ruined walls.

St George's Southwark   **6 Q 27**
Borough High St SE1. A Georgian building with fine ornamental plaster ceiling. 'Little Dorrit's' church. Rebuilt 1734-6 by J. Price.

St Giles Cripplegate   **6 L 31**
Fore St EC2. 14th cent church restored 1952 after bombing. Contains Milton's grave. Remains of London Wall in churchyard.

St Giles in the Fields   **3 H 23**
St Giles High St WC2. 01-240 2532. Flitcroft 1731-3. Well restored 1952.

St Helen's Bishopsgate   **6 N 32**
Gt St Helen's EC3. 01-283 2231. The 'Westminster Abbey of the City' built about 1212. Has two naves, northern originally a nunnery, southern parochial. Contains fine monuments of many city worthies and some excellent brasses.

St James's   **2 C 13**
Sussex Gardens W2. Contains an unusual stained glass memorial to Alexander Fleming showing him at work in his laboratory. The discovery of penicillin was made nearby at St Mary's Hospital.

St James Clerkenwell   **3 I 29**
Clerkenwell Green EC1. Rebuilt 1788-92 by Carr. Fine Wren-like steeple.

St James Garlickhythe   **6 N 29**
Garlick Hill EC4. 01-236 1719. Fine city church by Wren, 1687, well-restored steeple 1713. Good ironwork.

St James's Piccadilly   **2 I 18**
Piccadilly W1. 01-734 5244. Wren 1684. Restored by Sir Albert Richardson in 1954 after serious bomb damage. Reredos, organ casing and font by Grinling Gibbons. Famous 'Father Smith' organ preserved by Queen Mary in 1691 and brought from Whitehall Palace.

St James the Less Westminster   **5 O 16**
Thorndike St, Vauxhall Bridge Rd SW1. G. E. Street, 1860, largely unaltered.

St John the Evangelist   **5 O 19**
Smith Sq SW1. Dramatic remains of unique church by Archer 1721-8. Blitzed, now restored and used as concert hall. View from Lord North Street.

St John's Clerkenwell   **3 I 29**
St John's Sq EC1. 01-253 6644. Originally a round church. Present nave 1720 restored after bombing. Well-preserved crypt dating from 1140, used by the Order of St John and its foundation — the Ambulance Brigade — for ceremonies and services. *Application to curator for entry.*

St John's Wood Church
St John's Wood High St NW8. 01-722 4378. Thomas Hardwick, 1813. White and gold interior with carved ceilings supported by Ionic columns.

St John Waterloo Road   **6 O 24**
Waterloo Rd SE1. Bedford, 1824. Four walls, steeple

and portico remain after bombing. Restored by Ford in 1951. Fine reredos.

St Katherine Cree   **6 O 32**
Leadenhall St EC3. 01-283 5733. Rebuilt under Archbishop Laud 1631 in hybrid Gothic and Classical style.

St Lawrence Jewry   **6 M 30**
Gresham St EC2. 01-600 9478. Wren, 1670-86. Tower and four walls remain after bombing. Restored in 1957. Replicas of steeple and original Wren ceiling. Official church of City Corporation.

St Leonard Shoreditch
Between 118 & 119 High St E1. Rebuilt 1736-40 by Dance senior. Fine steeple. *OPEN 12.30-14.00.*

St Luke Chelsea   **4 K 9**
Sydney St SW3. 01-352 9171. Savage, 1824. Sumptuous early-Gothic revival.

St Magnus the Martyr   **6 P 30**
Lower Thames St EC3. 01-636 4481. Wren, 1671-87. Restored by Lawrence King. One of Wren's finest steeples, 185 ft high, added 1705-6. Anglo-Catholic. Baroque interior.

St Margaret Lothbury   **6 N 31**
Lothbury EC2. 01-606 8330. Wren 1686-93, Steeple 1698-1700. Fine fittings, including an open-work screen. Bust of Ann Simpson by Nollekens.

St Margaret Pattens   **6 P 31**
Rood Lane, Eastcheap EC3. 01-623 6630. Church by Wren 1684-9. Fine spire 1698-1702. Unusual canopied pews and punishment bench.

St Margaret's Westminster   **5 M 20**
Parliament Sq SW1. 01-222 6382. Rebuilt 1504-18. Splendid early 16th cent east window and an excellent series of stained glass windows by John Piper. The parish church of the House of Commons.

| St Mary Le Strand | St Margaret's Westminster | St Martin in the Fields |

St Martin-in-the-Fields   **5 K 22**
Trafalgar Sq WC2. 01-930 1862. James Gibbs. 1726. Famous spire and portico. Fine venetian east window and white and gold moulded plaster ceiling. Lunchtime music *13.00-14.00 Mon & Tues.*

St Martin Ludgate   **6 L 28**
Ludgate Hill EC4. 01-248 6054. Wren 1677-87, now restored. Elegant spire, fine interior, notable woodwork.

St Mary Abbotts Kensington   **1 C 8**
Kensington Church St W8. 01-937 5136. Scott 1872. Transitional between early-English and decorated style.

St Mary Abchurch   **6 O 30**
Abchurch Yard EC4. 01-626 0306. Wren, 1681-7. Fine ceiling by Wm. Snow. Reredos by Grinling Gibbons.

St Mary Aldermary   **6 M 29**
Watling St EC4. 01-248 4906. Late Gothic rebuilt by Wren. Early 18th cent. Fine fan vaulting with saucer domes.

St Mary-at-Hill   **6 P 31**
Lovat Lane EC3. 01-626 4184. Wren, 1676. Tower, 1788. Box pews and magnificent fittings.

St Mary-at-Lambeth   **5 P 21**
Beside Lambeth Palace, Lambeth Rd SE1. Rebuilt (except tower) by T. Hardwick, 1850. The tomb of Captain Bligh ('Mutiny on the Bounty') has been recently restored.

St Mary Islington   **3 E 32**
Upper St N1. 01-226 3400. Launcelot Dowbiggin, 1750. Restored 1956, after bomb damage. Fine Baroque steeple.

St Marylebone Parish Church   **2 B 17**
Marylebone Rd NW1. 01-935 7315. Thomas Hardwick, 1813-17. Thomas Harris added the chancel in 1884. Imposing white and gold interior.

St Mary-le-Bow   **6 M 29**
Cheapside EC2. 01-248 5139. The church of 'Bow Bells' fame by Wren, 1680. Restored by Lawrence King after bomb damage. Superb steeple.

St Mary-le-Strand   **6 K 24**
Strand WC2. James Gibbs, 1714-17. A perfect small

Baroque church in the middle of the road.

St Mary Magdalen Bermondsey   **6 R 29**
Bermondsey St SE1. Rebuilt 1680. Charming classical interior. Gothic west end, 1830.

St Mary Magdalene Munster Square   **2 C 22**
58 Osnaburgh St NW1. Carpenter, 1852. Handsome Victorian Gothic. Completely restored 1967.

St Mary Somerset   **6 M 28**
Upper Thames St EC4. Wren, 1694. Only the imposing 8-pinnacled tower remains.

St Mary Woolnoth (Guild Church)   **6 N 30**
Junction of Lombard St & King William St EC3. 01-626 9701. Remarkable 1716-27 Baroque church by Hawksmoor. Church of England services on weekdays.

St Michael Chester Square   **5 L 14**
Chester Sq SW1. 01-730 2015. Cundy, 1846. War memorial chapel added in 1920. Fine coloured alabaster.

St Michael Paternoster Royal   **6 N 29**
College Hill EC4. Wren, 1694, steeple 1713. Recently restored. Dick Whittington buried here. Tower used as office by The Missions to Seamen.

St Michael-upon-Cornhill   **6 N 31**
Cornhill EC3. 01-626 8841. Wren, 1677, much restored by Scott. Handsome Gothic tower added 1722. Twelve magnificent bells which always ring on Sundays. First rate choir and organ.

St Nicholas Cole Abbey   **6 M 28**
Queen Victoria St EC4. 01-248 5213. Wren, 1671-81. Restored after bombing, with spire similar to original. Rich stained glass by Keith New.

St Olave Hart Street   **6 P 32**
8 Hart St EC3. 01-488 4318. Pre-'fire', Samuel Pepys church, 1450. Restored by Glanfield after bomb damage. Fine vestry and crypt.

St Olave Old Jewry   **6 M 30**
Ironmonger Lane EC2. Wren, 1679. Only the tower remains.

St Pancras New Church   **3 D 25**
Upper Woburn Place WC1. 01-387 6460. W. and H. Inwood, 1822. Sumptuous neo-Grecian style.

St Pancras Old Church   **3 B 26**
Pancras Rd NW1. 01-387 8818. Church with country atmosphere. Added to and transformed 1848. 4th cent foundations. Saxon altar stone (AD 600). Third oldest Christian site in Europe.

St Paul Covent Garden   **6 J 23**
Covent Garden WC2. 01-836 5221. Fine 'ecclesiastical barn' by Inigo Jones. Rebuilt by T. Hardwick after fire of 1795. Pleasant gardens at western (entrance) end.

St Paul Knightsbridge   **2 I 14**
32a Wilton Place SW1. 01-235 3460. Victorian church by Cundy, 1843. Rich, colourful interior.

St Paul Shadwell
Next to 302 The Highway E1. First built 1656; rebuilt 1817-21 by John Walters. Good steeple.

St Peter Eaton Square   **5 K 14**
Eaton Sq SW1. Classical church by Blomfield 1875. Fine mosaics in sanctuary.

St Peter-ad-Vincula   **6 Q 32**
1 Tower Green, H.M. Tower of London EC3. 01-709 0765. Much restored church built about 1512. Many historic monuments.

St Peter-upon-Cornhill   **6 N 31**
Bishopsgate Corner EC3. 01-626 9483. Very fine church by Wren, 1677-87. Oldest church site in City, reputedly AD 179. Famous for Elizabethan music: organ built by Schmidt. Fine carved screen. 14th and 15th cent plays performed at Christmas.

St Philip Stepney
Archer St E1. Splendid Victorian-Gothic by Arthur Cawston 1888-92.

St Stephen Walbrook   **6 N 30**
Walbrook EC4. 01-626 2277. Masterpiece by Wren, 1672-79; steeple 1714-17. Dome, with eight arches, supported by Corinthian pillars, all beautifully restored. Fine fittings. Glass by Keith New. Lord Mayor of London's church and the home since 1953 of 'The Samaritans' to help the suicidal and desperate.

St Vedast   **6 L 29**
4 Foster Lane EC2. 01-606 3998. Wren, 1695-1701; spire 1709-12. Recently restored. Fine rich interior.

Bevis Marks Synagogue   **6 O 33**
Heneage Lane (off Bevis Marks) EC3. Avis, 1700. Fine windows. Brass chandelier from Amsterdam.

The Temple Church   **6 K 26**
Inner Temple Lane EC4. Completely restored. 12th cent round nave and 13th cent choir. Fine effigies. Reredos by Wren.

Modern architecture

The following are some of the best modern buildings either in London or within easy distance. Few pre-war modern buildings of quality have survived, but the post-war concern with functionalism is well reflected in redeveloped areas such as the Barbican Project. Some 4 million new houses have been built in London since the war, by private enterprise or with state assistance, and much pioneering architecture can be found in the new towns outside London. New redevelopment projects on a massive scale in central London have been threatened recently by two forces; the concern of preservationist groups such as SAVE, 3 Park Sq West NW1, 01-486 4935, and the 1975 Community Land Act coupled with the declining economic climate. Emphasis is now on modernising and adapting existing buildings and on building up small sites to blend in with their surroundings. Further information on modern buildings may be obtained from:

The Architectural Association Bookshop   **3 G 23**
34 Bedford Sq WC1. 01-636 0974. Architectural Press publications and a specialist library.

Dept. of Architecture & Civic Design   **5 N 22**
Information Group. GLC Room 177, North Block, County Hall SE1. 01-633 5000. Supply a free map detailing 100 GLC schemes developed since the 1960's. Will provide technical data.

Royal Institute of British Architects   **2 D 21**
66 Portland Place W1. 01-580 5533. Various publications including a free list of modern buildings. Fine specialist library.

Some interesting publications are:
The Architect 4 Addison Bridge Place W14. 01-603 4567.
The Architectural Review 9 Queen Anne's Gate SW1. 01-930 0611.
'The City of London; Its Architectural Heritage' by David Crawford (Woodhead-Faulkner. £2.95).

Local authority housing

Alton West Estate (Roehampton)
Roehampton Lane SW15. LCC 1955-61. One of the LCC's most dramatic post-war achievements in mixed development with tall slabs of flats open at ground level onto parkland. See also the stepped terraces, shopping centre and the high and low point and slab blocks.

Barbican Project   **6 K 30**
London Wall EC2. Chamberlain Powell & Bon 1955-73. Pedestrian decks, water gardens and cultural and educational institutions provide a splendid example of architectonic environment. The projected Arts Centre will provide a home for the LSO and RSC.

Churchill Gardens   **5 P 14**
Grosvenor Rd SW1. Powell & Moya 1946-62. Competition winning scheme for flats and maisonettes, housing 6,500 people and heated by discharged cooling water from Battersea Power Station across the river.

Foundling Estate (Bloomsbury)   **3 F 25**
Marchmont St WC1. Patrick Hodgkinson's design succeeded by Bickerdike Allen, Rich & Ptners. 1970. A revolutionary housing and shopping complex with an underground cinema.

St-Katherine-by-the-Tower   **6 R 32**
An £80m project by Taylor Woodrow to redevelop this part of the dockland. The complex is dominated by the London World Trade Centre and the Tower Hotel (by Renton Howard Woods) while the dock forms the new Yacht Haven with private moorings, yachtclub and quayside facilities. There will be a floating museum of historic boats. Ivory House, an elegant Italianate warehouse retaining its original machinery, is surrounded by 19th cent buildings that are being restored and reconstructed. A large housing development for the GLC is underway to provide badly needed homes in this area and to stabilize the community.

Thamesmead
Erith, Kent, GLC Department of Architecture and Civic Design, 1967. This massive housing scheme on reclaimed marshland south of the Thames and just below Woolwich is so large as to justify the description 'New Town'. Some very fine stepped large balcony housing and a determined effort to provide pedestrian segregation.

Private enterprise housing & houses

Old Church Street   **4 M 8**
SW3. No. 64 by Mendelsohn & Chermayeff. No. 66 by Gropius & Fry. 1936. Good pioneer examples of modern house design of the thirties.

125 Park Road, (Marylebone)   **2 A 18**
Flats NW1. Farrell/Grimshaw Partnership. 1970. Built

for a housing co-ownership society, this sophisticated point block overlooks Regent's Park. The superficially bland architecture reveals exciting skill and sensitivity on more careful inspection. The use of corrugated metal cladding and restrained industrial quality express a new movement in British architecture towards a less 'hand-made' image, accepting the mass-produced component.

34-36 Lime St EC3   6 O 31
Completed in 1973 by Richard, Sheppard, Robson & Ptnrs. A superb example of modern 'infill' architecture where a new building has been designed to blend with the old buildings surrounding it. Inserted between two Victorian houses, the upper storeys are stepped back in sympathy with their design, while the bronze-tinted windows and emphasised stories serve to preserve a completely modern appearance.

Vickers' House
Millbank SW1. Erected 1963 for Vickers Armstrong. 387ft high. By Ronald Ward & Ptnrs.

Offices, shops & commercial developments

Centrepoint   3 H 23
New Oxford St WC1. R. Seifert & Partners. 1965-6. A spectacular 36-storey high office block using strongly modelled pre-cast concrete cladding — spoilt by crude detailing at ground level. Still unoccupied when going to press.

Commercial Union and P & O Buildings   6 O 32
Leadenhall St EC3. Winners of the 1970 Civic Trust Award for Architecture, these buildings represent a unique occurrence in city redevelopment. The two companies, finding that they both needed rehousing, merged to jointly hire the Gollins, Melvin, Ward Ptnrship to design two seperate but complementary buildings. Deliberately contrasted, the tall, sheer C.U. building stands in an open piazza next to the smaller horizontally emphasised P & O building and creates a striking effect.

Economist Building   5 J 19
25 St James's St SW1. Alison & Peter Smithson. 1964-6. A very beautiful and harmonious group of buildings with its own raised piazza. The design was intended to demonstrate a general principle for the redevelopment of dense commercial areas and is a rare example of new building in an area with traditional street pattern.

Hoover Factory Building
Perivale on the A40 just outside London. Wallis, Gilbert & Ptnrs 1932. Splendid example of Art Deco streamline design with lavish coloured decoration.

New Zealand House   5 J 21
Haymarket SW1. Robert Mathew, Johnson-Marshall & Ptnrs. 1963. A finely modelled 15-storey glass tower on a 4-storey podium. Good materials and detailing and an exciting entrance hall. A focal point in the heart of London, and a particularly interesting foil to its flamboyant Victorian neighbour — 'Her Majesty's Theatre'.

Public buildings

GPO Tower   2 E 22
Howland St W1. Ministry of Public Building & Works. 1966. 580-ft tower housing telecommunications equipment, offices and a revolving restaurant. A dramatic landmark which provides a spectacular panorama of London and a wonderful bird's-eye view of the Bloomsbury squares and parks.

Regent's Park Zoo   2 A 21
North side of Regent's Park NW1. Contains a number of interesting and uninhabited buildings: Gorilla House by Lubetkin & Tecton 1935; Penguin Pool by Tecton 1935; Aviary by Viscount Snowdon, Cedric Price & Frank Newby 1965-6; Elephant House by Casson, Conder & Ptnrs 1965-6; Small Mammal House by Design Research Unit 1967; Sobell Apes & Monkeys Pavilion 1972; and the New Lion Terraces 1976.

Museum of London   6 L 30
London Wall EC1. One of the worst blitz areas of the city, London Wall has been completely rebuilt since 1960. The newest addition is the museum, designed by Powell & Moya, which is scheduled to open in 1977. From the outside, part of the building looks like a concrete ring surrounded by traffic, but inside is ingeniously housed the museum's garden and restaurant.

South Bank Arts Centre   6 M 23
Between Waterloo Bridge and Hungerford Footbridge SE1. GLC Architect's Department. 1951-72. Has now reached the third stage of its development with the completion of the National Theatre. Conceived as a project to revitalise the South Bank of the river, these buildings form a linear statement of three phases in British Architecture from 1951 to the present day. The

buildings are:

Hayward Art Gallery   6 M 23
South Bank SE1. GLC Architect's Department. 1967. Part of the Queen Elizabeth Hall complex, sited between the Royal Festival Hall and Waterloo Bridge, the Gallery provides a series of exhibition galleries at different levels together with open-air sculpture balconies, for a series of high quality changing exhibitions.

Queen Elizabeth Hall & Purcell Room   6 M 23
Linked to the Royal Festival Hall & Waterloo Bridge by pedestrian decks. GLC Architect's Department. 1967. A 'purist' building of a highly introverted character built and finished only in pre-cast and in-situ concrete, but the interiors of the small concert halls have a beautiful, relaxed simplicity which focuses on and enhances the music.

The Royal Festival Hall   6 M 24
Junction of Waterloo Rd & Belvedere Rd SE1. LCC. Robert Mathew & Leslie Martin. 1951. Built to form the music centre of the Festival of Britain, this building expresses so well the excitement and uncertainty of the end of post-war austerity.

National Theatre   6 M 23
South Bank SE1. 01-633 0880. Completed in 1977 more than 125 years since its inception. Three auditoria: open stage Olivier Theatre; proscenium arch Lyttleton Theatre; studio Cottesloe Theatre. Foyer space, bars and terraces used for exhibitions, music or fringe performances. By Denys Lasdun & Ptnrs.

The National Film Theatre   6 M 24
Under Waterloo Bridge. Built in 1957 by LCC Architect's Department, updated in 1970.

St Paul's Church (Bow Common)
Burdett Way, Stepney, Robert Maguire. 1958-60. One of the very few notable modern churches, in purple brick with a central altar and dramatic top lighting.

Schools & colleges

Bousfield Primary School   1 I 6
South Bolton Gdns, Old Brompton Rd SW5. Chamberlin, Powell & Bon. 1955. An imaginative and cheerful environment with an open-air auditorium.

Imperial College of Science & Technology   1 G 10
Prince Consort Rd SW7. Various new buildings including: Biochemistry building. Architects Co-partnership. Halls of residence.
Princes Gardens SW7. Richard Sheppard. Robson & Ptners. 1963. A cleverly planned and strongly modelled building housing over 400 students. See also Weeks Hall, across the gardens, by the same architects.

Pimlico School   5 P 15
Lupus St SW1. GLC Department of Architecture. 1970. An exciting and adventurous project to fit a large comprehensive school on a tight city site. Interesting as architecture and as an educational innovation.

Royal College of Art   1 F 10
Kensington Gore SW7. H.T. Cadbury Brown, Sir Hugh Casson & R.Y. Goodden. 1962-4. The 8-storey studio and teaching block faces Hyde Park beside the Royal Albert Hall. Fine skyline of penthouse studios. Good interiors, particularly the foyers and Gulbenkian Hall.

Royal College of Physicians   2 C 22
Outer Circle, Regent's Park NW1. Denys Lasdun & Ptners. 1964. A bold and severe solution to the problem of being a neighbour to the Nash Terraces. Interesting interiors with a very successful inclusion of some salvaged interior fittings from the former College.

Universities

Some of the best post-war architecture is within universities. The following can be visited on a day trip from London:

Cambridge University
Variety of beautifully integrated new extensions to ancient college buildings. History Faculty Library by Stirling, 1968.

Leicester University
Faculty of Engineering Building by Stirling & Gowan completed 1964. One of the most formative and exciting post-war buildings in Britain with each part expressed as a separate entity.

Oxford University
As at Cambridge, the bold contrast between old and new increases the pleasure of inspecting the university buildings.
Contributions made by influential architects, g. Powell & Moya's Wolfson College 1974 & Jacobsen's St Catherine's College 1962-4.

Sussex University
Brick and vaulted concrete buildings by Basil Spence in association with Bonnington & Collins. Sited on pleasant landscaped parkland on the Downs above Brighton. Gardner Centre Theatre by Spence, 1969.

Museums and parks

Museums and galleries

London's national museums and galleries contain some of the richest treasures in the world. Access to special items or collections not on show is willingly and trustfully given. In addition, they offer a service of advice and scholarly reference unequalled anywhere in the world. Note that their reference libraries and print collections are further described under 'Reference Libraries'.

The British Museum, the V & A and other national galleries give expert opinion on the age or identity of objects or paintings — they will not however give you a valuation. Apart from the museums owned by the nation, London is further enriched by other collections open to the public. Most were started as ·specialist collections of wealthy men or associations but are now available to all, by right or courtesy. They are continually being improved and extended and are an invaluable part of our culture and history. National museums and galleries are free. Special exhibitions and shows usually charge a small entrance fee.

Artillery Museum
The Rotunda, Woolwich Common SE18. 01-854 2424. The Rotunda was an architectural 'tent' once erected in St James's Park (1814). Little known collection of guns and muskets. OPEN 10.00-12.45 & 14.00-17.00 Mon-Sat, 14.00-17.00 Sun. CLOSED 16.00 Oct-Mar, G. Fri, Xmas, Box, New Year's. Free.

Bear Garden Museum
Bear Garden Alley SE1 (between Park St and the Thames). 01-928 4229. Converted 18th cent warehouse on site of 16th cent bear baiting ring and The Hope Playhouse. Permanent Elizabethan Theatre exhibition and a condensed version of the popular Southwark exhibition 'In the Clink'. OPEN 12.00-16.00 Tues-Fri, 13.00-17.00 Sat & Sun. CLOSED Mon. Free.

Bethnal Green Museum
Cambridge Heath Rd E2. 01-980 2415. A branch of the V & A, opened in 1872. Gallery of 19th cent continental sculpture and decorative arts. 18th-20th cent English ceramics, glass and silver. Fine display of Rodin sculpture. Textiles display illustrating history of Spitalfields silk. Interesting 18th-20th cent costume collection. Historic dolls toys, dolls houses and model theatres. OPEN 10.00-17.50 Mon-Sat, 14.30-17.50 Sun. CLOSED G. Fri, Xmas, Box, New Year's. Free.

British Museum   3 **G 24**
Gt Russell St WC1. 01-636 1555. One of the largest and greatest museums in the world. Contains famous collections of Egyptian, Assyrian, Greek and Roman, British, Oriental and Asian antiquities. Among many outstanding and unique items are the Egyptian mummies, the colossal Assyrian bulls and lions in the Nimrud gallery. Cambodian and Chinese collections, the Elgin Marbles and the Rosetta Stone. Building 1823-47 by Sir Robert Smirke; the domed reading room 1857 is by Sidney Smirke. OPEN 10.00-17.00 Mon-Sat, 14.30-18.00 Sun. CLOSED G. Fri, Xmas, New Year's. Lecture tours. Free.

British Museum: Dept. of Ethnography   2 **I 19**
6 Burlington Gardens W1. 01-437 2224. Exciting collection of primitives, including the Benin bronzes. Opening times as the British Museum.

British Theatre Museum   1 **D 4**
Leighton House, 12 Holland Park Rd W14. 01-602 3052. British theatre from 18th cent to present day. Special collections of Henry Irving, Pauline Chase, English Stage Company archives and the Debenham photo collection. OPEN 11.00-17.00 Tues-Thur. CLOSED B. Hols. Free.

British Piano & Musical Museum
368 High St Brentford, Middx. 01-560 8108. A unique collection of automatic musical instruments which can be heard as well as seen. OPEN 14.30-17.00 Sat & Sun. CLOSED Dec-Feb. Admission charge.

Chartered Insurance Institute's Museum   6 **M 30**
20 Aldermanbury EC2. 01-606 3835. Collection of Insurance Companies' fire marks. Fire-fighting equipment, helmets, etc. OPEN 09.15-17.00 weekdays. CLOSED Sat & Sun, G. Fri, B. Hols, Xmas, Box, New Year's. Free.

Commonwealth Institute   1 **D 5**
230 Kensington High St W8. 01-602 3252. Scenery, natural resources, way of life and industrial development of Commonwealth countries. Reference library of current Commonwealth literature. Cinema, art exhibitions. OPEN 10.00-17.30 Mon-Sat, 14.30-18.00 Sun. CLOSED G. Fri, B. Hols, Xmas, Box, New Year's. Free.

Courtauld Institute Galleries   3 **F 24**
Woburn Sq WC1. 01-580 1015. The Courtauld Collection of French Impressionists (including fine paintings by Cézanne, Van Gogh, Gauguin) and the Lee, Gambier-Parry and Fry Collections. OPEN 10.00-17.00 Mon-Sat, 14.00-17.00 Sun. CLOSED G. Fri, Xmas, Box, New Year's. Free.

The Cuming Museum
Newington District Library, Walworth Rd SE17. 01-703 3324. The archaeology of the history of Southwark from earliest times to the present. Houses, too, the Lovett collection of London superstitions. OPEN 10.00-17.30 Mon-Sat. CLOSED Sun, G. Fri, B. Hols, Xmas, Box, New Year's. Free.

Dulwich College Picture Gallery
College Rd SE21. 01-693 5254. English, Italian, Dutch and French paintings exhibited in one of the most beautiful art galleries in England. Notable works by Rembrandt, Rubens and Gainsborough. Building by Sir John Soane 1811-14. OPENING times vary throughout the year. CLOSED Mon, B. Hols. Free.

Embroiderers' Guild   2 **E 19**
73 Wimpole St W1. 01-935 3281. Unusual collection in a private house. Library and museum of historical and contemporary embroideries. Advisory body available by appointment. Also embroidery classes. OPEN 10.00-12.00 Mon-Fri. CLOSED weekends and public hols. Appointment only. Free.

Fenton House
Hampstead Grove NW3. 01-435 3471. The Benton Fletcher collection of early keyboard instruments and the Binning collection of porcelain and furniture. OPEN 11.00-17.00 Wed-Sat, 14.00-17.00 Sun. CLOSED G. Fri, New Year's, all Dec. Small admission charge.

Foundling Hospital   3 **F 26**
40 Brunswick Sq WC1. 01-278 1911. Small gallery of 18th cent English painters, including Hogarth, Gainsborough and Kneller. Founded by Hogarth. OPEN 10.00-16.00 weekdays. CLOSED B. Hols and public hols. Small admission charge.

Geffrye Museum
Kingsland Rd E2. 01-739 8368. 18th cent almshouses. Period rooms and furniture from 1600 to the present day. OPEN 10.00-17.00 Tues-Sat, 14.00-17.00 Sun. CLOSED G. Fri, Xmas, Box, Free.

Geological Museum   1 **H 9**
Exhibition Rd SW7. 01-589 3444. Physical and economic geology and mineralogy of the world; regional geology of Britain. Models, dioramas and a large collection of gems, stones and fossils. OPEN 10.00-18.00 Mon-Sat, 14.00-17.00 Sun. CLOSED G. Fri, Xmas, Box. Free.

Goldsmiths' Hall   6 **L 29**
Foster Lane WC2. 01-606 8971. Fine collection of antique plate. The largest collection of modern silver and jewellery in the country. By appointment.

Gordon Medical Museum   6 **Q 29**
St Thomas St SE1. 01-407 7600. Collection of specimens and models dealing with diseases in humans. By application to curator.

Guildhall Gallery   6 **M 30**
King St EC2. 01-606 3030. Selections from the Guildhall's permanent collection, loan exhibitions and shows of Art societies. OPEN 10.00-17.00 Mon-Sat. CLOSED Sun, B. Hols. Free.

Gunnersbury Park Museum
Gunnersbury Park W3. 01-992 2247. Local history

museum documenting the social history and archaeology of Chiswick, Brentford and Ealing. Interesting topographical collection. *OPEN Apr-Sept 14.00-17.00 weekdays, 14.00-18.00 Sat & Sun; Oct-Mar 14.00-16.00. CLOSED Xmas, Box, G. Fri. Free.*

Hampton Court Palace
Hampton Court, Middx. 01-977 8441. Individual collection of Italian masterpieces. Giorgione, Titian, Tintoretto and early primitives. Also wall and ceiling paintings by Thornhill, Vanbrugh and Verrio. *OPENING times vary throughout the year. CLOSED B. Hols.*

Hayward Gallery   6   M 23
Belvedere Rd SE1. 01-928 3144. Changing exhibitions of major works of art arranged by the Arts Council. Fine modern building and river setting. *OPEN 10.00-20.00 weekdays, 10.00-18.00 Sat, 12.00-18.00 Sun. CLOSED G. Fri, Xmas, Box, New Year's. Approx. 1 month between exhibitions. Admission charge.*

Heinz Gallery   2   D 17
RIBA Drawings Collection, 21 Portman Sq W1. 01-580 5533. Regular exhibitions of architectural drawings. *OPEN 11.00-17.30 weekdays. Free.*

Horniman Museum
100 London Rd SE23. 01-699 2339. Natural history, ethnography, musical instruments. The building (1901) by C. Harrison Townsend is 'Art Nouveau'. Aquarium and reference library. *OPEN 10.30-18.00 Mon-Sat, 14.30-17.30 Sun. CLOSED public hols. Free.*

Imperial War Museum   Natural History Museum

Imperial War Museum   6   Q 23
Lambeth Rd SE1. 01-735 8922. Very popular national museum of all aspects of war since 1914. Collection of models, weapons, paintings, relics. The building was once a lunatic asylum. *OPEN 10.00-17.50 Mon-Sat, 14.00-17.30 Sun. CLOSED G. Fri, Xmas, Box, New Year's. Free.*

Institute of Contemporary Arts   5   K 20
Nash House. The Mall SW1. 01-839 5344. Changing exhibitions to explore new themes and mediums in contemporary art. *OPEN 10.00-20.00 Mon-Sat, 14.00-18.00 Sun. Free.*

The Iveagh Bequest, Kenwood
Hampstead Lane NW3. 348 1286. Fine house by Robert Adam. Paintings by Rembrandt, Vermeer, Reynolds and Gainsborough. *OPEN Apr-Sept 10.00-19.00; Oct-Mar times vary. CLOSED G. Fri, Xmas Eve, Xmas. Free.*

Jewish Museum   3   E 25
Woburn House, Upper Woburn Place WC1. 01-387 3081. A comprehensive collection of ritual objects and other antiquities illustrating Jewish life and worship. *OPEN 14.30-17.00 Mon-Thur, 10.30-12.45 Fri & Sun. CLOSED Sat, B. Hols, Jewish hols. Free.*

Leighton House   1   D 4
12 Holland Park Rd W14. 01-602 3316. Centre for Victorian studies and special exhibitions. Arab hall with decorations of 14th-16th cent oriental tiles. Paintings by Leighton and Burne-Jones. Watts and De Morgan pottery. *OPEN 11.00-17.00 Mon-Sat. CLOSED B. Hols. Free.*

London Transport Collection
Syon Park, Brentford, Middlesex. 01-560 0881. Every type of Public Transport to be found here from trams to underground railways spanning almost 150 years, including a replica of the first horse-drawn omnibus. *OPEN Apr-Sept 10.00-19.00 daily; Oct-Mar 10.00-17.00. CLOSED Xmas. Admission charge.*

Madame Tussaud's   2   B 19
Marylebone Rd NW1. 01-935 6861. Waxworks effigies of the famous and notorious. 'Battle of Trafalgar': reconstruction of gun-deck of 'Victory' at height of battle. *OPEN 10.00-17.30 Mon-Fri, 10.00-18.30 Sat & Sun. CLOSED Xmas. Admission charge.*

Martinware Pottery Collection
Public Library, 9-11 Osterley Park Rd, Southall, Middx. 01-574 3412. Collection of Martinware, including birds, face mugs and grotesques. *OPEN 09.00-20.00 Mon-Fri, 09.00-17.00 Sat. CLOSED Sun, B. Hols, Xmas. Free.*

Museum of London   6   L 30
London Wall EC2. 01-600 3699. Combined collections of the former London Museum and Guildhall Museum with extra material. A 3-dimensional biography of the

City and London area, with models, reconstructions and even the Lord Mayor's Coach. *OPEN Tue-Sat 10.00-18.00, Sun 14.00-18.00.*

M.C.C. Memorial Gallery
Lord's Cricket Ground NW8. 01-289 1611. The history of cricket. *OPEN 10.30-17.00 Mon-Sat & matchdays; weekdays only when no cricket. Appointment only. Small admission charge.*

National Army Museum   4   N 10
Royal Hospital Rd SW3. 01-730 0717. The story of the Army from 1480 to 1914, its triumphs and disasters, its professional and social life all over the world. Uniforms, pictures, weapons and personal relics. *OPEN 10.00-17.30 Mon-Sat, 14.00-17.30 Sun. CLOSED G. Fri, Xmas. Free.*

National Gallery   5   J 21
Trafalgar Sq WC2. 01-930 7618. Very fine representative collection of the various schools of painting. Includes many world famous pictures. Rich in early Italian (Leonardo da Vinci, Raphael, Botticelli, and

Titian). Dutch and Flemish (Rembrandt, Rubens, Frans Hals, Van Dyck), Spanish 15-18th cent (Velasquez and El Greco), British 18th and 19th cent (Constable, Turner, Gainsborough and Reynolds). Building 1838 by W. Wilkins. *Open 10.00-18.00 Mon-Sat, 14.30-18.00 Sun. CLOSED public hols. Free.*

National Maritime Museum
Romney Rd SE10. 01-858 4422. The finest maritime collection in Britain. Extensive collections of ship models, paintings, navigational instruments, costumes and weapons. The museum incorporates the Queen's House by Inigo Jones 1616 and the Old Royal Observatory. *OPEN 10.00-18.00 Mon-Sat, 14.00-18.00 Sun. CLOSED public hols. Free.*

National Portrait Gallery   5   J 22
2 St Martin's Place WC2. 01-930 8511. Historical collection of contemporary portraits of famous British men and women from early 9th cent to the present day. Excellent reference section of engravings and photographs. *OPEN 10.00-17.00 Mon-Fri, 10.00-18.00 Sat, 14.00-18.00 Sun. CLOSED B. Hols. Free.*

National Postal Museum   6   L 29
King Edward St EC1. 01-432 3851. Superb displays of stamps including the Phillips collection and the 'Berne' collection. Reference library. *OPEN 10.00-16.30 Mon-Fri, 10.00-19.00 Thur. CLOSED Sat & Sun, B. Hols. Free.*

Natural History Museum   1   H 9
Cromwell Rd SW7. 01-589 6323. The national collections of zoology, entomology, palaeontology and botany. Particularly notable are the bird gallery, the 90-ft model blue whale and the great dinosaur models. Built 1881 by A. Waterhouse. *OPEN 10.00-18.00 Mon-Sat, 14.30-18.00 Sun. CLOSED G. Fri, Xmas. Free.*

Passmore Edwards Museum
Romford Rd, Stratford E15. 01-534 4545 ext. 376. Collections of Essex archaeology, local history, geology and biology. Good collection of Bow porcelain. *OPEN 10.00-18.00 Mon-Fri, 10.00-20.00 Thur, 10.00-17.00 Sat. CLOSED Sun. Free.*

Percival David Foundation of Chinese Art   3   E 24
53 Gordon Sq WC1. 01-387 3909. Chinese ceramics from Sung to Ch'ing dynasty. Reference library. *OPENING times vary throughout the year. CLOSED Sun, B. Hols and public hols. Free.*

Pharmaceutical Society's Museum   3   H 24
17 Bloomsbury Sq WC1. 01-405 8967. Collection of 17th and 18th cent drugs, pharmaceutical ceramics, bell-metal mortars and historical apparatus. *Appointment only.*

Photographers' Gallery   5   J 22
8 Great Newport St WC2. 01-836 7860. A new and exciting venture contributing to the establishment of photography in the art world. *OPEN 11.00-19.00 Tues-Sat, 12.00-18.00 Sun. CLOSED Mon. Free.*

Planetarium   2   B 19
Marylebone Rd NW1. 01-486 1121. Representation of the universe, with commentary. *OPEN Oct-Mar 11.00-17.00 Mon-Sat; Apr-Sept 11.00-18.00. CLOSED Xmas. Presentations every hour. Admission charge.*

Public Record Office   6   K 26
Chancery Lane WC2. 01-405 0741. National archives and records of the Courts from 11th cent. Contains the Domesday book, Nelson's log and the signatures of the Kings and Queens of England. *Open 13.00-16.00 Mon-Fri. CLOSED B. Hols.*

Queen's Gallery   **5 K 17**
Buckingham Palace, Buckingham Palace Rd SW1. 01-903 4832. Pictures and works of art from all parts of the Royal collection. Exhibitions changed at intervals. *OPEN 11.00-17.00 Tues-Sat, 14.00-17.00 Sun. CLOSED Xmas. Small admission charge.*

RAF Museum
Aerodrome Rd, Hendon NW9. 01-205 2266. *(10 mins walk from Colindale station on the Northern Line).* The first national museum covering all aspects of the RAF and its predecessor the RFC. Opened November 1972 on a former wartime airfield. Aeroplanes, bits of aeroplanes, equipment, paintings, documents, etc. Prize exhibit is a complete — though battered — Avro Lancaster heavy bomber. *OPEN 10.00-18.00 Mon-Fri, 14.00-18.00 Sun. CLOSED Xmas, Box. Free.*

Royal Academy of Arts   **2 I 19**
Burlington House, Piccadilly W1. 01-734 9052. Holds its yearly summer exhibition *in May* (the work of present-day artists). *Holds special exhibitions open to the public during the year.*

Royal College of Music   **1 G 10**
Prince Consort Rd SW7. 01-589 3643. A collection of instruments, incorporating the Donaldson collection and including a 1531 harpsichord. *OPEN term-time 10.30-16.30 Mon & Wed. Appointment only.*

Royal College of Surgeons   **6 J 25**
The Hunterian Museum, Lincolns Inn Fields WC2. 01-405 3474. Physiology, anatomy and pathology. Includes most of John Hunter's famous experiments. *OPEN 10.00-17.00 Mon-Fri. CLOSED Aug. For medical profession only or by appointment.*

Royal Observatory
See Flamsteed House.

Science Museum   **1 H 10**
Exhibition Rd SW7. 01-589 6371. The history of science and its application to industry. A large collection of very fine engineering models, steam engines, motor cars, aeroplanes and all aspects of applied physics and chemistry. Instructive children's gallery. *OPEN 10.00-18.00 Mon-Sat, 14.30-18.00 Sun. CLOSED B. Hols. Free lectures 13.00 Mon, Wed & Fri, 15.00 Sat. Free.*

Sir John Soane's Museum   **3 I 25**
13 Lincolns Inn Fields WC2. 01-405 2107. Soane's personal collection of antiquities, paintings and drawings, including Hogarth's 'Election' and the 'Rake's Progress', original Piranesi drawings and most of the architectural drawings of the Adam brothers. Building designed by Soane 1812. *OPEN 10.00-17.00 Mon-Sat. CLOSED B. Hols. Library by appointment only.*

St Bride's Crypt Museum   **6 L 27**
St Bride's Church, Fleet St EC4. 01-353 1301. Interesting relics found during excavations. A unique continuity of remains from Roman London to the present day. *OPEN 09.00-17.00 daily. Free.*

St Bride Printing Library   **6 L 27**
St Bride Institute, Bride Lane EC4. 01-353 4660. A permanent exhibition of early printing equipment, machinery and books in the exhibition and lecture hall of the library. *OPEN 09.00-17.30 weekdays. CLOSED B. Hols. Free.*

Tate Gallery   **5 P 18**
Millbank SW1. 01-828 1212. Representative collections of British painting from the 16th cent to the present day; fine examples of Blake, Turner, Hogarth, the pre-Raphaelites, Ben Nicholson, Spenser and Francis Bacon. Also a particularly rich collection of foreign

paintings and sculpture from 1880 to the present day, including paintings by Picasso, Chagall, Mondrian, Pollock, Lichtenstein, Moore, Hepworth, Degas, Marini and Giacometti. Built 1897 by Sidney H. J. Smith. *OPEN 10.00-18.00 Mon-Sat, 14.00-18.00 Sun. CLOSED G. Fri, Xmas, Box. Lectures at various times. Free.*

Television Gallery   **1 I 11**
70 Brompton Rd SW3. 01-584 7011. Here you can find out how your favourite television programme reaches your TV screen. You will see models of the earliest sets, cameras and how television could look in the future. *OPEN Mon.-Fri; guided tours last 1½ hrs at 10.00, 11.30, 14.30. 15.30. CLOSED B. Hols. Free.*

Tower of London, the Armouries   **6 Q 32**
Tower Hill EC3. 01-709 0765. The Crown Jewels (heavily guarded). Largest collection of armour and arms in Britain. 10-20th cent. *OPEN 09.30-17.00 Mon-Sat, 14.00-17.00 Sun. CLOSED B. Hols and public hols. Admission charge.*

University College: Department of Egyptology Museum   **3 E 23**
Gower St WC1. 01-387 7050. Includes the collections of Amelia Edwards, Sir Flinders Petrie and part of Sir Henry Wellcome's collection. *OPEN 10.00-17.00 Mon-Fri. CLOSED B. Hols, Easter, Xmas hols. Appointment only.*

Victoria & Albert Museum   **1 H 10**
Cromwell Rd SW7. 01-589 6371. A museum of decorative art, comprising vast collections from all categories, countries and ages. Over 10 acres of museum! Each category is extensive and choice. It includes important collections of paintings, sculpture, graphics and typography, armour and weapons, carpets, ceramics, clocks, costumes, fabrics, furniture, jewellery, metalwork and musical instruments. Fine Art collections include Sandby, Girtin, Cotman, Constable Turner and some Raphael cartoons. The Prints and Drawings Dept has extensive collections dealing with art, architecture, pure and applied design, graphics, typography and craft. *OPEN 10.00-18.00 Mon-Sat, 14.30-17.50 Sun. CLOSED B. Hols, public hols. Free lectures at various times. Free.*

Wallace Collection   **2 D 18**
Hertford House, Manchester Sq W1. 01-935 0687. A private collection of outstanding works of art which were bequeathed to the nation by Lady Wallace in 1897. Splendid representation of the French 17th and 18th cent, including many paintings by Boucher, Watteau and Fragonard. There are also several Rembrandts, a Titian, some Rubens, and paintings by Canaletto and Guardi. Important collections of French furniture. Sèvres porcelain, Majolica, Limoges enamel and armour. Also a fine collection of Bonnington oils and watercolours. *OPEN 10.00-17.00 Mon-Sat, 14.00-17.00 Sun. CLOSED G. Fri, Xmas. Free.*

Wellcome Historical Medical Museum   **3 D 24**
183 Euston Rd NW1. 01-387 4477. The history of medicine and allied sciences from the earliest times. *OPEN 10.00-17.00 Mon-Sat. CLOSED B. Hols and public hols. Free.*

Wellington Museum
See under 'Houses of famous people' Section.

Whitechapel Art Gallery
80 Whitechapel High St E1. 01-247 1492. Frequent public exhibitions of great interest. The Whitechapel has successfully introduced new ideas in modern art into London. *OPEN 11.00-18.00 Tues-Sat. Free.*

Parks and gardens

London is particularly rich in parks, gardens, commons, forests and heathland. There are over 80 parks within 9 miles of Piccadilly. They are all that remain of early London's natural surrounding countryside. Many follow river courses and contain lakes and ponds. Left by accident, gift, or longsighted social intention, they are a welcome breathing space for the Londoner. The 10 Royal parks are still the property of the Crown and were originally the grounds of Royal homes or palaces. See under 'Children's London' for Playparks and One O'Clock Clubs. For general information telephone the following: Royal Parks — Dept of Environment 01-212 3434. GLC Parks — 01-633 1716.

Alexandra Park & Palace N22
01-883 9711. 200 acres, of which 8 acres are occupied by the Palace, a late Victorian building where exhibitions and concerts are held. Roller-skating rink, artificial ski-slope and a boating pool. Bands, children's concerts and miniature golf. *OPEN 24 hrs.*

Avery Hill
Bexley Rd SE9. 01-850 3217. The Winter Garden is a second smaller Kew. Tropical and sub-tropical Asian and Australian plants in greenhouses. Tennis courts. *OPEN summer 11.00-17.00, 11.00-18.00 weekends and B. Hols; winter 13.00-16.00. CLOSED first Mon in month. Park OPEN 07.00-dusk.*

Battersea Park SW11
01-228 2798. An interesting riverside park of 200 acres. Boating lake, deer park and children's zoo. Also contains a botanical wild-flower garden. Pleasure gardens and occasional fairs. *OPEN Easter-Sept 12.00-late evening. Playing fields, running track, tennis courts OPEN 06.00-dusk.*

Bayhurst Wood Country Park
Breakspear Rd, Harefield, Middx. 01-848 9662. 98 acres

of mixed woodland with fine views over open farmland. Facilities include barbecue and picnic sites, and a nature trail. *OPEN 24 hrs.*

Bostall Heath SE2
01-854 1674. Woods and heath. Fine views of London and the river's dockland. *OPEN 07.30-22.00; winter 07.30-dusk.*

Brockwell Park
Dulwich Rd SE24. 01-674 6141. Fine old English garden. Yew hedges and unusual trees and flowers. *OPEN 07.00-dusk; mid Dec-mid Jan 07.00-19.30.*

Crystal Palace, SE19
01-778 7148. Named after Paxton's 1851 Great Exhibition building removed here from Hyde Park and unfortunately burnt to the ground in 1936. Now a National Youth & Sports Centre with an Olympic swimming pool and fine modern sports stadium in an open park of 70 acres on a hill with fine views. Has boating and fishing lake. Four islands in the lake are 'colonised' by 20 life-sized replicas of primaeval animals; iguanodon, megalosaurus, pterodactyls and primitive reptiles — designed by Richard Owen 1854. Artificial ski slope. Bands in summer. *OPEN 08.00-dusk.*

Danson Park
Bexleyheath, Kent. 01-303 7777. Pleasant 200-acre park with large lake. 'Old English' garden, rock garden, bog garden, aviary. Landscaped about 1760 by Capability Brown, Georgian mansion by Sir Robert Taylor, 1756. Wide variety of recreational facilities, including boating. *OPEN 07.30-dusk weekdays, 09.00-dusk Sat & Sun. Mansion closed to public at present.*

Dulwich Park SE21
01-633 1718. Famous for its rhododendrons and azaleas. A favourite garden of the late Queen Mary. Boating lake and tennis courts. Tree trail. *OPEN 07.00-22.00 summer; 07.30-dusk winter.*

Greenwich Park SE10
01-858 2608. A Royal park of 200 acres with pleasant avenues lined with chestnut trees, sloping down to the Thames. Impressive views of the river, the shipping and the two classical buildings; the Queen's House by Inigo Jones and the Royal Naval College (once a Tudor Royal Palace). Contains also the old Royal Observatory and its pleasant garden. 13 acres of wooded deer park, a bird sanctuary and Bronze-age tumuli. *OPEN 07.00-22.00 summer; 07.00-18.00 or dusk winter.*

Hainault Forest, Essex
01-500 3106. Formerly part of the great forest of Essex, or Waltham Forest. Now a Country Park or 1,100 acres of extensive woodland, with a lake, two 18-hole golf courses, a playing field and facilities for angling, riding, picnicking, cross-country running and orienteering. *OPEN 24 hrs.*

Hampstead Heath NW3
01-485 4491. Open, hilly 800 acres of park and woods. Foxes can sometimes be seen. Crowded on Bank Holidays with visitors to the famous fair and the equally famous pubs — the Bull & Bush, The Spaniards and Jack Straw's Castle. Includes Parliament Hill, Golders Hill (containing a fine English town garden) and Kenwood. Ponds, concerts in summer, 10 tennis courts, Olympian track, orienteering, grass ski-ing. *OPEN 24 hrs, Kenwood and Golders Hill CLOSED at night.*

Hampton Court & Bushy Park, Middx
01-977 1328. 1,100 acres of Royal park bounded on two sides by the Thames. Hampton is the formal park of a great Tudor palace with ancient courts, superb flower gardens, the famous maze and the 'great vine' planted during Queen Anne's reign. Bushy Park is natural farmland, artificial plantation, watercress and ponds. Both parks have many fine avenues including the mile-long Chestnut Avenue with 'Diana' fountain in Bushy Park. Hampton Court, itself is described under 'Historic Buildings'. *OPEN 7.45-dusk.*

Holland Park W8   **1 B 5**
01-602 2226. Behind Kensington High Street. 55 acres of calm and secluded lawns and gardens with peacocks. Once the private park of Holland House (partially restored after bombing during the war). Dutch garden dating from 1812 with fine tulip displays. Also iris and rose gardens, yucca lawn and orangery. On the north side is a remarkable woodland of 28 acres containing 3,000 species of exotic British trees and plants, full of birds, woodpeckers, owls, peafowl and British birds generally. Open-air theatre in summer. Squash and tennis courts. *OPEN 07.30-22.00 summer; 07.30-dusk winter. Flower garden OPEN to 24.00 and illuminated at night.*

Hyde Park W1   **2 E 14**
01-262 5484. A Royal park since 1536, it was once part of the forest reserved by Henry VIII for hunting wild boar and bulls. Queen Elizabeth I held military reviews

here (still held on special occasions). It was the haunt of highwaymen until 1750 and even today is patrolled at night by police. The Great Exhibition of 1851 designed by Paxton was held opposite Prince of Wales Gate. Hyde Park now has 340 acres of parkland, walks, Rotten row with horse-riders, and the Serpentine — a fine natural lake for fishing, boating and swimming. The Serpentine Bridge is by George Rennie 1826. The famous 'Speaker's Corner' is near Marble Arch — public executions were held at Tyburn gallows nearby until 1783. Good open-air bar and restaurant overlooking the lake (near the bridge). *OPEN 05.00-24.00. No cars after dusk. The Lido OPEN May-Sept & hols 06.00-09.00 for swimming. Small admission charge.*

Kensington Gardens W2   **1 D 10**
01-262 5484. A formal and elegant addition to Hyde Park. 275 acres of Royal park containing William III's lovely Kensington Palace, Queen Anne's Orangery, the peaceful 'Sunken Garden' nearby, the Round Pond with its busy model sailing-boats, and, on the south, the magnificently Victorian 'Albert Memorial'. The famous Broad Walk, until recently flanked by ancient elms is now replanted with fragrant limes and maples and the nearby 'Flower Walk' is the home of wild birds, woodpeckers, flycatchers and tree-creepers. Queen Caroline produced both the Long Water (Peter Pan's statue is here) and the Serpentine by damming the Westbourne river. Good children's playground. *OPEN 05.00-dusk.*

Kew Gardens, Surrey
01-940 1171. Superb botanical gardens of 300 acres. Founded in 1759 by Princess Augusta. Delightful natural gardens and woods bounded by the river on one side, and stocked with thousands of flowers and trees. Many fascinating hothouses for orchids, palms, ferns, cacti and alpine plants. Hothouses OPEN at 11.00. Also a lake, aquatic garden and pagoda were designed by Sir William Chambers in 1760 and the magnificent curved glass palm house and temperate house 1844-8, are by Decimus Burton. Its scientific aspect was developed by its two directors Sir William and Sir Joseph Hooker and the many famous botanists who worked here. Known throughout the world for its botanical research and plant identification. 17th cent Queen's garden with formal rosebed. *OPEN 10.00-20.00 daily.*

Lesnes Abbey Woods SE2
01-310 2777. Commemorates the former 800 year-old abbey, now excavated. Woods and open ground with good views. 20 acres of wild daffodils in the spring. *OPEN 07.30-16.30 winter; 07.30-20.00 or dusk summer.*

Peckham Rye Park SE15
01-693 3791. Open park with good English, Japanese and water gardens. *OPEN 07.00-22.00 summer; 07.00-dusk winter.*

Primrose Hill NW8
01-486 7905. A very minor Royal park of simple grassy hill 200 ft high giving a fine view over London. *OPEN 24 hrs.*

Regents Park NW1   **2 B 21**
01-935 1537. A Royal park of 470 acres, it was originally part of Henry VIII's great hunting forest in the 16th cent. The Prince Regent in 1811 planned to connect the park (and a new palace) via the newly built Regent Street to Carlton House. Although never fully completed the design by John Nash (1812-26) is of great distinction, the park being surrounded by handsome Regency terraces and imposing gateways. Contains also the Zoo, the Regent's canal, a fine boating lake with 30 species of birds and the very fine Queen Mary's rose garden within Nash's Inner Circle. Open-air theatre. *OPEN 05.00-dusk.*

Richmond Park, Surrey
01-940 0654. A Royal park of 2,500 acres first enclosed as a hunting ground by Charles I in 1637. Retains all the qualities of a great English feudal estate — a natural open park of spinneys and plantations, bracken and ancient oaks (survivors of the great oak forests of the Middle Ages) and over 600 red and fallow deer. Badgers, weasels and the occasional fox can be seen. The Pen Ponds are well stocked with fish. Fine views of the Thames valley from White Lodge (early 18th cent and once a Royal residence) and the restaurant of Pembroke Lodge. Golf, riding, polo, football. *OPEN Mar-Sept 07.00-dusk; 07.30-dusk winter.*

St James's Park & Green Park SW1   **5 K 18**
01-262 5484. The oldest Royal park, acquired in 1532 by Henry VIII, laid out in imitation 'Versailles' style by Charles II; finally redesigned in the grand manner for George IV by John Nash in the 1820's. A most attractive park, with fine promenades and walks, and a romantic Chinese-style lake, bridge, and weeping willows. The bird sanctuary on Duck Island has some magnificent pelicans and over 20 species of duck and

geese. Good views of Buckingham Palace, the grand sweep of Carlton Terrace, the domes and spires of Whitehall and to the south, Westminster Abbey. The Mall and Constitution Hill are frequently part of ceremonial Royal occasions. *OPEN 05.00-24.00*

Shooters Hill SE18
01-856 3610. Hundreds of acres of woods and open parkland containing Oxleas Woods, Jackwood and Eltham Parks. Castlewood has a folly erected 1784 to Sir William James for his exploits in India. *OPEN 24 hrs.*

Streatham Common SW16
01-769 7634. The Rookery was formerly the garden of an 18th cent mansion; rockery, wild garden, a 'white' garden and splendid old cedars. *Common OPEN 24 hrs. Rookery 09.00-22.00 summer; 09.00-dusk winter.*

Trent Park, Enfield
01-449 8706. Formerly part of the royal hunting forest Enfield Chase. Now a Country Park of 400 acres of woodland and grassland, with a golf course, water garden, two lakes, a nature trail, farm trail, horse rides and a covered riding school. *Picnic facilities and a trail for the blind. OPEN 24 hrs.*

Victoria Embankment Gardens WC2   5   M 21
The joy of the lunchtime office worker on a fine summer day. Banked flowers, a band, shady trees, deckchairs and a crowded open-air café.

Waterlow Park N6
01-435 7171. Presented by Sir Sidney Waterlow to the people of London in 1889. Contains Lauderdale House (Nell Gwynne lived here) and the house of Andrew Marvell. 26 acres. Park, ponds. Aviary and a disconcerting mynah bird who talks to visitors. Band in summer. OPEN 07.30-dusk.

Wimbledon Common SW19
01-788 7655. 1,100 acres, including Putney Heath, comprising wild woodland, open heath and several ponds. Golf courses. 16 miles of horse rides. Playing fields. Bronze age remains. Rare and British flora. Protected by act of 1871 as a 'wild area' for perpetuity. Famous old 19th cent windmill, composite smock and post type, now restored to original design. Queensmere, nude bathing (tradition since Victorian era) *06.00-09.00* men only. *OPEN 24 hrs. Cars not admitted after dusk.*

Botanic gardens and arboreta

Remember that many of the London Parks have living botanical collections; Holland Park has a good arboretum, and others have bog gardens, rock gardens, and extensive rose gardens. Most of the 'Great Houses' have fine collections of plants, often specialising in one botanical aspect. Also some of the specialist commercial nurseries are almost miniature botanical gardens; for instance Sunningdale Nursery in Surrey has one of the finest collections of 'old-fashioned' roses in the world.

Avery Hill
Bexley Rd SE9. 01-850 3217. A second smaller Kew. Good collection of tropical and temperate Asian and Australasian plants in glasshouses, including a selection of economic crops. *OPEN Apr-Oct 13.00-17.00 weekdays, 11.00-18.00 Sat & Sun, B. Hols; Nov-Mar 13.00-16.00. CLOSED first Mon in month. Park OPEN 07.00-dusk. Free.*

Bedgebury National Pinetum
Goudhurst, Kent. First planted in 1924. The forest consists of over 200 species of temperate zone cone-bearing trees laid out in genera. Of great use to foresters and botanists, it is sited in the lovely undulating countryside of the Weald of Kent. *OPEN 10.00-20.00 or dusk. CLOSED Xmas. Free.*

Borde Hill Arboretum
Haywards Heath, Sussex. Haywards Heath 50326. Created by Col. Stephenson R. Clarke at the end of the 19th cent. The garden and park now extend to 350 acres. Comprehensive collections of native and exotic trees and shrubs from Eastern Asia. *OPEN Apr-Aug 30th 14.00-19.00 Wed, Sat & Sun, B. Hols; Jun-Jul 11.00-19.00. Small admission charge.*

Cambridge University Botanic Garden
Bateman St Cambridge. Cambridge 50101. The first garden was established in 1761; moved to its present 40-acre site ¾ mile south of the city in 1846. Extensive collection of living plants, fine specimens of trees and shrubs, glasshouses, pinetum, ecological area, chronological bed, scented garden and geographically arranged alpine garden. *OPEN 08.00-19.30, Glasshouse 14.00-17.00. CLOSED Sun, Xmas, Box. Free.*

Chelsea Physic Garden   4   N 10
Swan walk, Chelsea SW3. 01-352 5646. Founded in 1673 by the Society of Apothecaries; second oldest botanical garden in UK. Contains fine old trees. Plants grown. mainly for teaching purposes. *Appointment only.*

The Garden Centre
Syon Park, Brentford, Middx. 01-560 0881. A brand-new one-million pound project opened in 1968. The Great Conservatory houses cacti, orchids and indoor plants. Machinery and implements on show. Large rose collection. Fruit and vegetable gardens. A centre for gardeners with information and advice. *OPEN 10.00-17.00. CLOSED Xmas, Box. Small admission charge.*

Grayswood Hill Arboretum
Grayswood, Haslemere, Surrey. Fine flowering trees and shrubs informally planted. Good views over the Weald of Sussex.

Oxford botanic garden
Oldest botanic garden in Britain founded in 1621 by Henry, Lord Danvers. About 3 acres within high stone walls, another 3 acres outside pleasantly situated by the river. Glasshouses, rock garden, some notable trees. Entrance arch by Inigo Jones. *OPEN summer 08.30-17.30 Mon-Sat, 10.00-12.00 & 14.00-18.00 Sun; winter 08.00-16.30 Mon-Sat, 10.00-12.00 & 14.00-dusk Sun. Greenhouses OPEN 14.00-16.00 daily.*

Royal Botanic Gardens, Kew
Kew Rd, Richmond. 01-940 1171. One of the world's great botanic gardens. Famous for its natural collections, identification of rare plants, economic botany and scientific research. Nearly 300 acres of pure aesthetic pleasure. Arboretum; alpine, water and rhododendron gardens. Magnificent tropical orchid, palm and Australasian houses. Herbarium contains Sir Joseph Hooker's famous H.M.S. 'Erebus' and Indian plant collections. Library of rare books on botany and exploration. Kew has been associated with many famous botanists; the Aitons, Sir Joseph Banks, the Hookers and others. *OPEN 10.00-19.00 or dusk. CLOSED Xmas, New Year's. Small admission charge.*

Savill Garden, Windsor Great Park
Egham 5544. Approach by Englefield Green. Created by Sir Eric Savill in 1930's. Outstanding woodland garden together with a large collection roses, herbaceous plants and alpines, in 35 acres and with a lake. *OPEN Mar-Oct 10.00-18.00, 10.00-19.00 Sat & Sun. Free.*

Sheffield Park Gardens
Near Uckfield, Sussex. Danehill 231. Gardens with five lakes and house by James Wyatt. Magnificent rhododendrons and azaleas in May and June. Brilliant autumn colours with maples and other shrubs. Rare specimen conifers and eucalyptus. *OPEN Apr-Nov 19th. Apr 11.00-19.00 Wed & Sat, 14.00-19.00 Sun; May-Sept 11.00-19.00 Tues-Sat, 14.00-19.00 or dusk Sun; Oct-Nov 11.00-17.00 Tues-Sat, 14.00-17.00 or dusk Sun; B. Hols 11.00-15.00. CLOSED G. Fri. Admission charge.*

Wakehurst Place
Ardingly, Sussex. A very lovely 500-acre 'satellite' garden to the Royal Botanic Garden at Kew; chosen because of its humid climate, clear air, lakes and running streams, and its variety of soils. The open woodland and high forest contain large numbers of rare trees, shrubs and plants from all over the world, particularly from Chile and New Zealand. *OPEN 10.00-19.00 daily in summer; 10.00-16.00 in winter. CLOSED Xmas, New Year's.*

Winkworth Arboretum
Hascombe Rd, Godalming, Surrey. Hascombe 336. 95 acres of steep hillside planted with trees and flowering shrubs; many rare species and many modern introductions. Fine views of the North Downs. Two lakes and many wild birds.

Wisley Royal Horticultural Gardens
Wisley, Surrey. A fine 200-acre botanic garden originally created by C. F. Wilson as a wild and woodland garden, acquired by Royal Horticultural Society in 1904. Famous for its trials and improvements of new varieties. Green-houses and pinetum. Notable collections of old fashioned and new roses, rhododendrons, camelias, heathers, rock garden plants and bulbs from the Near East. *OPEN Apr-Sept 10.00-19.00; Oct-Mar 10.00-16.30. CLOSED Xmas. Admission charge.*

Zoos and aquaria

This list extends outside London to distances near enough for a day's outing. All zoos ask visitors not to bring dogs.

Aquaria

Chessington Zoo has a good aquarium. The most comprehensive however is:

The London Zoo Aquarium
Regent's Park NW1. 01-722 3333. Marine and Tropical Halls. Excellently lit and displayed. A well-stocked aquarium of both sea and freshwater fish and amphibians from European and tropical waters. Particularly notable are the fine sea fish, the octopus, stingrays and sharks. *OPEN 09.00-dusk; Nov-Feb 10.00-16.00, 09.00-19.00 Sun & B. Hols. CLOSED Xmas. Admission charge.*

Brighton Aquarium
Marine Parade & Madeira Drive (opp Palace pier) Brighton, Sussex. Brighton 64233. Oldest public aquarium in Britain containing 48 tanks of marine and freshwater fish. Main feature is the Dolphinarium; at feeding times the dolphins perform, including 'walking' on the waters of the pool. *OPEN 09.00-18.30; Nov-Mar 09.00-17.30. Admission charge.*

Zoos

The London Zoo
Regent's Park NW1. 01-722 3333. This famous zoo has one of the largest collections of animals in the world. Excellent aviary designed by Lord Snowdon and a new 'Moonlight Hall' where day and night is reversed and rarely seen nocturnal animals are awake. The zoo was originally laid out by Decimus Burton in 1827; since then many famous architects have designed special animal houses. A large ape and monkey house opened in May '72, houses Guy the gorilla, and his mate Louie. *OPEN 09.00-dusk; Nov-Feb 10.00-16.00, 09.00-19.00 Sun & B. Hols. CLOSED Xmas. Admission charge.*

Chessington Zoo
Leatherhead Rd, Chessington, Surrey. Epsom 27227. A zoo of 65 acres on outskirts of London; most animals including lions, giraffes and elephants. 'Great Ape' house with gorillas, orang-outangs and chimps. Small aquarium of tropical and coldwater fish; reptiles and amphibians. Also has a circus, a pets corner and a Punch & Judy show. *OPEN 09.30-18.30; Nov-Feb 10.00-16.00. Admission charge.*

Colchester Zoo
Standway Hall, Colchester, Essex. Colchester 330 253. A good general collection, including an aquarium and reptile house, 40 acres. London 50 miles (A12). *OPEN 09.30-dusk. CLOSED Xmas. Admission charge.*

Cotswold Wild Life Park
Bradwell Grove, nr. Burford, Oxon. Burford 3006. Tropical birds, rhinos, zebras, pumas and otters. Reptile house. Tropical marine aquarium. *OPEN Mar-Oct 10.00-dusk. Admission charge.*

Linton Zoo
Handstock Rd, Linton, Cambridgeshire. Cambridge 891 308. Set in 10 acres of grassland. Lions, tigers, bears, wolves, porcupines, pheasants and tropical birds. Pets corner. *OPEN 10.00-dusk. CLOSED Xmas. Admission charge.*

Longleat Lion Reserve
Warminster, Wilts. Maiden Bradley 328. Visitors to the magnificent Renaissance house can choose to drive through the game park where lions roam at will! You can

stop your car and watch in safety but it is extremely toolhardy to get out, however friendly the lions. Also has a chimpanzee island. No soft-topped cars allowed. *OPEN 10.00-dusk. Admission charge.*

Mole Hall Wildlife Park
Mole Hall, Widdington, Nr Newport, Essex. Newport 40400. An interesting collection including monkeys (especially a fine colony of woolly monkeys), chimpanzees, otters, flamingoes and waterfowl. 12 acres. London 35 miles (A11). *OPEN 10.30-19.00 or dusk. Admission charge.*

Verulamium British Wildlife Zoo
Verulamium Park, St Albans, Herts. St Albans 66100. Small collection of British fauna maintained by St Albans City Council. London 20 miles (M1). *OPEN Apr-Oct 11.00-13.00 & 14.00-18.00. Small Admission charge.*

Weyhill Wildlife Park
Near Andover, Hampshire. Weyhill 2252. Specialist collection of wildlife of Europe. Children's corner containing cockatoos, parrots, etc. *Admission charge.*

Whipsnade Park Zoo
Dunstable, Bedfordshire. Whipsnade 471. A 500-acre 'natural' Zoo of woods and downland in the Chilterns. 2,000 animals in large open-air enclosures. Some species roam freely throughout the park. You can

picnic in the grounds — take binoculars or use the telescopes provided. Travel within the park in your own car or by miniature motor-coach train. London 35 miles (M1). *OPEN 10.00-19.00 or dusk. CLOSED Xmas. Admission charge.*

Windsor Safari Park
St Leonards, Windsor. Windsor 69841. Drive round the park in the car (long queues in summer). Lion and baboon reserves, monkey jungle, zebra, camels, giraffes, and lakes with waterfowl and a reptile house. Dolphins give hourly performances in the Dolphinarium. *OPEN 10.00-dusk. CLOSED Xmas. Admission charge.*

Woburn Abbey Zoo
Woburn, Bedfordshire. Woburn 666. 3,000-acre park surrounding the fine 18th cent house. Rare European bison, wallabies, llamas, rheas and other animals roam freely. Contains the original herd of Père David deer, saved from extinction by the 11th Duke of Bedford. Also a bird sanctuary. London 40 miles. (M1). *OPEN 10.00-17.00 or dusk. Admission charge.*

Children's Zoos and animal enclosures in parks
See under 'Children's London'.

Aviaries and wildfowl reserves

There are good aviaries at London Zoo and Chessington. Several London parks have small aviaries, notably Brockwell, Clissold, Dulwich, Victoria and Waterlow parks.

Bentley Wildfowl Collection
Halland, Lewes, Sussex. Halland 260. Private wildfowl collection of 23 acres with accent on conservation. London 50 miles (A22). *OPEN Apr-Oct 11.00-18.00. CLOSED G. Fri. Small admission charge.*

Birdworld Zoological Bird Gardens
Holt Pound, on A325 nr Farnham, Surrey. Bentley 2140. Birds from all over the world living almost naturally in landscaped gardens. Flamingoes, Lories, Indian peafowl and penquins among many species. *OPEN 10.00-dusk. Admission charge.*

Flamingo Gardens & Tropical Bird Zoo
West Underwood, Olney, Bucks. Bedford 711 451. Mammals, including bison, yaks, llamas, alpacas and rare mountain sheep. Magnificent collection of waterfowl, pheasants, cranes, pelicans and flamingoes, birds of prey and many exotic species in delightful surroundings. London 50 miles (M1). *OPEN Easter-Sept 14.00-20.00. CLOSED Mon, Tues, Fri. Admission charge.*

Stagsden Bird Zoo
Stagsden, Bedford. Oakley 2745. Large collection of exotic pheasants, also waterfowl, old English poultry breeds, flamingoes and jays. 1,300 birds. London 45 miles (A6). *OPEN 11.00-19.00 or dusk. CLOSED Xmas. Admission charge.*

Wicken Fen
Wicken, nr Ely, Cambridgeshire. Ely 720464. A last surviving remnant of the Great Fen that once covered the 2,500 square miles bounded by the Wash, Lincoln, Huntingdon and Kings Lynn. It is the haunt of 5,000 species of insects (many quite rare) including many butterflies and moths and 200 species of spiders. Alive with birds: herons, many species of duck, waders, bittern and owls — most breed in the sedge and marsh. A vigorous policy of preservation and maintenance keeps the fen a unique natural habitat. Parties should contact the warden. Watchtower overlooking the mere. *OPEN 10.00-18.00. CLOSED Thur, Xmas, Box.*

Birdwatching

The number of excellent birdwatching sites in or near London is surprisingly high. Largely because of its reservoirs and its proximity to the marshes of the Thames estuary, it has very good places for observing wildfowl. Winter is the most rewarding time if you are hardy enough.
Many of the more common birds can be seen in London parks, where they are comparitively tame, including wood pigeon, jay, great tit, blue tit, gulls, coot and moorhen.

Barns Elm Reservoir SW13
Sometimes well over 1,000 ducks can be seen. Waders and tern (numerous), tufted duck, pochard, gadwall, wigeon, smew (fare). Admission by permit only from: The Metropolitan Water Division 01-837 3300, ext 26.

Regent's Park NW1
Best areas for watching migrants are the Sanctuary and the woods in the N.E. corner. Willow warblers,

chiffchaff, whitethroats, flycatchers, redstart, pipits, redpoll.

Walthamstow Reservoir N17
Access Ferry Lane N17. A chain of waters formed by the River Lea. The wooded islands are breeding places for heron and the great crested grebe. Smew and tufted duck in winter. Permit only from MWB.

Wimbledon Common and Putney Heath SW19
Popular heath with gravel pits, marsh, lake and oak woods. Skylark, woodpeckers, willow warbler, cuckoo, whitethroat, blackcap, spotted flycatcher.

The following places are all within an easy day's journey of London:

Abberton Reservoir, Essex
Nr Chelmsford. The reservoir with the heaviest population of wildfowl in England. Four square miles which in Oct-Nov have thousands of mallard, teal, wigeon, pintail, shoveler, pochard, goldeneye, goosander, smew and mute swan. Also Bewick's swan, white-fronted goose, gadwall, red-crested pochard and many other varieties. No public access but view from nearby roads. London 35 miles (A12).

The Blackwater & Crouch Estuaries, Essex
A vast flat, windy and immensely rich area for the birdwatcher. Includes the Bradwell Bird Observatory and Dengie flats (vantage point — 16 miles of sea wall). Waders, brent geese, oyster catchers, wigeon, redshank, greenshank, shelduck, etc., but also practically any other sea bird. London 40 miles (A12).

Berkhamsted Common, Hertfordshire
5 miles north of Hemel Hempstead. Woods and heath in the Chiltern Hills. Fieldfares and redwings (numerous in winter). Also woodcock, nightjar, grasshopper warbler, redpoll, brambling. London 25 miles (A41).

Broxbourne Woods, Hertfordshire
2 miles west of Hoddesdon. Woodland and heath. Nightingale, nightjar, warblers, woodcock, tree pipit.

Canvey Point, Essex
Despite its proximity to Southend, a good place to see terns, skua, brent goose and wader. Also wigeon, shelduck, plovers, redshank. London 30 miles.

Chobham Common, Surrey
1,600 acres of heath and woodland. Tree and meadow pipit, skylark, carrion crow.

Epping Forest, Essex
5 square miles of oak and hornbeam woods. Redstarts, nightingale, tree pipit, warblers, hawfinch.

Frensham Ponds, Surrey
Sandy wooded common south of Farnham with hills and ponds. Buzzards, woodlark, nightjar, nightingale, warblers, redstart, goldcrest, siskin, great shrike, wildfowl generally. London 30 miles (A3).

Ham Island Bird Sanctuary, Berkshire
100-acre island in the Thames near Windsor. Canada goose, sandpipers, ringed plover, dunlin, waders.

Hanningfield Reservoir
Large area of water where you can see gadwall, garganey, little grebes, black-necked grebes and terns. Also teal, wigeon, shoveler, pochard, goldeneye, smew, divers, dunlin, waders, plover, whimbrel, sandpipers, curlew, redshank, greenshank, little stint, ruff. Good views from public roads. London 30 miles (A12).

Hilfield Park Reservoir, Hertfordshire
Near Elstree airfield. Many thousands of ducks. Pochard, wigeon, smew, goldeneye, goosander.

Northaw Great Wood, Hertfordshire
Just North of Potters Bar. 750 acres of oak woods. Redstart and nightingale (numerous). Also redpoll, warblers, lesser whitethroat, hawfinch and tree pipit.

Staines Reservoir, Middx.
The central causeway is the best vantage point. The reservoir is rated high for birdwatching, particularly waders and grebe. Also smew, goosander, wigeon, shoveler, goldeneye, pochard, terns, black-necked grebe.

Swale Estuary, Isle of Sheppey, Kent
Shell Ness Point, the mudflats of Harty and Queensborough cover a vast attractive area excellent for the very best kind of birdwatching. Noted for waders, oyster catchers, bar tailed godwit and grey plover. The winter resort of about 15,000 knot. everything else too. London 40 miles (A2).

Thames & Medway Estuaries, Kent
Twenty miles of sea wall skirt the marshes and the mudflats at Cliffe, Egypt Bay and Yantlet Creek — a marvellous winter's walk, with the busy Thames shipping, the melancholy of Dickens' 'Great Expectations' country, and literally thousands of duck, waders, white fronts, and enormous variety of other wildfowl. The Nature Reserve at Northward Hill at High Halstow contains a heronry of over 100 birds. Access by permit from RSPB. London 30 miles (A2).

Tring Reservoir, Hertfordshire
The waters feed the Grand Union canal and are now a Nature Reserve. Famous as the breeding grounds of the little ringed plover. Also teal, wigeon, shoveler, pochard, tufted duck, goosander, waders, terns, great crested grebe, sandpipers, greenshank, curfew, stint. London 30 miles (A41).

Virginia Water, Surrey
Attractive lake and woodland. Manderin duck, garganey, wigeon, shoveler, pochard, great crested grebe, goosander, smew, siskin, goldcrest, warblers, woodpeckers, hawfinch, woodcock. London 25 miles.

Windsor Great Park, Berkshire
Huge park with woods and plantations. Great Meadow Pond is good for mandarin and passage garganey, wigeon and shoveler. Also nightjar, woodpecker, warblers and pipits.

Nature reserves

These are maintained to preserve fast-disappearing kinds of natural vegetation and wild life. Conservation and control of this type requires expert management to maintain these precious parts of the countryside for the enjoyment of the public. Where permits are required write to:
Nature Conservancy Zealds Church St, Wye, Kent.
For Herts, Kent, London, Middx, Surrey, Surrey.
Nature Conservancy Foxhold House, Thornford Rd, Crookham Common, Newbury, Berks.
For Berks, Bucks, Hants, Oxon and Wilts.
Nature Conservancy 60 Bracondale, Norwich
For Beds, Essex, Cambs, Norfolk and Suffolk.

Blean Woods, Kent
NW of Canterbury. Fine mixed woods containing several unusual insects including the Heath Fritillary butterfly. Fine views across Swale river and the Isle of Sheppey. Permit required away from footpath.

Bure Marshes, Norfolk
9 miles NE Norwich. Four broads and unsurpassed typical marsh, fen and aquatic habitats. Excellent plant and bird-life. Permit required.

Cavenham Heath, Suffolk
1 mile W of Icklingham. One of the last remaining tracts of Breck heathland. Free access but permit required for some parts.

Chippenham Fen, Cambridgeshire
3½ miles N of Newmarket. Valley fen, scrub and mixed fen woodland. Many insects including some rarities. Permit required away from footpath.

Cothill, Berkshire
5 miles SW of Oxford. A small fen and swamp rich in flora and fauna. Shows the succession of open water to swamp and woodland of alder, ash and birch. Permit required.

Hales Wood, Essex
2½ miles NW of Saffron Walden. Ash-oak woodland on chalk and clay. Oxlips grow here. Permit required

Ham Street Woods, Kent
5 miles S of Ashford. Typical Kentish woodland rich in flowers and insects. Permit required away from footpath.

Hickling Broad, Norfolk
10 miles NW of Great Yarmouth. Broads, fen and marshland rich in plant and animal communities. Many unusual insects including the swallowtail butterfly. Rare birds include bitterns, several uncommon waders and bearded tits. Boating access but permit required for marshland.

High Halstow, Kent
6 miles NE of Rochester. A gaunt wood overlooking the Thames estuary supports a heronry. Access only by permit from RSPB.

Holkham, Norfolk
11 miles E of Hunstanton. Very large reserve of sand dunes, mud flats and salt marshes. Many wildfowl: little terns at High Cape, sandwich terns are nesting and increasing on Stiffkey Binks. Permit required away from shore and footpaths.

Kingley Vale, Sussex
4 miles NW of Chichester. Famous yew woods in all stages of development. Contrasting acid heath overlying the chalk near Bow Hill. Free access.

Lullington Heath, Sussex
4 miles NE of Seaford. One of the largest areas of chalk heath left on the South Downs. A fascinating mixture of shallow-rooted acid-loving plants and deep-rooted lime-lovers. Permit necessary away from footpaths.

Orfordness-Havergate, East Suffolk
Large shingle spit with typical vegetation and some rare insects. Famous for its Avocet colony. Permit required.

Pagham Harbour, Sussex
Mud flats, pools and reed beds rich in bird life.
Ruislip, London
The reservoir has a good area of reeds and fen plants at
the north end. Large variety of birds. Permit from Sec:
Ruislip Natural History Society, 62 Briarwood Drive,
Northwood.
Scolt Head, Norfolk
1 mile NE of Brancaster Staithe. An island famous for
its colonies of sandwich and common terns. Permit
required.
Stanpit Marshes, Hampshire
SE of Christchurch. Water meadows, saltings, mud
flats and reed beds. Many birds. Free access.

Temple Ewell Downs, Kent
Fine area of chalk grassland rich in plants and insects.
Restricted access. Apply A. P. Brown, Beech Hill,
Cryals Rd, Tonbridge, Kent.
Weeting Heath, Norfolk
1 mile NW of Brandon. Heath plants and an enclosure
showing how rabbits existed before myxomatosis.
Wheatear and stone curlew occur. Permit required.
Winterton Dunes, Norfolk
8 miles N of Yarmouth. Very wide coastal sand dunes
with some heath and bogs. Rare maritime grasses.
Permit required away from rights of way.
Wychwood, Oxfordshire
7 miles W of Woodstock. 600 acres of ancient oak
forest formerly royal forest. Interesting plants and
insects. Permit required.

Children's London

Looking at London

The obvious choices are usually the most rewarding —
as much for the accompanying adult as for the child.
There are also many new things to do — like looking at
windmills or going to a puppet show. For more ideas on
what to do during school holidays ring 'Stewpot' 01-246
8007. The section 'Historic London' includes the places
that are usually visited.
'Cutty Sark' Gardens
Greenwhich pier SE10 (Information centre) 01-858
6376. The old and romantic 'Cutty Sark' is joined by
'Gipsy Moth IV', the boat in which Chichester sailed
around the world. OPEN daily 11.00-18.00 Sun 14.30-
18.00. Admission charge.
Evening Standard   **6 K 27**
47 Shoe Lane EC4. 01-353 3000. General tour following
production of newspaper from start to finish. 2 months
waiting list. Mon-Fri 14.00-15.00. Minimum age 15
(parties of 10). Free. Contact the Works Manager.
Daily Express   **6 K 27**
Fleet St EC4. 01-353 8000. 6 months waiting list.
Minimum age 16. Contact the Group Tech. Dept. Tours
on Sun-Wed 20.30-23.00.
Daily Mail   **6 L 26**
Northcliffe House, Carmelite St EC4. 01-353 6000. 3
months waiting list. Minimum age 14. Contact the
Production Manager. Tours 21.00-23.15 Tues, Wed &
Fri. 12 people max.
Daily Mirror   **6 J 28**
Holborn Circus EC1. 01-353 0246. 3 months waiting list.
Minimum age 16. Contact the Production Dept. Tours
21.00-23.15
Fire!
Be right on the spot when the siren goes. For
permission to visit your local fire station write to the PR
Dept, London Fire Brigade HQ, Albert Embankment
SE1.
Ford Motor Co.
Dagenham Essex. 01-592 4591. Fascinating conducted
tours of the factory, from glass furnace through to final
assembly building with completed cars. 09.45-12.00,
13.30-15.45. Adult supervision required for children
aged 10-16. Free. 3 month waiting list for parties.
GPO Mount Pleasant   **3 G 28**
Rosebery Avenue EC1. 01-837 4272 Ext 118. If you
write, address it to the Controller. You will be shown
round this enormous sorting house which is now fully
mechanised, and see the underground railway.
Minimum age is 14. Tours 14.30-16.30, 19.30-21.30.
Please give 3 weeks notice.
Houses of Parliament   **5 H 20**
St Margaret St SW1. 01-219 3000. Tour of Parliament
admission at Sovereign's entrance. House of Lords
admission at St Stephen's entrance (Old Palace Yard
side) or by Westminster Hall if wet. House of Commons
admission write to MP or queue on day outside St
Stephen's entrance. When neither House is sitting
OPEN 10.00-16.30 Sat; Easter Mon & Tues; Spring hol
Mon & Tues; Mon, Tues, Thur in Aug; Thur in Sept.
Conducted tours Sat. During session queue admitted
from 16.15 Mon-Thur, 11.30 Fri to House of Commons

and from 14.40 Mon-Wed, 15.10 Thur to House of
Lords. Westminster Hall OPEN when Parliament is in
session but neither House is sitting 10.30-13.30 Mon-
Thur, 10.00-17.00 Sat. During recess 10.00-16.00 Mon-
Fri, 10.00-17.00 Sat. CLOSED G. Fri, Xmas, Box. All
free.
London Airport (Heathrow)
From the roof garden you can watch the massive
planes landing and taking off and listen to a
commentary over the loudspeakers. There is a
children's playground and refreshments are available.
London Symphony Orchestra   **3 G 24**
1 Montague St WC1. 01-637 2622. An annual
subscription of £1.50 (open to children) to the LSO club
gives free attendance at final rehearsals.
Maxwell J. T.   **2 G 13**
The Boathouse, Serpentine, Hyde Park W2. Hire out
sailing boats, rowing and outrigger skiffs and cycle
crafts on the Serpentine and other London park lakes.
Reasonable hourly rates plus deposit.
Observatory
Hampstead Heath (nr Jack Straw's Castle). Owned by
the Hampstead Scientific Society and maintained by
their Astronomy Section. OPEN Sept-May at weekends
weather permitting. Apply to the Society's Secretary,
22 Flask Walk NW3. 01-794 7341.
Old Bailey   **6 L 28**
Old Bailey EC4. 01-248 3277. Trials in the Central
Criminal Court can be watched from the public gallery.
OPEN Mon-Fri 10.30-13.00, 14.00-16.00. Minimum age
14. Free.
River Trips
See under that heading in the 'Sightseeing' section
Boats, like trains, planes and cars fascinate youngsters,
so seeing London from the water is double fun. On the
Thames you can take a trip downriver to the docks to
see the 'big ships' or up-river to Battersea or further up
towards Hampton Court. All along the banks there are
sights to see and small boats 'messing about on the
river'. Or you can take to the canals and travel from
Little Venice to Regent's Park Zoo in one of the original
painted barges, which often tows a tender.
Round Pond   **1 D 10**
Kensington Gardens W2. Model yachts abound: usually
sailed by proud fathers. Kite flying nearby at weekends.
Royal Philharmonic Orchestra   **2 G 19**
If you write several weeks beforehand to the RPO
office, 97 New Bond St W1. 01-629 4078 you may be
able to join a party (12-20 people) to attend a rehearsal.
Minimum age is 10.
Season Ticket to History
If you like to visit places like the Tower of London,
Hampton Court and so on several times it's worth-while
writing for a season ticket. These cost £2.00 for adults,
75p for children under 16, free for children under 5 and
mean that you can visit as many preserved buildings as
you like as often as you like during a certain length of
time. Write to Dept. of the Environment, D.A.M. H.
B/P. Room G.1. 25 Savile Row W1.
Stock Exchange   **6 N 32**
Old Broad St EC2. 01-588 2355. Entrance to public
gallery at corner of Threadneedle St and Old Broad St.
Running commentary and questions answered by

patient guides. Films shown in adjoining cinema. Gallery *OPEN Mon-Fri 10.00-15.15. CLOSED G. Fri, B. Hols, Xmas & New Year's Day.* Parties up to 40 ring or write to PR Dept. *Free.*

Trafalgar Square   5 **J 21**
Always popular with children who like to chase and feed the pigeons, climb the lions and watch the fountains. Parents will enjoy the bustling, colourful crowd which always congregates here.

Museums for children

For a full list see the separate section 'Museums and parks'. Most museums will arrange special tours for children as long as arrangements are made well in advance.

Baden-Powell House   1 **H 8**
Queens Gate SW7. 01-584 1671. Exhibition of the life-history of Baden-Powell, founder of the scout movement. *OPEN daily 09.00-22.00. CLOSED Xmas, Box. Free.*

Bethnal Green Museum
Cambridge Heath Rd E2. 01-980 2415. Fine display of historic toys, dol's and dolls' houses and model theatres, including an 18th cent Venetian marionette theatre. Special collection of children's costume. Saturday work shop *(11.00-13.00, 14.00-16.00)* provides facilities for drawing, puppetry and modelling. Holiday activities include painting competitions, story-telling and Punch and Judy shows with traditional figures. *OPEN 10.00-17.50 Mon-Sat, 14.30-17.50 Sun. CLOSED G. Fri, Xmas, Box, New Year's. Free.*

Geffrye Museum
Kingsland Rd E2. 01-739 8368. 18th cent almshouses with period rooms and furniture from 1600 to present-day. Activities for children over 7 include drawing, painting, puzzles, plays, model-making, outings and classes in pottery and basketry. *OPEN 10.00-17.00 Tues-Sat, 14.00-17.00 Sun. CLOSED G. Fri, Xmas, Box. Free.*

Geological Museum   1 **H 10**
Exhibition Rd SW7. 01-589 3444. Real gold, diamonds, minerals, rocks, fossils including an impressive collection of gem stones. Demonstrations, dioramas and films throughout the year. Special feature exhibition 'Story of the Earth' is a complete account of the origin of the universe. *OPEN 10.00-18.00 (Sun 14.30-18.00). Closed G. Fri, Xmas, Box.*

Horniman Museum
London Rd, Forest Hill SE23. 01-699 2339. Exhibits include many fascinating stuffed animals such as foxes and birds, also less common animals like the giant walrus. Fish from all over the world in the aquarium. *OPEN daily 10.30-18.00 (Sun 14.30-17.30). CLOSED G. Fri, Xmas.* Free. The Children's Centre provides craft facilities for children over 8 or they can borrow drawing materials and wander round the museum. *Every Sat and daily during school holidays. 10.30-16.30. CLOSED Sun.*

London Transport Collection
Syon Park, Brentford, Middx. 01-560 0881. Every type of Public Transport to be found here from trams to underground railways spanning almost 150 years, including a replica of the first horse-drawn omnibus. *OPEN Apr-Sept 10.00-19.00 daily; Oct-Mar 10.00-17.00. CLOSED Xmas, Box. Admission charge.*

Madame Tussaud's   2 **B 19**
Marylebone Rd NW1. 01-935 6861. (Adjoins Planetarium). Life-size wax figures of historic, notorious or famous people. Murderers, royalty, statesmen and astronauts all under the same roof, looking incredibly life-like. 'Battle of Trafalgar': reconstruction of gundeck of 'Victory' at height of battle. *OPEN 10.00-17.30 Mon-Fri, 10.00-18.30 Sat & Sun. CLOSED Xmas. Admission charge.*

National Maritime Museum
Romney Rd SE10. 01-858 4422. Vast collection of ship models, navigational instruments, costumes and weapons. *OPEN 10.00-18.00 (Sun 14.30-18.00). CLOSED G. Fri, Xmas, Box. Free.*

Natural History Museum   1 **H 9**
Cromwell Rd SW7. 01-589 6323. Fossilised remains and reconstructions of prehistoric monsters like the dinosaur. Marvellous displays of birds, beasts and reptiles from all over the world and a 91-ft (full-size) cast of the blue whale in the Whale Room. *OPEN 10.00-18.00 Mon-Sat, 14.30-18.00 Sun. CLOSED G. Fri, Xmas. Free.*

Old Royal Observatory
Greenwich Park SE10. 01-858 4422. Houses the Greenwich Planetarium which shows projections of the sky and stars. During school holidays this is *OPEN Mon, Tue, Thur & Fri 10.30-15.30. CLOSED Wed, Sat & Sun.* For Planetarium bookings ring 01-858 1167. During the school year parties must book. (Minimum number 12.) Contact the Education Officer.

Planetarium   2 **B 19**
Marylebone Rd NW1. 01-486 1121. A fascinating look into outer space and at our neighbours in the galaxy. *Presentations daily every hour on the hour from 11.00 to 18.00.* Joint ticket with Tussaud's as above. *Admission charge.*

Pollock's Toy Museum   2 **F 22**
1 Scala St W1. 01-636 3452. Old toys, theatres and dolls crammed into two floors. On the ground floor there is gingerbread for sale. The oldest teddy bear in England sits in state here. *OPEN Mon-Sat 10.00-17.00. CLOSED B. Hols. Small admission charge.*

Science Museum   1 **H 10**
Exhibition Rd SW7. 01-589 6371. The main gallery has the finest collection of scale working models of steam engines, mine pumps, early aeroplanes and other machinery. The Children's Gallery is full of exciting press button models and dioramas showing the development of scientific techniques. Daily lectures (*not Sun*) and film shows *Wed-Sat.* Museum *OPEN daily 10.00-18.00. Sun 14.30-18.00. CLOSED G. Fri, Xmas, Box. Free.*

Telephone Museum   3 **I 32**
Ironmonger Row, Lever St EC1. 01-829 4005. A permanent exhibition of old and new telephones and all the associated systems. There are models for the children to work. *OPEN Mon-Fri 10.00-16.30. Minimum age 10. Free.*

Tower of London   6 **Q 32**
Tower Hill EC3. 01-709 0765. Fascinating collection of armour for man and horse and a vast display of old pikes, halberds, muskets, swords and pistols, also the most extensive collection of Japanese armoury in Europe. Almost better than the Crown jewels is the room which houses them, with thick walls, well below ground and completely steel lined. *OPEN 09.30-17.00 Mon-Sat, 14.00-17.00 Sun. CLOSED Pub. Hols & B. Hols. Admission charge.*

Animals in parks

Battersea Park   4 **P 9**
SW11. 01-228 2798. Animals and birds chosen to be of special interest to children. Exotic birds. Pony. rides. *OPEN Easter-Sept 13.30-17.30 weekdays, 11.00-18.00 Sat & Sun, school hols & B. Hols. Small admission charge.*

Brockwell Park
SE24. 01-674 6141. Quail, touracos, toucans, jays and many other exotic birds.

Clissold Park
N16. 01-800 1021. Fallow and Chinese water deer, rabbits, peafowl, crane, mynah birds, guinea fowl, doves, black-necked swans and a large collection of other water fowl.

Crystal Palace
SE19. 01-778 7148. Small zoo where children can handle the animals as they wander about; penguins, squirrels, otters, monkeys. Also caged birds. Pony rides. *OPEN Easter-Sept term-time 13.30-17.30, holidays weekends and B. Hols, 11.00-18.00.* The Open Dog Show and obedience test for domestic and working dogs is held here in August.

Dulwich Park
SE21. 01-693 5737. Quail, touracos, mot-mots, toucans and many exciting birds as well as a good collection of waterfowl on the lake.

Golders Hill Park
NW11. 01-455 5183. Fallow and Chinese water deer, sheep, rabbits, guinea pigs, pheasants, ducks, swans, cranes, rheas and guinea fowl.

Hainault Forest
Essex. 01-500 3106. Donkeys. Welsh mountain ponies, sheep peafowl, cows and llama.

Holland Park   1 **B 5**
W8 01-602 2226. Peafowl, junglefowl, pheasants, geese and crane.

London Natural History Society
Secretary: 21 Green Way, Frinton-on-Sea, Essex. Birdwatching excursions each weekend. Worth becoming a member for the regular outings and meetings.

Maryon Wilson Park
SE7. 01-854 0446. Ponies, fallow and Chinese water deer and Jacob sheep.

Mobile Zoo
Visits many London parks during the summer. Very popular. Tame animals are in small enclosures so that

children can handle them. Shetland and Welsh pony rides. Details from the GLC Parks Dept. 01-633 1716/7.

Regent's Park Zoo
NW1. 01-722 3333. As well as the excellent main zoo there is a children's zoo for pony and camel rides, chimps and small friendly animals. Also a nocturnal section and an aquarium. The **XYZ club** for children 9-18 can be joined for £1.00. This includes 6 free tickets to either London zoo or Whipsnade Park, 3 copies of the zoo magazine, news letters, meetings, lectures, films and competitions during the holidays.

Sydenham Wells
Wells Rd SE26. 01-699 8914. Large and colourful collection of waterfowl including flamingoes.

Victoria Park
E2. 01-985 1957. Fallow and Chinese water deer, guinea pigs, rabbits, guinea fowl, bantams and crane.

Waterlow Park
N6. 01-272 2825. Touracos, jays, quail, pheasants, black swans, geese, ducks, doves, mynah birds and many others.

Nature trails

These are carefully selected walks in rich natural habitats such as forest, bog or chalk grassland where the country is still in an uncultivated state. Unusual ecological features (points of interest about the plant, animal, bird and insect life) are pinpointed by an explanatory leaflet or by signposts.
Don't forget to visit the Children's Centre at the Natural History Museum where there is an interesting indoor trail on the museum's own exciting collection. OPEN 10.30-12.30, 14.00-16.30 daily.
The following are those trails nearest London.

Aston Rowant Oxfordshire
A nature showing the succession of chalk grassland to scrub and woodland. Flora and insects. Guide obtainable on trail. *Summer only.*

Barfold Copse Reserve Haslemere Surrey
Permit only. Mixed woodland. Guide and permit from R.S. Protection of Birds, The Lodge, Sandy, Beds.

Butser Hill Petersfield Hampshire
Large tracts of open downland with superb views across to the Isle of Wight. Leaflets at head of trail at Butser Hill picnic site (off A3). *All year round.*

Chinner Hill Oxfordshire
Chalk grassland and woodland. Plants and birds. Guide at car park at the end of the lane up the hill. *All year round.*

Coombe Hill Bucks 1½ miles W. of Wendover
Chalk grassland and beechwood with fine view. Guide from County Museum, Aylesbury, Bucks. *All year round.*

Finchhampstead Berks.
Plants and geology. Starts 1 mile E of village on B3348. Guide from local Shell petrol station. *Summer only.*

Fingringhoe Essex
Nature reserve. Flora and fauna of salt marshes, reclaimed marsh and ponds. Guide from Secretary, Essex Naturalist Trust, 9 Buryfields, Felstead, Essex. *All year round.*

Halton Wood Wendover Forest Bucks.
Pleasant forest walks. Guide from Forest Lodge, Aston Clinton Bucks. *All year round.*

Hickling Broad Norfolk
A fine nature reserve N.E. of Norwich. Water trail by boat to sedge and reed beds and woodland trail. Start Pleasure Boat Inn, Hickling. *May-Sep Mon & Thur only 10.00-14.30. Small admission charge.*

Holme Nature Reserve N.E. of Hunstanton, Norfolk
Birds and plants on sand dunes, shingle spits, marsh and lagoon. Starts from 'The Firs' on reserve. *May-Sep Wed & Thur 10.00-17.00.* Admission charge.

Hothfield Common Ashford, Kent
Heath and bog in original state. Guide from Secretary Kent Trust for Nature Conservation, Beech Hill, Cryals Rd Matfield Kent. *All year round.*

Kingley Vale West Stoke Chichester
Chalk downland, the famous yew woodlands and acid heath. Flora and fauna. Start on footpath N of West Stoke. Guide from kiosk. *All year round.*

Old Winchester Hill Hampshire
2 miles S of West Meon. Chalk downland, yew, juniper scrub and iron age fort. Guides at start of trail. White Trail easy. Red Trail has steeper slopes. *All year round.*

Thetford Forest Santon Suffolk
Downham Forest walk starts at church in village. Guide from Head Forester, District office, Santon Downham, Suffolk.

West Stow Suffolk
Mixed woodland badgers, deer and birds. Starts at

Forest Lodge. Guide from car park. *All year round.*

West Wycombe Hill
Lovely Chiltern countryside of chalk downs and woods. Guide at local Shell petrol stations or National Trust. *Summer only.*

Hill figures

The following are the most noteworthy hill figures nearest to London. The best are in Wiltshire. Children find them strange and fascinating. One of the best books on the subject is: 'Discovering Hill Figures' by Kate Bergamar. 40p. Shire Publications.

Alton Barnes Horse, Wilts
Just north of village. A fine horse cut in the early 19th cent. A most elegant and spirited figure.

Cherhill Horse, Wilts
Cherhill Down. Beneath the primitive fortress of Oldbury castle and near Cherhill village. Cut in 1780, it is 150 ft long. Originally it had a sparkling eye of a 4 ft circle inset with the bases of bottles.

Hackpen Hill, Wilts
On the Marlborough Downs, near Winterbourne Bassett. A fine horse cut in the early 19th cent.

Litlington Horse, Sussex
This horse was cut in 1925 to replace an earlier 'lost' horse to commemorate the coronation of Queen Victoria. It is on Hindover Hill and can also be seen clearly from Beachy Head.

Longman of Wilmington, Sussex
A threatening figure of a man holding two staffs over 200 ft high on Windover Hill. Restored in the 19th cent, it is almost certainly very much earlier in origin, and much speculated on. Supposed to have previously held a rake & scythe — possibly even Roman standards.

Marlborough Horse, Wilts
On Granham Hill, near Marlborough. About 60 ft long, this horse was cut in 1804 and has a curiously angular and symbolic grace.

Pewsey New Horse, Wilts
Just south of the village, this horse is the second one to be cut — the first, nearby, has now virtually disappeared. Cut in 1937.

Uffington White Horse, Berks
2-3 miles south of the village on the lovely Berkshire downs. Close to an iron-age fortress and other primitive earthworks and barrows. History unknown but attributed to King Alfred or Hengist or even earlier. Over 350 ft long, it is vigorous and flowing and very impressive, and surrounded by mystery & legend: stand in the eye with eyes closed, turn around 3 times and wish.

Westbury Horse, Wilts
A very fine horse with slender nose and legs and an unusual undocked tail. It is 180 ft long and 100 ft high. On Bratton Down a mile from the village.

Whipsnade White Lion, Beds
Below the zoo is a huge lion nearly 500 ft long, cut into the chalk in 1935. Replaces a vanished earlier horse of about mid 18th cent.

Wye Crown, Wye, Kent
A mile from the village, this 240 ft wide crown was cut for the coronation of Edward VII in 1902.

Fossil hunting

Start by visiting the Geological Museum and the National History Museum in South Kensington. They both have superb collections and often state where the fossils were found. They have guide books to fossil hunting in districts. Fossils are found most easily in newly exposed strata in quarries, road cuttings, cliffs and excavations. Ask permission where these are obviously private. Heavily built-up London offers a few opportunities — the following are outside and represent a small personal selection.

Chalk pits, Surrey & Kent
Numerous quarries at the base of the North Downs escarpment. They yield echinoids, brachiopods, sponges and ammonites. Quarries at Dorking, Oxted, Bletchworth and the Medway valley. A good selection are sited along the Pilgrim's way.

Cotswolds
The great oolite yields many fossils. There are quarries at Burleigh and at Kirtlington — a thick bed of brachiopods here.

Cromer 'forest beds', Norfolk
Found spasmodically along the coastal cliffs between Pakefield and Weybourne. Abundant fossils of the remains of trees and the bones and teeth of mammals

such as the rhino, elephant, sabre-toothed tiger and bear.

Easton cliffs, Suffolk
North of Southwold. Full of fossils of shells and some bones of prehistoric animals. Look out for semi-precious stone (cornelian and agates).

Ford Place nr Wrothan and Greatness Lane pits
Sevenoaks, Kent. Brick pits of blue gault clay containing ammonities, belemites, gasteropods, marine worms and the occasional shark's tooth and fish bone. Don't go on a wet day — the clay gets very sticky.

Herne Bay, Kent
Abundant specimens of bivalves and gasteropods in the cliffs. Nearer to Reculver there is a good bed of corbula shells.

Peterborough, Hunts
The brick pits here contain large numbers of vertebrate fossils, plesiosaurs and ichythyosaurs. Go and see the famous collection of these in the Natural History Museum, donated by two local geologists.

Poton, Beds
Remains of the dinosaur iguanodon are reputed to be a common find here in the lower greensand wherever you can find it exposed.

Sheppey, Kent
The cliffs of London clay are famous for fossils of plant, fruit and seeds particularly cinnamon, magnolia and palm. Look on the beach under the cliffs where the sea has done most of the work of cleaning away the clay from the fossils.

Shenley Hill, Leighton Buzzard, Beds
Sandpits around here contain ventricles of fossiliferous limestone 2-10 ft in length. They contain fossils and brachiopods, many kinds of primitive shells and the occasional ammonite.

Walton on Naze, Suffolk
Many fossils of the Miocene period in cliffs.

Woodham, Bucks
Brick pits here produced numerous ammonites.

Brass rubbing

A fascinating hobby which can take one all over the country! A helpful book is 'Discovering Brasses and Brass Rubbing' by Malcolm Cook. Brass rubbing materials can be obtained from:

Philips & Page 1 C 8
50 Kensington Church St W8. 01-937 5839.
Outstanding brasses are to be found in the following places:

Bedfordshire
Aspley Guise, Bromham, Cardington, Copie, Elstow, Marston Moretaine, Shillington, Wymington.

Berkshire
Ashbury, Blewbury, Bray, Childrey, Cookham, Shottesbrooke, Sparsholt, Wantage, West Hanney, Windsor, St George's Chapel.

Buckinghamshire
Chenies, Denham, Drayton Beauchamp, Edlesborough, Eton College chapel, Hambledon, Lillingstone Lovell, Middle Claydon, Pitstone, Quainton, Stoke Poges, Taplow, Thornton, Twyford, Upper Winchendon, Waddesdon.

Cambridgeshire
Balsham, Burwell, Cambridge: St John's Chapel, Trinity Hall, King's College; Ely Cathedral, Fulbourne, Hildersham, Horseheath, Isleham, Little Shelford, Trumpington, Westley Waterless, Wisbech, Wood Ditton.

Essex
Arkesden, Avely, Bowers Gifford, Chigwell, Corningham, Dagenham, Gosfield, Great Bromley, Latton, Little Easton, Little Horkesley, Pebmarsh, Stifford, Wimbish, Wivenhoe.

Hertfordshire
Albury, Baldock, Berkhampsted, Broxbourne, Digswell, Furneaux Pelham, Hemel Hempstead, Hunsdon, Knebworth, North Mimms, St Alban's Abbey, St Albans St Michael, Sawbridgeworth, Standon, Watford, Watton-at-Stone.

Kent
Ashford, Bexley, Bobbing, Brabourne, Chartham, Cobham, Faversham, Herne, Hever, Lydd, Margate, Saltwood, Seal, Sheldwich, Woodchurch, Wrotham.

London: inner
All Hallows-by-the-Tower, St Dunstan-in-the-West, Westminster Abbey, St Giles Camberwell, St Helens Bishopsgate.

London: outer
Enfield, Fulham, Harrow, Hillingdon, Hackney, Hadley, Harefield, Ruislip, St Mary's Willesden.

Norfolk
Aylesham, Blickling, Elsing, Felbrigg, Forleston, Hunstanton, Kings Lynn, Narborough, Norwich: St George Colegate, St John Maddermarket, St Lawrence, Southacre, Upwell.

Oxfordshire
Brightwell Baldwin, Chinnor, Dorchester, Great Tew, Mapledurham, Oddlington, Oxford: Merton College chapel, New College chapel, Queen's College chapel; Thame.

Suffolk
Acton, Barsham, Burgate, Ipswich: St Mary Tower; Letheringham, Long Melford, Mendlesham, Playford, Stoke by Nayland, Yoxford.

Surrey
Beddington, Carshalton, East Horsley, Lingfield, Stoke d'Abernon, Thames Ditton.

Sussex
Amberley, Ardingly, Battle, Cowford, Etchingham, Fletching, Trotton, West Grinstead, Wiston.

Traction engines

Once common, these early steam engines have now become collectors' pieces. Rallies are held periodically by area clubs in various parts of the country. They are colourful and unusual and the engines themselves are superb. Write for information of clubs to:

National Traction Engine Club
127 Greensted Rd, Loughton, Essex.
There are various museums and collections including the Science Museum in S. Kensington, and a useful book is 'Discovering Traction Engines' by Harold Bonnett (Shire Publications).

Thursford, Norfolk
Laurels Farm, Thursford. Tel 238. Mr George Cushing's private collection. *OPEN every Sun 16.00-18.00 (Summer every day except Sat).* Donations to Cancer Research.

National Motor Museum
Beaulieu, Hampshire. Beaulieu 12123. *OPEN 10.00-17.00 (18.00 summer).*

Windmills

There are very few windmills now left with a few, believe it or not, still in London. The rest are all within an easy day trip. Buy the excellent 'Discovering Windmills' by J. N. T. Vince (Shire Publications), for more detailed information.

London
Quite a famous one on Wimbledon Common.
A pumping mill on Wandsworth Common on the corner of Windmill Rd.
An early 19th cent tower mill at Blenheim gardens, Brixton.

Bedfordshire
A very fine post mill at Stevington, 1770.

Buckinghamshire
A fine 17th cent mill at Brill.
A smock mill of the mid 17th cent at Lacey green, with its original wooden machinery.
The oldest mill in England (1627) is at Piston green.
A tower mill at Wendover 60 ft high with a large cap. Late 18th cent.

Essex
A good smock mill with its machinery, at Upminster. Early 19th cent.

Kent
The graceful smock mill 80 ft high dominates the village of Cranbrook. Shuttered sails. Early 19th cent.
A hexagonal smock mill built 1800 with 5 floors. On the lovely village green at Meopham.

Surrey
The oldest mill still working, at Outwood. Built in 1665.

Sussex
Restored as a memorial to Hilaire Belloc, this fine mill at Shipley, Horsham, was originally built in late 19th cent.
An open trestle mill at Nutley with sails.
Pollgate has an interesting mill of early 19th cent with all its internal mechanism intact.

Learning

Crafts

Several museums have craft classes for children including Geffrye Museum, Horniman Museum and the Natural History Museum. Also try the following:
Chelsea Pottery **4 M 10**
13 Radmor Walk SW1. 01-352 1366. A club for pottery making. Annual membership fee plus small hourly rates (for lessons only). Cost of materials extra. *OPEN 09.00-18.00 Mon-Fri. Special Sat groups for children.*

Cricket

Gover Cricket School
172 East hill SW18. 01-874 1796. A unique all-year-round school for anyone over the age of 8, with a lively club and social facilities.

Drama

The Anna Scher Children's Theatre at Islington
25b Elsworthy Rd NW3. 01-722 9835. (Theatre at Bentham Court Hall, off Essex Rd N1.) Mime, improvisation, poetry, dance (tap and modern), production in plays, stage technique and theory of the theatre for children aged 6-17. *OPEN Mon-Fri.* Phone for details.
National Youth Theatre **3 D 22**
Shaw Theatre, Euston Rd NW1. 01-388 0031. Age 14-21. Auditions are held in *Feb and Mar* to select the casts of plays to be rehearsed and performed during the summer holiday. Only cost is your own food and accommodation during the summer and sometimes a few weekends in between.
The Questors
Mattock Lane, Ealing W5. 01-567 5184. An excellent amateur theatre club with an 'Under 14' and a 'Junior drama' workshop. *Classes Mon-Fri 17.00 & 17.30. Some Sats.*

Dancing

English Folk Dance and Song Society
Cecil Sharp House, 2 Regent's Park Rd NW1. 01-485 2206. Dancing and folk singing for children over 7.
Rambert School of Ballet **1 A 8**
31 Pembridge Rd W11. 01-727 7233. Classes after school and on *Sat morning* for children from 4 upwards. This is the junior school of the internationally famous Ballet Rambert.
The Royal Academy of Dancing **4 P 4**
48 Vicarage Crescent SW11. 01-223 0091. General classes for toddlers as well as graded classes for older children. First-class tuition.
Royal Ballet School
White Lodge, Richmond Park, Surrey. 01-878 3929. This is the Lower school for children age 11 and over. Auditions are held to determine physical aptitude for training. Accepted children receive a full-time general education in addition to being taught ballet. Probably the most famous school of its kind.

Gymnastics

Ladywell Sports Centre
Ladywell Rd SE13. 01-690 2887. Exceptional centre for all age groups including the under 5's who have free usage of all facilities. *OPEN Mon-Thur 15.00-22.00. Small admission charge.*

Ice skating

Richmond Ice Rink
Richmond Bridge, Twickenham, Middx. 01-892 3646. Coaching for children *10.00-12.30, 14.30-17.00 Sats.* General skating *10.00-12.30, 14.30-17.00, 19.00-22.00. CLOSED Aug.*
Silver Blades Ice Rink
386 Streatham High Rd SW16. 01-769 7861. Coaching *09.00-10.00 Sat & Sun.*

Music

National Youth Orchestra of Great Britain
94 Park Lane, Croydon. 01-686 6237. Children between 11 and 16 can apply for audition to be trained, and once a member of the orchestra remain so until they are 21.
The Orchestral Association **2 I 21**
13 Archer St W1. 01-437 1588. Will recommend music teachers for any kind of instrument.

Painting & drawing

Camden Arts Centre
Arkwright Rd NW3. 01-435 2643. Classes in painting, pottery, printmaking, etching, sculpture. *OPEN 10.00-17.00 weekdays plus regular evening classes. Special children's courses on weekends.* Detailed prospectus available on request.

Puppetry

Educational Puppetry Association **3 H 25**
Battersea Town Hall, Lavender Hill SW11. 01-223 5356. *OPEN Wed & Thur until 19.15.*

Road Safety

Road Safety Classes
Organised by the individual boroughs. There are 'Tufty' classes for 3-7-year-olds and cycle-training classes for 9-12-year-olds. All classes are free.

Riding

For a list of approved riding schools write to the:
British Horse Society and Show Jumping Association
National Equestrian Society, Stoneleigh, Kenilworth, Warwickshire, Coventry 27192. Supply information about approved riding schools, breeding and events.

Ski-ing

CCPR National Recreation Centre
Norwood SE19. 01-778 0131. Here there is a dry ski slope and tuition.

Sport

Sports Council **2 E 21**
(London and South East Region). Portland Court, 158-176 Great Portland St W1. 01-580 9092. Can help with advice on various courses for children (such as judo, badminton, swimming, tennis and so on) which are held at their various centres throughout the year. As well as the Crystal Palace centre they also maintain residential centres at Bisham Abbey, Marlow (on the Thames); Lilleshall Hall, Shropshire; Plas y Brenin, Snowdonia and a National Sailing Centre at Cowes.

Swimming

Enquire at your local municipal baths for details of classes for children after school. Otherwise there is the:
CCPR Easter Holiday Course
at the National Recreation Centre, Norwood SE19. 01-778 0131. Graded classes from 5-year-old non-swimmers to those who want to improve at any age. Crash courses held also during summer and Christmas holidays.

Tennis

Tennis in the Parks
Apply to the Chief Officer of the Parks Dept, Cavell House, 2a Charing Cross Rd WC2. Will send details of classes for children over 15.

Scouts and guides

Associated with these are the Sea, Land and Air Scout and Ranger companies which are senior branches of the Scout and Guide Associations for those aged 15-21.
The Scout Association **I G 9**
Baden Powell House, Queensgate SW7. 01-584 2030. Headquarters of the movement. They will give you the address of your nearest company. Boys aged 8-11 become 'Cubs' and above that age Scouts.
Girl Guides Association **5 M 14**
17 Buckingham Palace Rd SW1. 01-834 6242. The equivalent movement to the above. For girls aged 7-10 there are 'Brownie' packs and at the age of 10 girls become Guides.

Helping others

Genuine help is welcomed in most communities; the following organisations will help to direct your efforts most usefully.
Task Force **1 F 2**
Clifford House, Edith Villas W14. 01-603 3100. Practical help welcomed wherever possible. Volunteers wanted for visiting the elderly, doing odd jobs, etc. Over 14 year-olds preferred.
Shelter **6 O 24**
157 Waterloo Rd SE1. 01-633 9377. Volunteers wanted for fund-raising to support Housing Aid Centres which assist families with emergency housing problems. Contact the Field Secretary.
Oxfam
4 Replingham Rd SW18. 01-874 7335. Will put you in touch with your local 'Young Oxfam Group'.
Friends of Animals League
Foal Farm, Jail Lane, Biggin Hill, Kent. Biggin Hill 72386. Send postage stamps to help them rescue animals.

Community Service Volunteers   **3 E 29**
237 Pentonville Rd N1. 01-278 6601. Produce a variety of publications full of unusual suggestions for helping in the community.

Playgrounds

Many London parks offer free play and educational activities under the control of experienced staff; for children of various age groups (mostly during the school holidays). Over 600 shows are held in London's parks each summer. Punch & Judy shows, puppets, children's hour, plays and open-air cinema are all popular and go round all the parks in special caravan theatres. Consult 'Looking for Leisure' published by GLC Parks Dept. 285 Albany Rd, Camberwell SE5. 01-701 3148/3151, or the local borough council.

Adventure Playgrounds
Consist of odd pieces of timber, canvas, old cars and various creative constructions to help children climb and become confident and adventurous. Run by Play Leadership staff who, together with the local community, organise Holiday Schemes for children otherwise unable to go away. *OPEN 11.30-20.00.*

Conventional Playgrounds
Found in most parks. Contain mostly swings, roundabouts, swingboats, slides and seesaws. *OPEN 07.00-19.00 or dusk.*

One O'clock Clubs
These are for children under five and are staffed and equipped like playparks. Various hobbies and educational creative activities are taught. Mothers are expected to remain with under fives. *OPEN weekdays 13.00-16.30. CLOSED 2 weeks at Xmas.*

Playparks
The general aim of the playpark is towards free play. Generally intended for children from 5 to 16. Usually have children's lavatories and wet weather shelters for indoor recreation. Parents are encouraged to enter the playpark except in the case of handicapped children. *OPEN 11.30-20.00 in summer, 09.30-dusk in winter or the same hours as the park.*

Fairs

There are over 200 fairs a week held in England during the summer; the following is a selection of some in London.

Bank Holiday Fairs
Blackheath, Hampstead Heath and Wormwood Scrubs *(Easter, Whitsun & Summer B. Hol.).*

Other Occasional Fairs
Clapham Common *(mid Apr)*, Crystal Palace *(early May & Aug)*, Tooting Common *(early May)*, Victoria Park *(early May).*

Children's theatre

Audiences at the BBC
Write to the ticket unit, Broadcasting House W1. Send an S.A.E. and state what type of programme you wish to see. Minimum age limits vary according to what type of programme is on, so state children's age.

Cockpit Theatre
Gateforth St NW8. 01-262 7907. *OPEN Sat 10.00-13.00 Sept-July.* Minimum age is 14. Free.

Curtain Theatre
26 Commercial St E1. 01-247 6788. ILEA drama centre catering for the whole educational age range. Junior Theatre Club on *Sat mornings.* No need to have acting ability, there are courses in Do-it-Yourself backstage work. Summer schools.

Dogg's Troupe
Interaction Trust, 14 Talacre Rd NW5. 01-267 1422. The Troupe aims to involve children in street theatre and interest them in more community projects. Participatory indoor theatre is organised for children of all ages.

Dolphin Theatre Company   **3 D 22**
Shaw Theatre, 100 Euston Rd NW1. 01-388 1394. A professional company formed by the National Youth Theatre. Productions by Shakespeare as well as new playwrights are performed by such exciting young actors as Helen Mirren, John Stride and Simon Ward. Age range 14-21.

Greenwich Young People's Theatre
Stage Centre, Burrage Rd SE19. 01-854 1316. Occasional performances by the Bowsprit Company at the Greenwich theatre during the day. Evening and weekend workshop activities at the Stage Centre, a converted church. Drama and art classes.

Little Angel Theatre   **3 D 33**
14 Dagmar Passage, Cross St N1. 01-226 1787. A really excellent puppet theatre which performs both traditional and modern fairy tales and stories. Shows every day *at 15.00* (school holidays). Otherwise on *Sat and Sun only 15.00 (and 11.00 Sat morning).*

Mermaid Theatre Molecule Club   **6 M 27**
Puddle Dock EC4. 01-236 9521. Visually exciting theatrical experiment aiming to bridge the gap between science and art by illustrating principles of light, heat, sound, etc., through sketches, song and dance routines, demonstrations and plays. 7-11-year-olds. *Performances in spring & autumn.* Phone for details.

Thames Television
Live audiences for several children's hour programmes. Write stating age to the Ticket Office, Thames TV, Television House, 306 Euston Rd NW1.

Unicorn Theatre Club   **2 I 22**
Arts Theatre, Gt Newport St WC2. 01-836 3334. Plays for 4-14-year-olds. Improvisation sessions during holidays and at weekends. Films and occasional concerts. (M).

Young Vic   **6 O 24**
The Cut, Waterloo SE1. 01-928 6363. Young repertory company putting on a good choice of revivals and new experimental theatre. Specially written children's plays and adaptations of Shakespeare.

Children's holidays

Some of the holidays listed under 'Students' London' will also be suitable for older children.

Children's Holidays
PGL Adventure House, Ross-on-Wye, Hereford. Ross-on-Wye 3311. For 7-18-year-olds. Canoeing, pony trekking, sailing and cruising under expert and responsible guidance in Britain and abroad.

Council for Colony Holidays
Linden Manor, Upper Colwall. Colwall 40501. Group holidays for children 9-14. Held at large centres in England, Wales and Scotland. Games, musical, handicraft and adventure activities are organised.

Junior Holidays
25 Ludlow Way N2. 01-883 0177. Seaside holidays at Littlehampton for 6-13-year-olds costing £24.00 excluding fares.

John Ridgeway School of Adventure
Ardmore, Rhiconich, By Lairg, Sutherland. Kinlochbervie 229. Mountaineering, rock climbing, canoeing, sailing and orienteering in isolated countryside. Dormitories in wooden buildings on the shores of a remote sea loch.

Knight Bridge Stables
Sway, Hants, Sway 2271. British Horse Society approved riding school on the edge of the New Forest. Specialise in residential riding holidays and courses for children of all nationalities, in small groups. 10-18 yrs.

Outward Bound Trust   **2 G 21**
14 Oxford St W1. 01-637 4951. Strenuous, tough and adventurous 4-week holiday course for 14-20-year-olds.

Youth Hostel Association
National Office, Trevelyan House, 8 St Stephens Hill, St Albans, Herts. Have a large selection of open-air holidays for youngsters which are specially geared to their age, ability and interests. Or you can set off on your own and make use of their hostels which are spartan but safe, cheap and well supervised.

Exchanges

Amitié Internationale des Jeunes
Beaver House, 10a Woodborough Rd SW15. 01-788 6857. Exchanges between French and British schoolchildren 10-20 years old. Escorts are provided on the journey between London and Paris.

Educational Interchange Council   **3 F 24**
43 Russell Square WC1. 01-580 9137. Groups of children travel under escort to stay *en famille* in France and Germany.

Robertson's Educational Travel Service
144 Willoughdy Rd NW3. 01-435 4907. Long established. Careful matching up of families for exchanges mainly between France and England, though arrangements are made for exchanges with other countries. Also take children as paying guests.

For parents

Useful organisations which will help you to keep children occupied and happy.

Children's parties

Arnold Stoker's Entertainment Agency
3? Kings Rd SW19. 01-540 1191. Every type of entertainment: puppets, clowns, films, cartoons, conjurors and ventriloquists for children aged 3-14.

Children's Party Agency   **1 B 8**
32 Edge St W8. 01-727 8476. Provide entertainers according to age groups: conjurors, Punch and Judy and puppet shows for 3-7-year-olds; film shows for over 7's.

The Kensington Carnival Co   **4 J 4**
123 Ifield Rd SW10. 01-370 4358. Provide entertainers, film shows, presents and toys. Hire out slides, see-saws, roundabouts and children's equipment. Also low tables and chairs, paper table ware etc.

Piet Tovenaar
5a Sedgemere Ave N2. 01-444 9215. A true professional, with 25 years' experience of organising parties. Games, magic, films, puppets, Punch and Judy and ventriloquism.

Advisory Centre for Education ·
32 Trumpington St, Cambridge, Cambridge 51456. Subs include 12-monthly issues of 'Where?' Advice on courses, schools, methods and further education.

Children's Book Centre   **1 C 8**
140 Kensington Church St W8. 01-229 9646. Publish lists of children's books several times a year.

Junior Jaunts   **1 I 3**
Children's Tours, 13a Harriet Walk SW1. 01-235 4750. Organise carefully supervised river trips, sight-seeing and 'energy outlet' tours. From £8. Parties of 6 or 7. Library story-telling sessions.

Nursery schools and kindergartens

House-on-the-hill Nursery
33 Hoop Lane NW1. 01-455 0856. 2-6 years.

Stepping Stones Kindergarten
33 Fitzjohn's Avenue NW3. 01-435 9641. 3½-8½ years.

Walton Day Nursery   **2 H 13**
239 Knightsbridge SW7. 01-584 9847. (Near Harrods.) 1 year-5 years.

World's End Montessori School   **4 L 5**
Congregational Hall, Edith Grove SW10. 3-5 years.

Nursery schools: play centres

Held on existing school premises. Provide a safe place for children of 5-11 yrs to play and take part in educational games, music and dancing under skilled supervision. Evenings only during term-time; all day during holidays. Write for list of schools to:

Inner London Education Authority.   **5 N 22**
County Hall, Westminster Bridge SE1. 01-633 5000.

Pre-school Playgroups Association   **2 H 20**
57-59 Beak St W1. 01-434 1798. Organised by the ILEA. Will put you in touch with an approved playgroup in your area.

Children's shopping

Bookshops

Harrods have an excellent children's book department.

The Children's Book Centre   **1 C 8**
229 Kensington High St W8. 01-937 0862. The largest selection in London with 7,000 titles.

G. Heywood Hill   **2 I 17**
10 Curzon St W1. 01-629 0647. Good general collection of new and second-hand books including a large stock of children's books.

Hatchards   **2 I 20**
187 Piccadilly W1. 01-734 3201. Good variety of children's books well-displayed.

The Owl and the Pussy Cat
11 Flask Walk NW3. 01-435 5342. Good selection.

Carnival novelties

Barnum's   **1 D 2**
67 Hammersmith Rd W14. 01-602 1211. Masks, costumes, fair-ground novelties, balloons, flags, barrel organs and fancy dress.

The Theatre Zoo   **5 J 22**
28 New Row, St Martin's Lane WC2. 01-836 3150. Animal costumes, grotesque and unusual face masks, false feet, hands and moustaches.

Cigarette cards

London Cigarette Card Co
34 Wellesley Rd W4. 01-994 2346. An authority on picture-card collecting. Has the biggest stock in the world — 10,000 different series of cigarette, tea and other picture-cards dating from 1880 to the present day.

Universal Cigarette Card Co
228 London Rd, Twickenham, Middx. 01-892 3577.

Doll's hospitals

Dolls' Hospital   **4 J 1**
16 Dawes Rd SW6. 01-385 2081. Casualty department for broken limbs; spare part surgery.

Dolls' houses

The Dolls' House   **2 A 16**
4 Broadley St NW8. 01-723 1418. Every kind of dolls house from cardboard cut-outs to handmade scale models, antique and modern.

Fireworks

Meierhans   **5 Q 22**
113b Kennington Rd SE11. 01-735 5689. Stock fire works all the year round.

Hairdressers

D H Evans   **2 G 21**
318 Oxford St W1. 01-629 8800. Good department for boys up to 5 and girls up to 15. *OPEN Mon, Wed & Sat.*

Harrods   **2 I 14**
Knightsbridge SW1. 01-730 1234. Boys up to 10, girls up to 14.

Meenys   **4 K 11**
163 Draycott Avenue SW3. 01-581 2163. A painless way to get cropped amid pinball machines, light shows, penny arcades, milk shakes and a juke box.

Magic, jokes and tricks

Barnums   **1 D 2**
67 Hammersmith Rd W14. 01-602 1211.

Davenports   **3 H 23**
51 Great Russell St WC1. 01-405 8524.

The Theatre Zoo   **5 J 22**
8 New Row, St Martin's Lane WC2. 01-836 3150. A selection of furry bodies and rubbery heads to change you into a multitude of creatures, including Messrs Heath and Wilson. Good value children's make-up pack.

Models

Cherry's
62 Sheen Rd, Richmond, Surrey. 01-940 2454. Second-hand model steam engines & ships.

Chuffs Model Railway Specialists   **2 A 17**
116 Lisson Grove NW1. 01-402 4021. New and second-hand to swap or buy. *OPEN 10.00-18.00, Mon-Sat.*

Hamblings Models   **2 I 22**
29 Cecil Court, Charing Cross Rd WC2. 01-836 4704. More complex models for the enthusiast.

Model Aircraft Supplies Ltd
207 Camberwell Rd SE5. 01-703 4562.

Pet shops

See 'Animals' under the 'Shopping' section.

Battersea Dogs Home   **4 R 8**
4 Battersea Park Rd SW8. 01-622 4454. Unwanted and stray dogs and cats are kept here. Visitors only welcome when purchasing or claiming a stray animal. For claiming dogs *OPEN 09.30-17.00, 14.00-16.00 Sat, Sun & pub hols.* For purchasing dogs *OPEN 09.30-17.00 Mon-Fri.* Care for cats *Tues & Thur 15.30-16.00.*

Harrods Pet Shop   **2 I 14**
Knightsbridge SW1. 01-730 1234. The famous selection of animals and pets varies according to availability. *OPEN Wed until 19.00.*

Regent Pet Stores
33-37 Parkway NW1. 01-485 5163. Sell a large variety of birds, reptiles and fish as well as pups and mice.

Stamps

Stanley Gibbons   **6 K 23**
391 Strand WC2. 01-836 8444.

Toys

Most of the following stores will send mail order catalogues on request. Harrods, Selfridges and Heals all have good toy departments.

Abbatt   **2 E 19**
74 Wigmore St W1. 01-487 4382. Educational toys for children up to 8 years old. From small wooden puzzles to building blocks and climbing frames.

Davenports 3 H 23
51 Great Russell St WC2. 01-405 8524. Jokes, tricks and puzzles for the practical joker.

James Galt 2 G 20
30 Great Marlborough St W1. 01-734 0829. Sensible, simple toys for up to 8 years old.

Hamleys 2 H 20
200 Regent St W1. 01-734 3161. Have nearly everything. All ages. See also the 'First Five Room' in Kingly St W1.

The Owl and the Pussycat
11 Flask Walk NW3. 01-435 5342.

Pollocks Toy Shop 2 F 22
1 Scala St WC1. 01-636 3452. Good traditional and modern toys. Toy theatres.

Tridias Toy Shop 3 I 23
44 Monmouth St WC2. 01-240 2369. Modern, wooden toys.

Children's clothes

Laura Ashley 5 K 12
40 Sloane St SW1. 01-235 9728. Pastoral prints on Welsh cotton lawn, corduroys and drills, make-up aprons, smocks, shirts and dungarees. Straw boaters with lots of flowers.

C & A Modes 2 E 17
501-519 Oxford St W1. 01-629 7272. (Main branch) Good selection of inexpensive clothes for children up to 14.

Children's Bazaar 5 K 12
162 Sloane St SW1. 01-730 8901. Good quality second-hand clothes for 1 year-olds to teenagers.

Colts
5 Hampstead High St NW3. 01-435 7387. An ex-theatre

critic runs this boys' boutique. Imported continental casual clothes.

Mary Davies 2 H 17
12 Queen St W1. 01-499 1696. Delightful children's wear in Irish wools and wool blends. Arran jumpers.

Hand in Hand
149 Broadhurst Gardens NW6. 01-624 4466. Design their own unusual clothes for children up to 16 years. Laura Ashley and Liberty fabrics. Also suede, leather and imported French and Scandinavian clothes.

Harrods 2 I 14
Knightsbridge SW1. 01-730 1234. Traditional source of children's clothes for every purpose.

Kids in Gear 2 H 20
51 Carnaby St W1. 01-437 6009. Trendy clothes and denims for 1-14 year olds.

Littlewoods 2 G 21
207 Oxford St W1. 01-437 4171. Good cheap range of children's clothes. Many branches.

Marks and Spencer 2 G 21
Marble Arch Store, 458 Oxford St W1. 01-486 6207. (Largest branch, first to get the new ranges.) French mums flocks to buy the reasonably priced kilts, sandals, jumpers, macs and underwear; English ones tend to take M & S for granted as being best value for children's clothes.

Mothercare 2 E 17
461 Oxford St W1. 01-629 6621. (Main branch) Good quality clothes at reasonable prices for children under 5. Free catalogue available for mail order.

Rowes 2 G 19
170 New Bond St W1. 01-734 9711. Young children's riding and tailored clothes.

Small Wonder 4 L 4
296 Kings Rd SW3. 01-352 9608. Up to date clothes from France, Spain and Finland. Toddlers can play on the merry-go-round, or with stuffed toys.

Scholar's London

Reference libraries

There are over 400 specialised libraries in London. The following selection are the most important and have been classified in sections to help both the enquiring visitor and the serious research worker. The British Museum can usually finalise problems of research because of its vast collections. It is however, busy and understaffed, so try other libraries first. Public Libraries, maintained by each Borough, offer access to magazines, newspapers and reference books. Some have large reference departments specialising in certain subjects.

General

Government Departments
Extensive collections. Available by appointment only. Official publications, history and information associated with the department. The following few (of many) have particularly large libraries: Treasury; Home Office; Foreign Office; Colonial Office; Board of Trade; Army Dept; Navy Dept; Dept of Environment.

The British Museum 3 G 24
Great Russell St WC1. 01-636 1555. More than 8 million volumes. European printed books on all subjects, oriental books, manuscripts from 3rd cent BC, maps, music and large collections of prints and drawings. It is also a National Copyright Library and holds one copy of every printed book published in the UK. Ticket. *OPEN 10.00-17.00 Mon-Sat, 14.30-18.00 Sun. CLOSED G. Fri, Xmas, Box, New Year's.* Lecture tours. Free

The British Museum Newspaper Library
Colindale Avenue NW9. 01-205 6039. National collection of newspapers from the UK and overseas countries. London newspapers prior to 1801 hled at British Museum main building. *OPEN 10.00-17.00 Mon-Fri to adults over 21.* Free.

London Library 5 J 20
14 St James's Square SW1. 01-930 7705. A writers' and scholars' library with many distinguished authors

among its members. Permanent collection of standard and authoritative works dating from the 16th cent including a unique stock of foreign language books. 700,000 vols, most of which are on open shelves. Annual membership fee enables readers to take out 10 books at a time.

Art & Architecture

Courtauld Institute of Art 2 D 17
20 Portman Square W1. 01-935 9292. (Interesting Robert Adam interiors.) 66,000 volumes on the history of art. *Appointment only.* Also the Wick Library, a collection of a million photographs, reproductions of paintings and drawings. *OPEN 10.00-18.00 Mon-Fri.*

Fine Arts Library 5 J 21
Central Reference Library, St Martin's St WC2. 01-930 3274. English and European books. Painting, drawing and sculpture. Periodicals, reproductions, transparencies. Also the Preston Blake Library, which contains about 600 vols on and about William Blake. Ticket. *OPEN 10.00-19.00 Mon-Fri, 10.00-17.00 Sat.*

National Monuments Record 2 H 20
23 Savile Row W1. 01-734 6010. The historic architecture of England. Library of over 800,000 photographs, measured drawings and prints. *OPEN 10.00-17.30 Mon-Fri. CLOSED Easter, B. Hols, Xmas.* Free.

Royal Academy of Arts 2 I 19
Burlington House, Piccadilly W1. 01-734 9052. Fine Arts. 15,000 volumes, original drawings, mainly 18th-19th cent. *OPEN to students and researchers Mon-Fri 10.00-13.00 & 14.00-17.00.*

Royal Institute of British Architects 2 D 21
66 Portland Place W1. 01-580 5533. 80,000 volumes. Architecture and related arts, from 15th cent to the present day. The most extensive collection of architectural drawing in the world, including practically all the surviving drawing of Palladio. *OPEN Mon 10.00-17.00, Tue-Fri 10.00-20.00, Sat 10.00-13.30. CLOSED 3 weeks in summer.* Free.

Royal Society of Arts   6   K 23
8 John Adam St WC2. 01-839 2366. 11,000 books on industrial art and design. Pictures. *Appointment only.*

St Bride Printing Library   6   L 27
St Bride Institute, Bride Lane, EC4. 01-353 4660. A public reference library of typography and printing. *OPEN Mon-Fri 09.30-17.30. CLOSED B. Hols.* Free.

Sir John Soane's Museum Library   3   I 25
13 Lincolns Inn Fields WC2. 01-405 2107. Art and architecture, 15th-19th cent architectural drawings, including many of the drawings from the office of Robert and James Adam and those from Soane's own office. *By appointment.*

Victoria & Albert Museum   1   H 10
Cromwell Rd SW7. 01-589 6371. Nearly half a million volumes on fine and applied arts of all countries and periods. Sculpture, ceramics, silver, furniture, musical instruments, English costume. Prints and drawings department has extensive collections dealing with art, architecture, pure and applied design, graphics, typography and crafts. *OPEN 10.00-18.00 Mon-Sat, 14.30-17.50 Sun. CLOSED Pub & B. Hols.* Free lectures but times vary. Free.

British Museum
The Department of Prints and Drawings contains a very extensive collection of original drawings, etchings and engraving from all sources.

Ecclesiastic

Dr Williams Library   3   E 24
14 Gordon Square WC1. 01-387 3727. Modern and 17th-18th cent books on theology, Byzantine history, Dissenting history. 112,000 volumes. *OPEN 10.00-17.00 Mon-Fri (18.30 Tue & Thur). CLOSED B. Hol.* Free.

Jews' College   3   G 24
11 Montague Place W1. 01-723 9974. Hebraica and Judaica. 50,000 books and manuscripts. *OPEN 10.00-16.45 Mon-Thur, 10.00-13.00 Fri. CLOSED Aug, B. Hols, Jewish Hols.* Free.

Lambeth Palace   5   P 21
SE1. 01-928 6222. The archives of ecclesiastical history from medieval times, 120,000 books, 2,500 manuscripts records. *OPEN to students on production of a letter of introduction.*

Sion College   6   L 26
Victoria embankment EC4 (entrance in John Capenter St). 01-353 7983. Theological books from 17th cent to present day. 100,000 volumes. *OPEN 10.00-17.00 Mon-Fri. Check closing times.* Free.

St Paul's Cathedral   6   M 28
St Paul's churchyard EC4. Cathedral library of 17th-18th cent. Archives from 1099. Drawings, models and manuscripts on the Great Plague and Fire. 1,300 volumes. *Appointment only.*

Westminster Abbey Chapter Library & Muniment Room   5   M 20
The Cloisters, Westminster Abbey SW1. 01-222 4233. 16th-18th cent theology and history of Westminster Abbey. Archives from before the Norman Conquest. 14,000 volumes. *Appointment only. OPEN Mon-Fri 10.00-13.00 & 14.00-17.00.*

British Museum
Extensive collection of books and manuscripts from all sources. Dept. Oriental printed books + mss.

Film, sound, photo

British Film Institute   2   H 22
81 Dean St W1. 01-437 4355. The National archive. Over 20,000 films, 750,000 original stills, 19,000 books and scripts 1,300 on the cinema, periodicals. *OPEN Tue-Fri at various times.* Free.

British Institute of Recorded Sound   1   H 10
29 Exhibition Rd SW7. 01-589 6603. National archive of sound recordings. 180,000 discs, tapes and cylinders. Also a library, consisting mainly of microfilms, but some books relating to sound. *OPEN for research by appointment only. 10.00-18.00 Mon-Fri.* Free.

Central Film Library
Government Buildings, Bromyard Avenue, Acton W3. 01-743 5555. 2,000 titles of documentaries and shorts on a wide range of subjects from arts to industry, on hire.

Imperial War Museum   6   Q 23
Lambeth Rd SE1. 01-735 8922. 3½ million photographs of both world wars. 20 million ft of film dealing with all aspects of war since 1914. Free cinema shows *Tue-Fri 12.00. Sat, Sun 14.30.* 100,000 books and pamphlets, collections of British and foreign documents.

Mansell Collection   1   A 9
42 Linden Gardens W2. 01-229 5475. Will lend prints and photographs of engravings for reproduction purposes. Specialise in antiquarian and historical subjects. *Appointments only.*

Radio Times Hulton Picture Library   2   D 19
35 Marylebone High St W1. 01-580 5577. Six million photographs and prints on every conceivable subject. Available for reproduction. *By appointment.*

Geography

British Museum
Map room holds 10,000 volumes of maps and 500,000 sheet maps. *OPEN Mon-Sat 09.30-16.30.*

Royal Geographical Society   1   G 11
1 Kensington Gore SW7. 01-589 5466. Geography in all aspects, 100,000 books, 500,000 maps together with several thousand atlases. Public Map Room *OPEN Mon-Fri 09.30-17.30. CLOSED B. Hols, & Jun-mid Jul.* Library open to Fellows and associates of the RGS or by appointment for reading — £1.00 per day.

History

British Museum
Dept of Manuscripts; over 200,000 items from 3rd cent BC (but Egytian papyri kept in Dept of Egyptian Antiquities). Dept of Printed Books; extensive collections. *OPEN Mon-Fri 10.00-17.00, Sat 10.00-13.00.*

Guildhall Library   6   M 30
Baring Hall Ct EC2. 01-606 3030. A general reference library, 200,000 volumes and documents of London topography and history, general reference works and City Business library. *OPEN 09.30-17.00. CLOSED Sun & B. Hols.*

Institute of Archaelogy   3   E 24
University of London, 31-34 Gordon Square WC1. 01-387 6052. Archaeology, particularly Europe, Western Asia, Latin America, world prehistory and human environment. 20,000 volumes. *OPEN Mon-Fri 09.30-18.00, Sat 10.00-17.00.* Free.

Institute of Classical Studies   3   E 24
31-34 Gordon Square EC1. 01-387 7697. Includes the Hellenic and Roman Societies Library. 40,000 volumes. Classical Antiquity. *OPEN Mon-Fri 09.30-18.00, Sat 10.00-17.00. CLOSED at various times in summer.*

Institute of Historical Research   3   G 24
University of London, Senate House W1. 01-636 0272. 100,000 volumes. Seminar libraries providing the principal printed sources of British and foreign history. *OPEN 09.00-21.00 Mon-Fri, 09.00-17.00 Sat.* Free.

National Maritime Museum Library
Romney Rd, Greenwich SE10. 01-858 4422. Large collection of prints and drawings. 50,000 books, maps, charts. Portraits. *OPEN Mon-Fri 10.00-13.00 & 14.00-17.00. (Sat open by prior application.)* Ticket only.

Society of Antiquaries   2   I 19
Burlington House, Piccadilly W1. 01-734 0193. Archaeological and antiquarian research only. 130,000 volumes. *Appointment only.*

Law & public records

Inns of Court
The principal law libraries, only available by special permission.
Inner Temple: 80,000 volumes.
Middle Temple: 95,000 volumes.
Lincoln's Inn: 100,000 volumes.
Gray's Inn: 10,000 volumes only (most were destroyed in the last war).

Institute of Advanced Legal Studies   3   F 24
University of London, 25 Russell Square WC1. 01-580 4868. Centre for legal studies. 105,000 volumes. *Appointment only to academic researchers at postgraduate level.*

Public Record Office   6   K 26
Chancery Lane WC2. 01-405 0741. Government archives and records of the Courts from 11th cent. Ticket. *OPEN 09.30-17.00 Mon-Fri. CLOSED B. Hols.*

British Museum
State Paper Room. *OPEN to 21.00 Tue-Thur, to 17.00 Mon, Fri, Sat.*

Literature

Arts Council of Great Britain
Poetry Library 105 Piccadilly W1. A reference and lending library. *OPEN 10.00-17.00 Mon-Fri, 10.00-19.00 Thur.* Free.

British Museum
Great Russell St WC1. 01-636 1555. The most comprehensive literary collection in London of printed books and manuscripts. *OPEN to 21.00 Tue-Thur, 17.00 Mon, Fri & Sat.*

Medicine

British Medical Association Library   3   E 24
Tavistock Square WC1. 01-387 4499. Over 80,000 books and 2,000 modern medical periodicals, British and foreign. *OPEN 09.00-17.00 Mon-Fri, until 21.00*

Wed. By appointment only to doctors and BMA members. Free.

Institute of Psychiatry
De Crespigny Park, Denmark Hill SE5. 01-703 5411. Comprehensive collection of books and journals on psychiatry, psychology, neurology, biochemistry and allied subjects. More than 20,000 volumes and 20,000 reprints. *OPEN times vary.* For members only.

Medical Research Council
The Ridgeway NW7. 01-959 3666. All branches of medical science. 60,000 books and reprints. *Members only, or by application to director.*

Pharmaceutical Society   **3   H 24**
17 Bloomsbury Square WC1. 01-405 8967. Pharmaceutical research. Historical collections of pharmacopoeias, herbals and botanical works. 40,000 volumes. *Appointment only.*

Royal College of Physicians   **2   C 22**
11 St Andrews Place NW1. 01-935 1174. History and biography of medicine. Medical portraits. 40,000 volumes and pamphlets. *Appointment only.*

Royal College of Surgeons   **6   J 25**
Lincoln's Inn Fields WC2. 01-405 3474. Medical and surgical books and journals including large historical collections on anatomy and surgery. 140,000 volumes. Portraits. *OPEN 10.00-17.00 Mon-Fri. CLOSED Aug. For medical profession only or by appointment.*

Royal Society of Medicine   **2   E 19**
1 Wimpole St W1. 01-580 2070. All aspects of medicine. 500,000 volumes. *OPEN Mon-Sat. Letter of introduction from a Fellow necessary.*

Wellcome Institute of the History of Medicine   **3   D 24**
183 Euston Rd NW1. 01-387 4688. History of medicine and allied sciences. Original texts. 250,000 volumes. *Mon-Sat 10.00-17.00. CLOSED Pub. Hols. Free.*

Westminster Public Library (Medical)   **2   B 17**
Marylebone Rd NW1. 01-828 8070 ext 4039. Includes nursing, dentistry, psychiatry, speech and music therapy. Textbooks and periodicals. *OPEN Mon-Fri 09.30-20.00, Sat 09.30-17.00. Ticket.*

British Museum
Historical medical books. All current British clinical publications and foreign periodicals. *OPEN to 21.00 Tue-Thur, to 17.00 Mon, Fri & Sat.*

Music & drama

BBC Music Library   **2   E 21**
156 Great Portland St W1. 01-580 4468. All forms of printed music. *OPEN by appointment only 09.30-17.30. Free.*

British Museum
Printed music and books about music held in the Department of Printed Books. MSS material in Dept of MSS.

British Theatre Centre   **2   D 22**
9-10 Fitzroy Square W1. 01-387 2666. Comprehensive collection of plays and critical works on the theatre. 200,000 volumes. *OPEN Mon-Fri 10.00-17.00 (Wed 19.30). Members only. Free*

Central Music Library   **5   M 14**
Buckingham Palace Rd SW1. 01-730 8921. (Westminster Public Library). Books on music, scores, sheet music, song collections. *Ticket 09.30-19.00 (Sat. 09.30-17.00).*

Natural science

British Museum
The Sir Hans Sloane collection and the library of Sir Joseph Banks is rich in natural history.

Commonwealth Institute of Entomology   **1   G 9**
56 Queen's Gate SW7. 01-584 0067. Applied entomology. 17,000 books, reprints, periodicals, 61,000 pamphlets. *OPEN 09.00-17.00. CLOSED Sat, Sun. Free.*

Institute of Geological Sciences   **1   H 10**
Exhibition Rd SW7. 01-589 3444. Formerly the Geological Survey Museum. Geology and mineralogy. 100,000 books, maps, photographs. *OPEN 10.00-16.30 Mon-Sat. (ClOSED 13.00-14.00 Sat.) Free.*

Geological Society   **2   I 19**
Burlington House, Piccadilly W1. 01-734 5673. Geology. 300,000 volumes and papers. 100,000 maps. *OPEN by appointment only. 9.30-17.00 Mon-Fri. (Wed 20.00).*

Linnean Society   **2   I 19**
Burlington House, Piccadilly W1. 01-734 1040. Botany and zoology. Historical manuscripts. 90,000 volumes. Portraits of naturalists. *Appointment only.*

Natural History Museum   **1   H 9**
Cromwell Rd SW7. 01-589 6323. Botany, zoology, entomology, palaeontology, mineralogy and anthropology. Large collection of manuscripts, drawings and prints. 370,000 volumes. *OPEN 10.00-18.00 Mon-Sat,*

14.30-18.00 Sun. CLOSED G.Fri, Xmas. Free.

Royal Botanic Gardens
Kew, Surrey. 01-940 1171. Botany and travel. Prints and drawings. Extensive and historical record of millions of dried specimens of plants from all over the world. 100,000 volumes. *OPEN to scientists only 10.00-17.00 approx. CLOSED at times varying with season. Free.*

Royal Entomological Society   **1   G 9**
41 Queen's Gate SW7. 01-584 8361. Entomology. 50,000 early works, monographs and journals, pamphlets. *Appointment only.*

Royal Horticultural Society   **5   N 17**
Lindley Library, Vincent Square SW1. 01-834 4333. 36,000 volumes of horticultural and botanical books. Collection of original 18th and 19th cent plant drawings. Large number of periodicals. *Appointment by written application to the Secretary.*

Zoological Society
Regent's Park Zoo NW1. 01-722 3333. 120,000 volumes on zoology and related subjects, original zoological drawings and prints. Photographic library. *OPEN to members or by appointment only.*

Politics, economics & social sciences

British Library of Political & Economic Science   **6   J 25**
London School of Economics, Houghton St WC2. 01-405 7686. Social science. 50,000 books and manuscripts. *OPEN to research scholars by special permit at various times during term, Aug 10.00-17.00 daily. CLOSED Sat, July-Aug. Free.*

British Museum
Extensive collections of historical and current works. *OPEN to 21.00 Tue-Thur; to 17.00 Mon, Fri & Sat.*

House of Lords   **5   N 20**
Palace of Westminster SW1. 01-219 3000. Law and parliamentary history. 100,000 volumes, and manuscripts. *OPEN to persons undertaking research of volumes not available elsewhere. By application to Head Librarian.*

Institute of Banker's Library   **6   N 30**
10 Lombard St EC3. 01-623 3531. Comprehensive professional library on social scieces. 30,000 volumes. *Appointment only to non-members.*

Science

Chemical Society   **2   I 19**
Burlington House, Piccadillly W1. 01-734 9971. Chemistry. Early works, periodical. 70,000 volumes. *Appointment only.*

Institution of Civil Engineers   **5   M 20**
Great George St SW1. 01-839 3611. All branches of engineering; 19th cent engineering history. Film library. 100,000 books and pamphlets. *OPEN 09.15-17.30 Mon-Fri. Members only.*

Ministry of Agriculture   **5   L 22**
Whitehall Place SW1. 01-839 7711. Agriculture, fisheries and food. 150,000 volumes.

National Reference Library of Science & Invention   **6   J 26**
Holborn Division, 25 Southampton Buildings, Chancery Lane WC2. 01-405 8721. Formerly known as the Patent Office library. *OPEN Mon-Fri 09.30-21.00. Sat 10.00-13.00.*
Bayswater Division, 10 Porchester Gardens W2. **1   A 10**
OPEN 09.30-17.30 Mon-Fri. CLOSED Sat.
Contemporary literature of science and technology. Nearly 30,000 periodicals, over 10 million patent specification from many countries available for reference.

Royal Aeronautical Society   **2   I 16**
4 Hamilton Place W1. 01-499 3515. One of the finest collections in the world of historical and modern aeronautical books, prints and photographs. *OPEN 09.30-17.00 Mon-Fri. Appointment only.*

Royal Astronomical Society   **2   I 19**
Burlington House, Piccadilly W1. 01-734 4582. 25,000 volumes. Astronomy and geophysics. Photographic library. Portraits. *Letter of introduction from a Fellow necessary.*

Royal Institution of Gt Britain   **2   I 19**
21 Albemarle St W1. 01-493 0669. General science and history of science since 1799. Many complete scientific periodicals. Biography. Portraits. 50,000 volumes. *OPEN to the public for reference purposes, 10.00-17.30 Mon-Fri. CLOSED B.Hols. Free.*

Science Museum   **1   H 10**
Exhibition Rd SW7. 01-589 6371. The national library of pure and applied science. Holds all the important scientific publications. British and foreign. Portraits. More than 400,000 volumes. *OPEN 10.00-18.00 Mon-Sat, 14.30-18.00 Sun. CLOSED B.Hols. Free lectures at 13.00 Mon, Wed & Fri, at 15.00 Sat. Free.*

Student's London

London's students are as vital and active as students anywhere in the world. Nowhere is it more exciting to be a student than in London. Cheap theatre and entertainment abound (see the section 'Theatres, cinemas and music') and there are many restaurants offering unusual and inexpensive food ranging from macrobiotic to Indian (see 'Eating and drinking'). London has some of the best stocked reference libraries in the world (see the section 'Reference libraries'). For additional practical information a useful book is 'Nicholson's Students' London' 75p.

Grants & charitable trusts

Advisory Centre of Education
32 Trumpington St, Cambridge. Publishes 'Grants for Higher Education' which gives detailed information of ILEA grants, educational charities and trusts. Sponsorship by industry.

Association of Commonwealth Universities 3 E 24
36 Gordon Sq WC1. 01-387 8572. Publishes 'Scholarships Guide for Commonwealth Postgraduate Students' which gives details of awards to all Commonwealth and UK postgraduates studying in UK and Commonwealth countries.

British Council   **2 G 18**
65 Davies St W1. 01-499 8011. Publishes 'Scholarships Abroad' listing scholarships to British students by overseas governments and universities. Also offers grants to mature foreign postgraduate students wishing to study in the UK.

National Union of Students   **3 E 24**
3 Ensleigh St WC1. 01-387 1277. Maintains an educational grants advisory service and publishes an invaluable booklet 'Educational Charities' which gives details of the type of grant made by individual charities throughout Britain and what qualifications are necessary. Also publishes 'Grants' Handbook and Local Education Authority Awards with a breakdown of what constitutes eligibility for ILEA grants and an analysis of ILEA attitudes to particular circumstances.

Useful organisations

British Council   **2 G 18**
65 Davies St W1. 01-499 8011. Cultural body with language courses for overseas students. Will meet the student on arrival in GB, help find accommodation and assist generally with student welfare and education. Hostels and student centre.

British Youth Council   **3 D 25**
57 Chalton St NW1. 01-387 7559. Co-ordinating agency for all national voluntary youth organisations specialising in international youth work.

Hillel Foundation   **3 E 24**
1-2 Endsleigh St WC1. 01-388 0801. National federation of Jewish students in the UK; helps Jewish students with accommodation, meals and all sorts of other problems.

Inner London Education Authority   **5 N 22**
County Hall SE1. 01-633 3441. General information about education for British and overseas students in the inner London area.

National Union of Students   **3 e 24**
3 Endsleigh St WC1. 01-387 1277. 770,000 students are members. Represents students' rights. Organises social, cultural and educational events.

Centre of Help and Advice for Newcomers to Nursing Education and Life in the UK   **2 4 19**
Royal College of Nursing, Henrietta Place W1. 01-580 2646. Advisory Service, orientation courses and hospitality schemes.

Student Christian Movement
Wick Court, Wick nr Bristol. Abson 3377. Interdenominational and open to all students. Local and international branches. Meetings, reference library and monthly magazine.

Social clubs & societies

Federation of University Women   **4 M 8**
Crosby Hall, Cheyne Walk SW3. 01-352 5354. Membership open to women graduates of all nations. Club facilities and hostel.

International House   **2 I 21**
40 Shaftesbury Avenue W1. 01-437 9167. Nightly social programme. Educational and cultural trips and activities. Dances, restaurant. English-teaching theatre. All nationalities welcome. Information bureau.

International Students' House   **2 E 21**
229 Great Portland St W1. 01-636 9471. Open to all full-time students. Excellent social and recreational facilities — billiards, tennis. Inexpensive visits and theatre outings arrange in vacations. Also a hostel.

National Association for Youth Clubs
P.O. Box 1, Pond Gate, Nuneaton, Warwickshire. 0682-61921/2. Will provide details of local youth clubs with social, recreational and community facilities for teenage students.

Victoria League   **5 K 22**
18 Northumberland Ave WC2. 01-930 1671. Hospitality in British homes arranged for Commonwealth students and nurses. Comfortable club and programme of social activities.

YMCA   **3 I 23**
640 Forest Rd E17. 01-520 5599. Social activities. Games and physical recreation facilities. Discussion groups. Help with accommodation. Moving late 1974 to 112 Gt Russel St WC1.

YWCA   **3 H 23**
16 Gt Russell St, WC1. 01-636 7512.

Students' accommodation agencies

Help and advice in finding temporary and permanent lodgings. Also apply to the lodgings' bureau of your university or the welfare office of your London embassy. (See under 'Embassies'.) A useful booklet is 'London: A Guide to Inexpensive Accommodation' (British Tourist Authority, 64 St James's St SW1). Also see 'Time Out' for reasonable offers.

En Famille Agency
Westbury House, Queen's Lane, Arundel, Sussex. 0903 882450. Recommends overseas families to English students wishing to stay abroad as paying guests, and English families to overseas students who want to live with an English family. Fee £12.00.

London YWCA Accommodation & Advisory Service   **3 H 23**
16 Gt Russell St WC1. 01-580 0478. Not an agency but a charity. Publishes an annual handbook about all hostels in London for girls and advises about accommodation for women from 16 to 60. Also help with personal problems.

London Accommodation Bureau   **2 F 19**
102 Queensway W2. 01-727 5062 & 130 Blackstock Rd N4. 01-359 5291 for cheaper flats. Has very extensive selection of cheaper flats and bedsitting rooms in all parts of London and the suburbs.

International Students' House   **2 D 21**
229 Great Portland St W1. 01-636 9471. Accommodation advisory service for students. Finds cheap temporary lodgings for students in private houses, hostels or on mattresses in schools.

Truman & Knightley Educational Trust   **1 A B**
76-78 Notting Hill Gate W11. 01-727 1242. Will supply names of families who will accommodate students for short stays. Also has families in France and Germany. Free service.

Careers Guidance

Careers Research and Advisory Centre (CRAC)
Bateman St, Cambridge 69811. Non profit making educational charity. Wide range of publications on courses of study, training facilities, job openings, etc. Write for catalogues.

Tavistock Institute of Human Relations
Tavistock Centre, 120 Belsize Lane NW3. 01-435 7111. Help you to assess your own capabilities. Aptitude and intelligence testing and interviews. Fee.

Vocational Guidance Association   **2 C 20**
Upper Harley St NW1. 01-935 2600. Cases of occupational misfits exhaustively investigated and alternative careers explored. They'll recommend drastic changes if they think it's necessary. Fee.

Students' hostels

William Goodenough House   **3 F 27**
Mecklenburgh Square WC1. 01-278 5131. Postgraduate families and single women from the Commonwealth, EEC and USA. Single study rooms and flats available. Minimum stay 6 months.

GLC   **5 N 22**
Director of Housing (H.5), County Hall SE1. 01-633 5000 Ext 7736. Six hostels for men and women, including students. Single rooms, sharing or dormitories. £14.00 pw with board.

Hong Kong House   **2 C 12**
74 Lancaster Gate W2. 01-262 3056. Mostly dormitories. Long or short stays. B&B.

International Friendship League
Peace Haven, 3 Creswick Rd W3. 01-992 0221. All ages and nationalities. Temporary or permanent stays. No single rooms. From £1.50 with breakfast, showers & no curfew.

International Students' House   **2 D 21**
1-6 Park Crescent W1. 01-580 2765. Mixed hostel for all nationalities. Single, double and treble rooms. Social facilities. Double room £6.30 pw with breakfast.

Lee Abbey International Students' Club   **1 H 6**
27 Courtfield Gardens SW5. 01-373 7286. All nationalities. Single, double and treble rooms for long term residents £9.65 pw. Temporary stays £14.00 pw.

London House   **3 F 27**
Mecklenburgh Square WC1. 01-837 8888. The brother to William Goodenough House. Similar facilities for USA and Commonwealth single postgraduate men.

Malaysia Hall   **2 C 17**
46 Bryanston Square W1. 01-723 0188. Only students from the Malay states. 2 weeks or yearly stays. £1.00 per night with breakfast.

Methodist International House   **1 B 11**
4 Inverness Terrace W2. 01-229 5101. All nationalities. Full time students in single, double or dormitory rooms. Short or long stays.

Pakistan Students Federation   **1 H 5**
5 Barkston Gardens SW5. 01-370 5859. Exclusively for Pakistani male students. Double and single rooms. Maximum stay a few weeks. 36 beds, cooking facilities.

Sussex Gardens International
Students' Club   **2 C 14**
208 Sussex Gardens W2. 01-262 1641. Full-time students of all nationalities in a mixed hostel. Single, double and dormitory rooms. B&B and cooking facilities.

William Temple House   **1 G 4**
29 Trebovir Rd SW5. 01-370 1081. Mixed hostel for British and overseas students doing full-time studies. Single, double and treble rooms. Cooking facilities.

Youth Hostels Association   **5 K 22**
Enquiries to the Youth Hostel Shop, 29 John Adam St WC2. 01-839 1722. Four hostels in central London offering cheap dormitory accommodation. All ages and nationalities. Maximum stay 4 nights. Very cheap.

YWCA   **2 D 20**
2 Weymouth St W1. 01-636 9722. Permanent hostels for girls under 23. Also transient hostels with no age limit. Special hostels for Scandinavians.

Holidays

Also refer to 'Unusual holidays'.

BI Educational Cruises   **6 O 33**
P & O Pass. Div, Beaufort House, St Botolph St EC3. 01-283 8000. Educational cruises for students at very reasonable prices.

Camp America   **1 G 9**
37 Queen's Gate SW7. 01-589 3223. Summer vacation jobs for British and European students working in American summer camps. Free travel and board. Pocket money.

Central Bureau for Educational Visits
& Exchanges   **2 C 18**
43 Dorset St W1. 01-486 5101. National office giving information on educational travel, working holidays abroad and in Britain, and certain official student exchange schemes.

Common Cold Research Unit
Harvard Hospital, Coombe Rd, Salisbury, Wilts. You get paid but there is no work to do.

Concordia (Youth Service Volunteers)   **2 I 19**
11a Albemarle St W1. 01-629 3367. International work camps in Britain and Europe. Fruit picking in Britain; archaeology in Italy and Spain; wine harvesting in France; also social projects. *Book ahead.* SAE.

Farm Work Camps   **6 N 29**
Ministry of Agriculture, Fisheries and Food, Eagle House, 90-96 Cannon St EC4. 01-626 1515 ext 2810. Will send a list of farm work camps run under private management which organise help for local farmers with fruit picking, harvesting, etc.

Friends Service Council (Quakers)   **3 D 25**
Friends House, 173 Euston Rd NW1. 01-387 3601. Holiday work camps, mainly in the field of social services, for anyone over 16 years. *Book ahead.*

Holiday Fellowship
142 Great North Way NW4. 01-203 3381. Enormous range of good holidays at reasonable prices. Archaeology, birdwatching, pony trekking, painting, folk singing and many others.

Kibbutz Representative and Hechalutz
B'Anglia   **5 J 19**
1 King St, St James' SW1. 01-930 6181. Not an easy holiday but a challenging way to see a completely different way of life.

Youth Hostels Association   **5 K 22**
29 John Adam St WC2. 01-839 1722. Provides list of Youth Hostels in Britain and Europe where students who are touring and walking can stay the night at very low charges. Also list of active holidays.

Exchanges & group visits

Obtain the UNESCO information booklet 'Handbook of international exchanges'.

Educational Interchange Council   **3 F 24**
43 Russell Square WC1. 01-580 9137. Educational exchanges of students on a world-wide scale. Group visits to USSR, Bulgaria, Rumania and Hungary.

English Home Holidays
30 Rue Notre-Dame-des-Victoires, 75 Paris (2e), France. Exchanges arranged between French and English boys and girls in families during the summer holidays.

IAESTE   **2 C 18**
c/o Central Bureau for Education Visits & Exchanges, 43 Dorset St W1. 01-486 5101. Student exchanges with technical firms in a large number of countries.

Institute of Directors (Group Visits Dept)   **5 J 14**
10 Belgrave Square SW1. 01-235 3601. Technical study tours in this country from European and Latin American universities, by prior arrangement.

Environmental fieldwork

Friends of the Earth   **2 H 21**
9 Poland St W1. 01-434 1684. Effective ecological group believing in action rather than words. Responsible for the famous doorstep dumping of the Schweppes bottles. More recent concern for the decline in the whale population, increased use of indestructible packaging and open-cast mining in National Parks. Also concerned about nuclear power and transport policies.

The Victorian Society
1 Priory Gardens, Bedford Park W4. 01-994 1019. Fight for the preservation of Victorian architecture with interests that extend to Victorian fine and applied arts. Lectures, study tours, visits, exhibitions, etc arranged. Subs.

Student employment

Britain does not encourage her students to work. Full-time overseas students staying here are forbidden to do so, unless the work complements their studies. Students studying in other countries may do so if they obtain a work permit. The Central Bureau for Educational Exchange (see 'Holidays') publishes 'Working Holidays'. This is a list of useful addresses with branches in foreign countries.

Hotel & Catering Trades Employment
Service Agency   **3 H 23**
1-3 Denmark St WC2. 01-836 6622.

National Union of Students Employment
Service   **3 E 24**
3 Endsleigh St WC1. 01-387 1277.

Professional & Executive Register   **5 J 15**
4-5 Grosvenor Place SW1. 01-235 7030. An employment service for those seeking professional or executive appointments.

Students' welfare

Also refer to the 'Cry for help' section.

London Council for Welfare of
Women & Girls   **3 H 23**
16 Great Russell St WC1. 01-580 0478. Helps newcomers to London with difficulties over accommodation, employment, etc. Also advice on personal problems.

London Youth Advisory Centre   **2 C 19**
Nottingham Place W1. 01-935 8870. Help and advice on all problems for people 13-25.

NUS Education and Welfare Department   **3 E 24**
3-5 Endsleigh St WC1. 01-387 1277. Deals with all grant problems, social security, course entrance, transfer problems and all other career or accommodation troubles.

Release
1 Elgin Ave W9. 01-289 1123. Help with almost any troubles. Cases referred to professionals. Specialise in legal advice on drug prosecution. 24-hr emergency telephone service 01-603 8654.

Political and minority interest groups

In London, whether you're a Maoist, Zen Buddhist, or just an old True Blue, you're sure to find someone who shares your commitments. Joining an organised group enables you to air your views in sympathetic surroundings.

Anti-Apartheid   **2 F 22**
89 Charlotte St W1. 01-580 5311. Works in Britain against the system in South Africa. Issues newspaper *Anti-Apartheid News*. (M).

British Humanists Association   **1 E 8**
13 Prince of Wales Terrace, W8. 01-937 2341.

Campaign against forces which threaten to undermine individual liberty: over-population, censorship, bureaucracy, etc. Wide range of activities — conferences, meetings, counselling service.

Campaign for Nuclear Disarmament (CND)
Eastbourne House, Bullards Place E2. 01-980 0937. Long-established group, now rather depleted. Activities have diversified; they still march but concentrate more on supplying information. Emphasis on general peace movements. Publish bi-monthly *Sanity*.

Communist Party of Britain (Marxist-Leninist)
155 Fortress Rd NW5. Supports Peking, Albania, Vietnam. Publishes fortnightly 'The Worker'. Militant working class though quite small membership.

Communist Party of Great Britain   **6 J 23**
16 King St WC2. 01-836 2151. Marxist. Party programme — *British Road to Socialism*. Over 1,000 branches, including those in factories, large number of industrial militants. Daily *Morning Star*.

Conservative and Unionist Party   **5 O 19**
32 Smith Square SW1. 01-222 9000. Active young Conservative groups throughout the country.

Fabian Society   **5 M 19**
11 Dartmouth St SW1. 01-930 3077. Gradualist socialism. Renowned for excellent pamphlets on social issues, home and abroad, especially education and the environment. Good summer and weekend residential schools. (M).

Friends of the Earth   **2 H 21**
9 Poland St W1. 01-434 1684. Activist organisation devoted to defending the environment from pollution and waste. Very keen on 'recycling' materials and goods; dedicated enemy of producers of 'disposable bottles and unnecessary packaging. (M).·

Gingerbread   **2 H 21**
9 Poland St W1. 01-734 9014. An association of one parent families. Publishes *'Ginger'* fortnightly.

International Socialists
6 Cottons Gardens E2. 01-739 1878. Aims to overthrow capitalism by revolution through 'independent action of the working class'. Publish *'Socialist Worker'* and *'International Socialism'*.

Labour Party   **5 O 19**
Transport House, Smith Square SW1. 01-834 9434. Local branch addresses supplied from here.

Liberal Party   **6 K 23**
7 Exchange Court. Strand WC2. 01-240 0701. Dedicated to boosting interest in Liberalism; particularly active Young Liberals Group.

Minority Rights Group   **5 K 22**
Benjamin Franklin House, 36 Craven St WC2. 01-930 6659. Charity with the aim of preventing discrimination against minority and majority groups. Investigate complaints and publicise results.

Mothers in Action   **2 H 21**
9 Poland St W1. (No telephone). Pressure group for unsupported mothers (single, divorced, widowed or wives of prisoners). Campaigns for better. housing, day nurseries, etc.

National Peace Council   **3 H 26**
29 Great St James St WC1. 01-242 3228. Promotes the study and care of the ways of peace and the prevention of war.

Socialist International
88a St John's Wood High St NW8. 01-586 1101. Social democrats whose aim is to end all forms of exploitation between men and nations. Publish 'Socialist Affairs'.

Women's Liberation Front
58 Lisburne Rd NW3. 01-485 3609. Fights against all discrimination against women. International, Maoist and closely allied to the Workshop.

Women's Rights Campaign
Flat 2, 40 Menelik Rd NW2. 01-794 9510. To fight for equal rights for women in all spheres. Both men and women interested in the cause welcome.

Travel and holiday information

Passports

Applications and renewals for the 10-year passport can be handled by your bank or travel agency for a small charge, or by the local office of the Department of Employment. British 'Visitors' passports, valid for one year, can be obtained from a post office. These are for holidaymakers only and may be used for Canada and most European countries, usually those that don't require a visa. They are issued upon production of NHS medical card, birth certificate, pension book or an expired but uncancelled passport.

Passport Office   **5 L 18**
Clive House, Petty France SW1. 01-222 8010. *OPEN Mon-Fri 09.00-16.30. Emergencies Mon-Fri 16.30-18.30. Sat, Sun & Public Hols 10.00-12.00. CLOSED Xmas.*

Immigration Office
Lunar House, Wellesley Rd Croydon Surrey. 01-686 0688. Deals with questions concerning the granting of British visas to foreigners and entry under the Commonwealth Immigration Act. Subject to approval, visas are then supplied by the

Foreign Office   **5 L 18**
Clive House Petty France SW1. 01-930 2323.

Passport photographs

These can be done by any photographer, who will know the size and other requirements. Basically, you should submit two identical black and white, full face photographs of yourself without a hat. The size should be no more than 2½ in. by 2 in., no less than 2 in. by 1½ in. The paper should be ordinary photographic paper, unglazed and unmounted. It is possible to have the photos taken in one of the street photograph machines. The Passport office will accept photos taken in machines which have marked on them somewhere the words 'Passport' or 'Passport approved'. These machines are often available at the airport for a day passport.

Passport Photo Service   **2 F 18**
449 Oxford St W1. 01-629 8540. (Opposite Selfridges). *OPEN 09.00-18.00, Sat to 13.30.* £1.20 for 3 prints — 10 mins.

Thomas Cook   **2 I 18**
Polyphoto, 45 Berkeley St W1. 01-499 4000. *OPEN 09.00-17.00. Closed Sat.* 95p for 2 instant prints — 5 mins.

Inoculations and vaccinations

Can be carried out by your own doctor under the National Health Scheme free — though the doctor may charge for signing the certificate. The certificate should then be taken for stamping to the Health department of the local authority in which the vaccinator practises. International certificates are required for smallpox, cholera and yellow fever. The Department of Health and Social Security, Alexander Fleming House Elephant & Castle SE1 01-407 5522, will send you details of international requirements.

Unilever House   **6 M 27**
Blackfriars EC4. 01-353 7474. *OPEN 14.20 Tues & Fri for Yellow Fever* £2.00; *14.20 Mon, Wed & Thur for Smallpox* £1.50; *Cholera* £2.00; *Typhoid* £2.00; *Gamma Globulin* £3.50. *By appointment.*

Vaccinating Centre   **2 D 16**
53 Gt Cumberland Place W1. 01-262 6456. A centre for vaccinations and inoculations. *OPEN Mon-Fri 09.00-17.00. By appointment.*

Money: currency exchange

Thomas Cook
100 Victoria St SW1. 01-828 0437. Exchange bureau at Victoria Station. *OPEN 09.00-17.00 Mon-Fri, 09.00-12.00 Sat.*

Lost property

British Rail

All Regions except Southern
Property held at station where handed in for 7-14 days, then sent to Central Unclaimed Goods & Lost Property, Marylebone Station 01-387 9400. North of border to Glasgow Central Depot.
Southern Region
Covering Blackfriars, Cannon Street, Charing Cross, Holborn Viaduct, London Bridge, Victoria and Waterloo. Apply at the nearest railway station or at the main terminal. It will be held there for 3 days and then sent to the central holding depot at
Waterloo Station   **6 N 23**
York Rd SE1. 01-928 5151
Sealink trains
Property lost, phone 01-283 7535.

London Transport

Lost Property Office   **2 B 19**
200 Baker St W1 (next to Baker Street Station). For enquiries about lost property please call in person (or send another person with written authority) or apply by letter. No telephone enquiries. *OPEN Mon-Fri 10.00-18.00. CLOSED B. Hols.*

Air Travel

This is held by each individual airline (see list of airline offices). Property lost in the main airport buildings enquire: British Airport Police Lost Property Office, London Airport, Heathrow, Middx..01-759 4321.

Taxis   **3 E 30**
Apply 15 Penton St N1 or nearest police station.

Lost anywhere

Apply to the nearest police station. Lost property found in the street is usually taken there by the finder.

Lost children

Will be cared for by the railway police if lost on British Rail, otherwise ask at the nearest police station if lost elsewhere.

Lost dogs   **4 R 8**
May have been taken to Battersea Dogs Home, 4 Battersea Park Rd SW8. 01-622 4454. Unwanted dogs should be taken to the same address by the owner only. *OPEN 09.30-17.00 Mon-Fri. 14.00-16.00 Sat, Sun. Pub Hols.*

Embassies

All embassies have Consular Departments in the same building unless a separate address is given. All these offices deal with emigration.
Afghanistan   **1 G 11**
31 Prince's Gate SW7. 01-589 8891.
Algeria   **1 F 9**
6 Hyde Park Gate SW7. 01-584 9502.
Argentina   **5 J 14**
9 Wilton Crescent SW1. 01-235 3717.
Consulate: 53 Hans Place SW1   **5 J 12**
01-584 1701.
Austria   **5 J 14**
18 Belgrave Mews West SW1. 01-235 3731
Belgium   **5 K 14**
103 Eaton Square SW1. 01-235 5422.
Bolivia   **5 K 14**
106 Eaton Square SW1. 01-235 4248.
Consulate: 106 Eccleston Mews SW1. 01-235 4255.
Brazil
32 Green St W1. 01-629 0155   **2 F 17**
Consulate: 6 Deanery St W1. 01-499 7441.   **2 H 16**
Bulgaria   **1 G 8**
12 Queens Gate Gardens SW7. 01-584 9400.
Burma   **2 H 17**
19a Charles St Berkeley Square W1. 01-499 8841.
Cameroon   **1 A 5**
84 Holland Park W11. 01-727 0771.

Chile   **2 D 20**
12 Devonshire St W1. 01-580 6392.
Consulate: 01-580 1023.
China   **2 E 20**
31 Portland Place W1. 01-636 5637.
Colombia
Flat 3a, 3 Hans Crescent SW1. 01-589 9177   **2 I 13**
Consulate: Suite 10. 140 Park Lane W1.   01-493
4565   **2 G 16**
Costa Rica   **1 G 7**
1 Culross St W1. 01-493 9761.
Cuba   **1 E 8**
57 Kensington Court W8. 01-937 8226.
Czechoslovakia   **1 D 8**
25 Kensington Palace Gardens W8. 01-229 1255.
Denmark   **5 J 12**
67 Pont St SW1. 01-584 0102.
Dominican Republic   **1 G 7**
4 Braemar Mansions. Cornwall Gardens SW7. 01-937
1921. Consulate: 01-937 7116.
Ecuador   **2 I 13**
Flat 3b, 3 Hans Crescent SW1. 01-584 1367.
Consulate: 01-584 2648.
Ethiopia   **1 G 11**
17 Prince's Gate SW7. 01-589 7212.
Egypt   **2 H 17**
26 South St W1. 01-499 2401.
Finland   **5 L 14**
66 Chester Square SW1. 01-730 0771.
France
58 Knightsbridge SW1. 01-235 8080   **2 I 14**
Consulate: 24 Rutland Gate SW7. 01-584 9628.   **2 H 12**
Gambia   **1 E 8**
60 Ennismore Gardens SW7. 01-584 1242.
Germany   **5 J 14**
23 Belgrave Square SW1. 01-235 5033.
Greece   **1 A 5**
1a Holland Park W11. 01-727 8040.
Haiti   **1 H 8**
17 Queens Gate SW7. 01-581 0577.
Honduras   **2 D 17**
48 George St W1. 01-486 4880.
Hong Kong   **2 H 19**
6 Grafton St W1. 01-499 9821.
Hungary   **5 K 14**
35 Eaton Place SW1. 01-235 4048.
Consulate: 35b Eaton Place SW1. 01-235 2664.
Iceland   **5 L 13**
1 Eaton Terrace SW1. 01-730 5131.
Indonesia   **2 F 17**
38 Grosvenor Square W1. 01-499 7661.
Iran   **1 G 11**
Embassy: 16 Princes Gate SW7. 01-584 8101.
Consulate: 50 Kensington Court W8.   **1 E 8**
01-937 5225.
Iraq   **1 G 9**
21-2 Queens Gate SW7. 01-584 7141.
Ireland   **5 J 15**
17 Grosvenor Place SW1. 01-235 2171.
Israel   **1 D 8**
2 Palace Green, Kensington Palace Gardens W8. 01-937 8050.
Italy
14 Three Kings Yard W1. 01-629 8200.   **2 G 18**
Consulate: 38 Eaton Place SW1. 01-235 4831.   **5 K 14**
Ivory Coast   **5 K 15**
2 Upper Belgrave St SW1. 01-235 6991.
Japan   **2 G 18**
46 Grosvenor St W1. 01-493 6030.
Jordan   **1 C 6**
6 Upper Phillimore Gardens W8. 01-937 3685.
Korea   **5 K 12**
4 Palace Gate W8. 01-581 0247.
Kuwait   **2 D 20**
40 Devonshire St W1. 01-580 8471.
Laos   **1 C 8**
5 Palace Green, Kensington Palace Gardens W8. 01-937 9519.
Lebanon   **1 D 8**
21 Kensington Palace Gardens W8. 01-229 7265.
Consulate: 15 Palace Gardens Mews W8.
01-229 8485.   **1 B 9**
Liberia   **1 G 11**
21 Prince's Gate SW7. 01-589 9405.
Libyan Arab Republic   **1 G 11**
58 Prince's Gate SW7. 01-589 5235.
Luxembourg   **5 J 14**
27 Wilton Crescent SW1. 01-235 6961.
Mexico   **5 J 15**
8 Halkin St SW1. 01-235 6393.
Monaco   **2 H 17**
Consulate: Audley Square W1. 01-629 0734.
Morocco   **1 H 8**
49 Queens Gate Gardens SW7. 01-584 8827.

Muscat & Oman   1   F 9
64 Ennismore Gardens SW7. 01-584 6782.
Nepal   1   D 8
12a Kensington Palace Gardens W8. 01-229 1594.
Netherlands   1   F 9
38 Hyde Park Gate SW7. 01-584 5040.
Nicaragua   1   17
8 Gloucester Rd SW7. 01-584 3231.
Norway   5   J 14
25 Belgrave Square SW1. 01-235 7151.
Pakistan   2   I 13
35 Lowndes Square SW1. 01-235 2044.
Panama   2   H 12
39 Montpelier Sq SW7. 01-589 8751.
Consulate: 4 Carmelite St EC4. 01-353 4792.   6   L 26
Paraguay   1   G 7
Braemar Lodge, Cornwall Gardens SW7. 01-937 1253.
Consulate: 01-937 6629.
Peru   5   K 12
52 Sloane St SW1. 01-235 1917.
Consulate: 01-235 6867.
The Philippines   1   D 8
9a Palace Green, Kensington Palace Green W8. 01-937 3646.
Poland   2   E 20
47 Portland Place W1. 01-580 4324
Consulate: 19 Weymouth St W1 01-580 4324.   2   D 20
Portugal   5   J 14
11 Belgrave Square SW1. 01-235 5331.
Consulate: 62 Brompton Rd SW3. 01-235 6216.   5   J 14
Romania   1   D 8
4 Palace Green, Kensington Palace Green W8.
01-937 9666.
Salvador   2   E 20
9b Portland Place W1. 01-636 9563.
Saudi Arabia   5   K 14
30 Belgrave Sq SW1. 01-235 0831.
Senegal   1   C 6
11 Phillimore Gardens W8. 01-937 0925.
Somali   2   E 20
60 Portland Place W1. 01-580 7148.
South Africa   5   K 21
South Africa House, Trafalgar Square WC2. 01-930 4488.
Spain   5   J 14
24 Belgrave Square SW1. 01-235 5555.
Consulate: 3 Hans Crescent SW1. 01-589 8852.   2   I 13
Sudan   5   J 19
3 Cleveland Row, St James's SW1. 01-839 8080.
Sweden   2   E 17
23 North Row W1. 01-499 9500.
Switzerland   2   C 17
18 Montagu Place W1. 01-723 0701.
Thailand   1   G 9
30 Queens Gate SW7. 01-589 0173.
Consulate: 01-589 2857.
Tunisia   1   G 11
29 Prince's Gate SW7. 01-584 8117.
Turkey   5   J 14
43 Belgrave Square SW1. 01-235 5252.
Consulate: Rutland Gardens SW7. 01-589 0363. 2   H 12
United Arab Republic (Egypt)   2   H 17
26 South St W1. 01-499 2401.
Uruguay   5   J 12
48 Lennox Gardens SW1. 01-589 8835.
Consulate: 01-589 8735.
U.S.A.   2   F 17
24 Grosvenor Square W1. 01-499 9000.
U.S.S.R.   1   D 8
13 Kensington Palace Gardens W8. 01-229 3628.
Consulate: 5 Kensington Palace Gardens W8. 01-229 3215.
Venezuela   2   I 13
3 Hans Crescent SW1. 01-584 4206.
Consulate: 71a Park Mansions, Brompton Rd SW1. 01-589 1121 (Shipping Dept). 01-589 9916 (Visas Dept).
Vietnam   1   F 8
12-14 Victoria Rd W8. 01-937 3765.
West India Committee   2   G 18
18 Grosvenor St W1. 01-629 6353.
Yemen Arab Republic   2   H 17
41 South St W1. 01-499 5246.
Yemen People's Democratic Republic   1   I 19
57 Cromwell Rd SW7. 01-584 6607.
Yugoslavia   1   F 6
5 Lexham Gardens W8. 01-370 6105.
Consulate: 7 Lexham Gardens W8.
Zaire   5   K 13
26 Chesham Place SW1. 01-235 6137.

Commonwealth offices

These are the Commonwealth countries and colonies with offices in London. All deal with emigration.
Australia   6   K 24
Australia House, Strand WC2. 01-438 8000.
Bahamas   5   J 19
39 Pall Mall SW1. 01-930 6967.
Barbados   5   K 15
6 Upper Belgrave St SW1. 01-235 8686.
Bangladesh   1   G 9
28 Queens Gate SW7. 01-584 0081.
Botswana   5   L 17
162 Buckingham Palace Rd SW1. 01-730 5216.
Canada   5   J 21
Canada House, Trafalgar Square SW1. 01-930 9741.
Cyprus   2   F 17
93 Park St W1. 01-499 8272.
Eastern Carribean Commission & Grenada
Kings House, 10 Haymarket SW1. 01-930 7902   5   J 21
Fiji   2   F 16
34 Hyde Park Gate SW7. 01-584 3661.
Ghana   5   J 14
13 Belgrave Sq SW1. 01-235 4142.
Guyana   5   K 21
3 Palace Court, Bayswater Rd W2. 01-229 7684.
India   6   J 24
India House, Aldwych WC2. 01-836 8484.
Jamaica   2   G 18
48 Grosvenor St W1. 01-499 8600.
Kenya   2   E 20
45 Portland Place W1. 01-636 2371.
Lesotho   5   J 19
16a St James's St SW1. 01-839 1154. Entrance in Kings St on weekdays.
Malawi   2   D 16
47 Great Cumberland Place W1. 01-723 6021.
Malaysia   5   J 14
45 Belgrave Square SW1. 01-245 9221.
Malta   5   J 21
Malta House, 24 Haymarket SW1. 01-930 9851.
Mauritius   5   K 22
32-33 Elvaston Place SW7. 01-581 0294.
New Zealand   5   J 21
New Zealand House, 80 Haymarket SW1. 01-930 8422.
Nigeria   5   K 22
Nigeria House, 9 Northumberland Avenue WC2. 01-839 1244.
Sierra Leone   2   E 20
33 Portland Place W1. 01-636 6483.
Singapore   5   J 14
2 Wilton Crescent SW1. 01-235 8315.
Sri Lanka (Ceylon)   2   D 14
13 Hyde Park Gardens W2. 01-262 1841.
Swaziland   5   J 12
58 Pont St SW1. 01-589 5447.
Tanzania   2   I 16
43 Hertford St W1. 01-499 8951.
Tonga   5   J 12
New Zealand House, Haymarket SW1. 01-839 3287.
Trinidad & Tobago   5   J 14
42 Belgrave Sq SW1. 01-245 9351.
Uganda   5   K 21
Uganda House, 58 Trafalgar Square WC2. 01-839 1963.
Zambia   2   F 20
7-11 Cavendish Place W1. 01-580 0691.

Institutes of culture

Will tell you all you need to know about the way of life in a particular country. Most organise language tuition, exhibitions, filmshows and some run summer courses and exchanges.
Austrian Institute   2   H 12
28 Rutland Gate SW7. 01-584 8653.
German Institute   1   G 11
45 Prince's Gate SW7. 01-589 7207.
Greek Institute
34 Bush Hill Rd N21. 01-888 9538.
Italian Institute   5   J 14
39 Belgrave Square SW1. 01-235 1461.
Polish Cultural Institute   2   D 20
16 Devonshire St W1. 01-636 6032.
Spanish Institute   5   K 14
102 Eaton Square SW1. 01-235 1484.
Swedish Cultural Dept.   2   E 17
23 North Row W1. 01-499 9500.

Tourist offices

The following is a list of all the National Tourist Offices and information centres in London. Advice, specialised knowledge of the particular country and literature are available. Nearly all offices are within walking distance of Piccadilly Circus.

Australia 2 I 19
Australian Tourist Commission, 22 Old Bond St W1. 01-499 2247.

Austria 2 H 19
Austrian National Tourist Office, 30 St George's St W1. 01-629 0461.

Bahamas 2 I 19
Bahama Island Tourist Office, 23 Old Bond St W1. 01-629 5238.

Barbados 5 K 15
Barbados Tourist Board, 6 Upper Belgrave St SW1. 01-235 8686.

Belgium 5 J 21
Belgian National Tourist Office, 66 Haymarket SW1. 01-930 9618.

Bermuda 2 B 18
Bermuda Dept of Tourism, 84 Baker St W1. 01-487 4391.

Britain 5 J 19
British Travel, Queen's House, 64 St James's St SW1. 01-629 9191.

Bulgaria 2 H 20
Bulgarian National Tourist Office, 126 Regent St W1. 01-437 2611.

Canada 5 K 21
Canadian Government Travel Bureau, Canada House, Cockspur St SW1. 01-930 0731.

Czechoslovakia 2 I 19
Czechoslovak Travel Bureau Cedok (London), 17-18 Old Bond St W1. 01-629 6058.

Denmark 2 H 20
The Danish Tourist Board, Sceptre House 169-173 Regent St W1. 01-734 2637.

Egyptian Tourist Centre 2 I 18
62a Piccadilly W1. 01-493 5282.

Finland 5 J 21
Finnish Tourist Board, Finland House, 56 Haymarket SW1. 01-839 4048.

France 2 I 18
French Government Tourist Office, 178 Piccadilly W1. 01-493 3171.

Germany 2 H 19
German National Tourist Office, 61 Conduit St W1. 01-734 2600.

Gibraltar 5 J 22
2 Grand Buildings, Trafalgar Square WC2. 01-930 2284.

Greece 2 I 20
The National Tourist Organisation of Greece, 195-7 Regent St W1. 01-734 5997.

Holland 2 G 19
Netherlands National Tourist Office, 143 New Bond St W1. 01-499 9367.

Hungary 2 H 19
Hungarian Travel Centre, 6 Conduit St W1. 01-493 0263.

Iceland 2 G 18
Iceland Tourist Information Bureau, 73 Grosvenor St W1. 01-493 7661.

Ireland 2 G 19
Irish Tourist Office, Ireland House, 150 New Bond St W1. 01-493 3201.

Israel 5 J 19
Israel Government Tourist Office, 59 St James's St SW1. 01-734 4631.

Italy 2 I 20
Italian State Tourist Dept (ENIT), 201 Regent St W1. 01-439 2311.

Jamaica 2 H 18
Jamaica Tourist Board, 6-10 Bruton St W1. 01-493 3647.

Japan 2 I 20
Japan National Tourist Organisation, 167 Regent St W1. 01-734 9638.

Jersey 5 J 22
Jersey Tourist Information Office, 118 Grand Buildings, Trafalgar Square WC2. 01-930 1619.

Lebanon 2 I 18
Lebanese Tourist Office, 90 Piccadilly W1. 01-409 2031.

Luxembourg 5 J 21
Luxembourg National Tourist Office, 66 Haymarket SW1. 01-930 8906.

Malta 5 J 21
Malta Government Tourist Office, Malta House, 24 Haymarket SW1. 01-930 9851.

Mexico 5 L 15
Mexican National Tourist Council, 52 Grosvenor

Gardens SW1. 01-730 0128.
Morocco 2 H 20
Moroccan Tourist Office, 174 Regent St W1. 01-437 0073.

New Zealand 5 J 21
New Zealand Government Tourist Bureau, New Zealand House, 80 Haymarket SW1. 01-930 8422.

Northern Ireland 2 I 18
Northern Ireland Tourist Board, 11 Berkeley St W1. 01-493 0601.

Norway 5 J 20
Norwegian National Tourist Office, 20 Pall Mall SW1. 01-839 6255.

Poland 2 I 20
Polish Travel Office, 313 Regent St W1. 01-580 8028.

Portugal 2 G 19
Casa de Portugal, 1-5 New Bond St W1. 01-493 3873.

South Africa 5 J 20
South African Tourist Corporation, 13 Lower Regent St SW1. 01-839 7462.

Soviet Union 2 H 20
Intourist Moscow, 292 Regent St W1. 01-580 4974.

Spain 2 I 19
Spanish National Tourist Office, 70 Jermyn St SW1. 01-930 8578.

Sweden 2 G 18
Swedish National Tourist Association, 21-22 Grosvenor St W1. 01-499 9500.

Switzerland 2 I 22
Swiss National Tourist Office, Swiss Centre, 1 New Coventry St W1. 01-734 1921.

Tunisia 2 I 19
7a Stafford St W1. 01-493 2952.

Turkey 2 H 19
Turkish Tourism Information Office, 49 Conduit St W1. 01-734 8681.

United Arab Republic 2 I 18
62a Piccadilly W1. 01-493 5282.

U.S.A. 2 I 20
United States Travel Service, 22 Sackville St W1. 01-439 7433.

Yugoslavia 2 H 20
Yugoslavia National Tourist Office, 143 Regent St W1. 01-734 5243.

Travel agents and tour operators

The following list is a recommended choice of travel agents and tour operators of experience with a reputation for courtesy and efficiency. All are members of the Association of British Travel Agents (ABTA) and a few are members of the Tour Operators Study Group (TOSG).

Barry Aikman Travel 4 J 10
213 Brompton Rd SW3. 01-584 8121. Good selection of package tour holidays by air.

American Express 5 J 21
6 Haymarket SW1. 01-930 4411. Large, world-wide and efficient. Operate their own money cards and travellers cheques.

Thos Cook & Son 2 I 18
45 Berkeley St W1. 01-499 4000. The biggest. World famous for travel efficiency.

Kuoni Travel 2 G 19
33 Maddox St W1. 01-499 8636. Impressive list of exotic centres for luxury tours, popular with those who can afford to go further afield.

Erna Low 1 I 9
21 Old Brompton Rd SW7. 01-584 4545. Good personal service. Specialise in holidays for young people and ski holidays.

Wings
124 Finchley Rd NW3. 01-794 0483. Inclusive air tours, world-wide.

Youth Hostels Association 5 K 22
29 John Adam St WC2. 01-839 1722. Inexpensive individual travel arrangements in this country and abroad. Hostel or hotel accommodation. Cheap train travel. Special rambling, mountaineering, corn dolly and brass-rubbing holidays.

Unusual holidays

Some organisations cover a very wide range of unusual holidays — especially write for the brochures of the YHA, the Ramblers Association and Holiday Fellowship. Refer also to 'Students London' (75p, Nicholson) for low cost holidays. Most of the firms offering the holidays listed here are members of ABTA.

and some of them are also members of TOSG. If you want to receive compensation if the holiday you have booked collapses due to negligence or financial difficulties on the part of the agent, then make sure that the firm you are booking with is a member of one of these organisations (they make available a common emergency fund.).

Adventure Holidays

See 'The Sunday Times' and 'Time Out' for interesting holiday offers.

Kuoni Travel   **2 G 19**
33 Maddox St W1. 01-499 8636. Out of the way holidays, tours to S. America, SE Asia, Himalayas.

Kuoni-Houlders
Deepdene, Dorking Surrey. Dorking 5954. A wide choice of safari holidays, Nile cruises and many other unusual tours.

Air France Welcome Tours   **2 G 19**
158 New Bond St W1. 01-499 8611. Luxury tours to South America, Indian Ocean, Far East, Persia and Mexico.

John Ridgeway School of Adventure
Ardmore, Rhicanich by Lairg, Sutherland, Scotland. Test your courage and strength with sailing, climbing and camping holidays designed especially for various age groups. Ages 12-15, 15-18, 18-30 & 30-70.

Archaelogical cruises

Swans Hellenic Cruises   **3 G 23**
237/8 Tottenham Court Rd W1. 01-636 8070. Luxurious but scholarly cruises to archaeological sites in the Mediterranean, accompanied by prominent lecturers. Also Roman Britain tour.

Archaeological digs

Council for British Archaeology   **2 C 20**
7 Marylebone Rd NW1. 01-486 1527. Publish a monthly calendar of excavations in Britain, where helpers are wanted (£2.50).

The Holiday Fellowship
142 Great North Way NW4. 01-203 3381. Holiday courses which include lectures, accommodation and meals in their prices, Costs of excursions extra. Digs mostly in Dorset.

Art and architecture

Some of the most unusual and interesting art and architecture holidays are organised by specialised art societies. A small membership fee is required.

Brompton Travel   **4 J 11**
206 Walton St SW3. 01-584 6143. European opera holidays arranged.

Cadogan Travel   **5 K 12**
159 Sloane St SW1. 01-730 0721. Mainly study Malta, Gibraltar, Morocco and Tunisia.

Contemporary Art Society   **5 P 18**
Tate Gallery, Millbank SW1. 01-828 0650. Subs £4.00.

Friends of the Tate Gallery   **5 P 18**
Millbank SW1. 01-834 2742. Subs £8.00.

National Trust   **5 L 19**
42 Queen Anne's Gate SW1. 01-930 1841.

The Holiday Fellowship
142 Great North Way NW4. 01-203 3381. Week-long photographic course and holiday in the Isle of Arran. Tuition by a distinguished photographer. Price includes full board and instruction. Beginners and the experienced welcome.

Bicycling

Hire a bike and tour England or the Continent. Information and a list of hiring companies from:

The Cyclists Touring Club
Cotterell House, 69 Meadrow, Godalming Surrey.

Boating and sailing abroad

PGL Adventure
Station Rd, Ross-on-Wye, Hereford & Worcs. Sail in a barge along the Dutch canals from Amsterdam. Large barges with a skipper and 28-40 passengers. 4-berth cabins, meals provided.

Blue Line Cruises
59 High St, Braunstone, Pugly, Warwickshire. Hire 4-berth cruisers for the Canal du Midi, France.

Boating & Sailing in Great Britain

Boat Enquiries
7 Waltonwell Rd Oxford. Tel 48765. Hire of boats arranged on the Thames, other British waterways, Holland and many parts of Europe. 24-hr brochure service Tel 511161. Helpful with last-minute bookings. They also publish an excellent booklet, 'A lazy man's guide to holidays afloat', giving a list of all firms doing cruising holidays on rivers and canals in GB and Europe.

Holiday Fellowship
142 Great North Way NW4. 01-203 3381. A week's study of the canal system of the Midlands by foot and boat.

British Waterways Board
Chester Rd Nantwich, Cheshire. Pleasure craft base. Will send a complete list of firms' offering hire craft on canals and rives. Tel Nantwich 65122.

Brass rubbing

Tour the churches of England and collect beautiful brass rubbings. Information from:

Brass Rubbing Centres
48a Ashcroft Rd, Cirencester Gloucestershire. 0285 3971.

Businessmen

Kendall Travel Service   **3 F 23**
35-37 Alfred Place, Store St WC1. 01-637 2300. Visits to international conferences and exhibitions. Sightseeing usually included.

The John Ridgway School of Adventure
Ardmore, Rhicanich by Lairg, Sutherland. Tel Kinlochbervie 229. Adventure week for businessmen; camping in the highlands. Sailing, fishing, walking, ornithology – a complete physical 'get away from it all'.

Camping

The Camping Club of GB & Ireland   **5 K 16**
11 Lower Grosvenor Place SW1. 01-828 1012. Publish two site lists well worth the annual subscription. The 'Year Book & Sites List' details 2,500 sites in GB. The 'International Camping List of Recommended Sites' covers overseas. Organises camping tours abroad.

Country cottages in Britain

Taylings Holiday Cottages
14 High St, Godalming Surrey. 048 68 28522. Wide range of fully inspected cottages, farmhouses and chalets. Rental varies with season.

National Trust   **5 L 19**
42 Queen Anne's Gate SW1. 01-930 0211. A limited number of properties are let out as holiday cottages in N. Ireland, Isle of Wight, Dorset, Devon and Cornwall, and the Lake District. Book in advance as they're understandably popular. Also have campsites, nature walks & guide books.

Diving

Allways Travel Service   **3 H 25**
17 Sicilian Avenue WC1. 01-242 6436. 7-day holiday based at the Forte Holiday Village on Sardinia. Beach barbecues and night dives, sea-bed sight-seeing; excursions for non-divers. All equipment on the site.

Fishing

Bennett Travel Bureau   **2 H 20**
229 Regent St W1. 01-437 8223. Escorted coach tours in Norway. 8-13 days from £252.

Sports Council
70 Brompton Rd SW3. 01-589 3411. Fly fishing instruction in Wales.

Gastronomy & wine tasting

Costa Line Cruises   **2 G 18**
64-5 Grosvenor St W1. 01-409 0118. Caribbean cruises of 11 or 12 days exploring gourmet and wine-tasting delights.

Golfing

Global Tours   **3 F 23**
200 Tottenham Court Rd W1. 01-637 3333. Golfing holidays at famous courses in Spain, Portugal and Majorca.

Mountaineering

Sports Council
70 Brompton Rd SW3. 01-589 3411. Weekend to 7-day courses in mountaineering, rock climbing, canoeing and ski-ing in the heart of Wales' Snowdonia National Park.

Ramblers Association Services
Wings House, Bridge Rd East, Welwyn Garden City, Herts. Welwyn Garden 31133. Walking and hiking tours in Europe.

Natural History

Country Holidays Association
Birch Heys, Cromwell Range, Manchester M14. One week's birdwatching in Scotland for £19.50.

Kuoni-Houlders
Deepdene, Dorking, Surrey. Dorking 5954. A wide choice of safari holidays, Nile cruises and other unusual tours.

Ramblers Association Services
Wings House, Bridge Rd East, Welwyn Garden City, Herts. Welwyn Garden 31133. Birdwatching and flora and fauna holidays in Spain and Majorca. Intended for the informed amateur.

Scotland's Garden Scheme
26 Castle Terrace, Edinburgh. Tel. 031-229 1870. 6-day tours of Scotland's most famous and unusual gardens. May & Jun, Sep & Oct.

Outdoor Holidays

The following specialise in a general range of all sorts of sporting and outdoor holidays.

Club Méditerranée   **2 F 19**
5 South Molton St W1. 01-499 1965. Organise holidays to 15 Club Méditerranée villages on the Mediterranean coast. Sports, water ski-ing and aqualung schools. Children's staff in some villages.

Holiday Fellowship
142 Great North Way WC1. 01-203 3381. Enormous range of attractive and unusual holidays, particularly for young people. Canoeing, riding, camping, climbing in Britain and abroad.

Hosts Students Travel Service   **2 E 21**
161 Great Portland St W1. 01-580 7733. Holidays in Beer Sheba, Israel. Concession on flight plus free board and lodging. £10.00 registration fee. Similar arrangements made for 'kibbutz' holiday which incorporates a tour of Israel. Also archeological trips.

Painting

Wayfarers Travel Agency   **3 G 25**
97-107 Southampton Row WC1. 01-580 8222. Painting holidays in Bedrun, Spain. Flight, full board and tuition included in price. Beginners welcome.

Riding

Wayfarers Travel Agency   **3 G 25**
97-107 Southampton Row WC1. 01-580 8222. Riding holidays in Spain and Hungary. Price includes flight, board and use of horses.

The British Horse Society
National Equestrian Centre, Kenilworth, Warwickshire. Will send you, free of post, 'Where to Ride' (75p) which gives a list of approved riding schools in Britain.

Ponies of Britain
Brookside Farm, Ascot, Berkshire. Information on pony trekking in Britain.

Ski-ing

There is excellent ski-ing in the Austrian Tyrol, the Swiss Alps, Italian Dolomites, France, Norway, the High Tatras in Czechoslovakia, Sallent in the Spanish Pyrenees, the Scottish Highlands and the Troodos mountains in Cyprus (where you can drop down to the coast for warm sea bathing). See also under 'Sport' for lessons on the Crystal Palace slope and elsewhere in London before you go. Cooks and Erna Low are specialists.

Club Méditerranée   **2 F 19**
5 South Molton St W1. 01-499 1965. Organise ski-ing holidays to Club Méditerranée resorts in Switzerland, Austria, France and Italy.

Ski-ing in Scotland

Special areas are the Cairngorms, Glencoe and Glenshee. For literature and further information write to:

Highlands and Islands Development Board
Bridge House, Bank St, Inverness. Tel. Inverness 34171. They publish a brochure 'Spey Valley — Ski Valley' and supply information about facilities in the Cairngorms.

Scottish Council of Physical Recreation
1 St Colne St, Edinburgh 2. 031-225 8411. Publish a book 'Winter sports in Scotland' and have a complete information service including sale or hire of equipment.

Scottish Tourist Board   **2 I 14**
137 Knightsbridge SW1. 01-589 2218. Besides general information on Scotland and ski-ing they also provide an accommodation guide.

Scottish Youth Hostels Association
28 South Tay St, Dundee. Dundee 22150. Lists of hostels convenient for the slopes and details of SYHA ski-ing courses.

Sunshine cruises

Kuoni-Houlders
Deepdene, Dorking Surrey. Dorking 5954. Expensive but off the usual tourist track. Holidays in the Seychelles, Indonesia, the Far East, Caribbean, Latin America and more.

P & O Lines   **6 O 33**
St Botolph's St EC3. 01-283 8000. Thirty one cruises, with sailings to the Mediterranean, Caribbean and Canaries starting 30th Mar. One class ships.

Union Castle   **2 I 19**
Rotherwick House, 19-21 Old Bond St W1. 01-493 8400. Cruises to Southern & Eastern Africa.

Villa and chalet holidays

'The Sunday Times' and other daily papers often carry individual offers of villas, farmhouses or apartments for rent during holiday seasons. This can often prove cheaper than an agency offer, and more interesting for those who prefer a holiday away from other tourists and pre-arranged time schedules. Otherwise try:

Aegina Club
25a Hills Rd Cambridge. Cambridge 63256. Join them on the Greek mainland and islands in Turkey. Social & cultural activities. Food in local restaurants. Holidays tailored to individual needs.

OSL Villa Holidays   **6 J 23**
39 King St WC2, or an ABTA Travel Agency, or phone Hoddesdon 67211. Villas and apartments in Spain, Malta, Rhodes, Crete and more.

Walking and climbing

Thomas Cook   **2 I 18**
Special Promotions Dept, Tel. 0733 264000 ext. 290. Treks in the Himalayas with porters and Sherpa guides. Camping. Medical certificate needed. 5 weeks approx. £780.00.

Ramblers Association Services
Wings House, Bridge Rd East, Welwyn Garden City, Herts. Welwyn Garden 31133. Unique walking holidays in the mountain areas of Europe — Italy, Yugoslavia, Lapland.

Youth Hostels Association   **5 K 22**
29 John Adam St WC2. 01-839 1722. Walking tours and inexpensive accommodation in hostels throughout the world.

Wildlife tours and safaris

Kendall Travel Service   **6 M 32**
18 Eldon St EC2. 01-638 0771. World-wide tours and package holidays.

National Trust   **5 L 19**
42 Queen Anne's Gate SW1. Royal Society for the Protection of Birds, The Lodge, Sandy, Bedfordshire. Will supply lists of British nature reserves and bird watching facilities.

Passenger shipping lines

These are the main offices of the passenger shipping lines. Voyages are more expensive in July and August. Passengers may book direct with the line or through a travel agent.

Blue Star Line   **5 J 20**
34 Leadenhall St EC3. 01-488 4567. South America, South Africa, Australia, New Zealand and Pacific coast, Canada and USA. Also cargo passenger service. Las Palmas, Tenerife.

British India Steam Navigation   **6 O 33**
P & O Passenger Division (BI Educational Cruises). P & O Building, St Botolph's St EC3. 01-283 8000. Educational cruises throughout year to Mediterranean and Scandinavia. Xmas cruises to Holy Land. Cargo passenger service to India and East Africa.

Chandris Line   **5 J 21**
66 Haymarket SW1. 01-930 0691. Cruises to Mediterranean and Atlantic, Madeira, Canary Islands, Australia, New Zealand, round the world. No vehicles.

Compagnie des Messageries Maritimes   **5 K 21**
Compagnie Générale Transatlantique, 20 Cockspur St SW1. 01-839 9040. South America.

Cunard Line   **5 J 20**
Cunard Buildings, 15 Lower Regent St SW1. 01-930 7890. USA. Cruises throughout year to Mediterranean, Canary Islands, Caribbean.

DFDS Travel   **2 H 18**
8 Berkeley Square W1. 01-629 3512. Denmark. Also world-wide.

Ellerman & Bucknall Line   **6 N 32**
12-20 Camomile St EC3. 01-283 4311. South Africa.

Fred Olsen — Bergen Line   **2 H 20**
229 Regent St W1. 01-437 7315. *Mid-Sep to mid-May,* weekly cruises to Canary Isles.

French Paquet Cruises   **2 I 18**
177 Piccadilly W1. 01-493 4881.

Holland-America   **5 J 21**
56 Haymarket SW1. 01-930 1972. Singapore, New York, Miami, Vancouver, Greece, Nice & Venice.

Mediterranean Passenger Services   **2 G 20**
18 Hanover St W1. 01-629 1336.

Ned Lloyd Amsterdam   **6 O 32**
Phs van Ommeren (London), Baltic House, Leadenhall St EC3. 01-488 3242. South and East Africa, Persian Gulf.

Royal Netherlands Steamship Co   **6 O 32**
Phs van Ommeren (London), Baltic House, Leadenhall St EC3. 01-488 3242. West Indies, Guyana, west coast South America. Also cargo passenger service.

Swedish Lloyd: UK   **2 D 18**
94 Baker St W1. Spanish bookings: 01-289 2151. Swedish bookings: 01-289 2511. Car ferries to Spain and Sweden.

Union Castle Line   **2 I 19**
Rotherwick House, 19-21 Old Bond St W1. 01-493 8400. South Africa.

Car ferries

The price shown with each entry is the cheapest single passenger fare (return fares are usually double). Cars are shown as single fares for the shortest length car i.e. a Mini.

Booking agency

Car Ferry Advice & Booking Service
418 Hale End Rd, Highams Park E4. 01-531 3524. Advice and bookings on every ferry or hovercraft that leaves Britain.

Sea ferries

BELGIUM: Dover-Ostend   **5 L 15**
Sealink Continental Car Ferry Centre, 52 Grosvenor Gardens SW1. 01-730 3440. 3¾ hrs. 9-12 sailings daily (winter 3). Belgian Marine Line and British Rail. £6.60. Cars from £7. Reduction on cars for short stay trips.

BELGIUM: Dover-Zeebrugge
Townsend Car Ferries. 127 Regent St W1. 01-437 7800. 4 hrs. 6 sailings daily. £6.60. Cars from £8. Comfortable.

BELGIUM: Folkestone-Ostend   **5 L 15**
Sealink Continental Car Ferry Centre, P.O. Box 303, 52 Grosvenor Gardens SW1. 01-730 3440. 4 hrs. Up to 4 sailings daily. British Rail. From £6.60, cars from £7 (summer). Minitour reduced fares.

BELGIUM: Felixstowe-Zeebrugge   **2 H 20**
Townsend Thoresen Car Ferries, 127 Regent St W1. 01-734 4431/437 7800. 5 hrs. Up to 3 sailings a day from £7.60, cars from £8.

DENMARK: Harwich-Esberg   **2 H 18**
DFDS Travel, 8 Berkeley Square W1. 01-480 7651/4. 18 hrs. 1 sailing daily all year. Passenger berths from £22, cars free with 4 passengers or £20 with one. 01-481 3211 for tours, etc.

FRANCE: Dover-Boulogne or Calais   **5 L 15**
Sealink Continental Car Ferry Service, 52 Grosvenor Gardens SW1. 01-730 3440. 1¾ hrs. Up to 12 sailings daily to Boulogne (winter 1 daily) and up to 11 daily to Calais (winter 1 daily). British Rail and French Railways. £6.60. Cars from £7. Reduction on cars for short stays.

FRANCE: Dover-Calais   **2 H 20**
Townsend Thoresen Car Ferries, 127 Regent St W1. 01-734 4431/437 7800. Up to 12 sailings daily (6 in winter) from £6.60, cars from £8.

FRANCE: Dover-Dunkerque   **5 L 15**
Sealink Car Ferry Centre, 52 Grosvenor Gardens SW1. 01-730 3440. 3¾ hrs. Up to 6 sailings daily. British Rail from £6.60, cars from £7 (summer). Cheap minitour rates.

FRANCE: Folkestone-Boulogne or Calais   **5 L 15**
Sealink Car Ferry Centre, 52 Grosvenor Gardens SW1. 01-730 3440. 1½ hrs. Up to 6 sailings daily. British Rail. From £6.60, cars from £7 (summer). Minitour reduced fares.

FRANCE: Newhaven-Dieppe   **5 L 15**
Sealink Continental Car Ferry Centre, 52 Grosvenor Gardens SW1. 01-730 3440. 3¾ hrs. Up to 6 sailings daily (winter 4 daily). British Rail and SNCF. Reduction on cars for short stays. From £9, cars from £9 (summer).

FRANCE: Portsmouth-Cherbourg   **2 H 20**
Townsend Thoresen Car Ferries, 127 Regent St W1. 01-734 4431/437 7800. 4 hrs. Summer only. 1-2 sailings daily. From £9.30, cars from £11.

FRANCE: Southampton-Cherbourg and Le Havre
Townsend Thoresen Car Ferries, 127 Regent St W1. 01-734 4431/437 7800. Southampton-Cherbourg 5 hrs. Summer only. 1-2 sailings daily. From £9.60, cars from £11.50.
Southampton-Le Havre 6¾ hrs (8 at night). Up to 3 sailings daily. From £9.60, cars from £11.50. Special

reductions on short stays.

GERMANY: Harwich-Bremerhaven   **2 G 18**
Prins Ferries, 13-14 Queens St W1. 01-629 7961. 16 hrs. 1 sailing every alternate day. £21 (cabin and meals extra). Cars from £13.10.

HOLLAND: Felixstowe-Rotterdam   **5 L 21**
Transport Ferry Service, P.O. Box 7, The Ferry Centre, The Docks, Felixstowe, Suffolk. Felixstowe 78711. Up to 3 sailings daily. From £9.75 excluding cabin & meals, cars from £10.50.

HOLLAND: Harwich-Hook of Holland (day service)   **6 M 33**
Sealink Continental Car Ferry Centre, P.O. Box 303, 52 Grosvenor Gardens SW1. 01-730 3440. 6¼ hrs by day. 1 sailing daily. British Rail separate fare. Ferry from £9, cars from £7 (summer).

HOLLAND: Harwich-Hook of Holland (night service)   **6 M 33**
Sealink Continental Car Ferry Centre, P.O. Box 303, 52 Grosvenor Gardens SW1. 01-730 7334. 8 hrs. 1 sailing daily. British Rail. Quiet ships on this night service. Ferry fare from £11.

NORWAY: Harwich-Kristiansand   **2 G 20**
Fred Olsen Lines, 229 Regent St W1. 01-437 7315. 22 hrs. 24 hrs summer only.

NORWAY: Newcastle-Kristiansand-Stavanger-Bergen   **3 G 20**
Fred Olsen Lines, 229 Regent St W1. 01-437 7315. 2 sailings a week all year round. 24 hrs.

NORWAY: Newcastle-Oslo   **2 G 20**
Fred Olsen Lines, 229 Regent St W1. 01-437 7315. 36 hrs. Summer only.

SPAIN: Southampton-Bilbao   **6 P 32**
International Hoverlloyd, Pegwell Bay, Ramsgate Kent. Travel Lloyd, 8 Berkeley Sq W1. 01-629 3512. 37 hrs. Seasonal fares vary from £19. Meals extra, cars from £18 (free with 4 passengers in winter).

SWEDEN: Tilbury-Gothenburg   **6 P 32**
Swedish Lloyd UK, International Hoverlloyd, Pegwell Bay, Ramsgate Kent. Travel Lloyd, 8 Berkeley Sq W1. 01-629 3512. Seasonal fare rates. Spring £29.50. Cars free with 4 passengers.

Hovercraft

DOVER - BOULOGNE or CALAIS   **2 B 22**
Seaspeed. British Rail Hovercraft. Reservations & Information, 7 Cambridge Terrace NW1. 01-606 3681. Boulogne 7 flights daily (2 in winter). Calais 6 flights daily, check for winter times. Cars from £11 (8 in winter), passengers £7.10.

RAMSGATE-CALAIS   **S M 14**
Hoverlloyd, Victoria Coach Station, 164 Buckingham Palace Rd SW1. 01-499 9481 or 8 Berkeley Sq W1: 01-629 3512. Coach links to Brussels and Paris. 40 mins. 20 flights daily (4 in winter). Cars from £17.50, passengers free. London-Paris coach connections 4 daily (check for winter). Passenger fare £10.50.

Air ferries

BRITISH AIR FERRIES
Southend Airport, Essex. Southend-on-Sea 545751 (office hours) and 48601 (at other times). Freight and passenger service.

BELGIUM: Southend-Ostend
45 mins. Average 6 flights daily. £42 return.

FRANCE: Southend-Le Touquet
35 mins. 2 flights daily. £23 return.

HOLLAND: Southend-Rotterdam
65 mins. 3 flights daily. £58 return.

Taxis and mini cabs

Taxis

A few of the most useful telephone numbers of taxi ranks are:

Baker St Station NW1. 01-935 2553.	**2 B 19**
Islington, Liverpool Rd N1. 01-837 2394.	**3 O 32**
Kensington, Wright's Lane W8. 01-937 0736.	**1 E 7**
Moorgate EC2. 01-606 4526.	**6 M 31**
Russell Square WC1. 01-636 1247.	**3 F 24**
St George's Square SW1. 01-834 1014.	**5 Q 16**
Sloane Square SW1. 01-730 2664.	**5 L 12**
South Kensington, Harrington Rd SW7. 01-589 5242.	**1 I 9**

or try:
Radio Taxicabs (Southern) Ltd. 01-272 3030.
London-wide Radio Taxis. 01-286 6010.

Mini Cabs

All the following have a 24 hr service:

A1 Mini-cabs   2   D 18
45b Blandford St W1. 01-935 9958.
A1 Mini-cabs   5   O 15
21a Denbigh St SW1. 01-834 3961.
Ambassador Radio Cars   2   A 16
61 Lisson St NW1. 01-262 0171.
BAB Mini-cabs Tours   4   K 2
296 Fulham Rd SW10. 01-352 7889.
City & Suburban Operations
30 Filmer Rd SW6. 01-385 8555.
Express Car Service   6   Q 27
16 Borough High St SE1. 01-407 7381.
Mini-cabs Brunswick Car Hire   3   B 30
163 Caledonian Rd N1. 01-837 7205.
Mini-cabs City Car Service   6   J 29
416 St John St EC1. 01-837 0221.
Mini-cabs (Kensington)   1   I 17
149 Earls Court Rd SW5. 01-370 2371.

Car hire

Self-drive car hire

Price depends on season and size of car, plus mileage.
Avis Rent-a-Car
35 Headfort Place SW1. 01-245 9862. *07.00-22.00.*
                                                    5   J 15
Also Thurloe Place, Cromwell Rd SW7.   1   I 10
01-581 2252. *08.00-18.00.*
68 North Row W1. 01-629 7811.   2   E 17
OPEN 07.00-20.00.
28-32 Wellington Rd NW8. 01-722 3464. *OPEN 08.30-
18.00 Mon-Fri, 08.30-14.00 Sat.*
World-wide reservations at Trident House, Station Rd,
Hayes, Middx. 01-848 8733.
Car Hire International   2   I 20
23 Swallow St W1. 01-734 7661. Free reservation
centre for all British car-hire groups. Arrange hire in GB,
W Europe, Madeira, Canaries, Turkey, N Africa.
J. Davy   1   F 5
9 Logan Place W8. 01-373 6000.
*OPEN 08.30-18.00 Mon-Fri, 08.30-13.30 Sat, 09.00-
11.00 Sun.*
Dove Group
115 Addiscombe Rd, Croydon, Surrey. 01-654 8111.
OPEN 09.00-17.30 Mon-Fri, 09.00-12.00 Sat.
Godfrey Davis   5   M 16
Davis House, Wilton Rd SW1. 01-834 8484. *24-hr
service.* Rental stations throughout GB.
Hertz, Rent a Car   2   D 16
35 Edgware Rd W2. Daimlers particularly. Self or
chauffeur _ driven. Stations throughout GB and
Continent.
Kenning   1   A 5
84-90 Holland Park Avenue W11. 01-727 0123. Self-
drive cars. Stations throughout GB, at airports and
abroad. *OPEN 08.30-18.00 Mon-Fri, 09.00-13.00 Sat &
Sun.*
Sportshire   1   I 8
6 Kenrick Place, Reece Mews SW7. 01-589 8309. MGB,
E-type, Morgan, Jensen, Healey & Triumph Stag for
hire. *OPEN 09.30-19.00. Sat until 16.00.*
Travelwise Car Hire   5   K 12
77 Pavilion Rd SW1. 01-235 0751.

Chauffeur drive

Patrick Barthropp   5   K 15
1 Dorset Mews, Wilton St SW1. 01-245 9171. Rolls-
Royce Phantoms and Silver Clouds with liveried
chauffeurs, cocktails, TV and stereo. *OPEN 07.30-
23.00.*
Hanover Car Hire   2   E 19
6 Wigmore Place, Wigmore St W1. 01-580 0505. A fleet
of chauffeur-driven limousines and saloons. *OPEN
08.00-19.00 Mon-Sat.*
Horseless Carriage Hire   5   N 15
59 Eccleston Square Mews SW1. 01-834 9922. Sports
and vintage cars for self-drive. *OPEN 09.30-17.30. 24 hr
telephone service.*
Arthur Monk
677 Finchley Rd NW3. 01-794 8111. Chauffeur-driven
Volvo saloons and 12 passenger minibuses for hire.
*OPEN 07.45-18.30 Mon-Fri. 10.00-13.00 Sat. 24 hr
telephone service.*

Coach hire

Beeline
20-26 Nunhead Lane SE15. 01-639 5261.
George Ewer (Grey-Green)
53-55 Stamford Hill N16. 01-800 4549.
Garners
39 South Ealing Rd W5. 01-567 8031.
Greens
213a Hoe St E17. 01-520 1138.
London Transport   5   J 15
Private Hire Office, 10-11 Grosvenor Place SW1. 01-235
5432.
Sheenway Coaches
66 Stanley Rd SW14. 01-876 4243.

Buses and coaches

London Transport buses
Enquiries: 01-222 1234.
Free maps of all London bus routes from underground
station ticket offices.
Other information and LT publications from
Public Relations Officer   5   M 18
55 Broadway SW1. 01-222 5600.
Green Line Coaches
Enquiries Reigate 42411.
Operate a regular service to approx 30 miles from
London. The main picking up points are at Baker St,
Buckingham Palace Rd, Eccleston Bridge and the
Minories Coach station.

Coach stations

Kings Cross Coach Station   3   E 29
National Travel, 250 Pentonville Rd N1. 01-278 7081.
Coach services to East Anglia, Southend and Stansted
airports.
Victoria Coach Station   5   M 14
164 Buckingham Palace Rd SW1. 01-730 0202. The
main provincial coach companies operate from here,
travelling all over Britain and Continent. Booking
necessary.

Rail terminals

British Rail Travel Centre   5   J 20
12 Lower Regent St SW1. Personal callers only.
Booking centre for rail travel in Britain and rail and sea
journeys to the Continent and Ireland. Several
languages spoken. See also under 'Information
centres'.
Blackfriars *(South)*   6   M 27
Queen Victoria St EC4. Information 01-928 5100.
Broad Street *(North)*   6   M 33
Liverpool St EC2. Information 01-387 7070.
Cannon Street *(South)*   6   O 29
Cannon St EC4. Information 01-928 5100.
Charing Cross *(South)*   5   K 22
Strand WC2. Information 01-928 5100.
Euston *(North)*   3   C 24
Euston Rd NW1. Information 01-387 7070.
Fenchurch Street *(East)*   6   P 32
Railway Place, Fenchurch St EC3. Information 01-283
7171.
Holborn Viaduct *(South)*   6   K 28
Holborn Viaduct EC1. Information 01-928 5100
King's Cross *(North)*   3   D 27
Euston Rd N1. Information 01-837 3355.
Liverpool Street *(East & Continental)*   6   M 33
Liverpool St EC2. Information 01-283 7171. Continental
01-247 9812. Car bookings 01-623 1831.
London Bridge *(South)*   6   Q 29
Borough High St SE1. Information 01-928 5100.
Marylebone *(North)*   2   A 17
Boston Place, Marylebone Rd NW1. Information 01-
387 7070.
Paddington *(West)*   2   A 13
Praed St W2. Information 01-262 6767.
St Pancras *(North)*   3   D 26
Euston Rd NW1. Information 01-387 7070.
Victoria *(South & Continent)*   5   M 15
Terminus Place, Victoria St SW1. Information 01-928
5100. Continental 01-834 2345. Car ferry 01-730 3440.
Waterloo *(South)*   6   N 23
York Rd SE1. Information 01-928 5100.

Airports

Gatwick Airport
Horley, Surrey. Tel Crawley 28822.
London Airport (Heathrow)
Bath Rd, Heathrow, Middx. 01-759 4321.
London Heliport   4 Q 3
Lombard Rd SW11. 01-228 0181.
Luton Airport
Luton, Beds. Tel Luton 36061.
Southend Airport
Southend-on-Sea, Essex. Tel Southend 40201.
Stansted Airpot
Stansted, Essex. Tel Stansted 502380.

Air terminals

British Airways   5 M 14
Victoria Air Terminal, Buckingham Palace Rd SW1. 01-834 2323. Reservations 01-828 9711. British Airways Overseas Division, most inter-continental and world airlines. *OPEN 24 hrs.*
Air Lingus   1 E 8
Tara Hotel, Wright's Lane, Kensington High St W8. 01-734 1212.
Pan American Air Terminal   5 M 13
Semley Place SW1. 01-759 2595. Pan Am flights, National & Malaysian Airlines. Coaches for Varig and Qantas, to and from Heathrow. *OPEN 06.45-18.30.*
TWA Town Terminal   1 D 3
380 Kensington High St W8. 01-602 0141. Flights only. Coaches to and from Heathrow. *OPEN 07.00-15.30.*
British Caledonian   5 M 15
Central London Air Terminal, Victoria Station SW1. 01-834 9411. Departures only. To West Africa & South America. *OPEN 24 hrs.*
West London   1 G 7
Cromwell Rd SW7. 01-370 5411. British Airways European Division, operating coaches to London (Heathrow) Airport. *OPEN 06.00-22.30.*

Air lines

Aer Lingus   2 H 21
52 Poland St W1. 01-734 1212. Cross channel & European. Transatlantic reservations 01-437 8000.
Aerolineas Argentinas   2 G 19
18 New Bond St W1. 01-493 6941. South, Central and North America, Europe.
Air Canada   2 I 19
39 Dover St W1. 01-629 7233. Canada, USA, Bahamas, France, Germany, Switzerland, Austria, Denmark, USSR, Ireland, the Caribbean.
Air Ceylon   5 M 14
166 Piccadilly W1. 01-493 4881. All flights from Paris. Connections through UTA French Airlines. Reservations 01-629 6114.
Air France   2 G 19
158 New Bond St W1. 01-499 9511. World-wide.
Air India   2 G 19
17-18 New Bond St W1. 01-493 8100. World-wide.
Alitalia   2 I 20
251-9 Regent St W1. 01-734 4040. World-wide.
British Air Ferries
Southend Airport, Rochford, Essex. Tel. Southend-on-Sea 545751. Ferries to Belgium, France and Holland.
British Airways European Division   1 G 7
West London Air Terminal, Cromwell Rd SW7. 01-370 5411. Traffic Handling Agents for the following airlines: Air Malta, Cyprus Airways, Gibraltar Airways.
British Caledonian Airways   2 I 20
65 Regent St W1. 01-734 3153. Scheduled and charter flights Europe, Africa and America.
British Island Airways
Berkeley House, 51-3 High St, Redhill, Surrey. Redhill 65941. Flights to Jersey, Guernsey, Dublin, Belfast, Antwerp, Paris.
British Airways Overseas Division   2 I 20
75 Regent St W1. 01-834 2323. World-wide.
British Airways Regional Division   5 K 22
West London Air Terminal, Cromwell Rd SW7. 01-370 5411. Paris & UK.
Delta Airlines   5 J 19
43 Pall Mall SW1. 01-839 3156.
Eastern Airlines   2 I 19
Qantas House, 49 Old Bond St W1. 01-493 5764. USA inland & to London.

Egyptair   2 I 18
31 Piccadilly W1. 01-734 2395. To Cairo.
El Al Israel Airlines   2 H 20
185 Regent St W1. 01-437 9277. Israel, New York, Europe, Teheran, Nairobi, Johannesburg.
Ghana Airways   2 I 19
12 Old Bond St W1. 01-499 0201. W. Africa & Rome.
Iberia   2 H 20
169 Regent St W1. 01-437 5622. Europe, Scandinavia, N. Africa, USA, S. America and S. Africa.
International Air Bahamas, Icelandic Airlines & Icelandic Air/Lofleidir   2 G 17
73 Grosvenor St W1. 01-499 9971. New York, Chicago, W. Indies, Iceland & Scandinavia.
Japan Air Lines   2 G 20
8 Hanover St W1. 01-408 1000. To Japan via Siberia or the North Pole.
KLM Royal Dutch Airlines   2 G 19
Time & Life Building, 153-7 New Bond St W1. 01-492 0336. World-wide.
Lufthansa   2 I 18
28 Piccadilly W1. 01-437 9797. World-wide.
Luxavia   5 K 21
11 Grand Buildings, Trafalgar Square WC2. 01-839 5221. Johannesburg from Luxembourg.
Pakistan International Airlines   2 I 18
45 Piccadilly W1. 01-734 5544. Far East.
Pan American World Airways   2 I 18
193 Piccadilly W1. 01-734 7292. World-wide.
Qantas Airways   2 I 19
49 Old Bond St W1. 01-995 1361. Australia via Eastern route. Reservations 01-995 1344.
Dan-Air Services   5 L 14
33 Elizabeth St SW1. 01-730 9681. Paris, S. France, Ostend & Scandinavia. World-wide chartering.
South African Airways   2 I 20
251-9 Regent St W1. 01-437 9621. South Africa, Rhodesia, Australia.
Trans World Airlines   2 I 20
214 Piccadilly W1. 01-636 4090. USA and Germany.
United Airlines   2 H 20
20 Savile Row W1. 01-493 6321.
UTA French Airlines   2 I 19
177 Piccadilly W1. 01-493 4881. World-wide.
Varig   2 G 20
235 Regent St W1. 01-734 8981. Flights to Japan, Brazil, USA.

Specialist air charter

All the big airlines operate charter flights subject to aircraft being available. Additional charter specialist firms are:
Clark Air International   6 Q 30
Clark Air House, 85 Tooley St SE1. 01-407 8831. Planes & helicopters.
Instone Air Transport   6 L 31
St Alphage House, 2 Fore St EC2. 01-628 5491. Freight specialists, air brokers & aviation consultants.
Cabair
Elstree Aerodrome, Elstree, Herts. 01-953 4411. Piper, Aztec & Navajo air-taxi operators. Telex 934573.
London Airtaxi Centre   6 M 32
18-25 Eldon St EC2. 01-588 3578. Executive jets with a cruising speed of 400 mph for charter at £400-500 per flying hour. Also larger aircraft, light aircraft and helicopters.

Helicopter charter

Autair International   2 E 18
75 Wigmore St W1. 01-935 1151. Have a flight of jet executive helicopters for sale or hire. Phone Luton 22661 for bookings.
British Executive Air Services   4 Q 3
West London Heliport, Lombard Rd SW11. 01-223 2323. Fleet of helicopters & aircraft for all types of charter: Jet Ranger £125 per flying hr, plus landing fee & VAT. Pilot training in Bell 47 £65 per flying hr.
British Airways Helicopters
Gatwick Airport South, Horley, Surrey. Tel Crawley 28822, Ext 6455. Operate 22-seater craft at £750 per flying hour and 4-seater helicopters at £130.
Alan Mann Helicopters
Fairoaks Airport, Chobham, Surrey. 09905 7471/7037. Operates a fleet of 6 4-seater Jet Ranger helicopters & 2 3-seaters. Contact Mr G Adams for bookings.
Helicopter Hire   2 D 18
Aviation Way, Southend Airport, Essex. Southend 545821. Two passenger Bell & Enstroms or 4-passenger Alouettes & Bell Jet Rangers for hire.

Point to Point Helicopters
Denham Airfield, Denham nr Uxbridge, Bucks.
Denham 2417. Single- and twin-engined planes with
pilot can be hired. Piper Twin Comanches and Aztecs.
Helicopters: Hughes 300 from 55, Jet rangers from
£120, Gazelles from £140 per flying hour.

Crane helicopters
London Airtaxi Centre   **6 M 32**
18-25 Eldon St EC2. 01-588 3578. Have executive
passenger helicopters and provide crane helicopters to
lift heavy loads over impassable obstacles.

Accommodation

Hotel booking agents

Hotac   **2 E 19**
80 Wigmore St W1. 01-935 2555. Bookings from
London are free. Also take advanced bookings from
provinces. OPEN 09.30-18.00 Mon-Fri.
Hotel Bookings International
Globegate House, Pound Lane NW10. 01-459 1212. All
types of hotel reservations mainly in London. Theatres,
coaches, conference rooms booked if required.
Reception offices at Gatwick and Heathrow. No
charge.
Hotel Booking Service   **2 H 20**
137 Regent St W1. 01-437 5052. Excellent and
knowledgeable service to business firms. OPEN Mon-
Fri 09.30-17.30. Sat 09.30-13.00.
Hotel Guide   **2 I 22**
Faraday House, 8-10 Charing Cross Rd WC2. 01-240
3288. First class hotel accommodation service. No
charge.
**Accommodation Service of the London
Tourist Board**   **5 K 15**
4 Grosvenor Gardens SW1. 01-730 9845. Free. Budget
accommodation. OPEN 09.00-22.00 mid June-mid Oct.
Expotel Hotel Reservations
Dial 01-568 8765 for immediately confirmed hotel
reservations. A new computerised system which covers
the whole of Great Britain. No charge.

Hotels: luxury

*Over £15 per night, single room with continental
breakfast. Not usually inclusive of service charge and
VAT.*
Athenaeum Hotel   **2 I 18**
166 Piccadilly W1. 01-499 3464. Comfortable modern
hotel in good taste. 112 rooms. T.V. £16.
Berkeley   **2 I 14**
Wilton Place SW1. 01-235 6000. New modern building.
£27.00.
Britannia   **2 F 17**
Grosvenor Square W1. 01-629 9400. Modern inter-
national hotel. 432 rooms. £18.30.
Browns   **2 I 19**
Albemarle St W1. 01-493 6020. Traditional, restful, oak
panelled. Courteous service. 165 rooms. £20.50.
Carlton Tower   **5 K 13**
Cadogan Place SW1. 01-235 5411. International
standards of luxury and service in this sophisticated
hotel. Excellent food in the Rib Room and Chelsea
Room restaurants. 319 rooms. £30.00.
Cavendish   **2 I 19**
Jermyn St SW1. 01-930 2111. New, modern,
sophisticated. Excellent restaurant (OPEN 24 hrs). 275
rooms. £21.00.
Churchill   **2 D 17**
30 Portman Square W1. 01-486 5800. Modern
international type hotel. 489 rooms. £18.00.
Claridges   **2 G 18**
Brook St W1. 01-629 8860. Quiet luxury and lavish
traditional atmosphere. First-class cuisine in the
'Causerie' and restaurant. Secretarial service. 250
rooms. £25.00.
Clifton-Ford   **2 E 19**
Welbeck St W1. 01-486 6600. Quiet, efficient and
friendly. 220 rooms. £13.50.
Connaught   **2 G 18**
Carlos Place W1. 01-499 7070. Dignified and
distinguished. Excellent service. 110 rooms. £19.50.

Cumberland   **2 E 16**
Marble Arch W1. 01-262 1234. Large, busy, modern-
ised. Valeting service. 920 rooms. £18.00.
Dorchester   **2 H 16**
Park Lane W1. 01-629 8888. Luxury with courteous,
efficient service. Dinner dances in the Terrace
restaurant. Outstanding cuisine. 290 rooms. £29.00.
Dukes   **5 J 18**
35 St James's Pl SW1. 01-493 2366. Unique situation
on secluded gas-lit courtyard. All rooms named after a
Duke. Excellent restaurant. 46 rooms. £19.30.
Elizabetta   **1 G 6**
Cromwell Rd SW5. 01-370 4282. Opened 1973. Interesting Louis XV style decoration. 84 rooms. £13.50.
Europa   **2 F 17**
Grosvenor Square W1. 01-493 1232. Modern and
efficient. Good restaurant. 290 rooms. Conference and
banqueting facilities for up to 1,000 people. £17.80.
Grosvenor House   **2 G 16**
Park Lane W1. 01-499 6363. Unobtrusive luxury and
service. Swimming pools, sauna baths, banqueting
suites, shopping arcade and garage. Excellent
restaurant. 500 rooms. £24.00.
Hilton   **2 I 16**
22 Park Lane W1. 01-493 8000. Modern luxurious
American-international hotel overlooking Hyde Park.
Good roof restaurant with views and dancing. 510
rooms. £29.00.
Hyde Park   **2 H 14**
66 Knightsbridge SW1. 01-235 2000. Traditional luxury
and comfort. Good international restaurant. 187 rooms.
£25.00.
Inn on the Park   **2 I 16**
Park Lane W1. 01-499 0888. Luxurious new hotel, with
every comfort. Two haute-cuisine restaurants and
dancing. Views over Hyde Park. Parking available. 230
rooms. Rates on request.
Inter-Continental   **2 I 16**
Hyde Park Corner W1. 01-409 3131. Good modern
hotel. Excellent location. 500 rooms. £26.00.
The Londoner   **2 E 19**
Welbeck St W1. 01-935 4442. Well appointed, friendly
and modern. Conference facilities. Valeting service. 125
rooms. £13.50.
Londonderry   **2 I 16**
Park Lane W1. 01-493 7292 (formerly Londonderry
House). New modern hotel with good decor. Valeting.
140 rooms. £29.00.
May Fair   **2 I 18**
Berkeley St W1. 01-629 7777. Smart, modern and
sophisticated. Polynesian restaurant. Theatre. Cinema
Club. 390 rooms. £20.50.
Meurice   **5 J 19**
16 Bury St SW1. 01-930 6767. Luxurious and graceful
small hotel. Faultless service. Banqueting room. 41
rooms. £21.00.
Park Lane   **2 I 17**
Piccadilly W1. 01-499 6321. Spacious, comfortable
hotel. 400 rooms. £17.25.
Portman   **2 D 17**
22 Portman Square W1. 01-486 5844. Large open-plan
hotel, suitable for tourists and business functions. Valet
service. Rotisserie, Coffee shop and Normande
Restaurant. £24.00.
Ritz   **2 I 18**
Piccadilly W1. 01-493 8181. Grandeur with elegance.
Period rooms. Unobtrusive efficient service. 130 rooms.
£18.00.
Royal Garden   **1 E 8**
Kensington High St W8. 01-937 8000. Sumptuously
modern. Impeccably run. 4 restaurants. Valet and
secretarial services. 420 rooms. £18.50.

Royal Lancaster   2 C 12
Lancaster Terrace W2. 01-262 6737. A tall new block geared for businessmen and conferences. Magnificent views over Kensington Gardens and Hyde Park. Valet, secretarial and interpreting services. 435 rooms. £23.00.

Royal Trafalgar   5 J 21
Whitcomb St WC2. 01-930 4477. Recently opened hotel above an Angus Steak House. 68 rooms. £15.12.

Russell   3 F 24
Russell Square WC1. 01-837 6470. Older type hotel. Banqueting facilities. 330 rooms. £16.00.

St George's   2 F 20
Langham Place W1. 01-580 0111. Tall, new and faultless. Efficient service. Good views of London from public rooms. Outstanding cuisine. 85 rooms. £21.00.

Savoy   6 K 23
Strand WC2. 01-836 4343. World-famous in reputation and clientele. Edwardian in atmosphere and service, yet still faultlessly up to date. Impeccable standards. Outstanding cuisine. Secretarial service. 300 rooms. £25.00.

Stafford   5 J 19
16 St James's Place SW1. 01-493 0111. Elegant and comfortable. Good restaurant. Small banqueting suite available. Valet and secretarial service. 63 rooms. £18.50.

Strand Palace   6 K 23
Strand WC2. 01-836 8080. Large, practical accommodating hotel. 780 rooms. £15.00.

Waldorf   6 J 24
Aldwych WC2. 01-836 2400. Edwardian type casual comfort. Suitable for the business executive. Modernised, central. Templars Grill has outstanding cuisine. 310 rooms. £14.00.

Westbury   2 H 19
Corner of Bond St and Conduit St W1. 01-629 7755. Modern with American standards of luxury and efficiency. Anglo-American grill room. Good restaurant. 285 rooms. £24.80.

Hotels: medium prices

£7-£15 per night, single room with continental breakfast. Not usually inclusive of service charge, VAT or private bath unless otherwise stated.

Barkston Hotel   1 H 5
Barkston Gdns SW5. 01-373 7851. Victorian hotel nr Earls Court. 74 rooms. TV £9.00

Basil Street Hotel   2 I 13
Knightsbridge SW3. 01-730 3411. Victorian décor, country house atmosphere. 120 rooms. £10.75.

Bayswater Post House   1 B 10
104 Bayswater Rd W2. 01-262 4461. Competent, modern hotel overlooking Hyde Park. Secretarial service. 175 rooms. £13.00.

Bedford   3 G 25
83 Southampton Row WC1. 01-636 7822. Modernised hotel and garden suitable for businessmen. 181 rooms. £9.90.

Bloomsbury Centre   3 F 25
Coram St WC1. 01-837 1200. Newly built tourist hotel. Pizza room, good food. Conference facilities. 247 rooms. £9.25.

Bonnington   3 G 25
Southampton Row WC1. 01-242 2828. Modernised well-established hotel. 270 rooms. £8.50.

Burns   1 H 5
Barkston Gardens SW5. 01-373 3151. Victorian building. 104 rooms. £7.50.

Cadogan   5 K 12
75 Sloane St SW1. 01-235 7141. Comfortable and friendly. 85 rooms. £6.50.

Charing Cross   5 K 22
Strand WC2. 01-839 7282. Victorian, spacious but modernised and comfortable. Excellent international restaurant. 210 rooms. £15.00.

Clive
Primrose Hill Rd NW3. 01-586 2233. Modern newly built hotel. Valeting service. Banqueting facilities. 84 rooms. £9.50.

Coburg   1 B 10
129 Bayswater Rd W2. 01-229 3654. Overlooks Kensington Gardens. Older-type modernised hotel. Banqueting facilities. Specialise in wedding receptions. Car park nearby. 120 rooms. £9.50.

Cora   3 E 25
Upper Woburn Place WC1. 01-387 6473. Close to Euston Station. Straightforward older type hotel. 150 rooms. £8.00.

Cordova House   2 B 12
14 Craven Hill W2. 01-262 0111. Small modernised and comfortable b & b hotel. 60 rooms mostly with private baths. £8.00.

De Vere   1 E 8
1 De Vere Gardens W8. 01-584 0051. Victorian, spacious, modernised. Wedding receptions. 90 rooms. £11.70.

Durrant's   2 D 17
George St W1. 01-935 8131. Elegant family owned hotel. 86 rooms. £9.50.

Ebury Court   5 M 13
26 Ebury St SW1. 01-730 8147. Comfortable small hotel with good restaurant. No lift. 39 rooms. Doubles have bathrooms. £9.50.

Eccleston   5 N 15
Eccleston Square SW1. 01-834 8042. Modernised. Near Victoria Station. 150 rooms. £9.50.

Eccleston Chambers Hotel   5 N 15
30 Eccleston Square SW1. 01-828 7924. Small and select. 17 rooms, all with colour TV. £8.50.

Embassy House   1 G 9
31 Queens Gate SW7. 01-584 7222. Modernised terraced hotel for the business visitor. 100 rooms. £7.25.

Flemings   2 I 18
Half Moon St W1. 01-499 2964. Older type central hotel. 100 rooms. £8.50.

Goring   5 K 16
15 Beeston Place, Grosvenor Gardens SW1. 01-834 8211. Quiet, family-type hotel. All rooms have private bath. Garden. Valeting service. 90 rooms. £15.00.

Great Eastern   6 N 32
Liverpool St EC2. 01-283 4363. Spacious, modernised older-type hotel. Good service. 163 rooms. £9.00.

Great Northern   3 D 27
King's Cross N1. 01-837 5454. Spacious, comfortable older-type hotel. New décor. 70 rooms. £8.80.

Great Western Royal   2 B 13
Paddington Station W2. 01-723 8064. Older type, spacious and modernised. Efficient service and comfort. 168 rooms. £9.75.

Imperial   3 G 25
Russell Square WC1. 01-837 3655. Entirely new hotel on old site. Coffee shop. 499 rooms. £9.00.

Kensington Close   1 E 7
Wright's Lane W8. 01-937 8170. Good value hotel with plenty of facilities: conference room, swimming pool, sauna baths and squash courts. 539 rooms. £14.50.

Kensington Palace   1 E 9
De Vere Gardens W8. 01-937 8121. Restful and modernised older type hotel. Barrie Room restaurant excellent. 292 rooms. £12.25.

Kingshill   2 A 12
55 Westbourne Terrace W2. 01-723 3434. New hotel near Paddington. Also let rooms during the day for conference and interviews. £10.00 per day. Sauna. 150 rooms. £7.50. All with bath.

Kingsley   3 H 24
36-37 Bloomsbury Way WC1. 01-242 5881. Modernised hotel for the businessman and tourist. 173 rooms. £8.50.

London International   1 G 7
Cromwell Rd SW5. 01-370 4200. Opposite West London Air Terminal. Large transit hotel geared for air travel. Cavalier Restaurant with banqueting facilities. Attractively decorated. 425 rooms. £13.50.

London Embassy Hotel   1 B 10
Bayswater Rd W2. 01-229 1212. Modern hotel overlooking Kensington Gardens. Banqueting and conference facilities. Secretarial service. 194 rooms, all with colour TV. £15.00.

Milestone   1 E 8
Kensington Court W8. 01-937 0991. Comfortable old-style hotel opposite Kensington Gardens. Banqueting facilities. 90 rooms. £7.50.

Mount Royal   2 E 16
Marble Arch W1. 01-629 8040. Businesslike and functional. Coffee shop, banqueting and conference facilities. 750 rooms. £13.50.

Piccadilly   2 I 20
Piccadilly W1. 01-734 8000. Victorian, calm and comfortable and very central. Valet service. Carving table. TV in all rooms. £14.58.

President   3 G 25
67-73 Russell Square WC1. 01-837 8844. Modern and functional. Businessman's hotel. TV in all rooms. £9.90.

Prince of Wales   1 F 8
De Vere Gardens W8. 01-937 8080. Efficiently converted terrace-type hotel. Pleasant and comfortable. Banqueting facilities. 340 rooms. £7.50.

Regent Palace   2 I 20
Piccadilly Circus W1. 01-734 7000. Reasonably priced, busy central hotel. Well run and business-like. Three restaurants including an excellent 'Carvery'. 1070 rooms. £9.25. (No private baths).

Royal Angus Hotels
39 Coventry St W1. 01-930 4033. 100 rooms with bath & TV. £14.58.

Royal Court   **5 L 12**
Sloane Square SW1. 01-730 9191. Straightforward and practical older-type hotel. 101 rooms. £9.50.

Royal Kensington   **1 D 4**
380 Kensington High St W14. 01-603 3333. Transit hotel over TWA terminal, next to Olympia and near the motor rail terminal. Coffee shop and banqueting room. 400 rooms. £11.00.

Stratford Court   **2 F 19**
350 Oxford St W1. 01-629 7474. Central, practical and efficient. Recently modernised. 130 rooms. £11.88.

Tavistock   **3 E 24**
Tavistock Square WC1. 01-636 8383. Businessman's hotel, practical and comfortable. TV in all rooms. 300 rooms. £9.00.

Washington   **2 I 17**
Curzon St W1. 01-499 7030. Up-to-date fashionable hotel. Efficient service. 162 rooms. £13.50.

White House   **2 C 22**
Albany St NW1. 01-387 1200. Formerly an apartment hotel now an hotel with full service. Overlooking Regent's Park. First-class public rooms. Restaurant with outstanding cuisine. 550 rooms. £11.25. Coffee shop.

Whites   **1 C 11**
Lancaster Gate W2. 01-262 2711. Charming, unobtrusive modernised, overlooking Hyde Park. Excellent restaurant. 50 rooms. £14.50.

Hotels: low prices

Under £7 per night, single room. Not usually inclusive of service charge, VAT or bath.

Alexandra National
330 Seven Sisters Rd N4. 01-800 8090. Modern hotel close to Finsbury Park underground station; useful for car arrivals from the north. Extensive banqueting and conference facilities. 200 rooms. £6.75.

Arden   **1 F 6**
112-116 Lexham Gardens W8. 01-373 7788. Comfortable hotel suitable for tourists and businessmen. 66 rooms. £4.25.

Atlas   **1 F 6**
24-30 Lexham Gardens W8. 01-373 7873. Pleasant hotel for tourists and businessmen. 69 rooms, doubles with bath. £4.50.

Baileys   **1 I 7**
140 Gloucester Rd SW7. 01-373 8131. Near Earls Court. Modernised hotel near air terminal. 130 rooms. £6.50.

Bedford Corner   **3 G 23**
11-13 Bayley St WC1. 01-580 7766. Reasonably priced modernised hotel.85 rooms. £5.75.

Berners   **2 G 22**
10 Berners St W1. 01-636 1629. Spacious Edwardian modernised hotel. 240 rooms. £7.02.

Clarendon Court
Maida Vale W9. 01-286 8080. Near Lord's cricket ground. Pleasantly redecorated and comfortable. Sauna and swimming centre. Little Venice Restaurant. 155 rooms. £6.50.

Crofton   **1 G 9**
14 Queens Gate SW7. 01-584 7201. Plain but pleasant terraced hotel.120 rooms. £6.00.

Grand   **3 G 25**
126 Southampton Row WC1. 01-405 2006. Modernised hotel. 80 rooms. £5.40.

Green Park   **? I 18**
Half Moon St W1. 01-629 7522. Modernised hotel with good efficient service. 175 rooms. Sauna bath and men's hairdresser. £6.50.

Hobbs Belgravia   **5 N 15**
80-86 Belgrave Rd SW1. 01-828 8661. Simple friendly hotel near Victoria. No restaurant. 76 rooms. £6.48.

Ivanhoe   **3 G 23**
19 Bloomsbury St WC1. 01-636 5601. Modernised comfortable. 250 rooms. £5.75. With bath.

Kenilworth   **3 H 23**
97 Gt Russell St WC1. 01-636 7632. Modernised, reasonably priced and comfortable. 210 rooms. £6.21.

Mandeville   **2 E 18**
Mandeville Place W1. 01-935 5599. Well run, comfortable. Conference facilities. 160 rooms. £6.48.

Mount Pleasant   **3 G 27**
53 Calthorpe St WC1. 01-837 9781. Reasonable-priced tourist hotel. Clean and modern. Mostly single rooms without bath. 439 rooms. £5.30 with bath.

New Ambassadors   **3 E 25**
Upper Woburn Place. 01-387 1456. Modernised,

efficiently run and friendly. Valeting service. 100 rooms. £6.00.

Pastoria   **5 J 21**
St Martin's St, Leicester Square WC2. 01-930 8641. Cosy and comfortable. Outstanding cuisine. 50 rooms. £6.50.

Rembrandt   **1 I 10**
Thurloe Place SW7. 01-589 8100. Modernised, well run. Good service. 170 rooms. £6.80.

Royal Adelphi   **5 K 22**
21 Villiers St WC2. 01-930 8764. Tourist hotel. 57 rooms (with bath). £7.00.

Royal Bayswater   **1 B 10**
122 Bayswater Rd W2. 01-229 8887. 36 rooms. £5.50.

Royal Norfolk   **2 B 13**
25 London St W2. 01-402 5221. Reasonable hotel near Paddington. 59 rooms. £5.94.

Rubens   **5 L 15**
37-39 Buckingham Palace Rd SW1. 01-834 6600. Pleasantly modernised old-type hotel. 130 rooms. £7.02.

St James   **5 L 17**
Buckingham Gate SW1. 01-834 2360. Completely remodelled hotel in quiet location. 520 rooms. £6.25.

Shaftesbury   **3 I 23**
Monmouth St WC2. 01-836 4422. Modernised and efficient hotel, giving straightforward service and comfort. Suitable for businessmen. 200 rooms. £6.50.

Wilbraham   **5 K 12**
1-3 Wilbraham Place SW1. 01-730 8296. Old-type hotel with charm. Good restaurant. 40 rooms. £7.00.

Hostels

There is a large selection of hostel accommodation in London. This list is primarily for young men and women. Rooms are spartan but very clean and usually shared. Booking is advisable. Also refer to the booklet 'Hostels & Residential Clubs in London' published by the London Council for the Welfare of Women and Girls and the YWCA. It lists 200 hostels in central London.

Fitzroy Hostel   **2 E 22**
41 Fitzroy St W1. 01-387 7919. Mixed. Colour TV and central heating. B&B£2.48 per night.

GLC Hostels   **5 N 22**
The Director of Housing, County Hall SE1. 01-633 7736. There are 6 hostels for men and women in employment or studying in London. Mostly long term residents. Visitors £3.80 per day.

London Musical Club   **1 A 5**
21 Holland Park W11. 01-727 4440/7094. 50 beds, also music practice and concert rooms. B&B.

London Hostels Association   **5 N 15**
54 Eccleston Square SW1. 01-834 1545. Chiefly for permanent civil servants — students — young men and women coming into London. 15 hostels. Book in advance.

St Louise's Hostel   **5 N 18**
33 Medway St SW1. 01-222 6225. Hostel for working girls and students 17-22 years. B&B.

YMCA   **3 I 23**
Central Headquarters, 83 Endell St WC2. 01-836 3201. Hostel accommodation available at:
184 Tottenham Lane, Hornsey N8. 01-340 2345.
King George's House, Stockwell Rd SW9. 01-274 7861.
Wimbledon, 200 Broadway SW19. 01-540 7255.
Ealing, 14 Bond St W5. 01-567 4038.
Indian, 41 Fitzroy Square W1. 01-387 0411.   **2 D 22**
Dockyard, Church St, Woolwich SE18. 01-854 1630.
Dormitory accommodation, summer only.
66 West Hill, Dartford Kent. 32 20521.
Barbican, Fann St EC2. 01-628 0697.   **6 J 31**
(women also)

YWCA Accommodation and Advisory Service
16 Great Russell St WC1. 01-580 0478/9. An accommodation and advisory service for girls. Also help with personal problems.

YWCA Phone 01-580 0478 for current information on all London hostels.
Number of meals provided varies, but usually includes breakfast and possibly one main meal a day. A few of the hostels in central London are at:
East Acton Lane W3. 01-743 3285.
31 Draycott Avenue SW3. 01-589 6017. Residential only. Self-catering.
12-14 Endsleigh Gardens WC1. 01-387 3378.   **3 D 24**
57 Great Russell St WC1. 01-242 2757.   **3 H 23**
39 Ennismore Gardens SW7. 01-584 3060.   **1 H 11**
Goldsmith House, Park Village East NW1.   **3 A 23**
01-387 4501.

YWCA: Danish
43 Maresfield Gardens NW3. 01-435 7232. B&B £1.05 in dormitories. 17-30 year olds

YWCA: Norwegian   **1 A 4**
52 Holland Park W11. 01-727 9346. Single, double and 4 bedded rooms.(inc br and 1 meal).
Youth Hostels Association
Members only. Maximum stay 4 nights. Cost per night varies with age. Closes at 23.30.
Holland House, Holland Walk W8. 01-937 0748. **1 C 6**
84 Highgate West Hill N6. 01-340 1831.
38 Bolton Gardens SW5. 01-373 7083.   **1 H 5**
Zebra Trust   **2 I 12**
46a Cheval Place SW7. Head office. 01-589 0852. Living accommodation for students of all nationalities and their families. Long-term accommodation only. Long waiting list.

Lodgings

Bed and breakfast. Mostly found in streets around main line stations, but also scan notice boards outside newspaper shops.

Motels

Prices given are for a single person with breakfast, unless otherwise stated.
Bridge House
Reigate Hill, Reigate, Surrey. Reigate 46801. 20 miles from central London on A217. Swimming pool. 74 rooms. Open to 01.00. £4.25.
Epping Forest Motel
High St, Epping, Essex. Epping 73134. 15 miles from London on A11, 28 rooms. £9.18.
Esso Motor Hotel
South Mimms, Potters Bar, Herts. Potters Bar 43311. Just off the M1 and 20 miles from central London. 132 rooms. £8.70.
Harleen Motel
162 Romford Rd E15. 01-534 7861. On the main road to Tilbury. 20 miles from central London. 25 double rooms. £6.00 per double room.
Master Robert
366 Great West Rd, Hounslow, Middx. 01-570 6261. 2 miles from London airport on A4; and 12 miles from central London. 64 rooms (soundproofed). £9.95 excluding breakfast.
Post House Hampstead
215 Haverstock Hill, Hampstead NW3. 01-794 8121. Newly built and pleasantly decorated motel caters for families near Belsize Park. 140 rooms (40 single) £6.40 per person and £11.00 for a single room.
Saxon Inn
Southern Way, Harlow, Essex. Harlow 22441. 20 miles from central London on the A11. 100 single and double rooms have bath and TV. £8.80, breakfast extra.

Hotels near Heathrow airport

Recommended hotels near London Airport (Heathrow). All these are air conditioned and provide free transport to and from the airport. Prices are for a single room with bath.
The Ariel
Bath Rd, Hayes, Middx. 01-759 2552. Circular in design, post-war hotel with 180 rooms. £12.80.
Arlington
Shepiston Lane, Hayes, Middx. 01-573 6162. Transit hotel for the airport. 80 rooms. £9.75.
Centre Airport
Bath Rd, Longford, Middx. 01-759 2400. New hotel built as near as possible to the airport, and geared to cater for transit visitors. 360 rooms. £9.25.
Excelsior
Bath Rd, Hayes, Middx. 01-759 6611. New airport hotel, fully soundproofed. Swimming pool. 24-hr service. 666 rooms. £14.50.
The Heathrow
London (Heathrow) Airport. Bath Rd, Hounslow, Middlexex. 01-897 6363. Pleasant modern exterior design. Conference facilities; swimming poolive group nightly. 681 soundproofed rooms. £15.50.
Sheraton-Heathrow
Colnbrook by-pass. West Drayton, Middlesex. 01-759 2424. Built in 1973, with a well-designed interior. Free courtesy transport into central London. Night club; shops; swimming pool; sauna; 24-hr coffee shop. 440 rooms, all with colour TV and soundproofing. £13.37.

Skyways
Bath Rd, Hayes, Middx. 01-759 2535. Built 1971. 360 well-designed, soundproofed rooms. Swimming pool. £13.50.

Hotels near Gatwick airport

Airport Hotel
Tushmore Roundabout, Crawley, Sussex. Crawley 29991. Modern, efficient airport hotel. 230 rooms. £8.50.
Chequers Hotel
Brighton Rd, Horley, Surrey. Horley 6992. Well-converted black and white timbered Tudor coaching house, fully modernised. 78 beds. £9.50.
George Hotel
High St, Crawley. Crawley 24215. 15th cent Trust House retaining original features yet providing modern, well-equipped bedrooms in the rear extension. 75 rooms. £9.00.
Post House
Povey Cross Rd, Horley. Horley 71621. New, spaciously-styled hotel. Open-air heated swimming pool. 149 rooms. £11.50.

Estate agents

The following list covers most classes of property and gives the specialists in each field. Anyone interested in property as an investment should subscribe to:
The Property Letter   **2 H 20**
13 Golden Sq W1. 01-437 4923. Gives up-to-date property prospects of places and districts in Great Britain and Europe. £25.50 per year.

House property

Allsops   **2 H 12**
20 Montpelier St SW7. 01-584 6106.
Roy Brooks   **4 L 7**
Moravian Corner, 359 Kings Rd SW3. 01-352 0061.
Chesterton & Sons   **1 D 8**
116 Kensington High St W8. 01-937 1234.
Connells   **2 G 18**
62 Grosvenor St W1. 01-493 4932.
Hampton & Sons   **2 I 19**
6 Arlington St St James's SW1. 01-493 8222.
Jackson-Stops & Staff   **2 I 17**
14 Curzon St W1. 01 499 6291.
Knight, Frank & Rutley   **2 G 19**
20 Hanover Square W1. 01-629 8171.
Winkworth & Co.   **2 I 17**
48 Curzon St W1. 01-499 3121.
Strutt & Parker Lofts & Warner   **2 H 18**
13 Hill St W1. 01-629 7282.
John D Wood   **2 H 18**
23 Berkeley Square W1. 01-629 9050.

Commercial property

Office, commercial and investment property.
Chamberlain & Willows   **6 M 31**
23 Moorgate EC2. 01-638 8001. Factories and warehouses.
Donaldson & Sons   **2 I 19**
70 Jermyn St SW1. 01-930 1090. Industrial and investment property.
Healey & Baker   **2 G 19**
29 St George St W1. 01-629 9292. Office and industrial property. Specialises in shops.
Hillier Parker May & Rowden   **2 G 18**
77 Grosvenor St W1. 01-629 7666. Shops, factories and warehouses.
Jones Lang Wootton   **6 M 30**
16-17 King St EC2. 01-606 4060. Office property.
Matthews & Goodman   **6 M 28**
Malvern House, 72 Upper Thames St EC4. 01-248 3200. Factories, shops and city offices.
Pepper, Angliss & Yarwood   **2 G 18**
6 Carlos Place W1. 01-499 6066. Factories, shops and offices.
Bernard Thorpe   **5 M 14**
1-5 Buckingham Palace Rd SW1. 01-834 6890. Shops and office property.

Estate agents: property abroad

Goddard & Smith   **2 B 13**
104 Westbourne Terrace W2. 01-773 1299. Australia and Europe.
Hampton & Sons   **2 I 19**
Overseas Dept. 6 Arlington St, St James's SW1. 01-493 8222. Europe.

Knight, Frank & Rutley   **2 G 19**
International Dept. 20 Hanover Square W1. 01-629 · 8171. France, Portugal, Sardinia, Switzerland.
Palmer & Parker (Overseas)   **2 G 19**
63 Grosvenor St W1. 01-499 4801. Bahamas, Malta, Portugal, Spain, South of France, Switzerland, Majorca.
Bernard Thorpe & Partners   **5 M 14**
1-5 Buckingham Palace Rd SW1. 01-834 6890. Australia, Malta, Cyprus.
Tufnall
Private address. Tel Ascot 24211. Minorca.

Flat-sharing Agencies

Will help place you in a ready established flat, or else find you a kindred spirit to search with. They do try to match up carefully according to age, interests, background, etc.
Flatmates Unlimited   **1 I 11**
313 Brompton Rd SW3. 01-589 5491.
Flat-Share   **2 I 18**
213 Piccadilly W1. 01-734 0318.
Share-a-Flat   **2 I 18**
175 Piccadilly W1. 01-493 1265.

Furnished and unfurnished flats

The address will generally indicate the district in which the agent specialises.
Around Town Flats   **1 A 5**
120 Holland Park Ave W11. 01-229 9966. Luxury furnished property-specialise in short lets.
Britton, Poole & Burns
2 Wellington Rd NW8. 01-722 1166.
Keith Cardale Groves   **2 F 17**
43 North Audley St W1. 01-629 6604.
Chesterton & Sons   **D 8**
116 Kensington High St W8. 01-937 1234.

Cluttons   **5 N 18**
5 Great College St, Westminster SW1. 01-839 7800.
Gilland & Co
12 Finchley Rd NW8. 01-586 2701.
Norman Hirschfield, Ryde & Browne   **2 D 17**
85 George St W1. 01-486 4601.
Knight, Frank & Rutley   **2 G 19**
20 Hanover Square W1. 01-629 8171.
Marsh & Parsons   **1 D 8**
5 Kensington Church St W8. 01-937 6091.
Benham & Reeves
17 Kings Well, Heath St NW3. 01-328 1000. Expensive furnished and unfurnished flats and houses. Minimum let of 6 months.

Accommodation Agencies

London Accommodation Bureau   **2 F 19**
102 Queensway W2. 01-727 5062. Extensive selection of flats and bedsitting rooms in all parts of London and the suburbs.
Boyd & Boyd   **2 I 12**
40 Beauchamp Place SW3. 01-584 6863.

Surveyors and valuers

Most of the estate agents listed carry out surveys and valuations. A few other recommended specialist firms are listed here.
Collier & Madge   **6 K 27**
5 St Bride St EC4. 01-353 9161.
Daniel Smith, Briant & Done   **5 J 19**
32 St James's St SW1. 01-930 9385.
Daniel Watney, Eioloart, Inman & Nunn   **6 J 30**
The Charterhouse, Charterhouse Square EC1. 01-253 4414.
Humbert & Flint   **3 I 25**
6 Lincolns Inn Fields WC2. 01-242 3121.

Eating and drinking

Tipping

Should be an expression of one's pleasure for service rendered, never a duty. Some restaurants automatically add a service charge to the bill — so beware of inadvertently tipping twice. These are suggestions only, there is no rule.
Restaurants 10p in the £1.00. More if you are pleased with the service.
Taxis 5p for a 30p fare — rest in proportion.
Women's hairdressers 15p in the £1.00.
Men's hairdressers 15p in the £1.00.
Cloakroom attendants 5p to 10p per article when you collect.
Washroom services If clean towels provided and individual attention is given 5p.
Commissionaires For getting a taxi 5p to 10p depending on the effort expended.
Inns & Pubs Never at the bar. 5p in the £1.00 for waiter service in the lounge.
Hotels Tip individuals for special service. The rest is on your bill anyway — up to 15%.

Restaurants

These have been chosen primarily for authentic food and good cooking. No restaurant is included just because it is expensive or pretentious — alternatively some of the cheaper ones here give very good value and the cooking is excellent.

Average prices for a meal without wine:

£	*Under £3.00 per person*
££	*Under £6.00 per person*
£££	*Over £6.00 per person*
Children	*Children welcome, sometimes with a reduction in price.*
Reserve	*It is advisable to reserve*
A	*Access cards accepted*
Ax	*American Express*
B	*Barclay Card*

Cb	*Carte Blanche*	L	*Lunch*
Dc	*Diners Club*	D	*Dinner*
E	*Eurocard*		

Service charge: in a few restaurants about 10% is added on top of the total price. This should be declared clearly on both the menu and the bill. Question it if the charge is hidden or ambiguous (for instance 's/c') so that you might unknowingly pay the tip twice.

Cover charge: not to be confused with the service charge. This is usually about 25p for napkins, bread and water. Note that outstanding restaurants in their own right are also indicated in 'Hotels' and 'Pubs'.

American

American Haven
190 Kings Rd SW3. 01-352 7182   **4 L 9**
70-71 New Bond St W1. 01-493 2913   **2 G 19**
291 Finchley Rd NW3. 01-794 5707
The same basic hamburger menu, chicken in a basket, steaks, chilli con carne. The Bond St branch runs old silent comedy movies. *LD OPEN to 24.00.* **£.**
Drones   **5 J 12**
1 Pont St SW1. 01-235 9638. Stylishly spread over two floors, offering an uncomplicated menu featuring different hamburgers, shakes and ices. *LD OPEN to 24.00.* A. Ax. B. Dc. **£.**
Gatsby's   **2 F 19**
17 South Molton St W1. 01-408 2349. Relaxed atmosphere, and an interesting menu of inventive versions of the hamburger. *LD OPEN to 24.00.* A. Ax. B. Dc. **£.**
The Hungry Years   **1 G 5**
208 Earls Court Rd SW5. 01-370 5823. Friendly service. The outside window depicts a Depression bread queue. They serve 14 different hamburgers, steaks, spare ribs. *LD OPEN to 02.00.* A. Ax. B. Cb. Dc. **£.**
McDonald's Hamburger
57 Haymarket SW1. 01-930 9302.   **5 J 21**
47 Strand WC2. 01-839 6086.6086.   **6 K 23**
108-110 Kensington High St W8. 01-937 3705.   **1 D 4**
American answer to the Wimpy. Bright, fast, popular and spreading rapidly. *OPEN 10.00-23.30.* **£.**

Maxwells
76 Heath St NW3. 01-794 5450. Eat country style fried chicken, steaks and salads with a Hawaiian touch, delicious sweets, all very good value. *LD OPEN to 00.30.* **£.**

Parsons 4 **K 8**
311 Fulham Rd SW10. 01-352 0651. Lively cafe with rock music. Generous helpings and free seconds of spaghetti, hot sandwiches, ice creams and shakes. *LD OPEN to 01.00.* **£.**

The Widow Applebaum's Deli and Bagel Academy 2 **F 19**
46 South Molton St W1. 01-629 1776. American-Jewish delicatessen with a lengthy menu offering 101 dishes. Chopped liver, matzo balls, good hot pastrami, and a large selection of sandwiches, salads, burgers, ice cream sodas and giant sundaes. *LD OPEN to 22.30. CLOSED Sun.* **£.**

International

Many of the top class hotels have excellent restaurants with international cuisine, in particular the Savoy, Dorchester, Carlton Tower and the Connaught. Often forgotten, the British Rail hotels at main line stations frequently have restaurants with very good food indeed. Refer to 'Hotels' section.

Alonso's 4 **Q 11**
32 Queenstown Rd SW8. 01-720 5986. Imaginative food with charming and efficient service. Champagne and Camembert soup, lamb with cherries and tangerines, cold caramel apple soufflé. *LD Reserve. OPEN to 23.30. CLOSED Sat L & Sun.* Ax. Dc. **££.**

Andrea's 4 **L 11**
8-9 Blacklands Terrace SW3. 01-584 2919. Small comfortable and intimate. Filmed in Antonioni's 'Blow-Up'. Steak Diane au poivre, veal kebab, chicken à la Kiev. *LD Reserve. OPEN to 23.45. CLOSED Sun.* A. Ax. B. Cb. Dc. E. **££.**

Borshtch N'Tears 2 **I 12**
45 Beauchamp Place SW3. 01-589 5003. Loud, musical and very popular Slav restaurant. Unofficial dancing and much cheer. Large menu — boeuf strogonoff, chicken kiev, lamb kebabs in vast portions. Advisable to arrive before 20.00 or after 22.00. *D Reserve for parties over 7. OPEN to 02.00.* A. Ax. B. Dc. **£.**

Brompton Grill 4 **J 11**
243 Brompton Rd SW3. 01-589 2129. Consistently good food and service. Lobster bisque, tournedos rossini, good fish and grills. Fresh fruit. *LD Reserve. OPEN to 23.00, Sun to 22.30. CLOSED Sun L.* Ax. Dc. E. **£££.**

Carrier's 3 **E 32**
2 Camden Passage N1. 01-226 5353. Owned by the gourmet Robert Carrier. Eat in either a French 19th cent inn or a gothic greenhouse in the garden. Classic dishes from the famous cook book: lamb in Greek pastry, roulade of red caviar, petit pôt au chocolat à l'orange. Table d'hôte only. *LD Reserve. OPEN to 23.30. CLOSED Sun.* **£££.**

Chanterelle 1 **I 7**
119 Old Brompton Rd SW7. 01-373 7390. Attractive décor, friendly service. Dim lights and huge helpings. Mousse of Stilton, grilled steak of lamb. Reasonable set lunch. *LD Reserve. OPEN to 24.00, Sun to 23.00. CLOSED Sun L.* Ax. **£.**

Connaught Hotel 2 **G 17**
Carlos Place W1. 01-499 7070. Smooth, discreet and unchanged. Panelled dining room or à la carte grill. Mainly English and French cuisine. Oeufs en surprise Connaught, silverside of beef, tournedos cendrillon. *LD OPEN to 22.00. CLOSED Sat D, Sun.* A. E. **£££.**

Daphne's 4 **K 11**
112 Draycott Avenue SW3. 01-589 4257. Small and dimly lit. Theatrical clientele. Very good soups. Roast grouse, veau au romarin. *LD Reserve. OPEN to 24.00. CLOSED Sun.* **££.**

Inigo Jones 5 **J 22**
14 Garrick St WC2. 01-836 6456. Extremely popular restaurant in an old mission school reputedly built by the architect of the same name. First-rate food on a regularly-changed menu: smoked salmon and sour cream blinis, rognonnade d'agneau mâconnaise, soufflé chaud à la Riki. *LD Reserve. OPEN to 24.00. CLOSED Sat L, Sun.* A. Ax. B. Dc. E. **£££.**

Lacy's 2 **E 22**
26 Whitfield St W1. 01-636 2323. Mr Lacy and cookery writer wife Margaret Costa serve truly international gourmet fare in this exquisite white-vaulted dining-room. Sorrel and cucumber soup, turbot en brioche with smoked salmon purée & fennel sauce. *LD Reserve. OPEN to 23.00. CLOSED Sat L & Sun.* A. Ax. B. Dc. E. **£££.**

Leith's 1 **A 8**
92 Kensington Park Rd W11. 01-229 4481. Tastefully offbeat décor in this converted private house complements the originality of the menu. Preparation, presentation and service are excellent. Leith's duckling, trout mousse, ginger syllabub. *D Reserve. OPEN to 24.00, Sun to 23.15.* A. Ax. B. Dc. E. **£££.**

Mirabelle 2 **I 17**
56 Curzon St W1. 01-499 4636. A famous Mayfair restaurant, renowned for fine cooking and a magnificent wine cellar. Homard Mirabelle, aiguillettes de canetons aux truffles. Must book. *LD Reserve. OPEN to 23.00. CLOSED Sun & B. Hols.* A. Ax. B. Cb. Dc. E. **£££.**

Nick's Diner 4 **J 4**
88 Ifield Rd SW10. 01-352 5641. Vital and enthusiastic cooking usually generous and original. Menu spiced with jokes. Smoked mackerel pâté, filet de boeuf en croûte, spare rib of pork. *D OPEN to 23.30. CLOSED Sun.* Ax. B. Dc. **£.**

Odin's 2 **D 20**
27 Devonshire St W1. 01-935 7296. Décor of umbrellas and Roman busts. Individual menu inspired by various traditions of cooking. Seasonal food: game and mussels in winter, lobster in summer. *LD Reserve. OPEN to 23.15. CLOSED Sat L & Sun.* **£££.**

Parkes 2 **I 12**
4 Beauchamp Place SW3. 01-589 1390. Cooking of outstanding distinction. Small and expensive. Table d'hôte only. Cheaper à la carte *L* in 'Mr Benson's Bar'. *LD Reserve. OPEN to 23.00. CLOSED L Sat, all Sun.* **£££.**

Quaglino's 5 **J 19**
16 Bury St SW1. 01-930 6767. Luxury and style combined with excellent cooking. Escargots, quail lobster. *LD Reserve. OPEN to 00.30. CLOSED Sat L, Sun.* A. Ax. B. Cb. Dc. E. **£££.**

Le Relais du Café Royal 2 **I 20**
Regent St W1. 01-930 6611. Spacious and grand with little to remind one of the former literary associations of this famous café. The food is excellent. Lengthy menu and excellent wine list. Tournedos Mme St Ange, escalope de veau Albert, tatre fatin. *LD Reserve. OPEN to 23.20 Sun to 22.20.* A. Ax. B. Cb. Dc. E. **£££.**

Salamis 4 **L 4**
204 Fulham Rd SW10. 01-352 9827. Comfortable & relaxing offering an imaginative menu including some excellent Greek dishes. *LD Reserve. OPEN to 24.00. CLOSED Sun.* Ax. B. Dc. **£.**

Savoy Grill and Restaurant 6 **K 23**
Strand and Embankment WC2. 01-836 4343. World famous reputation for near-perfect service in a traditional, dignified atmosphere. Good, entertaining night out. River restaurant *L* Reserve. *OPEN to 14.30. CLOSED Sun.* **££.** *D* Reserve. Dancing to 21.00, cabaret 23.30. *CLOSED Sun.* **£££.** Savoy Grill *LD Reserve. OPEN to 22.30. CLOSED Sat.* Ax. B. Dc. **£££.**

Chinese Cantonese

The cooking of Canton and Southern China. Nearly all Chinese restaurants in this country are Cantonese and nearly all have unfortunately made many concessions to English taste. Cantonese when authentic is very good indeed. It differs from Pekingese mainly by being more liquid. It is steamed, boiled or braised — herbs and sauces are widely used.

Chuen Cheng Ku 2 **I 21**
17 Wardour St W1. 01-437 1398. Unpretentious and totally authentic restaurant, well patronised by Chinese. Good fish dishes and excellent value lunches. *LD OPEN all week to 03.30.* A. Ax. B. E. **£.**

The Friends 6 **L 28**
The City Friends, 34 Old Bailey EC4. 01-248 5189. The Good Friends, 139 Salmon La E14. 01-987 5541. A family concern of excellent Cantonese restaurants. Home grown beanshoots and raw materials. Try black eggs, belly of pork with oyster, savoury duck, eels, chicken in lemon sauce, Chinese cheese. *OPEN to 24.00. Reserve.* **£.**

Lee Ho Fook 2 **I 22**
15 Gerrard St W1. 01-734 9578. Patronised by numerous Chinese for the good cooking and reasonable prices. Duck stew with abalone, sliced steak in oyster sauce, suckling pig. LD OPEN to 24.00 (Sun) LD). **£.**

Lido 2 **I 22**
41 Gerrard St W1. 01-437 4431. Large menus of typical Cantonese specialities in the heart of the Chinese quarter of Soho. Baked crab in ginger, eel and seabass cooked in the Chinese manner. *LD OPEN to 24.00 (Sun LD).* **£.**

Marco Polo 4 **L 11**
95 King's Rd SW3. 01-352 0306. An attractive, smart restaurant with a large Cantonese menu and excellent house specialities. Fish in ginger and soya sauce,

Chung Yau chicken. *LD OPEN to 23.45.* Ax. B. Dc. E. **£.**.

New Hong Kong **2 I 21**
58 Shaftesbury Ave W1. 01-437 6847. Extremely good value with lots of set meals. Modern décor. Over 100 different dishes. *LD OPEN to 23.30.* A. Ax. B. **£.**

Sun Luk **2 I 22**
2 Macclesfield St W1. 01-734 5161. Cantonese cooking of a high standard — most of the customers are Chinese too. Excellent for quelling hunger pains after midnight. Wonton soup, roast duck, steamed crab, eels. *LD OPEN to 04.30.* **£.**

The Young Friends
11 Pennyfields, Limehouse E14. 01-987 4276. Sweet and sour mullet, barbecued spare ribs, pork with eels. *LD OPEN to 23.30 (Sat & Sun LD 24.00).* **£.**

Chinese: Pekingese

The dishes of Peking, Formosa and Northern China are considered to be the highest form of Chinese cuisine and often equal in quality to the best French cooking. There are only about 20 genuine Pekingese restaurants in England (mostly in London). The food is drier and sharper than Cantonese (often roasted or quick fried) and the 7 to 8 courses are all eaten separately as a 'banquet'— a leisurely ceremonial occasion ideally shared between 4 to 6 people. If possible order the day before — you can leave the choice to the restaurant. The great dishes are Peking duck and Mongolian hot-pot.

Chantecler **2 H 22**
42 Dean St W1. 01-437 9455. One of London's first Shanghai restaurants. Unusual and tasty dishes include chicken blood soup, pancakes with pork and spring onions and rice dumplings in wine and rice soup. *LD OPEN to 24.00.* A. Ax. B. **£.**

Mr Chow **2 H 13**
151 Knightsbridge SW1. 01-589 7347. Pekingese food, with Italian overtones. Modern décor and paintings. Peking duck, sole in wine. *LD Reserve. OPEN to 23.45.* A. Ax. B. Cb. Dc. E. **£££.**

Dumpling Inn **2 I 22**
15a Gerrard St W1. 01-437 2567. A Soho branch of Richmond Rendezvous with similarly genuine Pekingese cooking. The place for 'food', but not an intimate chat. Crowded. Prawns in chili sauce, beef in oyster sauce. *LD OPEN to 23.30.* Ax. B. Dc. **££.**

Fung Tse Yuan
133 Wembley Park Drive, Wembley. 01-902 2391. Near the television studios and patronised by TV stars. Cheerful willing waiters; comfortable seating. Food usually excellent but can vary. Imperial hors d'oeuvres. Mongolian hot-pot, gong-bao prawns in hot sauce. *LD OPEN to 23.30.* **££.**

Gallery Rendezvous **2 H 20**
53-55 Beak St W1. 01-734 0445. One of the Richmond Rendezvous group. Eat either among Ching dynasty paintings or in a Chinatown banqueting suite. Delicious food, and many specialities. Snow prawn balls, barbecued Peking duck. *LD Reserve. OPEN to 23.30.* Ax. Dc. **££.**

Golden Duck **4 K 6**
6 Hollywood Rd SW10. 01-352 3500. Casual, and dimly lit. Calls itself 'London's first Chinese bistro'. Pop-art walls. Food genuinely good (banquet or à la carte). *D OPEN to 24.00. L Sat & Sun only.* Ax. B. Dc. **££.**

Kuo Yuan
217 Willesden High Rd NW10. 01-459 5801. Shabby, in an 'out-of-the-way' area, but some of the best Pekingese food in London. Try the Peking duck. *LD OPEN to 23.00. CLOSED L Mon-Fri.* **£.**

Lee Yuan **1 E 5**
40 Earls Court Rd W8. 01-937 7047. Small and unsmart but has a first-class Peking chef. Toasted prawns with sesame seeds, Peking duck, spiced crispy chicken. Clear the palate with jasmine tea. *LD Reserve. OPEN to 23.45.* A. Ax. B. Cb. Dc. **£.**

Richmond Rendezvous
1 Paradise Rd, Richmond, Surrey. 01-940 5114 and nearby at 1 Wakefield Rd Richmond. 01-940 6869. An old favourite for authentic Peking cooking. Best to order a banquet in advance rather than à la carte. Sliced sole in Chinese wine sauce, scampi Peking style, chicken and walnut in bean sauce. *LD OPEN to 23.30.* Ax. B. Dc. **££.**

The Singing Bamboo **1 H 6**
15 Courtfield Gardens SW5. 01-373 3410. Nine-course August Moon Festival dinner including barbecued spare ribs, king prawns, chicken wan ton soup. Normal à la carte in the basement. *LD Reserve. OPEN to 23.00.* A. Ax. B. Dc. **££.**

Soho Rendezvous **2 I 22**
21 Romilly St W1. 01-437 1486. A branch of the Rendezvous chain, with properly cooked classic Peking

dishes. Beancurd with minced beef and chilli, sole in wine sauce, mashed red bean pancake. *LD. OPEN to 23.45.* A. Ax. B. Dc. E. **££.**

English

Many pubs also serve good lunches based on traditional English cooking. Refer to the section 'Pubs'.

Baker & Oven **2 C 19**
10 Paddington St W1. 01-935 5072. A restaurant in a converted Victorian bakery. Original bakers' ovens still used to cook enormous portions of English food. Soups, pies, roasts and game, all very good. *LD Reserve. OPEN to 23.00. CLOSED Sun & Sat L.* A. Ax. B. Dc. **££.** Children.

The Bargee
Commercial Complex, Camden Lock, Chalk Farm Rd NW1. 01-485 6044. Situated in an old stable building and pleasantly decorated. Pheasant pâté with rum, prawn and mushroom salad, fresh peach mousse. *D Reserve. OPEN to 23.15, L Sat & Sun. CLOSED Mon.* A. Ax. B. Dc. **££.**

Baron & Beef **6 M 29**
Gutter Lane (off Gresham St) EC2. 01-606 6961. First-class variety of English food eaten in great comfort. Impeccable service. Roast Scotch beef, braised oxtail, steak and kidney pie, fresh fruit. *LD OPEN to 22.00. CLOSED Sat & Sun.* A. Ax. B. **££.**

Hungry Horse **4 K 7**
196 Fulham Rd SW10. 01-352 7757. A mirrored ceiling, wooden tables and modern décor. English cooking at its best. Home-made soups, onion and anchovy salad, calves brains, kedgeree. *LD Reserve. OPEN to 24.00. Closed last 10 days of Aug.* **££.**

Hunting Lodge **5 J 20**
16 Lower Regent St SW1. 01-930 4222. Reconstruction of cosy, 'old world' England. Luxurious and traditional English food, highly priced but generally very good. Quails' eggs, jugged hare, sea bass. *LD OPEN to 23.30. CLOSED Sun, L Sat.* B. Cb. Dc. E. **££.**

Huntsman
15 Flask Walk, Hampstead NW3. 01-435 0769. Unusual English country style foods. Pickled pigeon and walnuts, gamekeeper's pie, jugged hare. Bring your own wine. *D OPEN to 22.30. CLOSED Sun.* A.B. **££.**

Lockets **5 O 18**
Marsham Court, Marsham St SW1. 01-834 9552. Richly panelled and dignified; popular with MPs from round the corner. Attractively presented medieval dishes. Saddle of hare, spiced beef cooked in strong ale. Fine wine list. *LD OPEN to 23.00. CLOSED Sat & Sun.* A. Ax. B. Dc. E. **££.**

Maggie Jones **1 D 8**
6 Old Court Place, Kensington Church St W8. 01-937 6462. Homely and pleasant with scrubbed tables. Enormous helpings; home-made pâtés and soups, roast venison, oxtail stew. *LD Reserve. OPEN to 23.30. CLOSED Sun.* B. Dc. **££.**

Massey's Chop House **2 I 12**
38 Beauchamp Place SW3. 01-589 4856. Simple, pleasant old-style chop house. All meats charcoal grilled; home-made pâté. T-bone steak, apple pie. *LD OPEN to 23.00. CLOSED Sun.* A. Ax. B. Cb. Dc. **££.**

Rules **6 J 23**
35 Maiden Lane, Strand WC2. 01-836 5314. Genuine Edwardian eating house with very good traditional English food. Jellied and smoked eels, grouse pie, duckling with orange sauce. *LD OPEN to 23.15. CLOSED Sat & Sun.* **££.**

Shirreff's Restaurant & Wine Parlour **2 F 20**
15 Great Castle St W1. 01-580 2125. English dishes at their best; oxtail, jugged hare, steak and kidney pies and puddings, braised beef. Good wine at shop prices. *LD Reserve. OPEN to 22.00. CLOSED Sat & Sun.* Ax. Dc. **£.**

Simpson's-in-the-Strand **6 K 23**
100 Strand WC2. 01-836 9112. A famous restaurant with an Edwardian club atmosphere. The attentive service and the large carvings from enormous joints of beef and lamb are the best feature. Draught beer. *LD Reserve. OPEN to 22.00. CLOSED Sun.* **£££.**

Stone's Chop House **5 J 21**
Panton St SW1. 01-930 0037. Victorian chop house, rebuilt after the war and given authentic atmosphere with brass, black leather seating and Victoriana. Excellent English cooking with generous helpings. Grilled meats, steak and kidney pudding and pie, roast saddle of mutton. *LD OPEN to 23.15. CLOSED Sun.* A. Ax. B. E. **££.**

Tetthers **1 A 5**
6 Portland Rd W11. 01-727 6167. Galleried restaurant decorated with stripped pine and olive green hessian. Old English recipes used for smoked haddock mousse, feather fowlie, lamb in tansy sauce and wardonies in

syrup. *LD* Reserve. *OPEN to 24.00. CLOSED D Sun, L Sat.* A. Ax. B. Dc. **££.** Children.

Tiddy Dol's   **2 I 16**
2 Hertford St W1. 01-499 2357. Gillray and Rowlandson cartoons of the 18th cent gingerbread maker who gave his name to this cheerful eating house. Amiable waitresses serve generous helpings of well-cooked food. Chicken in cream and cheese sauce, fisherman's pie, gingerbread and blackcurrant fool. *D OPEN to 02.00.* A. Ax. B. Cb. Dc. E. **££.**

Turpins
118 Heath St, Hampstead NW3. 01-435 3791. Restaurant in a bow-windowed 18th cent house near the Heath. Duck and cherry pie, steak and kidney pudding. Good Sun roast beef lunch. *D* Reserve. *OPEN to 23.00. L on Sun only. CLOSED D Sun, Mon.* A. Ax. B. Dc. **££.** Children.

The Vine Grill   **2 I 20**
3 Piccadilly Place (off Swallow St) W1. 01-734 5789. Comfortable restaurant with personal atmosphere. Aperitifs at the bar. Choose you own steak, chop or cutlet to be cooked on the grill. *LD OPEN to 22.00. CLOSED Sat & Sun.* A. Ax. Dc. E. **££.**

Wiltons   **5 J 19**
27 Bury St SW1. 01-930 8391. Small distinguished and Edwardian with art nouveau décor. Simple and delicious English food. Oysters, lobsters, roast beef and excellent game. *OPEN to 23.00 LD. CLOSED Sun.* **£££.**

French

The following restaurants all serve classical and famous French cooking at its best. Some specialise in simple French provincial dishes, others in highly sophisticated cuisine.

Ark
122 Palace Gardens Terrace W8. 01-299 4024.   **1 C 8**
35 Kensington High St W8. 01-937 4294   **1 E 8**
Good French provincial food. Onion soup, noisette d'agneau, foie de veau. *LD OPEN to 23.30 (Sun D).* **££.**

L'Artiste Affamé   **1 I 5**
243 Old Brompton Rd SW5. 01-373 1659. An extensive menu offering excellent provincial food. Plain surroundings nicely set off by unusual 'rustic' antiques and a log fire downstairs in winter. Carafes. Filet dijon, crespolini. *D OPEN to 23.15. CLOSED Sun.* A. Ax. B. Dc. **££.**

L'Artiste Assoiffé   **1 A 8**
122 Kensington Park Rd W11. 01-727 5111. Informal corner restaurant with fairly authentic French food. Eat outside in the summer. *D OPEN to 23.30. L Sat only. CLOSED Sun.* A. Ax. B. Dc. **££.**

Le Bistingo   **2 I 22**
57 Old Compton St W1. 01-437 0784. Excellent Soho bistro serving provincial French cooking from a blackboard menu. Fresh sardines, coquille de homard et scampi venison, banana au rhum. Carafes. *LD OPEN to 24.00, Sun to 23.00.* A. Ax. B. Cb. Dc. E. **£.**

Café Royal   **2 I 20**
68 Regent St W1. 01-437 9090. The days of Oscar Wilde and the 'old' Café Royal still linger in the grill room. Good pâtés, steak burgundy, paupiette de veau Josephine. *LD Reserve. OPEN to 23.30. CLOSED Sun, L Sat.* **£££.**

Capital Hotel Restaurant   **2 I 13**
22-24 Basil St SW3. 01-589 5171. Small, conveniently situated new hotel with first class French cuisine. Sole soufflé cardinale, carré d'agneau aux herbes, sorbet au fine Champagne. *LD Reserve. OPEN to 22.45.* A. Ax. B. Dc. E. **£££.**

Le Carrosse   **4 K 10**
19 Elystan St SW3. 01-584 5248. Chic and intimate with an art nouveau setting by David Hicks. Distinctive menu: pâté de saumon et turbot, lamb Shrewbury, apricot sorbet. *D Reserve. OPEN to 23.30. CLOSED Sun.* Ax. **££.**

Casse-Croute   **4 K 9**
1 Cale St SW3. 01-352 6174. Wide variety of provincial dishes. Smooth service by French waiters in a comfortable atmosphere. Seafood pâté, escalope de veau, coq au vin, fresh trout. *LD OPEN to 23.30. CLOSED L Mon.* A. Ax. B. Cb. Dc. E. **££.**

Le Cellier du Midi
28 Church Row NW3. 01-435 9998. Good, well flavoured typical Midi and Languedoc food served in the cellar of a fashionable Hampstead house. Pot au feu, pousse bedaine, crème brûlée. *D* Reserve. *OPEN to 23.30.* A. Ax. B. Dc. **££.**

Chez Solange   **5 J 22**
35 Cranbourn St WC2. 01-836 0542. Busy but roomy. Typical French cuisine with service entirely by women. Cerville au beurre noir, mignons de veau gratinée Lyonnaise, coq au vin. *LD Reserve. OPEN to 02.00.* A. Ax. B. Cb. Dc. **££**

Claridges   **2 G 18**
Brook St W1. 01-629 8860. Distinguished French cooking in luxurious surroundings. The atmosphere is typical of the sedate thirties. Polished service and notable wine list. *LD Reserve. OPEN to 23.00.* A. E. **££.**

Le Coq Hardi   **1 D 4**
353 Kensington High St W8. 01-603 6951. Attractive, quiet, genuinely French establishment. Pâté, onion soup, lobster. *LD Reserve. OPEN to 23.00. CLOSED Sun, L Sat.* A. Ax. B. Dc. **££.**

A L'Ecu de France   **2 I 19**
111 Jermyn St SW1. 01-930 2837. Superlative food. Fruits de mer, ris de Veau clarence. Notable wine list. *LD OPEN to 23.30. CLOSED Sun. L Sat.* B. Dc. **£££.**

L'Escargot Bienvenu
48 Greek St W1. 01-437 4460. Typical bourgeois French cuisine and décor with quiet and efficient service. Fresh sardines, escargots, carbonade de boeuf flamande, brochette St Jacques. Well chosen wine list strong in Alsace. *LD Reserve. OPEN to 22.30. CLOSED Sun, L Sat.* A. Ax. B. Dc. **££.**

L'Etoile   **2 F 22**
30 Charlotte St W1. 01-636 7189. Typically French in atmosphere and style. Top-quality food and attentive service. Caldeirada, rognons sautés au vin rouge, turbot à la Monégasque. Better at lunch. *LD Reserve. OPEN to 22.00. CLOSED Sat & Sun.* **£££.**

Au Fin Bec   **4 K 11**
100 Draycott Avenue SW3. 01-584 3600. Small but roomy and pleasant, with a visibly immaculate kitchen. Oeufs Bénédictine, suprême de volaille à l'estragon, pilaff de fruits de mer. *LD Reserve. OPEN to 23.00. CLOSED Sun.* Ax. Dc. **££.**

Le Français   **4 K 7**
259 Fulham Rd SW3. 01-352 3668. Comfortable, with excellent service. Serious minded approach to its excellent French provincial cooking. The ambitious menu changes fortnightly to different regions. Also basic à la carte. Frogs' legs and plover (imported), mousseline de sole. Private room available for parties. *LD OPEN to 23.15. CLOSED Sun & usually all July.* Ax. Dc. **££.**

Le Gavroche   **5 M 12**
61-3 Lower Sloane St SW1. 01-730 2820. Luxury restaurant with haute cuisine. Soufflé suissesse, caneton Gavroche, omelette soufflé Rothschild. Cooking variable but service faultless. *D* Reserve. *OPEN to 24.00. CLOSED Sun.* Ax. **£££.**

Genevieve   **2 E 19**
13-14 Thayer St W1. 01-486 2244. Comfortable, roomy. Specialises in French cuisine bourgeoise. Coq au vin, médaillon de morilles. *LD OPEN to 23.00. CLOSED Sun.* A. Ax. B. Dc. E. **££.**

Au Jardin des Gourmets   **2 H 22**
5 Greek St W1. 01-437 1816. Unassuming but impeccable French classical cuisine. Good wines. *LD Reserve. OPEN to 23.00.* A. Ax. B. Dc. E. **££.**

Keats
3-4 Downshire Hill NW3. 01-435 1499. Pleasant relaxed service and top-quality cuisine. At Xmas and the New Year and at other special times, it provides a bookable feast for gourmets of about 12 dishes, lasting 3-4 hrs. Turbot soufflé amiral, filet de boeuf Wellington, riz a l'impératrice. *D Reserve. OPEN to 24.00, L Sun only.* A. Ax. B. Dc. E. **£££.** Children.

Kettners   **2 I 22**
29 Romilly St W1. 01-437 3437. A 100-year old comfortably plush establishment with courteous leisurely service. Try their daily special dish. *LD OPEN to 23.15, Sun to 22.15.* A. Ax. B. Dc. **££.**

Langan's Brasserie   **2 I 19**
Stratton St W1. 01-493 6437. Vast L-shaped room seating 200. Popular and very trendy. Small menu, erratic service. *LD OPEN to 23.00.* Reserve. No cards. **££.**

Marcel   **2 I 13**
14 Sloane St SW1. 01-235 4912. Provincial, with 'slate' specialities. Boeuf bourguignonne, coeur de filet en croûte. *LD OPEN to 22.30. CLOSED Sun.* Ac. B. Dc. **££.**

Minotaur   **4 K 11**
Chelsea Cloisters, Sloane Avenue SW3. 01-584 8608. Spacious and comfortable, with classic French provincial dishes. Oeuf en soufflé, sole minotaur, tournedos en croûte. *LD OPEN to 23.00. CLOSED L Sat.* Ax. Dc. **££.**

Mon Plaisir   **3 I 23**
21 Monmouth St WC2. 01-836 7243. Small, spartan, typically French bistro. Unobsequious but friendly service. Escalope à l'estragon, veau Marengo, poulet au vinaigre. *LD Reserve. OPEN to 22.00. CLOSED Sat L, Sun.* **£.**

L'Opéra   **3 I 24**
32 Great Queen St WC2. 01-405 9020. Plush interior

with Victorian opera posters and intimate alcoves. French and North African cooking Bouillabaisse, couscous, steak bordelais. *LD Reserve. OPEN to 24.00. CLOSED Sun, L Sat.* A. Ax. B. Dc. E. **££**.

Le Petit Montmartre   2 **E 19**
15 Marylebone Lane W1. 01-935 9226. Good French cooking: cassoulet toulousaine, demoiselles de Cherbourg. *LD Reserve. OPEN to 23.30. CLOSED Sun, L Sat.* A. Ax. B. Dc. **££**.

Le Poulbot   6 **M 29**
45 Cheapside EC2. 01-236 4379. Expense account lunches downstairs, less expensive fare upstairs in this City partner of 'Le Gavroche'. Excellent food; poulet sauté à la nantaise, escargots de l'abbaye and poulet chasseur. *L Reserve. OPEN to 15.00. CLOSED Sat & Sun.* Ax. **££**

La Poule au Pot   5 **L 14**
231 Ebury St SW1. 01-730 7763. Casual and friendly, with reasonable prices. Flan de poireaux, canard à la solognote, lapin aux deux moutardes. *LD Reserve. OPEN to 23.15. CLOSED Sun.* B. **££**.

Pimlico Bistro   5 **O 15**
22 Charlwood St W1. 01-828 3303. Small menu but well-prepared food at reasonable prices. Whitebait, mackerel, barbecued lamb, stuffed veal. *LD OPEN to 23.30. Closed Sun, L Sat.* A. Ax. B. Dc. **£**. Children.

Au Savarin   2 **F 22**
8 Charlotte St W1. 01-636 7134. One of the last original pre-war restaurants with service to match. Classical French cuisine. *LD OPEN to 22.30. Closed Sun.* **£££**.

Trencherman
271 New Kings Rd SW6. 01-736 4988. Tiled floor, French tavern decor. Family run restaurant. Bouillabaisse, suprême de volaille à la Périgord, good wine selection. *LD Reserve. OPEN to 23.15. CLOSED L Sat, D Sun.* A. Ax. B. Dc. E. **££**.

German and Austrian

Kerzerstuberl   2 **E 18**
9 St Christopher's Place W1. 01-486 3196. Authentic Austrian food and music on the accordion, with yodelling. You are expected to join in, so be prepared for a noisy evening. *D Reserve. OPEN to 23.00. CLOSED L and Sun.* A. Ax. B. Dc. **££**.

Old Vienna   2 **G 19**
94 New Bond St W1. 01-629 8716. Gay Austrian atmosphere, music and excellent cooking. Rindsbraten sacher Art, paprika Huhn Franz Lehar, sacher torte. *LD OPEN to 23.00. CLOSED Sat L, Sun.* **££**.

Tiroler Hut
27 Westbourne Grove W2. 01-727 3981. Tyrolean atmosphere with waitresses in national dress. Dancing, yodelling. Good value and excellent cooking. Leberknodel suppe, jagerschnitzel and apfel strudel. *D OPEN to 00.30. CLOSED Mon.* A. Ax. Dc. **£**.

Greek
Many Greek restaurants are run by Cypriots who have absorbed the best of both Greek and Turkish dishes into their style of cooking. For this reason many of the restaurants listed under the 'Turkish' section may offer similar dishes to those found in some Greek restaurants.

Beotys   5 **J 22**
79 St Martins Lane WC2. 01-836 8548. Comfortable establishment with authentic Greek cooking. Taramasalata, dolmadakia, arnaki. *OPEN to 23.30. CLOSED Sun.* **££**.

Blue Dolphin   2 **F 22**
40 Goodge St W1. 01-636 4874. Simple Greek restaurant. Charcoal grilled meats and kebabs, humous, kakoretsi and salad. Good Greek wine and coffee. *LD OPEN to 00.45. CLOSED Sun L.* **£**.

Cypriana Kebab House   2 **G 22**
11 Rathbone St W1. 01-636 1057. Greek Cypriot food. Pleasant and not too expensive. Friendly service. Specialities range from talatouri salad to sheftalia. *OPEN to 24.00. CLOSED Sat.* Children. B. Dc. **£**.

Hellenic   2 **E 19**
30 Thayer St W1. 01-935 1257. Genuine inexpensive Greco-Turkish food. Fried mussels with garlic, suckling pig, loukomades. *LD Reserve. OPEN to 23.30. CLOSED Sun.* **£**.

Kalamaras Taverna   1 **A 11**
1 Queensway W2. 01-727 9122. True taverna atmosphere. Bouzouki players. Superb national dishes ranging from xolmades to baklava. *D Reserve. OPEN to 24.00. CLOSED Sun.* Ax. Dc. Children. **££**.

Trojan Horse   4 **J 11**
3 Milner St SW3. 01-589 4665. Excellent Greek-Cypriot food in Chelsea atmosphere. Humous, avgolemono, psito, moussaka. Bouzouki music. *D OPEN to 22.45. CLOSED Sun.* **£**.

White Tower   **G 22**
1 Percy St W1. 01-636 8141. Elegant; first class cuisine. Agreeable and leisurely service. Lemon soup, moussaka, dolmades. *LD Reserve. OPEN to 22.30. CLOSED Sat & Sun.* **£££**.

Hungarian
Hungarian food is distinguished by unusual but extremely tasty dishes. Fish are all of the freshwater variety. Carp and pike are presented in an impeccable style.

Gay Hussar   2 **H 22**
2 Greek St W1. 01-437 0973. Excellent Austro-Hungarian cooking. Good, enthusiastic service. Cold wild cherry soup, bulgar salata, roast partridge with lentils. *LD Reserve. OPEN to 23.30. CLOSED Sun & B. Hols. No credit cards.* **££**.

Le Mignon   1 **A 11**
2 Queensway W2. 01-229 0093. Typical Hungarian food, cheerful atmosphere and live gipsy orchestra. House sulz, chicken hongroise, fantanyeros, goulash. *LD OPEN to 24.00. CLOSED Mon.* **£**.

Indian
The farther south in India the hotter the spices. Madras, Bendi and Vindaloo mean climbing degrees of heat. For the European however there is no particular virtue in an excess of hotness — many Indians also enjoy (and prefer) mild curries. Hindu cooking uses vegetables in rich liquid juices; Muslims use more meat and the food is drier. The best cooking uses the traditional mud oven and adds spices individually to each dish, giving a distinctive and piquant flavour.

Ashoka   5 **J 22**
22 Cranbourn St WC2. 01-836 5936. Good Punjabi food at sensible prices. *LD OPEN to 23.15.* A. Ax. Cb. Dc. E. **£**.

The Ganges   2 **I 22**
40 Gerrard St W1. 01-437 0284. Specialises in authentic Indo-Pakistani dishes — some are newly introduced and unobtainable elsewhere. Tandoori dishes (baked in a clay oven) and tikkas. Indian music. *LD Reserve. OPEN to 23.00. Closed Sun.* A. Ax. B. Dc. Children. **£**.

The Gaylord   2 **F 21**
79-81 Mortimer St W1. 01-580 3615. Authentic Punjabi food. Spices added individually to each dish giving some delectable flavours. Tandoori chicken, lentils in cream and interesting Indian sweetmeats. *LD OPEN to 23.30.* A. Ax. B. Dc. E. **£**.

Jamshid's   1 **I 9**
6 Glendower Place SW7. 01 584 2309. Classic Indian dishes. Clean, agreeable but small. Kashmiri curries and kebabs. *LD OPEN to 23.30. CLOSED Sun.* Ax. B. Dc. Cb. E. **££**.

Light of India   2 **A 18**
59 Park Rd NW1. 01-723 6753. Specializes in curry dishes. Pleasant, roomy. Roghan josh, prawn patia, Persian pilau. *LD Reserve. OPEN to 23.30.* A. B. Dc. E. **£**.

Mumtaz   2 **A 18**
4-10 Park Rd NW1. 01-723 0549. Palms, gold filigree lamps. Excellent food in an unusual atmosphere. Seekh kebab. Mumtaz pasinda, tandoori chicken. Special buffets on Sun. *LD OPEN to 23.15.* A. Ax. B. Dc. E. **£**.

Sardar   3 **F 23**
60 Tottenham Court Rd W1. 01-636 0382. Good Punjabi cooking in an unpretentious setting. Tandoori chicken, shami kebab. *LD OPEN to 23.45.* **£**.

Shafi   2 **I 22**
18 Gerrard St W1. 01-437 2354. The oldest Indian restaurant in London. Some original dishes not found elsewhere. Samosas, chicken cucu-paka, potato chops. *LD OPEN to 23.30. CLOSED Sun L.* A. Ax. B. Cb. Dc. E. **£**.

Sri Lanka   1 **G 5**
19 Childs St SW5. 01-373 41-16. Tasty Ceylonese dishes in an oriental atmosphere. Risam, pittu prawns, biriani. *LD OPEN to 24.00.* A. Ax. B. Cb. Dc. E. **£**.

Star of India   1 **I 7**
154 Old Brompton Rd SW5. 01-373 2901. Excellent Indian food and good service. Mughlai dishes, prawn biriani, kebab. *LD OPEN to 24.00. Sun to 23.30.* **£**.

Tandoori   4 **J 10**
153 Fulham Rd SW3. 01-589 7749. North-west frontier cooking of very high quality by Pathan chefs in the traditional clay ovens. Pleasant décor with soft music. Tandoori chicken, kebab, roghan josh. *D OPEN to 00.30, Sun to 23.30. Sun L.* A. Ax. B. Cb. Dc. E. **££**.

Veeraswamy's   2 **I 20**
99-101 Regent St (entrance in Swallow St) W1. 01-734 1401.. Authentic food in 'Indian Empire' atmosphere. Moglai, Delhi, Madras, Ceylon and Vindaloo curries. *LD OPEN to 23.00. Sun to 22.00.* A. Ax. B. Dc. Cb. E. **££**.

Vijay
49 Willesden Lane NW6. 01-328 1087. Southern Indian cuisine with good vegetarian specialities. Masala dosai, vegetable pilau. *LD Reserve. Open to 22.45*. **£**.

Italian
The largest group of foreign restaurants in London. One can eat cheaply or expensively and almost always get good food. These are some of the best:

Alvaro 4 M 1
124 King's Rd SW3. 01-589 6296. Crowded. Some Amalfi specialities such as filet sole Bianca Nelve, spaghetti Don Lello. *LD OPEN to 24.00*. **££**.

Angelo's 2 I 19
42 Albemarle St W1. 01-499 1776. Popular trattoria with friendly service. Fresh grilled sardines, plat du jour, profiteroles. *LD Reserve. OPEN to 23.30. CLOSED Sat L & Sun.* A. Ax. B. Dc. E. **££**.

Bertorelli's
19 Charlotte St W1. 01-636 4174 2 F 22
70-72 Queensway W2. 01-229 3160. 1 A 11
Busy straightforward Italian eating places. Good food at reasonable prices. Scampi, veal cutlet royal, filets de sole Bertorelli, zabaglioni. *LD OPEN to 22.00. CLOSED Sun & B Hols.* **££**.

Biagi's 2 D 16
39 Upper Berkeley St W1. 01-723 0394. Well run, intimate small trattoria with fishing décor. Good varied Italian dishes. Scaloppine altla crema, entrecote alla pizza iola, saltimbocca. *LD Reserve. OPEN to 23.30.* A. Ax. B. Dc. E. **££**.

Bianchi's 2 H 22
21a Frith St W1. 01-437 5194. Good traditional Italian food and service. Pleasant and friendly atmosphere. Veal marsala, filetto Rossini, chicken marescalla. *LD Reserve. OPEN to 23.30. CLOSED upstairs Sun.* A. Ax. B. Dc. **££**.

Borgo Santa Croce 4 M 6
112 Cheyne Walk SW10. 01-352 7534. A branch of San Frediano's. Spacious, friendly trattoria with an original menu. Fresh salmon pâté en croûte, crespoline florentina, venison steaks. *LD Reserve. OPEN to 23.30. CLOSED Sun.* A. Ax. B. Dc. E. **££**.

La Capannina 2 I 22
24 Romilly St W1. 01-437 2473. Popular typical Soho trattoria. Music in the evening. Petto di pollo, vitello alla pianni. *LD Reserve. OPEN to 23.30. Ax. B. Dc.* **££**.

Casa Cominetti
129 Rushey Green, Catford SE6. 01-697 2314. An exceptional restaurant for South London run by two Italians . Home made cannelloni, scaloppine oggi. *LD OPEN to 21.00. CLOSED D Sun.* A. Ax. B. Cb. Dc. E. Children. **££**.

Chez Franco 1 A 10
3 Hereford Rd W2. 01-229 5079. Good menu of Italian dishes in small, neat restaurant. Settina di Manzo, pizza iola, fettucine al burro alla Romano. *LD OPEN to 23.30. CLOSED Sun.* **££**.

Colossea 5 J 22
12 Mays Court, St Martin's Lane WC2. 01-836 6140. Popular with theatre-goers. Large menu and good service. *LD Reserve. OPEN to 23.30. CLOSED Sat L, Sun & B. Hols.* A. Ax. B. Dc. E. **££**.

Como Lario 5 M 12
22 Holbein Place SW1. 01-730 2954. Lively and crowded trattoria. Generous helpings. Mussel soup, petto di pollo sorpresa, fritto misto di mare. *LD Reserve. OPEN to 23.30. CLOSED Sun.* **£**.

Gennaro's 2 H 22
44 Dean St W1. 01-437 3950. Busts of Roman heroes and contemporary figures. Wide menu of good Italian dishes. Tortalloni Marina Mia. *LD Reserve. OPEN to 23.30. Sun to 22.30.* A. Ax. B. Dc. E. **£££**.

Gondoliere 1 F 8
3 Gloucester Rd SW7. 01-584 8062. Food served by Venetian gondoliers. WElcoming, festal atmosphere. Authentic cooking. Cartoccio del gondoliere, Dover Sole del gondoliere. *LD OPEN to 23.30. CLOSED Sat L & Sun.* A. Ax. B. Dc. Bank Americard. **££**.

Hostaria Romana 2 H 22
70 Dean St W1. 01-734 2869. Boisterous and busy, consistently good Roman cuisine. Regularly changed menu. Crespoline alla Romana, agnellino al forno, torta mela. *LD Reserve. OPEN to 23.30.* A. Ax. Cb. E. **£**.

Medusa 1 C 8
38c Kensington Church St W8. 01-937 2005. Good pasta dishes, penne a la carbonara, rack of lamb with herbs and white wine. *LD Reserve. OPEN to 24.00. CLOSED Sat L & Sun.* A. Ax. Dc. B. **££**.

Mimmo d'Ischia 5 L 14
61 Elizabeth St SW1. 01-730 5406. Intimate, comfortable and busy. Original and imaginative dishes. Good spigola and spare ribs Casanova. *LD Reserve. OPEN to 23.45. CLOSED Sun.* A. Ax. B. Dc. **££**.

Peter Mario 2 I 22
47 Gerrard St W1. 01-437 4170. Carefully cooked food in a friendly setting. Generous helpings. Excellent soups, scaloppini Peter Mario. *LD OPEN to 23.30. CLOSED Sun.* A. Ax. V. Dc. E. Children. **££**.

Portofino 3 E 32
39 Camden Passage N1. 01-226 0884. Small, popular. Good friendly service and excellent cooking. Cannelloni, escallopine portofino. *LD Reserve. OPEN to 23.30. CLOSED Sun. Ax. B. Dc. E.* **££**.

San Frediano 4 L 4
62 Fulham Rd SW3. 01-584 8375. Bright and lively trattoria with friendly service. Excellent Italian dishes, particularly good fish and a tempting sweet trolley, all at reasonable prices. Clam salad, scallopino uccellato. *LD Reserve. OPEN to 23.30. CLOSED Sun.* A. Ax. B. Dc. E. **££**.

San Lorenzo 2 I 12
22 Beauchamp Place SW3. 01-584 1074. Very popular and friendly restaurant offering a different menu every day. *LD OPEN to 23.30. CLOSED Sun.* **££**.

Terraza Est 6 J 26
125 Chancery Lane WC2. 01-242 2601. Expensive but good Italian restaurant, with modern tiled décor and bar. Superior food with particularly delicious pastries and strawberry and raspberry flans. *LD Reserve. OPEN to 23.30. CLOSED Sat L & Sun.* A. Ax. B. Dc. **£££**.

Tiberio 2 H 17
22 Queen St W1. 01-629 3561. Top-quality Roman cooking in popular, crowded atmosphere. Band for dancing. *23.30-02.00.* Tripe 'Petronius', fettucine alla panna, duck and quail. *LD Reserve. OPEN to 01.30. CLOSED L Sat & Sun.* A. Ax. B. Cb. Dc. E. **£££**.

Trattoo 1 E 6
2 Abingdon Rd W8. 01-937 4448. Excellent food under a glass roof, surrounded by greenery. Vongole with clams, pollo surpresa, sweet Trattoo. *LD Reserve. OPEN to 23.30. Sun 22.30.* A. Ax. B. Dc. E. **£££**.

Trattoria Piedmonte 2 H 22
48 Frith St W1. 01-437 7444. Unpretentious Italian trattoria; good value for money. Pastas and veal dishes. *LD OPEN to 23.30.* A. Ax. B. Cb. Dc. E. **£**.

Verbanella 2 D 18
35 Blandford St W1. 01-935 2174. Cheerful, efficient, popular and inexpensive; good cooking. Scaloppine alla Borromeo, petto di pollo alla Milanese. Also branch at 145 Notting Hill Gate W11. 01-229 9882. *LD Reserve. OPEN to 23.30. CLOSED Sun.* A. Ax. B. Dc. **£**.

Japanese

Ginnan 6 L 28
5 Cathedral Place EC4. 01-236 4120. Crowded; polite and efficient service. Raw fish sachimi, excellent soups, soba and domburi dishes. Food fried in front of you. Traditional Tempura (deep fried sea food with subtle sauces). *LD Reserve. OPEN to 22.00. CLOSED Sat & Sun.* **££**.

Hiroko 2 E 18
6-8 St Christopher's Place W1. 01-935 1579. The first authentic Japanese restaurant in London. Service by graceful and charming Japanese girls in kimonos. Completely oriental atmosphere. Try the complete dinner, Sukiyaki or Tempura. Saké or Japanese beer. *LD OPEN to 22.30. CLOSED Sun.* Ax. B. Cb. Dc. E. **££**.

Hokkai 2 I 21
61 Brewer St W1. 01-734 5826. Japanese prints and red lanterns. Traditional dishes. *LD Reserve. OPEN to 23.00. CLOSED Sun L.* A. Ax. B. Dc. E. **££**.

Jewish

Bloom's
90 Whitechapel High St E1. 01-247 6001.
130 Golders Green Rd NW11. 01-455 1338.
Authentic Kosher restaurants. Busy and popular. Probably the best Jewish cooking in London. Large helpings; lockshen and meat balls, salt beef, stuffed kishka. *LD Open to 21.30. CLOSED Fri from 15.00, Sat & Jewish hols. OPEN B. Hols.* **£**.

Goody's Original Kosher Restaurant 2 H 21
55 Berwick St W1. 01-437 6050. 60 year old Kosher restaurant of good value. Comfortable and friendly. Generous helpings. Braten (braised beef) and lockshen pudding. *LD Reserve. OPEN to 22.00.* A. Ax. B. Dc. Cb. E. **££**.

Mendel's
8-10 Monkville Parade NW11. 01-455 8288. Small Kosher restaurant with a relaxed atmosphere. Also delicatessen and snack bar. Traditional Jewish cooking with some international additions. *LD OPEN to 20.30. CLOSED D Fri & Sat.* **£**.

Polish and Russian

Luba's Bistro   **1 | 11**
6 Yeoman's Row SW3. 01-589 2950. Individual, down to earth spartan atmosphere. Good peasant-style cooking at low prices. Borscht, beef Stroganoff, shashlik, pojarsky. *LD OPEN to 24.00. CLOSED Sun.* **£.**

Polonia   **5 L 15**
27 Grosvenor Gardens SW1. 01-834 4614. Plain, basic Polish cooking to high standard. Zrazy à la Nelson, tripe Polish style and stuffed cabbage, bigos. *LD OPEN to 22.00. CLOSED Sat.* E. **£.**

Portuguese

O Fado   **2 | 12**
50 Beauchamp Place, SW1. 01-589 3002. A genuine Portuguese restaurant with music in the basement. Sardines and the chicken speciality, franguintos a Fado, are superb. Good carafe wine. *D OPEN to 24.30, Sun to 23.30.* E. **£.**

Scandinavian

Dania
293-5 Railton Rd SE24. 01-274 9163. Authentic Danish dishes, including medaillons Copenhagen, frikadeller with red cabbage, chicken silkeborg. *LD OPEN to 23.00. CLOSED Sun.* E. **£.**

Hungry Viking   **1 B 9**
44 Ossington St W2. 01-727 3311. All the food here is home-made and includes pâtés, marinated herring and the traditional Smorgasbord. Good hot dish of the day *D Reserve. OPEN to 23.00, Sun to 23.00.* Ax. B. Dc. **££.**

Norway Food Centre   **1 | 11**
166 Brompton Rd SW3. 01-584 6062. Smorgasbord, cold table of fish and meats and some hot dishes. Help yourself from a vast selection of delicacies assisted by attractive girls in national costume. Norwegian beer or akvavit. *LD Reserve. OPEN to 22.30. CLOSED Sun L. Children.* **££.**

Spanish & Mexican

El Bodegon   **4 L 6**
9 Park Walk SW10. 01-352 1330. Intimate, cool and popular. Mainly Spanish dishes, excellently cooked. Gambas al pil-pil, pechuga de pollo noche de gala (stuffed chicken breasts in raisins and champagne), trenera sacromonte. *LD Reserve. OPEN to 23.30.* A. Ax. B. Dc. E. **££.**

La Cucaracha   **2 H 22**
12-13 Greek St W1. 01-734 2253. London's first Mexican restaurant, in the cellars of a converted monastery. Raw fish cocktail, arroz à la poblana, enchiladas. Spicy and delicious. *LD OPEN to 23.30. CLOSED Sat L & Sun.* A. Ax. b. Cb. Dc. E. **££.**

Martinez   **2 | 20**
25 Swallow St W1. 01-734 5066. Old-fashioned, beautifully decorated Spanish-style restaurant. Courteous service; guitarist. Gazpacho, paella Valencia, good tortillas. *LD Reserve. OPEN to 23.30. Sun to 22.30.* A. Ax. B. Dc. E. **££.**

La Parra   **4 K 11**
163 Draycott Avenue SW3. 01-589 2913. Good Spanish and Latin American dishes. Gazpacho, gambas pil-pil, Basque crab, chicken Marrakesh. *D. Reserve. OPEN to 23.00. CLOSED Sun.* Ax. B. Dc. E. **££.**

Simple Simon   **1 | 6**
234 Old Brompton Rd SW5. 01-370 2421. French-Spanish food with authentic specialities. Mushrooms cooked in garlic and chillies, poussin, quails and paella. *LD Reserve. OPEN to 23.30. CLOSED Mon.* A. Ax. B. Dc. **££.**

Valencia   **1 | 2**
1 Empress Approach, Lillie Rd SW6. 01-385 0039. Authentic restaurant with singing waiters, guitarists, sherry on the house and flamenco on Sundays. Good seafoods and wines. *D Reserve. OPEN to 24.00.* **££.**

Swiss

The Swiss Centre   **2 | 22**
1 New Coventry St (Leicester Square) W1. 01-734 1291. Four different restaurants of varying prices, of which the Taverne seems the most popular. Imaginative decoration. Fondue, Swiss country hams, pasta and delicious pastries. *LD OPEN to 24.00.* A. Ax. B. Dc. **£.**

Turkish

Adana Kebab Centre
17 Colomb St SE10. 01-858 1913. Busy, thriving Turkish restaurant with excellent Mediterranean foods. Chicken with lemon and bay leaves, humous, yogurtlu. Drink retsina or buzbag. *D. Reserve. OPEN to 24.00. CLOSED Sun.* Dc. **£.**

Gallipoli   **6 N 32**
8 Bishopsgate Churchyard EC2. 01-588 1922. Once a Turkish bath, with original gold décor and tiles; now an exotic restaurant with plump belly dancers. Excellent Turkish food. 20-dish hors d'oeuvre, shashlik and kebabs. Two shows nightly *22.00 and 01.00. LD Reserve. OPEN to 03.00. CLOSED Sun.* A. Ax. B. Cb. Dc. E. **£££.**

Nibub Lokanta   **2 D 16**
112 Edgware Rd W2. 01-262 6636. Fairly authentic Turkish dishes, usually tasty. Good variety of kebabs. Karisik mezze, kuzu but (lamb fillets) and plenty of yoghourt dishes. *LD Reserve. OPEN to 23.30.* A. Ax. B. Dc. E. **££.**

Fish

As well as those restaurants, some of which are listed here, that specialise in elaborately cooked fish dishes, London has a large number of fish and chip 'take away' shops, mostly to be found in residential areas. Fish and chips is a national dish which you can take away soused with vinegar, salt and pepper. Eaten hot it can be delicious and good value. (The following restaurants are not fish and chip shops.)

Bentley's   **2 | 20**
11-15 Swallow St W1. 01-734 6210. Famous seafood restaurant and oyster bar. Lobster Newburg, sole meunière, prawns, crabs and fish of many sorts. *LD Reserve. OPEN to 22.45. CLOSED Sun.* A. Ax. B. Cb. Dc. E. **££.**

Fisherman's Wharf   **2 D 18**
73 Baker St W1. 01-935 0471. Modern décor in orange, black and white. Some strangely named but palatable dishes: 'sole speckled band'. *LD Reserve. OPEN to 23.00.* A. Ax. B. Dc. E. **£££.**

La Croisette   **4 J 4**
168 Ifield Rd SW10. 01-373 3694. Excellent fish menu with produce imported fresh from Boulogne. Raw mussels, oysters, whole baby crabs, cockles, clams and prawns. Recently opened Le Suquet, Draycott Pl SW3. *D OPEN to 23.15. L Sun only. CLOSED Mon.* **££.**

Geale's   **1 B 8**
2 Farmer St W8. 01-727 7969. Going since 1919, this is fish and chips with a difference. Cod's roe, scampi, sole, trout, skate delivered fresh daily. Soup, fruit salad and, surprisingly, a wine list (featuring champagne!) *LD OPEN to 22.45. CLOSED Sun & Mon.* **£.**

Manzi's   **2 | 22**
1-2 Leicester St WC2. 01-437 4864. Typical busy provincial Italian fish restaurant with bar and marble-topped tables. Street-level room is best. Good swift service and cooking. Jellied eels, mussels, lobster. *LD Reserve. OPEN to 23.40. CLOSED L Sun.* A. Ax. B. Dc. E. **££.**

Overton's   **5 J 19**
5 St James's St SW1. 01-839 3774. Long-established fish restaurant of character. 'Old world' atmosphere in the nicest sense. Oysters, lobsters, Dover sole. *LD Reserve. OPEN to 23.00. CLOSED Sun.* A. Ax. b. Dc. E. **£££.**

Poissonnerie de l'Avenue   **4 K 11**
82 Sloane Avenue SW3. 01-589 2457. Beautifully cooked, simple fish dishes in a French bistro atmosphere. Sit at tables or on stools at the long fish bar. Coquilles St Jacques au vin blanc, moules, sole and turbot dieppoise. *LD Reserve. OPEN to 23.30. CLOSED Sun.* Ax. Dc. **££.**

Scott's   **2 G 17**
20 Mount St W1. 01-629 5248. Well-known and long-loved Edwardian restaurant, originally at Piccadilly Circus, now in modern premises. Still very good fish dishes and service, but lacks the old sparkle — perhaps it will return! Lobster bisque, scallops meunière, sole Véronique. *LD Reserve. OPEN to 23.00. CLOSED L Sun.* A. Ax. B. Dc. **£££.**

Sheekey's   **5 J 22**
28-32 St Martin's Court WC2. 01-836 4118. Family-owned since 1896. Fresh salmon, steamed turbot with lobster sauce, stewed eels. Crowded. *LD OPEN to 20.30. CLOSED Sun, D Sat.* A. Ax. B. Dc. **££.**

Sweeting's   **6 N 29**
39 Queen Victoria St EC4. 01-248 3062. Echo of a vanished age. Fish parlour, with excellent service. Sit at the bar and eat herrings with mustard, whitebait, fish pie of excellent quality. Good carafe and port. *L OPEN to 15.00. CLOSED Sat, Sun.* **£.**

Trattoria dei Pescatori   **2 F 22**
57 Charlotte St W1. 01-580 3289. Bustling and hectic. Excellent Italian fish dishes in nautical atmosphere. Sauces especially tasty. Red mullet, lobster, fish soup, fried octopus. *LD Reserve. OPEN to 23.30. CLOSED Sun. Children.* **££.**

Wheeler's Fish restaurants

A group of restaurants specialising in expertly cooked fish dishes. Welcoming atmosphere with sophistication. Scallops, lobster Normande, sole Egyptian and shellfish. They are:

Alcove　　　　　　　　　　　　　　**1 D 4**
17 Kensington High St W8. 01-937 1443. As in all Wheeler's restaurants, only fresh ingredients of high quality are used in the preparation of fish dishes; whitebait, sole bonne femme, prawn thermidor. *LD Reserve. OPEN to 23.00. CLOSED Sun.* A. Ax. B. Cb. Dc. **£££.**

Antoine　　　　　　　　　　　　　　**2 F 22**
40 Charlotte St W1. 01-636 2817. Small restaurant on 3 floors specialising in sea food. Lobster, smoked salmon, moules marinière and many ways of serving sole and halibut. *LD Reserve. OPEN to 23.00.* A. Ax. B. D. Cb. **£££.**

Carafe　　　　　　　　　　　　　　**5 J 13**
15 Lowndes St SW1. 01-235 2525. *LD Reserve. OPEN to 23.00. CLOSED Mon.* A. Ax. B. Cb. Dc. **£££.**

City
19 Great Tower St EC3. 01-626 3685. *LD Reserve. OPEN to 23.00. CLOSED Sat & Sun.* A. Ax. B. Cb. Dc. **£££.**

George & Dragon
256 Brompton Rd SW3. 01-584 2626. *LD Reserve. OPEN to 23.00.* A. Ax. B. Cb. Dc. **£££.**

Wheeler's
19 Old Compton St W1. 01-437 7661. *LD Reserve. OPEN to 23.00.* A. Ax. B. Cb. Dc. **£££.**

Vegetarian and health food

These places serve mainly salads, omelettes and savouries. Some people eat in them for religious reasons, others because it's healthy and less fattening. Prices are not rock bottom but the queues are evidence of good value and helpings are generous.

Cranks　　　　　　　　　　　　　　**2 H 21**
William Blake House, Marshall St W1. 01-427 9431. Modern, attractive décor; background of classical music. Home-made soups, hot vegetable savoury, mixed salads with fruit and nuts, good cheeses and sweets, and bread from their own bakery. *OPEN to 20.30, Sat to 16.30. CLOSED Sun.* **£.**
Also branch in Heal's, Tottenham Court Rd W1. 01-636 2230. *OPEN Mon-Sat 10.00-17.00.* **£.**

Food for Health Restaurants　　　　　**6 L 30**
15 Blackfriars Lane EC4. 01-236 7001.
85 Blomfield House, London Wall EC2. 01-588 3446.
Lunches only. Seven different fresh salads, omlettes, soufflés and savouries. Crowded. *OPEN 08.30-15.30. CLOSED Sat & Sun.* **£.**

Food for Thought　　　　　　　　　　**3 I 23**
31 Neal St WC2. 01-836 0239. Vegetarian wholefood in a cheerful Covent Garden basement. Occasional 'music and poetry evenings'. *LD OPEN to 20.00. CLOSED Sun.* **£.**

Nuthouse　　　　　　　　　　　　　**2 H 20**
26 Kingly St W1. 01-437 9471. Buffet service vegetarian health food on two floors. Nut roasts, quiches, blackberry pie, fresh raspberry juice. *LD OPEN to 20.00. CLOSED Sat & Sun.* **£.**

Oodles
31 Cathedral Place EC2. 01-248 2550/2559.
128 Edgware Rd W2. 01-723 7548.
3 Fetters Lane E4. 01-353 1984.
14 Fulwood Place WC1. 01-242 6165.
113 High Holborn WC1. 01-405 3838.
26 James St W1. 01-486 2363.
42 New Oxford St WC1. 01-580 9521.
Very popular; clean scrubbed tables. Well-balanced salads and savoury foods. Generous hot dishes. *OPEN 10.30-18.00. CLOSED Sun.* **£.**

Raw Deal　　　　　　　　　　　　　**2 B 17**
65 York St W1. 01-262 4841. Hot dishes, special food for slimmers. Fruit and vegetables all organically grown. Guitarist on *Thur & Sat. LD OPEN to 22.00, Sat to 24.00. CLOSED Sun.* **£.**

Sharuna Restaurant　　　　　　　　　**3 H 23**
107 Great Russell St WC1. 01-636 5922. An elegant South-Indian vegetarian restaurant. The highest quality and cleanliness. Vegetarian curries, delicately spiced, yogurt and fruit. *LD OPEN to 21.45. Sun 13.00-21.00.* **£.**

Slenders　　　　　　　　　　　　　**6 M 28**
41 Cathedral Place EC4. 01-236 5974. In a modern square beside St Paul's Cathedral. Many daily specialities including macaroni cheese, tomato and cheese flan. Excellent minestrone, fruit pies. *LD OPEN to 18.15, CLOSED Sat & Sun.* **£.**

Wholefood Farm Bar　　　　　　　　**2 D 18**
110 Baker St W1. 01-486 8444. Delicious quiches, salads, pâté and wholemeal bread all made from organically grown ingredients. Farm Bar *OPEN 08.00-20.00, Sat to 15.00. CLOSED Sun.* **£.**

Carveries

The four carveries below are excellent value for money. The price includes a 3-course meal. Customers carve as much and as often as they like from enormous succulent joints of beef, lamb and pork.

Cumberland Hotel Carvery　　　　　　**2 E 16**
Marble Arch W1. 01-262 1234. *LD OPEN to 21.00.* A. Ax. B. Cb. Dc. E. **£.**

Regent Palace Hotel Carvery　　　　　**2 I 20**
Piccadilly Circus W1. 01-734 7000. *LD OPEN to 20.30.* A. Ax. B. Dc. **££.**

Strand Palace Hotel Carvery　　　　　**6 K 23**
Strand WC2. 01-836 8080. *LD OPEN to 20.30. CLOSED Sun.* A. Ax. B. Cb. Dc. E. **££.**

Inexpensive eating

Places where you can eat well for under £3.00 (in some cases under £1.00). The café serving 'sausage, egg and chips' is not included here, however excellent some may be. This list prizes distinctive or unusual cooking and atmosphere — but particularly good value for money.

Al Ristoro　　　　　　　　　　　　　**1 B 8**
205 Kensington Church St W8. 01-727 3184. Genuine very good value Italian food. Canelloni, saltimbocca Romana. Italian ices. *LD OPEN to 23.30. CLOSED L Sun.* **£.**

Alpino restaurants
3 Lower Grosvenor Place SW1. 01-834 0722.　**5 K 16**
42 Marylebone High St W1. 01-935 4640.　　**2 D 19**
43 New Oxford St WC1. 01-836 1011.　　　　**3 H 23**
29 Leicester Square WC2. 01-839 2939.　　　**5 J 22**
102 Wigmore St W1. 01-935 4181.　　　　　**2 E 18**
Busy and popular with Italian atmosphere. Service efficient and quick. Good selection of Alpine dishes. *LD OPEN to 23.30. CLOSED Sun.* A. Ax. B. Dc. **£.**

Bistro Vino
1 Old Brompton Rd SW7. 01-589 3888.　　　**1 I 9**
303 Brompton Rd SW3. 01-589 7898.　　　　**4 J 10**
5 Clareville St SW7. 01-373 3903.　　　　　**1 I 8**
2 Hollywood Rd SW10. 01-352 6439.　　　　**4 K 6**
Started in 1958, this 'chain' shows no signs of breaking, judging by their fame for good simple bistro food at very reasonable prices in cheerful if noisy surroundings. *LD OPEN to 24.00.* **£.**

Casserole　　　　　　　　　　　　　**4 L 7**
338 Kings Rd SW3. 01-352 2351. Popular candlelit bistro with horse-box décor and pop music. Steak and mango casserole, baby chicken stuffed with chestnuts. *LD OPEN to 00.30.* A. Ax. B. **£.**

Casserole　　　　　　　　　　　　　**3 G 23**
67 Tottenham Court Rd W1. 01-636 1099. A basement room with good dishes served by cheerful and attractive girls. Quick service. Cheese and baked potato and many tasty dishes under 45p. Carafe 80p. *LD OPEN To 23.00, Sun to 22.00.* **£.**

Ceylon Tea Centre　　　　　　　　　**2 I 20**
22 Regent St SW1. 01-930 8632. Good, varied and unusual salads, savouries and cheese flans. The different sorts of tea are first class. *L OPEN to 18.00. CLOSED Sun.* **£.**

Chelsea Kitchen　　　　　　　　　　**4 L 10**
98 Kings Rd SW3. 01-589 1330. Part of the Stockpot group. The daily menu offers a good choice of hot cheap dishes. Soup, moussaka, spaghetti, ice cream and hot chocolate sauce. *LD OPEN to 24.00.* **£.**

Costas Grill　　　　　　　　　　　　**1 B 8**
14 Hillgate St W8. 01-229 3794. Good Greek meals of avgolemono (lemon, chicken and egg soup) and steak stewed in wine. Eat outdoors in summer. *LD OPEN to 22.30. CLOSED Sun.* **£.**

Daquise　　　　　　　　　　　　　　**1 I 9**
20 Thurloe St SW7. 01-589 6117. Simple, very cheap Polish food. Pierozki, shashlik, bitok. Many Polish customers. *LD OPEN to 23.45.* **£.**

Great American Disaster　　　　　　　**1 I 12**
9 Beauchamp Place SW3. 01-589 0992. Very popular. Hamburgers and traditional American fare . Several branches. *LD OPEN to 24.00, Sat & Sun to 01.00.* **£.**

Hamburger Products   **2 I 21**
1 Brewer St W1. 01-437 7119. Small fish bar. Cockney atmosphere. All fish freshly caught and home smoked. Smoked eel with pepper salad . Trout with beetroot salad 63p. *L OPEN to 15.00. CLOSED Sat & Sun*. **£**.

Hard Rock Café   **2 I 16**
150 Old Park Lane W1. 01-629 0382. One of the best hamburger places in London with relaxed, colourful atmosphere. Check tablecloths, wooden tables, rock music. A shorts bar and good hamburgers, sandwiches and steaks. Schlitz beer. *LD OPEN to 00.30*. **£**.

Jimmy's   **2 H 22**
24 Frith St W1. 01-437 9521. Crowded Turkish basement restaurant, very popular with students. Large helpings of meat, greens and haricot beans plus fresh salad and as much bread as you want. *LD OPEN to 22.00*. A. Ax. B. Dc. **£**.

Mermaid Theatre   **6 M 27**
Puddle Dock, Upper Thames St EC4. 01-236 9521. Lunchtime snackbar in the foyer of the theatre. Crowded with journalists and actors. Excellent cold dishes and salads. Very good pâté. *LD OPEN to 21.30. CLOSED L Sat & Sun*. **£**.

Nineteen   **4 J 11**
19 Mossop St SW3. 01-589 4971. Very popular with the young. Bistro atmosphere with scrubbed tables and candles. Bistro atmosphere with scrubbed tables and candles. Food consistently good value. Some Polish dishes. Borscht, pork fillet Stroganoff, sernic. *OPEN to 23.30 D* . **£**.

Parsons   **4 L 4**
311 Fulham Rd SW10. 01-352 0651. Trendy and crowded Edwardian-style spaghetti house; potted palms and bentwood chairs. Spaghetti with two sauces, garlic bread and wine. *LD OPEN to 01.00*. **£**.

Pasticceria Amalfi   **2 I 22**
31 Old Compton St W1. 01-437 7284. Good Italian food at reasonable prices. Cheerful and crowded. Pastas, pizzas and excellent pastries. *LD OPEN to 23.30*. **£**.

Pizza e Pasta
57 Haymarket SW1. 01-839 2129.   **5 J 21**
108 Queensway W2. 01-727 0176.   **1 A 11**
These smart modern eating houses serve hamburgers, Italian ices and good coffee. *LD OPEN to 23.30*. **£**.

Pizza Express   **3 H 24**
30 Coptic St WC1. 01-636 3232. Modern pizza parlour with a large red pizza oven in the middle. Many varieties. Good ice creams. Many branches. *LD OPEN to 24.00*. **£**.

Pizza House   **2 F 22**
56 Goodge St W1. 01-636 9590. Excellent pasta dishes at sensible prices. Pizza pies, pasta and meat dishes. *LD OPEN to 23.00. CLOSED L Sun*. **£**.

Romano Santi   **2 H 22**
50 Greek St W1. 01-437 2350. The set lunch is probably the finest value in London. A choice. Also excellent set dinner. *LD OPEN to 23.00. CLOSED Sun*. A. Ax. B. Dc. E. **£**.

Spaghetti House   **2 F 22**
15-17 Goodge St W1. 01-636 6582. Very busy, friendly restaurant. Separate kitchens on all three floors. Reasonably priced. Very good pastas and spaghettis. Cervella di vitello Milanese, saltimbocca alla Romana. Many branches. *LD OPEN to 23.00. CLOSED Sun*. **£**.

Stockpot
6 Basil St SW3. 01-589 8627. *D only*.   **2 I 13**
40 Panton St SW1. 01-839 5142.   **5 J 21**
Crowded, noisy and excellent value. Home-made soups, casseroles and puds at popular prices. *L OPEN 11.30-15.30. CLOSED Sun*. **£**.

Unusual eating

Beachcomber (Polynesian)   **2 I 18**
Mayfair Hotel, Berkeley St W1. 01-629 7777. Hawaii and the South Seas, complete with alligators and tropical atmosphere. Chinese and Polynesian food. Polynesian pâté, chicken momi, steak luau. *D Reserve. OPEN to 23.30. Dancing 20.30-02.00. CLOSED Sun*. **££**.

Dizzy's Diner (Victorian fantasy)   **2 I 13**
25 Basil St SW3. 01-589 8444. All in honour of Benjamin Disraeli. Victorian styled eating place. Not expensive. *LD OPEN to 23.30*. A. Ax. B. Dc. **£**.

1520 A.D. (Mediaeval Banquets)   **5 J 22**
St Martin's Lane WC2. 01-240 3978. Jesters and troubadours entertain while you eat your 7-course meal. Specialities include old English beef, not roast but stewed. *D Reserve. OPEN to 24.00*. A. Ax. B. Cb. Dc. E. **££**.

Flanagan's (Victorian Fantasy)
100 Baker St W1. 01-935 0287.   **2 C 18**

37 St Martin's Lane WC2. 01-836 5358.   **5 J 22**
Completely phoney (but enjoyable) Victorian 'dining rooms', with sawdust for spitting on, stalls, cockney songs and colourful signs, notices and extravaganza. Elegantly costumed waiters and serving girls (usually pleasantly independent Aussies). Tripe, jellied eels, game pie, enormous plates of fish and chips, golden syrup pudding. *LD OPEN to 23.15*. A. Ax. B. Cb. Dc. E. **£**.

Gallipoli (Belly dancers)   **6 N 32**
8 Bishopsgate Churchyard EC2. 01-588 1922. Exotic and unusual. Twice nightly cabaret of enjoyable and erotic Eastern belly dancing. Excellent Turkish food. Shish kebab, buryan Gallipoli, red mullet. *LD Reserve. OPEN to 03.00. CLOSED Sun. Cabaret 22.30-01.00*. A. Ax. B. Cb. Dc. E. **£££**.

Hispaniola (Dinner afloat)   **6 L 23**
The Thames at Victoria Embankment, Charing Cross WC2. 01-839 3011. A restaurant floating on the Thames. Romantic setting. Good Spanish food on upper or lower deck. *LD Reserve. OPEN to 23.20, Sun to 21.50*. A. Ax. B. Dc. **£££**.

Trader Vic's (South Seas)   **2 I 16**
London Hilton, 22 Park Lane W1. 01-493 8000. Atmosphere of Pacific Islands and the Orient in décor and food. South sea drinks. Tahitian fish soup, duckling barbecued, quenelles de Mahi Mahi. *LD OPEN to 23.45. CLOSED L Sat*. A. Ax. B. Dc. E. **££**.

Villa dei Cesari (Decadent Roman Empire)   **5 Q 15**
135 Grosvenor Rd SW1. 01-828 7453. Converted warehouse with good river views and decorated like a Roman villa. Two bands and dancing. Menu in Latin. Gallinorum-ora-pronobis. Forus dibolicum. *D Reserve. OPEN to 02.30. CLOSED Mon*. Ax. B. Dc. E. **£££**.

Outdoor eating

The continental habit of eating outside can be very pleasant on a hot summer's day. The following places have a few tables on the pavement or in the garden. There are also several in Charlotte St and Wigmore St W1.

Alpino
102 Wigmore St W1. 01-935 4181.   **2 E 18**
29 Leicester Square WC2. 01-839 2939.   **2 J 22**
Cheap, well cooked Italian food eaten on the pavement in warm weather. Canelloni, vitello and delicious Italian sweets. *LD OPEN to 23.30. CLOSED Sun L*. A. Ax. B. Dc. **£**.

Anemos   **2 F 22**
34 Charlotte St W1. 01-580 5907. Friendly, crowded and noisy, with customers and waiters singing and dancing on the tables. Eat outside at the pavement tables in summer. Humous, excellent kebabs, moussaka. *LD OPEN to 24.00. CLOSED Sun*. **£**.

Artiste Assoiffé
306 Westbourne Grove W11. 01-727 4714. French food can be eaten under the trees of a small front garden during fine weather. Filet de Dijon, caramalised poulet stuffed with mushrooms in pastry. *D Reserve. OPEN to 23.30. Sat L. CLOSED Sun*. A. Ax. B. Cb. Dc. E. **££**.

Au Bon Accueil   **4 K 10**
27 Elystan St SW3. 01-589 3718. Tables set out on the pavement in summer. Comfortable French restaurant with excellent cuisine. Escalope au rhum et orange, filet mignon sauce béarnaise. *LD Reserve. OPEN to 23.30. CLOSED Sat L & Sun*. A. Ax. Dc. **£**.

Costas Grill   **1 B 8**
14 Hillgate St W8. 01-229 3794. Eat good cheap Greek food in a courtyard in the summer. Taramosalata, avgolemono, steak stewed in wine. *LD OPEN to 22.30. CLOSED Sun*. **£**.

Dukes   **2 E 18**
55-58 Duke St W1. 01-499 5000. Café/restaurant with a fountain and tiled patio for open-air eating. Continental menu. *LD Reserve. OPEN to 23.15. CLOSED Sun*. A. Ax. B. Cb. Dc. **££**.

Froops
17 Princess Rd NW1. 01-722 9663. Bistro restaurant with a proper garden, partially covered and very full in summer. French provincial and 'Franglais' dishes. *D Reserve. OPEN to 23.30. CLOSED Sun*. Ax. B. Dc. **££**.

New Kebab House   **2 F 22**
12 & 14 Charlotte St W1. 01-580 1049. Pavement tables in hot weather. Very good cheap humous, kebabs and yogurt. *LD OPEN to 24.00. CLOSED Sun*. **£**.

The Rose Garden   **2 A 20**
Queen Mary's Rose Garden, Regent's Park NW1. 01-935 5729. Open-air eating in a London park at tables with parasols. Unadventurous English food. *LD OPEN To 23.00 in summer, to 18.00 in winter*. A. Ax. B. Dc. **£**. *Cafeteria open to 19.00*.

San Lorenzo Fuoriporta
Worple Road Mews SW19. 01-946 8463. Cheerful, lively trattoria with tables in the garden during summer. The SW19 branch has boules in the courtyard, and is ideal for Sunday lunches with children. Scaloppine di vitello alla San Lorenzo, petti di pollo, good fresh vegetables. *LD Reserve. OPEN to 23.30.* A. Ax. B. Dc. E. **££.**

Turpins
118 Heath St NW3. 01-435 3971. Good English food eaten in a tiny garden in good weather. Game, steak and kidney pudding, roasts. *D Reserve. OPEN to 23.00. Sun L. CLOSED Sun D & Mon.* A. Ax. B. Dc. **££.**

Afternoon teas

Afternoon tea is a British institution: fashionable, sociable, leisurely, gossipy. The following list gives the remaining strongholds.

Teas in hotels

Always good with excellent service and a comfortable sense of welcome. Often some quiet background music and usually a reasonable bill at the end. British Transport Hotels serve good quality blended teas in a pleasant atmosphere. Trust Houses are particularly concerned to give good service and good value tea in comfort.

Charing Cross Hotel   **5 K 22**
Strand WC2. 01-839 7282. Pleasant and comfortable lounge tea with delicate sandwiches and good pastries. *Until 18.00.*

Dorchester   **2 H 16**
Park Lane W1. 01-629 8888. Sandwiches and pastries in the main lounge. *Until 17.45.*

Ritz   **2 I 18**
Piccadilly W1. 01-629 8181. A good comfortable hotel tea in the Winter Garden, with dainty sandwiches and cream cakes.

Waldorf   **6 J 24**
Aldwych WC2. 01-836 2400. Opulent tea lounge with comfort and good service. *Until 18.00.*

Tea and cakes

Bendicks   **2 E 18**
55 Wigmore St W1. 01-935 7272. Good cream tea with all the trimmings.

Ceylon Tea Centre   **2 I 20**
22 Regent St SW1. 01-930 8632. A choice of several excellent pure Ceylon teas freshly made. Good sandwiches, salads and cakes.

Kardomah   **3 E 23**
162 Tottenham Court Rd W1. 01-387 8802. (other branches). Excellently made tea. Finest quality and blend. *OPEN to 20.00.*

Maison Sagne   **2 D 19**
105 Marylebone High St W1. 01-935 6240. Traditional tea shop with its own bakery and delicious patisserie. Serves cakes & croissants from 09.00, lunch & teas. *OPEN to 17.00, Sat to 12.30. CLOSED Sun.*

Patisserie Valerie   **2 I 22**
44 Old Compton St W1. 01-437 3466. Soho patisserie with tea, coffee and hot chocolate. Good cream cakes and sandwiches. *OPEN to 19.00. CLOSED Sun.*

Teas in stores

D. H. Evans   **2 F 19**
318 Oxford St W1. 01-629 8800. Restaurant serves teas with excellent cream cakes.

Fortnum & Mason   **2 I 19**
181 Piccadilly W1. 01-734 8040. Tea with toast, anchovy paste and gentleman's relish.

Thé dansant

Café de Paris   **2 J 21**
3 Coventry St W1. 01-437 2036. Dancing every afternoon from 15.00-17.45, and every evening 19.30-01.00, Fri & Sat until 02.00

Coffee shops

Ever since the first coffee shops opened in London in the early 18th cent, drinking coffee rapidly became a British habit. Most of those early shops became thriving businesses. (The most famous example is probably Lloyd's brokers.) A few modern places to drink coffee are:

Chelsea Drug Store & Snack Bar   **4 L 4**
49 Kings Rd SW3. 01-730 7513. A hall of mirrors where you can have a coffee or an ice-cream soda and watch the colourful people along the road. *OPEN to 23.00.*

Great American Disaster   **4 L 4**
335 Fulham Rd SW10. 01-351 1188. For hamburgers,

real American soda-fountain fare and good coffee.

Garden Café   **1 D 4**
Royal Garden Hotel, Kensington High St W8. 01-937 8000. Excellent coffee. *OPEN to 24.00.*

Torino   **2 E 17**
214 Oxford St W1. 01-636 1312. Excellent fresh cream cakes and coffee. *OPEN to 23.00.*

Way In at Harrods   **2 H 13**
Knightsbridge SW1. 01-730 1234. For a quick coffee while shopping. Lively and colourful coffee bar in the boutique.

Ice-cream

Baskin-Robbins
Delicious American ice-cream. 31 flavors. *OPEN 10.30-23.00.*
259 Finchley Rd NW3.
4 Marble Arch W1.   **2 E 16**
54 Haymarket SW1.   **5 J 21**
Highroad, North Finchley.

Dayvilles Original American Ice Cream
More delicious ice-cream. 31 flavors plus 'flavor of the month'. *OPEN 10.00-24.00.* More branches opening.
56 Edgware Rd W2.   **2 D 16**
144 Finchley Rd NW3.
10 Heath St NW3.
106 Kensington High St W8.   **1 D 4**
4 Carnaby St W1.   **2 H 20**

Marine Ices
8 Haverstock Hill NW3. 01-485 8898. Huge choice of Italian ice-cream and water ices. *OPEN 10.00-22.15.*

Pubs

Most London pubs date back to the 19th cent but many are up to 400 years old. Some take on the character and needs of the locality and are aptly called 'locals' while others provide cheerful places to relax for workers, shoppers or theatre-goers. Of the 7,000 pubs in London we have selected some of the most interesting, but there are many more to be discovered by the thirsty or the curious. The Pub Information Centre, Elliot House, 10-12 Allington St SW1, 01-828 6633, run by Chef & Brewer Ltd, will answer questions on their own pubs and help with general enquiries. Open Mon-Fri 09.30-17.30, messages recorded Sat & Sun.

*Pubs are usually divided into two bars: the **Public Bar** for darts, bar billiards or shove ha'penny, more rudimentary furniture and often cheaper drinks, and the **Saloon Bar** for a comfortable chair and a quieter chat. Some pubs also have a **Lounge Bar** which is more sophisticated and sometimes has waiter service and a **Private Bar** for a quiet, secluded drink. the **Off Sales** or '**Jug & Bottle**' is where you buy beer, wine or spirits to take away.*

Open hours vary but usually 11.00-15.00 and 17.30-23.00 with earlier closing on Sun.

L-lunch; D-dinner; B-buffet. Most pubs serve snacks, some have hot buffet lunches and many have restaurants. These are indicated in the following list.

Admiral Codrington   **4 J 11**
17 Mossop St SW3. 01-589 4603. Good Chelsea pub with a large collection of toby jugs and over 100 different whiskeys! **B D**

Anglesea Arms   **4 J 8**
15 Selwood Terrace, Onslow Gdns SW7. 01-373 1207. Free house. Try Ruddles County, Samuel Smith, Theakson's Old Peculiar, Charles Wells and Young's cask bitters. Trendy spot for young executive types. **B**

Antelope   **5 L 13**
22 Eaton Terrace SW1. 01-730 7781. Hearty, companionable Victorian atmosphere with a more intimate dining room upstairs. **B D**

Argyll Arms   **2 G 20**
389 Colharbour Lane SW9. 01-274 2832. Good Victorian pub. Mainly West Indian customers and barmaids. Delicious spiced patties. **B**

Baker and Oven   **2 C 19**
10 Paddington St W1. 01-935 5072. Small colourful orange and green pub with cosy basement alcoves and bars. Mouth watering home-made pies from 100 year old baker's ovens. **B D**

Becky's Dive Bar   **6 P 28**
24 Southwark St SE1. 01-407 2335. Built over cellars of old Marshalsea debtors' prison. Over 300 varieties of bottled beer. **B**

Black Friar   **6 M 28**
174 Queen Victoria St EC4. 01-236 5650. Triangular building in the shadows of Blackfriars railway bridge. Stunning shades of Art Nouveau mixed with Gothic; excellent buffet if you can get your eyes off the decor. **B**

Britannia   1 E 6
1 Allen St W8. 01-937 1864. Warm friendly pub with a secluded beer patio. Large bar with plenty of tables and chairs. **B** *lunch only.*

Bull & Bush
North End Way NW3. 01-455 3685. The famous Victorian pub of the Florrie Forde song. Full of Cockneys when Hampstead fair is on. **B**

Bunch of Grapes   1 I 11
207 Brompton Rd SW3. 01-589 4944. Popular Victirian pub with finely engraved 'snob-screens' separating the bars and impressively carved wooden pillars. **B**

Cartoonist   6 K 27
76 Shoe Lane EC4. 01-353 2828. In the heart of the newspaper world, this Victorian pub is lavishly wall-papered with cartoons, some famous and all amusing. Headquarters of the Cartoonist Club of Great Britain. **B**

Captain's Cabin   5 J 21
7 Norris St, Haymarket SW1. 01-930 5748. A cosy nautical pub well situated for a pre-theatre or cinema drink. **B**

Chelsea Potter   4 L 10
119 King's Rd SW3. 01-352 9479. Trendy meeting place for the locals. Tequila Sunrise is the specialty. **B**

Cheshire Cheese, Ye Olde   6 K 26
145 Fleet St EC4. 01-353 6170. Rebuilt after the Great Fire with low ceiling'd interiors, oak tables, sawdust on the floor. The pub probably hasn't changed much since Dr Johnson used to drop in. No snacks but good traditional English cooking for those in search of a meal.

Cheshire Cheese   6 K 25
5 Little Essex St WC2. 01-836 2347. Intimate Jacobean pub with original oak beams and friendly bars. **B**

Cock Tavern   6 K 26
22 Fleet St EC4. 01-353 8570. Small but good journalist's tavern with literary and Dickensian associations and mementoes. **B**

Cockney Price   2 I 19
6 Jermyn St W1. 01-930 5339. A nostalgic reconstruction of the cockney Victorian pub even down to the bubble and squeak! **B D**

Cross Keys   4 M 8
2 Lawrence St ·SW3. 01-352 1893. Popular Chelsea local with very friendly staff and an extensive cold table. Enclosed garden. **B D**

Dandy Roll   6 M 29
Bread St EC4. 01-236 5453. Good modern City pub. Huge selection of different cheeses and bread. **B**

De Hems   2 I 22
11 Macclesfield St, Shaftesbury Ave W1. 01-437 2494. Victorian pub popular with visitors — over 150 different bank note s dangle from the ceiling. **B**

Dirty Dick's   6 N 33
202-4 Bishopsgate EC2. 01-283 5888. The original pub named after Nat Bentley, well known 18th cent miser of the ballad. Lives up to its name with cobwebs and musty stuffed cats. **B D**

Dover Castle   2 D 20
43 Weymouth Mews W1. 01-636 9248. Mews pub patronised by the BBC. **B**

Duke of Cumberland
235 Kings Rd SW6. 01-736 2777. Edwardian elegance that won the 'Evening Standard Pub of the Year' award in 1971. Popular ,young and trendy. Summertime drinking on Parson's Green. **B**

Duke of Wellington   5 L 13
63 Eaton Terrace SW1. 01-730 3103. Traditional pub — pictures of the Iron Duke abound as does brass and copperware. Used by shoppers and workers as well as Chelsea locals. **B D**

Eagle   3 I 33
2 Sheperdess Walk N1. 01-253 3561. Victorian music-hall pub immortalised in the song 'Pop goes the Weasel'. Marie Lloyd associations. **B**

Empress of Russia   6 J 29
362 St John St EC1. 01-837 1910. Cheerful pub with an excellent cheese board. **B**

Ennismore Arms   1 H 11
2 Ennismore Gdns Mews SW7. 01-854 9116. Pretty mews pub with neo-Georgian décor and comfortable seating. **B**

Finch's (Kings Arms)   4 L 7
190 Fulham Rd SW3. 01-352 7469. Solid Victorian interior. Very arty crowd. **B**

Fitzroy Tavern   2 F 22
43 Windmill St W1. 01-636 6775. Famous literary and artistic pub. **B**

George   2 E 21
55 Great Portland St W1. 01-636 0863. Popular Victorian pub frequented by members of the BBC and rag trade. **B**

George   6 K 23
213 Strand WC2. 01-353 9238. Fine old timbered George III inn. **B**

George and Vulture   6 O 31
3 Castle Court EC3. 01-629 9710. 14th cent inn mentioned in the 'Pickwick Papers'. Beer is served in silver tankards. **B**

George Inn   6 Q 27
77 Borough High St SE1. 01-407 2056. Galleried Dickensian coaching inn mentioned in 'Little Dorrit'. Excellent beer, dispensed from an unusual 'beer engine', mussels, sprats, cockles and jellied eels. **B C**

Gilbert and Sullivan   6 K 23
John Adam St WC2. 01-839 2580. Strictly a G & S lovers pub. Programmes, playbills, photographs, scores and stage settings — and of course the music. **B D**

Golden Lion   5 J 19
25 King St, St James's SW1. 01-930 7227. Theatrical and literary pub. Oscar Wilde and Lily Langtry associations. **B**

Green Man
Putney Heath SW15. 01-788 1313. 15th cent ale house overlooking Putney Common. Associated with duels and highwaymen.

Greyhound   1 E 7
1 Kensington Sq W8. 01-937 7140. 'Pub of the Year' award winner in 1975. Warm and friendly in the front bar, quiet and relaxing in the back. Watch the experts on two full size billiard tables. **B**

Guinea (Ye Old One Pound One)   2 H 18
30 Bruton Place W1. 01-629 5613. Pleasant old pub hidden away in a narrow cobbled Mayfair mews. **B D**

Henekey's Long Bar   3 I 23
22-3 High Holborn WC1. 01-242 7670. A huge pub in the Victorian grand manner with cosy cubicles for discreet couples. This is where lawyers used to have confidential chats with their clients. **B**

Henekey's (Portobello)
281 Westbourne Grove W11. 01-229 4689. Bohemian Victorian pub with beer garden. Good snacks. **B**

Hole in the Wall   6 N 23
5 Mepham St SE1. 01-407 1204. Free house. Bass Worthington, Brakspear Ruddle County and Young's cask bitters. Built into the arches by Waterloo Station with bar-loads of beer fanatics.

Horse and Groom   2 E 21
128 Great Portland St W1. 01-580 4726. Attractive 200-year-old mews tavern. **B**

Intrepid Fox   2 I 21
99 Wardour St W1. 01-437 6513. Soho pub named after statesman Charles James Fox. **B**

Island Queen   3 F 32
87 Noel St N1. 01-226 5507. Two looming papier maché figures dominate the bar in this popular local. **B**

King of Bohemia
10 Hampstead High St NW3. 01-435 5962. Bow-fronted Georgian pub — a fashionable local. **B**

Lamb   3 H 26
94 Lamb's Conduit St WC1. 01-405 5962. A quiet Bloomsbury local with some intriguing music hall photographs and Hogarth prints. **B**

Lamb and Flag   6 J 23
33 Rose, St Covent Garden WC2. 01-836 4108. Originally called 'The Bucket of Blood' because the pub was the centre for fighting in the area (Dryden apparently got the 'once over' here). Now a popular mellow bar. **B**

London Apprentice
62 Church St, Old Isleworth, Middx. 01-560 3538. Thames-side 15th cent pub with fine Elizabethan and Georgian interiors. Prints of Hogarth's 'Apprentices'. **B L D**

Markham Arms   4 L 10
138 Kings Rd SW3. 01-589 2021. Popular with real and would-be Chelsea trendies. Crowded. **B**

Marquis of Anglesey   6 J 24
39 Bow St WC2. 01-240 3216. Newly expanded and popular with local workers and journalists. Good beer. **B L D**

Museum Tavern   3 H 23
49 Great Russell St WC1. 01-242 8987. Located opposite the British Museum, the tavern attracts students and sightseers. Victorian interior with a vast collection of bowler hats and umbrellas! **B**

Nag's Head
79-81 Heath St NW3. 01-435 4108. Crowded every night with dedicated beer swillers sampling the impressive selection offered. Small patio. **B**

Olde Mitre Tavern   3 I 28
1 Ely Place EC1. 01-405 4751. Built in 1546 by the Bishops of Ely for their servants. Associations with Elizabeth I and Dr Johnson. **B**

Orange   5 M 12
37 Pimlico Rd SW1. 01-730 5378. Nell Gwen once sold oranges here. Cheerful atmosphere. **B**

Printer's Devil   6 K 26
98 Fetter Lane EC4. 01-242 2239. A printers' and
journalists' pub named after the traditional printers'
apprentice. Notable collection of early printing curios.
B

Punch Tavern   6 L 27
99 Fleet St EC4. 01-353 8338. A brass figure of Mr
Punch, fascinating cartoons and framed old newspapers. **B**

Queen's Elm   4 K 4
241 Fulham Rd SW3. 01-352 9157. So-called because
Elizabeth I took shelter under a nearby elm in 1567.
Lively and popular with writers — buy books signed by
authors over the bar. **B**

Railway Tavern   6 M 32
15 Liverpool St EC2. 01-283 3598. Railway relics —
models, prints, posters and timetables. **B**

Red Lion   5 J 20
2 Duke of York St SW1. 01-930 2030. Plenty of
Victoriana in this friendly pub. Beautifully preserved
mirrors and rich mahogany panelling. **B**

Red Lion   2 H 17
Waverton St W1. 01-499 1307. 17th cent inn with
forecourt. Frequented by models, actors and young
businessmen. **B D**

Rossetti
23 Queen's Grove St John's Wood NW8. 01-722 7141.
Airy pub-trattoria with Rossetti etchings on the walls.
English beer, good Italian food. **B D**

Running Footman   2 H 17
5 Charles St, Mayfair W1. 01-499 8239. Pub with the
longest name in London: 'I am the Only Running
Footman'. Popular with band-boys and croupiers. **B**

Scarsdale Arms   1 E 5
23a Edwardes Sq W8. 01-937 1811. Country kitchen
décor with old clocks and frosted glass windows in
front of an open fire. **B**

St Stephen's Tavern   5 M 21
10 Bridge St SW1. 01-930 2541. The local for Members
of Parliament. Political journalists' gossip might be
worth hearing. **B D**

Salisbury   5 J 22
90 St Martin's Lane WC2. 01-836 5863. Glittering
Edwardian pub in the heart of theatreland. Cut-glass
mirrors and good buffet. **B**

Sherlock Holmes   5 K 22
10 Northumberland St WC2. 01-930 2644. Perfect
replica of Holmes's study at 221b Baker St. **B D**

Sir Richard Steele
97 Haverstock Hill NW3. 01-722 1003. Imposing
Edwardian décor — faded plush wallpaper, oil lamps
and a stained glass window of Richard Steele, the
essayist. American pool upstairs. **B**

Spotted Dog
212 Upton Lane, Forest Gate E7. 01-472 1794. 17th cent
inn used by City merchants during the great plague.
Dick Turpin associations though the décor is mostly
Tudor. Oak beams, plaster whitewash, prints. **B D**

Sun in Splendour   1 A 8
7 Portobello Rd W11. 01-727 5444. A lively place on Sat
after the market. Pretty courtyard in back. **B**

Swiss Cottage
98 Finchley Rd NW3. 01-722 4747. Ramgling Victorian
farm-type inn — you can't miss it. Loud and full of
youngsters 7 nights a week. **B D**

Tattersall's Tavern   2 H 13
Knightsbridge Green SW1. 01-584 7122. Filled with
mementoes of the old Tattersall's horse auction rooms
and other equine fripperies. **B**

Victoria Tavern   2 C 14
10a Strathearn Place W2. 01-262 7474. Victoriana and
theatre trivia. Pleasant forecourt. **B D**

Watling (Ye Olde)   6 M 29
29 Watling St EC4. 01-248 6235. Oak beamed tavern
rebuilt by Wren after the Great Fire of 1666. **B**

Williamson's Tavern   6 M 29
1-3 Grovelands Courts, Bow Lane EC4. 01-248 6280.
Inviting City tavern built after the Great Fire. **B**

York Minster (The French)   2 I 22
49 Dean St W1. 01-437 2799. Good wines and snacks.
French aperitifs and an antique dispenser for adding
water to your Pernod. **B**

Musical pubs

Folk

The Elgin   1 A 6
96 Ladbroke Grove W11. 01-727 4192. *Wed evenings.*

Half Moon
Lower Richmond Rd SW15. 01-788 2387. *Mon & Fri*
folk. *Sat & Sun* Country and Western.

Mathilda's   1 C 8
Old Swan, 206 Kensington Church St W8. 01-229 8421.
Every night with singers and musicians welcome. All
sorts of folk ranging from Aussie and blue grass to old
time. Free.

The Rising Sun, Granny's Folk Blues Club   2 F 23
46 Tottenham Court Rd W1. 01-636 6530. Friendly and
informal. Singers welcome. *Fri & Sat.*

Prince of Wales, Hammersmith Folk Centre
73 Dalling Rd W6. 01-748 1236. Residents and an
excellent array of guests *every Thur evening.*

Jazz

Bricklayer's Arms
Ealing Rd, Brentford Middx. 01-560 7841. Trad jazz and
good bars. *Tue, Thur & Sat.* Free.

Bull's Head
Barnes Bridge SW13. 01-876 5241. Modern jazz by top
English and visiting foreign players *every night.*

New Merlin's Cave   3 G 29
Margery St WC1. 01-837 2097. Barn-like pub offering
jazz *Wed-Fri,* and good *Sun lunchtime* sessions. Top
musicians drop in and play gratis.

Plough
90 Stockwell Rd SW9. 01-274 3879. Top quality jazz.
Different groups *Wed-Sun.*

Two Brewers   3 I 23
40 Monmouth St WC2. 01-836 7395. Warm and friendly
oak-panelled pub with a strong local following. Renown
jazz jam sessions Mon & Fri. A *must* for enthusiasts. **B.**

Prospect of Whitby
57 Wapping Wall E1. 01-481 1095. 600 year old Pepys
tavern overlooking the Thames. Nautical souvenirs and
excellent restaurant with balcony. Jazz *Tues-Sun.*

White Hart   3 I 24
191 Drury Lane WC2. 01-405 4061. Another pub that
claims to be the oldest in London. Friendly and loud
with jazz *every night* — mainly trad.

Music hall — piano and singing

The Londoner
2 East India Dock Rd E14. 01-987 3681. Cockneyland
pub with recently renovated large restaurant. Traditional pub entertainment *nightly* in the music lounge
except Tues which is jazz night. **B D**

Queens Head
83 Fieldgate St E1. 01-247 5593. Free and easy East End
pub. Seamen and vodka. Oldtime piano music.

Pindar of Wakefield   3 G 27
328 Gray's Inn Rd WC1. 01-837 7269. The pub to go to
for oldtime music-hall. *Thur, Fri & Sat* nights — book
first for an excellent show. **B**

Town of Ramsgate
62 Wapping High St E1. 01-480 5791. 17th cent tavern
with piano player and spirited community singing. *Fri,
Sat & Sun nights.* **B**

Rock

Greyhound
175 Fulham Palace Rd W6. 01-385 0526. *Every night.*
Excellent value with no entrance fee.

Hope and Anchor   3 E 32
207 Upper St N1. 01-359 4510. Beery pub with loud juke
box upstairs, live music in the cellar *Mon-Sat* nights.
Good food and open fires in winter.

The Kensington   1 B 3
54 Russell Gdns W14. 01-603 3245. Groups *Mon-Sat.*
Jazz *on Sun.*

King's Head   3 E 32
115 Upper St N1. 01-226 1916. Live music *every night*
from skiffle bands to trad jazz. Rock *at weekends.* **D**

The Nashville Room   1 E 2
171 North End Rd W14. 01-603 6071. Vast music bar,
two bands a night. *Open to 24.00 Fri & Sat.* Free Mon-
Thur.

Drag pubs

*Female impersonators enjoy an enormous popularity in
pubs with acts that are a combination of blue jokes and
songs. There is usually a central roster of artistes who
do the round of these better known pubs:*

Black Cap   3 A 25
171 Camden High St NW1. 01-485 1742. *Every night.*

Duke of Fife
35 Katherine Rd E7. 01-472 0963. *Fri-Sun.*

Elephant and Castle
2 South Lamberth Place SW8. 01-735 1001. *Every
night.* Also live bands.

Green Man   3 D 22
383 Euston Rd NW1. 01-387 6977. 4 bars, drag shows
and gay discos. Phone for details.

King's Head   **2 | 22**
48 Gerrard St W1. 01-437 5858. Drag shows *on Sat &
Sun* in one of the oldest Dive Bars in London.
Royal Oak
62 Glenthorne Rd W6. 01-748 2781. *Wed-Mon.* Live
groups.
Royal Vauxhall Tavern
372 Kennington Lane SE11. 01-582 0833. *Every night.*
Union Tavern
146 Camberwell New Rd SE5. 01-735 3605. Revues on
Tues, Wed, Thur and Sun in one of London's original
drag pubs. House band on *Fri & Sat.*

Open air pubs

*Where you can enjoy a drink outside — on a pavement,
in a courtyard or garden, or overlooking the river.*
Anchor   **6 O 28**
Bankside SE1. 01-407 1577. 18th cent replacement of
original destroyed by fire of 1676. Five beamed bars and
three restaurants — one with a minstrel's gallery. **B D**
Angel
101 Bermondsey Wall East SE16. 01-237 3608. 16th
cent Thames-side pub on piles with extensive views
over the river and the pool of London. Low ceilings,
wooden beams and fine French cooking. **B D**
Black Lion
2 South Black Lion Lane W6. 01-748 7056. Lovely old
riverside pub with a garden and grapevine. **B**
Bull's Head
Strand on the Green, Chiswick W4. 01-994 0647. 350-
year old water front tavern with Cromwell history. **B D**
City Barge
27 Strand on the Green, Chiswick W4. 01-994 2148.
15th cent riverside Elizabethan Charter Inn. **B**
The Crown   **5 O 21**
35 Albert Embankment SW1. 01-735 1054. Lovely view
over the river to the Houses of Parliament. **B**
Cutty Sark
Ballast Quay, Ladsell St SE10. 01-858 3146. Quiet
Georgian pub with wooden interior. Overlooks river and
wharves near 'Cutty Sark' in dry dock. **B D**
Dove
19 Upper Mall, Hammersmith W6. 01-748 5405. 16th
cent pub with verandah and good Thames view. **B**
Finch's (Duke of Wellington)   **1 A 8**
179 Portobello Rd W11. 01-727 6727. Cheerful pub with
trompe l'oeil windows painted on its outside. Pavement
drinking. **B**
Flask
77 West Hill, Highgate N6. 01-340 3969. Old tavern
named after the flasks which people used to buy here to
fill with water at the Hampstead wells. Crowded
forecourt for outside drinking.
Freemasons Arms
32 Downshire Hill NW3. 01-435 4498. Popular
Hampstead Heath pub with enormous garden,
courtyards, and a balcony. **B**
Grapes
76 Narrow St, Limehouse E14. 01-987 4396. Traditional
pub amid wharves and warehouses. **B**
Gun
27 Coldharbour Lane E14. 01-987 1643. Riverside pub
with Nelson history.
Mayflower
117 Rotherhithe St SE16. 01-237 4088. Tudor Thames-
side inn connected historically with the Pilgrim Fathers.
Good grills. **B D**
Old Caledonia   **5 M 22**
Victoria Embankment (under Waterloo Bridge) WC2.
01-240 2750. An old converted paddle-steamer. Ideal
for a hot summer's evening, but if you've got a queasy
stomach, then pray for no wind! **B D**
Samuel Pepys   **6 N 28**
Brooks Wharf, 48 Upper Thames St EC4. 01-248 3691.
Converted warehouse in Jacobean style. Two large
bars and a two-tier terrace overlooking the river. **B D**
Princess of Wales   **4 K 9**
145 Dovehouse St SW3. 01-352 7567. Classy pub set
back from the road with an attractive forecourt.
Smoked salmon and trout from the bar. **B**
Ship
Ship Lane, Mortlake SW14. 01-876 1439. 16th cent
Thames-side pub with terrace. **B**
Spaniards Inn
Hampstead Lane NW3. 01-455 3276. Famous 16th cent
inn with Dick Turpin and literary associations. Beer
garden. **B**
Swan   **1 B 10**
66 Bayswater Rd W2. 01-262 5204. Illuminated at night,
this popular beer garden opposite the park has become
a rendezvous for overseas visitors. **B**

Theatre pubs

Bush Theatre
Bush Hotel, Shepherd's Bush Green W12. 01-743 5050.
Theatre above a pub. Established by Brian McDermott,
John Neville and Andrew Barton to try to attract the
non theatre-going man in the street. Stage in rostrum
form with no curtain. Interesting experimental
productions. *Evening* performances. **B**
King's Head   **3 E 32**
115 Upper St N1. 01-226 1916. Probably the best
known and most widely reviewed of theatre pubs.
Decorated with theatre bills. You can have a meal
before you see the show and stay at your table for the
performance. *Lunchtime & evening* shows.
Membership. **B L D**
Nag's Head   **6 J 23**
10 James St, Covent Garden WC2. 01-836 4678.
Lunchtime performances *Fri-Sat.* Lively Covent Garden
pub decorated with theatre playbills and prints.
B D
The Orange Tree
45 Kew Rd, Richmond Surrey. Bookings 01-940 3633.
Popular performances by the excellent Richmond
Fringe Theatre Group above this friendly attractive pub.
Take your drinks upstairs to watch the plays at
lunchtimes and in the *evenings*. Small and informal. **D**

Wine Bars

*Cheaper and more informal than restaurants yet with
better food than most pubs, wine bars provide excellent
meeting places for locals and visitors alike. Wine is
served by the bottle or the glass and a selection of
cheese, pâtés and salads is usually available. Many bars
have their own restaurants. Booking is often advisable.*
D   Dinner
*Bars are open normal pub hours (see Pubs) except
where otherwise indicated.*
Balls Bros
One of the oldest wine bar chains in London, especially
useful for city workers. *OPEN Mon-Fri to 19.30.* Ten
branches:
142 Strand WC2. 01-836 0156.   **6 K 24**
3 Budge Row EC4. 01-248 7557.
5 Carey Lane EC2. 01-606 4787.
6 Cheapside EC2. 01-248 2708.   **6 M 29**
Gow's Restaurant, Old Broad St EC2. 01-588 2050.
                                                             6 N 32
Laurence Pountney Hill EC4. 01-283 2947.
Moor House, London Wall EC2. 01-628 3944.   **6 L 30**
2 Old Change Court EC4. 01-236 9921.
St Mary at Hill, Eastcheap EC3. 01-626 0321.
42 Threadneedle St EC2. 01-283 6701.   **6 N 31**
Bill Bentley's Wine Bar   **2 I 12**
31 Beauchamp Place SW3. 01-584 7714. Dark, cosy bar
in the old fashioned tradition with an excellent fish
restaurant upstairs. The wine, mostly good quality
French, is reasonably priced and well accompanied by
the delicious snacks from the oyster bar. **D**
Bow Wine Vaults   **6 M 29**
10 Bow Churchyard EC4. 01-248 1121. Victorian bar not
only within hearing of the Bow Church Bells, but next
to them! Popular with city gents, the bar offers a good
selection of well chosen French and German wines, a
large cheeseboard and a lunchtime restaurant. *OPEN
Mon-Fri to 19.00.*
Brahms & Liszt   **6 J 24**
19 Russell St WC2. 01-240 3661. Lively new addition to
Covent Garden's revival. Upstairs for food and
conversation, cellar bar for rowdier times, darts and bar
billiards. Popular with journalists and actors. Loud
music. *CLOSED Sun.* **D**
Capataz Wine Store   **6 N 32**
89 Old Broad St EC2. 01-588 1140. Dickensian wine
cellar that has been run by the same family for over 100
years. French and German wines and a selection of
about five sherries and ports. Popular city bar. No food.
OPEN lunchtimes only Mon-Fri.
Charco's   **4 L 11**
1 Bray Place SW3. 01-584 0765. Near Sloane Sq.
Interesting salads and game pies. Pavement tables in
summer. **D**
Coates   **6 M 32**
109 Broad St EC2. 01-638 4761. Crowded City bar on
two floors. Good port from the barrel. Branch in
London Wall EC1. *OPEN Mon-Fri to 19.00.*
Cork and Bottle   **5 J 22**
44-46 Cranbourn St WC2. 01-734 7807. Spacious
basement with unusual variety of top-class bargain
wines. Guitarist most evenings. *CLOSED Sun.*

Crawfords Wine Bar   2 C 17
10 Crawford St W1. 01-935 6744. Spanish style cellar bar and restaurant. Live music nightly. *OPEN Mon-Sat to 24.00.* **D**

Davy's Wine Bars
Dusty barrels, old prints and sawdust-covered floors create the Victorian image of these houses, the names of which date back to the wine trade of 100 years ago. The chain offers a good selection of wines and tasty fish appetisers. Normal pub hours but the City bars *close at 20.30. Most branches are closed Sat & Sun.*

The Boot and Flogger   6 Q 27
10-20 Redcross Way SE1. 01-407 1184.

The Bunghole   3 I 23
57 High Holborn WC1. 01-242 4318.

Davy's Wine Vaults
165 Greenwich High Rd SE10. 01-858 7204.

The Gyngleboy   2 B 13
27 Spring St W2. 01-723 3351.

Mother Bunch's Wine House
Arches F & G, Old Seacoal Lane EC4. 01-236 5317.

The Old Bottlescrue   6 K 28
Bath House, Holborn Viaduct EC1. 01-248 2157.

Downs   2 I 17
5 Down St W1. 01-491 3810. Excellent food and French wines. Two floors but crowded at lunchtime with Mayfair clientele. *OPEN Mon-Sat to 24.00. Sun to 23.30.* **D**

Ebury Wine Bar   5 M 13
139 Ebury St SW1. 01-730 5447. Stone and tile décor, distinguished restaurant. **D**

El Vinos   6 K 26
47 Fleet St EC4. 01-353 6786. Popular with male journalists — women not served at the bar. *OPEN Mon-Fri to 20.00. Sat lunch.*

Gordon's Wine Cellar   5 K 22
47 Villiers St WC2. 01-930 1408. 300 year-old barrel-lined cellar hidden in Watergate Walk. Upstairs bar overlooks Embankment. *OPEN Mon-Fri to 21.00.*

Gows Oyster Bar   6 N 32
81 Old Broad St EC2. 01-588 2050. Cask wines, fish appetisers. City atmosphere. *OPEN Mon-Fri to 19.30.*

Julie's Bar   11 A 5
137 Portland Rd W11. 01-727 7985. Intimate restaurant upstairs, wooden bar and mirrors downstairs. Pleasant informal lounge with mixture of sofas, Persian and Indian furniture and art nouveau décor. *OPEN Mon-Sat 12.30-23.00. Sun 13.00-22.30.* **D**

T.A. Layton's Wine Bar   5 O 17
12 Esterbrooke St SW1. 01-828 5211. Sole importers of their excellent French wines. The bar provides a cosy lunchtime meeting place for local office workers. Hot and cold food. *CLOSED evenings and weekends.*

Loose Box   2 I 12
7 Cheval Place SW7. 01-584 9280. Handy for Harrods shoppers and lively in the evenings. Upstairs restaurant. *CLOSED Sun.* **D**

Loose Rein Wine Bar   4 L 4
221 Kings Rd SW3. 01-352 9188. French basement bar, beneath wine shop, with good French food — moules, bouillabaisse. Live music evenings. *CLOSED Sun lunch.* **D**

Martha's Wine Bar
34 Rosslyn Hill NW3. 01-435 5203. Huge mirrors and old prints dominated by a full-size stuffed tiger in the middle of the room. Hot food, live music. **D**

Michael Gould's   2 A 18
1 Glentworth St NW1. 01-935 3827. Small but friendly atmosphere perhaps helped by the house champagne. *OPEN Mon-Fri to 22.00. CLOSED Sat evening and Sun.*

Charlie's Bar   4 L 4
52 Kings Rd SW3. 01-589 6640. Lively American style bar with wide range of tasty snacks. Live music Sun evenings.

Old Compton Wine Bar   2 I 22
37 Old Compton St W1. 01-437 0306. Modernistic and busy. Large choice of fresh hot and cold food. *CLOSED Sun.*

Osparas   5 N 16
46 Churton St SW1. 01-834 7311. Greek food, wines and dancing. Basement restaurant. Friendly, fun and very popular. *OPEN Mon-Sat. Sun 14.00-22.30.* **D**

Night life and clubs

Dinner dancing

These are not membership clubs. Booking is advisable.
£ = *inexpensive*
££ = *medium priced*
£££ = *expensive*

Anthea's   2 G 20
Foubert's Place, Carnaby St W1. 01-734 3630. Large, modern discotheque with three bars and a restaurant. French cooking. *OPEN to 03.00. Sun to 02.00.* Entrance fee. A. Ax. B. Cb. Dc. **£.**

Beachcomber   2 I 18
May Fair Hotel, Berkeley Square W1. 01-629 7777. Polynesian theme, tropical drinks, alligators in a pool. *OPEN 19.30-02.00. CLOSED Sun.* A. Ax. B. Dc. E. **£££.**

Celebrity   2 H 9
13 Clifford St, New Bond St W1. 01-493 7636. Resident groups. Cabaret stars at *22.30 and 01.30. OPEN 20.00-03.00. CLOSED Sun.* A. Ax. B. Cb. Dc. E. **££.**

Churchill's   2 G 19
160 New Bond St W1. 01-493 2626. Long established traditional night club. Cabaret (usually several acts) and floorshow at *23.00 and 01.00. OPEN 21.00-04.00. CLOSED Sun.* A. Ax. B. Cb. Dc. E. **£££.**

Eve   2 H 20
189 Regent St W1. 01-734 0557. Luxurious surroundings and glittering floor shows. Excellent French cooking. Floor show at *00.45, 24.45 & 01.45. D OPEN to 03.30.* A. Ax. B. Dc. E. **£££.**

Latin Quarter   2 I 21
13 Wardour St W1. 01-437 6001. Resident floor show and band. *OPEN 20.00-03.30. CLOSED Sun.* A. Ax. B. Cb. Dc. E. **£££.**

Quaglino's   5 J 19
16 Bury St SW1. 01-930 6767. Tasteful, professional and very much part of the 'establishment'. Two bands. Imaginative food. *OPEN 19.30-01.30. CLOSED Sun.* A. Ax. B. Cb. Dc. E. **£££.**

Roof Restaurant   2 I 16
Hilton Hotel, Park Lane W1. 01-493 8000. The view is all you would imagine, the décor light and modern. Two bands. French food. *OPEN 19.30-01.00.* A. Ax. B. Dc. E. **£££.**

Showboat   5 J 21
Trafalgar Square Corner House WC2. 01-930 2781. Theatre restaurant with revue, dancing. Popular prices. *OPEN 20.30-01.00. CLOSED Sun.* **££.**

Savoy Restaurant   6 K 23
Savoy Hotel, Strand WC2. 01-836 4343. Elegant, formal. Resident orchestra and cabaret (usually a big name singer). *OPEN 20.00-02.00. CLOSED Sun.* A. Ax. B. E. **£££.**

Talk of the Town   2 I 22
Hippodrome Corner, Charing Cross Rd WC2. 01-734 5051. Theatre restaurant with a resident revue and bands. International cabaret star at *23.00. OPEN 19.30 - 01.15. CLOSED Sun.* A. Ax. B. Cb. Dc. E. **£££.**

Terrace Restaurant   2 H 16
Dorchester Hotel, Park Lane W1. 01-629 8888. Pleasant atmosphere. Live music but no cabaret. *OPEN 20.00-01.00. CLOSED Sun.* Dinner à la carte. A. Ax. B. Dc. E. **£££.**

Tiddy Dol's   2 I 16
2 Hertford St W1. 01-499 2357. An 18th cent house in Shepherd Market. Excellent game and English dishes with dancing in the Minstrel's Gallery. *D OPEN to 03.00.* A. Ax. B. Cb. Dc. E. **££.**

Villa Dei Cesari   5 Q 15
135 Grosvenor Rd SW1. 01-828 7453. Converted riverside warehouse with a fine view over the Thames. Continental food. Dance floor with one band. *OPEN 19.30-02.30. CLOSED Mon.* Dinner à la carte. Ax. B. Dc. E. **£££.**

Night clubs

Differs from the previous section in that club membership (M) is usually necessary for entry.

Bristol Suite   2 H 18
14 Bruton Place W1. 01-499 1938. Hostesses, music and an international cuisine. *D OPEN 20.30-03.30 Mon-Fri.* A. Ax. B. Cb. Dc. E. **£££.**

Le Cercle   2 I 16
5 Hamilton Place W1. 01-499 5050. Elegant and exclusive. Dancing to an orchestra. *OPEN 18.30-02.30. CLOSED Sun.* (M). **£££.**

Chaplins   2 I 20
9 Swallow St W1. 01-734 2649. Dancing to live music, cabaret and lounge bar. No (M) for overseas visitors. Entrance fee and (M) for guests. *OPEN 20.30-03.30 Mon-Sat.* **£££.**

Charlie Chester Casino   2 I 21
12 Archer St W1. 01-437 7045.

Clermont   2 H 18
44 Berkeley Square W1. 01-439 5587. Excellent restaurant and wine list.

Crockford's   5 K 20
16 Carlton House Terrace SW1. 01-930 2721. A. Ax. B. Dc.

Curzon House Club   2 I 17
21-23 Curzon St W1. 01-493 3581. Ax. Dc. B.

La Dolce Notte   2 I 19
55 Jermyn St SW1. 01-493 2011. Dolce-Vita owned and with many of the same characterists. Lively, busy. No cabaret. *OPEN 12.00-15.00, 18.00-01.30 Mon-Fri, 18.00-02.00 Sat. CLOSED Sun.*

Gargoyle   2 H 22
69 Dean St W1. 01-437 6455. Dance partners. Cabaret 24.00. *OPEN 22.30-03.30.* (M) A. Ax. B. Cb. Dc. E. **£.**

Golden Horseshoe   2 I 21
4 Archer St W1. 01-437 5036.

Golden Nugget   2 I 21
Tiffany's 22-23 Shaftesbury Avenue W1. 01-734 6211.

Hertford Club   2 I 16
21 Hertford St W1. 01-493 1801. *OPEN 14.00- 04.00. Restaurant OPEN 19.00-04.00.* (M) A. Ax. B. Cb. Dc. E.

New Casanova   2 G 18
52 Grosvenor St W1. 01-629 1463. Roomy and comfortable. Regency décor. Not cheap but good value.

Palm Beach Casino   2 I 18
May Fair Hotel, Berkeley St W1. 01-493 6585.

Penthouse   2 I 17
11 Whitehouse St W1. 01-493 1977. *OPEN 18.30-03.00. CLOSED Sun.* (M) **£££.**

Playboy   2 G 16
45 Park Lane W1. 01-629 6666. All the facilities to soothe the tired executive. Bunnies (untouchable), bar with pin-ups, cabaret (in the Playroom), discotheque, *OPEN 12.00-04.00.* (M) varies. **£££.**

Sportsman   3 G 23
3 Tottenham Court Rd W1.01-636 9622. A. Ax. B. Dc.

Stork Room   2 I 20
99 Regent St W1. 01-734 1393. Well-established club which maintains strong nostalgic associations with the late owner, Al Burnett (noted entertainer of the '50's). Twice nightly shows with singers, dancers and two bands at 23.30 and 01.45. *OPEN 21.00-04.00.* Dinner, supper & breakfast.

Victoria Sporting Club   2 C 16
150-162 Edgware Rd W2. 01-262 2467.

Strip clubs

Soho has many back street strip joints with temporary membership. Not 'clip joints' so your money is safe but the shows are boring and unsexy, and the girls, tired from walking from club to club, are either too old or too young. The following list does not belong to this group and offers better value shows.

Casino de Paris   2 I 21
5-7 Denman St W1. 01-437 2872. *OPEN 14.00-23.15.*

Gargoyle   2 H 22
69 Dean St W1. 01-437 6455. *OPEN 23.00-03.30. Floorshow at 00.15 & 01.15.*

Nell Gwynne
69 Dean St W1. 01-437 3278. Theatre revue, continuous performance *18.00-24.00.* Topless bar.

Raymond Revuebar   2 I 21
Brewer St W1. 01-734 1593. The source of many a magazine feature — the art of strip at its best. Spectacular at *20.30 and 22.00. OPEN 19.00-23.00.*

Membership

The Clubman's Club   2 I 19
14 Oxford St W1. 01-636 3016. An annual subscription of £6.95 gives you membership to several hundred clubs all over Britain.

Jazz clubs

100 Club   2 G 22
100 Oxford St W1. 01-636 0933. Lively, noisy, British jazz and room to dance. *OPEN 19.30-24.00 Sun-Thur, 19.30-01.00 Fri & Sat.*

Madingly Club
Richmond Bridge, Surrey. 01-892 5828. Trad jazz on *Thur & Sun* in this lovely riverside club.

Ronnie Scott's   2 H 22
47 Frith St W1. 01-439 0747. The best jazz in London backed by the right blend of good food, comfort and subtle lighting. On the stand a succession of big name jazzmen, usually USA imports. *OPEN 20.30-03.00. CLOSED Sun.*

Discotheques

Discotheques generally cater for the affluent young, the new celebrities and the fashionable. They are very numerous; these are probably the best and most popular. Membership is often necessary.

Annabels   2 H 18
44 Berkeley Square W1. 01-629 2350. Fashionable but expensive club for sophisticated clientele. (M) *CLOSED Sun.* **£££.**

Countdown   2 F 21
78 Wells St W1. 01-580 2881. Live groups and disco. *OPEN 20.30-03.00 weekdays, Sun to 02.00.* (M) at door. **££.**

Crackers   2 I 21
201 Wardour St W1. 01-734 4961. Pub upstairs with a basement disco for a young crowd. *OPEN 20.00-01.00 Mon-Thur, Fri & Sat to 01.00. CLOSED Sun.* **£.**

Dingwalls
Camden Lock, Camden High St NW1. 01-267 4967. Long room with a reasonable restaurant at one end and stage and dance floor at the other. Groups and records. Very popular. **££.**

Fanny's Bistro   2 G 19
51 Maddox St W1. 01-629 6214. Provides a balanced diet of bistro-type dinner discotheque dancing. Pub-priced drinks. Membership unnecessary. *OPEN 19.30-02.00. CLOSED Sun.* **££.**

Global Village   5 K 22
The Arches, Villiers St WC2. 01-839 3641. Choice of bars, music or dancing for the energetic. *OPEN to 00.30 Wed, 01.00 Thur, 03.00 Fri & Sat.* **£.**

Marquee   2 H 21
90 Wardour St W1. 01-437 6603. More of a music club than a disco. Younger age group. *OPEN 19.00-23.00 only.* **£.**

Playground   2 I 17
Hatchetts, 67a Piccadilly W1. 01-629 2001. Distinguished by its incredible décor which won first prize in an international design competition; there are carpets on the walls, zebra fur upholstery and mirrors reflecting every action. Good discotheque with frequent live groups. Snacks or full meals available. *OPEN 20.00-03.30 Mon-Fri, 20.00-24.00 Sun.* **££.**

Rock Garden   6 J 23
67 Piazza, Covent Garden WC2. 01-240 3961. Hamburger restaurant on street level and upstairs with outside eating in summer. Live groups and records in the basement. Also lunchtime theatre. *OPEN Mon-Sat to 02.30.* **££.**

Thursdays   1 D 4
38 Kensington High St W8. 01-937 7744. Popular non-membership club. Large complex includes 4 bars, a good dance floor and restaurant. Jeans banned. *OPEN Mon-Sat 21.00-03.00.* **££.**

Saddle Room   2 I 16
1a Hamilton Mews W1. 01-499 4994. Popular disco and restaurant. *OPEN 21.00-04.00.* (M). **£££.**

Samantha's   2 H 20
3 New Burlington St W1. 01-734 5425. A well known and lively place with groups and discs. *OPEN 21.00-03.00 (till 04.00 Sat); (20.00-01.30 Sun).* **££.**

Sloop John D   4 N 9
River Thames, Cadogan Pier SW3. 01-223 3341. Intercepters whizz you across to the floating discotheque. Good restaurant. *OPEN 20.00-03.00 Tues-Sat.* Disco *22.00-03.00.* (M). **££**

Speakeasy 2 F 20
48 Margaret St W1. 01-580 7930. Discs and live groups every night. Restaurant. *OPEN 22.30-04.00. CLOSED Sun.* (M). ££
Tiffany's 2 I 21
22 Shaftesbury Avenue W1. 01-437 5012. Resident group and records. *OPEN 20.00-02.00 Mon-Thur, 20.00-03.00 Fri & Sat, 19.30-24.00 Sun.* ££

Dance halls

Large halls specialising in mass dancing (ballroom or modern style). Usually have resident bands and singers and attract mainly the 20-35 age group or the tweenies.
Café de Paris 2 I 21
3 Coventry St W1. 01-437 2036.
Empire Ballroom 5 J 22
Leicester Square WC2. 01-437 1446. *Members only Sun.* (M).

Hammersmith Palais 1 A 1
242 Shepherd's Bush Rd W6. 01-748 2812.
Lyceum 6 J 24
Wellington St WC2. 01-836 3715.
Royal
High Rd Tottenham N17. 01-808 4179.
Cats Whiskers
158 Streatham Hill SW2. 01-674 5868.
Tiffany's 2 I 21
22 Shaftesbury Avenue W1. 01-437 5012. A little more select than the others in this group.

Ticket agents

Keith Prowse 3 F 23
24 Store St WC1. 01-836 2184. Plus many other branches. *OPEN Mon-Fri 09.30-17.30.*

Theatres, cinemas, music and poetry

Theatres

London theatre is famous throughout the world for its diversity and quality. There has always been a group of favourites in the West End, but recently many avant-garde and experimental theatres have sprung up outside this traditional area. See the weekly 'Time Out' for reviews of fringe and experimental theatre and current programmes. The daily papers and 'What's On in London' have lists of current cinema and theatre.
Adelphi 6 K 23
Strand WC2. 01-836 7611. Musicals.
Albery 5 J 22
St Martin's Lane WC2. 01-836 3878. Was called the New Theatre until Jan 1973.
Aldwych 6 J 24
Aldwych WC2. 01-836 6404. Home of the Royal Shakespeare Company which is expected to move to the new Barbican Arts Centre in 1978.

Criterion 2 I 18
Piccadilly Circus W1. 01-930 3216. Small, comfortable theatre playing light comedy & plays.
Drury Lane (Theatre Royal) 6 J 24
Catherine St WC2. 01-836 8108. Opened under Royal charter by Thomas Killigrew in 1663 and has been burnt down and rebuilt 4 times. Nell Gwyn sold oranges there; Garrick, Mrs Siddons, Kean and others played there. General policy now is vast productions of musical plays.
Duchess 6 J 24
Catherine St WC2. 01-836 8243. Opened 1929. Plays, serious drama and light comedy.
Duke of York's 5 J 22
St Martin's Lane WC2. 01-836 5122. Built by 'Mad (Violet) Melnotte' in 1892. Associated with names like Frohman, G.B. Shaw, Granville Barker, Chaplin and the Ballet Rambert. Straight plays and comedies.
Fortune 3 I 24
Russell St WC2. 01-836 2238. Small compared with its neighbour, Drury Lane. Intimate revues (Peter Cook and Dudley Moore shot to fame here in 'Beyond the Fringe') and modern drama.

Ambassadors   Duke of York's   Globe

Ambassadors 2 I 22
West St WC2. 01-836 1171. Small theatre.
Apollo 2 I 21
Shaftesbury Avenue W1. 01-437 2663. Old tradition of musical comedy. Now plays both comedy and domestic drama.
Cambridge 3 I 23
Earlham St WC2. 01-836 6056/7040. Excellent theatre with varied programmes of plays, comedies and musicals.
Jeanetta Cochrane Theatre 3 H 25
Southampton Row WC1. 01-242 7040. Experimental new plays and student productions at sporadic intervals.
Coliseum 5 J 22
St Martin's Lane WC2. 01-836 3161. See under Opera, ballet and musicals.
Comedy 5 J 21
Panton St SW1. 01-930 2578. Good intimate theatre showing unusual comedy and small cast plays.
Covent Garden 6 J 23
Royal Opera House, Bow St WC2. 01-240 1066. Information & bookings 01-240 1911. *(24-hr service).* See under Opera, ballet and musicals.

Garrick   Haymarket   Lyric

Garrick 2 I 22
Charing Cross Rd WC2. 01-836 4601. Notable managers included Bourchier and Jack Buchanan. Varied bills.
Globe 2 I 21
Shaftesbury Avenue W1. 01-437 1592. A wide variety of successful plays and comedies. The third theatre of this name in London.
Half Moon
27 Alie St, Aldgate E2. 01-480 6465. Experimental political and popular plays, many with East End interest. Entrance hall hung with photographs.
Haymarket (Theatre Royal) 5 J 21
Haymarket SW1. 01-930 9832. A lively history – Walpole thrashed a slanderous actor; the Duke (or 'Butcher') of Culloden began a riot; tailors rioted at the performance in 1805 of Foote's satire 'The Tailors'.
Her Majesty's 5 J 21
Haymarket SW1. 01-930 6606. A fine Victorian baroque theatre founded by Beerbohm Tree. Successes included the stage version of 'West Side Story'.

King's Road Theatre 4 L 8
279 King's Rd SW3. 01-352 7488. Converted cinema. 'The Rocky Horror Show.' has been playing here since its opening.

Her Majesty's   Palace   Vaudeville

Lyric 2 I 21
Shaftesbury Avenue W1. 01-437 3686. Eleonora Duse. Sarah Bernhardt, Owen Nares and Tallulah Bankhead all had long runs here. Plays and small musicals.

May Fair 2 I 18
Stratton St W1. 01-629 3036. In the May Fair Hotel. A luxurious theatre not open permanently but taken by companies for short seasons.

Mermaid 6 M 27
Puddle Dock, Blackfriars EC4. 01-248 7656. Bernard Miles converted this river warehouse into an open-staged theatre. Excellent restaurants and bar. Unusual productions in a unique setting. Membership entitles you to reduced-price previews.

National Theatre 6 M 24
South Bank SE1. Box office 01-928 2252. New complex of three theatres, Olivier, the Lyttelton and the Coltesloe. Home of the National Theatre Company. Company. Stages a wide mixture of plays.

New London Theatre 3 I 24
Drury Lane WC2. 01-405 0072. Can convert from a 900-seat conventional theatre to an intimate theatre-in-the-round within minutes. Opened 1972 on the site of the old Winter Gardens. Large restaurant; parking for 500 cars.

Old Vic 6 O 24
Waterloo Rd SE1. 01-928 7616. Previous home of the National Theatre Company, now houses various groups.

Palace 2 I 22
Cambridge Circus W1. 01-437 6834. Originally intended by D'Oyly Carte to be the Royal English Opera House but it has always been a 'Variety Palace' despite the occasional performances by Pavlova and Nijinski.

Palladium 2 G 20
8 Argyll St W1. 01-437 7373. Second in size to the Coliseum; houses top variety shows and the annual Royal Command Performance.

Phoenix 2 I 22
Charing Cross Rd WC2. 01-836 8611. A large theatre showing comedies, plays and musicals.

Piccadilly 2 I 21
Denman St W1. 01-437 4506. A pre-war theatre which showed the first season of 'Talkies' in Britain. A chequered post-war history of light comedy, plays and musicals.

Prince of Wales 2 I 21
Coventry St W1. 01-930 8681. Rebuilt 1937, this large, modern theatre has housed many popular musicals.

Queen's 2 I 21
Shaftesbury Avenue W1. 01-734 1166. Very successful between wars. Still presents good drama and varied productions.

St Martin's   Wyndham's

Regent 2 F 20
Upper Regent St W1. 01-580 1744. Converted from a cinema.

Royal Court 5 L 12
Sloane Square SW1. 01-730 1745. Home of the English Stage Company which produces many major experimental plays.

Royal Festival Hall
See 'Concert halls'.

Royalty 6 J 25
Portugal St, Kingsway WC2. 01-405 8004. Now managed by Raymond of Revuebar fame, this theatre presents big name 'drag' shows and blue comedy.

Sadler's Wells 3 G 30
Rosebery Avenue EC1. 01-837 1672. See under Opera, ballet and musicals.

St Martin's 2 I 22
Cambridge Circus, West St WC2. 01-836 1443. Small intimate playhouse for good straight plays.

Savoy 6 K 23
Strand WC2. 01-836 8888. Entrance is in the forecourt of the Savoy hotel. It was the first London theatre to be fully electrically lit. Produces a variety of plays, comedies and musicals.

Strand   Shaftesbury

Shaftesbury 2 I 21
Shaftesbury Avenue WC2. 01-836 6596. See under Opera, ballet and musicals.

Shaw Theatre 3 D 26
100 Euston Rd NW1. 01-388 1394. Modern theatre showing many unusual productions.

Strand 6 J 24
Aldwych WC2. 01-836 2660. Home of the farce in its heyday, the 30's. Remains basically a comedy theatre.

Theatre Royal
Salway Rd, Stratford E15. 01-534 0310. Joan Littlewood's East End theatre workshop showing new plays and musicals.

Vanbrugh 3 F 24
62 Gower St WC1. 01-580 7982. Two theatres showing experimental productions and revivals.

Vaudeville 6 K 23
Strand WC2. 01-836 9988. Originally ran farce and burlesque (hence the name) then became 'straight' (which for the most part it remains).

Westminster Theatre 5 L 17
Palace St SW1. 01-834 0283. Arts Centre opened 1931. Plays and musicals.

Whitehall 5 L 21
14 Whitehall SW1. 01-930 6692. Brian Rix played his particular brand of farce here for many years. The theatre still specialises in popular theatre.

Wyndham's 2 I 22
Charing Cross Rd WC2. 01-836 3028. Successful theatre founded by Sir Charles Wyndham, the famous actor-manager. Edgar Wallace was manager for a while. Plays, comedy and musicals.

Young Vic 6 O 24
The Cut, Waterloo SE1. 01-928 6363. Young repertory company putting on a good choice of revivals and experimental theatre. Specially written children's plays and adaptations of Shakespeare.

Arts theatres & theatre clubs

Arts Theatre Club 2 I 22
Great Newport St WC2. 01-836 7541. Experimental theatre and films for all ages. Lounge, restaurant and gallery. Box office 01-836 3334.

Artists' Place 3 D 25
17 Duke's Rd WC1. 01-387 0161. Practice rooms and theatre for a young and adventurous company. Also workshops for drama, music and films.

Cockpit
Arts Centre Gateforth St NW8. 01-262 7907. Opened by the ILEA in Jan 1970. An adaptable 'round' with a varied programme of drama and music.

Greenwich Theatre
Crooms Hill SE10. 01-858 7755. Successful outer London company with a string of West End transfers to its credit. Go by boat from Westminster, Charing Cross or Tower Pier.

Hampstead Theatre Club
Swiss Cottage Centre, Avenue Rd NW3. 01-722 9301. Vigorous serious drama and revue. An established professional theatre fostering new drama.

ICA Arts Centre Theatre 5 K 21
ICA, Nash House, The Mall, SW1. 01-930 6393. Popular arts centre.

Little Theatre Club 5 J 22
Empire House, 16-19 Upper St Martin's Lane WC2. 01-240 0660. Small theatre for new plays. Lunchtime performances.

Mountview Theatre Club
104 Crouch Hill N8. 01-340 5885. Amateur theatre, drama school and social centre.

Open Space Theatre Club 3 G 23
32 Tottenham Court Rd W1. 01-580 4664. New experimental plays and lunchtime revues in an underground arena.

The Place 3 D 25
17 Duke's Rd WC1. 01-387 0031. Experimental drama, music and mixed media shows in an informal atmosphere.

Players' 5 K 22
Hungerford Arches, Villiers St WC2. 01-839 1134. Last stand of the Edwardian music hall tradition in this successful private theatre. Drinks and sandwiches are served during the show and there is a good restaurant. Members only

Questors
Mattock Lane, Ealing W5. 01-567 5184. An excellent amateur theatre club. Productions include English and foreign classics, modern plays, experimental work, films, concerts and other social activities. The club includes 'Under 14' and 'Junior drama' workshops and a Student training course.

Round House
Chalk Farm Rd NW1. 01-267 2564. An exciting experimental theatre in a converted railway shed. Always packed to capacity.

Theatre Upstairs 5 L 12
Royal Court Theatre, Sloane Square SW1. 01-730 2554. New plays and playwrights in a club-like little room above the main theatre.

Tower
Canonbury Place N1. 01-226 5111. Tavistock Repertory Company present 18 plays a year. Closed during the summer season

Unity 3 B 26
1 Goldington St NW1. 01-387 8647. The first theatre in England to stage Brecht and to have world premieres of Sartre and Adamov. This theatre continues to promote new work. Also films, music hall and folk.

Marionette theatre

The Little Angel 3 D 33
14 Dagmar Passage, Cross St N1. 01-226 1787. The first real puppet theatre in London for over 100 years. Excellent shows every day at *15.00 (school hols). Otherwise 15.00 Sat & Sun only, and 11.00 Sat.*

Open-air theatres

George Inn 6 Q 27
77 Borough High St SE1. Contact the Festival Box Office 28 Peckham Rd SE5. 01-703 2917 for tickets and programmes of the Sat afternoon performances of Shakespeare in the open courtyard of the inn. Arrive at *14.00* for show at *15.00. May-Jul.*

Holland Park Court Theatre 1 C 5
W8. 01-633 1707. Performances of opera, ballet and plays are given near the house. No advance booking. *Jun-Aug.*

Regent's Park Open Air Theatre 2 A 21
Inner Circle, Regent's Park NW1. 01-486 2431. Lovely in good weather. Plays of Shakespeare (sometimes others) during the summer. Book in advance.

Opera, ballet and musicals

Coliseum 5 J 22
St Martin's Lane WC2. 01-836 3161. Largest London theatre seating 2,700. Now houses both the resident English National Opera (formerly Sadler's Wells Company) and the touring one.

Covent Garden 6 J 23
Royal Opera House, Bow St WC2. 01-240 1066. Information & bookings 01-240 1911 *(24-hr service).* The world-famous Royal Ballet and Opera company maintain an international reputation.

Drury Lane (Theatre Royal) 6 J 24
Catherine St WC2. 01-836 8101. Famous theatre. General policy now is vast productions of musical plays. *See also under* Theatres.

Royal Albert Hall
Orchestral pop and choral concerts. Famous for the 'Proms' — *see also under* Concert halls.

Royal Festival Hall
See 'Concert halls'. Orchestral and choral concerts and modern music.

The Place 3 D 25
17 Duke's Rd WC1. 01-387 0031. Home of the London Contemporary Dance Theatre, an exciting and creative modern dance company. Immaculate production with interesting choreographic ideas.

Sadler's Wells 3 G 30
Rosebery Avenue EC1. 01-837 1672. Once a spa (the original well discovered by Thomas Sadler is under a trap-door at the back of the stalls). Birthplace of the Royal Ballet company now used by visiting opera and ballet companies *See also* Coliseum.

Shaftesbury 3 H 23
Shaftesbury Avenue WC2. 01-836 6596. The theatre is particularly well equipped for musical plays and housed the tribal rock musical 'Hair'.

Victoria Palace 5 L 16
Victoria St SW1. 01-834 1317. Musicals, variety shows and plays.

Poetry

Poetry enthusiasts should consider joining either the ICA, Greater London Arts Association (Dial-a-Poem 01-836 2872), National Book League or the Poetry Society. These four bodies have pooled resources and formed a 'Poetry consortium' with the aim of promoting more ambitious ventures.

Avatar Reading Room 1 F 8
52 Victoria Rd W8. 01-937 3324. Spontaneous readings, music and songs of variable quality contributed by the audience. Complete freedom of expression, no censorship but time limits imposed on ramblers. Bread, cheese and cider. *First Mon of every month 20.30.*

Barrow Poets
70 Parliament Hill NW3. 01-435 7817. Well-known band of six bards hold lively sessions of music and poetry during university term-time in Woolseys Wine Bar 52 Wells St W1. *Thur 20.00.*

Dulwich Group
Crown and Greyhound, Dulwich Village SE21. 01-693 2466. Established poets give readings *last Wed of every month. 19.45.* Free.

Institute of Contemporary Arts 5 K 20
Nash House, 12 Carlton House Terrace SW1. 01-930 0493. Occasional lectures and readings by distinguished poets followed by discussion.

London Poetry Secretariat 3 E 25
25-31 Tavistock Place WC1. 01-387 9541. Grant-aided by the Greater London Arts Association to promote poetry activities.

National Book League 2 I 19
7 Albemarle St W1. 01-493 9001. Organise poetry readings and provide publicity for Poetry Consortium. Send SAE for monthly diary of events.

The Poetry Society 1 H 5
21 Earls Court Square SW5. 01-373 7861. Produces a 'Poetry Review' journal in which both new and established poets can appear. Library and theatre room for readings and discussion. Regular meetings *on Tue, Wed & Fri.*

Concert halls

Central Hall 5 M 19
Storeys Gate SW1. 01-930 7197. A large hall seating 2,640. Organ recitals, orchestral concerts, public meetings.

Conway Hall 3 H 25
Red Lion Square WC1. 01-242 8032. Seats 500. A large and small hall. Chamber music, concerts, meetings, rehearsals and recordings.

Covent Garden Royal Opera House 6 J 23
Bow St WC2. 01-240 1066. Information & bookings 01-240 1911 *(24-hr service).* World-famous ballet and opera company.

Holborn Assembly Hall 3 H 27
John Mews WC1. 01-278 4444 Ext 2132. Concerts and meetings.

Old Town Hall
Haverstock Hill NW3. 01-278 4444 Ext 2132. Concerts and meetings.

Purcell Room 6 M 23
South Bank SE1. 01-928 3191. Chamber music and solo concerts. Generally performances which require even intimate surroundings.

Queen Elizabeth Hall 6 M 23
South Bank SE1. 01-928 3191. Symphony, orchestral and large band concerts. Also special events such as Poetry International take place here.

Royal Albert Hall   1 F 10
Kensington Gore SW7. 01-589 8212. Victorian domed hall named after Prince Albert, built 1871. Orchestral, choral, pop concerts and public meetings. Famous for the 'Proms'.

Royal College of Music   1 G 10
Prince Consort Rd SW7. 01-589 3643. Chamber and orchestral concerts.

Royal Festival Hall   6 M 23
South Bank SE1. 01-928 3191. Built in 1951 for the Festival of Britain. Seats 3,000. Orchestral and choral concerts. Forms the South Bank Arts Centre with the Queen Elizabeth Hall, Purcell Room, National Film Theatre and the Hayward Gallery.

St Pancras Assembly Rooms   3 D 26
25 Euston Rd NW1. 01-278 4444 Ext 2132. Opera, concerts and meetings.

Sadler's Wells   3 G 30
Rosebery Avenue EC1. 01-837 1672. Great ballet and opera by visiting companies. The original Sadler's Wells Company now play at the Coliseum, St Martin's Lane.

Wigmore Hall   2 E 19
36 Wigmore St W1. 01-935 2141. Instrumental, song, chamber music and orchestral recitals.

Cinemas

These are the main London cinemas with the type of film normally shown. For current programmes see the evening newspapers or 'What's on in London'.

ABC   4 K 7
Fulham Rd SW10. 01-370 2636. Four separate cinemas showing the latest releases. Handy for late night eating.

ABC 1 & 2   3 I 23
135 Shaftesbury Ave W1. 01-836 8861.

Academy One & Two   2 G 21
165 Oxford St W1. Academy One 01-437 2981. Academy Two 01-437 5129. Latest continental and Festival successes with occasional revivals. Has outstandingly good restaurant. 01-437 8774.

Academy Three   2 G 21
167 Oxford St W1. 01-437 8819. New serious films. Repertory cinema.

Berkeley 1 & 2   3 G 23
30a Tottenham Court Rd W1. 01-636 8150. Double feature 'pot-pourri' of second-run Festival successes and provocatives.

Biograph   5 M 16
47 Wilton Rd SW1. 01-834 1624.

Bloomsbury   3 F 25
Brunswick Square WC1. 01-837 1177. Modern classics.

Carlton   5 J 21
Haymarket SW1. 01-930 3711. Long-running British and American releases.

Casino Cinerama   2 I 22
Old Compton St W1. 01-437 6877. Cinerama 'block busters'. All seats bookable.

Centa   2 I 20
215 Piccadilly W1. 01-734 1449. Selected 'X' films.

Cinecenta   5 J 21
Panton St SW1. 01-930 0631. Four small cinemas under one roof showing very new films.

Cineclub 24   2 G 23
Tottenham Court Rd W1. 01-636 3228. Members only.

Classic
405 Kilburn High Rd NW6. 01-624 6767. Double feature revivals of box-office draws.

Classic   2 I 20
Glasshouse St, Piccadilly Circus W1. 01-437 2380. Revivals of recent sensational films.

Classic
Pond St, Hampstead NW3. 01-794 4000. Double feature classic revivals. *Late show Fri & Sat 23.00.*

Classic Charing Cross Rd   2 I 22
35-37 Charing Cross Rd WC2. 01-930 6915. Sensational, sometimes obscure, international films.

Classic Moulin   2 I 21
43 Great Windmill St, Piccadilly Circus W1. 01-437 1653. British nude films and erotica.

Classic Victoria   5 M 17
152 Victoria St SW1. 01-834 6588. Split week revivals.

Columbia   2 I 21
93 Shaftesbury Avenue W1. 01-734 5414. Selected long running releases in plushy new cinema.

Compton Cine Club   2 I 22
60-62 Old Compton St W1. 01-437 4555. Members only. Unabridged foreign nudes and peep-shows.

Continentale   3 G 23
36 Tottenham Court Rd W1. 01-636 4193. Second-run recent popular continental and bawdy revivals.

Curzon   2 I 17
Curzon St W1. 01-499 3737. Specially selected new films in very lush surroundings.

Dilly Ciné Club   2 I 21
41 Gt Windmill St W1. 01-437 6266. Uncensored sex fare. Cheap membership and bar.

Dominion   3 G 23
Tottenham Court Rd W1. 01-580 9562. Long-running spectaculars.

Empire   5 J 22
Leicester Square WC2. 01-437 1234. Bookable first releases in cavernous 'movie palace'. Adjustable seats, perfect vision.

Empire 2   5 J 22
Leicester Square WC2. 01-437 1234. Latest British and American releases.

Eros Cartoon   2 I 21
7 Shaftesbury Ave W1. 01-437 3839.

Essential Cinema Club   2 I 21
76 Wardour St W1. 01-439 3657. Promotion of independent feature films. Membership.

Everyman
Holly Bush Vale, opposite Hampstead Tube Station NW3. 01-435 1525. Weekly classic revivals.

Focus   2 I 21
Brewer St W1. 01-734 4205. The latest 'Xs'. Sometimes late-night showings on weekends.

Gala Royal   2 D 16
Edgware Rd W2. 01-262 2345. Recent revivals and new releases.

Gate Cinema   1 A 8
Notting Hill Gate W11. 01-727 5750. Repertory cinema of exceptional adventurousness and insight.

I.C.A.   5 K 19
Nash House, The Mall SW1. 01-930 6393. Occasional films by contemporary directors. Seats bookable.

Imperial (Electric) Cinema   1 A 8
191 Portobello Rd W11. 01-727 4992. Revives rare and undershown movies. Electric Cinema Club for vintage, continental and underground films.

Jacey Film Theatre   5 J 22
Leicester Square WC2. 01-437 2001.

Jacey   5 J 21
Trafalgar Square WC2. 01-930 1143. New erotica releases.

Leicester Square Theatre   5 J 22
Leicester Square WC2. 01-930 5252. First releases in a vast 'movie palace'.

London Pavilion   2 I 20
3 Piccadilly Circus W1. 01-437 2982. Popular and sensational films. New releases.

Metropole   5 M 17
160 Victoria St SW1. 01-834 4673. Long-running new releases. Bookable.

Minema   2 I 14
New Berkeley Hotel, 45 Knightsbridge SW1. 01-235 4225.

National Film Theatre   6 M 23
South Bank SE1. 01-928 3232. Members only. Serious museum studies of directors, styles, stars, retrospectives and movie history. Public shows on *Sats.* Two cinemas.

New Cinema Club   2 I 21
122 Wardour St W1. 01-274 6055. Old and modern classics, underground movies. (M)

North London Film Theatre
Mountview Theatre Club, 104 Crouch Hill N8. 01-340 5885. International films rarely seen elsewhere. (M) includes all shows.

Odeon   5 H 21
Haymarket SW1. 01-930 2738/2771. Handpicked new releases in separate performances.

Odeon   1 D 4
Kensington High St W8. 01-602 6644. Circuit releases in a comfortable 'movie palace'.

Odeon   5 J 22
Leicester Square WC2. 01-930 6111. Latest, handpicked releases.

Odeon   2 E 16
Marble Arch W2. 01-723 2011. Claimed to be the most advanced cinema in Britain, with escalators and closed-circuit TV. Premiéres and popular 'block-busters'. Separate performances.

Odeon   5 J 22
St Martin's Lane WC2. 01-836 0691. Popular 'Road show' releases in new intimate cinema. Advance booking.

Paris Pullman   4 J 7
65 Drayton Gardens SW10. 01-373 5898. New foreign subtitled releases and revivals.

Plaza 1 & 2   **5 J 20**
Lower Regent St W1. 01-839 6494. Separate cinemas
showing the latest releases.

Prince Charles   **5 J 22**
Leicester Place, Leicester Square WC2. 01-437 8181.
Small new cinema. Latest releases. *Late shows at
weekends.*

Rialto   **2 I 21**
3 Coventry St W1. 01-437 3488. 'Popular sophistication' in new releases and recent revivals. *Late show
Sats 23.00.*

Ritz   **5 J 22**
Leicester Sq WC2. 01-437 1234. New releases.

Scene 1, 2, 3 & 4   **2 I 22**
Swiss Centre, Leicester Square WC2. 01-439 4446. 4
cinemas in one showing handpicked new releases.

Starlight Club   **2 I 18**
May Fair Hotel, Berkeley St W1. 01-629 7777. Members
only. Vintage films.

Studio One   **2 G 20**
225 Oxford St W1. 01-437 3300. New releases.

Studio Two   **2 G 20**
225 Oxford St W1. 01-437 3300.

Times Centa   **2 B 19**
Baker Street Station NW1. 01-935 9772.

Victoria Cartoon   **5 M 15**
Victoria Station SW1. 01-834 7641.

Warner   **5 J 22**
Leicester Square WC2. 01-439 0791. Two cinemas in
one showing new Warner general releases.

Radio and TV shows

*Free tickets obtainable. Write enclosing stamped
addressed envelope and preference of programme.*

Associated Television   **2 D 16**
Great Cumberland Place W1. 01-262 8040.

BBC Radio & Television   **2 E 20**
Ticket Unit, Broadcasting House, Portland Place W1.
01-580 4468.

Granada TV Network   **2 H 20**
36 Golden Square W1. 01-734 8080

London Weekend Television
Station House, Harrow Rd, Wembley, Middx. 01-902
8846.

Thames Television   **2 D 22**
Ticket Unit, 306 Euston Rd NW1. 01-387 9494.

Church music

*The following churches generally have above average
choirs or organists singing and playing at regular church
services:*

All Hallows-by-the-Tower; Annunciation, Bryanston
St; St Bartholomew the Great, Smithfield; Brompton
Oratory; Chapel Royal; Holy Sepulchre, Holborn
Viaduct; St James, Piccadilly; St John's, Smith
Square; St John's Hampstead; St Martin-in-the-Fields,
Trafalgar Square; St Mary's, Bryanston Square; St
Michael, Cornhill; St Paul, Knightsbridge; the Temple
Church; Tower of London; Westminster Abbey;
Westminster Cathedral.

Lunchtime concerts

*Mostly held in the city churches on weekdays at midday
for the office worker. Chamber music, choral music,
violin, piano and organ recitals. The interiors of the
churches are also rewarding in themselves.*

All Hallows-by-the-Tower   **6 P 32**
Byward St EC3. 01-481 2928. Mainly classical hi-fi
recordings *Mon 13.00.* Organ recitals by Gordon Phillips
12.15 and 14.00 Thur.

Bishopsgate Institute   **6 N 33**
230 Bishopsgate EC3. 01-247 6844. Classical and
chamber music. *Tue 13.05, spring & autumn.*

Holy Sepulchre   **6 K 28**
Holborn Viaduct EC1. 01-248 1660. Live recital of vocal,
instrumental and organ music. *Wed. 13.15.* Stereo
recorded music *Tue & Fri 13.15.* Choral service *Thur
13.20.* Free.

St Botolph's Without   **6 N 33**
Bishopsgate EC2. 01-588 1053. Piano, organ, choral,
string recitals by young musicians. *Thur 13.10.* Free.

St Bride   **6 L 27**
Fleet St EC4. 01-353 1301. Organ and harp recitals
every Wed 13.15.

St John's   **5 O 19**
Smith Square SW1. 01-799 2168. Instrumental recitals
by well-known musicians and groups. Amadeus
quartet, English Chamber Orchestra. Stephen Bishop.
Mon 13.00. 44p.

St Martin-in-the-Fields   **5 K 22**
Trafalgar Square WC2. 01-930 0089. Chamber music
recitals and choirs. *Mon & Tue 13.05.*

St Mary-le-Bow   **6 M 29**
Cheapside EC2. 01-248 5139. Concerts of hi-fi stereo
recorded classical music. *Mon & Fri 13.05.* Free.

St Mary Woolnoth   **6 N 30**
Lombard St EC3. 01-626 9701. 'Singers workshop'
rehearses church music — visitors welcome. *Fri 13.05
(not Aug).* Free.

St Michael-upon-Cornhill   **6 N 31**
Cornhill EC3. 01-626 8841. Organ recitals. *Mon 13.00.*
Free.

St Olave   **6 P 32**
Hart St EC3. 01-488 4318. *Wed & Thur 13.05.* Free

St Stephen   **6 N 30**
Walbrook EC4. 01-626 2277. Recitals. *Fri 12.30.* Free.

Open-air music

*There is a surprising variety of summertime outdoor
music in London: lunchtime bands and light orchestral
music in the City squares and gardens for office
workers, more serious evening concerts and old-time
concert parties in famous gardens and parks, as well as
country dancing demonstrations after which everyone
dances too. Many of these entertainments are free, and
when there is a charge, it is generally nominal.*

Alexandra Park
Wood Green N22. Band concerts in a tree-sloped park
area. *Spring and summer B Hols and Sun 15.00.* Free.

Battersea Park   **4 P 9**
Concert Pavilion SW11. 01-633 1707. Varied musical
events throughout the summer. See 'Looking for
Leisure' or phone for details.

Crystal Palace
SE19. Booking 01-633 1707. Lakeside symphony
concerts in the Concert Bowl. *Jul & Aug Sun 15.00.*
30p.

Finsbury Circus Gardens   **6 M 32**
Moorgate EC2. Lunchtime music. *Wed only May-Sep
12.00-14.00.* Free.

Greenwich Park
SE10. Military and brass bands. *Sun & B. Hols in
summer 15.00.* Free.

Holland Park   **1 C 5**
W8. Varied programme in the Court Theatre nightly.

Hyde Park   **2 H 15**
W2. Military and brass bands. *Sun & B. Hols in summer
15.00 & 18.30.* Free.

Kenwood
Hampstead Lane NW3. 01-348 1286. Lakeside
symphony concerts by leading orchestras in fine park.
Jun-Aug Sat 20.00. Also recitals in the Orangery of the
18th cent house. *May-Jul Sun 19.30.* Booking 01-633
1707.

Lincolns Inn Fields   **3 I 25**
WC2. City workers' lunchtime military bands. Deck
chairs and standing in tree setting. *Summer Tue &
Thur.*

Parliament Hill
NW3. 01-485 4491. Fine heath setting. Usually standing
and deck chairs. Bands.

St James's Park   **5 L 19**
SW1. Military and brass bands. *Weekdays in summer,
12.30 & 17.30.*

Regent's Park   **2 B 21**
NW1. Military and brass bands. *Summer & B. Hols
15.00 & 18.00.*

Tower Place   **6 C 31**
EC3. Military bands play in a modern pedestrian square
with fine views of the Tower and the Thames. *May-Sep
Fri 12.00.* Free.

Victoria Embankment Gardens   **5 L 22**
near Embankment Tube Station WC2. Leading military
brass bands and light orchestras play beside the river.
*Mid May-beg Sep Mon-Fri 12.30 & 19.00 (Sat & Sun
15.00 & 17.00). Sep Mon-Fri 12.30 (Sat & Sun 15.00).*
Also *Jul* performance by massed bands.

Paternoster Square
EC4. Lunchtime military band concerts with occasional
performances by the City of London Girl Pipers. Eat
lunch at an open-air café and listen to the music.
Summer Thurs 12.00-14.00. Free.

St Paul's Steps   **6 M 28**
EC4. Delightful setting facing St Paul's. Military bands
play to lunch-time strollers. *May-Sep Thurs 12.30.*

Festivals

Various festivals are held in and around London during the summer months. All the following are held annually and offer an extremely high standard of performance — often in unusual and interesting localities. The provincial festival has become a feature of British life, bringing culture to the countryside. Details of times from the British Travel Association 01-629 9191.

Aldeburgh, Suffolk
Outstanding festival of music and arts in a converted maltings overlooking the River Alde. The programme is dominated by Benjamin Britten, Peter Pears, Imogen Holst and Richter. Also exhibitions and lectures. *Jun.* Programme from Festival office, Aldeburgh, Suffolk.

Bath Festival
Directed by Sir Michael Tippett. Orchestral concerts, choral and chamber music in the Guildhall, Assembly rooms, abbey and Wells cathedral. Also in famous country houses. Also exhibitions, lectures and puppet theatre. *Mid May — early Jun.* Programme from the Bath Festival, Linley House, Pierrepont Place, Bath.

Brighton Festival, Sussex
Festival of music, theatre and the visual arts, generally devoted devoted to a theme. Some events in the Regency Royal Pavilion. Frequent performances by Daniel Barenboim. Fine setting in Regency seaside town. *Early May 10 days.* Programme and tickets from the Dome Box Office, New Rd, Brighton.

Broadstairs, Kent
Charles Dickens festival. Performance of a play adapted from a Dickens novel. Garden party with a parade of Dickensian costume. Victorian musical evenings. Talks on Dickensian subjects. Festival dance. *Mid June one week.* Programme from the Information centre. Pierremont Hall, Broadstairs.

Cambridge Festival
Music, opera, drama, films and exhibitions. Concerts in college chapels and gardens. Pre-Edinburgh festival productions by the Cambridge Theatre Company. The Hallé orchestra often performs. *Mid Jul 2 weeks.* Programme from the Central Library, Wheeler St, Cambridge.

Cambridge Jazz Festival
Not a 'hippy' festival. Whole day performances in the Corn Exchange by people like Alex Welsh, Ken Collier, George Chisholm. *Aug B. Hol weekend.* Programme from the Central Library, Wheeler St. Cambridge.

Chichester, Sussex
Drama festival in fine modern theatre with revolving circular stage. Latest production techniques. Classics and best of modern plays. *May — Sep.* Programme and tickets from Chichester Festival Theatre. Oaklands Park, Chichester. Tel 86333.

Glyndebourne, Lewes, Sussex
Famous opera festival held in a beautiful house on the edge of the Sussex Downs. Lake and gardens — ideal for a picnic supper. Evening dress usually worn. Train from Victoria. *Usually late May — early Aug.* Programme from Glyndebourne Festival office, Glyndebourne, Sussex. Tel. Ringmer 321.

Haslemere, Surrey
Festival of early music sponsored by the Dolmetsch Foundation and held at Haslemere Hall *for about 1 week mid Jul.* Programme from Festival Secretary, Dolmetsch Foundation, Jesses, Grayswood Rd, Haslemere.

King's Lynn, Norfolk
Festival of music and the arts with a varied programme. Performances in the medieval Guildhall of St George, St Nicholas chapel and St Margaret's church. Poetry readings, ballet, sculpture and painting exhibitions. *For about 10 days late Jul or early Aug.* Programme from the Guildhall of St George, King's Lynn. Tel 4725.

London: Aldwych World Theatre
Production of classics and outstanding modern plays by theatre companies from all over the world. All performances in original language (audio translators for audience). *Usually mid Apr-Jun.* Programme and tickets from Aldwych Theatre, 49 Aldwych WC2. 01-836 6404.

London: Camden Festival
Rarely performed music and opera; also well-known choral and symphony concerts. Three weeks (*usually late Apr — late May*). Box office: St Pancras Library, 100 Euston Rd NW1.

London: City of London Festival
Mid Jul for about 2 weeks. Musical festival with great choirs and orchestras. Also chamber music and recitals. Concerts in St Paul's Cathedral, the Guildhall and the Mansion House. Exhibitions in City livery companies. Some outdoor activities and processions. Ox roasting.

London: London Film Festival
Many people's only chance to see some of the best British and foreign films of the year. *Mid Nov 2 weeks.* Programme and tickets from the National Film Theatre, South Bank SE1. 01-928 3232.

London: South Bank Poetry International
Twelve well-known poets read their works. Stephen Spender, Alan Tate. Organised by the Poetry Book Society. *June for three days.* Programme and tickets from the Royal Festival Hall SE1. 01-928 3191.

London: Southwark Shakespeare Festival
Duthy Hall Theatre
Great Guildford St SE1. Excellent performances of Shakespeare by amateur companies *during last two weeks in Aug.*
The George Inn Courtyard
77 Borough High St SE1. Shakespeare performances *Sat afternoons Jun — Jul.*
Southwark Cathedral
Borough High St SE1. 01-407 2939. *Special service on or about 23 Apr (Shakespeare's birthday).*
Tickets and programmes for the above from The Festival Box Office, 28 Peckham Rd SE5. 01-703 2917.

Stour Music Festival, Kent
In the fine country houses and churches of the Stour valley. Instrumental and choral music by Alfred Dellar. Piano and harpsichord recitals at the Colt collection of early instruments, Bethersden. Also excellent modern painting exhibitions. *June.* Details from the Festival secretary, Barton Cottage, The Street, Kennington, Kent. Tel Ashford 23838.

Stratford-upon-Avon, Warwickshire
Shakespeare season in the Royal Shakespeare Theatre. Plays with top quality production and acting. Town of Shakespeare's birthplace. *Apr — Dec.* Programme and tickets from Royal Shakespeare Theatre, Stratford-upon-Avon.

Sport

Sports stadiums

The major centres and stadiums in London for national and international sporting events are:

Crystal Palace National Sports Centre
Crystal Palace SE19. 01-778 0131. Beautifully situated in Crystal Palace Park. Opened in 1964, this is the largest multi-sports centre in the country. Superb facilities for over 50 different sports include a floodlit stadium (seating 12,000 spectators), Olympic-size swimming and diving pools, a large indoor sports hall and a 'dry-ski' slope. A yearly fee is charged to users of the centre, plus an additional small amount for use of equipment or teaching. Important national and international events are frequently staged, including swimming, water polo, athletics and basketball. Motor, motor-cycle and cycle-racing events staged on the road circuit in the park.

Empire Stadium & Pool
Wembley, Middx. 01-902 1234. The stadium holds 100,000 people under cover. Famous as the home of the FA Cup Final, also stages international football, hockey, ice shows, the Rugby League final, Gaelic football, hurling, boxing, ice hockey and skating, tennis, basketball, netball, the Horse of the

Year Show and the interesting new 6 day cycle races; also greyhound racing, speedway, and some ice shows and squash.

Royal Albert Hall   1 F 10
Kensington Gore SW7. 01-589 8212. Professional and amateur boxing, wrestling, tennis and gymnastics.

White City Stadium
Wood Lane W12. 01-743 5544. Speedway and greyhound racing. All spectators under cover.

Ticket agents: sport

For all tickets consult:

Keith Prowse   3 F 23
24 Store St WC1. 01-637 3131. Head office. They will give you the address of their nearest ticket agency.

Sport

London has facilities for nearly all types of sport and has a formidable number of clubs, sports grounds and associations. This list gives the main authorities, places and events not only to the spectator but also for those who want to take part. There are numerous facilities for inexpensive tuition and training; the Sports Council and GLC run hundreds of courses all over London. For sports equipment see the 'Specialist shops & services' section.

Sports Council (London and South East Region)
70 Brompton Rd SW3. 01-589 3411. Exists to promote and improve physical and mental health through physical recreation. They are always helpful and co-operative. Have an advisory service for individuals andclubs, an information service giving details of all Sports Council activities and organises varied training courses. Run five very successful 'National Recreation Centres' at Bisham Abbey, Marlow (on the Thames), Lilleshall Hall Shropshire, Plas y Brenin in Snowdonia, Crystal Palace, London and the National Sailing Centre, Cowes.

Archery

Twenty-one archery clubs in the county of London, each having its own ground. County of London championships held at Bowrings sports ground, Earlsfield SW8, last Sun in Aug. Indoor championships at Michael Sobell Centre, Islington in Feb. This is an increasingly popular sport and there are few places available for beginners.

County of London Archery Association   6 J 26
61 Carey St WC2. 01-228 3987. Will supply information on the sport in London. Write for vacancies.

English Field Archery Association
8 Bedford Rd, Marston, Morteyne, Beds. Lower Shelton 8053. Write for details of clubs.

Grand National Archery Society
National Agricultural Centre, Stoneleigh, Kenilworth, Warw. 0203 23907. Will supply information about archery.

Southern Counties Archery Association
102 Ashgrove Rd, Ilford, Essex 01-590 4282. Supplies information about London clubs.

Athletics

The major events are held at Crystal Palace. See under 'Parks and gardens' for some public running tracks.

Badminton

All England championship at Wembley in March; also many other tournaments throughout the country during the year. All England junior championships held at Wimbledon in Jan.

Badminton Association of England
44/45 Palace Rd, Bromley, Kent. 01-464 0031. Administer the game generally and supply details of games and events.

Ballooning

British Balloon & Airship Club
Kimberley House, Vaughan Way, Leicester. Leicester 51051. Will supply a list of clubs.

Baseball

National League and Southern Baseball League clubs at Sutton, Richmond, Hendon, Purfleet, and Wokingham.

Basketball

National championships held at Crystal Palace. Particularly worth seeing are the Harlem Globetrotters visits to Wembley.

English Basketball Association
Calomax House, Lupton Ave, Leeds. Leeds 496044. Will supply a club list.

London Premier League
Swiss Cottage Sports Centre NW1. Some of the highest standard basketball in England. *From Oct.*

Billiards & snooker

Clubs throughout London.

Bowls

National championships held at Beach House Park, Worthing. Public greens in Battersea Park, Finsbury Park, Ravenscourt Park and many other London Parks.

English Bowling Association
The Secretary, 4 Lansdowne Crescent, Bournemouth. Bournemouth 22233.

Canoeing

Pleasant rivers within easy reach of London which can be explored by the canoe enthusiast are mentioned below. Consult the excellent 'Guide to the Waterways of the British Isles' obtainable from the British Canoe Union for explicit details.

British Canoeing Union   2 I 12
70 Brompton Road SW3. 01-584 9229. For information and advice.

Thames
Start from Cricklade. 150 miles to Putney Bridge. Pretty and lonely above Lechlade, pleasant all the way to Oxford; tidal below Teddington.

Kennet
Enter at Hungerford. 30 miles to the Thames at Reading. A clear, fresh, fast, chalk stream.

Wey
Two sources for canoeing — either at Farnham or Frensham. Fast and clear above Godalming; canalised below. From Farnham 36 miles to the Thames at Weybridge.

Clay pigeon shooting

For safety reasons an out of London sport.

Clay Pigeon Shooting Association
107 Epping New Rd, Buckhurst Hill, Essex. 01-505 6221. For a list of clubs.

Cricket

County matches and Test matches at Lord's and the Oval. For latest Test scores dial 154. The season is from mid-Apr to early Sep.

Gover Cricket School
172 East Hill SW18. 01-874 1796. Private coaching by first-class cricketers. Club practice *in the evenings.*

Lord's
St John's Wood Rd NW8. 01-289 1615. The ground of the MCC, which is also the governing body for British cricket and supplies information about the game. Stages a Test match in *Jun.*

The Oval
The Surrey Ground, Kennington Oval, Kennington SE11. 01-735 2424/5. For latest scores 01-735 4911. Stages a Test match in *Aug.*

Croquet

Croquet Association
Hurlingham Club, Ranelagh Gardens SW6. 01-736 3148. For information and advice.

Cycling

Once a predominantly continental sport, now becoming increasingly popular in Britain. The professional, spectacular and incredibly fast 6 day indoor events staged at Wembley are well worth a visit, even for the uninitiated. Details from British Cycling Federation.

British Cycling Federation   2 I 12
70 Brompton Rd SW3. 01-584 6706. Information and touring service.

Cyclist Touring Club
69 Meadrow, Godalming, Surrey. Godalming 7217. Will send details of your nearest group and arrange training holidays.

Herne Hill Track
Burbage Rd SE24. Controlled by the GLC Parks Dept. 01-633 5000. Many 'big name' and club events throughout the year. Details of events from the BCF. Track available for practice when there are no meetings.

Road Times Trials Council
Secretary, 13 Hobbs Close, Colney Heath Lane, St

Albans Herts. St Albans 62151. For details of forthcoming time trials.

Youth Hostels Association   **6 K 23**
29 John Adam St WC2. 01-839 1722. Will prove useful for touring information generally.

Dancing and keep fit

Local newspapers and newsagents' windows carry announcements of classes in your area. Local council education authorities offer classes in dance, keep fit and yoga — details from your local library.

Lotte Berk   **2 D 18**
29 Manchester St W1. 01-935 8905. Exercises to get you into shape.

Body Control Studio   **3 D 25**
The Place, 17 Duke's Rd WC1. 01-387 3578. For all ages, men and women, amateur and professional. Based on Pilates method, the classes use light equipment for aligning the body and developing fitness.

Dance Centre   **6 J 23**
12 Floral St WC2. 01-836 6544. Various styles and calibres of dance for amateur and professional men and women. Also yoga and mime. Reasonable charge.

Drag racing

Events take place infrequently at various airfields around London.

British Drag Racing and Hot Rod Association
63 Trowley Rise, Abbots Langley, Herts. Kingslangley 67960. Arrange meetings at Santa Pod.

Santa Pod Raceway
95-97 Martin's Rd, Shortlands, Bromley, Kent. 01-464 5445. Europe's only permanent drag strip at Santa Pod Beds.

Fencing

Amateur Fencing Association   **1 G 1**
83 Perham Rd W14. 01-385 7442. For information and list of events.

Fishing

To fish anywhere in the Thames area it is necessary to hold a Thames Water Authority Rod Licence. An additional permit is needed to fish in Royal Parks. The season is between Jun 16 – Mar 14.

London Anglers' Association
183 Hoe St E17. 01-520 7477.

River Conservation Essex River Authority
Rivers House, 129 Springfield Rd, Chelmsford, Essex. 0245 64721. Division licence covers coarse and game fishing, reductions for children and OAPs. Regional licence covers wider area and is more expensive. Weekly licences available.

Southern Water Authority
Area Finance Officer, College Ave, Maidstone, Kent. 0622 55211. Kent river licences are granted for coarse fish only. Reduction for under 16s and OAPs free.

Fishing: lakes & ponds

To fish in these places it is necessary to hold a permit from the Royal Parks Dept, The Storeyard, Hyde Park W2. 01-262 5484. Reductions for children under 16 and OAPs. To fish anywhere in the Thames area you must hold a Thames Water Authority Rod Licence.

Battersea Park   **4 P 9**
Roach, tench, dace and gudgeon.

Chestnut Abbey Cross Pit, Herts
Good pike, perch, roach, tench. Crowded in summer.

Chingford Connaught Waters
All species. Crowded in summer.

Clapham Common Eagle Pond
Good carp, some roach, pike, bream.

Crystal Palace Boating Lake
Good carp, pike, roach and perch.

Epping, Copped Hall Estate Pond
Carp, tench, perch, gudgeon, some rainbow trout, *Summer only.*

Finsbury Park
Gudgeon, roach.

Hampton Court Ponds
Tench, pike, roach, perch. Beautiful water but often crowded.

Hampstead Heath Ponds
Good tench, roach, bream, pike.

Hollow Ponds
Whipps Cross E17. Tench, pike, eels *(but get there very early in the morning).*

Hyde Park Serpentine   **2 F 12**
Good roach, perch.

Osterley Park, Middx
Tench, perch, roach

Richmond Park Pen Ponds
Good roach and perch.

Rickmansworth Lakes, Herts (nr Grand Union Canal).
Good roach, perch, tench, bream, pike. **South Weald Park, Essex**
Good tench, crucian carp, roach, rudd, pike, perch.

Tooting Common Lake
Roach, perch, carp.

Victoria Park Lake E9
Good eels, pike, perch, bream, gudgeon.

Wandsworth Common
Carp, roach, tench, pike.

Windsor Great Park
Obelisk Pond, Johnson's Pond and Virginia Water. Carp, tench, pike, roach, rudd, perch. Good scenery. Permits from Crown Estate Office, Great Park, Windsor. (Enclose SAE.) 95 53747.

Wormley Northern Pit, Near Cheshunt, Herts
Good summer tench and winter pike, also perch, roach, rudd.

Fishing: reservoirs

These consist of the Metropolitan Water Board reservoirs of the Walthamstow and Barn Elms groups. Not always easy to fish, but monsters abound. Apply:

Metropolitan Water Board   **3 H 28**
Rosebery Avenue EC1. 01-837 3300 Ext 26/226. Day tickets for Walthamstow Season tickets for Barn Elms and Walthamstow are granted for *Mon-Fri* or *Sats and B. Hols.*

Fishing: rivers & canals

Grand Union Canal
Denham, Bucks. from Black Jack's Lock (No 85) to Denham Lock (No 87).

River Lea
Walthamstow to Hertford. Best fishing above Enfield Lock at Waltham Abbey, Cheshunt, Broxbourne, Rye House and St Margarets.

River Thames
Fishing starts above Kew. Probably England's best coarse fishing river. All species. Various stretches.

Fives

Rugby Fives Association
Fairbourne Lodge, Epping Green, Essex. Epping 72904. Write for information. No callers.

Flying

British Light Aviation Centre   **5 M 17**
75 Victoria St SW1. 01-222 6782. For information, help and advice on all aspects of light aviation.

London School of Flying
The Aerodrome, Elstree, Herts. 01-953 4343. Training and use of aircraft. Grumman American aircraft available for training.

Football

The FA Cup final is held at the Empire Stadium, Wembley, about the second Sat in May. Stadium holds 100,000 people under cover. The following clubs stage some of Britain's finest football. Crowd capacities shown. The season is from August to April, normal 'kick off' times are 15.00 on Saturdays, 19.30 for evening matches.

Football Association   **1 C 11**
16 Lancaster Gate W2. For amateur and professional.

Arsenal
Highbury Stadium, Avenell Rd N5. 01-226 0304. Cap. 60,000.

Chelsea   **4 K 3**
Stamford Bridge, Fulham Rd SW6. 01-385 5545. Cap. 50,000.

Crystal Palace
Selhurst Park SE25. 01-653 2223. Cap. 50,000.

Millwall
The Den, Cold Blow Lane SE14. 01-639 3143. Cap. 40,000.

Queen's Park Rangers
South Africa Rd, Shepherds Bush W12. 01-743 2618. Cap. 31,000.

Tottenham Hotspur
748 High Rd N17. 01-808 1020. Cap. 58,000.

West Ham United
Boleyn Ground Green St E13. 01-472 0704. Cap. 41,000.

Gliding

British Gliding Association
Kimberley House, Vaughan Way, Leicester. Leicester 51051. For information and help, club list and details of training courses.

London Gliding Club
Tring Rd, Dunstable, Beds. Dunstable 63419. The

home of British gliding. Contact the secretary for a familiarisation flight on a temporary membership basis so that you can see what it's about before committing yourself.

Golf

'Golf Course Guide' published by the Daily Telegraph and Collins, gives details and maps of all the courses in the British Isles. A useful book for the travelling golfer. Also the 'Golfers' Handbook' can be obtained from the reference section of most libraries if you don't feel like spending any money.
Municipal courses can be found at:
Addington Court
Featherbed Lane, Addington, Croydon. Two 18 hole courses, a 9 hole course and a pitch and putt course of 18 holes.
Coulsdon Court
Coulsdon, Surrey. 01-660 0468. 18 holes.
Hainault Forest
Chigwell Row, Hainault, Essex. 01-500 2097. Two 18 hole courses.
Home Park
Hampton Wick, Kingston-upon-Thames, Surrey. 01-977 6645. 18 holes.
Royal Epping Forest
Forest Approach, Station Rd, Chingford, Essex. 01-529 1039. 18 holes.

Golf clubs in and near London for which membership is necessary, although many will extend guest facilities to members of comparable clubs from overseas:
Berkshire GC
Swinley Rd, Ascot, Berks. Ascot 21496. Two 18 hole courses.
Hampstead GC
Winnington Rd N2. 01-455 0203. 9 holes. Lunches and teas served.
Highgate GC
Denewood Rd N6. 01-340 1906. 18 holes. Lunches served.
North Middlesex GC
Friern Barnet Lane, Whetstone N20. 01-445 1604. 18 holes. Lunches except Mon.
RAC Country Club
Wilmerhatch Lane, Woodcote Park, Epsom, Surrey. Ashstead 76311. 36 holes. Meals and accommodation by arrangement.
Richmond GC
Sudbrook Park, Petersham, Richmond, Surrey. 01-940 1463. 18 holes. Lunches except Mon.
Royal Mid-Surrey GC
Old Deer Park, Richmond, Surrey. 01-940 1894. 36 holes. Men's 6,435 yds; Ladies' 5,530 yds. Lunches served.
Sunningdale GC
Ridgemount Rd, Sunningdale, Berks. 0990 21681. 36 holes. Two courses. Also a Ladies' Club. Open all year. Lunches served.
Walton Heath GC
Tadworth, Surrey. 01-823 2060. Old 18 holes and new 18 holes. Lunches served.
Wentworth GC
Virginia Water, Surrey. 09904 2201. Two 18 hole and one 9 hole course. Open all year. Lunches served.
John Jacobs Golf School
Sandowne Park, More Lane, Esher, Surrey. 78 65921.

Grass ski-ing

A new sport employing the techniques of winter ski-ing. Also see under 'Parks'.
Ski Club of Great Britain   **5 K 14**
118 Eaton Sq SW1 01-235 4711. Events take place throughout the country during *Apr — Oct* with ski-ing at weekends.

Greyhound racing

It is advisable to check times with evening newspapers.
Catford Stadium
Catford Bridge SE6. 01-690 2261. *Thur & Sat and occasionally Tue 19.45.*
Hackney Stadium
Waterden Rd E15. 01-986 3511. *Tue 14.30, Sat 11.00.*
Harringay Stadium
Green Lanes N4. 01-800 3474. *Mon & Fri 19.45.*
Walthamstow Stadium
Chingford Rd E4. 01-527 2252. *Tue, alternate Thurs & Sat 19.45.*
Wembley Empire Stadium
Empire Way, Wembley, Middx. 01-902 1234. *Mon & Fri 19.45*
White City Stadium
Wood Lane W12. 01-743 5544. *Thur & Tues, Sat 19.45.*

Wimbledon Stadium
Plough Lane SW17. 01-946 5361. *Wed & Fri & alternate Mons 19.45.*

Gymnasiums

See 'Health clubs', *under* 'Specialist shops and services'.

Gymnastics

Competitions at the Royal Albert Hall and Crystal Palace.
British Amateur Gymnastics Association
23a High St, Slough, Bucks. Slough 32763. For information and list of local clubs.

Hang gliding

British Hang Gliding Association
Corston, Monksilver, Taunton, Somerset. Write for information.

Hockey

Hockey international played at Wembley and Headingley (women) and Lord's Cricket Ground (men).
The Hockey Association   **2 I 12**
70 Brompton Rd SW3. 01-584 2584.
All England's Women's Hockey Association **2 E 21**
160 Great Portland St W1. 01-636 0264.

Horse-racing

Courses in and near London: Ascot, Berks (famous for its Royal meeting in Jun); Epsom, Surrey (stages the world famous Derby in Jun and also the Oaks); Kempton Park, Sunbury-on-Thames, Middx; Lingfield Park, Surrey; Sandown Park, Esher, Surrey (famous for the Whitbread Gold Cup) and Windsor, Berks. Flat racing season Mar-Nov. Steeplechasing Aug-Jun.
Jockey Club (incorporating the National Hunt Committee)   **2 D 17**
42 Portman Square W1. 01-486 4921. For information on all matters concerning horse-racing in Britain.

Ice hockey

Matches played at the Empire Pool, Wembley.
British Ice Hockey Association   **6 J 23**
20 Bedford St WC2. 01-240 5222. For information on clubs and events.

Judo

National Team Championships and Open Individual Championships held at Crystal Palace. All the following clubs have excellent facilities for complete novices and international players. Instructors are of 4th Dan grade or above. Local councils also run clubs.
British Judo Association   **2 I 12**
70 Brompton Rd SW3. 01-584 3273. For information.
Judokan Club
Latymer Court W6. 01-748 6787.
London Judo Society
89 Lansdowne Way SW8. 01-622 0529.

Jujitsu

Judokan Club
Latymer Court W6. 01-748 6787.

Karate

AK Karate Federation   **2 B 16**
17 Homer Row W1. 01-723 6179. Instruction by world class Japanese experts.
Amateur Karate Association   **3 E 26**
Tunbridge Clubs, 80 Judd St WC1. 01-837 4406.
British Karate Control Commission
4 Deptford Bridge SE8. 01-691 3433.

Karting

Royal Automobile Club   **5 J 14**
31 Belgrave Sq SW1. 01-235 8601. Control karting and sell books on regulations and maintenance.

Kung Fu

British Karate Control Commission
4 Deptford Bridge SE8. 01-691 3433. For information and advice.

Lacrosse

The main events, staged Mar-Apr, are the Schools Tournament (at Merton Abbey, Surrey), an international and a clubs tournament (played in London).
All England Women's Lacrosse Association 2 I 12
70 Brompton Rd SW3. 01-584 2508. For list of clubs and details of events.
South of England Men's Lacrosse Association
57 Vincent Close, Orpington Kent. 01-850 9064.

Lawn Tennis

Public courts in about 60 London Parks. Tournaments are held at Beckenham: (Kent championships second week in June); Chingford (Connaught Club's Hard Court Tournament beginning Aug); Sutton (Surrey Hard Court championships, fourth week of Apr).

Lawn Tennis Association   **1 F 1**
Barons Court W14. 01-385 2366. The governing body of lawn tennis in Britain. Will supply a list of clubs.

All England Lawn Tennis & Croquet Club
Church Rd SW19. 01-946 2244. Stages the 'Wimbledon Fortnight' (perhaps the world's top event) in the *last week of Jun and first week of Jul.*

Queen's Club
Palliser Rd W14. 01-385 3421.

Motor racing

Over 100 clubs in the London area.

British Automobile Racing Club
Thruxton Racing Circuit, nr Andover, Hants. For fixture list.

British Racing & Sports Car Club
Empire House, Chiswick High Rd W4. 01-995 0345. Stages meetings at Brands Hatch and seven other car circuits. Also organises annual tour of Britain *Jul-Aug.*

Royal Automobile Club   **5 J 14**
Competitions Dept. 31 Belgrave Square SW1. 01-235 8601. Controls competitions.

Motor cycle racing

Road racing at Brands Hatch.

The Auto-Cycle Union   **5 J 14**
31 Belgrave Square SW1. 01-235 7636. Governs all motorcycle competitions. Publishes a handbook of forthcoming road racing and scrambling events.

Motor cycle speedway

Speedway racing held at the following:
Hackney Stadium
Waterden Rd E15. 01-985 9822
Rye House Stadium
Rye Rd, Hoddesdon, Herts. 61 61990.
Wimbledon Stadium
Plough Lane SW17. 01-946 5361. *Mar — Oct, Thur 19.45 and B. Hols.*

Mountaineering

British Mountaineering Council
Crawford House, Precinct Centre, Booth St, East Manchester. 061-273 5835. Supply a list of clubs, information on how to find the best equipment and even where to find mountain huts, etc.

Alpine Club   **2 G 17**
74 South Audley St W1. 01-499 1542. Climbing experience essential. Decorated with lumps of rock, picks and ropes from Everest expeditions.

Netball

Played lunchtimes in Lincolns Inn Fields WC2.
All England Netball Association   **2 I 12**
70 Brompton Rd SW3. 01-584 2578. For information and advice.

Orienteering

Rapidly growing in popularity, this sport can be enjoyed by people of all ages and involves map and compass work. Events take place most Sundays.
British Orienteering Federation
Lea Green, Matlock, Derbyshire. Dethick 561.
South East Orienteering Association
Dr D. Thomas, 16 Lambourne Drive, Bagshot, Surrey. For information (M)

Parachuting

British Parachute Association
Kimberly House, 47 Vaughan Way, Leicester. Leicester 59778. For information. A list of clubs and help.

Polo

Played at Smiths Lawn, Windsor, most summer weekends, at Ham House, Richmond, on summer Suns; Richmond Park (nr Roehampton Gate) Tues & Thur evenings and Sat afternoons in summer; Cowdrey Park, Sussex on Wed, Fri, Sat & Sun; Herts Polo Club, Woolmers Park on Tues, Thur evenings & Sun.
Hurlingham Polo Association
Pephurst Farm, Coxwood, nr Billingshurst, Sussex. 0403 752738.

Rackets

Tennis & Rackets Association
Stone Hall Balcombe Sussex. For help and information.

Queen's Club
Palliser Rd W14. 01-385 3421. Stages the most important events Feb — Apr, Nov — Dec.

Real Tennis

This interesting game is in danger of becoming extinct and there are only 5 clubs in the London area. A trial game can be played at:
Queen's Club
Palliser Rd W14. 01-385 3421.

Riding

British Horse Society
National Equestrian Centre, Stoneleigh, Kenilworth, Warwickshire. Coventry 27192. For information on riding and breeding.

Knightsbridge Riding School   **1 G 9**
11 Elvaston Mews SW7. 01-584 8474. Horse and pony riding in Rotten Row, Hyde Park. Special attention to children.

Lilo Blum   **2 I 15**
32a Grosvenor Crescent Mews SW1. 01-235 6846. Horses and ponies for riding in Rotten Row. Take special care with children.

Roehampton Gate Riding Stable
Priory Lane SW15. 01-876 7089. Lessons and rides in Richmond Park.

Rowing

Events take place in the summer months, the most notable being the Oxford and Cambridge boat race from Putney to Mortlake in Mar or Apr. Other events are the Head of the River event on the Thames, the Schools Head of the River race from Chiswick to Putney, the Sculling Head of the River from Mortlake to Putney, the Wingfield Sculls between Putney and Mortlake. Important regattas are held at Brent (Welsh Harp reservoir, Whit Mon), Chiswick, Hammersmith, Henley, Kingston, Putney (including the Metropolitan regatta) Richmond, Twickenham, Walton.
Amateur Rowing Association
6 Lower Mall, Hammersmith W6. 01-748 3632. Publishes the British Rowing Almanack which gives a list of clubs and coming events.

Rugby football

The principal association connected with the game of rugby is:
Rugby Football Union
Whitton Rd, Twickenham, Middx. Twickenham is the home and headquarters of rugby and the important matches, including internationals are played there.
Wasps FC
Repton Avenue Wembley Middx. 01-902 4220.

Shooting

The most important competitions held at Bisley Camp are: The National Small Bore Meeting in Jul & Aug, NRA Imperial Meeting in Jul and the British Pistol Championship in Aug & Sep.
The National Rifle Association
Bisley Camp, Brookwood, Woking, Surrey. Brookwood 2213. Will recommend a suitable club, but these are rare in London.

National Small-bore Rifle Association   **6 O 26**
113 Southwark St SE1. 01-928 3262. Will recommend a suitable club on receipt of a self addressed envelope.

Show-jumping

The two major events are: the Royal International Horse Show at Wembley in Jul and the Horse of the Year Show at Wembley in Oct. There are also notable events staged at Windsor, Richmond and Clapham Common. See also 'Riding'.
British Show Jumping Association
National Equestrian Centre, Kenilworth, Warwickshire. Coventry 20783.

Skating

Alexandra Palace Roller Rink
Wood Green N22. 01-883 9711. Roller skating. Admission charge and fee for skate hire. Outdoor rink *OPEN daylight hours.* Free. Bring own skates.

National Skating Association of Great Britain
Chaterhouse Sq EC1. 01-253 3824   **6 J 30**
For information and advice.

Queen's Ice Skating Club   **1 B 10**
17 Queensway W2. 01-229 0172. Membership fee. Fee for skate hire. Tuition available. *OPEN 10.00 — 12.00, 14.00 — 17.00. 19.00 — 22.00 Mon — Fri; 19.30 — 22.30 weekends.*

Richmond Ice Rink
Clevedon Rd, East Twickenham, Middx. 01-892 3646.
OPEN 10.00 – 12.30, 14.30 – 17.00, 19.00 – 22.00 Mon – Sat; 19.30 – 22.00 Tues; 10.00 – 12.30. 15.00 – 17.30, 19.30 – 22.00 Sun.

Silver Blades Ice Rink
386 Streatham High Rd SW16. 01-769 7861. Admission charge plus skate hire. *OPEN 10.30 – 12.30 Mon – Fri and 14.00 – 16.30 Mon, Wed & Fri, 14.30 – 18.00 Tues & Thurs and 19.30 – 23.00 Mon – Fri; 10.30 – 12.20, 14.30 – 17.00 and 19.30 – 23.00 weekends.*

Ski-ing

The National Recreation Centre at Crystal Palace runs classes on its fine outdoor artificial slope.
The National Ski Federation of Great Britain
118 Eaton Square SW1. 01-235 8228.   **5 K 14**
Publish a full list of dry-ski slopes.

Skittles

Freemason's Arms
32 Downshire Hill NW3. 01-435 4498. Played with a 'cheese', this is the original game of skittles. Must provide your own 'sticker'.

Squash

Holland Park
GLC Parks Dept, Kensington W8. 01-602 2226. One court. Registration fee. Book 7 days in advance. Another court being built.
Lansdowne Club   **2 H 18**
9 Fitzmaurice Place W1. 01-629 7200.
Squash Rackets Association   **1 I 11**
70 Brompton Rd SW3. 01-584 2506. Publish the 'Squash Rackets handbook' which gives a list of clubs and courts.
Wembley Squash Centre
Empire Way, Wembley. 01-902 9230. Book 7 days in advance. 14 courts and 1 championship court.

Stock car racing

Controlled by the RAC. Noisy, colourful, exciting and only slightly dangerous. Contrary to popular opinion, the drivers do actually try to avoid hitting each other. Events mostly staged Saturday evenings in the summer.
Harringay Stadium
Green Lanes N4. 01-800 3474.
Wimbledon Stadium
Plough Lane SW17. 01-946 5361.

Sub-aqua

British Sub Aqua   **1 I 11**
70 Brompton Rd SW3. 01-584 7164. For information of local branches where training courses are run. To join you will have to pass a swimming test, produce a certificate of fitness signed by your doctor, and evidence of a satisfactory chest X-ray. BSAC training is recognised world-wide as being of the highest order. Holborn branch and London branch are well equipped, active groups who train throughout the year and dive regularly. See also 'Sports equipment – sub aqua' in the shopping section.

Swimming

Magnificent new Olympic standard pool at the Crystal Palace National Recreation Centre. High standard competitions. Excellent tuition and facilities for members.
Public baths (indoor)
Caledonian Road N1. 01-837 4973   **3 B 30**
Chelsea Manor St SW3. 01-352 6985.   **4 M 9**
Great Smith Baths, St Ann's St SW1.
01-352 6985.   **5 N 19**
Ironmonger Row EC1. 01-253 4011.   **3 I 32**
Kensal Rd W10. 01-969 0772.
Kensington New Pools, Walmer Rd W11. 01-727 9747.
Marshall St W1. 01-437 7665.   **2 H 21**
Merlin St WC1. 01-837 1313.   **3 G 29**
Oasis, Endell St WC2. 01-836 9555.   **3 I 23**
Also an outdoor pool.
Porchester Rd, Queensway W2. 01-229 3226.   **1 A 11**
Seymour Place W1. 01-723 8018.   **2 D 16**
Swiss Cottage Centre, Adelaide Rd NW3. 01-278 4444.
Tooting Common Baths SW17. 01-769 4226.
Swimming in the parks (outdoors)
OPEN 06.30 - dusk summer; 07.00 – 10.00 winter (subject to demand).
Brockwell Park Lido SE24. 01-274 7991.
Eltham Park South Baths SE9. 01-850 9890.
Hampstead Ponds NW3. 01-435 2366. Free.
Highgate Ponds N6. 01-340 4044. Men only. Free.
Hornfair Baths, Woolwich SE18. 01-856 7180.
Kennington Park Baths SE11. 01-735 3574.

Kenwood Pond N6. 01-340 1033. Women only. Free.
London Fields Baths E8. 01-254 7494.
Parliament Hill Lido NW5. 01-485 3873.
Peckham Rye Park Baths SE22. 01-732 8157.
Serpentine Hyde Park W2.
Southwark Park Baths SE16. 01-237 6572.
Tooting Common Baths SW17. 01-769 4226.
Victoria Park Lido E9. 01-985 6774.
Amateur Swimming Association
Harold Fern House, Derby Square, Loughborough, Leics. Tel 30431. The authority governing national swimming events.
Southern Counties ASA
30 Tamworth Rd, Croydon. 01-688 3327. Publish the SCASA handbook and a list of clubs.

Table tennis

Tournaments are staged at Crystal Palace.
English Table Tennis Association
21 Claremont, Hastings, E. Sussex. 0424 433121.

Tennis

See 'Lawn Tennis'.

Ten pin bowling

The closing times given here are approximate: bowling alleys quite often stay open well past times shown.
ABC Cine Bowl
Broadway, Bexleyheath. 01-303 3325. *OPEN 10.00-22.00, later on Fri & Sat nights. CLOSED Xmas and Box.*
Airport Bowl
Bath Rd, Harlington, Middx. 01-759 1396. *OPEN Sun-Thur 10.00-01.30. Fri & Sat 10.00-04.00. CLOSED Xmas Day.*
British Ten Pin Bowling Association
19 Canterbury Ave, Ilford, Essex. 01-554 9173.
Mecca
142 Streatham Hill SW2. 01-674 5251. *OPEN 11.00-24.00. CLOSED Xmas.*
Piccadilly Bowl   **2 I 21**
30 Shaftesbury Avenue W1. 01-437 1580. *OPEN 10.30-early hours. Sats 04.00.*

Water polo

Occasional games at Crystal Palace
Amateur Swimming Association
Harold Fern House, Derby Square, Loughborough, Leics. Tel 30431. For details.

Water ski-ing

Public water ski-ing at Ruislip Lido, Reservoir Rd, Ruislip Common. Championships take place August Bank Holiday weekend at Bedfont Lake, behind London Airport.
British Water Ski Federation   **2 I 12**
70 Brompton Rd SW3. 01-584 8262. For information and club lists. Run residential courses in summer.
Princes Water Ski Club
Clockwork Lane, Bedfont, Middx. 01-695 3201. First class equipment and trainers. Subs. Reduced rate for juniors and husband and wife.
Princess Water Ski Club
Clockhouse Lane, Bedfont, Middx. 01-695 3201. First-class equipment and trainers.

Weight lifting

National championship held at Crystal Palace.
Len Sell Health Studio
43 St James St E17. 01-520 3944. A top London weight lifting and body building club.
National Sports Centre
Crystal Palace SE19. 01-778 0131. An excellent weight lifting and body building gym.
Wag Bennett Gymnasium
335 Romford Rd E7. 01-534 7972. Excellent weight lifting and body building facilities. 'Big names' such as John Hewlett (Mr Universe) and Rick Wayne train here. Supply 'protein supplements' for athletes.

Wrestling

Main professional bouts held at the Royal Albert Hall.
British Amateur Wrestling Association
2 Huxley Drive, Bramhall, Stockport, Cheshire. Write for information.

Yachting

For full details of events around London or abroad contact:
Royal Ocean Racing Club   **5 J 18**
20 St James' Place SW1. 01-493 5252. To become eligible you must have taken part in two Ocean races or one Fastnet race.

Royal Yachting Association and the International Yacht Racing Union
Victoria Way, Woking, Surrey. Woking 5022. Publish a yearly international fixture list of venues ranging from Hanko in Norway to Perth, Australia.

Coastal marinas
Unless stated otherwise all the following have car parks, phones, repair and servicing facilities, food store, restaurant, showers, chandleries, fuel supply, a boat valet service, slipways, launching ramps and boatlifts. All are within easy reach of London.
Camper & Nicholsons
Gosport, Hants. Gosport 80221. 7½ ft draft; 230 berths. No food store, restaurant or slipway. Book well in advance.
Cresta Marina
Newhaven, Sussex. Newhaven 3881. 650 berths; draft 6½ft constant. Minimum 25ft. Max 80ft.

Dart Marina
Sandquay, Dartmouth. Dartmouth 3351. 275 berths, draft up to 20ft. Max length 60ft. Own hotel on site. Special winter rates for long term moorings. No boat valet service or food store.
Essex Yacht Marina
Wallsea Island, Rochford, Canewdon 364. No launching ramp, phones or boat lifts. 150 berths, draft 10½ft. Max length 100ft.
Kemps Shipyard
Quayside Rd, Bitterne Manor, Southampton. Southampton 32323. 100 berths; draft 10ft and max length 200ft. Cost varies. Contessas, Seals and 470's.

Yoga

Your local newspapers and newsagents' windows carry announcements of classes in your area and local adult education authorities often offer yoga tuition — check your library for details. 'Time Out' is a useful source for classes in various types of yoga.

Shopping

Consumer protection

Always keep the receipt for goods you buy and, if you're not satisfied, take them back to the shop and ask to speak to the manager. If the fault is entirely theirs you don't have to accept a credit note: ask for cash. The Trade Descriptions Act protects the consumer against fraudulent claims made for goods — contact your Trading Standards Officer at the local Town Hall, your local Consumer Advice Centre or phone the Citizens' Advice Bureau at 01-636 4060.

Children's clothes

See 'Children's shopping' section in 'Children's London' for details of shops.

Men's clothes

The large stores
For good traditional ready-made and quality modern clothes and accessories.
Asquascutum   **2 I 20**
100 Regent St W1. 01-734 6090. Large selection of quality coats, raincoats, suits and jackets.
Austin Reed   **2 I 20**
103 Regent St W1. 01-734 6789. Five floors of English and Continental suits and all accessories. Accent on quality. Valeting and barber's.
Burtons   **2 H 20**
114 Regent St W1. 01-437 7194. Suits and accessories at modest prices.
C & A Modes   **2 E 17**
505 Oxford St W1. 01-629 7272. Reasonably priced shirts, jackets, overcoats.
Harrods   **2 I 14**
Knightsbridge SW1. 01-730 1234. Excellent quality range from young fashions to traditional. Stock everything.
Jaeger   **2 H 20**
204 Regent St W1. 01-734 4050. Well cut suits and coats.
Lillywhites   **5 J 20**
24-36 Lower Regent St W1. 01-930 3181. Sportswear of all sorts.
Marks & Spencer   **2 G 21**
458 Oxford St W1. 01-486 6151. Good value for money in pullovers, underwear, shirts and socks. Branches everywhere.
Selfridges   **2 G 21**
400 Oxford St W1. 01-629 1234. Good selection of fashionable as well as traditional styles.

Simpsons   **2 I 20**
203 Piccadilly SW1. 01-734 2002. Suits, sports clothes and holiday wear of good quality.

Beachwear

Good quality beachwear of all sorts at Lillywhites. For something out of the ordinary try John Michael branches and 'Way In' at Harrods.

Bespoke tailors

Savile Row for expensive but long-lasting hand-tailored clothes in the finest cloths.
Anderson & Sheppard   **2 H 20**
30 Savile Row W1. 01-734 1420.
Blades   **2 H 20**
8 Burlington Gardens, Savile Row W1. 01-734 8911.
Douglas Hayward   **2 G 17**
95 Mount St W1. 01-499 5574.
H. Huntsman & Sons   **2 H 20**
11 Savile Row W1. 01-734 7441. King of Savile Row from before 1800.
Kilgour, French & Stanbury   **2 I 19**
33a Dover St W1. 01-629 4283.
Henry Poole   **2 H 19**
10-12 Cork St W1. 01-734 5985.
Sandon   **2 H 20**
7-8 Savile Row W1. 01-734 1457.
Charles Stevens
53 Brick Lane E1. 01-247 9373. A good tailor in an unexpected area (near the Whitechapel Art Gallery) Same quality as Savile Row but lower prices.

Boutiques

Kings Road Chelsea   **4 L 4**
Well-known area for chic and avant-garde boutiques and people. Don't miss the Saturday fashion parade when the Chelsea trendies come out on show.
Carnaby Street W1   **2 H 20**
A narrow Soho street that became world famous as a centre of original fashion in the 1960's. Packed with jostling crowds and colourful boutiques.
Kensington High Street W8   **1 D 4**
The major centre for young fashion of the 1970's. Small and large boutiques, markets and department stores. Don't forget to take a look up Kensington Church Street which branches off towards Notting Hill Gate.
Carvil   **4 L 4**
103 Kings Rd SW3. 01-352 8665. Popular shetland and cashmere sweaters, continental suits and separates.
Cassidy   **4 L 4**
114 & 182 Kings Rd SW3. 01-584 0397. Make their own suits, trousers and shirts. Also import Italian and French clothes.
Cecil Gee   **2 I 21**
39-45 Shaftesbury Ave W1. 01-734 8651. Well-made, fashionable clothes.

Dandy 1 D 4
102 Kensington High St W8. 01-937 9906. All types of clothing for the fashionable young man. Several branches.

Geezers
32a Kensington Church St W8. 01-937 3816. Continental styles for the fashionable but not eccentric. Branch in the Strand.

John Michael 2 H 20
18 Savile Row W1. 01-734 0831. Top-quality international male fashion. Many other branches.

John Stephen 2 F 20
268 Oxford St W1. 01-734 1772. High fashion clothes. Branch in Carnaby St.

Just Men 4 L 11
7-9 Tryon St SW3. 01-584 1221. Everything from machine-made trousers to individual hand-made shoes, furs and shirts. Also has a top hairdresser on the premises.

Lord John
5 Warple Way W3. 01-749 1395. Suits, trousers, ties — everything. Branches in all main shopping areas.

Mates 2 F 19
356 Oxford St W1. 01-499 0769. Colourful and inexpensive fashion. Irvin Sellars group. Many branches.

Michael Barrie 4 L 4
174 Kings Rd SW3. 01-352 5000. Large selection of shirts, jackets and trousers.

Squire Shops 4 L 4
97 Kings Rd SW3. 01-352 9853. Huge selection of trousers; also suits, jackets and leather clothes.

Take 6 2 H 20
24 Carnaby St W1. 01-437 4617. High fashion at reasonable prices. Branches on Kings Rd and Kensington Church St.

Thackeray's 4 L 4
79 Kings Rd SW3. 01-352 8961. Suits, blazers, leather jackets and coats at sensible prices. Branch in Oxford St.

Village Gate 4 L 4
131 Kings Rd SW3. 01-351 1338. High fashion menswear in a good range of sizes.

Way In 2 I 14
Men's and women's boutique in Harrods. See under 'Women's clothes'.

Clothes Hire

Alkit 2 I 22
Cambridge Circus WC2. 01-836 1814. Tropical kits.

Kritz 2 D 18
192 Baker St NW1. 01-935 0304. Dinner and morning suits.

Moss Bros 6 J 23
Bedford St WC2. 01-240 4567. Men's and women's ceremonial and formal wear. Arrange to hire a week in advance.

Clothing fabrics

Also refer to the fabric shops under 'Women's clothes' for materials suitable for shirts, ties, etc.

Allans 2 E 18
56-58 Duke St W1. 01-629 3781. Specialise in men's light-weight suitings.

W. Bill 2 F 19
93 New Bond St W1. 01-629 2837. British tweeds, cashmeres and suitings. World-wide mail order.

Dormeuil 2 H 20
14 Warwick St W1. 01-437 1144. World-famous 'Tonik' cloths, tropical worsteds, etc.

Hunt & Winterbotham 2 I 19
4 Old Bond St W1. 01-493 0940. Wide range of quality suiting fabrics, tweeds, cashmere, etc.

Denim

Has been called 'the uniform of the young'. Most boutiques sell jeans but listed below are the main specialists who also carry denim shirts, jackets and accessories. These shops often sell cheesecloth shirts, casual corduroy and cotton trousers and T-shirts. Also see under 'Markets'.

Jean Junction 2 F 20
291 Oxford St W1. 01-629 2695. Branches in all main shopping areas.

Jean Machine 4 L 4
163 Kings Rd SW3. 01-352 0098. Many branches.

Millets 2 F 18
89 Oxford St W1. 01-437 2811.

The Panthouse 4 L 10
123a Kings Rd SW3. 01-352 2497.

Upwest 2 F 20
270 Oxford St W1. 01-493 9651.

Westerner 2 F 20
469 Oxford St W1. 01-499 3781.

Fur Coats

For second-hand furs see 'Markets'. If you can't afford to buy, Moss Bros rent men's and women's furs.

Furs-For-All 2 H 20
205 Regent St W1. 01-734 7770.

Gayfurs 2 F 20
70 Oxford St W1. 01-636 6969.

John Michael 2 H 20
18 Savile Row W1. 01-734 0831.

Hats

Herbert Johnson 2 H 19
13 Old Burlington St W1. 01-439 7397. Everything from crash-helmets to yachting caps.

James Lock 5 J 19
6 St James's St SW1. 01-930 8874. Famous for bowlers. Also top-quality riding hats.

High fashion clothing

Differ from boutiques in that these are internationally known names, very chic and on the expensive side.

Browns 2 F 19
23-27 South Molton St W1. 01-499 5630. Best selection in London of Europe's foremost ready-to-wear designers which the shop carries exclusively.

Bugatti 1 D 8
59 Kensington Church St W8. 01-937 2624. Elegant French and Italian clothes — Cerruti, Valentino, Cartier accessories. Sicom leather coats.

Gieves & Hawkes 2 H 20
1 Savile Row W1. 01-734 0186. Bespoke and ready-made suits for the fashion-conscious yet elegant.

Piero de Monzi 4 L 4
68 Fulham Rd SW3. 01-589 8765. Very chic French and Italian clothes. Cerruti suits.

Yves St Laurent 1 I 11
84 Brompton Rd SW3. 01-584 4993. Exclusive Paris clothes, own label. Branch in New Bond St.

Vincci 2 J 19
60 & 67 Jermyn St SW1. 01-493 4651. Top Italian designs made exclusively for the shop in unique materials.

Leather & fur-lined clothes

See under 'Women's clothes' and 'Second-hand clothes'. For a cheaper range of fashion leather coats and jackets try the markets, especially in Kensington, and boutiques.

Military & naval dress

Moss Bros 6 J 23
Bedford St WC2. 01-240 4567. Make uniforms for officers in any of the services. War medals and ribbons. Ceremonial dress can be hired.

Raincoats

Aquascutum 2 I 20
100 Regent St W1. 01-734 6090.

Burberrys 5 J 21
18 Haymarket SW1. Well-cut classic English weather-proofs. Also have a cleaning, proofing and dyeing service.

J.C. Cording 2 I 20
19 Piccadilly W1. 01-734 0830. Functional rainwear for sports and rough weather.

Second-hand clothes

Don't miss the markets, especially Antiquarius, Portobello Rd and Camden Lock for period clothes.

A. Alexander (and Marks next door) 2 B 14
79 Praed St W1. (No phone). Suits and tweed, leather and suede jackets. Very cheap.

Axfords 5 N 16
306 Vauxhall Bridge Rd SW1. 01-834 1934. Large stock of suits.

Barry Gee 5 M 16
82 Wilton Rd SW1. 01-828 1081. Buy and sell suits and coats in good condition. Do alterations.

Regent and Gordon 2 G 19
180 New Bond St W1. 01-493 7180. Not strictly second-hand but sell unclaimed Savile Row suits at half price or less.

Shirts

It is possible to get low priced custom-made shirts at many of the multiple stores which cost less if you bring your own material. Poplins, voiles and batistes are suitable (see 'Clothing fabrics'). The following firms make top-quality shirts to measure:

Coles 2 H 20
35 Savile Row W1. 01-434 1290.

Deborah & Clare 2 I 12
29 Beauchamp Place SW3. 01-584 2875.

Harvie & Hudson   **2 I 19**
77 Jermyn St SW1. 01-930 3949.

Hawes & Curtis   **2 H 19**
2 Burlington Gardens W1. 01-493 3803.

Turnbull & Asser   **2 I 19**
71 Jermyn St SW1. 01-930 0502. Ready-made and
bespoke English cottons and silks.

Shoes

*Refer to women's shoes — many also have a good
men's department.*

John Lobb   **5 J 19**
9 St James's St SW1. 01-930 3664. Top quality made-
to measure shoes. Also women's shoes.

Maxwell's   **2 G 19**
177 New Bond St W1. 01-493 1097. Hand-made
bespoke boots and shoes of the highest quality.

Pinet   **2 G 19**
47 New Bond St W1. 01-629 2174. Good casual shoes.

Toppers   **2 F 20**
237-239 Oxford St W1. 01-437 1767. Quality styles.

Trickers   **2 I 19**
67 Jermyn St SW1. 01-930 6395. Hand-made shoes at
cheaper prices.

Trousers

*See under 'Boutiques' and 'Denim' for ready-made
trousers. For custom-made go to Savile Row.*

Unusual sizes

Cooper's All Size   **2 D 16**
72 & 74 Edgware Rd W2. 01-402 8635. Ready-to-wear
clothes for the tall and small. Alterations service.

High and Mighty   **2 I 12**
177 Brompton Rd SW3. 01-589 7454. Main branch.
Everything ready-to-wear for the big or tall man. Chest
sizes 44-58 in up to 6ft 9in in height. Shoes to size 15.

Outsize Manshop
242 High Holborn WC1. 01-405 8566   **3 I 23**
145 Edgware Rd W2. 01-723 8754.   **2 C 16**

Women's clothes

The large stores

Aquascutum   **2 I 20**
100 Regent St W1. 01-734 6090. Classic English-style
clothes in tweed and plain colour cloth. Good rainwear.

Bourne & Hollingsworth   **2 G 21**
116 Oxford St W1. 01-636 1515. Inexpensive
underwear, haberdashery, hats: accent on fashion.
Unusual food department.

C & A Modes   **2 E 17**
505-519 Oxford St W1. 01-629 7272. Vast selection of
inexpensive fashionable clothes for the whole family.

Debenhams   **2 F 19**
344-348 Oxford St W1. 01-580 3000. Good lingerie and
knitwear, costume jewellery and shops within shops.

Dickens & Jones   **2 G 20**
224 Regent St W1. 01-734 7070. Everything from well-
made evening wear to fashion jewellery, handbags and
other accessories. Large fabric department. Children's
wear.

D.H. Evans   **2 F 19**
318 Oxford St W1. 01-629 8800. Women's and
children's wear, accessories, medium-priced fashion
fabrics. Excellent for corsetry. Hairdressing and beauty
salon.

Fenwick   **2 G 19**
63 New Bond St W1. 01-629 9161. High quality fashion
and accessories. Good coats and lingerie. Hair-dressing
salon.

Fortnum & Mason   **2 I 19**
181 Piccadilly W1. 01-734 8040. International smart-
ness for the older woman. French clothes and copies.
High quality handbags, hats and country wear.

Harrods   **2 I 12**
Knightsbridge SW1. 01-730 1234. French clothes and
copies, brides' department and all accessories. Carries
almost every major designer. Good sweater
department.

Harvey Nichols   **2 I 13**
Knightsbridge SW1. 01-235 5000. High quality in all
departments, especially fabrics. Young fashion in '21
Shop'.

Jaeger   **2 H 20**
204 Regent St W1. 01-734 4050. Well-cut, fashionable
English clothes. Cashmeres, camel and knitted
garments. Good swim and ski-wear.

Marks & Spencer   **2 G 21**
458 Oxford St W1. 01-486 6151. Very good value. No
garments can be tried on but everything can be brought
back for exchange or refund. New lines are tried out at

this branch. Also sell children's wear, food-stuffs and
accessories such as shoes, handbags, gloves, scarves
and underwear.

Peter Robinson's Top Shop   **2 G 20**
234 Oxford St W1. 01-636 7700. Quality separates and
sportswear — good fashion jewellery and cosmetics
departments. Basement complex of boutiques carrying
all major designers of young fashion — from the way-
out to the practical. All accessories.

Selfridges   **2 G 21**
400 Oxford St W1. 01-629 1234. Good selection of
clothes, accessories and cosmetics.

Simpsons   **2 I 20**
203 Piccadilly W1. 01-734 2002. Good casual and sports
wear.

Young fashion chains

*Differ from boutiques in that the clothes are less
individual or way-out while still being up-to-date. Main
branches only listed below:*

Chelsea Girl   **1 D 4**
124 Kensington High St W8. 01-937 0224. Popular
young styles at very reasonable prices. Good tops and
skirts, shoes, tights and handbags.

Etam   **2 F 18**
484 Oxford St W1. 01-629 1430. Specialise in cheap
separates and dresses. Pretty nightdresses.

Just Looking   **4 C 11**
88 Kings Rd SW3. 01-589 9329. High quality fashion
clothes. Good coats, jackets and evening wear.

Mates   **2 F 19**
356 Oxford St W1. 01-499 0769. Irvine Sellars fashion
group. Colourful range of styles, especially in skirts and
trousers.

Miss Selfridge   **2 E 18**
40 Duke St W1. 01-629 1234. Enormous selection of
fashionable clothes. Excellent sweaters and shirts.
Tights, jewellery, cosmetics and a good shoe shop.

Richard Shops   **2 E 17**
480 Oxford St W1. 01-629 2796. Large selection of
dresses, separates, coats and sportswear.

Wallis   **2 E 17**
490-492 Oxford St W1. 01-629 2171. Large range of
dresses, copies of Paris couture clothes and well-cut
quality fashions. Specialise in colour coordinates.

Young Jaeger   **2 H 20**
204 Regent St W1. 01-734 4050. Smart, top-quality
London look clothes.

Boutiques

*Kings Rd, Carnaby St and Kensington High — see
under men's clothes (boutiques).*
*From unique hand-made clothes to famous names in
design, these shops have been chosen for the quality
and individuality of their goods. Prices will vary, some
areas being particularly expensive such as South
Molton St and Knightsbridge. Boutiques are an integral
part of London life and there are many more than listed
here — have fun discovering your own!*

Bombacha   **4 K 8**
104 Fulham Rd SW3. 01-584 5381. French and Italian
fashions and accessories. Italian jeans.

Browns   **2 F 19**
23-27 South Molton St W1. 01-499 5630. Top British
and continental designs which the shop carries
exclusively. Beautiful but expensive clothes.

Bus Stop   **1 D 18**
3 Kensington Church St W8. 01-937 9694. Lee Bender's
distinctive up-to-the-minute fashions. Bright colours,
soft materials, lovely scarves and hats. Several
branches.

Che Guevara   **1 D 7**
44 Kensington High St W8. 01-937 3137. Exciting range
by leading designers of young fashion. Stirling Cooper,
Ossie Clark. Striking interior with a fountain, mirrors
and a large selection of colourful jewellery and shoes.

Conspiracy   **1 D 4**
170 Kensington High St W8. 01-937 9138. Eye-catching
sweaters and separates.

Crocodile   **2 I 12**
58 Beauchamp Place SW3. 01-589 4455. Beautiful
range of chic but expensive fashions.

Elle   **2 G 19**
12 & 92 New Bond St W1. 01-409 0430. Costly French,
Italian & English fashions by top designers. Clothes
often featured in Vogue and Harpers.

Feathers   **1 E 8**
43 Kensington High St W8. 01-989 0356. Well-chosen
but expensive collection of continental clothes and
accessories. Good knits, chiffons, bags and belts.
Several branches.

Fiorucci   **1 I 11**
15 Brompton Rd SW3. 01-584 3910. Unusual range of
accessories and 'crazy clothes' — gold boots, jeans

with snakes and sequins sewn on, silver jackets. Also
pillows, toys, aprons, baskets, etc.

Hedgehog   **4 K 8**
135 Fulham Rd SW3. 01-584 6114. Limited range of
skilfully made clothes.

Joseph   **4 L 11**
33 Kings Rd SW3. 01-730 7664. Clothes by top French
designers with prices to match.

Laura Ashley   **4 L 4**
175 Fulham Rd SW3. 01-584 6939. Romantically styled
dresses, skirts and nighties in distinctively patterned
cottons and corduroys. Amazingly cheap. Several
branches (see 'Fabrics').

Marian McDonnell   **4 K 11**
80 Sloane Ave SW3. 01-589 0717. Exclusive elegance.

Maryon   **1 I 11**
39 Brompton Rd SW3. 01-584 1341. Large range of
colourful separates and dresses at reasonable prices.

Parkers
13a Heath St NW3. 01-435 8629. Unusual flowing styles
in romantic materials.

Piero de Monzi   **4 K 7**
68-70 Fulham Rd SW3. 01-589 8765. Sporty but
expensive clothes from Italy. Immaculate knitwear.

Plaza 9   **1 I 11**
33 Brompton Rd SW3. 01-581 1818. French clothes —
chic and expensive.

Quorum   **4 M 10**
52 Radnor Walk SW3. 01-352 2962. Ossie Clark designs
— lovely evening wear.

Regamus   **2 I 12**
17 Beauchamp Place SW3. 01-584 7295. Beautiful
evening wear in original and exotic designs. Expensive.

Ronnie Stirling   **2 F 19**
94 New Bond St W1. 01-499 2675. Well-cut Stirling
Cooper clothes in the latest styles.

Spectrum   **1 I 7**
70 Gloucester Rd SW7. 01-584 7327. Romantic clothes
at reasonable prices — pretty dresses. Branch in
Kensington Church St.

Stop the Shop   **4 L 11**
126 Kings Rd SW3. 01-589 3956. Rotating first floor.
Latest fashion ideas.

Topaz   **2 G 21**
138 Oxford St W1. 01-636 8151. Full range of well-
styled clothes to suit the younger and older woman.

Wardrobe   **2 D 18**
42 Chiltern St W1. 01-486 5064. Good quality fashion
for all ages. Attractive lingerie and beachwear.

Way In at Harrods   **2 I 12**
Knightsbridge SW1. 01-730 1234. Fashionable, elegant
and well-made clothes for men and women. Music and
snack bar. Comprehensive range of accessories —
jewellery, cosmetics shoes, tights, etc.

Belts

Most boutiques and large stores stock belts.

Paris House   **2 F 19**
41 South Molton St W1. 01-629 5065. Make belts and
cuff links from their unusual button collection.

Couturiers

*These are the great internationally famous fashion
houses. Appointment necessary.*

Chanelle   **1 I 11**
23 Brompton Rd SW3. 01-589 6503.

Christian Dior London   **2 G 20**
9 Conduit St W1. 01-499 6255.

Hardy Amies   **2 H 20**
14 Savile Row W1. 01-734 2436.

Hazel Graeme   **1 I 11**
8 Rutland St (off Montpelier Walk) SW7. 01-584 1964.

Lachasse   **2 H 17**
4 Farm St W1. 01-499 2906.

Norman Hartnell   **2 H 18**
26 Bruton St W1. 01-629 0992.

Rahvis Couture   **2 G 18**
50 Grosvenor St W1. 01-629 8301.

Yves St Laurent 'Rive Gauche'   **2 G 19**
113 New Bond St W1. 01-493 1800.

Denim

See under 'Men's clothes'.

Ethnic fashions

Forbidden Fruit   **4 L 4**
325 Kings Rd SW3. 01-351 1157. Afghan tribal clothes,
some second-hand.

Hindu Kush   **1 A 8**
231 Portobello Rd W11. Embroidered Asian tribal
dresses. Branch in Kensington High St.

Mexicana   **5 M 12**
89 Lower Sloane St SW1. 01-730 3871. Cotton clothes
and knitwear from Mexico. Can be expensive.

Mitsukiku   **1 I 18**
15 Old Brompton Rd SW7. 01-589 1725. Everything
Japanese — bright satin jackets especially pretty.
Teapots, windchimes, slippers and crockery. Several
branches.

Monsoon   **2 I 12**
53 Beauchamp Place SW3. 01-589 7737. Indian cotton
clothes — bright and airy.

Thea Porter   **2 H 22**
8 Greek St W1. 01-437 6224. Exotic oriental clothes in
swirling gossamer fabrics and silks.

Fabrics

*The following are recommended for men's and
women's fabrics.*

Allan's   **2 E 18**
56-58 Duke St W1. 01-629 3781. English and
continental couture fabrics and lace.

W. Bill   **2 F 19**
93 New Bond St W1. 01-629 2837. British tweeds,
cashmeres and suitings. World-wide mail order.

Dickens & Jones   **2 G 20**
224 Regent St W1. 01-734 7070. Superb women's wool
and novelty fabrics.

Harrods   **2 I 12**
Knightsbridge SW1. 01-730 1234. Exclusive and
exquisite women's fashion fabrics.

Harvey Nichols   **2 I 13**
Knightsbridge SW1. 01-235 5000. Delightful range of
women's dress fabrics.

The Irish Shop   **2 E 18**
11 Duke St W1. 01-935 1366. Hand-woven Donegal
and superfine tweeds.

Jacob Gordon   **2 F 19**
19 South Molton St W1. 01-629 5947. Retail prices in
cottons, silks, suiting fabrics and tweeds.

Jane Halkin   **4 K 11**
45 Sloane Ave SW3. 01-589 2919. English tweeds and
silk and cotton prints. Resident dressmaker.

Jason's   **2 F 19**
53 New Bond St W1. 01-629 2606. Exclusive and
expensive silks.

John Lewis   **2 F 19**
278-306 Oxford St W1. 01-629 7711. One of the finest
general selections of fabrics in the world at very
reasonable prices.

Laura Ashley   **5 M 12**
71 Lower Sloane St SW1. 01-730 1771. Amazingly
cheap fabrics: calico, corduroy, cotton drills and lawns
in plain colours or rustic prints.

Liberty's   **2 G 20**
210-220 Regent St W1. 01-734 1234. Superb silk and
cotton fabrics. 'Art Nouveau' and flower prints.
Continental couture fabrics and Chinese silks.

Peter Jones   **5 L 12**
Sloane Sq SW1. 01-730 3434. Good general selection
of materials at low prices.

The Scotch House   **2 I 15**
2 Brompton Rd SW1. 01-581 2151
84-86 Regent St W1. 01-734 0203.
Excellent tartans.

Selfridges   **2 E 18**
400 Oxford St W1. 01-629 1234. Excellent general
selection.

Simmonds at Stanley Lowe   **2 G 19**
42 New Bond St W1. 01-629 9691. Exclusive selection
of novelty fabrics: French lace, printed silks and rayons,
hair fabrics and worsteds.

Furs

*Inexpensive younger-style furs can be bought from
'Way In' at Harrods, 'Young Jaeger' and Dickens &
Jones. Try second-hand shops and the markets as well.*

Calman Links   **1 I 11**
149 Brompton Rd SW3. 01-589 5411. Top-quality furs.

Femina Furs   **2 F 21**
13-14 Great Castle St W1. 01-580 4700. A boutique of
excellent furs.

Frank Cooney   **2 G 19**
23 Avery Row W1. 01-629 4664. Fashionable young
styles in quality furs.

Maxwell Croft   **2 G 19**
105 New Bond St W1. 01-629 6226. Luxurious modern
styles and some fabulous prices!

National Fur Co   **1 I 11**
195 Brompton Rd SW3. 01-589 4801. Excellent choice
at all prices.

Swears & Wells   **2 F 18**
374 Oxford St W1. 01-629 1273. Wide selection of coats
in all kinds of fur, leather and suede. Many branches.

Fur cleaning and valeting

Bradleys   **2 E 19**
27 Wigmore St W1. 01-580 4444. Fur valeting and
storage with insurance cover.

Fur Clean
3 Belsize Place NW3. 01-794 3242. Clean fur, suede and leather.

Gloves

Dickens & Jones and Harrods for top-quality gloves.

Haberdashery

MacCulloch & Wallis   **2 F 19**
25 Dering St W1. 01-629 0311. One of the best in London. All kinds of interlinings, zip-fasteners and sewing cottons. Will make labels and sharpen scissors.

R.D. Franks
Kent House, Market Place W1. 01-636 1244. All sewing accessories and materials as well as fashion and instruction magazines.

Hairpieces and Wigs

Most large stores have a small boutique which sells wigs and false pieces. C & A Modes have some excellent and very inexpensive hairpieces.

Teeda   **2 F 19**
63 South Molton St W1. 01-499 7282. Wigs, hairpieces and after-care service.

Handbags

Carried by most boutiques and shoe shops.

Alba Handbags   **2 B 18**
189 Baker St NW1. 01-935 3410. Good modern bags at all prices, exciting shapes and colours. Also luggage.

Gucci   **2 G 10**
172 New Bond St W1. 01-629 2716. Beautifully made top-quality leather and crocodile skin.

Susan Handbags   **2 G 19**
68 New Bond St W1. 01-629 8673. Smart but expensive English and foreign bags and shoes.

Hats

Herbert Johnson   **2 H 19**
13 Old Burlington St W1. 01-439 7397. Hats for all sizes and all ages.

Malyard: Hat Gear   **2 H 20**
3 Kingly St W1. 01-437 1848. Unusual and colourful hats in straw, fur, sealskin and silk. Top-quality fashion in young styles. Also men's.

Simone Mirman   **5 K 13**
9 Chesham Place SW1. 01-235 2656. Unusual high-fashion hats for very smart people.

Graham Smith   **2 F 19**
8 Blenheim St, New Bond St W1. 01-493 7982. Well-made, beautiful hats. Also obtainable at Fortnum & Mason.

Knitwear

Bond Street Boutique   **2 G 19**
99 New Bond St W1. 01-629 5326. Large collection of colourful cashmere sweaters and dresses.

Carolyn Brunn   **1 I 11**
287 Brompton Rd SW3. 01-589 1966. Brightly coloured heavy-knit sweaters, jackets and coats. Pretty slinky dresses. Branch in South Molton St.

Jaeger   **2 H 20**
204 Regent St SW1. 01-734 4050. Top-fashion knits.

Lewis Henry   **2 F 19**
36 South Molton St W1. 01-493 3628. All their clothes are hand crotcheted — even their bikinis. Very attractive and original styles.

Marks & Spencer   **2 G 21**
458 Oxford St W1. 01-486 6151. Very reasonably priced woollens of high-tested manufacturing standards.

Mary Farrin   **2 F 19**
9 South Molton St W1. 01-493 7363. Soft angora sweaters and dresses, knitted cotton bikinis, tammies and long scarves.

Noble Jones   **2 I 19**
12-14 Burlington Arcade W1. 01-493 3830.

The Scotch House   **2 I 15**
2 Brompton Rd SW1. 01-581 2151. Enormous range of Scottish knitwear — Shetland, cashmere and lambswool.

Westaway & Westaway   **3 H 24**
65 Gt Russell St WC1. 01-405 4479 Specialists in Scottish fabrics and knitwear of fine quality.

Leather & fur-lined clothes

Antartex   **2 I 14**
143 Knightsbridge SW3. 01-584 8410. Sheepskin coats and jackets for the whole family.

Bonnie Cashin at Liberty's   **2 G 20**
210-220 Regent St W1. 01-734 1234. Fabulous leather clothes designed by Bonnie Cashin from New York.

Cordoba   **2 G 19**
134 New Bond St W1. 01-629 5619. Haute couture leather coats and other clothes in subtle colours.

Loewe   **2 I 19**
25a Old Bond St W1. 01-499 0787. Quality hand-made Spanish leather and suede costs, dresses and suits for men and women.

The Sheepskin Shop   **2 E 17**
435-7 Oxford St W1. 01-629 1301. Inexpensive leather, sheepskin and pigskin clothes in all colours and sizes. Several branches.

Skin   **4 L 11**
120 Kings Rd SW3. 01-589 9474. Inexpensive coats and jackets in a variety of skins. Fashionable styles and colours.

Skincraft   **2 G 19**
100 New Bond St W1. 01-629 5454. High quality leather clothes by top designers — but not always top prices. Several branches.

Lingerie and nightwear

Marks & Spencer, Littlewoods and Fenwicks carry good, inexpensive lingerie and nightwear while Harvey Nichols, Liberty's and Fortnum & Mason are excellent for the more elegant, dreamy styles.

Bradleys   **2 I 14**
83 Knightsbridge SW1. 01-235 2903. Specialty shop for well-made lingerie and nightwear.

Courtenay   **2 G 18**
22 Brook St W1. 01-629 0543. French and Belgian nightdresses and underwear.

Le Trousseau   **2 D 18**
64 Blandford St W1. 01-935 9776. Glamorous styles.

Night Owls   **4 J 9**
78 Fulham Rd SW3. 01-584 2451. Unique little shop selling nightclothes so pretty they'd double as daywear.

Rigby & Peller   **2 F 19**
12 South Molton St W1. 01-629 6708. Made to measure underwear and exclusive French beach clothes.

S. Weiss   **2 I 12**
59 Shaftesbury Ave W1. 01-437 1821. Up-to-date styles. Also stock bikinis.

Maternity clothes

Just Jane   **2 I 13**
8 Sloane St SW1. 01-235 6639. Very distinctive maternity wear. Catalogue available for mail order. Several branches.

Mothercare   **2 E 17**
461 Oxford St W1. 01-629 6621. (Main branch). Good quality maternity and baby clothes and equipment at practical prices. Free mail order catalogue.

Raincoats

Many of the big stores' boutiques have good rainwear, i.e. Harvey Nichols, Dickens & Jones and Harrods. Try Fenwick for the latest macs; Selfridges have a large selection. See also under 'men's clothes'.

Second-hand clothes

Markets are your best bet for period clothes — especially Portobello Rd and Camden Lock.

Antiquarius Antique Market   **4 L 10**
15 Flood St SW3. 01-351 1145. Victorian nighties, fur coats, old Levis, '20's crepe dresses, art deco — you'll find them all here.

Chelsea Antique Market   **4 L 9**
253 Kings Rd SW3. 01-352 1425. Good selection of antique clothes, belts, bags, shoes, hats and buckles. Also new dresses from old materials.

Essenses   **4 L 9**
410 Kings Rd SW10. 01-352 0192. Vintage clothes from the late 19th century. Also made to measure.

Jenny   **1 D 7**
40 Gordon Place W8. 01-937 8493. Old and new clothes bought and sold, plus many accessories.

Mary Leigh   **2 F 19**
47 South Molton St W1. 01-629 3380. Buys and sells gowns, suits and furs from couturiers.

Pandora Dress Agency   **5 L 12**
54 Sloane Sq SW1. 01-730 5722. Very good used model garments bought and sold on commission.

Shoes

Good shops with branches everywhere are: Dolcis, Lilley & Skinner and Saxone. Other more individual shops are:

Anello & Davide   **2 I 24**
30 Drury Lane WC2. 01-836 6744. Beautifully made shoes and boots in long lasting styles and at good prices.

Bally   **2 I 19**
30 Old Bond St W1. 01-493 2250. Good quality shoes for men and women. Several branches.

Charles Jourdan   **2 I 19**
42-49 Brompton Rd SW3. 01-584 3258. Beautiful shoes imported from France for men and women.

Chelsea Cobbler 4 K 11
165 Draycott Ave SW3. 01-584 9794. High fashion shoes and boots in the latest sytles. Branches in boutiques such as 'Way In' and Top Shop.

Elliots 2 F 19
76-77 New Bond St W1. 01-629 3644. A wide range of high fashion boots and shoes. Specialise in narrow fittings. Several branches.

Ferragamo 2 I 19
18 Old Bond St W1. 01-629 5007. Italian shoemakers. Smart, comfortable shoes.

Frederick Freed 5 J 22
94 St Martin's Lane WC2. 01-240 0432. Specialists in theatrical and ballet shoes. Also make excellent boots to order.

Gamba 2 I 12
55 Beauchamp Place SW3. 01-584 4774. Good range of fashion shoes.

Kurt Geiger 2 F 19
95 New Bond St W1. 01-499 2707. Modern shoes and handbags.

Peter Lord 2 G 21
260 Oxford St W1. 01-629 0897. Stock quality shoes in wide fittings.

Ravel 2 G 19
103 New Bond St W1. 01-493 6111. Quality fashion shoes and boots. Branches throughout London.

Russell & Bromley 2 H 19
24 New Bond St W1. 01-629 6903. Fine hand-made shoes from Spain, Paris and Italy.

Sacha 2 E 17
227 Oxford St W1. 01-437 4981. Modern shoes in up-to-date styles for the younger woman. Several branches — four in Oxford St alone.

Stockings & tights

Fenwicks for extravagant patterns; Selfridges for a wide selection; Harvey Nichols for the more expensive; 'Way In' for Mary Quant and Marks & Spencer or the British Home Stores for an inexpensive range of colours.

Swimsuits

Most large stores stock a good selection. Harrods sell a variety of fashionable beachwear all the year round.

Unusual sizes

Berketex 2 F 19
309 Oxford St W1. 01-629 9303. Large outsize department of well-made ready-to-wear clothes.

Buy & Large 5 L 12
4 Holbein Place, Sloane Sq SW1. 01-730 6534. Full selection of clothes in fittings from 16-24. Good for evening wear.

Evans Outsizes 2 E 17
538 Oxford St W1. 01-499 5372. General selection of clothes for the larger woman.

Mary Fair 2 D 18
18 Baker St W1. 01-935 8618. Avant garde designs in small sizes.

Lilley & Skinner 2 F 18
356 Oxford St W1. 01-629 6381. Special department for large and small size fashion shoes at reasonable prices. Also long stockings.

Selfridges 'Wide & Narrow Shop' 2 E 18
400 Oxford St W1. 01-629 1234. Comfortable women's shoes in sizes 3-9½. Fittings range from AAA to D and some E.

Swan & Edgar 2 I 20
49-63 Regent St W1. 01-734 1616. Special '44 Room' for those with larger hips.

Tall Girls 2 G 19
17 Woodstock St W1. Everything for girls from 5ft 9in to 6ft 5in. Shoes from 9½ to 12½, lingerie, stockings and tights.

Specialist shops and services

London is an international centre of art, fashion, antiques and collectors' items. Many shops have specialised in certain goods and have become world famous names. The list below represents only a selection of some of the best shops in each category. Good general shopping areas are Oxford St, Regent St, Soho, Savile Row, Piccadilly and the nearby arcades, Bond St, Chelsea's Kings Rd, Knightsbridge and Beauchamp Place and Kensington High St. Some shops close on Sat afternoon and stay open late on Thursday evenings.

'Which?' Magazine 5 K 22
Consumers' Association, 14 Buckingham St WC2. 01-839 1222. The best subscription periodical for unbiased testing of all kinds of everyday products and services.

Acupuncture

Acupuncture Association 5 O 14
34 Alderney St SW1. 01-834 1012/3353. Dr Chen provides excellent treatment.

Austin Clinic of Acupuncture 2 A 18
28 Clarence Gate Gdns, Glentworth St NW1. 01-723 6354. By appointment.

Dr P. Charalambous
4 King Edward Rd, New Barnet, Herts. 01-449 8112. By appointment. Has worked with Acacia House healing centre.

Aerial photos

Aerofilms
Elstree Way, Borehamwood, Herts. 01-207 0666. An enormous stock of oblique and vertical aerial views of Isles.

Fairey Surveys
Reform Rd, Maidenhead, Berks. Maidenhead 21371. Aerial photos available of London, home counties, and world-wide. Special surveys carried out.

Animals

Harrods Pet Shop 2 I 14
Knightsbridge SW1. 01-730 1234. Famous selection of pets — will supply an elephant if asked nicely!

Palmers
35 Parkway NW1. 01-485 5163. Unusual animals like baby alligators, tree frogs and giant South American toads.

Regent Pet Stores
33-37 Parkway NW1. 01-485 5163. Sell a large variety of birds, reptiles and fish as well as pups and mice.

Antiques
English homes are still rich in antiques, as is reflected in the amount of 18th and 19th cent furniture, china and objets d'art available in the hundreds of antique shops in London. Good hunting grounds are the Kings Rd, Portobello Rd, Camden Passage in Islington, Kensington Church St, Fulham Rd and Camden Town.

Antique Fairs

Arms Fair 1 B 10
Royal Lancaster Hotel, Bayswater Rd W1. *Usually held twice yearly in May and Sept,* this fair attracts collectors and dealers in all types of arms, armour and militaria.

Chelsea Antiques Fair 4 L 4
Chelsea Old Town Hall, Kings Rd SW3. *Held twice yearly, usually in Mar and Sept,* this well-established fair offers a wide range of antiques and works of art.

Fine Art & Antique Fair of Great Britain 1 D 2
National Hall, Olympia, Hammersmith Rd W6. 01-603 5654. *Held annually in June,* the fair offers great variety in quality and price. Interesting for a casual browse.

Grosvenor House Antiques Fair 2 G 16
Grosvenor House Hotel, Park Lane W1. Founded in 1934, this fair is held *annually in June.* High quality goods — Edwardian and 20th cent antiques and works of art.

Antique hire

Michael Carleton
77-81 Haverstock Hill NW3. 01-722 2277. Furniture, pictures and decorative items available for hire for film,. TV or photographic use.

Dodo
185 Westbourne Grove W11. 01-229 3132. 19th cent advertisements and signs, posters and showcards. Also early 20th cent packets, tins and clothes for sale and hire.

Dunning's Antiques
58-62 Holywell Hill, St Albans, Herts. St Albans 51065. Hire of unusual and decorative period pieces.

The Obsolete Fleet 2 I 20
17 Air St W1. 01-437 8225. Hire of veteran and vintage vehicles, especially London buses. Also an agency for private owners wishing to hire out vehicles.

K. Paul
22-24 England's Lane NW3. 01-722 7553. Hire of antique props.

Geoffrey Van 1 A 8
105-107 Portobello Rd W11. 01-229 5577. Hire of wood carvings, porcelain and works of art. Also furniture.

Antique shops

Bluett 2 G 18
48 Davies St W1. 01-629 4018. Fine oriental antiques.

T. Crowther 1 G 2
282 North End Rd SW6. 01-385 1357. Period lead and stone figures, gates, mantelpieces.

Gallery 43 2 G 18
28 Davies St W1. 01-499 6486. Primitive and far Eastern works of art.

W. R. Harvey
67-70 Chalk Farm Rd NW1. 01-485 1504. English 18th and early 19th cent furniture and objets d'art.

Jeremy 4 L 8
255 Kings Rd SW3. 01-352 0644. Choice English and French furniture and objets d'art.

Park Antiques
62 New Kings Rd SW6. 01-736 6222. Small and unusual antiques; silhouettes, snuffboxes, etc.

Phillips & Harris 1 D 8
54 Kensington Church St W8. 01-937 3133. Oriental ceramics, 18th cent furniture, etc.

John Sparkes 2 G 17
128 Mount St W1. 01-499 2265. Oriental objets d'art.

Spink 5 J 19
5-7 King St, St James's SW1. 01-930 7888. Superb oriental pieces.

Antique supermarkets

These enclosed antique markets can be found in Camden Passage, Kings Rd and as follows:

Antiquarius 4 L 10
15 Flood St (off Kings Rd) SW3. 01-351 1145. Good for books, prints and period clothes.

Antique Hypermarket 1 D 8
26-40 Kensington High St W8. 01-937 7846. Antique furniture, books, coins and silver.

Antique Supermarket 2 E 18
3 & 5 Barrett St W1. 01-486 1439. A large and varied market.

Chelsea Antique Market 4 L 9
253-254a Kings Rd SW3. 01-352 9695. A large, busy market covering all collectors' items.

Furniture Cave 4 L 5
533 Kings Rd SW10. 01-352 5373. Comprehensive second-hand furniture market.

Marylebone Antique Market 2 L 17
43 Crawford St W1. 01-723 2727. General market dealing in pictures, china, Persian rugs, etc.

Antiquities

The following shops deal in ancient works of art and objects.

Antiques 5 M 12
90-92 Pimlico Rd SW1. 01-730 8681. Roman sculpture, textiles.

Ian Auld 3 E 2
1 Gateway Arcade, Camden Passage N1. 01-359 1440. Mixed stock of antiquities and ethnographical items, with an emphasis on the latter.

Berkeley Galleries 2 G 18
20 Davies St W1. 01-629 2450. Excellent general stock.

Charles Ede 2 G 18
37 Brook St W1. 01-493 4944. Roman, Greek, Egyptian and some middle Eastern sculpture.

Elgin Antiques 1 A 8
121 Portobello Rd W11. 01-727 9852. Mainly Roman, Greek and Egyptian.

Michel Dumez Onof 2 G 17
109 Mount St W1. 01-499 6648. Small stock of classical and gothic sculpture, but specialises in works of art and furniture.

Antiquities: restorations

P. Levi
20 Brook St Mews North W2. 01-723 1948. Terracotta and wooden sculptures repaired.

R. Wilkinson
45 Wastdale Rd, Forest Hill SE23. 01-699 4420. Expert restorations and reproduction of glass.

Aquaria

Aquapets
12 Spring Bridge Rd W5. 01-567 2748. Excellent general stock of fish, tanks and equipment.

Chiswick Aquaria
136 Chiswick High Rd W4. 01-994 6549. Tropical marine and fresh-water fish.

Fish Tanks 2 D 18
49 Blandford St W1. 01-935 9432. Make tanks and supply the fish to go in them. Mail order anywhere.

Tachbrook Tropicals 5 N 16
244 Vauxhall Bridge Rd SW1. 01-834 5179. Importers and growers of over 200 species of tropical water plants for the aquarium.

Architectural prints and dyelines

Times Drawing Office 2 G 20
11 Pollen St W1. (Off Hanover St) 01-629 5661. *OPEN* for dyelines *10.30 Sats*. Quick collection and delivery service.

Artists' Materials

Cass Art Materials 2 I 22
13 Charing Cross Rd WC2. 01-930 9940. Stock all leading brands of paints, papers and artists' materials.

Cornelissen 3 I 24
22 Gt Queen St WC2. 01-405 3304. Painting and etching materials.

Fulham Pottery 4 K 6
210 New Kings Rd SW6. 01-736 1188. All potters' materials from clays to kilns.

Hobby Horse
387 King St W6. 01-748 9636. Sells all types of artists' materials.

Langford & Hill 2 H 20
10 Warwick St W1. 01-437 0086. The only place in London where you can get a selection of the latest American and German commercial art materials, films, coloured papers, special inks, drawn curves, etc. Expert advice.

T.N. Lawrence 6 J 28
2 Bleeding Heart Yard, Greville St EC2. 01-242 3534. Everything for the engraver, etcher and printmaker.

Letraset 2 I 22
44 Gerrard St W1. 01-437 3242. Transfer lettering and graphic art products. Well laid-out and efficient shop.

George Rowney 2 G 22
12 Percy St W1. 01-636 8241. Large and varied stock of general artists' paints and materials.

Paperchase 3 G 23
216 Tottenham Ct Rd W1. 01-637 1121. Exciting collection of papers and card. All types of artists' papers, book papers, Japanese foils and display papers.

Alec Tiranti 2 F 22
21 Goodge Place W1. 01-636 8565. Large range of tools and material for wood and stone carving. Also plasters, resins and fibreglass.

George Whiley
Victoria Rd, South Ruislip, Mddx. 01-422 0141. Gold leaf, metallic foils and bronze powders.

Winsor & Newton 2 G 22
51-52 Rathbone Place W1. 01-636 4231. Good general selection of artists' materials, papers and paints.

Astrology

Astrological Lodge (Theosophical Society) 2 A 18
50 Gloucester Place W1. 01-935 9261. Free open meeting every *Mon* for elementary introduction. Also public lectures and classes.

Faculty of Astrological Studies
The Registrar, Hook Cottage, Vines Cross, Heathfield, Sussex. Send s.a.e. with enquiries. Non-profitmaking, world-wide correspondence courses leading to Certificate and Diploma. Evening classes held in London.

Auctioneers: general

W. & F.C. Bonham & Sons 2 I 12
Montpelier Galleries, Montpelier St SW7. 01-584 9161. Mainly fine art, carpets, jewellery and wine.

Christie, Manson & Woods 5 J 19
8 King St, St James's SW1. 01-839 9060. Internationally famous — handle almost everything.

Christie's South Kensington 1 I 19
85 Old Brompton Rd SW7. 01-581 2231.

Croydon Auction Rooms
144-150 London Rd, West Croydon, Surrey. 01-638 1123. Weekly miscellaneous sales.

Stanley Gibbons 6 J 23
Drury House, Russell St WC2. 01-836 8444.

Glendining 2 G 19
7 Blenheim St, New Bond St W1. 01-493 2445.

Harrods Auction Galleries
Arundel Terrace SW13. 01-748 2739.

Hollingsworths
4-7 Burford Rd, Stratford E15. 01-534 1967.

Lot's Road Auction Galleries
71-3 Lots Rd SW10. 01-352 2349.

Marylebone Auction Rooms 2 A 17
Hayes Place, Lisson Grove NW1. 01-723 1118.

Phillips 2 G 19
7 Blenheim St, New Bond St W1. 01-629 6602. General auctioneers who also have several specialist auctions yearly of rare books, prints, lead soldiers, etc.

Reeves Auction Rooms
110-120 Church St, Croydon Surrey. 01-688 3136.

Southeby's Belgravia 5 J 14
19 Motcomb St. SW1. 01-235 4311. Paintings and works of art. Also furniture and silver.

Sotheby Parke Bernet 2 G 19
34-35 New Bond St W1. 01-493 8080. Internationally famous, especially for antiques and works of art.

Bernard Walsh 5 L 15
29 Lower Belgrave St SW1. 01-730 9148.

Auctioneers' Lists

Auction List
25 Queens Rd, Enfield, Middx. 01-363 3199. Will supply a weekly list of every auction in GB except large London ones.

Auctions: books

Sotheby's (Hodgson's Rooms)   6 J 26
115 Chancery Lane WC2. 01-405 7238. Hold auctions of antiquarian books several times a year.

Auctions: carpets

Persian Carpet Galleries   1 I 11
152 Brompton Rd SW3. 01-584 5516. Regular auctions of rare and antique Oriental rugs. Catalogues issued.

Auctions: stamps

City of London Philatelic Auctions   6 N 33
170 Bishopsgate EC2. 01-283 7968.

London Stamp Exchange   5 K 22
5 Buckingham St SW1. 01-930 1413.

Rigby Philatelic Auctions
31 Richmond Hill, Bournemouth. Bournemouth 22515.

Robson Lowe   5 J 20
50 Pall Mall SW1. 01-839 4034. Fine stamps and postal history items.

Ballroom dancing classes

Classes are held by the ILEA — for details of these see 'Floodlight'. Other good schools in London are:

Imperial Society of Teachers of Dancing   2 A 18
70 Gloucester Place W1. 01-935 0825. Will send you a list of schols in your area.

Morgans School of Dancing
32 Parkhurst Rd N7, 01-607 1968. Evening classes.

Rosina Ross
Conservative Club, High Rd N11. 01-886 4602. Private lessons and general classes by appointment.

Top of the Stairs Dance Club
1334 London Rd, Norbury SW16. 01-764 2828. Graded evening classes and private lessons.

Baskets

Eaton   2 H 22
16 Manette St (off Charing Cross Rd) W1. 01-437 9391. Baskets and woven cane matting.

Habitat   2 F 23
156 Tottenham Ct Rd W1. 01-387 9021. Large, colourful selection. Several branches.

David Mellor   5 L 12
4 Sloane Sq SW1. 01-730 4259. Kitchenware shop with lots of baskets.

Beauty specialists

Madame Angèle Curtin   2 E 18
70 Duke St W1. 01-493 5619.

Agnes Balint & Mary Eggerton   2 E 19
25 Welbeck St W1. 01-935 1754. Specialise in electrolysis, acne, and the removal of warts, moles, broken veins and freckles.

Beauty Clinic   2 C 18
118 Baker St W1. 01-935 3405. Deal with skin trouble, figure problems and unwanted hair. While you're there arrange to have a facial, manicure and a pedicure.

Beauty without Cruelty   2 D 19
40-41 Marylebone High St W1. 01-486 2845. Produce and use a large range of cosmetics made purely of herbs, flowers and natural essences. Will advise on skin care.

Countess Csasky   2 I 16
5 Carrington House, Hertford St W1. 01-629 3732. Skin rejuvenation specialist.

Books: antique

The book collector is fortunate in having about 250 book shops in London, many specialising in particular subjects. The Charing Cross Rd, Cecil Court and around the British Museum are good areas for browsing.

Edward G. Allen & Son   3 H 23
14 Grape St WC2. 01-240 0993. Early scientific books and early parliamentary papers.

Bell Book & Radmall   3 J 23
80 Long Acre WC2. 01-240 2161. Modern first editions, literary periodicals, avant-garde literature. Catalogues issued.

Andrew Block   3 H 24
20 Barter St WC1. 01-405 9660. Drama, entertainment and ephemera. Prints.

Stanley Crowe   3 G 23
5 Bloomsbury St WC1. 01-580 3976. Topography and history — particularly London home counties.

Dance Books   5 J 22
9 Cecil Court WC2. 01-836 2314. All aspects of ballet, classical and folk dancing. Also posters, photos and biographies.

W.M. Dawsons & Sons   5 J 19
16-17 Pall Mall SW1. 01-930 2515. Large stock of early science and natural history. Catalogues issued.

David Drummond   5 J 22
11 Cecil Court WC2. 01-836 1142. 19th and early 20th cent juvenilia. Theatrical souvenirs and playbills and a large collection of classified postcards.

Peter Eaton   1 A 5
80 Holland Park Ave W11. 01-727 5211. Huge selection of antique books.

Francis Edwards   2 D 19
83 Marylebone High St W1. 01-935 9221. Early travel, natural history, old maps. Very large stock.

Otto Haas
49 Belsize Park Gardens NW3. 01-722 1488. One of the best stocks on music, musical literature and autographs in the world.

Hatchards   2 I 18
187 Piccadilly W1. 01-734 3201. Fine, illustrated books above a modern bookshop.

G. Heywood Hill   2 I 17
10 Curzon St W1. 01-629 0647. Books with fine coloured plates. Also an extensive collection of late and early 20th cent juvenilia.

E. Joseph   2 I 22
48a Charing Cross Rd WC2. 01-836 4111. Fine natural history. General collection of rare, beautiful and useful books.

Maggs Bros   2 H 18
50 Berkeley Sq W1. 01-499 2007. Rare books, illuminated manuscripts, fine illustrations.

Marlborough Rare Books   2 I 19
85 Old Bond St W1. 01-493 6993. Illustrated books: bibliography and architecture.

Pickering & Chatto
13 Brunswick Centre WC1. 01-278 5146. 17th to 19th cent English literature, books, plays, literary manuscripts, autographed letters.

Bernard Quaritch   2 H 20
5 Lower John St, Golden Sq W1. 01-734 0562. Illuminated manuscripts, fine sets of literature, natural history.

Books: children's

See under 'Children's shopping' in Children's London.

Books: new

Most major department stores have book departments, the better ones being Harrods, Selfridges, Bourne & Hollingsworth and Liberty's. The following bookshops are recommended:

Ashcroft & Daw   2 I 22
83 Charing Cross Rd WC2. 01-734 0950. Enormous selection of the latest paperbacks.

Barbican Business Book Centre   6 L 31
9 Moorfields EC2. 01-628 7479. Excellent stock of business books.

Baker Street Bookshop   2 D 18
33 Baker St W1. 01-486 6959. General books and records.

Cinema Bookshop   2 H 23
13-14 Gt Russell St WC1. 01-637 0206. Specialists in books, magazines and all material relating to the cinema.

Collet   2 I 22
52 Charing Cross Rd WC2. 01-836 2315. Large selection of Penguins and Pelicans.

Compendium
240 Camden High St NW1. 01-485 8944. Avant-garde and general shop specialising in political and feminist literature.

Denny's   6 J 30
2 Carthusian St EC1. 01-253 5421. General books.

Dillon's   3 F 24
1 Malet St WC1. 01-636 1577. Large academic stock including science and literature. Also antiquarian and second-hand books.

The Economists' Bookshop   6 J 25
Clare Market, Portugal St WC2. 01-405 5531. Specialists in social science and business books.

Fantasy Book Centre
43 Station Rd NW10. 01-965 3643. Specialists in science fiction.

Foyles   2 H 22
119-125 Charing Cross Rd WC2. 01-437 5660. The biggest — has practically every English book in publication.

French's Bookshop   6 K 23
26 Southampton St WC2. 01-836 7513. Books on the theatre.

Claude Gill   2 E 17
481 Oxford St W1. 01-499 5664. Excellent general bookshop.

The Government Bookshop   3 I 23
49 High Holborn WC1. 01-928 6977. HMSO publications on every subject from cooking to parliament. No fiction.

Grant & Culter   5 K 22
11 Buckingham St, Strand WC2. 01-839 3136. New and second-hand books in German, French, Spanish, Portugese and Italian.

Hachette   2 H 20
4 Regent Place (off Regent St) W1. 01-734 5259. French books and periodicals.

Hatchards   2 I 20
187 Piccadilly W1. 01-439 9921. Select books — good leatherbound editions.

London Art Bookshop   1 D 7
7 Holland St W8. 01-937 6996. Books and magazines on art and architecture.

A. Probsthain & Co   3 H 23
41 Gt Russell St WC1. 01-636 1096. Books in Eastern and African languages.

W.H. Smith
Branches throughout London and also at railway stations.

Travis & Emery   5 J 22
17 Cecil Court WC2. 01-240 2129. Music and books on music. Theatrical and musical prints. Catalogues issued.

Truslove & Hanson   2 I 13
205 Sloane St SW1. 01-235 2128. Good general bookshop.

J. M. Watkins   5 J 22
19-21 Cecil Court WC2. 01-836 3778. Comparative and oriental religions, mysticism, ecology.

Wholefood Bookshop   2 D 18
114 Baker St W1. 01-935 9903. Health foods, diet and ecology books.

A. Zwemmer   2 I 22
78 Charing Cross Rd WC2. 01-836 4710. Comprehensive stock of international books on art, architecture and design.

Book binding & restorations

Robert L Green
364 Kingsland Rd E8. 01-254 3098. Hand bookbinding in leather and other materials. Repairs and restorations.

W.T. Morrell   3 I 23
4-7 Nottingham Court, Shorts Gdns WC2. 01-836 6066. Fine quality bindings.

F. Sangorski & G. Sutcliffe   2 H 21
1-5 Poland St W1. 01-437 2252. Hand binding and repairs for rare books.

Zaensdorf
175 Bermondsey St SE1. 01-407 1244. Hand binding in all styles and materials, design service. Repair and restore leather bindings.

Brass rubbing
See under 'Craft shops'.

Buttons
Try the markets — Camden Lock for Art Deco styles.

A. Taylor
1 Silver Place W1. 01-437 5343. Largest variety of buttons in London.

The Button Queen   2 E 18
23 Christopher Place W1. 01-935 1505. Specialise in antique buttons. Will make them into cuff-links.

Paris House   2 F 19
41 South Molton St W1. 01-629 5056. Buttons hand-made to order.

Cacti

H.A. Auger
Waconsta, Bishops Ave N2. 01-455 6086. All kinds of cacti and succulents. Specialists in Epiphyllums — the orchid cactus.

Richelle   2 D 18
4 & 5 Station Approach, Baker St W1. 01-935 1863. The place for cacti and succulents. Will make you up a garden.

Cameras
See under 'Photographic equipment'.

Camping
See under 'Sports equipment'.

Caravans
The British Travel Association will send you a list of sites. The AA has a list of firms that rent caravans, and 'Which' has a free list of firms selling or hiring dormobiles. The following associations will give advice and help on where to buy, hire or equip a caravan.

Caravan Advice Bureau
Link House, Dingwall Ave, Croydon. 01-686 2599.

Caravan Club
For advice on touring and sites, contact East Grinstead House, East Grinstead, West Sussex. East Grinstead 26944.

National Caravan Council
43-45 High St, Weybridge, Surrey. 0932-51376/9.

Carpets: antique

Benardout & Benardout   1 I 10
7 Thurloe Place SW7. 01-589 7658. Persian rugs and carpets, tapestries and needlework. Some French and English stock. Expert cleaners and repairers.

David Black Oriental Carpets   1 A 5
96 Portland Rd W11. 01-727 2566. Kelims, soumaks, tribal rugs etc. Also embroidery. Textile and carpet restoration.

C. John   2 G 17
70 South Audley St W1. 01-493 5288. Oriental and Persian carpets.

Mayorcas   5 J 20
38 Jermyn St SW1. 01-629 4195. Outstanding stock of European carpets, textiles and tapestries.

Persian & Oriental Carpet Centre   2 G 17
63 South Audley St W1. 01-629 9670. Persian and oriental carpets.

Samad   2 I 14
33 Knightsbridge Rd SW1. 01-235 7512. Variety of 18th and 19th cent oriental carpets and textiles.

M. Sasson   2 I 12
4 Cheval Place SW7. 01-589 1133. Antique textiles, embroidery and carpets.

Vigo-Sternberg Galleries   2 I 20
6a Vigo St W1. 01-734 4951. Oriental carpets.

Carpets: modern
The big stores such as Heal's, John Lewis, Liberty's, Marshall & Snelgrove, Maples and Selfridges have large stocks of modern designs.

Casa Pupo   5 K 12
17-25 Sloane St SW1. 01-235 1991. Gaily coloured Spanish rugs.

Charles H. Hall   6 O 33
6 Creechurch Lane EC3. 01-626 3112. Carpets sold at reduced prices — you may be lucky and find a bargain.

Carpet & textile restorers

Anglo-Persian Carpet Co
6 South Kensington Station Arcade SW7. 01-589 5457. Oriental carpets and tapestries.

Armenian Carpet Repairing
12 Brushfield St E1. 01-247 8556. Oriental carpets, Aubussons.

Bernadout   5 M 14
31a Buckingham Palace Rd SW1. 01-834 8241. Oriental carpets.

S. Franses   2 I 14
71 Knightsbridge SW1. 01-235 1888.

Pontremoli   2 B 13
11 Spring St W2. 01-723 6664.

Ceramic restorations

Peter Boswell   2 H 20
67 Beak St W1. 01-734 7909.

Chinamend   4 J 11
54 Walton St SW3. 01-589 1182.

China Repairs
64 Charles Lane NW8. 01-732 8407.

Hall Bros
73 Kenton St WC1. 01-837 5151.

Robin Hood's Workshop   5 L 13
18 Bourne St SW1. 01-730 0425. Also tuition in ceramic restoration.

Charity shops
School and church halls often hold beneficiary jumble sales where both donatos and buyers are welcome.

Oxfam shops
202b Kensington High St W8. 01-937 0833.   1 D 4
91 Marylebone High St W1. 01-486 4111.   2 D 19
85 High Rd N15. 01-800 5207.
There are over a dozen of these shops in London which offer excellent value in second-hand clothes, jewellery, furniture and bric-a-brac in good condition.

Salvation Army Warehouse
124 Spa Rd SE16. 01-237 1107. Second-hand chairs, tables, wardrobes, 3-piece suites, gas-stoves, etc.

Chemists

Boots   2 H 20
182 Regent St W1. 01-734 4934. The most comprehensive chemist in London with four floors selling everything from soap to stationery. Their own range of toiletries are very good value. Smaller branches all over London.

D. R. Harris   5 **J 19**
29 St James's St SW1. 01-930 3915. A very old firm. Specialises in lavender water, their famous 'eau de Cologne' and the original 'Pick-me-up'.

Savory & Moore   2 **G 19**
143 New Bond St W1. 01-629 4471. The shopfront was designed by George Maddox in 1797. As well as pharmaceutical products they sell their own bath colognes and French perfumes. The beautiful bowls and pomanders on show are fine Coalport and Wedgwood china.

Chessmen

C. Barrett   2 **I 19**
51 Burlington Arcade W1. 01-493 2570.

Chess Centre   2 **B 16**
3 Harcourt St W1. 01-402 5393.

China, glass & porcelain

Chinacraft
499 Oxford St W1. 01-499 9881. Fine English china, crystal and figurines. Ten branches, most in central London.

Casson Gallery   2 **D 19**
73 Marylebone High St W1. Run by a potter Michael Casson, The gallery stocks contemporary pottery and holds regular specialists exhibitions.

Craftsmen Potters Shop   ·   2 **H 21**
William Blake House, Marshall St W1. 01-437 7605. Only members of the Craftsmen Potters Association can sell work here. This demands a high standard. Good stoneware.

General Trading Co   5 **K 12**
144 Sloane St SW1. 01-730 0411. Some of the best designs in contemporary English and continental glass. Large stock.

The Glasshouse   3 **I 23**
27 Neal St WC2. 01-836 9785. Here you can see craftsmen making glass — and everything is for sale. Glass blowing courses for beginners.

Reject China Shop   2 **I 12**
33 Beauchamp Place SW3. 01-584 9409. Reject export china at low prices — a bargain as the flaws tend to be hardly noticeable.

Rosenthal China Shop   2 **I 20**
137-141 Regent St W1. 01-734 3076. Specialises in Rosenthal china, glass and porcelain.

Wedgwood   2 **I 20**
158 Regent St W1. 01-734 7262. The famous bone china and earthenware.

Chiropodist

Scholls   2 **I 20**
254 Regent St W1. 01-734 3583. Excellent — reasonably priced and expert.

Cigarette cards
Try the markets — especially Portobello Rd.

London Cigarette Card Co.
34 Wellesley Rd W4. 01-994 2346. An authority on picture-card collecting. Has the biggest stock in the world — 10,000 different series of cigarette, tea and other picture-cards dating from 1880 to the present day.

Ceramics — antique
The principal areas for antique ceramic shops are Kensington Church St and Knightsbridge — remember to look in the back streets.

Antique Porcelain Company   2 **G 19**
149 New Bond St W1. 01-629 1254. Fine English and continental china and porcelain.

Jellinek & Sampson   2 **I 12**
156 Brompton Rd SW3. 01-589 5272. Early English and some medieval pottery.

Newman Antiques
17 Brondesbury Park NW6. 01-459 2506. Fine 18th cent porcelain and faience.

Vandekar   1 **I 11**
138 Brompton Rd SW3. 01-589 8481. Said to have the largest collection of pre-1830 pottery and porcelain in Europe.

Clocks: antique

Aubrey Brocklehurst   1 **G 7**
124 Cromwell Rd SW7. 01-373 0319. Specialise in long case and bracket clocks. Restorations.

Camerer Cuss   3 **H 23**
56 New Oxford St WC1. 01-636 8968. Antique watches, clocks and horological curios. Restorations.

E. Dent   5 **J 19**
41 Pall Mall SW1. 01-930 2811. They made 'Big Ben'. Fine and unusual clocks.

Daniel Desbois   6 **J 26**
51 Carey St WC2. 01-405 7935. Established 1730. Fine quality bracket and carriage clocks.

Phillip & Bernard Dombey   1 **D 8**
174 Kensington Church St W8. 01-229 7100. Mainly French 18th and 19th cent clocks.

E. Hollander   4 **L 4**
80 Fulham Rd SW3. 01-589 7239. French and English clocks, longcases and barometers.

Huggins & Horsey   2 **I 12**
26 Beauchamp Place SW3. 01-584 1685. Specialise in French clocks, particularly of the period Napoleon I-III. Restorations.

Clock restorations
See under 'Clocks: antique'.

D. Boulstridge   5 **L 15**
47 Lower Belgrave St SW1. 01-730 7548.

C. Frodsham   2 **G 17**
5 South Audley St W1. 01-493 7449.

A. Lee   6 **J 29**
122 St John St EC1. 01-253 6901.

Rowley Parkes   3 **I 29**
17 Briset St EC1. 01-253 3110.

Kenneth Philips   4 **L 5**
100 Edith Grove SW10. 01-352 6221.

J. Walker   2 **F 19**
1 South Molton St W1. 01-629 3487.

Clocks and watches: modern
Good selections at Harrods and Selfridges and at most leading jewellers such as Bentleys and Kutchinsky.

Asprey   2 **G 19**
165 New Bond St W1. 01-493 6767. High-class watches and clocks.

Pearl Cross   5 **J 22**
35 St Martin's Court WC2. 01-836 2814. Presentation gold watches from 1880 onwards.

Coins and medals

A.H. Baldwin   5 **K 22**
1-11 John Adam St WC2. 01-839 1310. Good general selection (inside the Adelphi building).

Coins & Antiquities   2 **G 19**
20-22 Maddox St W1. Every variety of coin and medal.

Dolphin Coins
2 England Lane NW4. 01-722 4116. Hammered coins in gold and silver. Rare colonial coins.

B.A. Seaby   2 **F 20**
11 Margaret St W1. 01-580 3677. One of the largest coin shops in the world with 12 coin experts.

Spink
5-7 King St SW1. 01-930 7888. They stock or can acquire literally any coin wanted by a collector. Also mint commemorative medals.

Costumes: antique
See 'Second-hand clothes' section under 'Women's clothes'.

Laurence Corner   3 **C 23**
62 Hampstead Rd NW1. 01-387 6134. Uniforms and accessories from the Second World War onwards; some earlier items.

The Frock Exchange   4 **L 4**
450 Fulham Rd SW6. 01-381 2937. Clothes and accessories of the Edwardian period, the 1920s, 1930s and later.

Mayorcas   2 **J 19**
38 Jermyn St SW1. 01-629 4195. A few 18th cent costumes or earlier. High quality.

Morris Angel   2 **I 21**
119 Shaftesbury Ave WC2. 01-836 5678. Military full dress uniform 1800 onwards. Only for hire.

Orange Box   3 **E 32**
33 Islington Green N1. 01-359 2328. Original clothes and accessories of the 1920s, '30s and '40s.

Crafts: materials and equipment

Candle Makers Supplies   1 **A 1**
28 Blythe Rd W14. 01-602 4031. Sell everything for making your own candles as well as equipment for batik.

Crafts Unlimited   3 **I 24**
21 Macklin St WC2. 01-937 5370. Wax, dyes and jewellery making equipment.

Dryads   1 **D 4**
178 Kensington High St W8. 01-937 5370. Think of a craft and they'll sell you the materials for it.

Eaton Bag Co
16 Manette St W1. 01-437 9391. Raffia, cane, beads, shells and some stones and minerals.

Elder Reed
Riverside House, Carnwath Rd SW6. 01-736 7511. Glass and other materials for mosaics.

Felt and Hessian Shop 3 **G 26**
34 Greville St EC1. 01-405 6215. Colourful range of toy-making materials.
Foamall
5 Crostan St E8. 01-254 6613. Granulated foam for filling cushions or soft toys.
The Handweaver's Studio & Gallery
29 Haroldstone Rd E17. 01-521 2281. Fleece, silks, yarns and other equipment for weaving.
Phillips & Page 1 **D 8**
50 Kensington Church St W8. 01-937 5839. The only stockists of proper brass rubbing equipment.
Prime Leathers 2 **F 22**
30 Tottenham St W1. 01-636 6637. All types of leather for bags, belts and clothing. Also leather dyes.
Thorp Modelmakers 3 **G 27**
98 Grays Inn Rd WC1. 01-405 1061. Balsa wood and all other materials for model making.
Selectasine 2 **E 19**
22 Bulstrode St W1. 01-935 0768. Silk-screen printing equipment. Catalogue available.

Craft shops

Best of British 3 **H 24**
25 Museum St WC1. 01-580 6285. Stock a great many hand-made goods.
Boadicea 2 **I 12**
19 Beauchamp Place SW3. 01-584 2682. Items for the home of specially selected British design.
Craftsmen Potters Shop 2 **H 21**
Marshall St W1. 01-437 7605. Hand-thrown pots from British potters, who exhibit their own selection.
Homebound Craftsmen 1 **D 7**
25a Holland St W8. 01-937 3924. Toys, baskets, bags, knitwear, pottery — all made by the disabled.
Marjorie Parr 4 **L 8**
285 Kings Rd SW3. 01-352 0768. Decorative items for the home — sculpture, ceramics and modern paintings.
V & A Craft Shop 1 **G 7**
Victoria & Albert Museum, Cromwell Rd SW7. 01-589 6371. High quality, modern hand-made crafts.
Warehouse 3 **I 23**
39 Neal St WC2. 01-240 0931. Indian baskets, Portuguese pottery, Dutch clogs and Chinese clothes are just some of the goods sold here.

Crafts: national

Australia 6 **K 23**
Australian Gift Shop, 115 Strand WC2. 01-836 2292.
Britain 3 **I 23**
The British Crafts Centre, 43 Earlham St WC2. 01-836 6993.
China 2 **D 18**
Arts & Crafts of China, 89 Baker St W1. 01-935 4576.
Commonwealth 5 **M 17**
Commonwealth Crafts Centre, 35 Victoria St SW1. 01-799 3950.
Denmark 2 **G 19**
Georg Jensen, 15 New Bond St W1. 01-499 6541.
Greece & Turkey 2 **F 22**
Byzantium, 1 Goodge St W1. 01-636 6465.
India 2 **G 22**
51 Oxford St W1 and branches. 01-437 3979.
Ireland 2 **E 18**
The Irish Shop, 11 Duke St W1. 01-935 1366.
Israel
Israeli Shop, 146a Golders Green Rd NW11. 01-455 4960.
Japan 5 **M 12**
Mitsukiku, 73a Lower Sloane St SW1. 01-730 1505.
Mexico 5 **J 14**
La Cucaracha Galleries, 6 Halkin Arcade, West Halkin St SW1. 01-235 6741.
Persian 2 **D 16**
The Persian Shop, 75 Edgeware Rd W2. 01-402 4710.
Peru 2 **E 18**
Casa Andes, 1 St Christopher Place W1. 01-935 2857.
Russia 3 **I 26**
The Russian Shop, 278 High Holborn WC1. 01-405 3538.
Scotland 1 **I 11**
The Scotch House, 2-11 Brompton Rd SW1. 01-589 4421.
Spain 5 **K 12**
Casa Pupo, 17-25 Sloane St SW1. 01-235 1991.
Switzerland 5 **J 22**
Swiss Centre, Leicester Sq WC2. 01-734 1032.

Cycles

Selfridges and Halfords are good for standard machines.
Wilkins
185-187 Markhouse Rd E17. 01-520 1580. Frames are hand-made to your own specification on the premises.

Cycle hire

Saviles
97-9 Battersea Rise SW11. 01-228 4279. No advance bookings necessary to hire bicycles.
South Cycle Centre
1 Ascot Parade, Clapham Pk Rd SW4. 01-622 4818.
Rent-a-Bike 1 **I 10**
Thurloe Place SW7. 01-584 7676.

Design

The Design Centre 5 **J 21**
28 Haymarket SW1. 01-839 8000. An exciting show-room of the best British domestic design — always up to date. Free and helpful advice from experts and a comprehensive design index — a photographic sample record of over 10,000 consumer goods.

Detective: private

Association of British Investigators
10 Bonner Hill Rd, Kingston upon Thames. 01-546 3368/9. Will supply particulars of investigation and enquiry agents subject to strict code of professional conduct.

Discount shopping

Cheap buys and bargains can often be found by looking in the local newspapers, at newsagents' notice-boards or in 'Time Out', 'The London Weekly Advertiser', 'Exchange & Mart' and 'The Evening Standard'. Charity shops, jumble sales and the markets are also useful for the low-budget shopper.
Cash & Carry Trading Centre
178 Bellenden Rd SE15. 01-639 1437. These shops are all over London and deal in wine, clothes, food, tableware and fashion jewellery. The idea is to buy in bulk and save.

Discount: books

Reduced price bookshops abound in London. Three notable ones are:
The Booksmith
148 Charing Cross Rd WC2. 01-836 3032. 2 **I 22**
36 St Martin's Lane WC2. 01-836 5110. 5 **J 22**
33 Maiden Lane WC2. 01-836 3341. 6 **J 23**
Remaindered books of all kinds — a vast selection as they have about 3/4 million books in their warehouse!
Notting Hill Books 1 **C 8**
132 Palace Gardens Terrace W8. 01-727 5988. Remaindered and second-hand. Good art selection.
Words and Music
120 Charing Cross Rd WC2. 2 **I 22**
5 Marble Arch W1. 2 **E 16**
66-74 Victoria St SW1. 5 **M 17**
21 Queensway W2. 1 **A 11**
174 Fleet St EC4. 6 **K 26**
147 Brompton Rd SW3. 1 **I 11**
172 Kensington High St W8. 1 **D 4**
128 Notting Hill Gate W11. 1 **A 8**
Remaindered books at discount prices and good selections of new books. The larger branches also sell records.

Discount: household appliances

Argos 3 **H 23**
80-110 New Oxford St W1. 01-637 1869. Huge discount house selling small and large household machinery. Branches throughout London.
Bargain Shop 6 **J 23**
21 Tavistock St WC2. 01-240 0883. New radios, stationery, toys, tools, cosmetics, kitchen articles.
Comet
190 London Rd, Hackbridge, Surrey. 01-669 4321. Largest discount warehouse in London. Many of the goods are advertised in 'The Evening Standard'.
H.J. Cooper Co 3 **I 28**
19-21 Hatton Garden EC1. 01-405 1015. Clocks, cutlery, typewriters and much more at cut-prices.
New Dimension
Manor Rd W13. 01-998 2900. Kitchen equipment and other household items.

Discount: furniture and linen

Barkers Bargain Basement 1 **D 4**
Kensington High St W8. 01-937 7272. Good cheap sheets.
Secondhand City 1 **F 2**
222 North End Rd W14. 01-385 7711. Lots of solid furniture. Delivery service.

Discount: records

Discurio 2 **I 17**
9 Shepherd St W1. 01-493 6939. One floor of deletion records — classical and foreign popular.

Farringdon Records   6 **M 29**
42 Cheapside EC2. 01-248 2816. The major shop for classical deletions.

The Virgin Warehouse   3 **H 23**
108 New Oxford St WC1. 01-580 6177. Vast collection of popular music — jazz, rock, reggae, classical, etc. Many deletions.

Drawing Office Equipment & Materials

Admel International
Admel House, 24 High St, Wimbledon SW19. 01-222 5656. Good selection of modern equipment and instruments.

Ozalid Co   6 **L 33**
15-16 Bonhill St EC2. 01-628 5311. Variety of modern equipment and materials.

Ear piercing

Many jewellers will pierce ears but it is better to try a doctor, a beauty specialist or:

Hobbit Enterprises   1 **E 8**
Stall 162, Kensington Market, Kensington High St W8.

Roberts Jewellers   2 **G 21**
527 Oxford St W1. 01-493 3082.
94 Brompton Rd SW1. 01-589 7797.   2 **I 14**

Electrical

Electrical Contractors' Association   1 **B 9**
32-34 Palace Court, Bayswater W2. 01-229 1266. 450 member firms in London area. High standard of work guaranteed.

Electronic shops

Tottenham Court Road and around St Giles Circus is a happy hunting ground for the electronics enthusiast — the area is packed with excellent shops selling all sorts of electronic, radio and tape-recording equipment.

Heathkit Electronics   3 **G 23**
233 Tottenham Court Rd W1. 01-636 7349. Kits for stereo, radios and car radios.

Henry's Radio   2 **A 15**
303 Edgware Rd W2. 01-723 1008. Electronic and radio components, amplifiers, hi-fi equipment. Specialist in transistor valves and parts. Excellent prompt mail-order service.

Lasky's   3 **F 23**
42 Tottenham Court Rd W1. 01-580 2573.

Lindair   3 **F 23**
Lindair House, 227 Tottenham Court Rd W1. 01-580 7383. Europe's first hi-fi department store. Four floors of Hi-Fi, radio and TV equipment. Four demonstration studios.

Teletape   2 **D 16**
33 Edgware Rd W2. 01-273 1942. Specialise in tape-recorders and hi-fi. Branch in Shaftesbury Ave.

Entertainers & lecturers

John Alexander
72 Eleanor Rd E8. 01-254 0416. Traditional show lasting half an hour or longer for children.

Len Belmont
48 Morland Estate E8. 01-254 8300. Children's entertainer with ventriloquist, magic and paper acts.

Children's Party Agency   1 **B 8**
32 Edge St W8. 01-727 8476. Provide entertainers according to age groups. Conjurors, puppet shows, etc.

Foyles Lecture Agency   2 **I 22**
125 Charing Cross Rd WC2. 01-437 8502. Includes many famous names in the academic world.

Junior Jaunts   2 **I 13**
Children's Tours, 13a Harriet Walk SW1. 01-235 4750. Organise supervised river trips, sightseeing and 'energy outlet' tours.

The Kensington Carnival Co   4 **J 4**
123 Ifield Rd SW10. 01-370 4358. Provide entertainers, film shows, presents and toys for children. Hire out playground equipment and child-size furniture.

Escorts: general

Visitors Welcome   1 **F 6**
17 Radley Mews W8. 01-937 9755. Will escort children and adults shopping and provide interpreter guides.

Escorts: social & business

Anina Spitzer Escort Services   2 **I 13**
140 Piccadilly W1. 01-493 5935.

Fabrics: furnishing

Most of the big stores have a large range of furnishing fabrics, particularly Peter Jones, John Lewis and Liberty's.

Afia   2 **D 18**
85 Baker St W1. 01-935 5013. Huge comprehensive stock. Will replace old curtains or covers and copy original design.

Laura Ashley   5 **J 13**
40 Sloane St SW1. 01-235 9728. Fabrics and wallpaper in simple, traditional designs. Excellent value.

Boussac   2 **E 17**
299 Oxford St W1. 01-493 9622. Showroom of excellent French fabrics. You choose and they tell you where to buy.

Distinctive Trimmings   1 **D 8**
17 Kensington Church St W8. 01-937 6174. Full range of furnishing trimmings which they will dye to match your décor.

The Fabric Shop   4 **K 9**
6 Cale St SW7. 01-584 8495. Internationally designed fabrics, many of them originals. Will custom-make and design.

Habitat   4 **L 4**
206 Kings Rd SW3. 01-351 1211. Selection of unusual modern fabrics. Other branches.

Heals   3 **F 23**
196 Tottenham Court Rd W1. 01-636 1666. A large, varied range of modern fabrics in every type of weave and design, all excellent quality.

Russell and Chapple   3 **I 23**
23 Monmouth St, Shaftesbury Avenue WC2. 01-836 7521. Cotton and jute twill in white and colours, and hessian.

Sandersons   2 **G 22**
56 Berners St W1. 01-636 7800. Famous group of modern and traditional fabrics in lovely prints and weaves. Wide price range for excellent quality.

Tamasa Fabrics   4 **L 4**
343 Kings Rd SW3. 01-351 1126. Colourful modern designs — many originals.

Family trees

See 'Genealogy and heraldry'.

Fancy dress hire

Morris Angel   3 **I 23**
119 Shaftesbury Ave WC2. 01-836 5678. Theatrical costume, fancy dress and early military costume.

Barnum's Carnival Novelties   1 **D 2**
67 Hammersmith Rd W14. 01-602 1211. Carnival heads and some costumes.

Berman's & Nathan's   5 **J 22**
18 Irvine St WC2. 01-839 1651. Vast range of costumes for men, women and some for children.

Charles Fox   3 **I 23**
25 Shelton St WC2. 01-240 3111. Costumes from the 16th cent. Also wigs, false beards, make-up, props, etc.

Theatre Zoo   5 **J 22**
28 New Row, St Martin's Lane WC2. 01-836 3150. All types of animal costumes and masks. Also wigs.

Fashion & model schools & agencies.

London Academy of Modelling   2 **G 19**
143 New Bond St W1. 01-499 4751. Established for 20 years having trained many successful models.

Lucie Clayton   1 **I 11**
168 Brompton Rd SW3. 01-581 0024. Secretarial, fashion or model courses. Has schooled many famous models including Jean Shrimpton, Celia Hammond and Maudie James.

Ugly Enterprises Model Agency   2 **I 22**
6 Windmill St W1. 01-636 6247. Strictly non-beautiful people on their books: they take the thin, wide, lumpy and bald — anything but the traditional idea of an elegant clothes peg — to go into advertising, film, etc.

Fireworks

Meierhans   5 **Q 22**
113b Kennington Rd SE11. 01-735 5689. Stock fireworks all the year round.

Fish

See under 'Aquaria'.

Fishing tackle

See under 'Sports equipment'.

Flowers

See under 'Cacti' and 'Gardening'.

Justin de Blank   5 **M 13**
114 Ebury St SW1. 01-730 2375. Fresh flowers delivered for you once a week.

Flower House   2 **E 19**
130 Wigmore St W1. 01-486 4500. Good exotic plants and flowers.

Flower Services (London)   2 **G 18**
2 Carlos Place W1. 01-629 0932. Supplies flowers for weddings, balls and showrooms on contract.

Constance Spry   2 G 17
64 South Audley St W1. 01-499 7201. Famous for exquisite displays of beautiful blooms. Specialise in weddings, balls, parties.

Moyses Stevens   2 H 18
Lansdowne House, Berkeley Square W1. 01-629 5211.

Food: health shops

Ceres Grain Shop   1 A 8
269a Portobello Rd W11. 01-229 5571. Complete range of chemical-free, macrobiotic foods, herbs, vegetables and grains.

Cranks   2 H 21
8 Marshall St W1. 01-437 2915. Appetising health foods, dried fruits and grains.

Culpeper   2 H 18
21 Bruton St W1. 01-629 4559. Sell mainly natural beauty products and herbal remedies, but some health foods and confectionary.

Health Foods   4 L 4
767 Fulham Rd SW6. 01-736 8848. Macrobiotic foods such as organically grown rice, millet, chick peas and soya. Also creams, honeys, fruit juices, cereals and biochemical remedies.

Health Food Shop & Bar   1 I 17
12 Gloucester Rd SW7. 01-584 0372. Foods, cosmetics and herbal remedies. Salads and savouries in the bar.

Holland & Barrett   2 F 22
19 Goodge St W1. 01-580 2886. Complete range of foods and herbs.

Real Foods   1 I 17
63 Cricklewood Bdwy NW2. 01-450 8359. Vegetarian and whole foods, herbal remedies.

Sesame
128 Regent's Park Rd NW1. 01-586 3779. Foods, dairy products and home-made flans, pies and cakes.

Wholefood   2 C 18
112 Baker St W1. 01-935 3924. Organically grown products, free-range eggs and chickens, groceries and even wines. Also a restaurant.

Food: national centres

African & West Indian
Dein's Food Stores, 191 Shepherds Bush Market W12. 01-743 5389.

Ceylon Tea Centre   5 J 20
22 Lower Regent St SW1. 01-930 8632.

Greek   2 F 22
Hellenic Provision Stores, 25 Charlotte St W1. 01-636 4406.

Danish   2 H 19
2-3 Conduit St W1. 01-499 7040.

Dutch   3 I 23
Dutch Dairy Bureau, Dutch House, High Holborn WC1. 01-242 3775. Advisory only.

German Food Centre   2 H 13
44 Knightsbridge SW1. 01-235 5760.

Indian Emporium   3 H 24
10 Coptic St WC1. 01-580 3470.

Indian Tea Centre   2 F 19
343 Oxford St W1. 01-499 1975.

Norwegian   2 I 12
166 Brompton Rd SW3. 01-584 6062.

Spanish   2 F 22
Products from Spain, 89 Charlotte St W1. 01-580 2905.

Swiss   5 J 21
Swiss Centre, Leicester Sq WC2. 01-734 3130.

Food shops

Soho is an area full of small continental shops crammed with exotic foods, wines and spices. See under 'Markets' for cheaper buys and fresh foods.

Justin de Blank   5 L 14
42 Elizabeth St SW1. 01-730 0605. Wide range of freshly prepared dishes and prime fruit and vegetables. Branch in Brompton Rd.

Camisa   2 I 22
61 Old Compton St W1. 01-437 7610. Good general continental delicatessen.

Charbonnel et Walker   2 I 19
28 Old Bond St W1. 01-629 5149. Make succulent numbered chocolates containing 'your own personal message'.

Le Charcuterie Français   2 I 14
7 Kinnerton St SW1. 01-235 7472. Excellent French charcuterie.

Floris   2 I 21
39 Brewer St W1. 01-437 5155. Hand-made chocolates and magnificent cakes.

Fortnum & Mason   2 I 19
181 Piccadilly W1. 01-734 8040. Exotic and unusual tinned and bottled foods from all over the world.

Hamburger Products   2 I 21
1 Brewer St W1. 01-437 7119. Smoked fish. A small

unassuming shop whose owner still home-cures and smokes fish of all sorts: salmon, haddock, buckling, mackerel, trout, sturgeon and kippers. Also snack bar with smoked salmon sandwiches.

Harrods   2 I 13
Knightsbridge SW1. 01-730 1234. Top-quality fresh food.

Maison Bouquillon   1 A 10
45 Moscow Rd W2. 01-229 8684. Good patisserie.

Maison Sagne   2 D 19
105 Marylebone High St W1. 01-935 6240. Croissants, superb sausage rolls, pastries, glacé fruits of all sorts.

Moore Bros   5 J 13
171 Sloane St SW1. 01-235 5145. Main branch. First-class tea and coffee merchants.

Parmigiani Figlio   2 H 22
43 Frith St W1. 01-437 4728. Italian pasta, excellent cheeses and a large variety of garlic sausages. Fresh continental bread.

Patak   3 C 23
134 Drummond St NW1. 01-387 8653. Drummond Street is full of Indian shops and restaurants. Pataks is one of the best — spices, curries and vegetables from India.

Paxton & Whitfield   5 J 20
93 Jermyn St SW1. 01-930 3380. Famous for superb English cheeses and home-cured hams.

Pierre Pechon
127 Queensway W2. 01-229 0746.   1 A 11
27 Kensington Church St W8. 01-937 9574.   1 D 8
High class patissier.

Randall & Aubin   2 I 21
16 Brewer St W1. 01-437 3507. Pâtés, cheeses of all sorts, assorted meats and game.

Richards   2 I 21
11 Brewer St W1. 01-437 1358. Nothing but fish; shellfish, live crabs and lobsters, squid, fresh salmon and sea trout.

Louis Roche   2 I 22
14 Old Compton St W1. 01-437 4588. Importers of French cheeses, fresh vegetables and coffee.

Food: take-away

Fish & Chip shops can still be found on almost every main street in London despite the rise of various rivals. Other common take-away shops are: American — hamburgers, chicken and chips; Greek — Doner kebabs or sheftalia (chunks of lamb or spiced minced meat with salad, in pitta bread); Chinese — full meals to pancake rolls, and Indian curries. Chinese and Indian restaurants often do take-aways. If you haven't walked past a place first, look under 'Take-Away Foods' in your local Yellow Pages. The larger chain shops are:

Bake 'N' Take. To be found mainly in the suburbs. Barbecue chicken, spare-ribs and curry.

Kellyburgers. Good hamburgers, hot chicken and chips.

Kentucky Fried Chicken. Over 60 branches in London. Hot chicken, chips and relish packed in a box.

McDonald's. The famous American hamburgers.

Pizza Express. Restaurants with good quality pizzas to take away.

Foreign newspapers & periodicals

Many of the Soho newsagents deal in foreign papers. European magazines are usually available at the larger newsagents and at the station and airport branches of WH Smith and John Menzies. The following shops stock a good selection of both:

Harrods   2 L 14
Knightsbridge SW1. 01-730 1234.

Librairie Parisienne   2 L 22
48 Old Compton St W1. 01-437 2479.

NSS Newsagents   1 A 8
6 Pembridge Rd W11. 01-229 8020.

Selfridges   2 G 21
Oxford St W1. 01-629 1234.

Solossy   2 L 22
53 Charing Cross Rd WC2. 01-437 2922.

Furniture: antique

See under 'Antiques'.

Furniture: modern

Abode   4 L 4
781 Fulham Rd SW6. 01-736 3161. Pine, cane and woven willow furniture made to order.

Ciancimino   4 L 4
307 Kings Rd SW3. 01-352 2016. Sculptor turned furniture designer — tables and chairs of aluminium and wood in an interlocking system that allows for adaptation in shape and size.

David Bagott Design   1 I 17
266 Old Brompton Rd SW5. 01-370 2267. Specialists in

well-designed pine furniture sold at below normal retail prices as they make the furniture themselves.

Habitat   **4 L 4**
206 Kings Rd SW3. 01-351 1211. Modern international furniture and colourful household goods. Other branches.

Harrods   **2 I 14**
Knightsbridge SW1. 01-730 1234. Widest range of every kind of furniture.

Heals   **3 F 23**
196 Tottenham Ct Rd W1. 01-636 1666. Big selection of the best British and continental designs.

Liberty's   **2 G 20**
210-220 Regent St W1. 01-734 1234. Good contemporary international furniture.

London Bedding Centre   **2 I 13**
26 Sloane St SW1. 01-235 7542. The largest range of beds in London.

Scandinavian Rooms   **2 D 16**
Marble Arch House, 32 Edgware Rd W2. 01-723 8114. Popular Scandinavian designs.

Zarach   **5 K 12**
183 Sloane St SW1. 01-235 6146. Ultra-modern furniture and fittings in chrome, leather, perspex, etc.

Furniture restorers

Peter Boswell   **2 H 20**
67-9 Beak St W1. 01-734 6543. Also cabinet makers.

G.F. Dyer   **3 H 24**
16 & 18 Barter St WC1. 01-405 6788.

Fernandes & Marche   **3 F 31**
80 Islington High St N1. 01-837 8767.

Charles Hammond   **5 K 12**
165 Sloane St SW1. 01-235 2151. Restore antique furniture. Also make fine upholstered furniture and have an interior design and decorating service.

P. Levi
20 Brook Mews North W2. 01-723 1948. As well as furniture, they restore mirrors, sculptures and give advice on framing.

Galleries: prints, paintings & sculpture

Most picture galleries are grouped in and around Bond St, South Kensington and St James's. Camden Lock is an interesting area for contemporary pictures and pottery, as are the open-air exhibitions by London's major parks.
These are a selection of specialist galleries often showing exhibitions of individual's work. See the daily papers, Time Out and the art press for current listings.

Agnew   **2 I 19**
43 Old Bond St W1. 01-629 6176. Outstanding selection of old masters.

Annely Juda
11 Tottenham Mews W1. 01-637 5517. Contemporary paintings and sculpture.

Angela Flowers   **2 E 17**
3 Portland Mews, W1. 01-734 0240. Interesting monthly exhibitions of all kinds of work by younger British artists.

Brook Street Gallery   **2 G 18**
24 Brook St, W1. 01-493 1550. 20th cent masters, paintings and sculpture.

Crane-Kalman   **1 I 11**
178 Brompton Rd SW3. 01-584 7566. 20th cent British and European paintings.

P. & D. Colnaghi   **2 I 19**
14 Old Bond St W1. 01-493 1943. Fine old master etchings and engravings and prints, and early photographs.

Cork Street Gallery   **2 H 19**
16 Cork St W1. 01-493 0745. 20th cent English and French paintings.

The D.M. Gallery   **4 J 9**
72 Fulham Rd SW3. 01-589 8202. Selection of modern art: Hockney, Warhol. Monthly exhibitions.

Editions Alecto   **1 F 7**
27 Kelso Place W8. 01-937 6611. Limited editions of prints and multiples — Hockney, Paolozzi, Dubuffet, Alan Jones, Proctor and Denny.

Editions Graphiques   **2 H 19**
3 Clifford St W1. 01-734 3944. 19th and 20th cent prints and graphics, art nouveau and art deco objects.

Electrum   **3 F 19**
21 South Molton St W1. 01-629 6325. Exhibition of outstanding modern jewellery design, showing brand new work 3 times a year.

Felicity Samuel Gallery   **2 H 20**
16 Savile Row W1. 01-734 8557. Contemporary British and American artists — emphasis on West Coast painters.

Gimpel Fils   **2 G 18**
30 Davies St, W1. 01-493 2488. Contemporary British, American and European art.

Hayward   **5 N 22**
Belevedere Rd, South Bank SE1. 01-928 3144. Important large exhibitions mounted by the Arts Council.

Institute of Contemporary Arts   **5 K 20**
Nash House, 12 Carlton House Terrace SW1. 01-839 5344. An active centre for new movements in all the media.

Marlborough Fine Art   **2 I 19**
6 Albemarle St W1. 01-629 5161. 19th and 20th cent French 'master' paintings and sculpture.

Marlborough Graphics   **2 J 19**
6 Albemarle St W1. 01-629 5161. Large selection of graphics: Kokoschka, Moore, Richards, Sutherland, Nolan, Kitaj, Pasmoore.

Mayor Gallery   **2 F 19**
14 South Molton St W1. 01-493 8778. Contemporary paintings and drawings.

Photographers Gallery   **2 G 22**
8 Gt Newport St WC2. 01-836 7860. Holds excellent photographic exhibitions.

Redfern Gallery   **2 H 19**
20 Cork St W1. 01-734 1732. Very large collection of European graphics. Picasso, Max Ernst.

Roland Browse & Delbanco   **2 H 19**
19 Cork St W1. 01-734 7984. Traditional and modern French and English paintings and sculpture.

Rowan Gallery   **2 H 18**
31a Bruton Place W1. 01-493 3727. Very modern top quality artists.

Royal Academy   **2 I 18**
Burlington House, Piccadilly W1. 01-734 9052. Large special exhibitions, and famous for the annual Summer Exhibition of paintings (May - Aug)

Serpentine Gallery   **1 F 11**
Kensington Gardens, W1. 01-402 6075. Interesting shows of contemporary work, often spreading outdoors.

Waddington and Tooth   **2 H 19**
2 Cork St W1. 01-439 1866. French impressionists, and 20th cent English, American and Continental paintings, drawings and watercolours.

Whitechapel
80 Whitechapel High St E1. 01-247 7125. A policy of orientation to its local community, it holds impressive exhibitions of all types of contemporary work.

Gardening

See also under 'Flowers' and 'Cacti'.

Chelsea Nurseries   **4 L 4**
408 Kings Rd SW10. 01-352 5519.

Clifton Nurseries
5a Clifton Villas W9. 01-286 9888. The best range of gardening plants in London; specialists in town gardens and window boxes.

Dig
Studio, Mills Yard, off Hugon Rd SW6. 01-736 8733. Young and enthusiastic firm tackling garden design. They'll take on any sized job down to window boxes or just tidying up a scruffy corner.

New Covent Garden Market
Vauxhall SW8. 01-720 2211. Cheapest way to buy plants in London — but you must buy by the box. Flower market *OPEN Mon-Fri until 11.00.*

Rassells   **1 E 5**
80 Earls Court Rd W8. 01-937 0481. Everything for greenfingered flat-dwellers; terracotta pots and fibreglass tubs, hanging baskets and window boxes, house plants and herbs, perennials and bedding plants.

Sunningdale Nurseries
London Rd, Windlesham, Surrey. Ascot 20496. Old-fashioned roses.

Thompson & Morgan
London Rd, Ipswich. Ipswich 214226. Seed usually ordered by mail — this is one of the very best for quality. Particularly good for vegetables and unusual varieties.

Tropical Plants Display
64 Emlyn Rd W12. 01-351 0195. Exotic plants and palms.

Garden furniture and ornaments

Crowther of Syon Lodge
Syon Lodge, Busch Corner, Isleworth. 01-560 7978. Famous; thousands of garden statues, fountains and columns in an enormous walled garden.

T. Crowther
282 North End Rd SW6. 01-385 1375. Antique lead, stone and marble garden ornaments and fountains.

Garden Crafts
158 New Kings Rd SW6. 01-736 1615. Ornaments and wrought iron work and furniture.

General Iron Foundry 6 R 29
156 Bermondsey St SE1. 01-407 5588. Specialises in metal gates of all sorts.
Mallett at Bourdon House 2 G 18
2 Davies St W1. 01-629 2444. Garden statuary and furniture.
Peter Jones 5 L 12
Sloane Square SW1. 01-730 3434.

Gemmology

Gemmological Association 6 J 25
St Dunstan's House, Carey Lane EC2. (Next to Goldsmith's Hall.) 01-606 5025. Supply crystal specimens and ornamental materials for students. Gem testing equipment.
Gemrocks 3 F 26
7 Brunswick Shopping Centre WC1. 01-837 7350. A vast stock of minerals, rocks and mounts. Specimens up to 2ft across; books and equipment for amateur lapidaries.
Max Davis Stones 2 G 22
38 Oxford St W1. 01-580 7571. Crystals and cut stones.

Genealogy & heraldry

To help you trace your predecessors and make up the 'family' coat of arms try:
College of Arms 6 M 28
Queen Victoria St EC4. 01-248 2762. Will undertake research and help identify coats of arms. Houses official records of all coats of arms ever granted.
Heirloom & Howard 2 H 18
1 Hay Hill W1. 01-493 5868. Specialists in armorial antiques and genealogical history.
The Heraldry Society 3 H 24
28 Museum St WC1. 01-580 5110. Membership open to all. Small library. Sell heraldic books.
Society of Genealogists 1 H 7
37 Harrington Gdns SW7. 01-373 7054. Help to trace your ancestors. Library if you want to do your own research.

Geology

Gregory Bottley 4 M 8
30 Old Church St SW3. 01-352 5841. The world's largest selection. Fascinating stock of minerals, fossils, meteorites, spread generously over two floors. Geology equipment; gem cutting. Extensive collections of rough uncut jewels and stones at reasonable prices.

Gift shops

Old Curiosity Shop 6 J 25
13 Portsmouth St WC2. 01-405 9891. Immortalised by Dickens, the shop now sells gifts and antiques.
Le Papillon 2 D 15
46 Connaught St W2. 01-402 6924. Lovely gifts which they wrap up specially for you.
Pewter Centre 1 E 6
87a Abingdon Rd W8. 01-937 4118. Anything pewter.
Suma's 2 C 19
31 Paddington St W1. 01-935 4076. Handmade pottery, Welsh tapestry, cushion covers, purses, screenprinted smocks and scarves.
Tortoiseshell & Ivory House 2 D 18
24 Chiltern St W1. 01-935 8031. Also jade.
Xanadu 4 K 10
17 Cale St SW3. 01-352 0536. Mexican animals, glass ornaments, Portuguese cache pots.

Glass: antique

Most antique dealers have good 18th-19th cent glass as part of their stock in trade. See also under 'Antiques'.
W.G.T. Burne 4 K 10
11 Elstan St SW3. 01-589 6074. English and Irish glass. Wine glasses, candelabra and chandeliers from the early 18th cent.
Denton Antiques 2 D 19
87 Marylebone High St W1. 01-935 5831. Victorian decanters, glasses and chandeliers.
Lloyd 5 J 14
11 Halkin Arcade, Motcomb St W1. 01-235 1010. Good stock of glass of all periods, including an enormous selection of 18th and 19th cent decanters.
Howard Phillips 2 F 19
11a Henrietta Place W1. 01-580 9844. English, Irish, Dutch, Venetian, Roman, German and Spanish glass. Outstanding varieties.
Leslie Scott 5 J 14
Halkin Arcade, West Halkin St SW1. 01-235 7395. 18th and 19th cent glass. Also guns and general objets d'art.
Alan Tillman 5 J 14
9 Halkin Arcade, Motcomb St SW1. 01-235 8235. 18th cent glass and French paperweights.

Glass: modern

See under 'China and glass: modern'.

Guns: antique

Also refer to 'Antiques'.
Angel Armstrong 3 E 32
320 Upper St N1. 01-226 5155. Huge stock of guns and militaria.
Collectors Arms Antiques 3 H 26
95 Lamb's Conduit St WC1. 01-405 9982. Assorted antique firearms.
Peter Dale 5 J 19
11-12 Royal Opera Arcade, Pall Mall SW1. 01-930 3695. Antique weapons, armour and militaria for the collector.
E. Fairclough 2 H 19
61 South Audley St W1. 01-493 3946. Fine pistols, swords and militaria. Oriental weapons.
J. Roberts & Son 5 J 22
53 St Martin's Lane WC2. 01-836 1108. Antique guns, pistols and high-quality second-hand shotguns.

Guns: modern

Thomas Bland & Sons 5 J 22
21-22 New Row, St Martin's Lane WC2. 01-836 9122. Representative selection of all types of modern arms.
Holland & Holland 2 H 18
13 Bruton St W1. 01-499 4411. One of the top London gunsmiths.
Cogswell & Harrison 2 I 19
168 Piccadilly W1. 01-493 4746. Excellent selection of modern arms. Good stock of used weapons.
James Purdey & Sons 2 G 17
57 South Audley St W1. 01-499 1801. Fine gunsmiths.

Hairbrushes

G. B. Kent & Sons 2 I 18
174a Piccadilly W1. 01-493 0021. Long established brush maker.

Hairdressers: women & unisex

Most modern hairdressers cater for men & women.
Elizabeth Arden 2 H 19
20 New Bond St W1. 01-629 1200. Create sophisticated styles to complete the effect of their make-up.
André Bernard 2 G 17
94 Mount St W1. 01-629 4314. Specialist in styling for both young and older women.
Molton Brown 2 F 19
58 South Molton St W1. 01-493 6959. Rival to Sassoon in trendy but expensive styling. For men too.
Ricci Burns 4 L 9
151 Kings Rd SW3. 01-351 1235. Eye-catching styles, particularly on short hair. Two branches.
Cheveux 1 E 6
15 Abingdon Rd W8. 01-937 8860. Good reliable styling.
Crimpers 2 D 18
80a Baker St W1. 01-486 4522. Trendy styles for the young of both sexes.
Ginger Group 2 I 13
47 Brompton Rd SW3. 01-584 4714. Up-to-date styling. Many branches.
Hairline 1 I 17
68 Gloucester Rd SW7. 01-584 7193. A good modern salon.
Jingles 2 D 18
125 Baker St W1. 01-935 3929. Trendy salon for fashion cuts. Unisex. Several branches.
Leonard 2 F 16
6 Upper Grosvenor St W1. 01-629 5757. High quality cut and style with top service. Top fashion models come here.
Locks 4 K 8
281 Fulham Rd SW10. 01-351 1123. Popular modern salon.
Mane Line 2 F 18
22 Weighhouse St W1. 01-493 4952. Trendy place for men and women, convenient if you work in the West End.
René of Mayfair 2 G 17
66 South Audley St W1. 01-499 3227. Expensive, fashionable, famous.
Vidal Sassoon 2 G 19
171 New Bond St W1. 01-629 9665. Famous avant garde styles. Will arrange appointments at their other London branches. For men too.
Sissors 4 L 11
46a Kings Rd SW3. 01-589 9491. High fashion styles for men and women.
Smile 2 I 11
15 Brompton Rd SW3. 01-589 8334. Young lively salon with emphasis on cutting to keep the shape.

Steiner   **1 D 4**
Royal Garden Hotel, Kensington High St W8. 01-937 1228. A world famous salon linked with well-known hair preparations. Branches in several hotels and at Victoria and Euston railway stations.

Hairdressers: men
Stanley Alwin   **2 I 21**
110 Shaftesbury Ave W1. 01-437 8933. Some of the leading London hairdressers come here to get their own hair cut.
Fishers   **6 L 28**
28 Cathedral Place, St Paul's Churchyard EC4. 01-236 1767. Modern and pleasant — convenient for city executives.
Michaeljohn   **2 G 18**
6 Carlos Place W1. 01-499 7529. High fashion styles. Also a shop, food and individual TV.
Sweeneys   **2 I 12**
48 Beauchamp Place SW3. 01-589 3066. Fashionable barber in an elegant club atmosphere salon.
Trumper   **2 I 17**
9. Curzon St W1. 01-499 1850. A very famous establishment. Superb shopfront and interior.

Hairdressing schools
Alan International Hairdressing School   **2 I 14**
54 Knightsbridge SW1. 01-235 9591.
21-3 Hammersmith Broadway W6. 01-748 9495. Instructors will cut and shampoo children's hair.
Vidal Sassoon School   **2 G 18**
56 Davies Mews W1. 01-629 4635.

Health clubs
Lotte Berk   **2 D 18**
29 Manchester St W1. 01-935 8905. Exercises to get you into shape prescribed by this lithe 60-year-old.
Body Control Studio   **3 D 25**
The Place, 17 Duke's Rd WC1. 01-387 3578. Specialised exercising for body conditioning. Individual tuition.
Medau Centre
220 Balham High Rd SW12. 01-673 7333. German method of rhythmic movement originated by Hinrich and Senta Medau. Movement room, sauna with plunge pool, massage and rest room. Clubroom with refreshment bar.
Ravelle's Health Centre   **3 E 26**
Clare Court, Judd St WC1. 01-837 3819.
Portsea Hall, Portsea Place W2. 01-402 5704.   **2 D 15**
Individual schedules worked out for a 3-month minimum period. Lates equipment, saunas.
Slim Jims   **2 G 19**
3 Hanover Sq W1. 01-629 3353. Weight reducing and toning up courses for businessmen. Sauna bath. Branch in London Wall.
Town & Country Health Club   **1 I 11**
2 Yeoman's Row SW3. 01-584 7702. Membership for ladies only which allows use of all the club's facilities, including sauna.
Weight Watchers
1 Thames St, Windsor, Berks. Windsor 69131. Write for details of meetings in your area. Group therapy technique with lecturers who are all successful slimmers.

Health farms
Enton Hall
Nr Godalming, Surrey. Wormley 2233. Choice of a detached chalet, a garden room with shower and loo or a double or single room to stay in. Treatments follow naturopathic lines under careful supervision.
Grayshott Hall Health Centre
Headley Rd, Grayshott nr Hindhead, Surrey. Hindhead 4331. Most of the rooms here (there are enough for 100 clients) have their own loo and bath or shower. Naturopathic treatments, hydro-therapy and ultra violet therapy.
Tyringham Naturopathic Clinic
Nr Newport Pagnell, Bucks. Newport Pagnell 610450. In a gorgeous Georgian house with beautiful·gardens, this clinic is also a nursing home.

Hearing aids
A very good hearing aid called 'the medresco' can be obtained from the National Health Service.
Royal National Institute for the Deaf   **3 F 23**
105 Gower St WC1. 01-387 0168. Has an excellent technical department giving advice. Will test free anyone's hearing aid for efficiency.

Herbalists
Culpeper House   **2 H 18**
21 Bruton St W1. 01-629 4559. Also specialists in pure cosmetics, pot pourri and pomanders.

Heath & Heather   **2 F 22**
19 Goodge St W1. 01-580 2886.

Hire shops
Hire Service Shops
1 Essex Rd W3. 01-992 0101. 6 other London branches. Will hire out anything from slimming machines to camping· equipment but specialise in building equipment. Minimum deposit £5; free catalogue.
Hire Services   **1 C 7**
192 Camden Hill Rd W11. 01-727 0897. Almost anything for hire including record players, prams, chairs, etc. 5 other branches.

Icons
Maria Andipa's Icon Gallery   **4 J 11**
162 Walton St SW3. 01-589 2371. Byzantine, Greek, Russian and Ethiopian icons.
Marina Bowater   **1 D 8**
32b Kensington Church St W8. 01-937 1594. Icons and Russian works of art.
Temple Gallery   **1 I 11**
4 Yeoman's Row, Brompton Rd SW3. 01-589 6622. Russian, Greek and Byzantine icons.

Interior decorating shops
Placed to get unusual and attractive household objects as an aid to your own decorating and furnishing schemes. See also under 'Furnishing', 'Furnishing fabrics' and 'Craft shops'.
Athena Reproductions   **2 G 21**
133 Oxford St W1. 01-734 3383. Large selection of posters and blocks. Several branches.
Boadicea   **2 I 12**
19 Beauchamp Place SW3. 01-584 2682. A select stock of British design. They have glass, ceramics, stainless steel and country kitchen wood and rushwork. Some garden and patio furniture.
Casa Pupo   **5 K 12**
17-25 Sloane St SW1. 01-259 1991. Spanish ceramics, glassware, rugs, ornaments and bedcovers.
Deans Blinds
13 Deodar Rd, Putney SW15. 01-789 0121. Make roller blinds to order from your own material.
Dodo
185 Westbourne Grove W11. 01-299 3132. Fascinating oddities, signs, decorated mirrors and old clothes.
General Trading Company   **5 K 12**
144 Sloane St SW1. 01-730 0411. A miscellany of antiques, china, Japanese lampshades and soft furnishings — all in an elegant 'private house' setting.
Liberty's Home Ideas Department   **2 G 20**
210-220 Regent St W1. 01-734 1234. Very attractive household department.
The Louvre Centre & Door Store   **3 E 26**
61-65 Judd St WC1. 01-387 0091. Panelled and decorated doors of all sorts.

Invalid Equipment
British Red Cross   **5 L 15**
34 Grosvenor Gardens SW1. 01-730 0672. For enquiries regarding hire of equipment for nursing at home.

Ironmongery
G. & S. Allgood   **2 D 22**
297 Euston Rd NW1. 01-387 9951. Well-designed architectural ironmongery.
J.D. Beardmore   **2 G 22**
3-5 Percy St W1. 01-637 7041. Very large selection of good reproduction and architectural ironmongery and cabinet fittings.
Comyn Ching   **3 I 23**
15 Shelton St WC2. 01-836 7799. An enormous range of ironmongery designs still produced from old patterns.

Jewellery & silver: antique
Many antique shops deal in silver and jewellery, particularly those in the Burlington Arcade, but the markets and antique supermarkets are best for a variety of choice and price.
Asprey   **2 H 19**
165 New Bond St W1. 01 493 6767. Unusual antique and modern jewellery. Also an excellent range of luxury gifts.
Bentley   **2 G 19**
65 New Bond St W1. 01-629 0651. Long established. Superb jewels and antique silver.
Bond Street Silver Galleries   **2 G 19**
111 New Bond St W1. 01-493 6180. 15 showrooms of antique, modern and second-hand jewellery and silver.
Cameo Corner   **3 H 24**
26 Museum St WC1. 01-637 0981. Victorian and antique jewellery. Also some excellent contemporary designs.

Collingwood 2 H 19
46 Conduit St W1. 01-734 2656. Long established
jewellers to the Queen — antique and modern gold and
silverware.
Garrard 2 I 20
112 Regent St W1. 01-734 7020. Jewellers to the
Queen. Fine antique silver.
Green's Antique Galleries 1 D 8
117 Kensington Church St W8. 01-229 9618. Victorian
jewellery and rings.
M. Hakim 2 G 19
4 The Royal Arcade, New Bond St W1. 01-629 2643.
Fine antique jewellery and objets d'art.
Langford Silver Galleries 6 J 26
46-7 Chancery Lane WC2. 01-405 6402. Antique and
modern silver and gold.
Sac Frères 2 I 19
45 Old Bond St W1. 01-493 2333. Antique amber
jewellery.
S.J. Phillips 2 G 19
139 New Bond St W1. 01-629 6261. Fine jewels, silver
and objets d'art. English and continental.
The Silver Vaults 6 J 26
Chancery House, Chancery Lane WC2. 01-242 3844.
Packed with antique silver and plate.
Tessiers 2 G 19
26 New Bond St W1. 01-629 0458. Fine old firm of
silversmiths. Antique jewels.
Armour-Winston 2 I 19
43 Burlington Arcade W1. 01-493 8937. Fine jewels.

Jewellery & silver: modern
*London is rich in fine specialist jewellery shops. Many
are world famous. Good areas to shop are: Bond St,
the Burlington Arcade, Shepherd Market, Knightsbridge.*
Anschels 4 L 11
33e Kings Rd SW3. 01-730 0444. Craft shop selling
jewellery with a peasant look. Chunky stones and rough
metals, unsophisticated clay pendants, and rings in
plaits and twists of gold and silver.
Argenta 4 J 9
84 Fulham Rd SW3. 01-584 1841. Stunning modern
silver wear from Denmark. Their silversmith will make
up pieces for individual customers.
Asta 5 J 22
31 St Martin's Lane WC2. 01-836 7314. Large selection
of inexpensive fashion jewellery. Good silver and gold
rings.
Cartier 2 H 19
175 New Bond St W1. 01-493 6962. Top-class,
internationally famous jewellers.
Ciro Pearls 2 I 19
48 Old Bond St W1. 01-493 5529. Specialists in pearl
jewellery of all kinds.
Crafts Centre 3 I 23
43 Earlham St WC2. 01-836 6993. Young jewellers'
work exhibited.
Electrum Gallery 2 F 19
21 South Molton St W1. 01-629 6325. Exciting jewellery
by modern designers. Also special exhibitions.
Emeline 2 I 12
45 Beauchamp Place SW3. 01-589 0552. Tiny shop
with well-displayed, exciting modern French costume
jewellery.
Andrew Grima 2 I 19
80 Jermyn St SW1. 01-839 7561. Avant garde.
Distinctive personal jewellery.
Georg Jensen 2 G 19
15B New Bond St W1. 01-499 6541. Modern Danish
jewellery and silver.
Kutchinsky 2 H 19
179 New Bond St W1. 01-629 2876. Fine jewels, and
top-quality Swiss watches.
Mappin & Webb 2 H 20
170 Regent St W1. 01-734 3801. High-quality jewellery
and silver.

Jewellery: hire
Cameo Corner 3 H 24
26 Museum St WC1. 01-637 0981. Hire out antique
jewellery for any occasion.
Robert White 3 I 23
25 Shelton St WC2. 01-836 8237. Magnificent artificial
jewellery for hire.

Jewellery: repairs and restorations
Chelsea Gems 4 L 10
178a Kings Rd SW3. 01-352 8798. Repair any kind of
jewellery and string beads rapidly and for a reasonable
price.
Hillwoods
148 Station Rd, Edgware, Middx. 01-952 5067. Repairs

and restoration to all types of jewellery. Also make
jewellery to order.
Speedy Stringing Service
41 Greville St EC1. 01-405 9985. Any kind of necklace
restrung well and quickly.

Knitting wools
See under 'Needlework'.

Kitchen equipment
*Try the small shops in Soho which supply the local
restaurants. Heals, Selfridges and Habitat have
excellent kitchen departments. The Design Centre in
the Haymarket exhibits the best designs. Also visit the
Building Centre in Store St WC1 for a pre-selection of
kitchen units and fittings. Also see under 'Discount
shops'.*
Elizabeth David 5 L 12
46 Bourne St SW1. 01-730 3123. Complete range of
kitchen pots, pans, knives and pastrycook's equipment
from France and elsewhere.
House & Bargain 2 I 21
31 Brewer St W1. 01-734 9628. Reject kitchenware sold
cheaply. The flaws are scarcely noticeable.
Leon Jaeggi & Sons 3 F 23
232 Tottenham Court Rd W1. 01-580 1957. General
kitchen equipment.
Merchant Chandler
72 New Kings Rd SW6. 01-736 6141. Baskets, china
and glass.
William Page 2 I 22
87 Shaftesbury Avenue W1. 01-437 6285. Excellent
functional 'down to earth' pots, pans and cutlery as
used by the local restaurant trade. (Very reasonable
prices.)
G. Rushbrooke 6 J 28
67-77 Charterhouse St EC1. 01-253 5501. Very exciting
and colourful baskets, scales, aprons, kitchen utensils
of all sorts and sizes.

Language tuition: English
**Association of Recognised English Language
Schools** 3 F 24
43 Russell Square WC1. 01-580 7665. There are many
schools in central and outer London of very high
standard. This association will advise on your individual
needs.
The Canning School of English 1 E 6
4 Abingdon Rd W8. 01-937 3233. Small classes.
Intensive audio-visual courses for continental
businessmen.
Davies School of English 5 N 15
57 Eccleston Square SW1. 01-834 4155. Excellent
language school.
Inner London Education Authority 5 N 22
County Hall, Westminster Bridge SE1. 01-633 5000.
Excellent subsidised long-term education for students
and au pair girls. See 'Floodlight' from newsagents.
The International Language Centre 2 I 21
40 Shaftesbury Avenue W1. 01-437 9167. Good tuition.
Reasonably priced. Social club.
Language Laboratory 2 D 22
114 Whitfield St W1. 01-387 3795. Principally for
diplomats and executives. Crash courses and
immersion courses. *OPEN all year.*
LTC 2 G 22
26-32 Oxford St W1. 01-637 0681. Very good training
centre. Also teach all foreign languages.
The Pitman School of English 2 F 22
46 Goodge St W1. 01-580 8341. Excellent tuition at
reasonable prices.

Language tuition: foreign
*Local adult education centres often hold evening
classes in foreign languages — check at your local
library for details.*
St Giles College
51 Shepherds Hill, Highgate N6. 01-340 0828.

Left-handed
Anything Left-Handed 2 H 20
65 Beak St W1. 01-437 3910. Potato peelers, pen nibs,
scissors — every gadget is designed for the left-
handed.

Lighting
*Good lighting departments at Heal's, Harrods, Habitat,
Selfridges and British Home Stores.*
Homelights 2 H 21
98 Berwick St W1. 01-437 3443. Lots of well-designed
lights.
Thorn Electrical 5 J 22
Thorn House, Upper St Martin's Lane WC2. 01-836
2444. Well designed modern fittings for domestic and
office use. Showroom only.

Christopher Wray's Lighting Emporium   4 L 6
600 Kings Rd SW6. 01-736 8008. Over 2,000 genuine, restored oil and gas lamps. Also a lamp workshop to service, restore, repair or convert to electricity any oil or gas lamp.

Linen

Christy & Son   2 F 20
15 Cavendish Place W1. 01-580 0718. Famous for their high quality towels in lovely colours.

Irish Linen   2 I 19
35 Burlington Arcade W1. 01-493 8949.

Linen Cupboard   2 F 20
21 Great Castle St W1. 01-629 4062. Cut-price household linen, baby linen and Indian bed linen.

London Bedding Centre   2 I 13
26 Sloane St SW1. 01-235 7542. Bed linen of all kinds — duvets, quilts, etc. Lots of beds too!

National Linen Co   2 G 18
20 Brook St W1. 01-629 5000. Table linen and initialled handkerchiefs sold in a rather grand atmosphere.

Locksmiths

Barry Bros   2 B 14
123 Praed St W2. 01-262 9009. Operates *09.00-21.00*.

Haybel & Hogg
Day: 01-229 6779. Night: 01-452 6208.

Maps: antique

Baynton-Williams   5 J 13
18 Lowndes St SW1. 01-235 6595. 100,000 old maps and prints, also charts, plans, views and atlases. Branch at:
424 Upper Richmond Rd West SW14. 01-876 9252. Local Surrey totography and decorative prints. Framing service.

Francis Edwards   2 D 19
83 Marylebone High St W1. 01-935 9221. Large collection of early maps and atlases.

The Map House   2 I 12
54 Beauchamp Place SW3. 01-589 4325. Antique English county maps and some foreign maps; also world-wide maps and guides both new and old.

Weinreb & Douwma   3 H 23
93 Great Russell St WC1. 01-636 4895. Very large selection of old maps, atlases and views.

Maps: modern

Cook Hammond & Kell   5 M 18
22-24 Caxton St SW1. 01-222 4945. Stockists of ordnance survey and other maps.

Stanfords   6 J 23
12 Long Acre WC2. 01-836 1321. Maps of GB and Europe; ordnance survey maps, globes. Will obtain any map, to any scale, of any part of the world — but it may take time. Also guide books.

Matchbox labels

KC Labels
144 Merton Rd, Wimbledon SW19. Large selection of matchbox labels.

Matchbox Label Society
'The Bungalow', Dineridge County School, Esher Rd, Camber, Surrey. Camberley 64884. Will give advice to those starting collections. Publish a quarterly magazine.

Militaria shops

See also under 'Antiques' and 'Guns'.

Call to Arms
79 Upper St N1. 01-359 0501. General range of Third Reich militaria.

Collectors Corner
1 Northcross Rd, East Dulwich SE22. 01-693 6285. Militaria of the world, covering all aspects.

Military war medals

Services war medals can be bought at Moss Bros military department. Also:

Pipe and McGill   6 J 23
44 Bedford St WC2. 01-836 3657. Campaign and World War medals and decorations.

J.B. Hayward   2 I 18
17 Piccadilly Arcade SW1. 01-493 5082.

Miniatures

Arcade Gallery   2 I 19
28 Old Bond St W1. 01-493 1879. A few Indian miniatures and African tribal sculpture.

Asprey   2 G 19
165 New Bond St W1. 01-493 6767. Fine collection.

Green's Antique Galleries   1 D 8
117 Kensington Church St W8. 01-229 9618. Miniatures and netsuke amid antique jewellery.

Limner Antiques   2 G 19
The Antique Centre, New Bond St W1. 01-629 5314. Portrait miniature specialists.

Models

Aeronautical Models
39 Parkway NW1. 01-485 1818. Wide range of kits and accessories. Expert staff.

Beatties   3 I 23
112 High Holborn WC1. 01-405 6285. Once Bassett-Lowke, now modernised. Large stocks of proprietary railway scale equipment, and model cars. Repairs and second-hand department.

BMW
329 Haydons Rd SW19. 01-540 7333. Specialists in good plastic model kits.

Cherry's
62 Sheen Rd, Richmond, Surrey. 01-940 2454. Second-hand model steam engines and ships.

Chuffs Model Railway Specialists   2 A 17
116 Lisson Grove NW1. 01-402 4021. New and second-hand to swap or buy.

Hambling   5 J 22
29 Cecil Court WC2. 01-836 4704. Long established shop well known to the scale layout enthusiast who constructs his own equipment. Very good shop with very helpful staff.

Hamleys   2 H 20
200 Regent St W1. 01-734 3161. Good stocks of commercial toys and train sets. Impressive working train system on show.

Hummel   2 I 19
16 Burlington Arcade W1. 01-493 7164. Collector's pieces. Also some historical dolls.

James Luck
34 High St Southgate N14. 01-886 0334. Large selection of old model soldiers.

Model Railway Manufacturing   3 C 28
14 York Way N1. 01-837 5551. Knowledgeable service and stocks for the enthusiast. Makes own top-quality scale equipment. Full stocks of EM gauge tools.

Motor Books & Accessories   5 J 22
33-36 St Martin's Court, St Martin's Lane WC2. 01-836 5376. Mixture of merchandise: motor books, accessories, models and aviation books.

Henry J. Nicholls & Son
308 Holloway Rd N7. 01-607 4272. A specialist model aircraft shop for the serious enthusiast. All types of aircraft models including the most sophisticated radio controlled models.

Parker Gallery   2 I 19
2 Albemarle St W1. 01-499 5906. Old ship models.

Steam Age   4 K 11
59 Cadogan St SW3. 01-584 4357. Steam models of all kinds, and railway, ship and traction engines.

Tradition   2 I 17
5a-5b Sheperd St, Mayfair W1. 01-493 7452. The best selection of old and new model soldiers in London.

W & H Models   2 D 19
14 New Cavendish St W1. 01-935 8835. Caters for the more expensive train sets, scale models and kits. Hand-built locos on display. English and foreign stocks. Experienced staff.

Motor cars: accessories

Marble Arch Motor Supplies   3 I 24
314 High Holborn WC1. 01-242 8655. Large selection of specialised racing equipment, safety belts and helmets. Specialise in motorists' clothing.

Motor cars: tuning & conversions

Adlards Rallye Sport Centre
Southside, Clapham Common SW4. 01-622 5494.

Allard Motor Co
51 Upper Richmond Rd SW15. 01-874 2333. Sun-roof specialists. Also superchargers and accessories.

Henly's
399 London Rd, Croydon. 01-684 4283. Special tuning dealers.

Chris Montague Carb. Co
380-382 Finchley Rd NW2. 01-794 7766. A Leyland special tuning dealer.

Standish Service Station
327-343 King St, Hammersmith W6. 01-748 0910. Leyland special tuning dealer.

Superspeed Conversions
482 Ley St, Ilford, Essex. 01-554 8307. The principal Ford conversion specialists in London.

Motor cars: used

Remember that the AA will give you a complete engineer's report on a used car (useful also in bargaining over the exchange value).

Berkeley Square Garages   **2 H 18**
Berkeley Square W1. 01-499 4343.

H. A. Fox   **2 I 19**
34 Dover St W1. 01-499 8962. Top-quality second-hand and new Rolls-Royces and Bentleys among others.

Henlys   **2 D 22**
385-387 Euston Rd NW1. 01-387 4444. Enormous stock of guaranteed used cars of all makes, all meticulously overhauled before re-sale.

H.R. Owen   **2 I 18**
17 Berkeley St W1. 01-629 9060. Used (and new) Rolls-Royces, Bentleys and other quality cars.

Motor cars: vintage

Vintage Autos   **2 C 12**
20 Brook Mews North, Lancaster Gate W2. 01-723 2731. Immaculate vintage thoroughbred cars, 1900-1960.

Motor cycles: competition

Alf Hagon Products
350-352 High Rd, Leyton E10. 01-556 9200. Hagon/Jap. The world's leading grass track and dragster manufacturer. Holders of two world speed records and seventeen National Championships.

Motor cycles: touring

Harvey-Owen
181-183 Walworth Rd SE17. 01-703 0282. Kawasaki, Triumph. The most modern and impressive motor-cycle showrooms in London.

D. Lewis   **2 E 21**
124 Great Portland St W1. 01-636 3214. Excellent for all equipment and clothing.

Motor cars and cycles: tuition

Royal Automobile Club   **5 J 20**
83-85 Pall Mall SW1. 01-930 4343. The RAC run training courses at 19 London centres. Will provide cars and bikes if necessary.

Musical automata & boxes

Keith Harding
93 Hornsey Rd N7. 01-607 6181. Cylinder music boxes, polyphons, barrel organs and musical clocks. Also manufacture special parts and do restorations of musical boxes. Stock of reference books.

David Tallis   **1 A 8**
Weaver Arcade, 73 Portobello Rd W11. 01-229 7762. Musical boxes among scientific instruments and watches. Has written a book on music boxes.

Graham Webb   **1 A 8**
93 Portobello Rd W11. 01-727 1485. Musical boxes, barrel organs and street pianos.

Musical instruments: antique

J. & A. Beare   **2 I 21**
179 Wardour St W1. 01-437 1449. Rare Italian violins, violas and cellos.

Bluthner   **2 H 19**
47 Conduit St W1. 01-734 5949. Pianos.

Peter Coutts
43 Perryn Rd, Acton W3. 01-743 8727. Handmade harpsichords.

Harpsichord Centre   **2 D 18**
47 Chiltern St W1. 01-935 3438. Handmade by Michael Thomas.

N.P. Mander
St Peter's Organ Works, St Peter's Close E2. 01-739 4747. Antique organs supplied all over the world. Also restorations.

Robert Morley
4 Belmont Hill SE13. 01-852 6151. Various antique instruments, as well as second-hand and modern.

Musica-Rara   **2 G 20**
2 Great Marlborough St W1. 01-437 1576. Renaissance recorders and reproductions of first editions of the classics.

J.F. Pyne
9-11 Leighton Place NW5. 01-485 1435. Makers of organs, harpsichords. Old pianos.

Steinway   **2 G 19**
1 St George St W1. 01-629 6641. Steinway pianos from 1853.

Musical instruments: modern

Boosey & Hawkes   **2 G 20**
295 Regent St W1. 01-580 2060. Brass.

J. Broadwood & Sons
1-5 Brunel Rd, East Acton W3. 01-749 1337. Pianos.

Dallas Musical   **3 C 23**
67-87 Hampstead Rd NW1. 01-388 7971. Every kind of electronic musical instrument and accessory. Also acoustic guitars.

T.W. Howarth   **2 D 18**
31 Chiltern St W1. 01-935 2407. Specialists in oboes and wind instruments.

Len Hunt   **2 D 16**
Portland House, 351 Edgware Rd W2. 01-724 1488. Famous drum maker. Does repairs for the army and BBC.

Henry Keats
32 Clarence Mews, Clarence Place E5. 01-985 5673. Some second-hand brass instruments; repairs. Manufacturers of bugles, hunting and coach horns.

Bill Lewington   **2 I 21**
144 Shaftesbury Avenue WC2. 01-240 0584. New and second-hand wind instruments.

Qalandar Music
53 West Ham Lane E15. 01-534 6539. Indian musical instruments, parts, accessories, books, tapes and kits. Also technical advice, repairs, workshops and tuition.

Rudall Carte   **2 I 21**
8 Denman St W1. 01-437 1648. Orchestral wind instruments. 200-year-old firm; the Carte is of 'D'Oyly Carte' fame.

Schott   **2 G 20**
48 Gt Marlborough St W1. 01-437 1246. Musical instruments for children; educational sheet music.

SMI Musical Instruments   **2 I 22**
114 Charing Cross Rd WC2. 01-240 3386. Guitars, brass, drums and electrical stage equipment.

St Giles Music Centre   **3 H 23**
16 St Giles High St WC2. 01-836 4080. All sorts of new and second-hand musical instruments. Some repairs.

Musical instrument restorations

J. & A. Beare   **2 I 21**
179 Wardour St W1. 01-437 1449. Restore violins, violas and cellos.

Music: printed, antique

Foyles sheet music department   **2 I 22**
119 Charing Cross Rd WC2. 01-437 5660. Second-hand sheet music.

Otto Haas
49 Belsize Park Gardens NW3. 01-722 1488. Rare collectors' items — Mss and printed music from the middle ages to the 20th cent.

John Hall   **1 I 19**
17 Harrington Rd SW7. 01-584 1307. Victorian lithographic music fronts.

Musica Rara   **2 G 20**
2 Gt Marlborough St W1. 01-437 1576. Unusual and rare old sheet music.

Travis & Emery   **2 I 22**
17 Cecil Court, Charing Cross Rd WC2. 01-240 2129. 19th and 18th cent printed music.

Music: printed, modern

Chappell   **2 G 20**
50 New Bond St W1. 01-629 7600. Long established publishers with a world-wide reputation.

Novello   **2 H 20**
38a Beak St W1. 01-734 8080. Famous publishers of educational, church, vocal, instrumental and orchestral music.

Needlework, embroidery and knitting

D.H. Evans and John Lewis have excellent needlework departments. Most big stores have good wool departments.

Ellis & Farrier   **2 G 20**
5 Princes St, Hanover Square W1. 01-629 9964. Sell all kinds of beads mostly for the embroidery trade; sequins, bugle beads; pearl drops, shaped stones; all colours and sizes. Will dye beads especially to customers' requirements.

Harrods   **2 I 22**
87-135 Brompton Rd SW1. 01-730 1234. Needlework department covers continental merchandise — specialises in tramme tapestries and counted embroidery. Good knitting wools.

Luxury Needlepoint   **2 I 12**
36 Beauchamp Place SW3. 01-584 0499. Everything to do with tapestries either to make yourself or ready-made.

MacCulloch & Wallis   **2 F 19**
25 Dering St W1. 01-629 0311. Large stock of cottons in all colours.

Needlewoman   **2 H 20**
146 Regent St W1. 01-734 1727. English and foreign tapestry and needlework materials, knitting yarns and equipment of all kinds.

Ries Wools   **6 J 27**
243 High Holborn WC2. 01-242 7721. Knitting wools on the ground floor and embroidery, tapestry and rugmaking equipment in the basement.

Seldon Tapestries   4 **M 8**
10 Kings Mansions, Lawrence St SW3. 01-352 7759
Studio specialising in handpainted and tramme
canvases designed for the customer. Will visit homes to
advise. *By appointment only.*

Office equipment

*Many manufacturers sell direct to users, not through
retail shops, and especially so when their equipment
forms part of a system requiring specialised advice. The
following, however, are nearest to supplying a
complete range.*
The Ryman Group   3 **F 23**
200 Tottenham Court Rd W1. 01-636 3388. Large
selection of modern equipment of every kind.
Wagstaff Bros.   6 **M 31**
87 Moorgate EC2. 01-628 7955

Optical instruments   3 **I 23**

Brunnings   3 **I 23**
133 High Holborn WC1. 01-405 0312. Excellent stock of
second-hand microscopes, telescopes and lenses.
Arthur Davidson   2 **J 19**
78-79 Jermyn St SW1. 01-930 6687. Antique tele-
scopes and scientific instruments.
Henry's Home Entertainment   3 **G 23**
227 Tottenham Court Rd W1. 01-637 1601. Latest
Japanese and British astronomical telescopes, binoculars and optical accessories.
Carl Zeiss   2 **E 21**
31-36 Foley St W1. 01-636 8050. Precision binoculars,
magnifiers and scientific instruments including
photometers and surveying equipment.

Opticians

Dollond & Aitchison   6 **K 23**
428 Strand WC2. 01-836 3775.
London Contact Lens Centre   2 **F 20**
66 New Cavendish St W1. 01-935 0542.

Patterns: dressmaking

*See also under 'Needlework'. Dickins and Jones has an
excellent pattern department. John Lewis are the only
store in London to have a dressmaking adviser in their
paper pattern department. Both stores also have good
fabrics, buttons, trimming and sewing accessories.*

Pens

The Pen Shop   2 **G 20**
281 Regent St W1. 01-493 2125. Quality fountain pens,
also repairs.
Pencraft   6 **J 25**
91 Kingsway WC2. 01-405 3639.

Perfume

*Stores and chemists usually stock a large range of all
the more popular perfumes. For something more
unusual try the shops listed below.*
Chanel   2 **I 19**
2 Old Bond St W1. 01-493 7171.
Floris   5 **J 20**
89 Jermyn St SW1. 01-920 2885. Perfumers to the
Court of St James since George IV, specialising in
English flower perfumes, matching toiletries and
preparations for men.
Parfums de Paris
7 Colville Rd W3. 01-992 6838. Stock most of the
famous French perfumes — and lots of less well-known
ones.
Taylor of London   5 **K 12**
166 Sloane St SW1. 01-235 4653. Established in 1887,
this shop still distils its own perfumes for men and
women. Pot pourri, pomanders, perfumes and toilet
waters.

Pest control

*Your local Council offers a free service for the disposal
of vermine and insects, or try:*
Rentokil   2 **I 19**
16 Dover St W1. 01-493 0061. Give free surveys for
rising damp, woodworm and dry rot. Also do the
remedial work as well as clearing out pests.
H. Tiffin & Son   3 **A 32**
125 Offord Rd N1. 01-607 5971. Have been controlling
pests since 1695! Also give advice and action on timber
decay and rising damp.

Pets

See also under 'Animals'.
Battersea Dogs Home   4 **R 8**
4 Battersea Park Rd SW8. 01-622 4454. Choose a non-
pedigreed but deserving pet.

Friends of Animals League
Foal Farm, Jail Lane, Biggin Hill, Kent. 29-72386.
Mainly dogs, cats and rabbits available for adoption by
carefully vetted homes.
National Canine Defence League   2 **D 16**
10 Seymour St W1. 01-935 5511. Provides accommo-
dation and information on other kennels.

Photography services

Atlas Photography   2 **H 20**
4 New Burlington St W1. 01-734 8746. Can enlarge up
to 20ft long with a maximum of 4ft width; anything
wider has to be done in separate pieces.
Express Photo Service
1a Kilburn High Rd NW6. 01-328 3232. Retouching.
Robert Young   3 **H 24**
Museum House, Museum St WC1. Superb technical
craftsmen in retouching and finishing photo prints.

Photographic equipment

Brunnings   3 **I 23**
133 High Holborn WC1. 01-405 0312. Very wide
selection of good second-hand photographic
equipment and cameras.
De Vere   6 **K 26**
1st Floor, 149 Fleet St EC4. 01-353 2783. Manufacturers and importers of professional and industrial
photographic equipment of all types.
Dixons   2 **G 22**
27 Oxford St W1. 01-437 2411. Photographic
equipment. Thirty branches in London all with excellent
stocks.
Dollond's Photographic   3 **I 23**
14 High Holborn WC1. 01-405 1792. Comprehensive
stocks.
Wallace Heaton   2 **G 19**
127 New Bond St W1. 01-629 7511. High-quality new
photographic, cine and projection equipment. Film
library of colour slides of London and Great Britain. All
equipment is tested before being offered for sale.
Kodak   6 **J 25**
246 High Holborn WC1. 01-405 7841. Informative
showroom for film, filters, paper and materials. Expert
advice. First-class photographic exhibitions.
Sidney Levy   3 **I 28**
17-19 Leather Lane EC1. 01-242 3456. Modern shop
adjoining the Leather Lane market — both worth
visiting.
Pelling & Cross   2 **D 19**
104 Baker St W1. 01-486 5411. Very large stocks of
professional cameras and equipment.
Vines   5 **K 21**
8-9 Grand Buildings, Trafalgar Square WC2. 01-839
2581. One of the few places you can buy film on a
Sunday. *(OPEN Sat & Sun.)*

Picture framing

Blackman Harvey   3 **I 23**
29-39 Earlham St WC2. 01-836 1904.
F.A. Pollak   5 **J 19**
20 Blue Bull Yard, St James's St SW1. 01-493 1434.
Scharf
145 Stoke Newington Church St N16. 01-249 6961.
Supplies interesting and varied mouldings to artists and
framers. Excellent stock.
H.J. Spiller   2 **H 20**
37-39 Beak St W1. 01-437 7084. Enormous selection of
genuine old frames from all periods.
J & L Tanous   4 **L 2**
115b Harwood Rd SW6. 01-736 6497. Modern and
antique framing of quality.

Picture restorations

C.P. Anthony   5 **J 19**
6-7 Crown Passage, St James's St SW1. 01-930 2274.
Restors old masters.
Chiltern Art Gallery   2 **D 18**
10 Chiltern St W1. 01-486 1788.
Drescher
17 Alverstone Rd NW2. 01-495 5543. Anything
connected with paper restoration.
Frost & Reed   2 **G 19**
41 New Bond St W1. 01-629 2457.
N. Mackmin
Brantwood, Putney Heath Lane SW15. 01-788 0988.
Moorland Gallery   2 **H 19**
23 Cork St W1. 01-734 6961.

Pipes

Astleys   2 **I 19**
109 Jermyn St SW1. 01-930 1687. Specialise in briar
and meerschaum pipes.
Charatan   2 **I 19**
18 Jermyn St SW1. 01-734 2877. Specialist pipe
makers.

Dunhill   **5 J 19**
30 Duke St St James's SW1. 01-493 9161. Exclusive quality pipes.
Inderwick   **2 H 20**
45 Carnaby St W1. 01-734 6574. Established in the 18th cent. Made pipes for Edward VII. *OPEN all day Sat.*

Plants

See under 'Flowers' and 'Gardening'.

Postcards

John Hall   **1 I 9**
17 Harrington Rd SW7. 01-584 1307. Extensive collection of fine postcards.
Pleasures of Past Times   **5 J 22**
11 Cecil Court WC2. 01-836 1142. Extremely large classified collection of early postcards, greeting cards, juvenilia and theatre data.

Posters & reproductions

The London art galleries usually sell reproductions of their more popular paintings.
The Arts Council Shop   **2 I 20**
28 Sackville St W1. 01-734 4318. Sell a wide range of posters on the arts — also books and specialities for children.
Ashcroft & Daw   **2 I 22**
83 Charing Cross Rd WC2. 01-734 0950. Huge range of posters of animals, stars, reproductions of paintings and book illustrations.
Athena Reproductions   **2 G 21**
133 Oxford St W1. 01-734 3383. Main branch. Good selection of cheap posters and reproductions. Mail order service.
Camden Graphics   **3 E 32**
43 Camden Passage N1. 01-226 2061. Posters from all over the world. Wholesale and mail order service.
Ganymede Press   **3 I 16**
11 Great Turnstile WC1. 01-405 9836. Quality reproductions of paintings from the art galleries.
Imperial War Museum
South Bank. 01-735 8922. Specialise in 1st World War recruitment and other patriotic posters.
London Transport
280 Old Marylebone Rd NW1. 01-262 3444. Excellent posters commissioned from famous artists. Mail order service.
The Lords Gallery
26 Wellington Rd NW8. 01-722 4444. Permanent exhibition of European and American posters (Lautrec to World War 2).
Medici Society   **2 H 19**
7 Grafton St W1. 01-629 5675. Reproduction of famous works of art.
Motif Editions   **2 H 22**
58 Frith St W1. 01-734 1592. Publish original prints and reproductions by well-known contemporary artists.
Pallas Gallery   **3 I 23**
28 Shelton St WC2. 01-836 1977. Large selection of quality reproductions of works of art by the masters.
Paperchase   **3 F 23**
216 Tottenham Court Rd W1. 01-637 1121. Modern and Art Nouveau posters.

Press cutting agencies

Durant Press Cuttings   **3 H 28**
8 Herbal Hill EC1. 01-278 1733.
International Press Cutting Bureau   **6 R 25**
Lancaster House, 17 Newington Causeway SE1. 01-403 0608.
National Press Survey   **3 E 26**
Media House, 8-16 Cromer St WC1. 01-837 2794. Close analysis and information gathering service from the principal UK newspapers.
Romeike & Curtice
Hale House, 290-296 Green Lanes N13. 01-882 0155. Extensive cuttings from newspapers, magazines, trade journals as well as advert checking and a foreign department.

Printing

There are many firms of course, but a personal recommendation is:
Copyrun
21 Tower St WC2. 01-240 1830.   **2 I 22**
25 Victoria St SW1. 01-799 5876.   **5 M 17**
26 Grays Inn Rd WC2. 01-405 8333.   **3 G 27**
Instant printing and copying at top speeds coupled with low prices.

Radio

See 'Electronic shops'.

Raffia

Eaton   **2 H 22**
16 Manette St, off Charing Cross Rd (near Foyles) W1. 01-437 9391. Raffia hats, bags, belts, baskets and mattings. A very mixed shop, it also has tropical shells and fossils at reasonable prices.

Record players

See also under 'Electronic shops'.

Records

Records can be bought very cheaply, because of mass sales, through one of the record clubs. Don't forget that records can be borrowed like books from local libraries — a particularly good one is, Westminster Public Library in Charing Cross Rd WC2. Also see under 'Discount shops'.
Collectors Corner
62 New Oxford St WC1. 01-580 6155 and at   **3 H 23**
63 Monmouth St WC2. 01-836 5614.   **3 I 23**
English and foreign, vocal and operatic and classical records, including some very early rare recordings.
Collets   **2 I 21**
180 Shaftesbury Ave WC2. 01-240 3969. Jazz and folk music.
James H. Crawley
246 Church St N9. 01-807 7760. Rare and unusual records from 1900 to 1945. Operatic (e.g. Carusoe, early film star recordings and even earlier actors such as Beerbohm Tree). World-famous. Over 200,000 records (all 78rpm). *Appointment only.*
Discurio   **2 I 17**
9 Shepherd St W1. 01-493 6939. Foreign and unusual records; classical.
Dobell's   **2 I 22**
75-77 Charing Cross Rd WC2. 01-437 3075. Complete stocks of jazz, folk and blues records.
Gramophone Exchange   **2 I 21**
80 Wardour St W1. 01-437 5313. Large stock of early collectors' records.
Harlequin Record Shops   **6 K 26**
167 Fleet St EC4. 01-583 3434. Many branches of this excellent shop all over London. Popular and classical.
HMV Record Store   **2 E 17**
363 Oxford St W1. 01-629 1240. Probably the most comprehensive stock in London.
The Record Exchange
90 Goldhawk Rd W12. 01-749 2930. Large stock of all sorts of records. You can exchange your old records or select from the hundreds of second-hand ones.
W.H. Smith
Branches throughout London have record departments.
Henry Stave   **2 H 22**
8 Dean St W1. 01-437 2757. Specialises in classical records but will obtain any popular disc to order.
Virgin Records   **2 G 22**
24 Oxford St W1. 01-580 5755. Progressive and popular music, blues, jazz, classical — almost everything at below the recommended price. Many branches.

Replicas

The Cast Service   **3 G 24**
British Museum Publications, 6 Bedford Sq WC1. 01-323 1234. Replicas of famous historical sculpture and works of art in the museum for sale.

Saunas

Telephone for appointment as times vary considerably. See also under 'Health clubs' and 'Turkish baths'.
Olive Beaucham   **1 E 6**
15 Abingdon Rd W8. 01-937 8659. A beauty salon where you can sauna for as long as you like and then have a massage.
City Saunas   **6 L 32**
City Wall House, 22 Finsbury St EC2. 01-628 7117. Men only.
Clarendon Court Hotel Sauna
Maida Vale W9. 01-286 7227. Sauna and massage for women.
Harrods Beauty Salon   **2 I 12**
Knightsbridge SW1. 01-584 8881. Excellent salon with sauna facilities.
London Sauna Cabins   **6 J 23**
47 Bedford St WC2. 01-240 2748.
Oasis   **3 I 23**
Endell St WC2. 01-836 3771. Swimming pools and mixed sauna.
Strand Sauna   **6 K 23**
396 Strand WC2. 01-240 1766. For men only.

Scientific equipment

Generally visit Wigmore St and neighbouring areas for most of the reputable scientific and medical shops. Also visit the Labex International Exhibition at Earls Court — the largest scientific exhibition in England.

A. Gallenkamp   6   L 33
6 Christopher St EC2. 01-247 3211. Extensive stocks of scientific apparatus, instruments and glassware. Laboratory furniture and fittings.

Scientific Supplies   3   H 28
Scientific House, Vine Hill EC1. 01-278 8241. Any small item of scientific equipment can be purchased here.

Secretarial services

See under 'Business information services'.

Sex supermarkets

Anne Summers   2   D 16
18 Edgware Rd W2 (near Marble Arch). 01-262 4357. The original sex supermarket, with all types of contraceptives, gadgets, and aids to being a super man or woman. Helpful staff and demonstrations.

The Pellen Centre
1a West Garden Rd N15. 01-802 7781. Lower prices than the West End shops. Helpful staff and an expert doctor on sexual problems comes in twice a week for private consultations.

Lovecraft   2   B 14
161 Praed St W1. 01-723 7115. Amusement arcade-like sex supermarket. Wide selection of products. Branch in Charing Cross Rd.

Harmony Time   3   E 29
287 Pentonville Rd N1. 01-278 9170. Several branches.

Silver

See under 'Jewellery & silver'.

Sound recording

'Contacts' is a paper available at newsagents that gives a comprehensive list of recording studios.

Sponges

Maitlands   2   I 18
175 Piccadilly W1. 01-493 1975. Marvellous selection of natural sponges in all sizes.

Sports equipment: general shops

Lillywhites   5   J 20
Lower Regent St SW1. 01-930 3181. Excellent general stock of top English and continental equipment. Archery, underwater equipment, and most other sports.

Gordon Lowes   5   K 12
173 Sloane St SW1. 01-235 8484. Continental and English clothes and equipment.

Pindisports   6   J 27
14-18 Holborn EC1. 01-242 3278. Good British and continental ski-ing, camping and mountaineering equipment.

Sports equipment: boating & yachting

Arthur Beale   3   I 23
194 Shaftesbury Avenue WC2. 01-836 9034. Excellent small yacht chandler.

Boat Showrooms of London   1   D 6
284 Kensington High St W14. 01-602 0123. All types of boats from cruisers to dinghies. Clothing and accessories. Specialists in inflatable boats.

Thomas Foulkes
Lansdowne Rd, Leytonstone E11. 01-539 5084. Probably the best selection in London of all types of gear and equipment.

London Yacht Centre   6   N 33
13 Artillery Lane E1. 01-247 0521. Very large stock of boating equipment with the advantage of being near Liverpool St Station — gateway to the East coast yachting resorts.

Capt. O.M. Watts   2   I 19
48 Albemarle St W1. 01-493 4633. World-famous. One can buy anything from a length of rope to a luxury yacht. They are also yacht brokers.

Sports equipment: camping and mountaineering

Pindisports have good camping stocks; Simpsons and Lillywhites have small camping sections.

Blacks of Greenock   3   H 27
22-24 Gray's Inn Rd WC1. 01-405 4426. Now amalgamated with the well-known firm of Edgington. Probably the most versatile camping shop in London. Make their own tents and also supply the best British and continental equipment and clothing: have equipped many mountaineering expeditions.

Camping Centre
20-4 Lonsdale Rd, Queens Park NW6 01-328 2166. Possibly the largest exhibition of tents in the country — also trailer tents.

Milletts   5   J 21
445 Oxford St W1. 01-491 7381. Inexpensive equipment and clothes. Many branches.

Robert Lawrie   2   D 16
54 Seymour St W1. 01-723 5252. Alpine and polar equipment. Hand-sewn boots for all purposes, mountaineering, ski-ing, walking. Repairs and re-nailings.

Youth Hostels Association   5   K 22
29 John Adam St WC2. 01-839 1722. Large stocks of climbing, ski-ing and camping clothes and equipment Also an outdoor holiday travel department.

Sports equipment: cricket

Lillywhites have a good stock of cricket bats and equipment and a cricket expert in charge.

Jack Hobbs   3   F 31
11a Islington High St N1. 01-837 8611. The son of the famous cricketer. The shop is steeped in cricket tradition.

Sports equipment: fencing

Leon Paul   3   H 25
14 New North St WC1. 01-405 3832. World-famous fencing equipment designed and tested to Olympic standards.

Sports equipment: fishing

Benwoods
60 Church St NW8. 01-723 9970. Impressive range of high-class gear.

Don's of Edmonton
246 Fore St N18. 01-807 5396. The proprietor Don Neish is a capable all-round angler. Good stock.

C. Farlow   5   J 19
5b Pall Mall SW1. 01-839 2423. Modern approach to anglers' needs. Specialists in game fishing tackle. Staff are all anglers. Established 1840.

Hardy Bros   5   J 19
61 Pall Mall SW1. 01-831 5515. Finest handmade rod makers in the world.

Sports equipment: riding & saddlery

Giddens of London   2   H 19
15d Clifford St W1. 01-253 2888. Top quality riding clothes. Manufacture their own saddles.

Moss Bros   6   J 23
Bedford St WC2. 01-240 4567. Stock saddles, equipment and riding clothes.

George Parker & Sons   5   J 22
12 Upper St Martin's Lane WC2. 01-836 1164. Make and sell every kind of saddlery, harness and horse clothing, also sell second-hand and unusual saddles: Spanish and Argentinian.

Bernard Weatherill   2   I 19
33a Dover St W1. 01-734 1344. Excellent sporting tailors. Specialists in breeches.

Sports equipment: shooting

See under 'Guns'.

Sports equipment: ski-ing

Pindisports, Lillywhites, Simpsons, Harrods and Moss Bros have good ski clothes and equipment.

Sports equipment: sub-aqua

The basic equipment needed is a wet suit, aqualung and harness, demand valve, weight belt, knife, fins, mask and snorkel. A life-jacket is also considered essential. There are numerous accessories from badges to sophisticated decompression meters. The following shops can fully equip you; they both have compressors (for refilling your aqualung).

Collins & Chambers
197-201 Mare St E1. 01-985 0752. Seibe-Gorman, Farallon, Aquastar and Pirelli concessionaires. Wide range of quality gear. Ten percent discount to BSAC members.

Sportsways
57-59 Balham High Rd SW12. 01-385 4874. Large, friendly shop with a wide range of equipment at discount prices.

Sports equipment: tennis & golf

Gordon Lowes   5   K 12
173 Sloane St SW1. 01-235 8484. Continental and English clothes and equipment for tennis, ski-ing and shooting.

Simpsons   2   I 20
203 Piccadilly W1. 01-734 2002. Good range of golf and tennis equipment. Expert and helpful staff.

Stamps

J.M. Banin   6 **K 23**
Manfield House, 376-9 Strand WC2. 01-240 1682. GB and the Commonwealth.

Bridger & Kay   6 **K 23**
86 Strand WC2. 01-836 2316. British, Colonial and Commonwealth stamps from Queen Victoria to Queen Elizabeth II.

Central Stamp Gallery   2 **H 20**
277 Regent St W1. 01-493 2467. Israel and the Middle East.

A. Constantine   5 **K 22**
124 Grand Blds, Trafalgar Square WC2. 01-930 6933. France, colonies, China, Russia and Western Europe.

David Field   2 **I 18**
42 Berkeley St W1. 01-499 5252. British and Commonwealth.

Stanley Gibbons   6 **K 23**
391 Strand WC2. 01-836 8444. World-famous for stamps and catalogues. New issues to classics.

W.E. Lea   5 **K 22**
1 The Adelphi, John Adam St WC2. 01-930 1688. Rare postage stamps of the world.

H.A. Wallace   6 **N 32**
94 Old Broad St (entrance London Wall) EC2. 01-588 5306. Classic issues of Gt Britain and the Commonwealth.

Stores

A list of the many large stores where you can buy practically anything. Most have restaurants and serve good reasonably priced lunches and afternoon teas.

Bourne & Hollingsworth   2 **G 21**
116 Oxford St W1. 01-636 1515. Fashion, accessories and large haberdashery and lingerie departments. Good food hall, catering service for weddings, etc.

Debenhams   2 **F 19**
344-8 Oxford St W1. 01-580 3000. Fashionable clothes at reasonable prices. Good departments for kitchenware, lingerie, hosiery and cosmetics.

Dickins & Jones   2 **G 20**
Regent St W1. 01-734 7070. American and continental women's clothes. Excellent corsetry department.

Fortnum & Mason   2 **I 19**
181 Piccadilly W1. 01-734 8040. World-famous. Luxury goods and exotic foods. Superb hampers for all occasions.

Harrods   2 **I 12**
Knightsbridge SW1. 01-730 1234. Vast selection of high quality goods. Expensive fabrics from Italy, Switzerland and France. Excellent needlecraft department of tapestry wool and silk threads. Large selection of handbags, often in unusual colours. 'Way In' boutique. Magnificent marbled Edwardian food department.

Peter Jones   5 **L 12**
Sloane Square SW1. 01-730 3434. Furniture, glass, china. Largest furnishing fabric department in London. Excellent linen department; bright coloured sheets in all sizes. Young boutique clothes.

John Lewis   2 **F 19**
Oxford St W1. 01-629 7711. Lively and forward-looking store good for pleasant browsing. Automatic lifts and all goods out on display. Largest dress department in London. Hairdressing salon (prompt, inexpensive and friendly service with snacks under the drier). Large furnishing fabric department.

Liberty's   2 **G 20**
Regent St W1. 01-734 1234. Fashionable. Printed fabrics department is famous. Modern furniture and kit kitchen goods.

Marks & Spencer   2 **G 21**
173 & 458 Oxford St W1. 01-734 4904. Excellent quality separates and accessories, coats, food, home furnishings, etc. Nothing can be tried on but everything can be brought back for exchange or refund. Good value. Many branches.

Harvey Nichols   2 **I 14**
Knightsbridge SW1. 01-235 5000. Stylish clothes, houseware and home furnishings.

Selfridges   2 **E 18**
400 Oxford St W1. 01-629 1234. Limitless household department. Furniture, fashion, toys.

Simpsons   2 **I 20**
203 Piccadilly W1. 01-734 2002. Five floors with good quality luggage, handbags and sportswear.

Tattooing

Jocks Tattoo Studio   3 **E 29**
287 Pentonville Rd N1. 01-837 0805. American colours used with hygienic methods. Removals on appointment.

Telephone answering service

Answering   2 **D 17**
16 Jacobs Well Mews (off George St) W1. 01-935 6655. 24-hour acceptance of calls.

Air Call   5 **O 16**
176-184 Vauxhall Bridge Rd SW1. 01-834 7946.

Theatrical suppliers

See also 'Fancy dress' 'Antique hire' and 'Furniture hire'.

Old Times Furnishings
135 Lower Richmond Rd SW15. 01-788 3551. Stage furniture on hire.

Robinsons   3 **I 23**
76 Neal St WC2. 01-240 0110. Stage property.

Tobacco & snuff

Good modern shops are Dunhill and Bewlay with branches everywhere. The following are, however, outstanding:

James J. Fox   2 **I 19**
2 Burlington Gardens, Old Bond St W1. 01-493 9009. Sell the finest Havana cigars.

Fribourg & Treyer   5 **J 21**
34 Haymarket SW1. 01-930 1305. One of London's 'historical' tobacconists; worth visiting for the architecture as much as for the excellent tobaccos and snuffs. Scales suspended from the ceiling.

Radfords   6 **K 26**
145 Fleet St EC4. 01-353 3700. Tobacco mixtures, cigars and snuffs as well as excellent briars. Established since 1700. Customers go right back to Samuel Johnson.

Smith's Snuff Shop   2 **I 22**
74 Charing Cross Rd WC2. 01-836 7422. Colourful blue and gold 19th cent shopfront. Inside has old Victorian tobacco adverts and rich snuff jars. A great snuff house. *OPEN Mon-Sat until 18.00.*

Tools

Buck & Ryan   3 **G 23**
101 Tottenham Court Rd W1. 01-636 7475. Very large stock of all essential tools.

Tyzack   6 **J 32**
341 Old St EC1. 01-739 8301. Also make their own high-quality machinery.

Toys

See under 'Children's shopping'.

Turkish baths

Epsom Municipal Turkish Baths
East St, Epsom, Surrey. Epsom 22111. For men and women on different days of the week.

Ladywell Baths
Lewisham High St SE13. 01-690 2123. Excellent and inexpensive.

Porchester Hall   1 **A 11**
Queensway, Bayswater W2. 01-229 3226. Public and cheap.

Veterinary clinics

Battersea Dog's Home   4 **R 8**
4 Battersea Pk Rd SW8. 01-622 4454. Free out-patients clinic.

Beaumont Animals Hospital   3 **A 26**
Royal Vetinary College, Royal College St NW1. 01-387 8134.

Blue Cross Animals Hospital   5 **M 14**
1 Hugh St SW1. 01-834 5556.

People's Dispensary for Sick Animals
PDSA House, South St, Dorking, Surrey. 0306-81691. For London enquiries write to The Secretary, PDSA, 5-7 Hurst Rd, Croydon, or phone 01-686 3972.

Wallpapers

Cole & Sons   2 **F 21**
18 Mortimer St W1. 01-580 1066. Exclusive and unusual French and continental prints. Fine modern and traditional English hand-blocked designs.

Elizabeth Eaton   2 **I 13**
25a Basil St SW3. 01-589 0118. Pretty American wallpapers in cottagey prints. Fabrics and furniture too.

Home Decorating   5 **J 12**
83 Walton St SW3. 01-584 6111. French and other continental papers with matching fabrics.

Osborne & Little   4 **L 4**
304 Kings Rd SW3. 01-352 1456. Range of stunning hand-printed designs, some on metallic backgrounds.

Plus Two   4 **J 11**
79 Walton St SW3. 01-589 4996. Excellent selection of wallpapers, floorings and fabrics.

Sandersons   2 G 22
52 Berners St W1. 01-636 7800. Very large and well-laid-out showroom displaying 'easy to see' English and continental papers — hand-printed, textural, flocks, imitation marbles and murals. Also good matching fabrics.

Wigs

See 'Hairpieces & wigs' under 'Women's clothes'.

Wine

Most chain store wine merchants in London belong to big organisations who buy in bulk — Harveys is one of the best. Also listed are some completely independent shops specialising in individual service and small excellent parcels of wine. Harrods have a good wine department which buys selectively and independently. Soho is well worth searching for passable cheap wines.

Berry Bros & Rudd   5 J 19
3 St James's St SW1. 01-930 1888. Charming old wine merchant's shop. First-class list. Independent merchant.

Christie's   5 J 19
8 King St SW1. 01-839 9060. Wine auctions usually held on Thursdays.

Christophers   5 J 20
4 Ormond Yard SW1. 01-930 5557. A good sound old-fashioned independent wine merchant.

Dolamore   2 A 15
16 Paddington Green W2. 01-723 2223. Small independent wine merchant who has been in business over 125 years.

Hampstead Wine Co
29 Heath St NW3. 01-794 5464. Free off licence. Helpful and knowledgeable service, excellent wines.

Harveys of Bristol   5 J 19
27 Pall Mall SW1. 01-839 4091. Long-established group with excellent list.

Hedges & Butler   2 H 20
153 Regent St W1. 01-734 4444. Long-established reliable wine merchants.

Justerini & Brooks   5 J 19
61 St James's St SW1. 01-493 8721.

Oddbins   6 K 28
41 Farringdon St EC4. 01-236 7721. (Other branches.) Jumbo bottles of perfectly drinkable plonk as well as bargains in more illustrious wines.

Soho Wine Market   2 H 22
3 Greek St W1. 01-437 9311. Cut-price wines and spirits — some excellent bargains.

Wine clubs

Justerini & Brooks, Harveys and some others (see under 'Wine') will lay down wine and will help customers invest in good wines.

Unit Wine Club   6 N 32
109 Old Broad St EC2. 01-638 4761. Members can have good wines put aside for future drinking or investment. Subscription includes storage and a report on maturing.

Wine making

W.R. Loftus   2 F 22
1-3 Charlotte St W1. 01-636 6235. Pioneers of home wine-making. Wide range of supplies and expoert advice.

Markets

There are two main sorts of markets: vast wholesale complexes which sell only in bulk and where the visitor will be entranced by the bright stabbing colours, the noise and the smells, and those where the stall-holders will mesmerise you into parting with your money under the impression that anything and everything is a bargain — try not to be deceived into believing them. There are literally hundreds of these markets: with their rich variety of goods and people they make shopping an event infinitely preferable to trailing round the chain stores buying canned goods in time to canned music. Some of London's best known markets are listed below: local Town Halls will supply full details of addresses and times. Remember that on wet days and Mondays markets tend to be fairly dead.
Also see 'Markets' and 'Supermarkets' under 'Antiques'.

Bermondsey and New Caledonian Market   6 R 29
Between Tower Bridge Rd and Bermondsey St SE1. A vast number of antique and junk stalls mostly aimed at collectors and dealers, although the large variety and specialist goods make for fascinating browsing. There is a large indoor market and comforting snack bars and cafés for cold early mornings. *OPEN Fri only.*

Berwick Street   2 H 21
Soho W1. It's worth braving the aggressive stall-holders: the fruit and vegetables are good, and prices reasonable, particularly at the southern end of the street. *Mon-Sat 08.00-19.00.*

Billingsgate (wholesale)   6 P 30
Lower Thames St EC3. 400 tons of fish are handled daily. There's been a market on the site since Saxon times, the rich, ripe tang that pervades the area seems adequate confirmation of this. The porters wear white smocks and strange leather helmets (which enable them to balance crates on their heads). *Mon-Sat from 06.00. Sun — shellfish only.*

Borough Market   6 O 26
8 Southwark St SE1. Wholesale fruit and vegetable market under the railway arches of London Bridge. *Mon-Sat from 06.00.*

Brixton
Radiating from Atlantic Rd SW9. Large general market with a distinct West Indian flavour; exuberant atmosphere heightened by the loud reggae music reverberating around the railway arches. *Mon-Sat.*

Camden Lock
Where Chalk Farm Rd crosses Regent's Canal NW6. Small antique, junk and bric-a-brac market. Also art and craft shops set in a cobbled courtyard beside the pretty lock and canal walks. Good hot food stand by the entrance. *Sat & Sun 08.00-18.00.*

Camden Passage   3 E 32
Islington High St N1. A paved walk lined with a mixture of shops and stalls; the haunt of the trendies, selling a mixture of antiques and attractive, but expensive, bric-a-brac. Particulary fine art-deco shop and opposite, a print shop which repays frequent visiting. *Mon-Sat 09.00-18.00.*

Camden Town
Inverness St NW1. Fruit, vegetables and a few junk stalls. *Wed, Fri & Sat.*

Chapel Market   3 E 31
White Conduit St, off Liverpool Rd N1. General market selling cheap fruit and vegetables and other tat; also pet stall. *CLOSED Thurs & Sun afternoons.*

Chelsea Antiques Market   4 L 4
253 Kings Rd SW3. Large confused market spreading back from the Kings Rd. Mostly general stock, but some specialists. Worth including on a visit to the area.

Cheshire St & The East End
Off Whitechapel Rd towards Houndsditch E2. Traditionally the East End is rich in markets, and the network of streets north of the Whitechapel Rd are filled on Sundays with stalls selling every kind of merchandise. Early on Sun morning the junk and second-hand dealers spread over the road into Cheshire St and nearby.

Church St & Bell St NW1.   2 A 16
Small general antiques and junk markets. *Mon-Sat.*

Club Row
Sclater St E1. Dealers have been selling animals of all kinds at Bethnal Green end for over 100 years. Farther up there are a few more animal stalls scattered between china and household goods. The R.S.P.C.A. see to it that the animals are well looked after. *Sun mornings.*

Columbia Road Market
Hackney E2. Flowers and plants. *Sun.*

Covent Garden   5 R 14
Nine Elms SW8. London's foremost wholesale fruit, vegetable and flower market which has only been in its present location since the end of 1974. Some of the old charm and vitality have been lost in the move from the age-old site in the centre of London, but it's still extremely lively and well worth a visit if you can get up in time. *Mon-Sat from 04.00.*

The Cut   6 O 24
Lower Marsh Rd, off Waterloo Rd SE1. Fruit, vegetables and all sorts of household items. *Mon-Sat.*

Cutler St   6 O 33
Houndsditch E1. This small market specialises in silver, jewellery and coins. It's a dealers' market so there are some good items. *Sun mornings.*

East Street
off Walworth Rd SE17. General items sold in the week, but mainly fruit, vegetables, plants and flowers *Sun mornings. Tues-Sun. CLOSED Thurs & Sun afternoons.*

Farringdon Road   3 G 28
Clerkenwell EC1. Old and rare books. *Mon-Sat.*

High Street
Walthamstow E17. Over a mile of stalls and shops selling literally everything. Crowded and noisy. *Thurs, Fri & Sat.*

Kensington Market   1 E 8
Kensington High St W8. A maze of off-beat clothes mingled with jewellery, antiques and records. Stall-

holders prepared to buy, sell and barter. *Mon-Sat 10.00-18.00.*

Kingsland Road
Hackney E8. Antiques, curios, clothes, fruit and vegetables. *Sat 09.00-18.00.*

Leadenhall Market **6 O 31**
Gracechurch St EC3. General retail market: vegetables, poultry, plants, fish and endless other items. The late Victorian glass and ironwork of the building is superb. *Mon-Fri 09.00-17.00.* Shellfish on *Sun.*

Leather Lane **3 I 28**
Holborn EC1. Vast range of goods, much of which may well have 'fallen off the back of a lorry'. *Mon-Fri 11.00-15.00.*

Petticoat Lane **6 N 33**
Radiates from Middlesex St E1. Huge bustling complex selling everything under the sun; some bargains, lots of rubbish but, most important, an atmosphere of fun. Some of the streets leading off the main road of stalls specialise in one type of thing e.g. **Club Row** deals in fish, birds, reptiles and mammals while neighbouring **Brick Lane** is good for furniture and electrical equipment. *Sun only.*

Portobello Road **1 A 8**
Nr Notting Hill Gate tube W11. Superb flea-market, though now too well known for many bargains to exist. Vegetables, fruit and flowers *Mon-Sat 07.00-18.00* plus antiques, bizarre clothes and a welter of glorious junk on *Sat.*

Royal Standard Antique Market
Royal Standard Hotel car park, Vanbrugh Park, Blackheath SE3. 01-858 1533. Antique market with variety of stalls. *Sat all day.*

Shepherds Bush
W12. Large general open-air market alongside the railway arcade. Food stalls have a strong West Indian bias. Pets, household goods and the usual market tat. *Mon-Sat.*

Smithfield (wholesale) **6 J 28**
Charterhouse St EC1. World's largest meat market; some interesting architecture and storage techniques but for most people 10 acres of horror. *Mon-Fri from 06.00.*

Spitalfields (wholesale)
Commercial St E1. Covered fruit, flower and vegetable market — 5 acres. Extensive underground chambers: one of the main centres for ripening bananas. *Mon-Sat from 05.00.*

Vallance Road
Whitechapel Rd E1. A popular junk market. *Mon-Sat 05.00-10.00.*

Wentworth Street
E1. Fruit, vegetables and bric-a-brac. *Sun-Fri 09.00-14.00.*

Westbourne Grove
W11. Clothes, especially leather goods, and some bric-a-brac. *Mon-Sat 10.30-18.00.*

Westmoreland Road
SE17. Flea market. *CLOSED Thurs & Sun afternoon.*

Home services

Builders

The Building Centre **3 F 23**
26 Store St WC1. 01-637 9001. Information on building materials, equipment and techniques. Large permanent exhibition and special heating and timber advisory service. *CLOSED Sat.*

Carpets: cleaning

London Carpet Cleaners & Patent Steam Carpet Cleaning
Frumage St, Wandsworth SW18. 01-874 4333. Will either collect the carpet or clean it in your own home.

Patent Cleaning Carpet Co
50 Eagle Wharf Rd N1. 01-253 6121. Collect and deliver.

Servicemaster **1 D 2**
3 Hammersmith Rd W14. 01-602 4411. World's largest carpet and upholstery cleaners.

Catering service

Anni et Jim **2 C 12**
29 Carrol House, Craven Terrace W2. 01-262 8645. French cooking for small or large parties.

Justin de Blank **5 L 14**
42 Elizabeth St SW1. 01-730 0605. Variety of delicious foods to take away — soups, salads, quiches and pâtés.

Dial-A-Meal **2 I 14**
173 Knightsbridge SW7. 01-584 9111. Hot 3-course dinners at reasonable prices.

Dial-A-Drink
01-351 3113. (10 lines). All off licence products available for delivery on the same day if you phone in time, or the next morning if you phone in the evening. Cash on delivery — very reasonable prices. Specialise in good wines.

Fortnum & Mason **2 I 20**
181 Piccadilly W1. 01-734 8040. Deliver packed lunches and superb picnic hampers.

London Domestic Services **2 I 12**
313 Brompton Rd SW3. 01-584 0161. Can supply all the staff — butlers, cooks, waiters and waitresses — for any function. Will arrange the menu.

Moveable Feasts
83-5 Holloway Rd N7. 01-607 2202. Vast selection of 3-course lunch and dinner menus. Cater for weddings, parties, etc and will supply staff, cutlery and plates.

Party Planners **1 A 6**
56 Ladbroke Grove W11. 01-229 9666. Provide food, drink and even music and cabaret for parties.

Searcy Tansley **2 I 12**
136 Brompton Rd SW3. 01-584 3344. High-class catering for cocktail parties, dances, etc.

Toastmasters Incorporated
6 Gladstone House, High Rd N22. 01-888 7098/2398. Professionals to officiate at any type of function can be supplied up to half an hour before needed.

United Kingdom Bartenders Guild **2 I 17**
70 Brewer St W1. 01-437 2113. Supply barmen or wine waiters for evening and day functions.

Do-it-yourself

Building Centre **3 F 23**
26 Store St WC1. 01-637 9001. Supply information on anything connected with building.

Central Handyman
30 Ballards Lane N3. 01-346 4460. All kinds of tools and materials.

Hire Service Shop **3 E 33**
Hire out every conceivable piece of DIY tackle/-scaffolding, sanders, strippers, etc.

Ideal Homecrafts
74 South Ealing Rd W5. 01-567 2767.

Michel & Polgar **2 D 18**
41 Blandford St W1. 01-935 9629. Have a wide range of plastic materials and will make anything to your specifications.

Parry & Son **6 J 32**
329 Old St EC1. 01-739 9422. Good selection of power tools.

Wallpaper & DIY Shop
220 St James's Rd SE1. 01-237 6300.

Whiteley's **1 B 10**
Queensway Bayswater W2. 01-229 1234. Kits for making roller blinds.

Domestic help

Au Pair
Buy the leaflet 'Au-pair in Britain' from the HMSO, 271 High Holborn WC1. Your local Borough council will have a list of thoroughly investigated and reputable agencies through which you can hire foreign girls to help in your home.

Babysitters Unlimited **1 I 11**
313 Brompton Rd SW3. 01-730 7777/8. Mostly trained nurses. Also supervise day outings — cheaper rates to members.

Belgravia Bureau **2 I 13**
35 Brompton Rd SW3. 01-584 4343. Supply cooks, cleaners, housekeepers, nannies or secretaries.

Brompton Bureau **2 I 12**
10 Beauchamp Place SW3. 01-584 6242. For 24 hour babysitting and mother's helps.

Childminders **2 D 19**
67a Marylebone High St W1. 01-935 9763. Babysitters supplied to the home and to hotels, minimum 4 hours. Also party staff and temporary nannies.

Domestics Unlimited **2 A 14**
494 Harrow Rd W9. 01-969 7495. Cleaners, barmen and general household help.

Doorsteps **5 L 13**
26 Eaton Terrace SW1. 01-730 9244. For all kinds of household maintenance — even decorating.

Gentle Ghost **1 A 5**
33 Norland Rd W11. 01-603 2871. Everything from moving house to babysitting services by a group whose aim is to bring people closer to a more caring society.

Universal Aunts **4 L 11**
36 Walpole St SW3. 01-730 9834. Babysitting, shopping, au pair, cleaning and removal problems solved.

We People
92 Tavistock Rd W11. 01-727 1228. A workers' co-operative providing most services including light removals.

Enamel repairs

Renubath
596 Chiswick High Rd W4. 01-995 5252. Re-enamel baths, tiles, etc. Good range of unusual colours.

Household services

Economic Drain & Flue Repairs   **2 B 18**
17 Linhope St, Dorset Sq NW1. 01-723 2273. On instant call for clearing blockages.
Problem   **5 O 16**
179 Vauxhall Bridge Rd SW1. 01-828 8181. Plumbers, electricians, secretaries, taxis — you name it, they help for an annual subscription fee.

Interior decorators

Godfrey Bonsack   **2 G 17**
14 Mount St W1. 01-629 9981. Well-known for his restoration and decoration of many English country houses. Specialises in luxury bathroom fittings.
Druce & Co   **2 G 22**
66 Newman St W1. 01-580 0462. Design service for not-too-expensive prices. Will do anything from structural alterations to carpets and finishing touches.
Heal's Contract   **3 F 23**
196 Tottenham Court Rd W1. 01-636 3399. Excellent individual schemes for offices, boardrooms, public buildings, ships and hotels.
John Siddeley   **2 I 13**
4 Harriet St SW1. 01-235 8757. Imaginative modern outlook and ideas. Good use of colour and furnishing.
Toynbee-Clarke Interiors   **2 G 17**
95 Mount St W1. 01-499 4472. Good modern designers with a large selection of wallpapers, fabrics and furniture on the premises.

Key-cutting

Selfridges, Harrods, many branches of Woolworths and other big stores have a while-you-wait service: also many small local ironmongers, shoe repairers and some of the larger tube stations.

Laundry & cleaning

There are many reliable dry cleaners and launderers in London, but for specialist treatment go to:
Collins Cleaners   **5 J 20**
88 Jermyn St SW1. 01-839 5172. Pressing while you wait and clothes cleaning the same day.
Jeeves   **5 J 12**
8-10 Pont St SW1. 01-235 1101. A personal service. Everything is hand-finished and the prices are reasonable. They collect in central London and have a postal service.
Liliman & Cox   **2 H 18**
34 Bruton Place W1. 01-629 4555. Highest quality cleaning of special garments such as beaded and embroidered dresses.
Suede Services
2a Hoop Lane NW11. 01-455 0052. Specialise in cleaning, restoring and repairing all skin garments.
Swears & Wells   **2 F 18**
374 Oxford St W1. 01-629 0640. Suede and leather cleaning.

Mail order

Mail order shopping is both convenient and economic. The three companies listed below are the principal mail order suppliers and each has several subsidiary companies with individual catalogues. Write to these addresses and ask for the catalogue you want.
The Littlewood Organisation
Derby Lane, Old Swan, Liverpool L70 1AD. General household goods, clothes, furnishings. Subsidiary companies: Janet Frazer, Peter Craig, Burlington, John Moores Home Shopping Service and Brian Mills Ltd.
J.D. Williams & Co
N. Brown Investments Group, 7 Dale St, Manchester M60 6ES. Household goods. Subsidiary companies: Oxendale & Co Ltd, Ambrose Wilson Ltd, Quality Post, Heather Valley, Halwins, Dale House Ltd.
Great Universal Stores
Devonshire St, Ardwick, Manchester M60 6EL. Subsidiary companies: British Mail Order Corp. Ltd, Key & Co Ltd, Marshall Ward, Chorlton Warehouses, John England, George Day, J.H. Jones, Bollin House, Royal Welsh, John Noble.

Removals

See under 'Domestic help' or look in 'Time Out' and your local newsagent's window. There are many removal services charging reasonable prices.

Night services

Most of London quietens down soon after midnight; some parts, however, remain very wide awake. Journalists, policemen and market porters work through the night; the 'in set' dance and drink the night away in clubs; lorry drivers and long distance travellers make full use of the empty roads. So one can still get service, a late bed or food at any time of the night — somewhere. Here is a list of places open all, or some of, the night.

Accommodation

Should you find yourself stranded in London without a hotel there are several alternatives to a peaceful night's sleep depending on your means and inclinations; late night bowling alleys, 24-hr restaurants and cafés and some very late nightclubs. If you do want some sleep, refer to the 'Crisis page' or try:
Embankments, open spaces & parks
A fine summer night is preferable if you want to actually sleep. Advantages: wide choice of benches and the dawn chorus; disadvantages: the police might move you on or charge you with vagrancy. *All Royal parks are closed at night and it is an offence to sleep in them.*
Hostels & doss houses
There are an enormous number of hostels available in London — all fairly spartan but quite adequate and cheap. (See 'Hostels' section). Lower down the scale are the working men's hostels and doss houses at very low prices.
Banks
The most time-saving method of cashing cheques after office hours is to use a cash dispensing machine found outside some branches of major banks. Ask your bank about this service, as it is necessary to obtain a special card to insert in the machines. The bank will also give you a list of branches with cash dispensers. The machines operate 24 hrs.
Barclays Bank   **5 M 14**
BA Airways Terminal, Buckingham Palace Rd SW1. 01-897 1296. 24-hr service for arrivals in No. 3 terminal. For departures the bank is open *06.30-21.30.* Bona fide air travellers only.
Buses
Excellent all night bus service from the centre to outer London throughout the night (except Sat-Sun morning). (See 'Night bus map and timetable'.)
Car hire
Godfrey Davis   **5 M 16**
Davis House, Wilton Rd SW1. 01-834 8484. *24-hr service 7 days a week.*
Avis Rent-a-Car   **2 E 17**
68 North Row, Marble Arch W1. 01-629 7811. *Daily 07.00-02.00. 24-hr service at airports.*
Cars: petrol
The following serve petrol 24 hrs a day:
Blue Star Garages
Branches all over London. Here are just two:
Monmouth St WC2 (nr Covent Garden). 01-994 2446.
88 Evershott St NW1 (nr Euston). 01-387 1714.
Chiswick Flyover Service Station
1 Great West Rd W4. 01-994 1119
Fountain
Mawson Lane W4. 01-994 2446.
Park Lane Underground Garage   **2 G 16**
Hyde Park W1. 01-262 1814.
Savoy Adelphi Garage   **6 K 23**
Savoy Place, off Savoy Hill WC2. 01-836 4838.
Cars: repairs and breakdowns
The following give a 24-hr breakdown, repair, vehicle recovery and roadside repair service, 7 days a week. All makes of vehicle.
Belsize Garage
27 Belsize Lane NW3. 01-435 5472.
Cavendish Motors
Cavendish Rd NW6. 01-459 0046.
Kensington Park Garage   **1 A 8**
53 Kensington Pk Rd W11. 01-229 3006.
Parkgate Service Station
15 Parkgate Rd SW11. 01-223 1962. Also petrol.
Cars: AA and RAC
Both organizations operate a 24-hr emergency service for motorists. They can help in practically any motoring emergency if you are a member.
Automobile Association   **5 J 22**
Fanum House, Leicester Square WC2. 01-954 7373.

Royal Automobile Club   **5 J 19**
85 Pall Mall SW1. 01-681 3611 for south of the Thames.
92-33555 for north of the Thames.

All-night cinemas

The warmth and darkness make it difficult to stay awake but they're good value even if you don't manage to concentrate for the full 7 hrs or so. Vintage movies often shown. Also see 'Time Out'.

Classic Cinemas
103 Wardour St W1. 01-734 7381   **2 I 21**
All-night programmes of four or five films shown in at least one of the 'Classics' each Sat; phone to find out which one.

Gate Cinema   **1 A 8**
Notting Hill Gate W11. 01-727 5750. Films start at 23.15 every night.

National Film Theatre   **6 M 24**
South Bank SE1. 01-928 3232. All-night sessions several times a year. *OPEN 24.00-07.30.*

Eating: open early, late or 24 hrs

Canton   **2 I 22**
11 Newport Place WC2. 01-437 8935. *OPEN 24 hrs.*

Cavendish Hotel   **2 I 19**
Jermyn St SW1. 01-930 2111. Restaurant *OPEN 24 hrs.*

Empire Grill   **1 H 7**
85 Gloucester Rd SW7. 01-370 4404. *OPEN 24 hrs.*

Ferrari's Restaurant   **3 H 28**
505 Central Market, Farringdon St EC1. 01-253 4190. *OPEN to 04.00.*

The Great American Success   **1 D 4**
100 Kensington High St W8. 01-937 3183. *OPEN to 06.00.*

Kentucky Fried Chicken
Most of these take-aways are open to 24.00 or later. The following are open 24 hrs.
71 Gloucester Rd SW7   **1 I 7**
246 Old Brompton Rd SW7
132 Uxbridge Rd W12
116a Holland Park Ave W11
95 Westbourne Grove W2.
245 Kilburn High Rd NW6

Londonderry House Hotel   **2 I 16**
The Pelican, Old Park Lane W1. 01-493 7292. *OPEN 24 hrs.*

Mick's Café   **6 K 26**
Fleet St EC4. Reporters' and printers' café. *OPEN to 24.00.*

Terminal Buffets
Terminals 1, 2 & 3, London Airport, Middx. 01-759 4321 *OPEN 24 hrs.*

Wimpy Bars
Most stay open late. Here are some *OPEN to 24.00:*
126 Baker St W1   **2 D 18**
24 Charing Cross Rd WC2   **2 I 22**
177 Edgware Rd NW9   **2 D 16**
148 Strand WC2   **6 K 24**

Food shops

Late night supermarkets and delicatessens can be found on Queensway W2, in Earls Court Rd W8 and SW5 and on King's Rd SW1.

Information

Nightline
01-387 0680. Out of hours telephone information service *18.00-07.00 daily.*

Post office

Trafalgar Square, 24 William IV St WC2.   **5 J 22**
24-hr service.

Ten pin bowling

See under 'Sports' section. All are open late and some all night.

24 hour casualty

Most large general hospitals have a casualty department but they are not always open 24 hrs. In an emergency or accident, wherever you are, dial 999. The operator will give you the name of the nearest hospital casualty department open at that time and probably arrange an ambulance if necessary.

Business information services

These are the major organisations available to help the businessman with trade enquiries and export and import information. Do not overlook the assistance you can get from your bank, your own trade association, or the trade sections of embassies, who do much to promote trade between countries.

Information and advice on exporting   **6 L 28**
Board of Trade, Export Services Branch, 50 Ludgate Hill EC4. 01-248 5757. Market assessments; specific opportunities (published daily in Export Service Bulletin, a subscription publication); appointment of overseas agents; reports on standing of overseas traders; foreign tariff and import regulations; resolving commercial disputes; 'Pick-a-back' and export partnerships; service for foreign business visitors wishing to buy British goods.

Export Intelligence
01-248 5757. Fast information service for British exporters.

Association of British Chambers of Commerce   **6 N 29**
68 Queen St EC4. 01-248 7211.

British Export Houses Association   **6 N 29**
69 Cannon St EC4. 01-248 4444.

Central Office of Information   **5 P 22**
Hercules Rd SE1. 01-928 2345.

Companies House
Companies Registration Office, Crown Way, Maindy, Cardiff. 0222-388 588. For enquiries concerning limited companies. Enquiries for other types of business: 55-71 City Rd EC1. 01-253 9253. For 5p search fee all details of companies and firms can be inspected, in person and without undue delay.

Confederation of British Industries   **5 M 19**
21 Tothill St SW1. 01-930 6711.

Council of Industrial Design   **5 J 21**
28 Haymarket SW1. 01-839 8000.

Chamber of Commerce   **6 N 29**
68 Cannon St EC4. 01-248 4444.

Institute of Export   **6 K 29**
Royal Trade Centre, East Smithfield E1. 01-488 2400.

Institute of Practitioners in Advertising   **5 J 14**
44 Belgrave Sq SW1. 01-235 7020.

National Economic Development Office   **5 O 19**
Millbank Tower, 21-41 Millbank SW1. 01-211 3000.

Business and secretarial services

Also see under 'Domestic help'.

Brook Street Bureau   **2 G 18**
Brook St House, 47 Davies St W1. 01-629 8866. Largest employment agency with 18 branches in central London.

Forum   **2 H 20**
15-16 New Burlington St W1. 01-493 1351. Typing, xeroxing, photography and litho printing.

Norma Skemp   **5 M 18**
14 Broadway SW1. 01-222 5483. Can let you have an office or just a desk, an accommodation address, telephone and receptionists to deal with messages and enquiries. A 24-hr telephone answering service can be arranged. Translations, duplicating and litho printing.

TIPS   **2 G 20**
310 Regent St W1. 01-580 7011/2/3. Also branch in The Hilton, Park Lane. 7 days a week comprehensive personal secretarial service.

Social Services

Police stations

These are the most important police stations within a 3-mile radius of Piccadilly Circus.

City of London 6 M 30
Headquarters & all departments, 26 Old Jewry EC2. 01-606 8866.

Bishopsgate 6 N 33
182 Bishopsgate EC2. 01-606 8866.

Snow Hill 6 K 28
5 Snow Hill EC1. 01-606 8866.

Wood Street 6 L 30
Wood St EC2. 01-606 8866.

Metropolitan

Battersea 4 Q 7
112-118 Battersea Bridge Rd SW11. 01-223 6611.

Bow Street 6 J 23
28 Bow St WC2. 01-434 5212.

Cannon Row 5 N 21
1 Cannon Row SW1. 01-434 5212.

Chelsea 4 K 10
2 Lucan Place SW3. 01-741 6212.

Hyde Park 2 F 14
North of Serpentine W2. 01-434 5212.

Kensington 1 G 5
72 Earls Court Rd W8. 01-741 6212.

Kings Cross 3 E 28
76 Kings Cross Rd WC1. 01-837 9121.

New Scotland Yard 5 M 18
Broadway SW1. 01-230 1212.

Rochester Row 5 N 17
63 Rochester Row SW1. 01-434 5212.

Southwark 6 Q 27
323 Borough High St SE1. 01-407 8044.

Wellington Arch 2 I 16
Hyde Park Corner SW1. 01-930 5757.

West End Central 2 H 20
27 Savile Row W1. 01-434 5212.

Hospitals

General hospitals: Central London

Guy's Hospital 6 Q 29
St Thomas' St SE1. 01-407 7600.

Lambeth Hospital 6 R 23
Brook Drive, Kennington Rd SE1. 01-735 4352.

London Hospital (Whitechapel)
Whitechapel E1. 01-247 5454.

Metropolitan Hospital
11 Kingsland Rd E8. 01-254 6862.

Middlesex Hospital 2 F 22
Mortimer St W1. 01-636 8333.

National Temperance Hospital 3 C 23
Hampstead Rd NW1. 01-387 9300.

New Charing Cross Hospital
Fulham Palace Rd W6. 01-748 2040.

Royal Free Hospital 3 F 27
256 Gray's Inn Rd WC1. 01-837 6411.

St Bartholomew's Hospital 6 K 29
West Smithfield EC1. 01-600 9000.

St George's Hospital 2 I 15
Hyde Park Corner SW1. 01-235 4343.

St Mary Abbots Hospital 1 F 6
Marloes Rd W8. 01-937 8201.

St Mary's Hospital 2 B 14
Praed St W2. 01-262 1280.

St Stephen's Hospital 4 K 6
369 Fulham Rd SW10. 01-352 8161.

St Thomas' Hospital 5 O 21
Lambeth Palace Rd SE1. 01-928 9292.

University College Hospital 3 E 23
Gower St WC1. 01-387 9300.

Westminster Hospital 5 O 19
Horseferry Rd SW1. 01-828 9811.

Chest hospitals

Brompton Hospital 4 J 9
Fulham Rd SW3. 01-352 8121.

Grove Park Hospital
Marvels Lane SE12. 01-857 1191.

London Chest Hospital
Bonner Rd E2. 01-980 1214.

St Marylebone Chest Clinic
St Marylebone Town Hall NW1. 01-935 2918.

Children's hospitals

Belgrave Hospital for Children
1 Clapham Rd SW9. 01-274 6222, ext 702. *24-hr minor casualty department.*

Children's Hospital Sydenham
321 Sydenham Rd SE26. 01-778 7031. *24-hr casualty.*

Evelina Children's Hospital 6 Q 26
(of Guy's Hospital) Southwark Bridge Rd SE1. 01-407 4747. *24-hr casualty.*

The Hospital for Sick Children 3 G 26
Great Ormond St WC1. 01-405 9200. *24-hr casualty.*

Paddington Green Children's Hospital 2 A 15
(St Mary's Hospital Teaching Group) Paddington Green W2. 01-723 1081. *24-hr casualty.*

Queen Elizabeth Hospital for Children
Hackney Rd E2. 01-739 8422. *24-hr casualty.*

Westminster Children's Hospital 5 N 17
(Westminster Hospital Teaching Group) 56 Vincent Square SW1. 01-828 9811. *24-hr casualty.*

Dental hospitals

Eastman Dental Hospital 3 F 27
252 Gray's Inn Rd WC1. 01-837 7251.

Royal Dental Hospital of London
32 Leicester Square WC2. 01-930 8831.

St George's Hospital
Tooting Grove SW17. 01-672 1255.

University College Dental Hospital 3 E 23
Mortimer Market (off Tottenham Court Rd) WC1. 01-387 9300. *OPEN 09.00-14.30, Sat 09.00-11.00. CLOSED Sun.* At other times, cases of real emergency may be treated at the University College Hospital, see under 'General hospitals'.

Drug dependence clinics

The following hospitals have special clinics to deal with sufferers from heroin or cocaine dependence. They will generally accept self-referred patients, but do not operate a 24-hr emergency service. Emergency cases should go to their nearest casualty department. Also see under the 'Cry for help' section where voluntary organisations giving assistance to addicts are listed.

Charing Cross Hospital 5 K 22
1a Bedfordbury WC2. 01-385 8834.

Hackney Hospital
230 Homerton High St E9. 01-985 5555.

Lambeth Hospital 6 R 23
Brook Drive SE11. 01-735 6155.

Maudsley Hospital
Denmark Hill SE5. 01-703 6333.

Queen Mary's Hospital
Roehampton Lane SW15. 01-789 6611.

St Clement's Hospital
2a Bow Rd E3. 01-980 4899.

St George's Hospital
Tooting Grove SW17. 01-672 1255.

St Mary's Hospital
Woodfield Rd W9. 01-286 4884.

University College Hospital 3 E 23
Gower St WC1. 01-387 9300.

West Middlesex Hospital
Twickenham Rd, Isleworth, Middx. 01-560 2121.

Westminster Hospital 5 O 19
52 Vincent Square SW1. 01-828 9811.

Foreign hospitals

French Dispensary 2 C 22
Jellicoe House, Osnaburgh St NW1. 01-387 5132.

Italian Hospital 3 G 25
Queen Square WC1. 01-831 6961.

Homoeopathic hospital

Royal London Homoeopathic Hospital 3 **G 26**
Gt Ormond St WC1. 01-837 7821.

Maternity hospitals

British Hospital for Mothers & Babies
Samuel St SE18. 01-854 8016.
City of London Maternity Hospital
Thoresby St N1. 01-253 2280.
Forest Gate Hospital
Forest Lane E7. 01-534 5064.
The Mothers' Hospital (Salvation Army)
143-153 Lower Clapton Rd E5. 01-985 6661.
Plaistow Maternity Hospital
Howard's Rd E13. 01-552 3311.
Queen Charlotte's Maternity Hospital
339 Goldhawk Rd W6. 01-748 4666.
St Teresa's Maternity Hospital
12 The Downs SW20. 01-947 3142.
Whipps Cross Hospital
Whipps Cross Rd E11. 01-539 5522.

Migraine clinics

Princess Margaret Migraine Clinic 6 **J 30**
22 Charterhouse Sq EC1. 01-253 8777. *OPEN 10.00-16.00 Mon-Fri. CLOSED Sat, Sun.*
New Charing Cross Hospital
Fulham Palace Rd W6. 01-748 2040.

Nursing & convalescent homes

The National Health Service can send you free or at very low cost to one of their many convalescent homes by the sea or in the country — consult your hospital doctor.
King Edward's Hospital Fund 1 **B 9**
14 Palace Court W2. 01-727 0581. for directory of convalescent homes serving Greater London.
The London Clinic 2 **C 20**
20 Devonshire Place W1. 01-935 4444. A top private clinic.

Psychiatric hospitals

Castlewood Day Hospital
25 Shooter's Hill SE18. 01-856 4970.
Halliwick House
58 Friern Barnet Rd, New Southgate N11. 01-368 8484.
Institute of Psychiatry
De Crespigny Park SE5. 01-703 5411.
Lebenoh Hospital for Mental Diseases
Drayton House, Garden St WC1. 01-387 2108.
Maida Vale Hospital for Nervous Diseases
4 Maida Vale W9. 01-286 5172.
The Maudsley Hospital
Denmark Hill SE5. 01-703 6333. Also drug clinics and drug in-patient facilities.
Paddington Centre for Psychotherapy 2 **A 14**
217-221 Harrow Rd W2. 01-286 4800. Also drug therapy by appointment only.
St Clement's Hospital
2a Bow Rd E3. 01-980 4899. Drug unit and drug in-patient facilities.
St Thomas' Psychiatric Day Hospital for Children
35 Black Prince Rd SE11. 01-735 1972.
Tooting Bec Hospital
Tooting Bec Rd SW17. 01-672 9933. Also drug in-patient facilities and geriatrics.

Seamen's hospitals

Albert Dock Seamen's Hospital
Alnwick Rd E16. 01-476 2234.
Dreadnought Seamen's Hospital
King William Walk SE10. 01-858 3433.

Specialist hospitals

London Foot Hospital 2 **D 22**
33 Fitzroy Square W1. 01-636 0602.
Metropolitan Ear, Nose & Throat Hospital 1 **F 6**
St Mary Abbots Hospital, Marloes Rd W8. 01-937 8206.
Moorfields Eye Hospital 3 **I 33**
City Rd EC1. Also High Holborn, *see 'Crisis page'*. 01-253 3411. *24-hr casualty.*
The National Hospital 3 **G 25**
Queen Square WC1. 01-837 3611. Diseases of the nervous system.
National Heart Hospital 2 **D 19**
Westmorland St W1. 01-486 0824.
Royal Eye Hospital
St Georges Circus SE1. 01-928 4477.
Royal Marsden Hospital 2 **E 21**
Fulham Rd SW3. 01-352 8171. Malignant diseases.
Royal National Orthopaedic Hospital 2 **E 21**
234 Great Portland St W1. 01-387 5070.
Royal National Throat, Nose & Ear Hospital 3 **E 27**
Gray's Inn Rd WC1. 01-278 6261.

St John's Hospital for Diseases of the Skin 2 **I 21**
5 Lisle St WC2. 01-437 8383.
St Paul's Hospital 3 **I 23**
Endell St WC2. 01-836 9611. Genito-urinary.
St Mark's Hospital for Diseases of the Rectum & Colon 3 **F 31**
City Rd EC1. 01-253 1050
St Peter's Hospital 6 **J 23**
Henrietta St WC2. 01-836 9347. Genito-urinary.
St Philip's Hospital 6 **J 25**
Sheffield St WC2. 01-242 9831. Genito-urinary.
Western Ophthalmic Hospital 2 **B 18**
(St Mary's Hospital Teaching Group) Marylebone Rd NW1. 01-402 4211. *24-hr casualty.*

Venereal diseases hospitals

Dreadnought Seamen's Hospital
King William Walk SE10. 01-858 3433.
Eastern Hospital
Homerton Grove E9. 01-985 1193. Out-patients only.
Guy's Hospital 6 **P 29**
St Thomas St, London Bridge SE1. 01-407 7600.
Miller General Hospital
Greenwich High Rd SE10. 01-692 1136.
London Hospital
Turner St E1. 01-247 7310.
Middlesex Hospital 2 **F 22**
73 Charlotte St W1. 01-636 8333.
Prince of Wales General Hospital
High Rd Tottenham N.15. 01-808 1081.
Queen Mary's Hospital for the East End
West Ham Lane E.15. 01-534 2616.
Royal Free Hospital 3 **F 27**
Gray's Inn Rd WC1. 01-837 6411.
Royal Northern Hospital
Holloway Rd N7. 01-272 7777
St Bartholomew's Hospital 6 **K 29**
West Smithfield EC1. 01-606 7777.
St George's Hospital 2 **I 15**
Hyde Park Corner SW1. 01-235 4343.
St John's Hospital
Morden Hill SE13. 01-852 4467.
St Mary's Hospital 2 **B 14**
Praed St W2. 01-262 1123.
St Thomas' Hospital 5 **N 21**
Lambeth Palace Rd, Westminster Bridge SE1. 01-928 9292.
South London Hospital for Women & Children
Clapham Common South Side SW4. 01-673 1221.
University College Hospital 2 **E 22**
Grafton Way W1. 01-387 9300.
Westminster Hospital 5 **O 19**
Dean Ryle St, Horseferry Rd SW1. 01-828 9811.

Cry for help ·

This section covers the main social services. London has many organisations available to give help and advice to anyone in need, and particularly to those who are ill, lonely or desperate Information or help is given willingly on practically any problem and most of it is free. These are the most useful organisations, but do not forget that the local borough has a wide range of free services and also that the Citizens Advice Bureaux can put you in touch with local voluntary societies. It is also worth remembering that at any time day or night, one can contact the local police station in an emergency. The following publications contain useful information and addresses:
Charities Digest
£2.25. Family Welfare Association 501-505 Kingsland Rd E8. 01-254 6251.
Consumer's Guide to the British Social Services
50p. Phyllis Willmot, Penguin.
Guide to the Social Services
90p. Family Welfare Association 501-505 Kingsland Rd E8. 01-254 6251.
Voluntary Social Services
£2.00 National Council of Social Service, 26 Bedford Square WC1. 01-636 4066.

General: local borough departments

Addresses from the local town hall or Citizens Advice Bureau.
Directorates of Social Services
Help with everything from day nurseries to advice for the homeless.
Directorates of Development, Housing & Planning
Let and maintain council homes. Advice and assistance.
Environmental Health Division
Public health inspectors for shops, homes, etc.

General

Church Army
CSC House, N Circular Rd NW10. 01-930 3763. Offers help to anyone in need: homes, hostels, holidays, youth services, prison welfare and social work.

Centrepoint   **2 I 22**
65a Shaftesbury Ave W1. 01-734 1075. Emergency night shelter for 16-25 year olds in central London. No alcoholics or drug addicts.

Citizens Rights Office   **3 I 24**
1 Macklin St WC2. 01-405 5942. Advice on housing and Welfare State benefits Free and confidential service.

Family Welfare Association
501-505 Kingsland Rd E8. 01-254 6251. Counselling service to families on all problems from financial to marital. Trained caseworkers.

Help Advisory Centre   **2 B 14**
10 South Wharf Rd W2. 01-402 5233. Free help and advice on all problems.

Help Line
Capital Radio runs several telephone services for listeners: Help Line, 24-hr information and advice on all sorts of problems; flat sharing; job finders; community projects, etc. listen in for telephone numbers.

Salvation Army   **6 M 28**
101 Queen Victoria St EC4. 01-236 5222. *24-hr telephone service.* Help on any problem.

St Giles Centre
Camberwell Church St SE5. 01-703 5841. 24-hr telephone service for general advice. Day shelter for single homeless. Emergency night shelter for single girls.

St Martin-in-the-Fields Social Service Unit   **5 J 22**
5 St Martin's Place WC2. 01-930 1732. Voluntary society to assist anyone in need. 24-hr telephone.

Women's Royal Voluntary Service   **2 L 16**
17 Old Park Lane W1. 01-499 6040. A nationwide service for all kinds of government and local community welfare work. Trained members to help in both local and national emergencies.

Abortion

The Abortion Act 1967, allows two doctors jointly to recommend abortion where, taking the woman's environment into account, they believe there is risk to her life and health, or risk to the life and health of her existing children. They may also recommend abortion where there is a substantial risk that a seriously handicapped child may be born. Always consult your doctor about abortion. The following organisations might also be of help.

Abortion Law Reform Association
88a Islington High St N1. 01-359 5209. For advice on the present legal position only. They cannot help you obtain an abortion.

Brook Advisory Centre   **3 G 23**
233 Tottenham Court Rd W1. 01-323 1522. Five other London centres. Pregnancy tests and help in obtaining an abortion provided by doctors, nurses and social workers. Free for most London areas (depending on local council), otherwise p&p charged.

Release
1 Elgin Avenue W9. 01-289 1123. Will give advice and help on where to obtain an abortion.

Adoption

Demand is always greater than supply. All adoption societies have to be registered and most prefer the adopting parents to be practising Christians. Their aim is to safeguard the welfare and future of the child. Either apply through the Social Services department of the local authority or direct to an agency (lists from the Association of British Adoption Agencies). Some of the better known agencies in London are given below:

Association of British Adoption Agencies   **3 H 25**
4 Southampton Row WC1. 021-242 8951. Publishes a list of agencies and other literature and information on adoption.

Church Adoption Society   **5 M 16**
282 Vauxhall Bridge Rd SW1. 01-828 6443.

The Crusade of Rescue Catholic Adoption Society
73 St Charles Square W10. 01-969 5305. At least one adoptive parent must be a Roman Catholic.

Independent Adoption Society
160 Peckham Rye SE22. 01-693 9611. Non-religious society.

National Children Adoption Association   **2 H 13**
71 Knightsbridge SW1. 01-235 6436. All denominations. Also runs an ante-natal and post-natal hostel.

The National Children's Home
85 Highbury Park N5. 01-226 2033 Practising Protestants only.

Alcoholics

Alcoholism is now widely recognised as an illness. Help and treatment can be claimed under the NHS either through your doctor or through hospitals. Other useful centres are:

Alcoholics Anonymous   **4 J 5**
11 Redcliffe Gardens SW10. 01-351 3344. Give help to people wishing to recover from alcoholism or in need of the support and companionship of fellow sufferers. Meetings. *24-hr telephone service.*

Helping Hand   **5 M 18**
8 Strutton Ground SW1. 01-222 6862. Runs rehabilitation hostels. Also 'Link' Centre for young people.

London Council on Alcoholism   **3 D 25**
68 Chalton St NW1. 01-387 2191. Information and advisory centre for alcoholics and their families.

Richmond Fellowship   **1 B 4**
8 Addison Rd W14. 01-603 6373. Has a special residential community for ex-alcoholics.

Ambulance

*Dial **999** for an emergency, otherwise:*

St John Ambulance Brigade   **2 D 20**
29 Weymouth St W1. 01-580 6762. Will arrange a private ambulance and will collect ambulance cases from airports, docks or rail terminals. *OPEN 09.00-17.00.*

Animals

RSPCA
The Causeway, Horsham, Sussex. All complaints of cruelty to animals investigated in strict confidence. 24-hr emergency rescue service for animals in distress. 24-hr clinic for sick animals. Take in strays. (See also 'Veterinary clinics' under 'Services').

The blind

Guide Dogs for the Blind Association
113 Uxbridge Rd W5. 01-567 7001. Provides dogs and trains owners to use them.

National Library for the Blind   **5 N 19**
35 Gt Smith St SW1. 01-222 2725. Free lending library of 300,000 'embossed and enlarged type' books. Also Braille books. Catalogue sent.

Royal National Institute for the Blind   **2 E 21**
224-8 Gt Portland St W1. 01-388 1266. Provides active help and advice on practically any problem involving the blind; occupational training, education, homes, holidays, Braille library, talking tapes, books.

St Dunstan's
P O Box 58, 181 Old Marylebone Rd NW1. 01-723 5021. Rehabilitation, training, housing and welfare scheme for people blinded during service in war or in peacetime.

Cancer

It is important that cancer is detected in the early stages. Take advantage of the cancer precaution units if they visit your area. Women should have a regular cervical smear test.

Family Planning Association   **2 F 21**
27-35 Mortimer St W1. 01-580 3077. Breast cancer tests and cervical smears carried out free of charge.

Marie Curie Memorial Foundation   **5 K 12**
124 Sloane St SW1. 01-730 9157. Homes, nursing and welfare service for the seriously ill.

Marie Stopes Memorial Centre   **2 E 22**
108 Whitfield St W1. 01-388 0662. Tests for breast cancer and cervical smears.

National Society for Cancer Relief   **2 B 18**
Michael Sobell House, 30 Dorset Sq NW1. 01-402 8125. Financial assistance for needy cancer sufferers and their families.

Women's National Cancer Control Campaign   **2 G 17**
1 South Audley St W1. 01-499 7532. Information on alternative treatments, mobile clinics and a list of clinics offering check-ups.

Children

All Borough Council Social Services Directorates offer services such as day nurseries, advice, child-minding and schemes for handicapped children.

Dr Barnardo's
Tanner's Lane, Barkingside, Ilford, Essex. 01-550 8822. Homes for children. Give services to prevent the breaking up of family life.

Invalid Children's Aid Association   **5 M 14**
126 Buckingham Palace Rd SW1. 01-730 9891. Trained social workers help parents of invalid or handicapped children in their own homes. Also special schools for asthmatic and non-communicating children.

National Association for Gifted Children 6 **K 23**
27 John Adam St WC2. 01-839 1861. Advice of all kind for parents and teachers of gifted children. Activities for the children. Newsletter.

National Society for Autistic Children
1a Golders Green Rd NW11. 01-458 4376. Advice on help. Special schools. Play-group. Publications.

National Society for Mentally Handicapped Children 1 **A 9**
Pembridge Hall, 17 Pembridge Square W2. 01-229 8941. Helps the mentally handicapped child and its parents. Care centres, day nurseries, leisure clubs, speech therapy, training schemes.

NSPCC 2 **F 21**
1 Riding House St W1. 01-580 8812. Helps parents with problems concerning their children, marriage and financial difficulties. Investigates reports of neglect or ill-treatment of children.

Shaftesbury Society 5 **O 17**
112 Regency St SW1. 01-834 2656. For physically handicapped children. Hostels for muscular distrophy sufferers (over 16 years of age). Residential schools. Holiday homes.

Contraception

Apart from the addresses below your own doctor can advise and direct you to one of the official clinics in Britain. Birth control is now freely available whether you are single or married, and fewer organisations are demanding parental consent for minors. Two of the best surveys of the merits of various methods are 'Sex with Health' by the Consumer's Association's 'Which' magazine and a cheaper publication by students, the 'Little Blue Book'.

Birth Control and Pregnancy Counselling 2 **E 21**
31 Langham St W1. 01-637 8271. Provide all methods of contraception, medical consultation and advice on unwanted pregnancy.

Brook Advisory Centre 3 **G 23**
233 Tottenham Court Rd W1. 01-323 1522. Provide contraception and advice. No age limit.

The Family Planning Association 2 **F 21**
Margaret Pyke House, 27-35 Mortimer St W1. 01-636 7866. Head office which will supply a list of clinics catering for men and women. General advice.

Marie Stopes Memorial Centre 2 **E 22**
108 Whitfield St W1. 01-388 0662. Complete advice and service on all aspects of birth control for men and women. Small fee.

The deaf

Over the past few years more advanced designs in electronic hearing aids and the emphasis on training deaf children early have greatly improved the deafs' opportunities to lead a normal life. Your Borough Council's Social Services Directorate can help.

British Association of the Hard of Hearing
16 Park St, Windsor, Berks. A self-help organisation with 220 branches for those with acquired hearing loss, total or partial. Social clubs, lipreading groups, advice on hearing aids, educational weekends, holidays, etc.

National Deaf Children's Society 2 **A 18**
31 Gloucester Place W1. 01-486 3251. Information and guidance for parents and all well-wishers of deaf children. Free literature. Regional branches.

Royal Association in Aid of the Deaf and Dumb
7 Armstrong Rd W3. 01-743 6187. Concerned with the spiritual, social and general welfare of the deaf and blind/deaf in London, Essex, Surrey and Kent; trained staff to act as interpreters and counsellors. Special social clubs.

Royal National Institute for the Deaf '3 **F 23**
105 Gower St WC1. 01-387 8033. Information, education, training, hostels, homes for the deaf. Hearing aids tested free.

Diabetics

The British Diabetic Association 3 **F 23**
3-6 Alfred Place WC1. 01-636 7355. Aims to educate the diabetic to come to terms with his condition and lead an active and useful life. Literature and advisory services available. Annual holiday camps for children.

Disabled

Two very useful publications are: 'London for the Disabled' by Freda Bruce Lockhart (Ward Lock) and 'Holidays for the Physically Handicapped' by the Central Council for the Disabled.

British Council for the Rehabilitation of the Disabled 3 **E 24**
Tavistock House, South Tavistock Sq WC1. 01-387 4037. Information and advice on education, training and employment of the disabled. Provides indivudual tutors, correspondence courses and a Learning College for people with dyslexia and other such problems.

British Red Cross 5 **J 15**
9 Grosvenor Crescent SW1. 01-235 5454. Offer auxiliary assistance to the disabled and run clubs, outings, holidays. Medical equipment for nursing in the home is often available on loan.

Central Council for the Disabled 5 **M 15**
34 Eccleston Sq SW1. 01-834 0747. Information and advice, particularly on travel, holidays, and housing.

Garden Centre
Syon Park, Brentford, Middx. Permanent demonstration garden for the disabled.

Spastics Society 2 **D 21**
12 Park Crescent W1. 01-636 5020. Information on care, treatment, education and training.

Waterloo Action Centre 6 **O 23**
14 Baylis Rd SE1. 01-261 1404. Occupational work centre for the handicapped.

Discharged prisoners

These organisations try to welcome the discharged prisoner back into society. Many of them have voluntary workers to act as friends. You can also go to your local court and ask for the Probation Officer who should give you advice and help.

Brixton Circle Trust Club
33 Effra Rd SW2. 01-737 2888. Social centre for discharged prisoners.

Circle Trust Club
25 Camberwell Grove SE5. 01-703 6545. Voluntary service and social centre for discharged prisoners and their families.

Golbourne Centre
92 Golbourne Rd W10. 01-969 1650. Accommodation and refuge for ex-prisoners and homeless men. 18 places.

National Association for the care and Resettlement of Offenders
125 Kennington Park Rd SE11. 01-735 1151. Services voluntary organisations providing facilities for offenders in the community; runs pilot projects to test out new ideas and educates the public about the care of offenders and prevention of crime.

New Bridge
373a Brixton Rd SW9. 01-274 7854. Employment bureau for ex-prisoners living in South London.

The New Bridge 6 **K 30**
St Botolph's Church, Aldersgate EC1. 01-606 3692. To help discharged prisoners resettle themselves in society. Voluntary associates build a relationship with a prisoner while he is still in prison and help him on release. Employment and advisory scheme for ex-prisoners. *By appointment only.*

Probation & After Care Service 6 **Q 27**
Resettlement Office, 289 Borough High St SE1. 01-407 4611. Helps rootless and homeless ex-prisoners coming to inner London.

Drug dependence

The 'Misuse of Drugs Act 1971' made it illegal to possess cannabis, LSD, cocaine, amphetamines, opium, morphine or heroin. The police can search suspects and their property and, with a warrant, their premises. Treatment for most types of drug dependence is best provided by a sympathetic family doctor or, for heroin and opium addicts, the clinics listed under 'Drug dependence clinics' in the 'Hospitals' section. The following voluntary organisations offer supportive help of various kinds to drug users:

Community Drug Project Day Centre
Burnett Hall, Wren Rd SE5. 01-701 1294. Day-centre for heroin addicts. Advice to social workers, parents and other interested people.

Featherstone Lodge Project
Phoenix House, 1 Eliot Bank SE23. 01-699 5748. Long term residential rehabilitation for ex-drug addicts. Therapeutic community staffed by ex-addicts and social workers.

Helping Hand 5 **M 18**
8 Strutton Ground SW1. 01-222 6862. Counselling service and a hostel for the after care of addicts who have undergone treatment.

The Hungerford 5 **L 22**
12 Northumberland Ave WC2. 01-930 4688. Counselling service, advice and information centre for people with drug related problems.

Institute for the Study of Drug Dependence (ISDD)
Kingsbury House, 3 Blackburn Rd NW6. 01-328 5541. Collects and give gives information on all aspects of the non-medical use of drugs. Education Research Unit engaged in evaluating and seeking to improve drugs education methods. Organises conferences.

Release
1 Elgin Ave W9. 01-289 1123. *Emergency 24-hr:* 01-603

8654. Specialise in legal advice for those arrested for drug offences. General advice on drugs; legal and practical help.

Dyslexia

Many children and adults are handicapped by dyslexia (word-blindness).

The British Dyslexia Association
18 The Circus, Bath. Tel: 0225 28880 encourages research into the disability.

British Council for Rehabilitation of the Disabled   **3 E 24**
Tavistock House South, Tavistock Sq WC1. 01-387 4037. Has a Learning College for dyslexics.

The Dyslexia Institute
133 Gresham Rd, Staines. Staines 59498. A charity which provides advice for parents and teachers, expert examination of difficulties, specialty teaching, training for teachers and performs research.

Elderly people

Abbeyfield Society
35a High St, Potters Bar, Herts. 43371. Family-sized houses where 6 or 7 live together with resident housekeeper responsible for main meals. Own bed/sitting room furnished by occupant.

Age Concern
Bernard Sumley House, 60 Pitcairn Rd, Mitcham, Surrey. 01-640 5431. The focal point of all voluntary welfare organisations for the old. Excellent.information service.

British Red Cross   **5 J 15**
9 Grosvenor Crescent SW1. 01-235 5454. Provides regular visitors who act as friends and helpers. Loans medical equipment for nursing in the home. Organises holidays for the elderly.

Contact   **6 J 23**
15 Henrietta St WC2. 01-240 0630. Volunteers take the elderly on monthly Sun afternoon outings.

Employment Fellowship   **3 E 24**
Drayton House, Gordon St WC1. 01-387 1828. Has a list of work centres for the elderly. Offers interest and compansionship.

Meals on Wheels
Lunches brought to the homes of invalids and pensioners. For services in your area, contact your local council.

Mutual Households Association   **6 J 25**
41 Kingsway WC2. 01-836 1624. For retired professional class. Communal country houses for the elderly.

Over Fifty Housing Association   **5 K 13**
43 Cadogan Place SW1. 01-235 7536. Single rooms with all meals and services for the over fifties.

The Over Forty Association for Women   **5 L 15**
Grosvenor Gardens House, Grosvenor Gardens SW1. 01-834 0733. Free help in finding employment and housing for women over forty.

Pre-retirement Association
19 Undine St SW17. 01-767 3225. Supply details of courses specially designed to help people face retirement successfully. Also publications.

Salvation Army   **6 M 28**
101 Queen Victoria St EC4. 01-236 7020. Special 'Eventide' homes for old people at very nominal charges.

Task Force   **1 F 2**
Clifford House, Edith Villas W14. 01-647 0826. Also local offices throughout London. Young volunteers visit the elderly and give practical help.

Wireless For the Bedridden Society   **2 E 19**
20 Wimpole St W1. 01-935 0949. Radios and TVs lent free to needy invalids, the housebound and the aged poor. Free batteries and licences in extreme need.

Epilepsy

British Epilepsy Association   **3 F 23**
3-6 Alfred Place WC1. 01-580 2704. Advisory service covering welfare, training, education, employment and social adjustment. Literature available.

Gambling

Gambling can be as compulsive as drug addiction and may cause extreme distress to both the addict and his family.

Gamblers Anonymous   **4 M 8**
17-23 Blantyre St, Cheyne Walk SW10. 01-352 3060. An organisation with several meetings in the London area (no treatment centres). Constructive help and advice to compulsive gamblers.

Haemophilia

Haemophilia Society   **6 R 26**
PO Box 9, 16 Trinity St SE1. 01-407 1010. A society for sufferers of haemophilia and those interested in their welfare. Advice and assistance given.

Homeless

Quite a number of organisations provide homes and hostels for the sick, the old, the poor and the destitute. These are a few of the most useful. Also apply to your local office of the Department of Health and Social Security.

BIT
146 Great Western Rd W11. 01-229 8219. For emergency one-night accomodation.

Camberwell Reception Centre for Men
Consort Rd SE15. 01-639 1023. For the genuinely desperate and homeless. *24-hr service.*

The Carr-Gomm Society
36 Gomm Rd, Bermondsey SE16. 01-237 2318. Small houses and flats with housekeepers for the isolated who can't or don't want to live on their own.

Cheshire Foundation Homes for the Sick   **2 I 17**
7 Market Mews W1. 01-499 2665. Homes for the chronic sick and disabled and for mental rehabilitation.

Church Army (Men)
CSC House, N Circular Rd NW10. 01-903 3763.
46 Acre Lane SW2. 01-274 9447.
10-12 Star Rd W14. 01-385 1557.   **1 G 1**
75 Great Peter St SW1. 01-222 7272.   **5 N 19**
Good hostels at reasonable prices.

Church Army (Women)
1-3 Cosway St NW1. 01-262 3818.   **2 A 16**
An emergency hostel for women in any sort of need.
Elgood House, 84 Bell St NW1. 01-402 4971.   **2 A 16**
Hostel flatlets for young working women.
Portman House, 10 Daventry St NW1. 01-723 0447.
                  2 A 16
Queen Mary Hostel, 28 Greencoat Place SW1. 01-834 0584. For working women.   **5 N 17**

Distressed Gentlefolk's Aid Association   **1 C 8**
Vicarage Gate House, Vicarage Gate W8. 01-229 9341. Maintains 12 nursing and residential homes. Helps 800 people to live in their own homes.

Hostels for Homeless Women   **2 H 22**
59 Greek St W1. 01-437 1685. Room for 45 homeless women for both short and long-term.

International Camping
Millfields Rd, Hackney Marsh E5. 01-985 7656. Camping site for tents and vans. All nationalities welcome. *Jun-Aug.*

London Lodging Houses for Men   **6 J 24**
Bruce House, Kemble St WC2. Cubicle accommodation — clean and cheap.

Salvation Army (Men)
SPA Home, 124 Spa Rd SE16. 01-237 1670. Referral point for all men's hostels.

Salvation Army (Women)
Hope Town Hostel, Hopetown St SE1. 01-247 2693. Accommodation for about 150 women and 20 children.

Shelter Housing Advisory Centre   **1 I 6**
189a Old Brompton Rd SW5. 01-373 7276. Advice on all aspects of housing including legal rights of tenants. New Town scheme to help people get jobs and housing in new towns.

SOS Society   **4 L 11**
14 Culford Gardens SW3. 01-584 3717. Homes for the elderly; hostels for the needy.

Tent City
Oak Hill Common W3. 01-743 5708. Accommodation in large tents. All nationalities welcome. *Jun-Aug.*

Homosexuality

The Centre   **2 A 17**
Broadley Terrace NW1. 01-723 5889. Gay counselling service with an evening drop-in centre, *Fri* disco and *Wed* women's group.

CHE   **2 I 21**
22 Great Windmill St W1. 01-437 7363. Campaign for Homosexual Equality. Work for law reform, better relations between homo and hetero-sexual societies. Phone or call in for advice, information or a chat.

Gay Switchboard
01-837 7324. *24-hr* telephone service giving information on accommodation, activities and entertainment for gay people. Also advice and referral service.

Sappho
c/o BCM/PETREL London WC1V 6XX. Monthly magazine. Meeting place for homo and hetero-sexual women in Chepstow Pub, Chepstow Place W2 every Tues at 19.30. Disco in Sols Arms, Hampstead, second and last Sat of every month at 10.00.

Injustice or persecution

If you feel very strongly about a public issue you should contact one of the following organisations. They campaign against those in power to press for a just deal for the individual. If it is a personal case of injustice or persecution, also visit your solicitor. Refer to 'Legal aid'.

National Council for Civil Liberties   **3 F 28**
186 Kings Cross Rd WC1. 01-278 4575. A membership organisation which campaigns for the rights of individuals and minorities.

Race Relations Board   **5 L 15**
5 Lower Belgrave St SW1. 01-730 6291. Investigate complaints of discrimination by race or colour. Bring cases to court if necessary.

Society for Individual Freedom   **2 G 16**
55 Park Lane W1. 01-499 6476. Right-wing pressure group for maintenance of the rule of law.

Insomnia

Therapy Tapes
The New Kings Hotel, Brighton, Sussex. Brighton 29133. Supply a hypno-therapy casette tape supposed to cure insomnia.

Legal aid and advice

There is a legal aid scheme whereby your legal costs can be subsidised on a means-tested basis. To find out about this and to get legal advice, go to your local Citizens Advice Bureau; to any solicitor displaying the Legal Aid sign; or to your Neighbourhood Law Centre.

Citizens Advice Bureau, National Headquarters   **3 G 23**
26 Bedford Sq WC1. 01-636 4060. Advice on legal aid, housing, rents and lists of local branches.

Mary Ward Legal Centre   **3 E 25**
9 Tavistock Place WC1. 01-387 8271. Free legal advice.

Release
1 Elgin Ave W9. 01-289 1123. Emergency: 01-603 8654. General legal advice and help for those arrested in drug offences.

Lonely people

London Linkup
01-531 7224. Arrange for people with similar interests to go out together.

London Village
37b Lilyville Rd SW6. 01-731 4336. Membership organisation created by young people for young people. All kinds of social activities arranged. Introductory evenings at Grosvenor Hotel, Victoria Station SW1, every *Tues, Wed 18.15 & 20.30.*

Marriage guidance

Catholic Marriage Advisory Council   **5 N 16**
33 Willow Place SW1. 01-828 8307. Help for those with marital problems. Meetings arranged for parents, teachers and engaged couples.

Institute of Marital Studies
Tavistock Centre, Belsize Lane NW3. 01-435 7111. Professional help with marital problems.

London Marriage Guidance Council   **2 E 21**
76a New Cavendish St W1. 01-580 1087. Confidential counselling and education service for those with difficulties in their personal relationships.

Marriage partners

Katherine Allen   **2 F 19**
7 Sedley Place, Woodstock St W1. 01-499 2556. Mostly professional and middle-class applicants. A few aristocrats. Personal approach.

Heather Jenner   **2 G 19**
124 New Bond St W1. 01-629 9634. Famous for creating successful partnerships. 5,000 members.

Matchmaker   **4 L 11**
25 Kings Rd SW3. 01-730 5142. Variety of social activities, dating and group events for members.

Mental health

If you have a severe emotional problem, the best person to see is your doctor who may recommend psychiatric help. The mental welfare officer and psychiatric social worker (contacted through the Health department of the local borough) can also advise on treatment and after-care.

Cope
11 Acklan Rd W10. 01-969 9790. Anti-psychiatric approach offering help and advice.

Counselling Centre   **2 A 16**
5 Cosway St NW1. 01-262 0756. Help for anyone with deep-rooted problems supervised by highly trained staff and a doctor.

Mental After Care Association   **5 J 19**
Eagle House, 110 Jermyn St SW1. 01-839 5953. Rehabilitation homes and hostels — short- and long-term care.

MIND (National Association for Mental Health)   **2 E 20**
22 Harley St W1. 01-637 0741. Advisory service on all aspects of mental disorder.

Neurotics Confidential
1 Clovelly Rd W5. 01-567 0262. An organisation of trained members for consultation by people with neurotic and emotional problems.

Richmond Fellowship   **1 B 4**
8 Addison Rd W14. 01-603 6373. Runs therapeutic communities for the mentally or emotionally disturbed.

The Samaritans   **6 N 30**
St Stephen's Church Crypt, Walbrook EC4. 01-626 2277. 'Suicides anonymous'. A voluntary organisation to help people who have thoughts of suicide or despair. *OPEN every day 09.00-22.00. Free 24-hr telephone service.* Many London branches.

Missing persons

It is advisable to inform the police, although they can do little unless there is suspicion of foul play.

'News of the World'   **6 L 26**
Bouverie St EC4. 01-353 3030. Missing relatives column. Person must have been missing for at least 6 months, and be a relative. One insertion £1 per word.

The Salvation Army Family Services Dept
280 Mare St E8. 01-985 1181. Enquiries for husbands and putative fathers are accepted here.

The Salvation Army International Investigation Dept   **6 N 33**
110-112 Middlesex St E1. 01-247 6831. Enquiries for all relatives are accepted.

Motorists: disqualified

St Christopher Motorists Security Association   **2 I 18**
45 Clarges St W1. 01-629 7324. For yearly fee of £15 will provide benefits of £15.00 per week in the event of disqualification.

Nursing

The NHS can provide a district nurse. Apply at the local health centre. For private nurses look in the telephone directory; at the advertisements in a nursing magazine; or contact one of the following:

British Nursing Association   **2 C 16**
470 Oxford St W1. 01-723 8055. Nursing agency supplying all types of nurses.

Langham Nurses Association   **1 A 10**
2 Porchester Gardens W2. 01-723 1444. Private, qualified nurses available (resident and non-resident).

One-parent families

Gingerbread   **2 H 21**
9 Poland St W1. 01-734 9014. Help one-parent families stay sane and solvent. Advice on housing, the law, social security, babysitting, etc.

National Council for One-Parent Families
255 Kentish Town Rd NW5. 01-267 1361. Will help and advise single parents and single pregnant women.

Pregnancy tests

A pregnancy test can always be done by your own doctor. Otherwise consult the FPA, one of the laboratories listed here or look down the advertisement columns of a magazine for addresses. Some chemists also do tests. See also 'Contraception' and 'Abortion'.

Ladycare
5 Norbreck Grove W10. 01-997 7425. Send or bring in urine samples.

Pharmacy & Professional Services
188 Brent Crescent NW10. 01-965 1477. Confidential service. Send or bring sample of urine in clean container and £3.00. Result while you wait. Free refreshment.

Pregnancy Advisory Service
40 Margaret St W1. 01-409 0281. Tests, advice and help.

Poverty

Child Poverty Action Group   **3 I 24**
1 Macklin St WC2. 01-242 3225. More a pressure group than a charity but they do advise on obtaining social security, etc.

Rape

See under 'Crisis page'.

Service & ex-servicemen

Royal British Legion   **5 J 19**
49 Pall Mall SW1. 01-930 8131. Will give assistance and financial aid to ex-servicemen and women and their dependants. Apply to local branch.

Soldier's, Sailor's & Airmen's Families Association   5 L 19
27 Queen Anne's Gate SW1. 01-839 4131. Financial advice and other aid for the families of service and ex-servicemen.

Smokers
GLC: Medical Dept
County Hall SE1. 01-633 5000. Ext 8133. Lectures for school children on the dangers of smoking.
Maudsley Hospital
Smokers Treatment Unit, Denmark Hill SE5. 01-703 5411, ext. 104. Help and advice for anyone wishing to give up smoking.
Ash
Margaret Pyke House, 27 Mortimer St, W1. 01-637 9843. Advice and addresses of withdrawal clinics in London area.

Unmarried mothers
About 50,000 illegitimate children are born in Britain each year. Consult the Social Services Directorate of the borough council about facilities in the area. Also see under 'One-parent families'.
Day nurseries
The Social Services Directorate can supply lists of registered child minders. They also operate day nurseries.

Venereal diseases
See list under 'Hospitals'. All treatment is free, anonymous if desired and completely confidential. You do not need an appointment or letter from your own doctor. 01-246 8072 is the London VD Telephone Service, which' gives advice on symptoms and treatment by taped message.

Widows
Cruse
Cruse House, 126 Sheen Rd, Richmond, Surrey. 01-940 4818. Brings widows together in a variety of social activities and holidays. General advice.

Charities

Giving away things
Dr Barnardo's
Gift-in-Kind Dept, Canada Hall, The Garden City, Woodford Bridge, Essex. 01-504 1010. Any useful or saleable gifts.
St John & Red Cross Hospital Library   2 J 15
6-7 Grosvenor Crescent SW1. 01-235 7131. Paperbacks wanted.
NSPCC   2 F 21
1 Riding House St W1. 01-580 8812. Send toys to Relief and Welfare department here or at your local office.
Notting Hill Housing Trust
All Saints House, 46 All Saints Rd W11. 01-229 9782. Good clean clothes and jumble needed, also second-hand furniture for tenants.
The Save the Children Fund
Warehouse, 120 Great Moor St, Bolton Lancs. Good clean clothes wanted for children up to 12 years old. No shoes.
The Spastics Society   2 D 21
12 Park Crescent W1. 01-636 5020. Send your old postage stamps and 'Green Shield' stamps here.

Donating your corpse
Legally your corpse does not belong to you but you can ask for it to be given to an anatomical school or hospital for medical use by students or doctors. Details available from:
Inspector of Anatomy   6 R 24
Dept of Health & Social Security, Alexander Fleming House, Elephant & Castle SE1. 01-407 5522. In office hours phone 01-636 6811, ext 3572.

Donating your eyes
Particularly valuable in corneal grafting. Details and forms from
Royal National Institute for the Blind   2 E 21
224 Great Portland St W1. 01-388 1266.

Donating your kidneys
Department of Health & Social Security   6 R 24
Division HS2B, Hanibal House, Elephant & Castle SE1. 01-703 6380 ext 3210. Will supply forms and information.

Voluntary social work

The voluntary worker no longer has a matronly do-gooder image but is welcome in many spheres of the social services. People of all ages, backgrounds and qualifications can help with anything from driving old people to the shops to sorting out files. An excellent book on voluntary work is 'Helping' by Caroline Moorehead (Macdonald & Jane's) which clearly describes the organisations that need help, the type of help they want and how to contact them. Also contact any of the organisation in the 'Cry for help' section and these below:
Camden Council for Social Service
Volunteer Bureau, 11 Tavistock Place WC1. 01-388 2071. Guides people into the type of voluntary work that they are most suited to.
Children's County Holiday Fund   2 C 17
1 York St W1. 01-935 8373. Takes children in need on summer holidays.
Community Service Volunteers   3 E 29
237 Pentonville Rd N1. 01-278 6601. Produce various publications full of unusual suggestions for helping in the community.
Ecumenical Youth Service
British Council of Churches, 10 Eaton Gate SW1. 01-730 9611. Organises summer work camps in Britain and Europe for volunteers aged 18-30. Information on long-term overseas voluntary work.
London Adventure Playground Association
25 Ovington St SW3. 01-581 2490. Helpers often needed, especially in school holidays.
London Council of Social Service   3 D 25
68 Chalton St NW1. 01-388 0241. Helpful booklet 'Someone like you can help' — lists nearly 200 charities in the London area. Also run a Voluntary Advisory Service whose aim is to allocate individuals to most suitable work.
Notting Hill Housing Trust
All Saints House, 46 All Saints Rd W11. 01-229 9782. Volunteers of all ages needed to help with all aspects of housing.
Oxfam
4 Replingham Rd SW18. 01-874 7335. Money raised for overseas projects. Many jobs from carol singing to pub collections.
Samaritans   6 N 30
St Stephen's Church, Walbrook EC4. 01-626 2277. Counsellors needed for potential suicide victims. Understandably stringent selection process; interviews, sensitivity tests, lectures and 6 months probation period.
Many London branches.
Toc H   6 Q 32
42 Crutched Friars EC3. 01-709 0472. Members work with old people, refugees, mentally handicapped, etc. Practical skills useful — driving, cooking. Local branches.
Voluntary Societies' Committee for Services Overseas
The Secretary, British Volunteer Programme, 26 Bedford Sq WC1. 01-636 4066. They provide the application form and details of all VSO programmes.
War on Want
467 Caledonian Rd N7. 01-609 0211. Gift shops manned by voluntary helpers. Gifts also needed for shops.
Westminster Council for Social Service
Volunteers' Organisation, 19 Marylebone Rd NW1. 01-486 5711. All kinds of community voluntary work.
Women's Royal Voluntary Service   2 L 16
Old Park Lane W1. 01-499 6040. Men and women volunteers welcome for all kinds of community work.

Lavatories

Parks, main railway stations, museums and art galleries generally have WC's. Closing times only are given. Owing to vandalism and staff shortage, lavatories are constantly being closed down (this applies especially to London Transport Underground).
M - Men. W - Women.

Aldwych Underground Stn. W	6 K 24
Babmaes St (off Jermyn St). MW. *23.00*	2 I 20
Baker St Underground. MW	2 B 19
Barret St W1. M *23.00*	2 F 18
Battersea Park SW11. MW. *Sunset*	4 P 9
Bayswater Rd W2. MW. *23.00*	1 B 10
Billingsgate Lower Thames St EC3. M	6 P 30

21.00 Sat 13.30, Sun 15.30. W 15.00.
CLOSED Sat & Sun.
Bishopsgate EC2. MW. *23.00 Sun 22.00*　　6　**N 33**
Bishopsgate Churchyard EC2. M. *17.00*　　6　**N 32**
CLOSED Sat & Sun.
Blackfriars Bridge Stn. MW　　6　**M 27**
Bond St Underground Stn. W　　2　**F 18**
Brick St W1. MW. *23.00*　　2　**I 17**
Broad Sanctuary SW1. MW　　5　**M 19**
Broadwick St W1. MW. *23.00*　　2　**H 21**
Brompton Rd SW3. MW. *23.00 Sun 22.30*　　1　**I 11**
Bruton Lane W1. M *23.00*　　2　**H 18**
Caledonian Rd Underground Stn. W　　3　**B 30**
Cambridge Circus WC2. M *23.00*　　2　**I 22**
Cannon St EC4. MW. *21.00, Sat 17.30,*
Sun 18.30.　　6　**O 30**
Cannon St Bridge Stn. MW　　6　**O 29**
Caxton St SW1. MW. *23.00*　　5　**M 18**
Chapel Market N1. MW. *18.00. Sun, Thur 15.00* 3　**E 30**
Fri, Sat 19.30.
Charing Cross Bridge Stn. MW　　5　**K 22**
Charing Cross Rd (by Old City Hall) WC2. MW
23.00　　5　**J 22**
Charter House St EC1. M *14.00 CLOSED Sat*　6　**J 28**
Circus Place EC2. M *17.00 CLOSED Sat & Sun* 6　**M 32**
Clerkenwell Green EC1. MW. *18.30.*
CLOSED Sat & Sun.　　3　**I 29**
Covent Garden WC2. M *24 hrs. CLOSED Sun*　6　**J 23**
Earls Court Rd. W. Cromwell Rd SW5. MW　　1　**F 5**
Eastcheap EC3. MW. *21.00, Sat 17.30, Sun 18.30*
　　6　**O 31**
Edgware Rd W2. MW. *23.00*　　2　**A 15**
Edgware Rd Underground Stn (Met). W　　2　**A 15**
Embankment. M *24 hrs* W *23.00*　　4　**N 11**
Essex Rd by Cross St N1. MW　　3　**D 33**
Euston Bridge Stn. MW　　3　**C 24**
Euston Rd NW1. MW. *24.00 Sun 23.00*　　3　**D 27**
Fenchurch St M *21.00, Sat 17.30*　　6　**O 31**
Fenchurch St Bridge Stn. MW　　6　**P 32**
Fleet St EC4. M *24 hrs*　　6　**K 26**
Foley St W1. M *23.00*　　2　**E 21**
Fulham Broadway Underground Stn M　　4　**K 2**
Gt Marlborough St W1. MW. *23.00*　　2　**G 20**
Gt Portland St W1. MW. *23.00*　　2　**D 22**
Gt Portland St Underground Stn. M　　2　**D 22**
Grosvenor Hill W1. MW. *23.00*　　2　**G 18**
Guilford St WC1. MW *23.00*　　3　**G 26**
Guildhall Yard EC2. MW. *17.00 Sat, Sun 18.00* 6　**M 30**
Hays Mews W1. MW. *23.00*　　2　**H 17**
High Holborn WC1. MW. *23.00*　　3　**I 23**
High St Kensington Underground Stn. W　　1　**E 7**
Holborn EC1. MW. *21.00, Sat, 17.30, Sun 18.30* 6　**J 27**
Holborn Viaduct Bridge Stn. MW　　6　**K 28**
Hyde Park Corner SW1. MW. *24 hrs*　　2　**I 15**
Islington Green N1. W. *22.30*　　3　**E 32**
Islington High St N1. M. *22.30*　　3　**F 31**
Kensington Rd SW7 (In Gardens). MW. *23.00*　1　**F 9**
Kings Cross Bridge Stn. MW. *23.30*　　3　**D 27**
Lambeth Bridge SW1 (Millbank) MW. *23.00*　5　**O 19**
Leadenhall Market EC3. M. *18.00, Sat 14.30.*
CLOSED Sun.　　6　**O 31**

Leicester Sq WC2. MW. *24 hrs*　　5　**J 22**
Leicester Sq Underground Stn. W　　5　**J 22**
Lillie Rd SW6. MW　　1　**I 2**
Lincolns Inn Fields WC2. MW. *23.00*　　3　**I 25**
Liverpool St Bridge Stn. W　　6　**M 33**
Liverpool St Underground Stn. W　　6　**N 33**
London Bridge Stn. MW　　6　**Q 29**
London St W2 (nr Praed St). MW. *23.00*　　2　**B 13**
Lupus St SW1. MW. *23.00*　　5　**O 14**
Marble Arch W2 (Cumberland Gate).
MW. *24 hrs*　　2　**E 16**
Marylebone Bridge Stn. MW　　2　**A 17**
Marylebone Rd NW1. MW. *23.00*　　2　**C 19**
Mason's Yard (by Duke St) SW1. MW. *23.00*　5　**J 19**
Mornington Crescent NW1. MW. *23.00*　　3　**A 24**
Notting Hill Gate Underground Stn. MW　　1　**A 8**
Old St EC1. MW. *22.30, Sun 16.00*　　6　**J 32**
Oxford Circus W1. MW. *23.00*　　2　**F 20**
Paddington Bridge Stn. MW. *24 hrs*　　2　**B 13**
Paddington St W1. MW. *23.00*　　2　**C 19**
Pancras Rd NW1. MW　　3　**D 27**
Parliament St SW1. MW. *23.00*　　5　**M 20**
Paternoster Sq EC4. MW. *22.00*　　6　**L 29**
Piccadilly W1 (nr Green Park Underground Stn) MW
23.00　　2　**I 18**
Pimlico Rd SW1 (by Ebury Rd) MW. *23.00*　5　**M 13**
Queensway W2. MW　　1　**A 11**
Regency Place SW1. M *23.00*　　5　**N 18**
Rochester Row SW1 (by Vauxhall Bridge Rd) MW
23.00　　5　**N 17**
Rosebery Ave EC1.MW. *18.00*　　3　**H 28**
Royal Exchange EC3. MW. *22.00*　　6　**N 31**
St Giles's Circus (Subway) M　　3　**H 23**
St James Gdns, Cardington St NW1. MW *Dusk* 3　**C 24**
St Pancras Bridge Stn. MW. *24 hrs*　　3　**D 27**
St Pancras Gardens NW1. MW. *Dusk*　　3　**B 27**
Salisbury St NW8 (by Church St) MW　　2　**A 16**
Sloane Sq SW1. MW. *23.00*　　5　**L 12**
Star Yard WC2 (By Carey St) MW. *23.00*　　6　**J 26**
Strand WC2 (by Law Courts) MW. *23.00*　　6　**K 25**
Sydney St SW3. MW. *23.00*　　4　**L 9**
Theobalds' Rd WC1. MW. *23.00*　　3　**H 25**
Three Kings Yard, Davies St W1. MW. *23.00*　2　**G 18**
Tottenham Court Rd W1. MW. *24.00,*
Sun 23.00　　3　**D 23**
Tower Hill EC3. MW. *23.00 (Winter 22.00)*　6　**Q 31**
Trafalgar Sq Subway WC2. MW. *23.00*　　5　**K 21**
Victoria Bridge Stn. MW. *24 hrs*　　5　**M 15**
Victoria Embankment Gdns WC2. MW. *23.00*　6　**K 23**
Victoria St SW1. (by Bressendon Place)
MW. *23.00*　　5　**M 16**
Warwick Way SW1 (by Ebury Bridge)
MW. *23.00*　　5　**N 14**
Waterloo Bridge SE1 (Foot of Bridge) MW　　6　**L 24**
Waterloo Bridge Stn. MW. *24 hrs*　　6　**N 23**
Wellington St WC; (by Strand) M *23.00*　　6　**J 24**
West Smithfield EC1. MW. *20.30 Sat 15.30,*
Sun 18.30　　6　**K 29**
Westminster Bridge SW1. MW　　5　**N 21**
World's End Passage SW10. MW. *23.30*　　4　**L 6**

Crisis Page

Emergency of any kind?
Dial 999 for police, fire or ambulance.

Desperate?

New Horizon   **3 I 24**
1 Macklin St WC2. 01-242 0010. Advice, referral and counselling for the young homeless in the West End.
The Samaritans   **6 N 30**
St Stephen's Church Crypt, Walbrook EC4. 01-626 2277. *On the telephone 24 hrs.* Just phone and talk out your problem.
St Martin-in-the-Fields Social Service Unit   **5 J 22**
5 St Martin's Place WC2. 01-930 1732. *On the telephone 24 hrs.* Phone for help and support.

Accident?

When in an accident with another car remember to take its licence plate number and the name of the other driver and his insurance company. Then report the accident to the police — dial 999 — and say where you are.

Arrested?

Always keep calm and remain polite. If you are innocent it often helps to explain the facts on the spot; if not say nothing until a written statement in your own words can be made. Ask to phone your lawyer. Appeals for legal representation, legal aid and bail can be made in court. See under 'Legal aid'.

Baby battering

NSPCC. 01-580 8812. 24-hr telephone service taking in all reports and complaints.

Wife battering

If you are being assaulted or become aware of a woman being beaten, phone your local Social Services department, the police (999) or the local Citizens Advice Bureau who will give advice and a local contact. Also try:
The National Women's Aid Federation
51 Chalcot Rd NW1. 01-586 0104/5192. Sympathetic advice.

Bombs

If you see a suspicious looking package:
1— **DON'T TOUCH IT**
2— Get people away from the area
3— Inform personnel in charge of the premises
4— Dial 999 and tell the police where it is.

Drinking too much?

Alcoholics Anonymous   **4 J 5**
11 Redcliffe Gardens SW10. 01-351 3344. Help and support available *24 hrs a day.*

Drug problem?

Go to your nearest casualty hospital for emergency treatment (see 'Hospitals') or phone:
Release
The emergency number is 01-603 8654 (the operator will refer you). Help legal and practical.

Nowhere to sleep?

Centrepoint   **2 I 22**
65a Shaftesbury Ave W1. 01-734 1075. Free night shelter for homeless young people aged 17-25 who are new to London and at a loss.

Gambling too much?

Gamblers Anonymous   **4 M 8**
17-23 Blantyre St, Cheyne Walk SW10. 01-352 3060. They help you to get things into perspective.

For more physical emergencies:

If you need a hospital
Dial 999 and ask for the ambulance service or go to casualty at:
Hackney Hospital
230 Homerton High St E9. 01-985 5555. *24 hr casualty.*
Middlesex Hospital   **2 F 22**
Mortimer St W1. 01-636 8333. *OPEN 24 hrs.*
Moorfields Eye Hospital
High Holborn WC1. 01-836 6611.   **3 I 24**
City Rd EC1. 01-253 3411.   **6 K 33**
Casualty. Deal only with eye injuries.
St Mary's Hospital   **2 B 14**
Praed St W2. 01-262 1280. *24 hr casualty.*

An emergency birth?

Phone the hospital at which the mother is registered — if any — failing this try one of the casualty hospitals under 'Maternity Hospitals'. If all else fails, dial 999 — the ambulance men are trained to cope.

All-night prescriptions

Bliss Chemist
54 Willesden Lane NW6. 01-624 8000.
Boots   **2 I 20**
Piccadilly Circus W1. 01-930 4761.
Both are open 24 hrs.

No petrol?

Stuck in town in the middle of the night? Most Blue Star garages have a 24-hr service. See also under 'Night services'.

Broken down?

See under 'Night services' for a list of garages providing 24-hr breakdown, vehicle recovery and roadside repair service.

Lost your car keys?

If you know the number of your key (keep a note of it somewhere in your wallet) the AA or RAC can probably help (see phone numbers under 'Night services') if a nearby garage or the police can't.

Stuck in town and nowhere to go?

Of course, if it's any night but Saturday night, you're not really stuck, because there's an excellent night bus service (see 'Night bus map and timetable'). Otherwise, ask a friendly policeman. If it is Saturday then you really are stuck (virtually no night buses) and you'd better try the following:
Classic Cinema   **2 I 21**
103 Wardour St W1. 01-734 7030. Phone this number to find out at which Classic cinema films are showing all night.

Rape?

If you have been raped or sexually assaulted, and need support, information or any other help — phone 01-340 6145. Rape crisis centre operate a 24-hr service.

Starving at 4 a.m.?

Look under 'Eating' and 'Food shops' in 'Night Services'.
Westminster stall   **5 N 20**
Outside Westminster Abbey. Pies and coffee.
Chelsea stall   **5 P 12**
South end of Chelsea Bridge. Hot dogs, pies, coffee.
Waterloo stall   **6 O 24**
Waterloo Rd SE1. Tea, coffee and sundries.

Home late and locked out?

Haybel & Hogg
01-229 6779. *24-hr emergency locksmith service.*

The police can help you

When you need a garage
Each police station keeps a list of local garages, emergency services and so on and the times they are open.
When you need a hotel
They keep up-to-date information on hotels and boarding houses in the area with prices — of course, they don't know if there are vacancies, but at least you'd have somewhere to try.
When you've lost property on the street
It may have been taken to them, or they will be able to tell you where to go for things lost in trains or taxis.
When your car has been stolen
Ring them up straight away — it may simply have been towed away to a police pound for a parking infringement.
When your dog is lost
It may have been taken to them at the station, in which case they will look after it for one night and then take it to the Battersea Dogs Home.
When you're stranded
If you've come to London from a provincial town and spent your return fare, they can take the name of someone in your home town who will deposit your fare at the local police station there and then the London police station will give you a travel warrant to get you home. *(This applies to British residents only — all other nationalities should apply to their own embassy for repatriation.)*

Index

Abbeys 55
Abortion 148
Accommodation 78, 89, 144
Adoption 148
Aerial photography 124
Afternoon teas 102
Air charter 88
Air ferries 86
Airlines 88
Airport 88
Air terminals 88
Alcoholics 148
Ambulance 148
Animals 148
Animals in parks 69
Annual events 36
Antiques 124
Aquaria 125
Arboreta 65
Archaeological digs 84
Archery 114
Architectural prints and dyelines 125
Architecture libraries 75
Art and architecture holidays 84
Art galleries 61, 132
Artists' materials 125
Art libraries 75
Athletics 114
Auctioneers 125
Au pair 143
Automobile Association 144
Aviaries 66
Babysitting 143
Badminton 114
Ballet 110
Ballooning 114
Ballroom dancing 126
Banks 144
Baseball 114
Basketball 114
Baskets 126
Beachwear 119
Beauty specialists 126
Belts 122
Bespoke tailors 119
Billiards 114
Bird watching 66
Birth control 149
Blind 148
Boating and sailing abroad 84
Boating equipment 140
Boats 140
Books 126
Botanical gardens 65
Boutiques 121
Bowls 114
Boxing 114
Boy scouts 72
Brass rubbing 71, 127
Builders 143
Building materials 143
Buses and coaches 87, 144
Business information services 145
Business and secretarial services 145
Businessmen's holidays 84
Bus map: day 31
Bus map: night 32
Bus map: red arrow routes 33
Bus map: timetable 33
Buttons 127
Cacti 127
Camera repairs 138
Cameras 127
Camping equipment 140
Camping holidays 84
Canal trips 42
Cancer 148
Canoeing 114
Caravans 127
Careers guidance 78
Car ferries 86
Car hire 87, 144
Car parks 34
Carpet cleaning 143
Carpets 127
Car repairs, breakdowns 144, 154
Carveries 100
Catering service 143
Cathedrals 56
Charities 152
Charter boats 43

Chemists 127
Chessmen 128
Chest hospitals 146
Children's aid 148
Children's clothes 75
Children's hairdressers 74
Children's holidays 73
Children's London 68
Children's shopping 74
Children's theatre 73
China and glass 128, 133
Chiropodist 128
Churches 56
Church music 112
Cigarette cards 73, 128
Cinema map 28
Cinemas 111, 145
Clay pigeon shooting 114
Climbing holidays 85
Clocks 128
Clothes cleaning 144
Clothes hire 120
Clothing fabrics 120, 122
Coach hire 87
Coach stations 87
Coach tours 42
Coastal marinas 119
Coins and medals 128
Commemorative plaques 53
Commonwealth offices 82
Concert halls 110
Consumer protection 119
Continental ferries 86
Cottages for hire 84
Couturiers 122
Craft classes 72
Craft shops 129
Cricket 72, 114, 140
Crisis page 154
Croquet 114
Cry for helf 147
Currency exchange 81
Cycling 114
Daily ceremonies 36
Dance halls 108
Dancing 115
Dancing classes 72
Day trips from London 43
Deaf 149
Dental hospitals 146
Design showrooms 129
Detectives 129
Diabetics 149
Dinner dancing 106
Disabled 149
Discharged prisoners 149
Discotheques 107
Discount shopping 129
Disqualified motorists 151
Diving holidays 84
Do-it-yourself services 143
Dolls 74
Domestic help 143
Donating your corpse 152
Drag pubs 104
Drag racing 115
Drama classes 72
Drama libraries 76
Drawing lessons 72
Drawing office equipment 130
Dressmaking patterns 138
Drinking 93
Drug addicts 149, 154
Drug clinics 146
Dyelines 125
Dyslexic 150
Ear piercing 130
Eating 93, 145
Ecclesiastic libraries 76
Elderly people 150
Electronic shops 130
Embassies 81
Embroidery 137
Emergency 145, 154
Employment (student) 79
Engravings 132
Entertainers 130
Environmental field work 79
Epilepsy 150
Escorts 130
Estate agents 92
Fairs 73
Family trees 130
Fancy dress 130

Fencing 115, 140
Ferries 86
Festivals 113
Film and sound libraries 76
Fireworks 73
Fishing 84, 115
Fives 115
Flats 93
Flowers 130
Flying 115
Food shops 130
Football 115
Foreign hospitals 146
Foreign newspapers 131
Fossil hunting 70
Fur cleaning, valeting 122
Fur coats 120
Furnishing fabrics 130
Furniture 131
Furniture removals and
    depositories 144
Furs 122
Galleries 61, 132
Gambling 150, 154
Gardening 132
Garden ornaments 132
Gardens 50, 63
Gastronomic holidays 84
Geography libraries 76
Geology 133
Genealogy 133
Gift shops 133
Gliding 116
Gloves 123
Golf 116, 140
Golfing holidays 84
Grants and charitable trusts 78
Grass-skiing 116
Great houses 50
Greyhound racing 116
Guide books 35
Guns 133
Gymnasiums 116
Gymnastics 72, 116
Haberdashery 123
Haemophilia 150
Hairbrushes 133
Hairdressers 133
Hairpieces 123
Handbags 123
Hats 123
Hearing aids 134
Helicopter charter 88
Helping others 72
Heraldry 133
Herbalists 134
Hill figures 70
Historic buildings 44
Historic London 44
History libraries 76
Hockey 116
Holiday information 80
Holidays 80
Homeless people 150
Home services 143
Homeopathic hospital 147
Homosexuality 150
Horse racing 116
Hospitals 146
Hostels 78, 91
Hotel booking agents 89
Hotels 89
Hotels near Gatwick airport 92
Hotels near Heathrow airport 92
Household emergencies 144
Houses of famous people 52
Hovercraft 86
Ice hockey 117
Ice skating 72
Icons 134
Inexpensive eating 100
Information centres 35
Information services 35
Injustice and persecution 150
Inns and pubs 102
Inoculations 80
Institutes of culture 82
Interior decorating shops 134
Interior decorators 144
Interior designers 144
Invalid equipment 134
Ironmongery 134
Jazz clubs 107

Jewellery 134
Jewellery hire 135
Judo 116
Jokes and magic 74
Jujitsu 116

Karate 116
Karting 116
Keep fit classes 115
Key cutting service 144
Kitchen equipment 135
Knitting wools 135
Knitwear 135

Lacrosse 116
Language tuition 135
Laundry 144
Lavatories 152
Law libraries 76
Lawn tennis 117
Learning 72
Leather clothing 123
Lecturers 130
Legal aid 151
Libraries 75
Lighting 135
Linen 136
Locksmith 136
Lodgings 92
London tours 42
Lonely people 151, 154
Lost property 81
Lunchtime concerts 112

Magic and jokes 74
Maps 136
Marionette theatre 110
Markets 142
Marriage guidance 151
Marriage partners 151
Matchbox labels 136
Maternity clothes 123
Maternity hospitals 147
Medical libraries 76
Men's clothes 119
Men's hairdressers 134
Mental health 151
Migraine clinics 147
Militaria shops 136
Mini cabs 86
Missing persons 151
Model aircraft 74
Model railways 74
Modern architecture 59
Modern outdoor sculpture 55
Motels 92
Motor car accessories 136
Motor cars 136
Motor car tuning and
conversions 136
Motor cycles 137
Motor cycle speedway 117
Motor racing 117
Mountaineering 84, 117
Museums 61
Museums for children 69
Music 137
Musical boxes 137
Musical instruments 137
Musical pubs 104
Music lessons 72
Music libraries 77
Music publishers 137

National food centres 131
Natural history holidays 84
Natural science libraries 77
Nature reserves 67
Nature trails 70
Needlework 137
Netball 117
Night clubs 107
Nightdresses 123
Night life 106
Night services 144
Nursery schools 74
Nursing 151
Nursing and convalescent
homes 147

Office equipment 138
One parent families 151
Open air music 112
Open air pubs 105
Open air theatre 110
Opera 110
Optical instruments 138
Optician 138

Orienteering 117
Outdoor eating 101
Outdoor holidays 83
Painting classes 72
Painting holidays 85
Paintings 132
Parachuting 117
Parking 34
Parks and gardens 63
Passenger lines 85
Passports 80
Patterns (dressmaking) 138
Pens 138
Perfume 138
Petrol 154
Pets 138
Pet shops 74
Photographic enlargements 138
Photographic equipment 138
Photographic film and paper 138
Photography 138
Photo retouchers 138
Picture cleaning 138
Picture frames 138
Picture hire 138
Picture research 138
Pipes 138
Playgrounds 73
Poetry 110
Police 154
Police stations 146
Politcal and minority interest
groups 79
Political libraries 77
Polo 117
Postcards 139
Posters 139
Post office 145
Poverty 151
Pregnancy tests 151
Prescriptions 154
Press cutting agencies 139
Printing 139
Prints 132
Psychiatric hospitals 147
Public records libraries 76
Pubs and inns 102

Rackets 117
Radio and T.V. shows 112
Radios 139
Raffia 139
Rail terminals 87
Raincoats 120, 123
Real tennis 117
Record players 139
Records 139
Reference libraries 75
Replicas 139
Restaurants 93
Riding 85, 117
Riding holidays 85
River trips 42
Road safety 72
Rowing 117
Royal Automobile Club 144
Rugby football 117

Saddlery 140
Sauna baths 139
Scholar's London 75
Science libraries 77
Scientific equipment 139
Scouts and guides 72
Sculpture 132
Sea ferries 86
Seamen's hospitals 147
Secondhand clothes 123
Secretarial services 145
Service and ex-servicemen 151
Sex supermarket 140
Sheet music 137
Shoes 121, 123
Shooting 117, 140
Shopping 119
Shopping map 29
Show-jumping 117
Sightseeing 35
Silver 134, 140
Skating 117
Ski-ing 85, 118, 140
Skittles 118
Smokers 152
Snooker 114
Snuff 141
Social clubs and societies 78

Social sciences libraries 77
Social services 146
Sound recording 140
Specialist shops and services 124
Specialist hospitals 147
Specialist air charter 88
Sponges and loofahs 140
Sports 72, 113
Sports equipment 140
Sports stadiums 113
Squash 118
Stamps 74, 141
Statues 54
Stock car racing 118
Stockings and tights 124
Stores 119
Street index 16
Street maps 4
Strip clubs 107
Student's London 78
Sub-aqua 118, 140
Sunshine cruises 85
Surveyors and valuers 93
Swimming 72, 118
Swimsuits 124

Table tennis 118
Tattooing 141
Taxis 86
Teas 102
Telephone answering services 141
Telephone services 35
Tennis 72, 118, 140
Tenpin bowling 118, 145
Thames river map 38
Theatre map 28
Theatre pubs 105
Theatres 103
Theatrical costume 141
Theatrical suppliers 141
Ticket agents 108, 114
Tipping 93
Tobacco 141
Tools 141
Tourist offices 83
Toys 74
Traction engines 71
Travel agents 83
Travel information 80
Trousers 121
Turkish baths 141

Underground map 30
Unusual eating 101
Unusual holidays 83
Unmarried mothers 152
Unusual size clothes 124

Vaccinations 80
Vegetarian and health food 100
Veneral disease 147, 152
Veterinary clinics 141
Victorian postcards 139
Viewpoints 36
Villa and chalet holidays 85
Vintage motor cars 137
Voluntary social work 152

Walking holidays 85
Walking tours 42
Wallpapers 141
War medals 136
Watches 128
Water polo 118
Water ski-ing 118
Weight lifting 118
Welfare (student's) 79
Widows 152
Wigs 123, 142
Wildfowl reserves 66
Wildlife tours and safaris 85
Windmills 71
Wine 142
Wine bars 105
Wine clubs 142
Wine making 142
Wine tasting holidays 84
Women's clothes 121
Women's hairdressers 133
Wren churches 57
Wrestling 118

Yachting 118, 140
Young women's shops 121

Zoos 65

FIND YOUR WAY AROUND LONDON WITH

Nicholson's Guides and Maps

LONDON GUIDES

Nicholson's London Guide
Pocket sized, packed full of information, plus many coloured maps.

Nicholson's Student's London
Pocket sized, directed specifically to the student's own needs. Maps and index.

Nicholson's Visitor's London
Specially for the tourist. Full colour picture maps and index.

Nicholson's London Restaurants
London's best restaurants, including cheap meals and pub lunches. Coloured centre maps.

Nicholson's London Nightlife
Not only the hot spots, but a practical guide to London after dark. Coloured centre maps.

Nicholson's American's Guide to London
Written by Americans for Americans in the famous Nicholson format. Coloured centre maps.

Nicholson's Guide to Children's London for Parents
All a parent needs to know to keep the kids happy and informed. Coloured centre maps.

LONDON MAPS

Nicholson's Central London Map and Index
30 square miles of central London in two colours and showing one-way streets.

Nicholson's London Street Finder
The famous and long established best seller. Two colours throughout, with large scale centre section showing one-way streets.

Nicholson's Large Street Finder
Large scale and two colour maps throughout for extra legibility.

Nicholson's Hard Back Street Finder
The handy, legible Street Finder for office or car. Two colour maps throughout.

Nicholson's Sightseer's London
An easy guide to localities wherever you are in London.

Nicholson's London Map
Large scale central London with index.

Nicholson's 2 London Maps
Central London map with index plus London route planning map.

Nicholson's Visitor's London Map
Handy full colour fold out map with main sights in 3D.

GREAT BRITAIN GUIDES & MAPS

Nicholson's Great Britain
An easy reference guide to all the family's interests and activities. Fully illustrated and with coloured relief maps.

Nicholson's Waterway's Guides
Five regional guides to the canals of England and Wales with detailed maps.

Nicholson's Thames
Complete from source to sea with detailed maps, drawings and photographs.

Nicholson's Real Ale Guide to the Waterways.
Over 1000 pubs on or near the waterways. Maps.

Nicholson's Great Britain Touring Map
Full colour map of Great Britain showing motorways and main roads.